A New Anatomy of Ireland

A New Anatomy of Ireland:
The Irish Protestants, 1649–1770

Toby Barnard

Yale University Press
New Haven and London

For information about this and other Yale University Press publications, please contact:
U.S. Office: sales.press@yale.edu   yalebooks.com
Europe Office: sales@yaleup.co.uk   www.yaleup.co.uk

Set in Bembo by SNP Best-set Typesetter Ltd., Hong Kong
Printed in Great Britain by St Edmundsbury Press

Library of Congress Cataloging-in-Publication Data

Barnard, T. C. (Toby Christopher)
A new anatomy of Ireland: the Irish Protestants, 1649–1770.
p.   cm.
Includes bibliographical references and index.
ISBN 0–300–09669–0 (cloth: alk. paper)
1. Ireland—History—18th century.   2. Ireland—History—17th century
3. Protestants—Ireland—History—18th century.   4. Protestants—Ireland—
History—17th century. I. Title.
DA947 B36 2003   305.6'40415—dc21   2002155553
A catalogue record for this book is available from the British Library.

2 4 6 8 10 9 7 5 3 1

Published with assistance from the Annie Burr Lewis Fund

Contents

Preface

The research and writing of this book have arisen from a wish – simple but naïve – to discover what it was like for Protestants to live in the Ireland of the later seventeenth and eighteenth centuries. In this period, Protestants, mainly from England, Scotland and Wales, twice reconquered Ireland, and took over property, office and power. The processes by which this system – in all but name a Protestant Ascendancy – was erected have been traced clearly. Also, the embryonic ascendancy has been shown in action. The excellence of these accounts has freed me to pursue my own enquiries. Thanks to the studies – notably those by David Hayton – of public policy, the interplay between governors in Dublin and government in London is well understood. More recently, Ivar McGrath, Paddy McNally and Eoin Magennis have narrated in convincing detail conventional 'high', parliamentary politics between 1690 and 1765. In parallel, the structures and dynamics of demography and the economy have been uncovered in a series of pioneering works by Louis Cullen and David Dickson. Equally helpful are two admirable books – David Dickson's *New Foundations* and Sean Connolly's *Religion, Law and Power* – which splice together the separate strands. Anyone keen to know what happened in Ireland between 1659 and 1800 should turn to those books, not to this.

My interests look tangential to those of most who have recently investigated Stuart and Hanoverian Ireland. This volume concerns itself little with the processes by which Protestants ensconced themselves but a great deal with the results. In many accounts, the few who ran the Dublin parliament or their counties bulk large, leaving in the shadows the majority who peopled Protestant Ireland. If, as has been suggested, mid-eighteenth-century Ireland contained approximately 400,000 Protestants, we can begin to discern fewer than 20,000, usually freeholders in the countryside and freemen of the boroughs. Most remain in darkness. Once before, I was sucked into a historiographical black hole: Cromwellian Ireland. As with that earlier study, so with this, the reasons for the void are quickly identified. For want of evidence, it is difficult to bring into focus many of the 20,000, let alone the mass outside those élites. The effort may seem disproportionate to the results. In the voluminous log of the exploration, this, the first stage, attempts to delineate the society. It tries to recover something of those customarily overlooked. Each chapter has obliged me to tackle a topic (or topics) which deserves a monograph to itself. The next instalment of my own investigations will show the members of the Protestant interest in action (and in repose or at play); probe their minds and values, and detail their material worlds. To separate these spheres falsifies what was united in their lives, and misleads by relegating recreation, domesticity and sociability to a distinct and – by implication – lower sphere. Unfortunately, to make it manageable, the fabric has been rent asunder.

My wish to make sense of this society arose after Paddy O'Flanagan invited me to contribute to a collection of essays on County Cork. His invitation obliged me to review and reorder diffuse researches. Many of the problems to which I then sought answers are pursued here – albeit in a larger space and over a longer period. South Munster still supplies a disproportionate amount of the evidence. I have attempted to correct it, but Ulster – particularly its distinctive Presbyterian society and economy – is under-represented. I have shown some of the overlapping activities of Protestant dissenters and conformists, and speculated on what developed separately and in parallel. Patient use of kirk session records and family papers may allow a detailed reconstruction of this society before 1770, but it has scarcely begun. There is also a view of the Protestant possessors to be reconstructed from the plaints of the dispossessed. Poetry and prose in the Irish language have started to be interpreted. The results do not always inspire confidence that startling new perspectives will be revealed. Inevitably, this account, like the sources on which it is grounded, is biased and uneven in what it covers. Numbers are offered from time to time, in a bid to show how many belonged to the distinct social and occupational groups. Levels of income are sometimes suggested. However, there is no sustained effort at quantification, since it would invest this exercise with a spurious statistical plausibility. Sir William Petty, the pioneer anatomist of Ireland, littered his speculations with numbers, all too many of which turn out to be guesses, and sometimes wild ones. Yet the homage to Petty indicated in my title is not entirely ironic, although Petty was alert to ironies. The arresting but untypical example has been favoured above the aggregation; the concrete before the generality. This is by intention. My interest is unashamedly in the people who lived in a particular place at a specific time.

Undoubtedly, in preferring the individual to the abstraction, I will offend historical ascetics and – more worryingly – ignore those who exist only as part of a statistic in bills of mortality or lists of tax-payers. To repeat the analogy of one of the most distinguished archers among current historians: I have reverted to the bow and arrow. There is a method in this, even if, since it is wearisome to all but a handful of professionals, I fail to rehearse it here. In the main, I have gone to the testimony of those whose lives form the subject of the study. Inevitably, what survives, by chance or design, relates to few. Moreover, it is a fabrication, whether deliberate or unconscious. Despite these shortcomings, the fragments of letters, journals and accounts offer a way into otherwise forgotten lives. Sometimes I have been obsessive in trying to track down and read what was written in seventeenth- and eighteenth-century Ireland. It is not pure whimsy to unfold a letter last read by the person to whom it had been addressed in 1699. The scatter of sand falling from the folds reminds that this was written and received. The physicality of these worlds was most strikingly conveyed to me in a library when I come across a hank of hair still pinned to a plaintive note from a grieving widow, asking a relation to include it in a mourning brooch. Perhaps it was; or maybe the request was ignored.

It is a happy thought that much that I have not had time to consult or which is not yet available will eventually offer alternative perspectives. Already, under its presently enlightened directorship, the National Library in Ireland is yielding up more of its secrets; collections in North American, British and continental European archives in time will do the same. Print, especially the newspapers produced in eighteenth-century Ireland, sampled very selectively, can also be expected to change considerably what is offered here.

Provisional as this sketch is, there comes a moment to exhibit it. And, sketch though it is, it has cost me dear. At the same time, the pleasures have been great. It is not perhaps enough to repeat that simple curiosity led me into an engagement with the history of Protestant Ireland. Insistence that this account is conceived as neither eulogy nor elegy, or that I have no wish vicariously to associate myself with the ascendant, will not convince doubters. Living in a village close to the intersection of Roman roads and favoured by the Romans and Normans, it seems natural enough to be curious about now almost vanished orders and immigrants.

As a result of those labours, I have acquired many new friends, and – I hope – lost none. Working in Oxford and teaching mainly the history of the British Isles and continental Europe pose obstacles which partly explain the long gestation. In Oxford, and particularly in my college, I have been indulged and stimulated in my Hibernian obsessions, notably by Geoffrey Ellis and Christopher Tyerman. Roger Pensom on journeys backwards and forwards has obliged me to clarify notions and approaches. Much to my surprise, Hertford, which had long tolerated my interests, during the 1990s became a centre for the study of Ireland and its culture. The enjoyment and stimulus of having first Roy Foster and then Tom Paulin as colleagues have also ensured that this has been far from a solitary quest. Earlier, my association with the Carroll Institute obliged me to widen my view to include more of the Irish midlands. I remember gratefully the comradeship of Ewan Broadbent, Peter Davies, Liz Fitzpatrick, Aoife Leonard, Tim Venning and – of course – the progenitor himself, Gerald Carroll.

The bulk of the research has inevitably taken me far from Oxford. What I owe to those who have invited me to speak and examine, baited and boarded me, shared their knowledge and ideas, can never be quantified. What I have received by way of subvention can. I am grateful to the Leverhulme Foundation for its award in 1993–94, to the British Academy first for a small grant in 1996–97 and then for the research readership in 1997–99, which allowed much of the study to be concluded, to the Modern History Faculty in Oxford and to the Harding Fund at Hertford for annual grants.

Different geographical bases in Ireland have helped me to see the diversity of the island. In West Cork, I think particularly of what I have learnt at Innis Beg, Castlehaven and Cunnamore, and so of Michael MacCarthy-Morrogh, Gwen and Peter Harold-Barry, Joyce Thallon, Margot Magill, Shiela and Micheal Sokolov Grant, Connie and Helen Desmond. In East Cork, the Falvey family, and especially Anne and Derry, have welcomed me and corrected any occidental bias. Olda and Desmond Fitzgerald at Glin, Brendan and Alison Rosse at Birr, Hanne and Christopher Gray at Higginsbrook, David and Deirdre Hayton, Anthony Malcomson and Bruce Campbell in Belfast, Michael and Anne Harnett in County Down, Paul Kelly and Daniel Beaumont in Dublin have all been generous in their hospitality. Also in Dublin it has been heartening to continue the friendships first established in the 1960s with Aidan and Mary Clarke, Paul Pollard and William O'Sullivan, and to come to know fresh generations of scholars. Indeed, just as there is virtually no writer on seventeenth- and eighteenth-century Ireland from whom I have not learnt something (even when disagreeing with them), there are few whom I have not come to know and be helped by. The generosity with which insights and information have been shared is a reminder of the reality of a commonwealth of scholars, not all bent on advancement and pre-eminence. Tony Aspromourgos, Daniel Beaumont, Eavan Blackwell, Christine Casey, Liam Clare, Christina Colvin, Sean Connolly, Jason Dorsett, Rowena Dudley, Arch J. Elias, Jr., Mihail Evans, Derry Falvey, Betsey Fitzsimons Taylor, David Fleming, Andrew Forrest, David Hannigan, David Hayton, Kevin Herlihy, David Hunter, Jimmy Kelly, Mary-Lou Legg, Patrick Little,

Rolf Loeber, Magda Stouthamer Loeber, Ian McBride, Gerard McCoy, Paddy McNally, Eddie McParland, Eoin Magennis, Anthony Malcomson, Finola O'Kane, Philip O'Regan, Harold O'Sullivan, Vivienne Pollock, Michael Port, Deana Rankin, Rosemary Richey, Nessa Roche and William Roulstone have all allowed me to read work either unpublished or in advance of publication, to my benefit. They and many more – Clare Asquith, Jane Clark, Helen Clifford, Anne Crookshank, Mairead Dunlevy, Jane Fenlon, Alison FitzGerald, Sarah Foster, Peter Francis, the Knight of Glin, David Griffin, Claudia Kinmonth and Joanna Macintyre – have willingly discussed questions of shared concern and directed me to material which otherwise I might have missed.

I have been lucky to benefit from the scholarship and friendship of Mary-Lou Legg. Her edition of Bishop Synge's letters to his daughter has illumined – as will her forthcoming editions of the Elphin census of 1749 and Nicholas Peacock's laconic journal – so much of humdrum existence in mid-eighteenth-century Ireland. By reading and commenting on the entire text in draft she has alerted me to errors and obscurities. David Hayton and Eddie McParland have welcomed me, seemingly a fugitive from the seventeenth century, into the congenial eighteenth. I and others have already recorded how – far beyond their publications – Bernadette Cunningham and Ray Gillespie have served Irish history. They have, times beyond count, offered a matchless combination of intellectual and physical refreshment. If, now and again, the conviviality has strained my resolve to be in the archives when they open, their talk has brought more enlightenment than another account book, inventory or improving sermon.

In a project of this scope and vagueness, my dependence on fellow hewers and drawers among academic toilers is heavy. Even greater is my debt to the owners and staff of the many libraries and archives in which I have worked. Indeed, as opinion and interpretation quickly pass from fashion, it is the residue of information which endures. Some documents which I consulted when in private hands are now in public collections. Thereby their future is secured, but I remember fondly the marvellous (and occasionally hazardous) conditions in which originally I read these papers. Accordingly I thank Mrs Eileen Barber, Viscount de Vesci, the Duke of Devonshire and the trustees of the Chatsworth settled estates, the Knight of Glin, Mr Michael Harnett, the Marquess of Lansdowne, Dr Mary-Lou Legg, the Duke of Leinster, the Earl of Rosse, Canon George Salter, the Earl of Shelburne, Mr Allen Synge, Major-General Marston Tickell, and Captain Richard Turner. I am fortunate, with one or two exceptions, to have been assisted politely, efficiently and often far beyond the call of duty by librarians and archivists throughout Ireland and Britain. Under pressure from employers obsessed with a modish managerialism (which will pass as surely as other ruling divinities) and from the many hot on the scent of Irish ancestors, these harassed custodians have met my often odd and exorbitant demands. Without them, quite simply this could not have been written. I remember with special gratitude: at PRONI, David Lammey, Ian Montgomery, Jean Agnew and Anthony Malcomson; in the Presbyterian Historical Society, Bob Balfour; Ray Refaussé, Heather Smith and Susan Hood (RCB); Catherine Fahy, Colette O'Flaherty, Elizabeth Kirwan and Tom Desmond (NLI); at Marsh's, Muriel McCarthy and Ann Simmons; Siobhan O'Rafferty and Bernadette Cunningham (RIA); Aileen Ireland (NA); David Griffin (IAA); Maire Kennedy of the Dublin Public Libraries; Mary Kelleher at the RDS; in the Dublin City Archives, Mary Clark; at the Friends' Historical Library, Mary Shackleton; at the King's Hospital, Leslie Whiteside; in the Cork Archives Institute, Patricia MacCarthy; at the Boole Library in Cork, Helen Davies and Julian Walton (as earlier in Waterford); and at Chatsworth, Peter Day. Mary-Lou Legg helped me to overcome a fear of heights by inducting me into the Registry of Deeds; Peter Busch similarly taught me to conquer suspicions of electronic gadgetry, while Greg Jennings and David Croxford have helped me to use this wizardry constructively. A literal-mindedness about the laptop has led to some demarcation disputes with successive pugs, not – contrary to myth – natural lap-dogs. Pym, Holles and Yorick have undoubtedly slowed production of this work, but by doing so have improved me and it. Anthony O'Connor has tolerated the drifts of paper and piles of books, the impromptu excursions to odd places, uproar, and the disconnected gossip about the long dead, out of which this book has come. I am very grateful to Robert Baldock and Diana Yeh at Yale University Press for their support and care in the later stages at this project.

The longer the engagement with a topic, the more one realizes how much has been achieved by predecessors. I am conscious of the shades which have gathered around this protracted enterprise. I like to think that Jennifer Loach, Angus Macintyre, Alistair Parker, Jeanne Sheehy and William O'Sullivan would have been interested in, even amused by, what follows. Had they lived to read it, they would certainly have improved it.

Abbreviations

Al. Dubl.	G. D. Burtchaell and T. U. Sadleir, *Alumni Dublinenses* (Dublin, 1935)
Barnard, 'Cork settlers'	T. C. Barnard, 'The political, material and mental culture of the Cork settlers, 1649–1700', in P. O'Flanagan and N. G. Buttimer (eds), *Cork: history and society* (Dublin, 1993), pp. 309–65
Barnard, 'Robert French of Monivea'	T. C. Barnard, 'The worlds of a Galway squire: Robert French of Monivea, 1716–1779', in G. Moran and R. Gillespie (eds), *Galway: history and society* (Dublin, 1996), pp. 271–96
Barnard, 'Sir William Petty'	T. C. Barnard, 'Sir William Petty, Irish landowner', in H. Lloyd-Jones, V. Pearl and A. B. Worden (eds), *History and Imagination: essays in honour of H. R. Trevor-Roper* (London, 1981), pp. 201–17
BL	British Library
Bodleian	Bodleian Library, Oxford
CARD	*Calendar of the Ancient Records of Dublin*, ed. J. T. Gilbert and R. M. Gilbert, 19 vols (Dublin, 1899–1944)
Chatsworth	Chatsworth House, Derbyshire
Christ Church	Christ Church Library, Oxford
CJI	*Journals of the House of Commons of the Kingdom of Ireland*, 20 vols (Dublin, 1796–1804)
[C] RO	[County] Record Office
CSP, D, Irel, etc.	*Calendar of State Papers, Domestic, Ireland*, etc.
Dickson, 'Economic history of the Cork region'	D. Dickson, 'An economic history of the Cork region in the eighteenth century', unpublished Ph.D. thesis, TCD, 2 vols (1977)
EHR	*English Historical Review*
GEC, *Complete peerage*	G.E.C., *The complete peerage of England, Scotland, Ireland, Great Britain and the United Kingdom*, ed. V. Gibbs and H. A. Doubleday 13 vols (London, 1910–40)
GO	Genealogical Office, Dublin

HJ	*Historical Journal*
HMC, *Dartmouth Mss*	Historical Manuscripts Commission. *The manuscripts of the earl of Dartmouth*, 3 vols (London, 1887–96)
HMC, *Egmont diary*	Historical Manuscripts Commission. *Report on the manuscripts of the earl of Egmont. Diary of Viscount Percival, afterwards first earl of Egmont*, 3 vols (London, 1920–3)
HMC, *Egmont Mss*	Historical Manuscripts Commission. *Report on the manuscripts of the earl of Egmont*, 2 vols (London and Dublin, 1905–9)
HMC, *Ormonde Mss*, n.s.	Historical Manuscripts Commission. *Calendar of the manuscripts of the marquess of Ormonde, K.P., preserved at Kilkenny Castle*, new series, 8 vols (London, 1902–20)
HMC, *Portland Mss*	Historical Manuscripts Commission. *The manuscripts of his grace the duke of Portland, preserved at Welbeck Abbey*, 10 vols (London, 1920–3)
IAA	Irish Architectural Archive, Dublin
IHS	*Irish Historical Studies*
JCHAS	*Journal of the Cork Historical and Archaeological Society*
JRL	John Rylands Library, Manchester
JRSAI	*Journal of the Royal Society of Antiquaries of Ireland*
KIAP	E. Keane, P. B. Phair and T. U. Sadleir (eds), *King's Inns Admission Papers 1607–1867* (Dublin, 1982)
Legg, *Synge Letters*	M. L. Legg (ed.), *The Synge Letters. Bishop Edward Synge to his daughter Alicia, Roscommon to Dublin, 1746–1752* (Dublin, 1996)
LJIre	*Journals of the House of Lords of the Kingdom of Ireland*, 8 vols (Dublin, 1779–1800)
Mulcahy, *Kinsale*	M. Mulcahy (ed.), *Calendar of Kinsale documents*, 7 vols (Kinsale, 1988–1998)
Marsh's	Marsh's Library, Dublin
NA	National Archives, Dublin
NAM	National Army Museum, London
NLI	National Library of Ireland, Dublin
NLW	National Library of Wales, Aberystwyth
NUI	National University of Ireland
P & P	*Past and Present*
Petworth	Petworth House, West Sussex
PRIA	*Proceedings of the Royal Irish Academy*
PRO	Public Record Office, Kew
PRONI	Public Record Office of Northern Ireland, Belfast
RCB	Representative Church Body Library, Dublin
RD	Registry of Deeds, Dublin
RDS	Royal Dublin Society
RIA	Royal Irish Academy, Dublin

RSAI	Royal Society of Antiquaries of Ireland, Dublin
Statutes	*The Statutes at large, passed in the Parliaments held in Ireland*, 21 vols (Dublin, 1796–1804)
TCD	Trinity College, Dublin
TRHS	*Transactions of the Royal Historical Society*
UCNW	Department of Palaeography and Manuscripts, University College of North Wales, Bangor
UL	University Library
V & A	Victoria and Albert Museum, London
Williams (ed.), *Swift Correspondence*	Harold Williams (ed.), *The correspondence of Jonathan Swift*, 5 vols (Oxford, 1963–65)
Writings of Petty	C. H. Hull (ed.), *The economic writings of Sir William Petty*, 2 vols (Cambridge, 1899)

Dates before 1752 are given in the old style, when the new year began on 25 March, with the modern year indicated in parentheses for dates between 1 January and 24 March. Prices are in £. s. d. sterling. I have followed the common compromise of using 'Derry' to refer to the city and 'Londonderry' for the county. I have also referred to the earls, marquess and first duke of Ormond as Ormond and Ormonds. After 1688, since the second duke was frequently known as Ormonde, I have adopted that spelling, and Ormondes when the ducal dynasty is discussed.

Illustrations

Plates

I am grateful to BL for plates 1 and 2; to the Bodleian for plate 16; to Christ Church Mansion and Ipswich Borough Council Museums and Galleries for plate 12; to Christie's Images Ltd for plate 8; to the Courtauld Institute, London and Eton College for plate 23; the National Gallery of Ireland for plates 5, 9 and 10; to the NLI for plate 6; to the National Portrait Gallery, London, for plates 3 and 4; to the RCB for plates 7 and 17; to Sotheby's Picture Library for plate 25; to The Treasures of Waterford and Waterford City Council for plate 15; to Michael Campbell for plate 11; and Derry Falvey for plate 18.

Maps

Tables

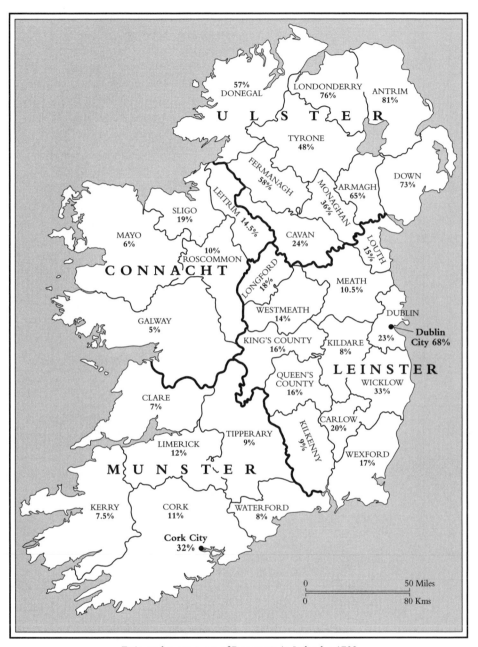

Estimated percentages of Protestants in Ireland, *c.* 1732

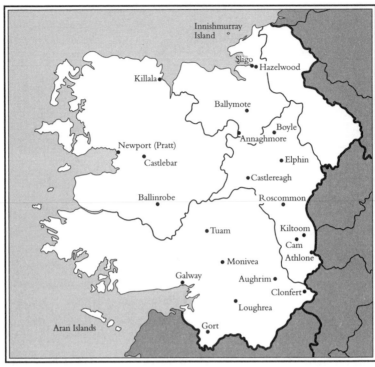

Province of Connacht

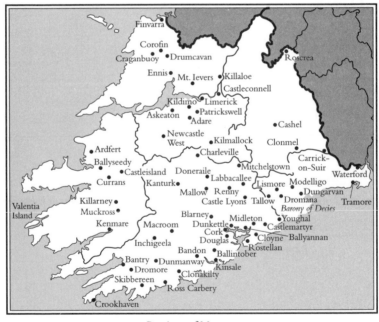

Province of Munster

Province of Ulster

Province of Leinster

Chapter 1

The Problems of Orders

I

In 1741, Sir Richard Cox contemplated writing the history of Ireland. Intending to focus on the reigns of Elizabeth I and James VI and I, together with the wars started in 1641 and 1688, he doubted 'if any revolutions of the world afford a more copious subject of history'.[1] Cox meant the English victories over the insurgent Irish, each of which had been followed by the transfer of property and power to Protestants, often recently arrived in Ireland from Scotland, Wales and England. Earlier in the eighteenth century, the archbishop of Dublin, William King, lamented the failure of his contemporaries to write an adequate history of the island. He conceded that it would be an intractable task, likely to yield 'a virulent libel, both on the conquerors and conquered'. King could recall 'no example of a country above 500 years in the possession of a people without settling it in a prospect of peace or bringing the conquered into the interest of the conquerors' other than Ireland.[2]

Neither Cox nor King undertook the taxing project. King himself and Cox's grandfather, the first Sir Richard, had earlier written to uphold the English title to and Williamite reconquest of the kingdom.[3] Each personified not just the prevalent attitudes among the Protestant population, but its different strands. Archbishop King, although a dignitary of the episcopalian Church of Ireland, descended from Scottish Presbyterians who had settled in seventeenth-century Ulster.[4] Cox's forebears had established themselves in the southern province of Munster early in the seventeenth century. There, his grandfather, the first Sir Richard Cox, had risen from modest beginnings, thanks to the law and public offices, to a position, adorned with a baronetcy, as a landed proprietor. Coming relatively late into the game, the elder Cox was edged towards the wilder uplands of West Cork.[5] Others had already grabbed the more accessible and fertile places. Indeed, Munster had one of the denser concentrations of Protestants. In 1641 there were an estimated 22,000; by 1660, perhaps

30,000.[6] Even so, if the newcomers commandeered property, they remained in a numerical minority and as a result felt vulnerable. Unevenly spread over the province, they tended – as elsewhere in Ireland – to congregate in the lush valleys, around the coast and in the relatively safe boroughs and ports. West of the River Shannon, the Protestant presence was even sparser. In 1732, there were supposed to be no more than 4,299 Protestant families in the province of Connacht. This was less than a tenth of the total population.[7] Again outposts such as the town of Sligo exerted a magnetic appeal to the Protestants. Sponsored townships, like Newport Pratt – named for its owner, the government functionary John Pratt – on the seaboard of Mayo, harboured others.[8]

Outside Munster, only in Ulster and Dublin were the total and proportion of Protestants in the population greater. In the seventeenth century, Ulster, like Munster, saw the dispossession of many existing owners and the assisted or voluntary arrival of substitutes. By the 1630s, the area may have had 15,000 British settlers, and double that number by 1660. Ulster, because close to Scotland and north-western England, and seemingly welcoming to Protestant newcomers, continued longer than Munster to attract immigrants. Particularly in the 1690s, grim conditions in western Scotland propelled more to the north of Ireland: perhaps 50,000 or even 80,000.[9] Some did not linger long. Recession and hardships propelled Ulster Scots further west, to north America.[10] Nevertheless, by 1732, Protestants formed a majority of the inhabitants in six of the nine counties of Ulster. In Antrim, they amounted to 81 per cent; in Down, 73 per cent. Overall, there were thought to be 62,624 Protestant families (or households) in the province, or nearly 60 per cent of all inhabitants.[11]

Dublin, thanks to its unique combination of functions – as capital, port, administrative, judicial, educational and cultural centre – enticed the ambitious or desperate from the rest of Ireland, as well as from overseas. In the first half of the eighteenth century, Protestants preponderated there. In 1732, they amounted to two-thirds of its recorded inhabitants. By 1706, its population was reckoned at 62,000; by 1760, perhaps 145,000. According to these estimates, it housed a concentration of between 44,000 and 75,000 Protestants.[12] This made it the Protestant stronghold within Ireland, as well as the second most populous city in the Hanoverians' empire. However, the Protestant majority was gradually but inexorably eroded over the eighteenth century, adding to the tensions within the metropolis. Elsewhere, no other town approached Dublin either in size or proportion of Protestants. The capital's nearest rival, Cork, numbered about 18,000 heads in 1706, around 37,570 by 1744, and approximately 55,640 in 1760. Of these between 33 and 40 per cent were Protestants.[13] Other towns, smaller than Cork, let alone

Dublin, also accommodated smaller proportions of Protestants in 1732: Limerick just under 30 per cent; Drogheda, 26.5 per cent; Kilkenny, 20.5 per cent and Galway, no more than 13 per cent.[14]

Estimated numbers of Protestant and Catholic families in Ireland, 1732

Province	Protestants	Catholics	Total
Connacht	4,299	44,101	48,400
Leinster	25,241	92,434	117,675
Munster	13,337	106,407	119,744
Ulster	62,624	38,459	101,083
Total	**105,501**	**281,401**	**386,902**

The revolutions benefited the forebears of Cox and King. Beneficiaries laboured to consolidate, celebrate and defend their gains, both through public activism and by their pens. Yet, despite the grandeur of the proposed theme, the younger Cox's history was never completed or published. Nor were the other schemes to write the natural and civil histories of Ireland mooted by Protestant profiteers and prophets.[15] This failure was symptomatic of the incurious and repetitive nature of most of what was printed about Ireland between the 1650s and 1760s. Numerous brochures purported to tell of Protestant Ireland. In general, they justified rather than regretted the sequence of reconquests and settlements, enforced and spontaneous, by and from Britain, which had created the dominant communities over which the likes of Cox lorded. Usually the older Ireland, with Gaelic social organization and Catholic loyalties, was decried. English and Scottish interventions were – for the most part – celebrated, although it was sometimes regretted that they had not achieved more. The literature, certainly abundant, was both partisan and derivative. Indeed, those from Ireland were tempted to devote more attention to exotic localities, such as Poland, the United Provinces or Denmark, than to their own kingdom.[16]

Two such travellers, Sir William Temple and Robert Molesworth, did look at aspects of Ireland, but cursorily. Their tracts aimed to lift Ireland to continental standards of industry and prosperity, rather than to describe its topography or classify its inhabitants.[17] Increased travel worsened the habit among some born in Ireland of belittling their island.[18] To the familiar lament that Ireland failed to meet the standards of lowland Britain was added dismay at how far Ireland lagged behind continental Europe.

Just as dazed or dazzled tourists wrote accounts which, when not simply filched from handy guides, followed conventions, entrenched stereotypes and hardly engaged with what had been seen, so reporters from Ireland fell into the same trap.[19] A treatise of 1673, promising to be fresh, repeated verbatim (and unacknowledged) what had been published earlier in the century by Sir John Davies.[20]

Themes of social and cultural change – whether projected or achieved (such as those identified by Cox) – thread through the disquisitions. Two, widely separated in time but both influential, suggest that much altered between the 1650s and 1760s. During the Cromwellian interregnum, Richard Lawrence, an army officer from England, followed numerous precedents in arguing that Ireland would be safe and prosper only when Protestants were everywhere substituted for the incumbent Catholics. Most urgently, the social, religious and military leaders of Catholic Ireland should be expropriated and expelled. Even the generality of the population, mere hewers of wood and drawers of water, were best removed to the distant and inhospitable regions beyond the River Shannon.[21] Universal exile, whether internal or external, proved impracticable, and the plan was quickly forgotten.[22] In time, too, Lawrence's own ferocity softened. By the 1680s, coming to know Ireland better as a resident, investor and trader, he realized that apparent underdevelopment was not explained solely by the shortcomings of the Catholic majority. Much responsibility rested with mistaken policies imposed from London. But he also blamed the recently settled Protestants. A few succumbed to luxury and vice; others, conspicuously in Dublin, sank into poverty. Ominously, traits previously ascribed to Catholic ignorance and indolence were appearing among the newcomers from England, Wales and Scotland. In analysing the causes, Lawrence traced much to the makers of policy. Attitudes hostile to trade and manufacture had a further depressing effect. Yet, his analysis was set in a frame in which economic torpor and social ills arose ultimately from moral failings and invited divine rebukes. Only obliquely, through strictures against selfish peers and pretentious merchants, did Lawrence address some of the structures in this world.[23]

Critiques of the behaviour of the Protestants in Ireland began even before Lawrence wrote. The shock of the 1641 uprising, when Irish Catholics rose, stimulated introspection. The Protestants' greed and selfishness had made them neglect their wider duties to the entire population in Ireland.[24] Over the next century, preachers, invited to ruminate on the past, present and future of the Protestants in Ireland, alternated between optimism and gloom. Some were cheered by evidence of peace, industry, prosperity, spreading Protestantism and even social change. Others were despondent when they detected only poverty, unrest (either open or latent), irreligion, emboldened and expanding Catholicism and a society seemingly impervious to the cultural and social forces animating Britain and continental Europe.[25] Secular commentary similarly veered between jubilation and dejection.[26] Firmly among the optimists was the author of a volume, published in 1759, which surveyed the state of Ireland.[27] Much, it seemed, had improved since Lawrence issued his jeremiads. In particular, the prosperous, whether peers, landowners or professionals, discharged their assorted functions conscientiously. In countries other than Ireland, it was conceded, might be found 'many of more popular bustle and éclat, more extensive commerce, greater opulence and pomp, but none of more general, solid and intrinsic worth'.[28] This encomium to the locals, no less than Lawrence's disparagement, spoke of the moment. In 1759–60, new moves were afoot to unite Ireland with England, and on terms detrimental to the smaller kingdom. It was important for the patriotic within Protestant Ireland to emphasize how successfully it was being run. Earlier, Lawrence had moved from demanding the absolute subordination of Ireland to English needs to an appreciation that it was better governed by those familiar with and interested in its affairs. He too, against the grain of his aggressive anti-Irishness of the 1650s, espoused Irish interests and bewailed English mistakes. He dreamed that Ireland might be turned into 'West England'.[29] By 1759, although that term was not used, some celebrated the solid progress towards that goal. Celebrants of material and ethical betterment expressed a popular variety of patriotism. The achievements, Irish Protestant patriots averred, were only possible thanks to the large measure of control which they exercised over their own affairs.[30]

Lawrence and later writers offered lengthy accounts of Ireland. Although they did not aim at the statistical precision of the contemporary political arithmeticians, they provided ample detail on economy and society. Their purposes and perspectives distorted their writings. Undoubtedly, in the intervening century, much had changed. But, according to the attitude of the commentator, the extent and speed of those changes might be either exaggerated or minimized. Nor did the attitudes themselves remain constant over a century. As the years of peace lengthened, some took a more relaxed view of the Catholic majority. Their world was no longer always regarded as threatening. Environments once described simply as dangerously primitive were compared either with the commonplace or the exotic. The imaginative saw the decaying splendours of the County Limerick town of Kilmallock as evidence of former grandeur, and likened it to Baalbek and Palmyra.[31] The younger Cox pricked the pretensions of colleagues by asserting that Ireland was no more important than Corsica.[32] Such comparisons set the kingdom securely in the context of European, not outlandish, civilizations. What once had been decried as barbarous was now thought merely backward. In part, this was because the presumptions of visitors had changed, as well as what they saw. Typical of the altered attitude was the injunction to treat the Irish as 'fellow subjects', with 'good manners, humanity and charity'.[33] By 1759, the consciously polite responded to the evidence that at least some among the leaders of Protestant Ireland had embraced the new codes of politeness. In contrast, back in the 1650s, criteria other than politeness and sociability were invoked to isolate Irish shortcomings. Yet, if the terminology (and perhaps the thinking behind it) changed, there were continuities. Certain enduring features – Catholicism, poverty or industry – still excited the same reactions. In consequence, any attempt to reconstruct the lineaments of Protestant Ireland between the 1650s and 1760s has not only to grapple with sparse or defective data but also with perplexing, cryptic and inconsistent approaches. Especially in questions of stratification and differentiation, what contemporaries thought rather than what, in retrospect, can be shown to have happened, helps more in reconstructing the contours of a changing society.

Topographical set-pieces, celebrations of change as 'improvements' and admonitions to speed those changes, took the place of social analysis. Yet the upheavals of seventeenth-century Ireland stimulated exact enquiries into who owned what. Large tracts of the island were mapped more accurately.[34] Property-owners were inventoried, usually as the prelude to their expropriation or taxation. In order to decide how inhabitants were to be treated they were classified according to confession.[35] The authorities worried that Ireland, even more than England, was underpopulated. Additionally, it contained too few Protestants and too many Catholics. In order to document these assertions, in 1736 there were published enumerations, county by county, of how many Catholic and Protestant families each contained.[36] If religion, the basis of power and property, obsessed the authorities, money also preoccupied them. Briefly in the 1660s and 1690s, parliamentary taxes were graduated according to different social orders. Cadastral enquiries promised more detailed occupational and social codifications of the population. Poll taxes and subsidies soon gave way to a hearth tax.[37] Assessment and collection required surveys of houses. Behind the levy lay an assumption that size of house, gauged by number of hearths or chimneys, accurately reflected wealth and status. It did, so the style and ambition of a residence can guide towards rankings; but in imprecise and even misleading ways.[38]

In this situation, although the state in Ireland became better informed about acreages, topography and people, it did not know how many belonged in most social categories below the parliamentary peerage. The indefatigable Sir William Petty speculated about how many might dwell in the various-sized houses. In time, revenue officers brought some precision to his conjectures. But those who assembled and analysed the statistics never engaged in the same exercises which enabled Gregory King or Joseph Massie to depict the hierarchies of late seventeenth- and eighteenth-century England.[39] This omission in Ireland was the more surprising given the abundant data generated by the upheavals under the Tudors and Stuarts. Moreover, at least one involved in this work, Petty, overseer of the land transfers during the 1650s, used it both to develop and demonstrate a method. He aimed to render his findings about Ireland and its inhabitants 'in number, weight and measure'.[40] Voluminous and innovative as his writings about Ireland are, he was as disappointingly incurious about structures as the intellectually unadventurous.[41]

II

Two traits distorted almost all accounts. Prescription was frequently confused with description. A consistent aim behind English actions in Ireland was to bring the island closer in character to England. One method was to introduce into Ireland the occupational and social template of England. Such distinctive and desirable features as peers, their titles passing to heirs by primogeniture, esquires and yeomen were imported. Once there in Ireland, it was often assumed that these groups were the exact equivalents of their English originals. This assumption can deceive. Moreover, even if some features of English society were successfully exported to Ireland, it does not follow that all were transplanted or that Protestant Ireland became an exact replica of England, with its full range of occupations and social types.

A second characteristic is the fondness of reporters for squeezing what they met in Ireland into the ready-made grid supplied by vivisectors of English society. On occasion, to be sure, the oddities of the Irish scene called for special treatment. During the 1680s, for example, the county of Westmeath was described. Among the occupiers were the *sculloges*. The want of any obvious English counterpart obliged this chronicler to retain the local coinage. Even so, for his Anglophone audience, he sought to 'English' the term, as 'farmer, or husbandman, or yet more properly, boors'. The comparison helped to place this group of strong farmers. However, the author was not content. He glossed what he had written. *Sculloges* were noteworthy because 'very crafty and subtle in all manner of bargaining, full of equivocations and mental reservations, especially in their dealings in fairs and markets, where, if lying and cheating were no sin, they make it their work to overreach anything they deal with'.[42] *Sculloges* were again considered in 1766. Nicholas, Viscount Taaffe, a panegyrist of a lost Ireland, equated them with 'that most useful body of people, called yeomanry in England'. Taaffe remembered the *sculloges* forming 'communities of industrious housekeepers . . . herded together in larger villages'. As a 'great nursery of labourers and manufacturers', their expulsion from their properties impoverished the whole island.[43] These *aperçus* typify the way in which seemingly dispassionate taxonomists of Irish communities slipped into the mode of moralists. This was not, of course, a failing unique to those contemplating Ireland.[44] Nevertheless, the habit should caution against using the occasional discussions of the Irish social structure as objective testimony to what existed.

The propensity for investing both descriptions, and the society being analysed, with moral worth runs through much of the writing on Tudor, Stuart and Hanoverian Ireland. Usages like *gneever, sculloge, scalpeen, squireen* and eventually 'middleman' acknowledged the peculiarities of the Irish scene. Otherwise, the classificatory systems already current in England were widely and uncritically employed. One term from that system, yeoman, serves to illustrate the resulting puzzles. In England itself, yeoman denoted an assemblage of laudable attributes rather than a precise occupational or tenurial category.[45] A yeomanry, because the repository of such excellent qualities as industry and loyalty, was seen as essential to Ireland. Successive plantations intended to root it there. Returns by clerks and surveyors suggested that yeomen were proliferating across the island, particularly in the areas intensively resettled from England, Wales and Scotland. By the eighteenth century, however, this optimism about the velocity and intensity of social and economic change evaporated. Instead, the worried lamented the failure of a yeomanry to develop, and proposed expedients – such as the sponsorship of tillage – which would foster it.[46] Yet, if by the mid-eighteenth century it was generally admitted that Ireland lacked a substantial yeomanry on the English model, many were styled 'yeomen'. They ranged from such improbable characters as the majordomo of Henry Ingoldsby, MP, to the notorious highwayman, James Freney.[47] As with other of these styles, notably 'gent' or 'gentleman', yeoman was more often applied by others than assumed by the holder. Frequently the listing of individuals or groups as 'yeomen' told of the inventiveness or exhaustion of harassed clerks, at a loss how to describe those with whom they were dealing and fearful lest they offend by applying a demeaning term. In flattering, they deceived: many were advanced in official documents beyond the value which they enjoyed in their immediate neighbourhoods.[48] These elisions by enumerators have to be remembered before we put too much trust in the accuracy of the terms with which they ornamented their contemporaries. The haphazardness of much commentary means that the peculiarities of the social structure evolving in early modern Ireland may be hidden behind an inappropriate English vocabulary of description. A lack of curiosity on the part of the investigators of Irish society about how the population divided other than along denominational lines largely explained the rarity of reliable classifications of the Irish Protestants (and of Catholics too).

A further obstacle to retrieving the way in which seventeenth- and eighteenth-century Ireland was ordered comes from the conflation of abstractions with persons. *Sculloges* and yeomen were expected to possess distinctive attributes. So, too, nobles properly ought to personify nobility; the gentry, gentility; the respectable, respectability. When it came to 'the quality', the imprecision of the qualities which they should display bewildered. Even with such apparently neutral categories as 'the middling' or 'lower rank', placing on the scale depended on where the appraiser stood. All codifiers brought prejudices to the task. The criteria by which they ordered their contemporaries varied. Pedigree, possessions, income or office all played a part. But which had the greatest importance was not so readily agreed. Moreover, all these distinctions might be erased by unfitting behaviour. Credit and reputation could be lost and with them public esteem. These mischances did not necessarily dethrone the offender from an eminence resulting from inheritance or wealth, but lessened their standing in the eyes of the conventional and exacting. A mother in Connacht remonstrated with a daughter-in-law about the misconduct of her husband. Mary Brabazon wailed, 'you are both, God help you, the table talk of the whole country . . . It has broke my heart to think the hopes of my family the most unfortunate man living as to reputation'.[49] Moses Leathes informed his brother in 1717 that a sister in the north of Ireland had become 'the common talk of the country'.[50] A similarly malodorous air surrounded a cadet in County Limerick in 1740s. Uncertainly located socially and economically among the 'mobbish' gentry and despised provincial attorneys, Hugh Massy was implicated in unedifying scrapes. These alone did not explain his local unpopularity. Rather, as a contemporary remarked, Massy 'has the misfortune of not being liked or regarded by any person of figure or character in this county'.[51]

Prisms refract the emergent Protestant Ascendancy in the early eighteenth century. Too often, the glasses resemble the distorting mirrors in a side-show. Nevertheless, three are worth looking in: not least to caution against accepting the verisimilitude of what they show of Queen's County, Fermanagh and the borders of Wicklow and Wexford. The operators, working while the descriptive terminology and methodologies were in flux, fully captured the inconsistencies and ambiguities of contemporary perception. Pole Cosby, squire of Stradbally (Queen's County), turned a baleful eye on his neighbours. Some attributes which he revered, such as lineage, lavishness in housekeeping, indifference to elementary economy

and a touchiness about personal honour, had an antique, even anachronistic feel. Yet, notwithstanding prejudices worthy of the untravelled who
never ventured beyond the local market, Cosby knew the continent. His
family sympathized with Protestant dissent long after most armigerous
families had embraced conformity.[52] Moreover, Cosby preserved a
hereditary antipathy towards the greatest aristocratic house of Ireland,
the Ormondes, and towards the Tories, many of whose views he seemed
to share. Inconsistent, irascible and often odd, Cosby's vignettes, if not to
be dismissed as the maunderings of a drunk, warn how subjective were
contemporaries' views of one another, perhaps because often seen through
a bibulous haze.[53] Cosby made no pretence of inventorying the entire
landed élite of his county. He seized on domestic habits or anecdotes about
political and personal conduct to delineate his neighbours. Those with
whom he had crossed swords or who had dared to usurp the supremacy
which the Cosbys sought in their locality were ridiculed as upstarts. Often
they were not; their histories in the county almost as long as that of the
Cosbys. Chief among those whom Cosby demonized was Ephraim
Dawson. The latter's misdemeanour had been to sink what he had earned
from government office into local property and then to build up, rapidly
and effectively, a political interest. To salve the wounds left when Dawson
ousted Cosby from the county seat in parliament in 1727, the latter wrote
him off as 'a mean, a very mean upstart', and circulated the canard that
Dawson's father had kept an alehouse, the Cock, in Belfast.[54]

The untrustworthiness of Cosby's account of Dawson cautions against
accepting the veracity of his (and others') thumbnail sketches. John Parnell,
a fashionable lawyer and judge, who purchased the estate of Rathleigh in
Queen's County, was recalled as 'good humoured and ready to oblige and
full of complaisance and fine speeches'. This agreeable mask hid a flawed
personality. Cosby damned the judge as having 'neither the parts nor
knowledge that his high post required'. In sum, Parnell 'was but a mushroom, a man of no family at all, at all'.[55] In so far as Parnell had bought
into county society recently, and, once the lawyer was dead, his descendants found it onerous to maintain their local prominence, Cosby was not
so wide of the target.[56] Cosby's animosity towards other neighbours led
him to invent failings. Conversely, his reasons for praise could be perverse.
He was struggling with the language at his disposal to express liking and
dislikes. The resulting discords nevertheless convey something of the
complex and confused responses of the time. Few conformed completely
to Cosby's idiosyncratic idea of the gentleman; but fewer were worthless.
Lancelot Sands of Kilcavan was personified as 'a mere county squire'.
Cosby seems to have meant by this one unpolished by training and travel.
Sands had 'no great parts or sense'. Although 'good humoured to his own',
he was also 'rough, unpolished and always spoke whatever was uppermost,

and a disobliging shocking thing he would never fail telling, even to a person's face'. He discharged his responsibilities to his family by providing adequately for them. Vital, perhaps, to the friendly portrait was the fact that Sands 'lived very plentifully and hospitably and did entertain his friends heartily and cheerfully'. Cosby also admired Squire Weldon, a reformed rake, as 'a well-bred [he was a cousin], agreeable, conversable man, and very agreeable companion'.[57] In the case of another – Colonel John Bland – recent arrival in the neighbourhood did not condemn him, as it did Dawson and Parnell. Bland sank his earnings from soldiering into an estate soon renamed Blandsfort. Cosby praised the colonel as 'a good substantial man'. Bland's son was also liked for being well read, 'a sensible and cunning artful man, a very complaisant facetious joking old man, very religious and mighty sober . . . he was universally loved by all parties, beloved and liked. He knew how to please well'.[58]

Partisanship, not solidarity, was one trait which (Cosby implied) ran through the Queen's County notables. Otherwise, the values which he most admired were not universally endorsed by his neighbours. By the 1750s, the Blands wearied of Irish life. In particular, Colonel Humphrey Bland (successor to his brother at Blandsfort) was disillusioned by financial dealings with neighbours, including Cosby. Bland vowed 'never to trust any of the country squires for the future' since they had proved so slippery. These encounters made him write off most country gentlemen in Ireland, because their estates are 'so overloaded with debts that they have scarcely a maintenance out of them, and yet never think of paying any of their creditors off, but go on the old extravagant way till the whole is gone and their families ruined'. To combat the casualness detected in Cosby and his kind, Bland urged 'a proper frugality and economy'. But such restraint, which linked credit and reputation with honest dealing and punctual payment, belonged (or so it was often argued) more to upright townsmen than feckless landowners.[59] The latter, in Bland's analysis, were afflicted by 'that foolish Irish pride, in appearing richer than they are in the eye of the world, [which] wont let them act the honest, just part'. Bland, coming late to Irish landed society, was unusually resistant to its blandishments. In his estimation, the characteristics revered as the marks of the stalwart squire by Cosby were the antithesis of gentility. Indeed, Bland thought that Scotland (where he had commanded) might suit him better.[60]

The angle from which T. Dolan approached Fermanagh's notables around 1719 differed from that of Cosby. Dolan, unlike most anatomists of early eighteenth-century Ireland, hailed from the long settled. Unsentimental about the vanquished and vanishing Gaelic order, he set out how land and power had been redistributed. Neither the once mighty – such as the Maguires and the Dolans – nor their values were forgotten. Indeed,

Dolan depicted the newcomers as taking over the principles as well as the
property of the supplanted. Customary behaviour – liberality, care for their
dependants, martial and sporting prowess – united with the novelties of
public-spiritedness and attachment to the new Hanoverian dynasty. He
extolled 'a nobility' addicted 'to recreation and pastimes of hunting,
hawking, riding, drinking, feasting and banqueting with each other'. He
detected further signs of what others might write off as undesirable
archaisms. The Fermanagh grandees delighted in the music of the harp,
played chess or at 'tables', and loved 'sciences and comical pastimes,
spending much for their credit and reputation [and were] free and boun-
tiful in spending and gifting on all necessary causes'.

'Credit and reputation' were bound up with the exercise of familiar
virtues. Many resembled those praised by Cosby. In Fermanagh, the commonalty, as far as their resources permitted, copied the expansiveness of
their betters. In addition, the newer settlers, originally Scots and English,
sometimes collected together under the umbrella of 'British', underwent
such thorough acculturation to indigenous ways that they became simu-
lacra of those whom they displaced. The newcomers' values harked back
to the old. Dolan remarked that 'they hold a liberal poor man at more
respect than a stingy rich man. Their chiefest extraordinary is drinking
strong waters, in which their commonalty are more expansive yearly
than their rent'.[61] Struggling with a sparse descriptive vocabulary, he
nevertheless conveyed ambiguities and paradoxes. Dolan read certain
indices as confirmation that the baronets, esquires and gentlemen were
fulfilling their wider obligations. Important among them was the willingness to build and entertain on a generous scale and to undertake public
office. Few would dissent from his singling out of these qualities as the
marks (and duties) of the important: again they suggested continuities
between the notables of Hanoverian Ireland and a now discredited past.[62]
Restraint and moderation were to be popularized, but somehow failed to
kindle the enthusiasm of most commentators.

Early in the 1730s, an agent, Hume, arrived from England to inspect
Lord Malton's estate astride southern Wicklow and northern Wexford.
Twenty years earlier, it had been taken in hand by the owner, who hoped
to fashion it into an exclusively 'Protestant colony'. This scheme repeated
larger-scale endeavours, notably in seventeenth-century Munster and
Ulster. Part of the problem in Wicklow reflected the presence of Protestants as head tenants. By the 1730s, having enjoyed generous terms since
at least the 1690s, many had built extravagantly and lived ostentatiously.
Among these fortunates, Hume identified several separate types. Clergy of
the established Church, lawyers and 'Irish esquires' all exhibited unwelcome features. Members of the first two groups could finance their show

from professional emoluments as well as agricultural income. However, the supplements would fail in succeeding generations. 'Irish gentlemen', meanwhile, lived at the expense of poor under-tenants whose rents were repeatedly increased. Also culpable were 'half-gentlemen', who devoted themselves to field sports and failed to teach their children any useful skills. Hume was singularly difficult to please. He decried both the survival of ways associated with the Gaelic past and Catholic present, and the craze for novelties. The latter – elegant furnishings, new beverages, foods and recreations – might have been applauded as signs that English civility was permeating the settlement. Instead Hume read the material culture of Malton's lucky tenants as evidence of self-indulgence, indolence and parasitism. Running through this critique is a belief that certain kinds of display inflicted ethical as well as economic harm.

Hume was not unique in approaching social analysis with such presuppositions. Especially those disappointed that Ireland had not become more evidently Protestant and prosperous looked for moral as much as physical explanations. The rulers and propertied were failing in their duties. What Hume spotted in his microcosm had been noted earlier by Lawrence, and struck other observers like Bishop Berkeley and Dr Madden.[63] Such commentaries, seemingly authoritative, created vivid images of Ireland which discredited some among its Protestant inhabitants. Agents sent especially unflattering reports back to absentee proprietors. Hume, fresh from the packet-boat from England, fortified his claims to permanent employment by disparaging what his predecessors had or had not accomplished. Sometimes, too, agents covered their own failures or frauds by exaggerating the disorder in their bailiwicks. Malton in Yorkshire, primarily concerned with what the Irish holdings yielded, was neither inclined nor equipped to check Hume's dispatches. Yet the jaundiced accounts of those who had seen conditions at first hand were seized upon, not just by outsiders, but by local patriots, to explain the malaise which beset the island.[64]

III

On the flimsy foundations of what partisans observed of the quirks and failings of individuals were raised more elaborate theories. Groups, such as the absent, middlemen, 'half' or 'half-mounted' gentlemen, bore special responsibility for the retarded nature of the Irish culture, economy and society.[65] Moralizing of this kind was based on the belief that certain elements in society were not pulling their weight. It discloses little of the underlying structures of the newer Ireland. From the skeletal remains, the striking rather than the typical stand out: peers, baronets, esquires and gentlemen. From this habit of taking the important and self-important at their own inflated estimations arises the notable oddity of equating Protestant Ireland with 2,000–3,000 landowners. By the mid-eighteenth century, the total Protestant population numbered at least 400,000. Yet, it would seem, less than 1 per cent of this contingent dominated Protestant Ireland. It is possible that wealth, public activism and cultural innovation may have conferred a disproportionate influence. In accepting this contention, there is a danger of taking the landed minority at its own high assessment, and so inflating its importance. Cosby, Dolan and Hume mentioned among local notables occasional clerics, lawyers, office-holders and even traders. Mostly, these professionals and merchants lived not in the towns but in the countryside where they had lately joined the landed order. Their assimilation implied that the community of country squires recruited itself from a variety of sources. This recruitment also suggests that those who prospered in towns wanted only to quit them as quickly as possible.[66] This exaggerated the eagerness to exchange the city for rural life. Furthermore, it belonged to a more general belief in the superiority of the landed over traders, craftsmen and artificers. The autonomous activities and distinctive values of the urban or metropolitan were consistently depressed. Anatomies of Ireland sometimes appreciated the strength and wealth of Dublin and a few larger ports, but did little to analyse their occupational and social structures. This problem was compounded by the early urban histories in Ireland. At best, they appended lists of civic office-holders.[67]

In 1687, a reasonably astute observer guessed that the freeholders in Ireland totalled 3,000.[68] The number crept upwards in the early eighteenth century, when extra freeholds were created for electoral purposes. This growth supports later estimates of a Protestant élite of perhaps 5,000.[69] However, it is clear that the great majority of Irish Protestants were not landed proprietors. Many – perhaps most – did not even live in the countryside. Towns had always been conceived in Ireland as bastions of English civility. Deliberately, in the aftermath of the uprisings of the 1640s and 1689–90, the boroughs were transformed into redoubts of the English and Protestant interests.[70] A much larger proportion of Protestants than Catholics dwelt in them. Petty said 50 per cent.[71] This being the case, although some doubled as country squires and urban *rentiers*, or as landed gentleman and office-holders or professionals, the majority followed callings remote from those of the leisured countryman. This was true of the bulk of more than 3,000 freemen in mid-eighteenth-century Dublin. As freemen, they enjoyed privileges of citizenship. In consequence they belonged to and benefited from the embryonic Ascendancy.[72] These freemen were a small fraction of the 45,000 in Dublin, whom enquirers in 1733 identified as conforming to the established Church of Ireland.[73] Few of the 3,000 freemen and fewer still of maybe 45,000 Protestants in Dublin were mentioned by the social codifiers.[74]

Dublin housed the densest concentration of Protestants. They ranged from recognizable notables, pseudo-gentry and simple citizens to the unenfranchised and property-less. Other towns added substantially to this total of these often disregarded Protestants. Across the island, there survived 54 boroughs in which the franchise was vested in the freemen or a wider body of Protestant and male householders.[75] In these municipalities, the citizenry numbered anything from 120 to almost 500. In 1729, the freemen of the city of Cork totalled more than 500. Non-residents were listed promiscuously alongside residents. The lord-lieutenant, together with almost forty peers, bishops, judges and knights, were honorific members of the civic body. How many of more than 100 esquires and forty-four gentlemen lived and worked in the city is more difficult to know. About 164 designated as merchants, twenty-five butchers, twenty-three clothiers, nine coopers, six brewers, six apothecaries, four bakers and four chandlers helped to complete the citizenry. Virtually all can be assumed to have been active in Cork life.[76] In the County Waterford port of Dungarvan, between 400 and 500 participated in the election of 1703.[77] At Youghal in 1721, 244 were named as freemen.[78] Further down the Cork coast, 175 freemen were listed at Clonakilty in 1725, and at Kinsale 159 voted in a by-election in the same year.[79] Four hundred and thirty were enumerated as freemen of the Kilkenny borough of Inistiogue in 1751. They included a bellman, boatman, cooper, gardener, smith, shoemaker and tailor.[80] In the midland borough of Athlone, 595 participated in the 1761 election.[81] Even where full political rights were more restricted, as in the Protestant enclave of Bandon, with the franchise confined to the provost (or mayor) and a dozen burgesses, a larger and more variegated Protestant community can be glimpsed. A Bandon 'patriot club' formed in 1753 included 'weavers, combers, shopkeepers, blue dyers, attorneys, farmers, &c.' At a meeting of its thirty-three members, the chair was taken by a writing master. Four shopkeepers, an apothecary, an innkeeper, butcher, miller, two barbers, two maltsters, a joiner and an attorney attended. But the bulk of the company was formed by weavers, drapers, combers and clothiers. Others present were involved in the drinks trade.[82] These, 'inconsiderable people' or 'the middling people', were sometimes blamed for fissures within the ruling Protestant interest.[83] 'Ungovernable woolcombers and low tradesmen' were thought to disturb an otherwise tranquil and united world.[84] Yet it was recognized that these laborious elements were necessary to a thriving Protestant Ireland. Moreover, just as some located the economic and ethical heart of a civilized and industrious Ireland in the towns, others went further and venerated the respectable town-dwellers.

The opportunities for the 'inconsiderable' to act on a national stage, primarily through parliamentary elections, were at best occasional.[85] Their leverage diminished during the eighteenth century as more non-resident freemen, largely drawn from the rural squirearchy, were enfranchised.[86] Numerous boroughs functioned only as devices to return a brace to the House of Commons. However, in the thirty to fifty which regulated their localities, the active freemen were taught the civic arts. The work – letting small plots of land, overseeing markets, appointing to corporation offices and policing the locality – was parochial. It could also be venal. Potentially valuable property was leased on advantageous terms to the burgesses and their cronies. At the same time, these groups did sometimes promote the prosperity, health and pleasure of their inhabitants.[87] In consequence, the surviving freemen boroughs were cherished as, 'in their institution, the best school for the vulgar to learn and to practise virtue and public spirit in'. Between 3,000 and 5,000 provincial townsmen were given a chance to participate, and so to learn of 'liberty, power, pre-eminence and distinction'.[88] Towns with their councils, guilds and courts replicated the outlets in the counties – magistracy, grand jury, shrievalty, militia, barony and manor – for the qualified to join in the business of running Protestant Ireland. The freemen of the towns, when those in Dublin are added, totalled perhaps 6,000 to 8,500. They considerably outnumbered the freeholders on whom so much of rural rule devolved.

Both in theory and practice, towns best accommodated the purpose and the personnel of the Protestant Ascendancy. Yet most of the participants remain, if not anonymous, unconsidered because seemingly 'inconsiderable'. The obscurity of individuals and occupational groups within the boroughs largely explains the scant attention paid to them in treatments of Protestant Ireland. A little of the collective activity, notably in the corporation and guilds, has recently been brought into the light.[89] Also, occasional town-dwellers, like the Dubliner John Putland, can be fleshed out. His multifarious activities, fitfully documented, reveal his importance as exemplar and executant of Protestant designs. Putland had risen through the exertions of his forebears in the trades of Dublin and the profitable offices of the Protestant kingdom.[90] By the 1740s he guided the Dublin Society, the Physico-Historical Society and the board of Mercer's Hospital. Wealthy and cultivated, he abstained from parliament and any recorded municipal office. His activism was possible only in the urban setting, although financed by the rents of farms and town tenements. Yet, such is the imbalance in surviving evidence and recent writing that

Putland is entirely eclipsed by the first duke of Leinster, whose contribution to Hanoverian Ireland was dwarfed by Putland's.

The crowded and vibrant spaces of the towns, in which the likes of Putland flourished, delighted enthusiasts. They also excited apprehensions. Some reporters, fearful of the towns as points of contagion, ignored or diminished their role. In addition, an often artificial opposition between the interests and values of town and country might be postulated. Further anxieties arose from the presence, particularly in Dublin and Ulster, of numerous Protestant nonconformists. The survival after 1660 of Protestant dissent embarrassed and split the Irish Protestant interest. Its persistence confused any simple picture of Protestant Ireland. Some denominations like the English Presbyterians and Quakers proved tenacious, but remained small. The latter may have had 6,500 members by the time of George I's accession. By 1725 the Baptists in Ireland, progeny of the mid-seventeenth century, had dwindled to perhaps 1,500 to 2,000.[91] The Scottish Presbyterians, centred in but spreading beyond Ulster, and (from the 1740s) the Methodists were resilient and more numerous.[92]

After 1704, when a Test Act was passed, Protestant dissenters were – in common with Catholics – denied full citizenship. Yet, at times of danger, especially in 1688–90, 1715 and 1745–46, security required that all Protestants unite. Furthermore, Protestant nonconformists were to the fore in promoting useful industries, particularly the manufacture of textiles. Also, as fecklessness and idleness came to be seen as Protestant as much as Catholic failings, Quakers and Presbyterians with their thrift and industry seemed proof against such infections. Some dissenters visibly prospered.[93] What should have reassured the champions of Protestant Ireland increasingly dismayed them. The success of nonconformists, often thought greater than was the case, reproved the adherents of the established Church. In describing the triumphs of the dissenters, especially the Presbyterians, there was a tendency to write only of undifferentiated aggregations. Again this left the middle ranks in shadows. By the early eighteenth century, a process of attrition and the pressures – legal and social – to conform to the state Church had virtually extinguished dissent among the peerage and squirearchy.[94] Instead congregations derived their strength from the towns, and the middle and lower people. As early as the 1690s, an observer in Dublin fretted because so few of the middling sort followed the state cult. Devotees of the Church of Ireland were said to be drawn either from the quality or from 'ordinary handicraftsmen'. In contrast, the dissenting congregations contained 'substantial shopkeepers and tradesmen'. At the same time, it was noted that the two eastern counties of Ulster, Down and Antrim, were well settled with Protestants of the middling and lower orders, many of them Scottish Presbyterians.[95] This impression of the solidity of urban nonconformity was confirmed from Dublin in 1749. A list of the enfranchised revealed that among more than 2,800 freemen, 14.5 per cent were Protestant dissenters. In the most prestigious of the guilds, that of the merchants, the percentage rose to 22.[96]

Pessimism about the weakness of the established Church of Ireland among the *menu peuple* ignored more hopeful signs. St Werburgh's parish in the shadow of Dublin Castle in 1716 was said to contain 'mostly shop-keepers and tradesmen'. The same conclusion is suggested by what is known of the pew-holders and functionaries of other city churches.[97] The poor and humble, however, posed an even greater problem for the Church of Ireland. In and around the capital it was acknowledged in George I's reign that there were seats for no more than a third of the possible wor-shippers, and these places were reserved chiefly for those who could pay. The near invisibility of this broad base of the Protestant interest is wors-ened by their effective exclusion from the city churches. In other towns, once churches were reordered with fixed seating, the difficulty recurred. The poor, without places, were most likely to absent themselves from Protestant worship. By staying away, they joined the majority, also mainly poor but in addition Catholic. Such behaviour encouraged a tendency to equate Catholicism with indigence and indolence, to regard it as a cause and consequence of poverty, and to fear that poor Protestants were being assimilated to popery and its ways.

The parish, although it acquired fewer secular functions than its counterparts in England and Wales, was nevertheless a principal nursery for civic concern.[98] Service as churchwardens, sidesmen, members of select vestries or assessors and collectors of rates differentiated a minority of activists from the generality. Often, these humdrum tasks were undertaken by the locally important (or self-important), who were also to the fore in the affairs of guilds, municipal corporations, Masonic lodges and voluntary associations. With occasional exceptions, Catholics and Protestant dissenters were denied these outlets through which to develop and refine public virtues. After 1704, the Test Act required communion according to the rites of the established Church of Ireland to qualify for full citizen-ship. Substantial dissenters bowed to legal and social pressures by practising occasional or full conformity. They even rented pews in Church of Ireland buildings, as with the Quakers at Edenderry in County Offaly.[99]

Especially in the countryside, dissenters of social eminence had all but vanished by 1714. Among the middling and lower sorts, principally in Ulster, nonconformity endured. Scottish Presbyterians no less than the Catholics were excluded from active citizenship of the parish, guild, corporation and county magistracy. The Presbyterians, subject to a sacra-mental test and despairing of concessions to comprehend them within the state Church, directed their energies into their own institutions. Parallel to the state Church an alternative Presbyterian structure was erected. It rose from the parish and kirk session, through synods, to the general assembly. Like the Church of Ireland vestries, the nonconforming congregations dealt with multifarious tasks. Presbyterians shut out of corporate affairs in towns like Belfast, Coleraine and Derry, instead dispatched the business, both secular and spiritual, generated by the meeting house and its members.[100] This dull administration, and those who did it, hardly detained observers of later seventeenth- and eighteenth-century Ireland, except as a possible seedbed of protest. Once more, activities and activists, certainly more numerous and arguably more representative of Protestant Ireland than the grandees of the countryside, were neglected. The extent to which an alternative Protestant society, even an embryonic free state, was fashioned by the Presbyterians of Ulster awaits elucidation alongside the republic of the Protestant conformists erected in Dublin and the bigger towns, which is described below.[101]

Even more shadowy, at present, than the alternative structures of Presbyterian Ireland are those of Catholic Ireland. Want of property, and so of money and free time, doomed almost all Catholics to the frustrations of a life outside the ken of official institutions. What secular tasks attached to the Catholic parish, especially when in Dublin and other towns it took on a fixed and continuing form, have hardly been discerned, so great has been the concentration on bishops, either absent and delinquent or heroic and laborious. Education, charity and even moral regulation may in the course of the eighteenth century have allowed the laity greater scope for useful and communal endeavours comparable to those of the select vestrymen in the Church of Ireland parishes. From time to time, knowing or nervous Protestants had spies report on what occurred in Catholic churches. Alarmist stories usually circulated as a result.[102] Otherwise, what is remarkable about the routine correspondence of Protestants is the lack of reference to the Catholics with whom they were surrounded. Comment tended to generalize about the threats of popery, priestcraft, Rome, and the Romans' designs for absolute monarchy. Catholicism in the abstract, whether as political, theological or ecclesiological system, not Catholics as individuals, was discussed. When, at moments of imagined or real danger, Catholics were personified they were given many of the attributes which elsewhere conventionally attached to the 'mob' or 'the rascal multitude'. They were feared more for their numbers and their poverty than for their religious principles.

The rarity of explicit comments on specific Catholic neighbours or acquaintances might suggest that the Protestants were able to seal themselves hermetically from these potential sources of pollution and competition. Except for the wealthiest peers and some settlements in eastern Ulster, any separation was not physical. Despite efforts during the

1650s to reserve all urban property for Protestants and to expel virtually all Catholics from walled towns and ports, all outside Ulster retained sizeable Catholic presences. Moreover, although Catholics were relegated to the poorer holdings and cabins, where possible outside the walls of the place, strict segregation was impossible. Even corporations with a reputation for Protestant bigotry, such as Youghal, appreciated the value of Catholic trade and custom, and so in 1729 readmitted some to the mercantile privileges of the borough.[103] In the streets and shops of the towns, Catholics were encountered daily. So, too, in the countryside, as tenants and labourers they were ubiquitous. Most importantly, they entered Protestant homes as servants. Protestant comments on Catholic foibles typically arose from debates about the character of possible tenants and domestics.[104]

Stereotyping instead of exact observation could cause Protestants to assume that the lazy, slatternly or poor must be Irish and Catholic. One who made this assumption, Edward Synge, bishop of Elphin, in 1751 had to confess his error. He resented giving a bed to a traveller because she looked like 'the errantest Irish trull', only to discover that his visitor was 'a protestant, of an English family, and a very creditable one, tho' now low in condition'.[105] On the one hand, the ease with which, at least in their recorded comments, Irish Protestants generally ignored the Catholics around them could be interpreted as evidence of growing Protestant confidence. By 1706, five out of every six Catholics could be described as 'poor, insignificant slaves, fit for nothing but to hew wood and draw water'.[106] The formerly mighty were dead, exiled or stripped of places and property. As a collective, Catholics, like the poor, were, alternately, objects of fear or contempt, projects of improvement, pity or indifference. How this degraded majority regarded its supplanters is a subject which, in time, will alter perspectives on the Protestants who engrossed power and positions. Irish and Catholic critics were no more sensitive to the minuter notations on the social scale than were the English and Protestant commentators. It did not take the anger of the dispossessed to identify the quirks and failings of the incumbents of Protestant Ireland.[107]

Groups which come momentarily into focus, notably freeholders and freemen, probably constituted no more than 5 per cent of the entire Protestant presence. The majority of conforming Protestants, no less than the generality of Catholics and dissenters, constitute a hidden Ireland. Succeeding chapters will try to bring more into the light. Among the newly established, no order aroused more criticism, as well as fawning, than that conventionally situated at the apex: the parliamentary peerage. Alone of the orders, its membership was precisely defined and therefore readily quantified. The lay peers irradiate the prevailing gloom, so it is with them that this survey begins.

Chapter 2

Peers

The peerage, despite an eagerness to depict Ireland as an *ancien régime* in an aristocratic century, has been strangely neglected. This neglect revives the suspicion, raised already, that formal rankings could vary from those current among contemporaries, and that qualities other than lineage and heredity (supposedly pronounced among the peerage) were esteemed more. Often hierarchies of regard and intrinsic worth diverged startlingly from the conventional table of ranks. This divergence, arguably sharper in Ireland than in Britain, may explain the meagre attention accorded to the peers there.

Ireland, as part of its gift from its conqueror, received a hereditary peerage. Because it had first been introduced as a device of foreign plantation, it might be repudiated for the same reasons. Indigenous Irish society had also been organized hierarchically, with hereditary attributes cherished. But the native lordships descended according to rules different from those which regulated the earldoms and baronies introduced from outside. Some of those alternative values around which nobility and gentility were organized survived into the late seventeenth and eighteenth centuries after the Gaelic lordships had been extinguished. These survivals could have denied legitimacy to the hierarchy, headed by peers, which the English had imposed on Ireland.

In practice, the peerage was regarded ambivalently. The idea that an alternative – if now spectral – aristocracy survived beneath the one overlaid by the interlopers was not the prime reason for this ambivalence. By the eighteenth century, the Irish lay peerage was composed of assorted elements. Old Irish, such as the Macarthys, Macdonnells and O'Briens, mingled with Old English, like the Barrys, Burkes, Butlers and Talbots, on the benches of the Irish House of Lords. An influential celebrant of the older Ireland, Geoffrey Keating, felt that these nobles admirably embodied the attributes of nobility. Nevertheless, Keating shared with other conservatives a disdain for some of more obscure and recent origins lately ennobled.[1] Undoubtedly, Irish honours were inflated in the early seventeenth century. Even so, a rough congruence was maintained between length of settlement in Ireland, landed wealth and place in the pyramid. This relationship persisted into the eighteenth century. By then only five of the active lords could trace their ancestry back to the indigenous Gaels of the island. Another nine could place their origins in Ireland among the Old English who had settled before the sixteenth-century Reformation. The presence of representatives of such venerable dynasties attested to the agility with which the canny had adjusted to radically altered conditions. But the bulk of the parliamentary peerage in Georgian Ireland now belonged to families which had established themselves in Ireland during the heyday of conquest and plantation between the 1530s and 1641. Of the fifty-nine families whose members were active in the House of Lords between 1692 and 1727, it has been calculated that thirty-nine had arrived in Ireland during this period of most intensive resettlement under the Tudors and early Stuarts. Only five of the peerage dynasties had come to Ireland after 1641. As in aristocracies everywhere, and contrary to what critics maintained, it took time for the thrusting to ascend the social ladder.[2]

A parliamentary peerage appeared in Ireland as part of the paraphernalia of conquest and attempted Anglicization. In the aftermath of invasion, Ireland, like England itself after the Norman conquest or parts of France during the Lancastrian occupation, endured the establishment of an imported aristocracy. By the sixteenth century, when England sought to set its authority over Ireland on more secure foundations, peerages were important in this artillery. Heads of local septs were invited to swap their customary lordships for English titles.[3] These were to be governed by primogeniture and would carry seats in the upper house of the Irish parliament. Some, notably Macarthy, Macdonnell, O'Brien (two lines), O'Donnell and O'Neill snatched what was on offer. Thus the earldoms of Clancarty, Antrim, Thomond, Inchiquin, Tyrconnell and Tyrone were inaugurated. Even so, these changes in designation were not always accompanied by the expected cultural and political mutations into Anglicized loyalists. The O'Briens, earls of Thomond, straddled this world awkwardly. In 1639, the fifth earl ordained that a monument to his father be erected in Limerick cathedral. The figures were to be portrayed 'in their parliamentary robes, swords and crownets, according to their degree'. Earlier, in 1617, this father had bequeathed to him the earldom, 'whose rightful inheritance it is', rather than relying simply on descent by primogeniture. The fourth earl had been determined that his sons be reared in the reformed religion to which he adhered. At the same time, he exhorted them to 'be true, respective and honourably affected towards the gentlemen and inhabitants of Thomond, whom I have ever found as honest, faithful followers to me as any nobleman had'.[4] As yet, while the Thomonds had adopted some of the ways approved by the new English government of Ireland, they had not entirely forsaken the old.[5]

Another, larger addition to the Irish peerage was made early in the seventeenth century. It paralleled a contemporary inflation of honours in England. James I and Charles I readily gratified suitors and favourites in England and Scotland, and eased their financial straits, by selling Irish titles. Between 1603 and 1641, eighty newcomers were elevated to Irish peerages. It has been reckoned that only twenty-four of the recipients were already closely linked with Ireland.[6] This unfamiliarity could lead to embarrassing incidents which did nothing for the credit of the Irish peerage as a whole. An English purchaser of an Irish title dithered over which to select. He was 'certain that there is such towns as Lucan and Granard, but can not find it in the map, but divers tell me for certain there is such a place . . . If it is possible we will change Granard for a whole county'.[7] By attaching so many strangers to Ireland through peerages with seats in the Dublin legislature, the early Stuarts may have planned to speed the integration of the élites in their kingdoms. In time, those previously unconnected with the distant kingdom of Ireland would assume its leadership.[8] But this did not immediately happen. Instead, the policy devalued Irish peerages, further divided the members of the Irish Lords and worsened the problems of parliamentary management. Not until later monarchs abandoned the early Stuarts' philosophy and awarded peerages more sparingly did Irish titles cease to be despised as pinchbeck versions of the genuine. Those with Irish peerages of some antiquity, such as Kildare or Ormond, were mortified to find honours that had once acknowledged service to the crown devalued.

Between 1641 and the 1770s, the Irish peerage was expanded more slowly. Greater care was taken to match creations to worth, as measured by revenues and adherence to the English sovereign. This restraint did something to restore the standing of Irish peers. Nevertheless, the trade in Irish creations did not altogether end. In 1661, a viscountcy was touted for £2,200, and in Queen Anne's reign another was alleged to be on offer for £1,200. Disquiet at what was accounted 'a traffic' in Irish titles still depressed demand and dimmed lustre.[9] A few with the requisite qualifications for ennoblement refused it. Sir Maurice Eustace, lord chancellor from 1660 to 1665, and Sir William Petty, the richest commoner in Charles II's Ireland, both rejected peerages on the not wholly specious grounds that they did not want to burden themselves with the extra expenditure that a peerage would inevitably bring.[10] This hesitancy persisted. In 1743, the lord chancellor, Thomas Wyndham declined a title. 'He thinks his fortune not sufficient for his son, in case any accident should happen to himself.'[11] Another rich and successful commoner after the Williamite revolution, William Conolly, resisted invitations to enter the Lords. In 1720, it was still confidently predicted that he was to be made an earl.[12] Conolly may have looked on a title as an unnecessary decoration when already he revelled in abundant power and wealth. In addition, his political mastery was based on the Irish House of Commons and a conscious cultivation of the ways of a bluff squire. This political idiom, aggressively non-aristocratic, was adopted by Conolly's political successor, Henry Boyle. The latter, although a cadet of an Irish aristocratic house, also played up his dual persona as provincial squire and Speaker of the Commons.[13] When, in 1756, Boyle finally accepted a remove to the upper house as earl of Shannon, many regarded it as a betrayal of the simpler, patriotic values which he had previously espoused. To cynics the elevation confirmed his reputation as 'a great pretended patriot and violent grumbler'.[14] Such reactions are reminiscent of the sometimes unfriendly feelings towards both the institution and specific members of the Irish peerage.

Hostility certainly existed. Some in eighteenth-century Ireland rejoiced that their county contained no resident peer to whom court must be paid. Thus, in 1757, a Protestant clergyman in County Waterford was pleased that he had 'no Leviathan to contend with. No lord, knight or esquire in my parish'. The landlord of Gloster in County Offaly, Trevor Lloyd, jibbed at obeying the joint governors of his county, Lords Belfield and Molesworth.[15] Earlier, a novice lawyer from a squirearchical family lamented the behaviour of nominal superiors. 'I could wish that our great men when they came to it could learn to jest and play as genteely as we inferiors'.[16] This unwillingness unthinkingly to honour the socially pre-eminent arose from contempt for particular peers. Personal failings, intrinsic to any hereditary system, induced scepticism when, either in theory or practice, peers aspired to lead Irish Protestant society. In the 1720s, both Jonathan Swift and his literary collaborator, Thomas Sheridan, voiced some of the obvious objections to the pretensions of the aristocracy.[17] Whatever merits had entitled the originals to ennoblement, over subsequent generations the hierarchies of revenues, virtue and service slipped further and further apart from the table of ranks. A willingness to apply other criteria of 'true' nobility accounts for something of the continuing disdain for Irish peers. Of the third earl of Orrery, a youth in the 1680s, it was acknowledged, that 'tho by the sweetness of his temper, a very amiable man', he 'was no ways conspicuous for knowledge or erudition'. More roundly, Lord Blessington was dismissed in 1696 as 'a man made of vanity and froth, and, except his being a bigot to superconformity, good for nothing'.[18] Another from the circle of Swift and Sheridan, Patrick Delany, don and fashionable Dublin preacher, regularly attacked behaviour characteristic of the aristocracy: duelling, gambling, excess in dress and diet, pride, avarice and a cavalier attitude towards debts. Delany, in many respects a defender of the existing social hierarchy, nevertheless rejected notions of inherited nobility as 'foolish and ill-founded'. He insisted that 'nothing but a man's merit can entitle to any degree of distinction and regard'. Some who vaunted their distinguished lineage frequently had 'much lower and meaner origins, from slaves and syco-phants, from robbers and murderers'. Furthermore, he located virtue, as well as piety, among those (like himself) of 'the middle state'.[19] These doubts were strengthened by a series of incidents, such as the trial and conviction of Lord Santry for murdering a servant or the brawl in which Lord Allen wounded the constable who had hauled him from a Dublin brothel in the early hours of the morning.[20]

So prevalent was this contempt thought to be that eighteenth-century Ireland, notwithstanding its character as *ancien régime*, accorded its nominal social leaders an attenuated role. In parliament, the initiative had passed by the 1690s to the Commons.[21] As the Lords dwindled in importance in the legislative and political processes, so did attendance. During the reigns of Anne and George I, of nearly 130 entitled to sit in the upper house, first about thirty and then perhaps forty did so. One result was to enhance the importance of the twenty-two bishops, already vital to a Protestant majority, in the business of the house.[22] Similarly, across the island, many counties and most parishes lacked a resident peer. In consequence, others led. Again, the spiritual peers more actively exhibited the benevolence, cultivation and hospitality intended to give Protestantism a benign face in the Irish provinces. Indifference to, if not outright hostility towards, lay peers cautioned the wise against insisting on their claims to consideration. When Santry was arraigned for his crime, Archbishop Boulter of Armagh counselled that the peer suffer the full consequences so that the nation would see that 'no man's quality can entitle him to destroy his fellow subjects with impunity'.[23] By 1767, Lord Southwell was realist enough to recognize the consequences of his own absence from, and shrinking rents in, County Limerick. He sensed that any intervention in the coming parliamentary contest would be counter-productive: 'a letter from a Lord could ruin the best election that ever was held for a county'.[24]

The notion that the beneficiaries of inherited privileges should earn respect was not unique to Ireland. Across Europe critiques of hereditary aristocracy proposed alternative criteria for evaluating and deciding who should head local society. Hostile assessments coexisted with outward def-erence and continuing enthusiasm for the hereditary principle. In Ireland, as elsewhere, the relative importance of lineage, merit, service and wealth in constituting the peerage was not universally agreed. Irish peers were also caught in the turbulence which agitated the kingdom throughout the centuries of conquest and resettlement. Swift vividly noted that 'the dunghill having raised a huge mushroom of short duration is now spread to enrich other men's lands'.[25] A system governed by strict primogeniture did not sit easily with the traditions of Gaelic Ireland. In 1745, Gerald Dillon contrasted the achievements of non-inheriting younger brothers with those of elder brothers who generally prove 'inactive, indolent and extravagant'. A common enough complaint, in Ireland it perhaps implied affection for the now proscribed practices which had not automatically favoured the eldest.[26]

The extent to which peers' 'title[s] and privileges outlive their estates' could be illustrated from the examples of numerous penurious aristocrats eking out a sorry existence in Dublin, the Irish provinces, England or cheap *pensions* on the continent. Subsidy assessments showed the extremes of wealth. In Charles II's reign, they ranged from £110 to be levied on the earl of Cork and Burlington or £100 on the duke of Ormond to a mere £2 10s. expected from Lord Cavan and £2 from Lord Castlehaven. Cork and Burlington and Ormond, each with rentals valued at between £25,000 and £30,000, inhabited different worlds from the impecunious.[27] By the early eighteenth century, the fortunate like Anglesey and Shelburne each drew about £6,000 annually from their Irish properties. But the average income of those with Irish peerages remained considerably lower. The straitened nagged the government for jobs or gratuities which might enable them to maintain suitable appearances. In 1720, George I succumbed to the pleadings of Lord Blayney. To an allowance of £182 10s. was added an annual pension on the Irish military establishment of £300. The king recognized the zeal and loyalty of Blayney, and that with 'the lowness of his circumstances, he can neither live suitably to his quality nor exert his endeavours so far as he is desirous for our service'. But the king was also inspired by a more general principle, 'being desirous to support the dignity of our nobility'.[28]

Typical of the pass to which peers might be reduced were the late seventeenth-century earls of Cavan and Roscommon, who depended on the charity of the state. Pensions of £150 or £200, although literally 'the bread' for the likes of the indigent Roscommon, did not finance any lordly establishment.[29] In the 1690s, the threadbare Lord Cavan, camping out in rooms in a back alley off the Dublin poultry market, begged a bishop not to visit since the lodgings were 'not fit for a person of your quality to come into'.[30] A successor of this Cavan, as impoverished as his forebear, tried to cash in one of the few finite assets of Irish peers: legal privilege during the parliamentary session. The resulting scandal, in which Lords Altham, Blessington and Roscommon were also implicated, tarnished the entire order.[31] Instead of a disinterested nobility, these peers were associated with cupidity. Again, in 1744, Cavan, together with Mayo and Rosse, each received an annual £300, 'to support a little their honour which they are not in any measure able to do without it'. However, they still teased and solicited for more.[32] In 1746, the death of the second Viscount Boyne brought the title to a cousin, said to be married to a blacksmith's daughter. It was predicted that the new viscount would apply 'for support of the same kind with that which many of his brother peers subsist by'. Sure enough, he was soon granted an annual pension of £200.[33]

The personal failings which reduced a peer to a suppliant were frankly admitted by Viscount Strangford. Given alms of £200 p.a. by the state from the age of eighteen, he was even housed in Dublin Castle. Having entered the established Church, he was nominated by the government as Swift's successor as dean of St Patrick's in Dublin only to be black-balled by the chapter. Soon he had conjured the valuable deanery of Derry from the administration.[34] With a show of candour, Strangford confessed to the 'former impudencies I was unwarily drawn into by an empty rank, I vainly imagined would infallibly lead to certain advancement'. These exaggerated expectations prevented his 'acting up to the strict rules of economy'. By 1760, he had arranged matters so as to leave only £300 p.a. to support himself, his wife and three children. With a dramatic flourish beloved of impoverished magnificoes, he announced, 'this moderate income requires a total retreat from the world'. Simultaneously, he rattled his begging bowl in the face of Dublin politicians. He hoped that the king might continue the pension of £250 allowed his mother and himself when the former died. He also solicited a commission in the dragoons for his nine-year-old son. A few years later he exchanged the deanery for the archdeaconry of Derry, so 'putting a large sum of money in their pockets' and defrauding those to whom tithes had been let. Strangford missed the bishopric which he craved and instead was expelled from the House of Lords in 1784 for accepting a bribe.[35] Equally importunate was Lord Mountcharles. In 1755 he wrote, 'I think I am greatly neglected by the viceroys of Ireland, for I never received a favour from any'. He had demanded the mastership of the ordnance from Dorset. From Dorset's successor he begged the alnagership and an advance in the peerage to a viscountcy. Mountcharles was mortified to see other peers, like the Hillsboroughs, 'loaded with favours both in England and Ireland without half my interest in either kingdom or the tenth part of my family pretensions'.[36]

The mismatch between peers' pretensions to nobility in conduct and their shabby stratagems may have been more striking in Ireland than elsewhere. Apart from the effects of the genetic lottery and temperamental incapacity, peers in Ireland suffered from a series of problems which, both individually and cumulatively, depressed their condition. The length and severity of warfare in the 1640s and 1689–91 not only deprived numerous landowners of their rents but also burdened them with extraordinary expenses as they raised and paid soldiers to defend their holdings. The lucky were recompensed with extra lands. Nevertheless, the debts which had been incurred, especially in the 1640s, dogged several aristocratic families, such as the Butler dukes of Ormonde and Macdonnell marquesses of Antrim, through successive generations.[37] The apparently more serious consequences of warfare for Irish than for English peers may owe much to more primitive methods of paying for fighting, which in Ireland threw the main burden on the resources of the notables, not on taxation. It is likely, too, that credit facilities for raising money and managing repayments were less developed in Ireland. A further effect of these wars was to doom the vanquished to financial penalties and even confiscation. In England and Scotland, peers (and others) who had chosen the losing side in the civil wars, while they were penalized at the time, recovered favour and might even be recompensed after 1660. In Ireland, those who were defeated, exiled and dispossessed were seldom completely reinstated in the 1660s and 1680s. Thereafter Catholics were stripped of lands and debarred from office. Peers were not alone in being treated so severely, but for the Catholic nobles these discriminations worsened their already formidable problems.

Already in the 1660s, one observer confessed, 'it troubles me to see men of worth incapable as well by their religion as education of those advantages and employments that would better become them than many that have them'.[38] Regret that Catholicism disabled some of talent from their customary roles did nothing to alter the official view that its adherents were too dangerous to be trusted. Pressure on the heads of great aristocratic dynasties to conform to the state Church intensified. Some, such as Ormond, Kildare and Inchiquin, by timely conversion, kept their families at the forefront of society and politics. It was hoped that other peers would follow. Efforts were concentrated on the young and impressionable heirs. Catholics, either before or after inheriting, were removed from their relations and dosed with bracing draughts of Protestantism. In the case of the youthful heir to the Ormond patrimony, this strategy had worked triumphantly in the 1620s, and would be repeated frequently thereafter. It was even suggested that this method of élite integration should be institutionalized. A school under the auspices of the Court of Wards and then Trinity College in Dublin would drill future leaders of Irish society. But the measures were never systematized, so that *ad hoc* arrangements had to be made for each heir.[39]

A process of attrition, sometimes natural, but also engineered, dramatically reduced the numbers and proportions of Catholic peers. In 1641, the sixty-nine peers resident in Ireland were exactly balanced between Catholics and Protestants.[40] Fewer than half attended the House of Lords. As a result of the upheavals of the 1640s and consequent political proscription of 'rebels', the confessional advantage passed decisively to the Protestants. After 1660, Charles II's covert sympathy for loyal Catholics resulted in ambivalence in Irish policies: he was unsure whether to value unswerving devotion to the Stuart cause above Protestantism. Ormond, the king's viceroy and premier peer of Ireland, sensed the dilemma. He noted, for example, a kinsman of his own, Lord Mountgarret, a Catholic whose outlawry in fighting for the Confederates during the 1640s had yet to be reversed. Mountgarret, although still possessed of substantial estates, was 'overwhelmed with a title', which obliged him to 'make shift to provide the most important superfluities, as coach, liveries, &c.' Another relation of Ormond, 'a very sad peer called Lord Dunboyne', was similarly embarrassed. By the 1670s, twelve peers, including Dunboyne and Mountgarret, had yet to have their sentences of outlawry, arising from their role in the fighting of the 1640s, reversed.[41] In the interim, five of these outlawed peers were pensioned.[42] In 1685, the accession of the Catholic James II brought nearer the readmission of all peers to their full rights. With a parliament likely, he was no longer preoccupied, as his predecessors had been since 1613, with excluding staunch Catholics from both houses. It was now expected that the remaining outlawries would be lifted. In addition, the dispossessed or impoverished looked hopefully to the state for more aid to support the expenses of their peerages.[43]

In 1682, the 119 Irish peers split between eighty Protestants and thirty-nine Catholics. Another catalogue listed sixty-seven Protestants and thirty-seven Catholics.[44] The Protestant majority was composed of many who lived habitually in England. By James II's reign, it was thought only nineteen of the sixty-seven Protestants were currently in Ireland, whereas all but two of the thirty-seven Catholics dwelt there.[45] The uncertain future for the Protestants in Ireland was already driving the prosperous from the island. But the English residence of so many revealed the consequences of the early Stuarts' prodigal creations. James's rule did not usher in any complete or permanent restoration of Catholic peers. Rather it doomed the remnant which had enthusiastically supported him to worse penalties. In 1716, survivors were excluded from the House of Lords simply because they were Catholic. This added to the economic and social pressures at the upper levels of society to embrace Protestantism. More peers, Clanricarde, Antrim and Inchiquin, having wavered, finally opted for the state religion and so were welcomed wholeheartedly into the ruling Protestant interest. By 1721, a listing of 119 lay peers noted eleven as Catholics. Another list of 127, compiled in 1725, returned only nine

Catholics.[46] Among this small group, penalties and persuasion had seemingly succeeded in reconciling most peers to the new Protestant interest in Ireland. This raised the prospect that the peerage would prove an effective instrument to fuse the élites of the two kingdoms. This may have been what the Stuarts had earlier intended when they ennobled Scots and English. In practice, few of these strangers took their seats in the Dublin House of Lords.[47] Instead, as the enquiries of the 1680s showed, the majority of Protestants with Irish titles lived for most of the time outside Ireland. This continued to be the case in the more settled conditions under the Hanoverians. Many of these nobles either had tenuous Irish links or, if periodically domiciled in Ireland, moved easily and frequently between the two kingdoms. This easy movement, of ideas and manners as well as individuals and remittances, need not have undermined the utility or reputation of the Irish peerage.

By the 1720s, at least superficially, the parliamentary peerages in Ireland and England had converged. For the most part, they shared a confession. Also, they participated in a common culture, similar to that of an increasingly internationalized high society throughout western Europe. In actuality, the peers of Ireland contributed less than might have been hoped to synchronize the two kingdoms. Those living in England suffered rebuffs as provincials with incomes and manners inadequate to their pretensions. However, notwithstanding irritations over precedence and occasional insults, affluent Irish peers, such as Cork and Burlington, Egmont, Mountrath and Palmerston, passed as grandees in England. Unfortunately, absent from Ireland, their influence there was at best limited and indirect. Colleagues who remained in Ireland might be hampered by meagre incomes. This partly explained another of their perceived deficiencies: want of public spirit. Convention extorted from underlings courtesy and deference to the titled. It did not always mask contempt or indifference. The absent could be largely ignored, or derided for their selfishness. The present had failings which some censured. Too many peers, it was felt, had been promoted beyond their deserts. In the early seventeenth century, the rapid advance of the rapacious adventurer Richard Boyle to an earldom (of Cork), together with the ennoblement of three of his sons as Lords Dungarvan, Kinalmeaky and Broghill, excited ribaldry if not fury. In the early eighteenth century when George Evans received a peerage as Baron Carbery, critics descanted on his supposed descent from 'an Oliverian shoemaker'.[48] Another analyst traced what he regarded as the supine conduct of most active in the Dublin House of Lords to their being 'new men, the late descendants of the subalterns or common soldiers of Cromwell's officers, or the newer of offspring of clerks in offices'.[49] In the mid-eighteenth century, Primate Stone cast a jaundiced eye over his lay colleagues in the House. He recognized the urgent need for recruits of solid worth. He conceded that 'our House of Lords' would not be dishonoured by the presence of either Sir John Rawdon, well travelled and rich, or Joseph Leeson. In doing so he hinted that lower standards than in England were inevitable '*in hoc faece reipublicae*'. He allowed nothing could be objected against Leeson other than 'the common failings of a *bourgeois gentilhomme*'. Leeson had to wait more than a decade for his peerage. Stone, the son of a London banker who as archbishop of Armagh affected a Polish splendour in Dublin, sneered at Leeson, whose main source of wealth made him an early member of the 'beerage'.[50]

These objections, familiar among conservatives in most countries, carried an extra charge in Ireland. Peerages rewarded – or encouraged – good affection. Those of a different kidney were inevitably dissatisfied. As a matter of course, after 1690, Catholics and partisans of an older Ireland could expect no refreshment from the fount of honour. Their criticisms of the new creations often conflated objections to lowly origins with an unspoken disapproval of heretics. An elegiast of the vanishing world of Old English Catholicism mourned its passing in the 1690s. Saddened that 'people very mean in their descent but endowed with wealth' lorded it over dethroned notables, this conservative pleaded for proper acknowledgement of the truly noble rather than merely rich.[51] Monarchs, inundated with aristocratic demands for help, did not willingly create more poor peers. After the recklessness of the early Stuarts, successors were more careful to match honours to worth, both political and pecuniary. When George St George was recommended for a peerage in 1714, his income of £2,000 p.a. was adduced in support.[52] Henceforward, £2,000 to £3,000 annually was treated as the prerequisite for ennoblement. More difficult was the linking of new creations with the subjective abstraction of nobility. Money, confession and politics more commonly qualified for a peerage. On all three counts, Catholics were cut off from this – as from other favours from the English monarch. Occasional voices objected not just to particular peers as intruders but to the institution itself as alien to indigenous society. In the 1720s, O'Connor in his translation of Keating's *General history* made this case.[53] Yet, despite the differences between Gaelic kingship and Anglo-Norman lordship, the Old Irish had never shunned the newfangled titles. There were larger reasons for impugning the system of stratification imposed by the conquerors – dispossession, confession, ethnicity, economic survival – so that the nature of the overwhelmingly Protestant peerage was not on its own an intolerable grievance.

Indeed, it was Irish Protestants themselves who most frequently criticized the prodigality and insensitivity with which these honours were distributed. Anxiety lest the locals be swamped by outsiders led the House of Lords to try to limit the influence of those from Britain. Efforts to do so permanently failed. By the 1720s, self-styled patriots focused on specific cases. Not only might peers be derided as agents of England, but fresh creations were a reminder of the continuing subjection of Irish institutions, including the peerage, to English needs.[54] Henry Temple came of a family at the ideological and physical centre of Protestant Ireland in the previous century. One forebear had presided over Trinity College in Dublin; another had compiled the apparently authoritative account of Catholic violence in and after 1641. A grandfather had helped implement, and enriched himself from, the Restoration land settlement.[55] In 1723, Temple was advanced to the Irish peerage as Viscount Palmerston and Baron Temple. Temple had removed himself permanently to England, but continued to draw Irish rents worth more than £3,000 p.a. and to occupy the remunerative patentee office of chief remembrancer of the Irish Exchequer. Because his elevation coincided with a moment of heightened Anglo-Irish antagonism, Palmerston was victimized.

Although the self-styled patriots in Dublin could not block Palmerston's peerages, an honour bestowed by the monarch for which the recipient by conventional measures was admirably equipped, they could mar his delight. Instead of the normal fees for a patent of nobility prepared by the Office of Arms in Dublin, Palmerston was to be charged double: once for the viscountcy and secondly for the barony. Until the money was paid, Ulster King of Arms prevented the passage of the patent. Behind an obstructive and mercenary herald, Palmerston detected the Irish Protestant incendiaries. In particular, William King, archbishop of Dublin and hammer of English interlopers, opined that 'honours were too easily got'. Palmerston was told, 'double fees (as I hear) are become the common talk of the people in our markets, and the archbishop of Dublin's cook had the modesty to say he and others should have them in spite of the viscount'.[56] The squabble had to be referred to the lord–lieutenant, who, reluctant to fan patriotic flames, upheld double fees. Palmerston's agent in Dublin, 'terrified or bamboozled', handed over the money.[57] The new viscount totted up the costs of his honour: fees of £70 2s. 6d. in England, but £414 15s. 4d. extorted in Dublin. He concluded, 'the money I don't value. The insult and the manner of picking my pocket I stomach'.[58]

This incident was an extreme example of Irish antipathy to the aristocracy. Anti-English feelings coalesced dangerously with anti-aristocratic sentiments. The problem was that the origins and continuing uses of Irish peerages meant that similar protests could recur. Not only did the sale of Irish titles to English, Welsh and Scots worsen the problems of absenteeism among those whose sonorous titles made them the natural leaders of Irish Protestant society, it failed to hasten Ireland's full assimilation into the British political and social systems. In 1729 when absentees were first publicly inventoried, twenty-six peers headed the shaming catalogue. Another fourteen were absent from Ireland for all but a couple of months, with a further five as occasional absentees.[59] In all, then, about a third of the lay peerage seldom or never took their places in local society.

The apparent want of public spirit among peers lessened respect for the order. Inactivity of most in parliament coincided with indifference to responsibilities in their localities and in voluntary spheres. Hanoverian Dublin abounded with institutions dedicated to improvement and charity. They, like their equivalents in London, sought the help of peers, but (as in London) few came regularly to their boards as trustees and governors before the 1750s.[60] Indicative of a situation in which commoners directed these organizations is Mercer's Hospital. This venture sought peers as sub-scribers or – better still – governors. Peers readily accepted nomination. Yet, at routine board meetings during the first twenty years of Mercer's, from 1736 to 1756, only Lord Tullamore appeared twice and Lord Mountjoy once. Bishops were hardly more assiduous and never rivalled the diligence of a few Dublin incumbents and civic worthies. Peers and bishops were more in evidence at the annual fund-raising concerts for the hospital. From time to time some, notably Tullamore, took on the organ-ization of this important event. They also headed the lists of stewards who each year lent tone to the proceedings. Throughout the 1740s, at most four peers assisted with the yearly event. Again, Mountjoy and Tullamore were the most regular.[61] Only in the 1750s did more peers volunteer as helpers. One, Lanesborough, came to twenty-two meetings between 1749 and 1757. This amounted to a small proportion of the 135 gatherings which he could have attended. Eleven lay peers were named as stewards for the fund-raising concert in 1755, and twelve in 1757. This greater involvement may be part of a conscious desire on the part of holders of Irish peerages to redeem the reputation of the entire order. Similar imperatives animated another engine of improvement, the Dublin Society. In 1733, during the first flush of enthusiasm for this design, many peers and bishops signed up. A few of the spiritual lords, such as Francis Hutchinson of Down and Connor, assiduously attended meetings. Lay peers came more rarely. In 1740, Dr Samuel Madden, aware of the need for the Society to appeal to the fashionable and grand if it were to survive, reorganized its activities. Persistent prodding persuaded a minority that nobility entailed activism, and that patriotism could best be demonstrated through public-spiritedness.[62]

The localities as well as Dublin looked to the peers for leadership: often in vain. As in England and Wales, so in Ireland noblemen were named in the commissions of the peace for the counties where they had property.

Even those regularly resident on their Irish holdings balked at this chore. In 1734 Lord Grandison, newly installed in County Waterford, repented of his enthusiasm to sit on a bench packed with the socially dim. Grandison's contemporary, Lord Castledurrow, congratulated himself on thirty years' service in the county magistracy.[63] In doing so, he confirmed that such drudgery was uncommon among men of his rank. However, for twenty-five of his thirty years he had been a commoner. Similarly, in 1749, when it was reported that six peers had sat on the bench during a trial at Kilkenny, it was an exceptional demonstration, as a notorious gang was brought to book.[64] In the counties, the posts which peers valued were the prestigious ones of governor and *Custos Rotulorum*, not magistrate: they offered or confirmed pre-eminence, as did the place of foreman of the grand jury (occasionally filled by a peer). Attached to these offices were chances of patronage.[65] Yet, as the appointments to county governorships regularly revealed, the pool of resident peers in which to fish was shallow. In about half the Irish counties, the absence of a resident and reliable peer necessitated the appointment of a non-noble.[66]

Non-residence did not always damage Ireland. By constantly shuttling between Britain and Ireland, the mobile could speed the assimilation of the inhabitants of the one kingdom to the ways of the other. The traffic in goods and tastes linked Ireland with the worlds of the consciously refined throughout western Europe and north America. Irish peers, familiar with the political and administrative mazes of Whitehall, Westminster and St James's, sometimes usefully served Ireland. In 1720 they petitioned against a measure which directly threatened their power and prestige: the Declaratory Act intended to dock the constitutional competence of the Irish House of Lords. While the bill was being debated, forty-five Irish peers were believed to be in London. Twenty-two signed a remonstrance against the measure directed to George I.[67] The peers' services, frequently covert and erratic, were hailed by one apologist, and compared with the feebleness of those resident in Ireland. The latter were derided as 'ringleaders of a low debauchery and dissolute extravagance', not as 'protectors of the liberties and properties of the nation'.[68] Yet the exertions of a minority in England hardly redeemed the entire order. The absence of so many, so often, from Ireland allowed commoners to act in place of these 'natural leaders' in parliament, Dublin society or the localities. In Stuart England, aristocrats were commanded to forswear the fleshpots of the capital and sink themselves in useful activities on their estates. However, resort to London was not reduced. In Ireland, too, lay and spiritual peers were reminded of what they could and should do in the provinces.[69] At the same time, the government needed the important in Dublin, particularly to attend the council or parliament. Late into the seventeenth century, the authorities licensed the absences from the kingdom of notables. Thereafter any attempt to inhibit their movement was abandoned.[70]

The presence of a peer on his Irish estate had more than symbolic value. A resident could oversee household, estate and county. A dynamic establishment quickened the economy and set physical and cultural patterns for others to copy. At Kilkenny, the town felt the chill as the absences of the dukes of Ormonde from the castle lengthened into permanent exile. Similarly, at Lismore and Youghal, the retreat of their principal owners, the earls of Cork and Burlington, to England depressed the neighbourhood. One expedient would be to let Lismore Castle to another grandee, the earl of Meath.[71] In the event, only the agents of the Cork and Burlingtons inhabited the premises and deputized – inadequately – for their masters. Proxies could nevertheless undertake some functions. Moreover, the residence itself stood permanently as a surrogate for the often non-resident lord. Increasingly, the splendour and ambition of a house announced, and sometimes enhanced, the standing of its possessor. This was a strategy open to others than the titled, if rich. The greatest prodigy house of the early eighteenth century, Castletown in County Kildare, was built for Conolly, an obstinate commoner. Nevertheless, the biggest establishments in the countryside in later Stuart and Hanoverian Ireland generally belonged to peers or to those who would soon become peers.

In the County Antrim of the 1660s, the most massive houses were owned by the earl of Donegall. His Belfast Castle and Carrickfergus mansion of Joymount were each returned as having forty hearths.[72] At Dunluce, the marquess of Antrim, impoverished by his military exploits and political miscalculations over the previous twenty years, had nineteen fireplaces. Viscount Conway at Portmore, high in royal favour, owner of valuable English properties and in the throes of ambitious building, had an adequate eighteen hearths. Two more in the county, rich and powerful but still commoners, lived in a grandeur equal to that of the peers whose number they would soon join. Rawdon at Lisburn had an impressive thirty-nine chimneys, and Robert Colvill at Galgorm a respectable twenty-four.[73] Since the majority of Ireland's inhabitants dwelt in cabins with a single or no hearth, the lavish accommodation of the few clearly differentiated them from the mass. Even in remote Sligo, where incentives to engage in this sometimes competitive display were less pressing, the newly elevated Lord Collooney owned a house with ten hearths. Thereby he easily excelled. Only Captain Robert Parke, recently an MP, lived in a castle with a modest complement of four hearths.[74] Remembering that five hearths were taken in England as the minimum to live in what was thought a genteel fashion, the rarity of houses of this size throughout most of provincial Ireland was a reason why its leaders were regarded as inferior to their English equivalents. In Devon during Charles II's reign, it has been reckoned that at least ninety members of the gentry owned mansions with fifteen or more hearths. In Warwickshire, the total with such grand establishments – fifty-five – was considerably smaller. However, it still far surpassed what was to be found in any part of Ireland outside Dublin, and so revealed either the relative poverty of the landed or their different aspirations towards material display.[75] Even in a remote and upland county such as Westmorland, knights and squires resided in houses as yet undreamt of by their counterparts in Ireland.[76] In Restoration Ireland, it was generally only peers who possessed conspicuous seats. In Tipperary and Louth, respectively, Ormond's house at Carrick-on-Suir and Drogheda's at Mellifont each had thirty chimneys. Nothing else in either county approached this scale.[77] This form of aristocratic superiority continued into the eighteenth century. In 1749, Lord Kingsborough at Boyle presided over a household of forty servants. His lavish *équipe* separated Kingsborough from the prosperous gentry of Roscommon and even from the stylish bishop at Elphin.[78]

In the rural hinterlands, few other than those aspiring to be peers built as sumptuously as the peers themselves. Their willingness to do so told of a wish – and the ability – to impress. In towns, the situation differed. The pre-eminence of the peerage through stone and lime diminished the nearer the populous heartland of the Protestant interest was approached. In County Wicklow during the 1660s the residences of Lord Ardee and Lord Castlecoote were scarcely bigger than those of a lawyer and another commoner.[79] The capital itself was thronged with well-to-do officials, professionals, merchants and clerics. Noblemen from the provinces, like other members of the landed interest, had yet to be bewitched by the city. Many regarded stays in Dublin, with the prospect of being cheated and insulted, as inescapable but costly and uncomfortable. Fifteen houses in Dublin are recorded shortly after Charles II's restoration as being owned by peers.[80] Of these, only Cork House in the shadow of the Castle proclaimed the pretensions and circumstances of its original proprietor, the first earl. His successor, having recovered it from the Cromwellian authorities, opened it up and entertained exuberantly during the first brilliant parliamentary winter of the new order. Soon, however, it was forsaken by its owner. Shopkeepers roosted in his place. Lord Cork and Burlington, thereafter a rare visitor to Dublin, lodged with his daughter and son-in-law, the Roscommons.[81] Lord Conway, needing to be in Dublin for a projected meeting of parliament in 1678, also rented.[82] Shrewd developers (including the future earl of Longford) catered for the growing demand among peers and visiting landowners for accommodation.[83] Most peers made shift with lodgings, even when business, fun and (from 1692) predictable sessions of parliament were bringing them more regularly to the city. Even the Ormondes, despite their wealth and long association with Dublin, lacked a suitable house of their own. Usually they counted on being in government and therefore able to lodge in the Castle or other viceregal berths. In 1697, the second duke, without an official residence, rented Clancarty House.[84] Billets could be found to suit all pockets. Lord Cavan, as we have seen, crouched in obscurity near the poultry market. When the earl of Drogheda died in 1727, it was at his Dublin digs on Bachelor's Walk.[85]

Peers, in the matter of housing themselves in Dublin, remained transients. Those needing from time to time to be in London usually adopted similar strategies. The purchase of a London house proclaimed either formidable resources, as with Cork and Burlington in the 1660s, or a pressing need of office-holders at the English court to make a show, in the cases of Conway, Ormond and Ranelagh.[86] By the early eighteenth century, wealthy Irish peers who had transferred their chief interests to England, such as Palmerston, Mountrath and Egmont, acquired town houses in London as well as English country seats.[87] The costs of bilocation quickly depleted the assets of even the most affluent, as the Ormondes ruefully discovered. Realistically, either England or Ireland had to be selected. A decision to lavish expenditure on a place in one country rather than the other did not prevent the priorities being reversed at a later date. The fifth earl of Orrery returned to live in Ireland, although not at Charleville, devastated during the Williamite campaigns, but at Caledon in County Tyrone, his wife's seat. The business of housing did not always oblige the functionally Anglo-Irish (those with estates and interests in both kingdoms) to choose definitively whether to act as English or Irish. Shuttered houses could be aired and reopened, servants engaged, improvements undertaken, and then the houses could be closed again. Most easily of all, when it suited, Dublin lodgings could be hired and an Irish identity assumed for a season.

During the eighteenth century, the magnetism of Dublin grew. Peers were affected by a general trend. In 1705, it has been estimated that twenty-five to thirty peers maintained Dublin residences; by the 1790s the total had risen dramatically to about 100.[88] Although, as the century passed, some peers took their public responsibilities more seriously, Dublin life hardly acquired a markedly aristocratic tenor. Still the majority of peers, while adopting the more exacting standards of comfort, lived in Dublin alongside and according to the same modes as affluent commoners.[89] Occasionally, aspirations to lead, whether politically, culturally or socially, were expressed in ambitious building. In the 1740s, a few peers –

Kildare, Powerscourt, Tyrone, Charlemont and Antrim – showed the way with costly free-standing town houses.[90] Motives varied. With Charlemont, aesthetic sensibilities refined by prolonged travel fused with patriotic concerns.[91] The Kildares most nakedly advanced public ambitions through architecture. The star of the Fitzgeralds, earls of Kildare, rose as that of their traditional rivals, the Ormondes, dimmed. The reviving popularity and fortunes of the Kildares were noted in 1714. Robert, nineteenth earl of Kildare, was said to add 'new honour to the most ancient and hereditary nobility' through his sincere piety, his exemplary behaviour as spouse, father and friend, his charity, constant residence in Ireland and as 'a lover of [his] country'.[92] By 1745, the current Lord Kildare could be lauded as 'the first earl of the kingdom, with the greatest estate'. Nothing trumpeted this more loudly than his Dublin mansion, Kildare (later Leinster) House, commanding alike in location, scale and modern style. Sycophancy alone did not explain its description in 1766 as 'perhaps the noblest city residence in the British Isles'. It aptly prefigured the advance of the Kildares to formal primacy within the Irish peerage when, in 1766, their head was created duke of Leinster.[93]

Building was one method, albeit a cumbersome and costly one, by which the peerage could demonstrate its economic and cultural primacy. Especially in Dublin, the habitations of most peers shaded into those of commoners. In the later seventeenth century, towns like Clonmel, Derry or Drogheda lacked any resident notable, and already their leading burgesses owned substantial dwellings.[94] To live like a lord consumed money. By the same token, those with the ready could lord it. This inescapable fact opened up the unnerving prospect of the customary boundaries in the social order being blurred or erased. Anxiety on this score reinforced suspicions that the actual peerage fitted badly with alternative rankings based on civic activism and moral worth. Military service and a personal fealty to the monarch had been integral to notions of nobility such as those entertained by Ormond in the seventeenth century.[95] These attributes had not been discredited. But, before the end of the seventeenth century, they were overlaid by more pragmatic criteria of service to the impersonal, notably the Protestant succession and the Protestant interest in Ireland.

Confessional exclusivity debarred some otherwise admirably qualified as nobles. Innate and nurtured nobility were further to be exhibited in a wider range of public duties. As has been emphasized, too many peers of Ireland failed to live on their holdings, participate in parliament or devil for charities and voluntary bodies. Notwithstanding the formal precedence and courtesies allowed to the titled, they were irrelevant to much that happened in Hanoverian Ireland. Isolated peers showed patriotism. Only in the 1750s did worry about the drooping reputation of the parliamentary peerage and indignation at crass British interventions unite to propel more lay peers into public life. One sign of this is their new enthusiasm for the work of the Dublin hospitals. Another was political engagement. Lord Kildare's self-interested participation in populist campaigns matched his showmanship at Kildare (as it was still) House and Carton, his mansion in the country. More disinterested was Lord Charlemont's espousal of patriotic causes. These belated stirrings among a minority of peers living in Ireland justified an assertion in 1759 that these paragons 'reflect true honour on nobility; and in reality derive their superior rank as much from the pre-eminence of their virtues, as from the constitutional dignity of their titles'.[96] In most spheres, however, peers were too few and reticent to be differentiated from the generality of the propertied and the quality in Hanoverian Ireland.

The long rule of the Ormondes, frequent viceroys between the 1640s and 1713, and the reappearance in high politics after 1714 of their arch-rivals, the Fitzgeralds, suggested an archaic and aristocratic timbre to Irish politics. The realities belied this impression. The Ormondes' fealty to the sovereign was backed by ideals of service and self-service. Loss of office threatened them with financial ruin. Their pre-eminent station, far from protecting them, added to their problems, obliging them to spend what they could no longer afford. The Kildares, especially in the 1750s, encouraged recollection of the past when they had ruled the kingdom and resisted meddlesome English politicians. Yet, the eighteenth-century heads of the house were not entrusted with the lord lieutenancy. Kildare was bought off with the 'sugar plum' of the mastership of Ordnance.[97]

In common with their equivalents in Britain, but unlike most continental aristocrats, it was argued that peers in Ireland suffered 'a happy disability to injure their inferiors'.[98] Not all took so sanguine a view. A visitor from Europe in 1732 was appalled by the condition of the peasantry, and thought them 'as great slaves to the Irish lords and gentry as the Russians are to the boyars'. Significantly, this traveller lumped together all landowners, seeing peers as essentially the same as other proprietors.[99] Accordingly, to take a narrow view of the aristocracy and restrict it to the holders of peerages entitled to sit in the Irish House of Lords, as this chapter has, risks separating a contingent which in all but hereditary membership of the legislature merged into a much larger and more powerful group of the landed. Yet, in this right, in the precedence which they were automatically accorded and – at least at the moment of ennoblement – in their revenues, lay peers differed from knights, esquires and simple gentlemen. But peers seldom acted in isolation. In establishing and exerting themselves in their districts, they allied with older and lesser families. The affinities constructed by the likes of the Ormondes, Cork and Burlingtons and Orrerys entrenched them more firmly in their regions, enabled them to operate in Dublin and added to their weight in England. Clienteles of these kinds brought a complex of reciprocal obligations. The peers derived precedence and some extra authority from their hereditary honours, but more from the extent and value of their holdings. On the social map, these alliances which encompassed peers, gentry, urban professionals, traders and even the 'inconsiderable' are not easily reconstructed. The relative ease with which peers can be identified and then isolated misrepresents a society in which, if they were to be effective, they had to act with others who were nominally their inferiors.

Chapter 3

The Quality

I

Lineages

In 1762 a jilted spinster exclaimed from Enniscorthy in County Wexford
that 'quality now abounds in every county'. In this instance 'the quality'
had been spotted at the local assembly room and consisted of the daughter of an earl.[1] Inseparable from this snob's assessment were the elegant
setting and polished gatherings in which the socially eminent revealed
their quality. Others, happy to use the term, understood it differently.
A clergyman, ordained in the 1680s, celebrated with a festive dinner to
which 'people of quality' were bidden. Another cleric, down on his luck,
remembered that he had once 'lived in good quality'. In 1690, pains had
been taken to distinguish 'gentlemen of quality and estates' from 'a parcel
of rabble'. The director of the Dublin Philosophical Society congratulated
himself that its meetings were attracting 'several persons of quality and
learning'. A character reference in 1706 was taken seriously because offered
'from one of the best quality in that country' of Cork. By 1742, 'persons
of quality and distinction' in Dublin had resolved to show a patriotic
benevolence by wearing only clothes of Irish manufacture.[2]

Characteristic of the uses of the term was Diarmaid O'Connor's appeal
in 1726 to the 'most noble personages of the kingdom of Ireland for birth,
quality and learning' to subscribe to his imminent publication of Keating's
General history of Ireland. O'Connor's trawl of the quality caught a
miscellany of peers, the titled, landed and obscure.[3] Yet, as early as 1703,
reservations were voiced about the quality. A clergyman confessed that he
thought it 'far more satisfactory and safe to deal with an honest plain gentleman than squeezing, shuffling quality'. In 1759, an agent, contemptuous
of the pretensions of tenants, wrote dismissively of 'the gentry as they call
themselves'.[4] Already, it would seem, some sensed that quality was a guise
assumed rather than always innate. Nor did outward looks invariably
match inner qualities. All concurred that the quality, in order to merit

admiration, had to behave appropriately. Ranking depended on merit. A manual, printed in Dublin in 1723, agreed that quality had to be respected. But by the same token, those 'of figure and quality' who overindulged 'metamorphosed into Bedlamites'. This produced a spectacle in which the 'quality and peasantry pig together'.[5] In 1738 Lord Santry was punished for his crime so as to demonstrate that 'no man's quality can entitle him to destroy his fellow subjects with impunity'.[6] In different hands, 'the quality' could encompass the peerage, squirearchy and gentry, and perhaps the professions, merchants and respectable of the towns. They possessed shifting and subjective attributes, among which gentility, politeness and civility featured. Unlike the peerage, with its fixed and legally defined membership, the quality could expand or contract, according to criteria variously and inconsistently applied. The noun *quality*, like its counterparts, nobility and aristocracy, implied a judgement, and so was not simply a neutral collective. It was closely connected, indeed sometimes overlapped, with the elusive idea of gentility.[7] But, just as the gentle or genteel were not confined to the gentry, so over time and in the mouths of social arbiters, the quality waxed and waned. Lineage could deposit the lucky among the quality, but as with nobility or gentility, personal traits, whether inherited or acquired, were increasingly emphasized.

What constituted gentility proved as mutable as the uses of 'quality'. Miscreants who died on the scaffold sometimes attested to having been educated 'as became a gentleman'. Although formulaic, these statements meant something, both to the condemned and their audience. Moreover, gentlemanly education could prepare for occupations such as those of barber surgeon and surgeon.[8] Upbringing and schooling were means to implant or nurture gentility. Thereafter, behaviour and possessions were most easily scanned for evidence that these lessons had succeeded in constructing the right figure. In 1721 Philip Perceval, an office-holder and conductor of polite Dublin society, thanked his brother, a peer, for procuring (in England) a coach. Painted with Perceval's armorials it was adjudged 'very genteel': reasonably so, since it had cost £100.[9] Andrew Crotty, floating uncertainly between squire and gentleman, agent to absent peers and well travelled in England and Europe, behaved 'very genteel' when he treated twenty or thirty neighbours to 'a merry bottle'.[10] Approval of the genteel was widespread, but subtly differed in the cases of Crotty and, for example, of William Crosbie, heir of Ardfert. Young Crosbie from Kerry was gratified when in Dublin to be entertained 'very genteely', and to be offered a seat in his coach by the Lord Chief Baron, also 'very genteely'.[11] Posts, whether in the army or administration, were commended in the same terms. In 1737, the holder of one office in the Dublin administration wheedled for another, 'of very genteel appearance, which must necessarily add to my expense in living'.[12] The diocesan schoolmaster at Limerick congratulated himself that he could attract a bride, the niece of the lord chancellor, and support her 'in a genteel way'.[13] In the Dublin of the 1760s, a linen factor was noted as living 'very genteel'.[14] Lodgings and how they were decorated and furnished might be commended as 'genteel'.[15]

Michael Smythe, a squire from Portlick in County Westmeath, displayed his gentility through dress. It was calculated to impress the freeholders and gentry and so second his political ambitions. Smythe, in desperation, asked a kinsman to bespeak in Dublin 'such as your genteel fancy shall point out'. Smythe equated this rig with what was 'most fashionable'. The outfit, when it arrived, was 'really most genteel, and well chose. Every one who sees them admires them'. He boasted how 'all the gentlemen of figure and fortune' in Westmeath and Longford did him 'the honour' of accompanying him to the poll in Athlone, where he emerged, defeated to be sure, 'with great credit and esteem'.[16] Dress often denominated the quality or would-be quality. Numerous social commentators decried the ease with which the proper striations were erased by the habit of dressing above one's rank. In the middle of the eighteenth century, a preacher issued a reminder of how clothing had been 'intended for distinction of the several orders, and stations of life'.[17] Over fifty years before, Sir Robert Southwell, vigilant about defending correct conduct among his prolific kindred and acquaintances from Protestant Ireland, rebuked a nephew for his 'fanciful dressing'. The youth retorted that, 'he desired to appear a gentleman'.[18] The proper look extended to mounts. From Dublin in 1730 came a request for 'a fashionable, genteel gelding'.[19] Even servants took on some of the appearances (if not the inner attributes) of the gentle and genteel. Of one recommended for employment early in the eighteenth century, it was admitted that 'he has nothing of the genteel or spruce, but sir, he's honest'. This translated as 'uncouth and awkward'. He compensated by being a 'sober, trusty, mettled fellow'.[20]

Faced with these puzzles, applicants for admission to the quality asked in vain for the requirements. The perplexed turned to such manuals as *The Gentleman Instructed*.[21] This popular guide appeared in a ninth edition in Dublin, apparently 'at the request of several of the nobility and gentry of Ireland'.[22] In 1753, when it was reissued in Dublin, it had arrived at its thirteenth edition. Purveyors of education, manners, polite accomplishments such as dancing, fencing, painting and musicianship and the décor of civility, rushed to assist the quality, and aspirants to it. Guides to the social labyrinth flourished. The supple, who took the fluid world of Protestant Ireland as it was, did better than the pedants. Prominent among the latter were the heralds. When, in sixteenth- and seventeenth-century Ireland, the Office of Arms tried to insist that the minute calibrations of the social gauge be maintained, it failed even more abjectly than its English counterpart.[23] This was not a society to be regulated by avaricious experts. Yet it was not unconcerned with precedence. Violent disputes might break out even at the council table, or over arrival and seating at Church of Ireland worship.[24]

Gentlemen and would-be gentlemen disliked paying fees to heralds who tried to regulate their styles and arms, yet bought escutcheons for their interments.[25] Resentful of the monopoly claimed by the functionaries of the Office of Arms in Dublin, they turned to cheaper alternatives. One was Aaron Crossly. A freelance heraldic painter and conductor of funeral pomps, Crossly undercut Ulster King of Arms. Well connected through the guilds and official and unofficial freemasonry of Protestant Dublin, his services were in demand. The best customers for his staple – hatchments and escutcheons – were the armigerous. Esquires, or 'squires', undisputed members of 'the quality', kept Crossly busy.[26] Ever the opportunist, he traded on the credulity and vanity of his contemporaries by publishing (in 1725) a ramshackle Irish *Peerage*.[27] Crossly's disappointments over the project were repeated with the next compiler, John Lodge. The nobility largely ignored Lodge's requests for help. His four volumes were eventually published in 1754, but in London. In this, as in other spheres, the peerage and its connections were incurious about origins and as yet formed only a small market in Ireland.[28]

Crossly, his rival Hawkins and other herald-painters necessarily serviced a larger clientele, perhaps coterminous with 'the quality'. They willingly tricked out achievements and traced descents for any who would pay.[29] As a result of his trade and (more importantly) the patentee office which he held from the crown, Hawkins enjoyed the status of an esquire. He joined fully in the public life of Dublin, serving as a churchwarden, and was also active in the early work of the Dublin Society before his death in 1736. Effectively he made the office of Ulster King of Arms hereditary in his family.[30] As an office-holder and professional, Hawkins was accepted into the urban squirearchy and was unequivocally of the quality. Crossly's social position, like his livelihood, was more precarious. For him, heraldry was essentially a craft, and membership (including office-holding) of the Dublin Painter-Stainers' Company important.[31] He never called himself anything other than 'herald-painter'; never adopted the style of 'gentleman'. Yet, at his own somewhat lower level, he participated exuberantly in the sociable rituals of the respectable through Masonic lodges and guilds as well as with kinsfolk, neighbours and acquaintances. This exuberance may have been his undoing. After one perhaps bibulous interment, he stumbled into a cellar and died soon afterwards. However he himself might rank, several of his circle were of the quality.[32]

Crossly advanced high claims for his calling. Heraldry, if properly practised, could order an otherwise confused world. Accurate genealogies, he
insisted, supplied the knowledge, 'wherein political distinctions between
man and man, family and family, for preserving order and subordination
in a monarchical government ought to be'.[33] Governments in Dublin
might share this sedative programme, but did nothing to protect Crossly's
arcane craft. However, even without official help, heraldry flourished.
Indeed, the gusto with which private patrons used professional genealo-
gists has been seen as a foible of settler society. Parvenus, it has been
suggested, sought to cover their sometimes unsavoury and usually shadowy
backgrounds with a veneer of antiquity.[34] This complaint was not unique
to Ireland: it occurred also in Wales.[35] In practice, the brisk Irish demand
for authenticated pedigrees came from customers with assorted backgrounds. The venerable and incontrovertibly grand, like the Ormondes and
Antrims, the recently ennobled Brodricks, Viscounts Midleton, the well-
established Edgeworths, squires in County Longford, and those freshly
emerged from obscurity such as Sir Richard Cox, briefly lord chancellor,
judge and baronet, all turned to the heralds and antiquaries.[36] Modest settlers in Ulster used heraldic devices on their tombstones in much the same
way as in seventeenth- and eighteenth-century Scotland.[37] The fondness
of the armigerous for heraldic obsequies echoed that of their counterparts
in Wales.[38] In Wales, too, the otherwise shabby revered long pedigrees.
The most imaginative reached back to the Greeks and Trojans.[39] In 1740
an Irish Catholic informed a relation, as for 'our coat of arms, I have got
one drawn on vellum, which makes a good figure'.[40] Members of the displaced élites of Old Ireland, adrift on the continent, clutched at pedigrees.
These comforted by reminding them of what they had forfeited, and but-
tressed requests for fresh ennoblement.[41] Above all they were guarantors
of essential qualities. In Gaelic society heredity and kinship governed the
distribution of power and occupations. Consequently, elaborate pedigrees
had long been constructed. But the wish to know kindred served practical purposes not unique to the Catholic Irish. Only by mapping the
intricate filigree of relations could these then be invoked as hosts and
helps. The propensity to parade armorials for other than utilitarian reasons
led the few manufacturers of pottery in mid-eighteenth-century Ireland
to offer to decorate their wares with the appropriate coats of arms.[42]

Utility as much as vanity stimulated even the eminent to commission
family trees. The Ormonde Butlers, hardly a line the length of which
could be doubted, had a professional chart their relationship through the
Boleyns with Queen Elizabeth.[43] By this device, history seconded suits for
favour and place. Some from the first duke of Ormond's circle, Sir William
Domville, successively solicitor- and attorney-general under Charles II, or

Sir George Lane, secretary of state and secretary at war during the same epoch, invoked the loyal service of their ancestors.[44] These claims were rarely authenticated with great strictness. The discontinuities in even the recent Irish past made proof difficult. Again, the propensity to embroider or fabricate was not unique to the lately arrived. Startling legerdemain was practised by Arthur Rochfort. Reasonably, Rochfort might boast of having been reared 'in the Glorious Revolution Principles'. Less plausible, remembering the arrival of the Rochforts in medieval Ireland, was his insistence that 'none of my family on any side can trace a drop of popery were [sic] amongst us, being Protestants so long as we are able to be traced'. Whether deliberately or through ignorance he had expunged fore-bears such as the thirteenth-century bishop of Meath and the Dominican who, in 1451, had been recommended for the bishopric of Down and Connor.[45]

Since credit conventionally attached to long settlement, it made sense to establish a venerable and complex lineage. Early in the eighteenth century, an inhabitant of Slane in County Meath imaginatively prefaced an appeal with the claim that his predecessors had lived in the locality 'this 600 years after the nature of freeholders to the knowledge of the best of the county'.[46] Later, when Morgan Jellett reminisced, he attributed the pre-eminence of his father in County Down to more than his position as Lord Moira's agent. Because the elder Jellett was one of the few land-owners left in the county who held under Oliver Cromwell's original patent, he was 'therefore respectable'.[47] In similar mode, William Conner, agent of the Boyles in south Munster in the 1750s, seconded his bid to be elected to parliament by reciting his ancestry. In recalling that his family 'have lived there [at Bandon] ever since the year 1641, when my great grandfather was slain by the rebels', Conner probably passed over an older past, at once Irish and Catholic.[48]

The Old Irish looked back to Adam as their progenitor. Newer settlers seldom sought to push back their own antecedents so far. A group of seventy-nine, designated the 'principal inhabitants' of County Waterford in 1746, contained only nineteen whose origins in Ireland reached back to the reign of Elizabeth I or earlier.[49] Investigations, even when inspired by the desire to locate oneself creditably and among the quality, could reach modest conclusions, as those of the Edgeworths and Warings demonstrated. Richard Edgeworth, of the eponymous Edgeworthstown in County Longford, belonged to the squirearchy of provincial Ireland in the mid-eighteenth century. As his annual income crept towards £1,500, he undertook both the burdens and pleasures of proprietorship. The family had been founded in Ireland early in the seventeenth century. Then two brothers had thrived: one in secular offices, the other as a Protestant bishop.[50]

Over succeeding generations, the mesh which united the Edgeworths with so many other similarly circumstanced families thickened. Whether in the locality and Dublin or on trips to England, these kindred helped to define Edgeworth's social and recreational rounds. Training as a lawyer added a professional circle to the family one. He moved easily between the establishments of the elevated, notably the Kildares in Dublin or his kinsman and neighbour recently created Lord Longford, fellow squires and barristers, prosperous doctors and merchants. Edgeworth methodically reconstructed the history of his family to confute 'the ill nature of some men [who] may possibly represent the family as of new growth or as upstart'. At the same time he would not endorse 'the vanity of some of the family [who] may possibly represent them as a more considerable family than they really ever were'. Edgeworth concluded unexceptionably from his researches that the Edgeworths were 'a good private gentleman's family, never masters of great fortunes, nor ennobled by the crown, but still lived in credit and above want, and . . . often favoured by the crown with honourable employments'.[51]

Edgeworth's self-assessment of his family's social placement involved several criteria. Important were 'credit', economic sufficiency and office-holding. Only the third, with membership of parliament, service as sheriff, magistrate and on voluntary boards, offered an agreed measure. 'Credit', like 'quality', mingled material and ethical evaluation.[52] For Edgeworth, the idea encompassed how he and his household lived. He approved and sometimes continued the expansive hospitality of his predecessors. In harking back to the amplitude of previous centuries, he echoed the enthusiasm for outward display expressed by Dolan in Fermanagh and Cosby of Stradbally. Externals, notably an enlarged and modernized house on to which carved armorials were affixed, mattered to Squire Edgeworth. Painstakingly he gathered a gallery of ancestral and contemporary portraits. He also commissioned heraldic tombs for ancestors in the graveyard.[53] Yet Edgeworth, aware of how the polite and genteel esteemed restraint and decorum, avoided excess.[54]

Edgeworth's researches included no obvious falsifications. He worked dispassionately until required to adjudicate between claims to seniority of different branches of his antecedents, the Huddlestones. He scanned the coats of arms of the rival lines. One consisted of three green dog turds on a white field; the other, three white dog turds on a green field. A heraldic expert, Edgeworth reported, had decided that the white were 'mouldy' dogs' turds, and therefore older than the green ones, which were depicted as 'fresh ones and even smoking ones'.[55] Edgeworth inadvertently threatened to reduce to absurdity the study advocated by Crossly as the likeliest to order society properly. Edgeworth, notwithstanding his modesty, worried about reputation, credit and standing. When he acted as high sheriff, he borrowed a more impressive equipage and coachman from a kinsman.[56] His position in county society as one of the quality looked assured by the 1740s. So he was mortified to be lampooned by a neighbour, John Piers of Tristernagh. Piers was aggrieved at the election to parliament of Edgeworth and his kinsman, Thomas Pakenham. Undoubtedly the family of the dotty Piers had been settled in the neighbourhood longer than either the Edgeworths or Pakenhams. Late settlement was not, however, the ground on which Piers attacked his neighbour. The libel, scabrous and obsessively scatological, lingered over Edgeworth's personal defects. Edgeworth and Pakenham went to court (fruitlessly) in order to protect 'their good name, fame and credit'.[57] Edgeworth's failure to find satisfaction from the law warned of the divergent assessments of credit and reputation among the quality.

Piers, Edgeworth's adversary, himself featured in other antiquarian researches. Henry Ware, an esquire living comfortably in one of the new and spacious houses on St Stephen's Green in Dublin, desultorily enquired into his forebears.[58] A thoroughly respectable provenance among the office-holding worthies of early Stuart Dublin was readily unearthed. A wider net, encompassing the Piers, enmeshed the townsman, Ware, in the landed society of the Irish midlands. Ware valued the link with the Piers of Tristernagh enough to buy Piers mementoes at auction.[59] Artefacts, thanks to their associations with kindred, could embody and recall cherished connections. Ware's researches, like Edgeworth's, were designed solely for his immediate family, so he did not hide forebears, who stretched across a spectrum from the anti-Catholic ferocity of Bishop Henry Jones and Robert Ware to some who had adopted Catholicism and even entered the priesthood.[60] The Wares, living as cultivated *rentiers* in the heart of smart Hanoverian Dublin, with an income approaching £1,000 p.a, were designated esquires. However, their lives had long focused on the city, office and the learned professions. These offered congenial outlets for the civility and gentility which differentiated them from the lowly. By the middle of the eighteenth century, the Wares frequented the library, the church, the Physico-Historical Society and eventually Bath.[61] Beside their cultivation, country cousins such as the Piers sometimes appeared bucolic, even uncouth.[62] Yet both, in contemporary estimates, were assigned to the quality.

In another family, the Warings of County Down, interest in ancestors and armouries told both of frank curiosity and of social aspirations. These preoccupations also revealed differences in outlook between generations. William Waring of Derriaghy in County Antrim had benefited, like numerous other Protestants in Ulster, from the recent upheavals. His parents had been attracted to the province early in the seventeenth century. They traded and manufactured in and around the town of Belfast Then, as Catholics paid the price for unsuccessful uprisings, Waring gained confiscated lands. He removed to County Down and established himself on a settlement, formerly owned by the Magennises, soon renamed Waringstown. By the 1690s, Waring commanded an annual £600, and had held office in the county as high sheriff and a magistrate. The son of a tanner, he had gradually progressed through the populous band of gentlemen into the select company of esquires.[63] Tenure of these prestigious posts, as well as income, assisted in this visible social ascent; ancestry had played little or no part.

In the mobile communities of later seventeenth-century Ireland, concealment of origins was neither possible nor necessary. Indeed, fables of sensational successes, such as Richard Boyle, first earl of Cork, Sir William Petty or (later) William Conolly, spurred others to emulate the freebooters. William Waring's story, albeit modestly, reprised the same theme. Self-help was admired; helping oneself, not. Contemporaries discriminated between legitimate and unsavoury methods of aggrandizement. Waring irritably scotched any rumour that he had behaved other than honestly. A reputation for plain dealing remained integral to his reputation. These personal qualities concerned him more than the standard material accompaniments of gentility. Even so, he did not disdain the latter. He used his wealth to house, clothe and train his family according to the norms current among those of his income and rank. By doing so, he helped his offspring to develop greater sensitivity to the nuances of status. For three sons, he purchased what he had lacked: university education.[64] Each child was helped into a calling, since only the eldest could be set up in succession to the parent as squire of Waringstown. Family traditions and networks brought one boy, John Waring, into trade, as a woollen draper in London.[65] Another, Richard Waring, bought (with parental help) an army commission, which he described as a 'genteel pretty post, fit for any private gentleman in England'.[66] Soldiering in the Low Countries alongside the young duke of Ormonde and on leave in London, where he married well, Richard Waring learnt modes rather different from his father's.

By 1701, now a lieutenant-colonel and himself an 'esquire', Richard Waring clashed over the seemingly risible issue of armorial bearings. Colonel Waring advised his father to have his arms registered by Ulster King of Arms. At the same time, he suggested a new crest. The son havered between the devices of the Warings, successful as London merchants, or of another branch in Liverpool, who had thrived in the fisheries there. The elderly Waring, nearing death, was uninterested in change. He proposed keeping his own crest: an outstretched hand. This emblem was a

constant reminder of 'God's providences, that hath attended me' from his
first entry into business. Early in his career, he had bespoken a seal, 'with
a hand cut in it which I have used to this day, owning that all I enjoy is
by the good hand of God'. He told his sons, if they insisted on a new
crest, 'that they take the hand of Providence'. The hand as depicted should
either be upright, as 'when we lift our hands to praise God, or else a hand
holding something in it that may signify that our family own all the blessings they enjoy from the good hands of God's Providence'. Despite these
forcefully expressed sentiments, within a month, Ulster King of Arms
entered the armorials of the Warings, esquires of County Down. Azure
lozenges had replaced the more expressive and personalized hand and
digits. The crest of the grebe's (or fisher's) head announced the link with
the prosperous fisherfolk of Liverpool.[67]

William Waring adopted by the 1690s many accoutrements of a squire
worth £600 a year. However, he was restrained from uninhibited enjoyment of his money and place by his religious outlook. The old man knew
that such gravity was now thought old-fashioned. Yet, he still prided
himself on it.[68] Among the fashionable, materialism was felt to be foster-
ing anti-clericalism, irreligion, libertinism and even atheism.[69] The sombre
dignity with which William Waring conducted himself was coming to
be associated more with the well-to-do in dissenting congregations. His
own heir, Samuel Waring, although orthodoxly pious, shed the austerity
of his father. He took his station in the county as improving squire,
ingenious connoisseur and public tribune. Education, travel, reflection and
money perfected a persona which could be replicated in many other
gentry families. Inheritance and revenue deposited Samuel Waring in the
County Down squirearchy: a group of hardly more than 100. He
earned high regard as an exemplar of 'the quality' by his civic energy and
accomplishments.

The Warings, despite recent arrival, were not sneered at by the unques-
tioned grandees of the locality, such as the Brownlows, Hamiltons and
Hills. Indeed, the notables, having availed of the elder Waring's financial
services, turned to Samuel Waring for aesthetic and political guidance. The
Warings, like the Edgeworths and Wares, neither hid nor invented ancestors. Samuel Waring, having visited Liverpool early in the 1690s, turned
the family link from a speculative one to something more solid.
The squires of Waringstown were uninterested in claiming descent from
the Anglo-Norman de Warennes. They answered politely a correspondent
from Kilkenny, also a Waring or Warren. The Kilkenny Waring had read
in the newspaper of 1725 that a Waring was serving as high sheriff of
County Down. He wanted to know whether they were related. (They
were not.)[70] Interest evaporated, and the answer was evidently forgotten.

In 1761, the enquiry was repeated. The Kilkenny correspondent reassured the Ulster squires that the question was not prompted by any wish to 'plume with borrowed feathers'.[71] Whether consciously or unconsciously, these Warings obeyed the social dictators. One manual produced in Dublin in 1723 advised, 'let not your family be the subject of your discourse, nor fling the registers of your genealogy on the table before all company; this topic is both fulsome and ungenteel'.[72]

II
Numbers and Income

Richard Edgeworth and Samuel Waring needed no busybodies to assign them to social stations or lecture them on fitting demeanour. Their annual rentals of, respectively, about £1,500 and £900 assured them of elevated positions. Income was linked with tenure of public offices, notably the country magistracy, shrievalty and service on the grand jury. What was not always clear was whether such offices conferred or simply resulted from rank. The Warings, as justices of the peace for County Down, belonged to a group which – by 1760 – would number eighty-five. In Edgeworth's Longford, it consisted of only twenty-six.[73] Furthermore, Samuel Waring and Richard Edgeworth when elected to parliament joined a national Protestant club with a membership of 300. For William Waring, making his way from obscurity to local eminence, office helped. He was first styled esquire when, briefly, he served the Cromwellians as a justice of the peace. Removed from the bench at Charles II's restoration, he dropped back into the undifferentiated body of gentlemen. Permanent elevation into the squirearchy was achieved only when he was pricked as sheriff and returned to the county commission of the peace.[74] In contrast, Edgeworth had been born into the squirearchy so that service as magistrate and sheriff simply consolidated an existing status. Convention did not immediately advance those named in the commission of the peace from gentleman or merchant to esquire. But service as high sheriff, the sovereign's man in the county for the year, did. Few declined this advancement. In this regard, George Macartney, a cousin of Waring, was unusual in scrupling over this vanity. Macartney, a leading trader in Belfast, during his term as high sheriff of County Down in 1680, instructed a Dublin correspondent, 'I pray you write me nothing but, *George Macartney merchant*, for the sovereign's [mayor of Belfast's] place or sheriff's is but for a year and then the esquire is gone, so I intend to continue as I was and will be after.'[75] Such disdain for worldly titles came to be associated with members of the dissenting churches, like Macartney.

By the 1740s, Daniel Mussenden occupied an eminence comparable to
Macartney's in Charles II's time. Mussenden prided himself on having
driven the most lucrative overseas trade in the port of Belfast for
twenty years. However, he was discomfited by the ambitions of his
heir who was reluctant to drudge in an urban counting-house. The
father scoffed at his son's pretensions which would probably deposit him
'at the tail of the country squires rather than the head of the merchants'.
Despite his protestations, the senior Mussenden was not wholly averse to
the life of a squire. He invested a portion of his mercantile fortune in
land. On his Larchfield estate in County Down, he conceded that
'farming and improvement is a very pleasant and useful study'.[76] Moreover, although sometimes addressed still as plain 'merchant', he did not
correct those who styled him 'esquire'.[77] By the early eighteenth century,
few squires were active in dissenting congregations: Mussenden was
unusual in this regard. Unconcerned with the precise gradations of county
society, and sometimes contemptuous of carnal distinctions, the dissenters
concentrated on the urban and spiritual hierarchies in which they stood
tall.[78]

Comparable conventions to those governing office elevated clergymen,
if not born gentlemen – as many had been – into the gentry. When one
punctilious divine protested, 'I am no gentleman, my father was only a
tanner', it was thought an eccentricity. The basis of the protest was that
the term, 'usually affixed to that of clergyman, he considered as highly
improper, it being of a worldly origin unsuitable to the spiritual nature
of his office'.[79] But the usages pleased too many to be ended by odd
objectors. In the case of public offices, the honorifics reminded that these
appointments derived from the crown. Among professionals, the styles
reflected liberal studies and the lettered nature of the callings. One group
traditionally denominated 'gentlemen' were the attorneys who devilled in
the four central courts in Dublin. An attorney questioned this prescriptive
right 'from time immemorial'. Often, he argued, the hackney attorneys
earned too little and were too narrow in their education to behave like
true gentlemen.[80] With 573 attorneys licensed to work there in 1734, the
practice simultaneously inflated and debased the style of gentleman.[81]
Further awkwardness was caused by the custom of terming holders of
patentee offices esquires. 'Even deputies in this age assume the style of
esquires, before they are known to be gentlemen.' It was noted sardonically in 1760 that there was 'scarcely a man of business in this kingdom,
who is not by some means or other dubbed an esquire and accordingly
they enlarge their ideas of themselves. Had every person who assumes that
ancient, honorary title really a right to it, there would be more esquires
here than in any three kingdoms in Europe.'[82]

Eagerness rather than reluctance to heighten standing predominated. Sticklers tried in vain to curb the promiscuous use of the appellation of 'gentleman'. The Recorder of Dublin explained that 'the word "gentleman" is a style, addition or designation whereby men of fashion, substance and education in this kingdom are distinguished and designed in deeds . . . from merchants or men of inferior callings'.[83] This liberality, even laxity, continued to worry. In 1721, a caustic eye was cast over a published list of subscribers to a proposed national bank. Of thirty-seven styled 'esquire', twenty were alleged to be so 'little known' that their qualifications should be referred to the King at Arms. Those who had assumed or been accorded the dignity were mocked as unworthy of it.[84] The confusion cried out for regulation, but with the heralds powerless to degrade upstarts, little could be done. Instead, alternative criteria for separating gentlemen from squires, the gentle or genteel from the unmannerly, and the quality from the rest were proposed. The trouble was that neither the group to be measured nor the measures to be used were universally agreed. Squires might form a discrete band; the 'gentry' or 'quality' did not. Ancestry offered one device for evaluation, but increasingly there was reluctance to accord precedence simply on grounds of pedigree. Office-holding or professional qualifications offered more solid evidence of substance. So, too, did income. At the same time, subjective qualities were invoked.

Because of these disagreements, uncertainty has continued about who constituted the quality in Irish counties. Indeed, not all accepted that income, ownership of freehold land or tenure of public places defined the élite. Despite these reservations, those who pushed themselves forward at the assizes and sessions tended to be equated with the notables of their counties.[85] In County Cavan in 1724, 156 signed a remonstrance against Wood's Halfpence. During the 1750s, when the notables of County Meath gathered for the assizes at Trim, 109 subscribed for a vellum map of the county. These signatories formed a self-defining county community of the important: approximately the same in numbers, if not always the same individuals, as in the commission of the peace.[86] Office-holders, either the county magistrates or the grand jurors, offered the quickest means to name and count the élite. Others deemed that possession of a residence of requisite size and encircled by a demesne announced membership of the quality. By the nineteenth century, more than 7,000 planned parks on this scale can be mapped.[87] All these measures ignored the larger towns where different offices – in corporation, guild and parish – entitled their holders to local regard.

These gauges allow county élites to be counted. Membership of the grand jury and commission of the peace overlapped. In many shires, more families supplied grand jurors, who, unlike magistrates, could change twice yearly. In Antrim between 1732 and 1747, 85 separate families provided grand jurors. In comparison, in the same county the commission of the peace only lengthened from 33 to 59 between 1720 and 1760. In Armagh, representatives of 84 families sat in the grand jury box from 1736 to 1751. Its commission of the peace increased from 26 in 1720 to 59 by 1760. In the small county of Louth, 142, from 97 families, were empanelled on the grand jury between 1716 and 1731: many more than were commissioned as magistrates. In Donegal, from 1753 to 1768, 80 individuals trooped into the grand jury box. In 1760, the commission of the peace had 67 names.[88] In Westmeath during George II's reign, 68 different men served as grand jurors. This differed little from the total in the commission of the peace: 61 at the start of the reign; 69 in 1760.[89] In most counties before the late eighteenth century, the quality, if identified by this method, numbered fewer than 100. Only in Cork (the largest county) did it edge above 200.

Size of county commissions of the peace[90]

County	1720	1760	1776–77	Protestant families, 1733
Antrim	33	59	68	14,899
Armagh	26	59	74	6,064
Carlow		36	52	1,000
Cavan	46	45	68	1,969
Clare		74	90	665
Cork	116	191	216	7,089
Donegal	34	67	66	5,543
Down		85	91	14,060
Dublin County	82 (1745)			1,928
Dublin City		92	109	8,823
Fermanagh		41	56	2,913
Galway		75	83	911
Kerry		74	86	1,073
Kildare		48	71	656
Kilkenny		93	92	970
King's County		48	80	1,237
Leitrim		33	57	735
Limerick		115	115	2,056
Londonderry		42	41	8,751
Longford		26	32	819
Louth		44	50	897
Mayo	32 (1686) 30 (1743)	43	66	697
Meath		77	115	1,691
Monaghan		39	56	2,838

Size of county commissions of the peace (*continued*)

County	1720	1760	1776–67	Protestant families, 1733
Queen's County		67	78	1,355
Roscommon		42	62	790
Sligo		27	42	1,166
Tipperary		99	111	1,627
Tyrone	39 (1765)	47	61	5,587
Waterford		40	48	827
Westmeath		69	93	1,139
Wexford		53	78	2,193
Wicklow		46	57	2,533

The problem of equating these office-holders with the quality is that it excludes many who, either voluntarily or – in the cases of rigid Protestant dissenters and Catholics – through legal incapacity, abstained from office. The government, needing drones, did not enquire too closely into the circumstances of candidates. Political tractability was all that was asked. After 1649, this was usually equated with Protestantism. The Test Act of 1704 further tightened requirements. It insisted – at least in theory – on communion with the established Church of Ireland as a prerequisite for important offices.[91] Otherwise, from the 1690s, nothing more onerous than devotion to the Protestant interest, enthusiasm for 'Revolution Principles' and (after 1714) adherence to the Hanoverians was needed. Those thus qualified and installed in prestigious places formed the most readily identifiable of the several élites which composed the embryonic Protestant Ascendancy. More were accepted as gentlemen or of the quality – sometimes grudgingly – than just the functionaries and freeholders of the counties. In particular, those who officiated in the humbler spheres of parish, manor, barony or borough were elevated above neighbours. In many cases, this was because they were already accounted gentlemen in their area. To be included among the gentry, even the parish or urban type, was to become eligible for duties. Often irksome and humdrum, these tasks nevertheless differentiated the substantial and reputable from the *hoi polloi*.[92] Neighbours knew better than distant governments whether, by background and behaviour, those set over them measured up to ideals of nobility, gentility and quality. Superiors were expected to display their superiority in their housing, dress, conversation, demeanour and diet. Notions of reputation and credit also came into play. Those with austere religious principles or attached to the dethroned of Catholic and

Gaelic Ireland honoured alternative hierarchies. But those rival systems are hard to retrieve, other than in outline.

Within the quality, the titled were known and easily ranked. Baronets were sparingly created. In Ireland, between 1698 and 1727, eleven were gazetted. However, between 1755 and 1766, another dozen were made.[93] As a reward, the hereditary title was coveted, since it did not force the recipient to live too opulently. Richard Cox, a lawyer (and eventually lord chancellor) of modest settler background, pestered Queen Anne's administration for a baronetcy.[94] The honour would signify to traducers that he still enjoyed favour. It also suited his finances. In 1720, he revealed that he had £2,000–£3,000 in leases and personalty, and another £560 p.a. not settled on any of his numerous progeny.[95] For Thomas Taylor, it was a staging post on a route from beginnings in Ireland as architects and executors of the Cromwellian land settlement to a marquisate. The dignity precipitated a flurry of activity to fit up houses in Dublin and County Meath in appropriate splendour.[96] Some observers derided the title as an empty vanity. In 1730, one of the Howard tribe, itself on course for a peerage, censured a Molyneux cousin for accepting a baronetcy. 'The money he paid for it would have done his family more good than the title'.[97] Ascetic Cork Quakers reproached a defector, who, 'coming into his father's inheritance young and foolish, became a prodigal, purchased at the heraldry office the title of knight and baronet, married and soon died'.[98]

Irish lords-lieutenant, as deputies of the sovereign, had the right to dub knights. How liberally they did so varied. In the heyday of the early Stuarts, knighthoods carried a price tag of £100. They were grabbed, like bargains from a bazaar. Between 1603 and 1641, 268 received this tawdry distinction.[99] Between 1641 and 1660, the honour was frequently used, both to reward past and to encourage future services. This prodigality provoked a royalist judge after 1660 to expostulate, 'what a parcel of knights have been made of late. Honour given to drummers and such low fellows'.[100] Thereafter, in more settled conditions, fewer received this accolade.[101] Among the brutally pragmatic Irish Protestants, non-hereditary titles lost ground to more solid favours. The lord-lieutenant was warned in 1757, 'neither feathers nor honours' would satisfy clamorous locals. Instead, they hungered after 'something more substantial', ideally a government pension or the governorship of a county.[102] Only belatedly did the English regime fashion silken fetters to bind Irish Protestant notables. An order of chivalry, the Knights of St Patrick, specific to Ireland was first mooted in Charles I's reign but instituted only in 1783.[103] Through the delay, a chance painlessly to assimilate the important into the Britannic system was missed.

Beneath the titled opened a large and perilous tract peopled with esquires, gentlemen, 'the genteel' and 'the quality'. Sometimes the same person slips within a few years between the social orders: now a gentleman, next an esquire, then back again to the gentry.[104] The suffix 'esquire' – in everyday usage conveyed by the complimentary prefix 'Squire' – was given more sparingly than that of 'gentleman'. It ornamented acknowledged leaders of Protestant Ireland, such as successive Conollys at Castletown. The greater selectivity in its use is shown by the few counties in which numbers and proportions of esquires and gentlemen were recorded. During and after the Cromwellian occupation, officials identified the landed and tax-payers. Ownership of land in Counties Antrim, Donegal, Down, Fermanagh and Londonderry was concentrated between 120 and 200 individuals. Within these propertied cliques, the percentage recorded as esquires varied from approximately 25 per cent in Londonderry, about 20 per cent in Antrim, Donegal and Down to maybe 16 per cent in Antrim and only 10 per cent in Fermanagh.[105] Similar social striations occur in Monaghan in 1660. Forty-six individuals apparently dominated this small and lightly settled shire. They divided between one non-resident peer, six esquires and thirty-nine 'gentlemen'.[106] The impression of an intimate group of county bigwigs is again conveyed by Dolan's peek at County Fermanagh in 1719. There the county was largely owned by three baronets, twenty-six esquires, twenty-three designated either as gentlemen or 'Mr', three given military titles, three clerics and an attorney.[107]

Enquiries necessitated by taxation continued. In 1662, rates for the subsidy were graduated according to rank and calling. Applotters had, therefore, to classify potential tax-payers. The parliamentary statutes under which they acted gave some guidance. Even so, as the returns from County Waterford warn, subsidy commissioners enjoyed much latitude. In consequence, terms were not used consistently. Householders in the barony of Decies were returned as a baronet, eight esquires, forty-six gentlemen, eight widows, four merchants and a butcher, together with 182 'yeomen' and 463 'husbandmen'. In fact, the authorities had permitted the designations of 'yeoman' and 'farmer' to be used interchangeably. Yet, in neighbouring baronies with similar economies, neither yeomen nor husbandmen were noted. All under the stratum of gentleman are called 'farmer'.[108] Such practices undermine efforts to deduce plausible taxonomies from these returns.

Different problems bedevil another inquisition: into County Clare in 1660. There, a landowning contingent of about 630 was itemized. It contained two peers, four baronets, one knight, forty-one esquires and an astonishing 582 'gentlemen'.[109] Maybe the clerks had soothed all below the squirearchy with the balm of being called 'gentleman'. Alternatively, the figures may tell how recent events had unbalanced Clare's social structure. During the 1650s, land in the county had been reserved for those punished for fighting on the losing side in the Confederate Wars by being uprooted from estates elsewhere in Ireland. Removed to Clare, these unfortunates received generally barren fragments.[110] The dispossessed, mainly Old Irish or Gaelicized Old English, formerly important in their counties, consoled themselves with the style if not the substance of gentlemen.

This humour connected with what others remarked of seventeenth-century Ireland. In 1612, Sir John Davies commented that 'every man, being born to land, as well bastard as legitimate, they all held themselves to be gentlemen'. In consequence 'they scorn to descend to husbandry or merchandize, or to learn any mechanical art or science'.[111] John Dunton, after touring Ireland in the 1690s, reported, 'you must know the Irish are all gentlemen, tho beggars and vagabonds, if they be of a name that has ever a gentlemen of it'.[112] Such attitudes if they persisted among reduced gentlemen stored up problems, both for the *ci-devant* gentry itself and for the authorities. 'The poor, proud gentry', herded into the least fertile regions, harboured hopes of 'the ever flying tomorrow' when they would be restored to their lost estates.[113] In the interim, they adopted a variety of strategies to survive. The continuing presence of these Catholic gentry alongside the newcomers disconcerted the latter. It fostered a suspicion that, even in periods of apparent quiet, these rival grandees were simply biding their time before resuming their rightful place.[114] Apprehensive Protestants traced the unruliness of rapparees, tories and brigands to this source. In contrast, friends of the displaced criticized what had overthrown them – the bad faith of Charles II, James II and the Irish Parliament in relation to the Treaty of Limerick. They also derided those installed as the new owners of the kingdom. Yet the critiques of the incumbents as par-venus, rapacious and negligent, bereft of true nobility or gentility, included nothing that was not voiced, and often more stridently, by alarmed Protes-tants.[115] Behind the hierarchies determined by inheritance, wealth or office were others, more spectral certainly but widely understood, based on merit. Ireland was unusual in harbouring so many whose sense of rank was completely at variance with wealth. But in Wales, too, many with no more than £5 or £10 a year from their freeholds treasured their gentle status. In 1730, all the inhabitants in one parish of the St Asaph's diocese were 'pretendedly and nominally gentlemen but as humble to live in cottages and huts'.[116]

The state and its auxiliaries lacked the authority and ultimately the inclination to distribute distinctions according to such tricky and inward criteria. Crude tests of loyalty, increasingly gauged by confession, sufficed. Otherwise, the government accepted rather than sought to alter the élites in the counties. So much was shown in County Wexford in 1686. It was surveyed, probably as a prelude to reconstituting the commission of the peace, and 101 notables were listed. They included a few survivors of Old Irish and Old English background. Among its landowners, Wexford boasted two peers, neither of whom resided. Next came two baronets, three knights, twelve esquires, nine gentlemen and eleven dignified with military ranks. The contingent was completed by nine merchants, six clergymen and a vintner. (Almost half the 101 were not described socially or occupationally.) Not just in social standing, but also in income, the Wexford worthies were diversified. The two non-resident peers had estates elsewhere, so their total revenues remain a mystery. The three richest residents each enjoyed estimated annual incomes of £800. Another three had £700 p.a. But thirteen of the fifty-three whose incomes were guessed were thought to live on less than £100 p.a. Two had no more than a yearly £40.[117]

Incomes of County Wexford notables, 1686

Income	Number
£800+	3
£700–799	3
£500–699	3
£400–499	7
£300–399	5
£200–299	8
£100–199	11
<£100	13

These figures accord with what can be recovered from other counties. They seem to diverge from what is known of even the remoter and poorer counties of Wales. In Merioneth in 1660, for example, the seven wealthiest landowners enjoyed rentals of between £600 and £1,200. On this evidence, a Welsh shire could support one or two who surpassed their Irish equivalents in income.[118] In Ireland, £40 seems often to have been taken as the minimum yearly competence to achieve a degree of respectability and consideration for official duties. Indeed, in 1698 only those with £40 p.a. from freehold land (or £1,000 personal estate) were permitted to hunt game.[119] This set a monetary qualification for gentility. Among the grand, particularly the esquires, incomes gradually edged upwards. But money alone did not dictate rank. Indeed, wealth and standing frequently and sometimes sensationally diverged. Squires and gentlemen, no less than peers, could be financially embarrassed. Furthermore, they embarrassed others by failing through poverty to maintain the port thought to be the essential, indeed defining, adjunct of their rank. The Wexford enquiry of 1686 showed that the government, in order to run the counties, had to look beyond peers, baronets, knights and esquires. A modicum of money was clearly vital to undertake any service for the state. In turn, it was widely appreciated that such service could bring money. Unscrupulous applicants, in order to persuade an innocent and ignorant administration remote in Dublin (or better still in London) to employ them, resorted to tricks. Some pretended to a substance which they manifestly lacked until state service supplied it. The same subterfuges, sometimes helpful in the quest for official favours, could assist to a prized place among the quality.[120]

On the peaks above the clouds, the precise altitudes of the eminent were accurately assessed. Owing to the need regularly to negotiate settlements with wives, children, trustees and creditors, assets were exposed. An Ulster squire, Cromwell Price boasted in 1746, 'my estate is known by every one in the country'.[121] Sir Richard Cox opened for inspection the details of his financial affairs as he sought spouses for his numerous brood.[122] It was possible for worth to be misrepresented. However, until paper transactions and stock-jobbing gained hold, the nature of the resources – based on property – militated against massive frauds. Naturally, the inclination was to talk up income, as with status. Thereby credit could be preserved and enhanced. Openness about income enabled both the government and individuals to calculate with reasonable accuracy who was worth what. Again, however, the lofty few were more readily described than the obscure majority.

Seventeenth-century Ireland, although famed as El Dorado, disappointed extravagant hopes. In 1686, Petty, a rarity whose expectations – at least in financial terms – had been satisfied, inventoried those in Ireland worth more than £2,000 p.a. Apart from himself, he listed only twenty-one. He overlooked several.[123] Thirteen of his twenty-one were already peers, and several of the others, including his own wife and heir, would soon be ennobled. This attests to the rough congruence between the formal gradations of society and wealth. He also implied what numerous successors found: the bulk of those who owned and ruled Ireland commanded markedly lower incomes than their counterparts in lowland England.[124] In 1689, a longer although still selective catalogue (of Protestant refugees from Ireland) found forty-four with revenues of or above £2,000 p.a.[125] Average incomes slowly rose.[126] In 1713, a well-informed official in Dublin again assessed notables.

He detailed the income of 80 per cent of 300 members of the Irish House of Commons. Sixty-one of those sitting for the counties had on average £1,585 p.a. This mean smoothed over startling disparities. It hid the £6,000 of Chaworth Brabazon, heir to the earl of Meath and member for County Dublin, or £5,500 for William Conolly, 'esquire', soon as Speaker to be the political boss and one of the wealthiest men in the kingdom. At the opposite pole was Sir Maurice Crosbie, knight of the shire for Kerry, worth (it was suggested) only £600 p.a. The 189 representatives of the towns enjoyed, on average, slightly more than an annual £900.[127] This put them well ahead of 'persons of moderate fortunes', said in 1719 to be £200 or £300 p.a.[128]

These figures are supported by what is known about individuals. John Blennerhasset of Ballyseedy in County Kerry, soon to sit in the Dublin parliament, in 1687 drew a notional £635 10s. from lands in Counties Cork and Kerry. In 1693, the sheriff of Donegal, Samson, was said to have £500 yearly.[129] In the 1690s, William Waring enjoyed about £600; by the 1730s, his successor, Samuel Waring, member for a borough between 1703 and 1727, had about £900 p.a. Jack Perceval, head of the Sligo branch of the ramifying Perceval tribe in Ireland, expected revenues of £650 to £800 early in the 1720s.[130] Between the 1660s and 1700, the Southwells received between £1,000 and £1,200 annually from their Kinsale holdings. In 1692 and 1697, the heir, Edward Southwell, sat for the borough of Kinsale. John Ormsby, MP, described at his death in 1721 as 'a wealthy man', had a yearly £1,800.[131] Swift, in *The Intelligencer* of 1728, introduced a country gentleman from Ulster, also a member of parliament, with £1,400 a year. Burke and his friends in their periodical of 1747, the *Reformer*, gave a 'gentleman of fortune' £2,000 p.a.[132] Back in 1721, a brother-in-law of Speaker Conolly declared that few gentlemen in Ireland enjoyed as much as £3,000 p.a.[133] Within the circle of the prosperous Conollys, £1,000 p.a. was thought a good fortune. An estate of £2,000 was conceived as the apogee of the landed squirearchy in south Wicklow early in the 1730s.[134] In 1751, it was recorded that Sir James Caldwell, the County Fermanagh baronet, could expect an annual £1,500 from his unimproved estates.[135] Such sums are in line with the incomes of other squires who entered parliament, such as Robert French of Monivea, Richard Edgeworth or the Balfours of Fermanagh and County Louth. Between the 1730s or 1740s and early 1770s, their rentals increased from about £1,500 to £2,500.[136] Yet a projector in 1762 still used £1,000 as the income of an archetypal gentleman in Ireland.[137]

By the 1770s, fresh investigations showed a denser settlement by the prosperous. Even so, when the undoubted notables were counted in three counties in 1775, they numbered at most (in Tipperary) 163. Tipperary now supported ten grandees reckoned to be worth more than £5,000 p.a.

The majority of them were peers, but several (Ashbrook and Bessborough) resided in England. Eighty per cent of those named enjoyed more modest incomes, ranging between £500 and £2,000 yearly. In Kilkenny fewer (75) were noted, perhaps because the observer knew less about the county. This may also explain why a larger proportion of those whose revenues were entered belonged to the higher bands, with over £3,000 p.a.; 50 per cent were recorded as having £500 to £2,000.[138] In the adjacent county of Waterford only fifty-eight individuals caught the attention of the enquirer. The three thought to have more than £5,000 p.a. were all peers: the habitually absent Devonshire, inheritor of the Cork and Burlington apanage, Tyrone, and Grandison. The majority of owners (47 of the 58) clustered below the £2,000 p.a. level. Indeed, twenty-six had less than £1,000 yearly.[139]

Incomes of notables in Counties Kilkenny, Tipperary and Waterford, *c.*1775

Income, p.a.	Kilkenny	Tipperary	Waterford
£5,000+	6	10	3
£3,000–£5,000	8	4	3
£2,000–£3,000	10	14	5
£1,000–£2,000	23	62	21
£500–£1,000	11	33	15
<£500	5	7	11

The slow increase in rents was merely one of several disadvantages under which the notables of Ireland laboured. Irish Protestants felt – and often were – poorer than their equivalents in lowland England. Using the estimates of income for assorted social and occupational groups furnished by King in 1688 and Massie in 1759 suggests that peers, knights, esquires and gentlemen in Ireland, close in revenues to the averages for their English counterparts late in the seventeenth century, had drifted further apart by the end of George II's reign. However, the accuracy of King's estimates – £650 for a knight, £450 for an esquire and £280 for a gentleman – has been questioned, so that the disparities between England and Ireland may not have widened so sharply but may long have existed.[140] At the same time, the generally sluggish performance of agricultural incomes in the first half of the eighteenth century may have depressed the standing of Irish landowners in relation to their English counterparts. Few peers in Ireland by 1760 could match the annual income of £20,000 posited by Massie, and virtually no esquires or mere gentlemen could equal the yearly revenues in England of (respectively) £4,000 and £2,000.[141] However, in English society, no less than in Ireland, it was acknowledged that within these bands there were considerable variations in circumstances.[142]

In remoter regions of Britain, revenues were often lower. Places like Cornwall, Cumberland and Westmorland, and indeed west Wales and Scotland, may be the more appropriate comparisons with Ireland. In the land-locked county of Montgomery, for example, although the conventional classifications of peer, squire and gentleman were used, the second and third were bandied about imprecisely. The four peerage families in the shire had incomes above £2,000 p.a., but were surpassed by a few commoners. A financial frontier between esquires and gentlemen has been detected, set – rather loosely – at the level of an annual £300 or £400. In manners reminiscent of much of provincial Ireland, Montgomeryshire had a landowning élite marked by discontinuities in membership, absenteeism among the richest and an uneven geographical distribution. By the end of the eighteenth century there had emerged a group of eleven leading families, each worth more than £1,000. A larger contingent, of perhaps thirty, dominated county offices.[143] This was a situation not so far removed from that in many Irish counties, although they tended to be larger in area. In Merioneth, a group of the seven wealthiest proprietors in 1660 had annual rentals worth between £600 and £1,200.[144] The manner in which these Welsh notables had come by their estates was more peaceful than the recent conquest and confiscation to which so many Irish Protestants owed their holdings. Nevertheless, in Wales, economic and cultural differences, sometimes with sectarian and even ethnic connotations, created antagonism between the few and the many. Similar patterns have been observed in the south-western triangle of Pembrokeshire, Cardiganshire and Carmarthenshire. The remoteness from metropolitan centres and generally modest yields from lands produced a social structure and range of incomes reminiscent of those in many Irish counties. Only two peerage families were to be found in the region. The summit of wealth was at £2,000 or £3,000.[145] Further east, in more affluent Glamorgan, the peak was higher: £3,000 to £5,000. There, at the end of the seventeenth century, the annual income which usually set an esquire apart from a gentleman was £500. Yet further east, in England, the apex in county society was occupied by those with £5,000 or £6,000.[146]

Scottish society, although undergoing rapid and enforced transformations in the later seventeenth and eighteenth centuries – especially along the western margin and Highlands and islands – did not otherwise closely resemble Protestant Ireland. A tripartite division into nobles, lairds and bonnet lairds, roughly corresponding to differences in income, has been proposed.[147] The nobles, it has often been suggested, retained a formidable battery of local powers while playing on the larger stage offered first by the regal union of 1603 and then by the Treaty of Union in 1707. The abolition of heritable jurisdictions in 1747 curtailed the legal powers of individuals. In addition, the tendency towards the concentration of massive estates in few hands was being reversed by the middle of the eighteenth century.[148] Proprietors, sometimes hated for their dominance, could be condemned in terms familiar in Wales and Ireland, as aliens, even as Norman freebooters.[149] Relatively simple occupational and social structures prevailed in the remoter districts, but – as in Ireland – the moves towards more commercial and legalistic dealings between owners and occupiers of the land had quickened by the eighteenth century. The resulting changes strained traditional relationships. Victims abounded, but hardly on the same scale as the casualties from the upheavals in seventeenth-century Ireland. Moreover, if some Scots were ousted and many grandees rode south, they were not replaced by strangers. In general, notwithstanding the dislocations, Scottish proprietors continued to share confession, language and lineage with tenants and servants.[150] It is more difficult to assess how the incomes of the landed in Ireland and Scotland compared.[151] Inhabitants of both countries, having once terrified their English neighbours, by the eighteenth century were ridiculed by the metropolitan.[152] But this contempt was as nothing compared to the scorn to which Dubliners, Palesmen and town-dwellers and lowlanders and urbane Presbyterians treated the provincials and backward in their own countries.[153] What seemed most obviously to unite those who inherited high stations in late Stuart and Hanoverian Ireland and Scotland was a need to supplement exiguous incomes, which drove many into the service of the crown outside their own kingdom.[154]

A position among the quality in any of the Stuarts' or Hanoverians' dominions depended on more than wealth. But lack of money or credit could prevent the elevated from maintaining the appropriate style. In South Wales, the Vaughans of Golden Grove, with 'the dignity of the peerage to support', worried about subsisting on £2,250 each year. Perhaps more pressing were the problems of a squire in the same vicinity who in 1780 revealed, 'I have but two pairs of stockings in the world. I am ashamed to go out, I am so shabby'.[155] What was needed to retain respect and ranking clearly varied. Discreet economies were practised so that the embarrassed could cut the grand figure for a spell in Dublin or even London.[156] In this particular, it was sometimes suggested that those in Ireland enjoyed an advantage, thanks to the lower costs of living. The smart certainly hoped to save money by wintering in Dublin rather than in London.[157] In turn, Dublin taxed resources more than provincial life.[158]

Savings could be achieved by shutting large establishments in the countryside and lodging in town, whether in Ireland, Britain or continental Europe. Any committed to public responsibilities, as active members of parliament or functionaries in their counties, found it hard to run an economical regime. Visitors to Dublin were struck by the rising rents for lodgings.[159] Those regarded or setting up as the quality had to differentiate themselves in dress, demeanour and diet. Most that was deemed stylish was imported at high cost, and often burdened with punitive dues.[160] Strenuous efforts were made to infuse these local leaders with a patriotic duty to shun the exotic and buy Irish. Notwithstanding the intermittent success of such campaigns, appearances being of the essence among the quality, bills for furnishings, foods and luxuries from abroad make nonsense of efforts to calculate average spending on the basis of a basketful of local staples. Furthermore, these urges to buy, thought irrational and wasteful by the austere, gripped others outside the quality or would-be quality.[161]

Land was traditionally treated as the sure path to social renown. This belief spoke more of the values of England than of the realities of late seventeenth- and eighteenth-century Ireland. Property was easily come by in Tudor and Stuart Ireland. Recompense for motley services – usually fighting but also pacifying – it was valued more by those who had lost it than by its new, and often absent, owners.[162] Job-lots scattered across the island seldom provided an income commensurate with the acreage. Unsentimentally, much was traded in, allowing others to set up on smaller plots and be admitted to the quality. Even those proprietors who held on to their sour and sodden parcels gave opportunities to locals. The latter, either as agents or tenants (or both), exploited these holdings, and hoisted themselves into polite society. The yield of all but the greatest estates failed to underwrite the expenses which those with comparable holdings in Britain confidently incurred. Since appearances – 'the grand figure' – decided rankings, the impecunious either lived on (or increasingly beyond) their credit or hunted for supplements. Projects of physical improvement were embraced. Paid employment was solicited. These needs turned many of the quality of rural Ireland into scavenging mongrels.

The known freeholders – between 3,000 and 5,000 – constituted an identifiable ascendancy. But to limit it to this landed group ignores too many whose claims to be of 'the quality' were endorsed by their contemporaries. Despite other, usually urban sources of wealth, income from land, in Ireland no less than England, brought special distinction. However, outright ownership was rarer in Ireland than in England and Wales. In consequence, the prejudice against land held by lease, although not absent, weakened. Most proprietors, even the lordly, had mixed portfolios.

Opportunists leased much on advantageous terms during the upheavals of the seventeenth century. Any who talked of a 'large estate of an ancient and unquestionable title', like one notable in eighteenth-century County Down, may have glossed over how and when it had been acquired.[163] In 1730, the inheritance of the younger Edward Southwell was admired as 'a great and clear estate'.[164] By 1736, the Boyles' holdings, the earliest acquired in the late sixteenth century, could be praised as 'ancient, on good foundation and the best of titles'. Again, this assertion disregarded the adventitious and often unscrupulous ways in which holdings had been assembled.[165] As well as the Boyles, the Temples, future Viscounts Palmerston, the Lanes, ennobled as Viscount Lanesborough, Sir William Ellis, a Dublin official in the 1680s, and the earls of Anglesey typified the opportunists who had grasped both Dublin and scattered rural properties when offered on favourable terms.[166]

Long ownership and a clear title, nevertheless, could add cubits to the stature of a landlord. Practical considerations as well as sentiment weighed heavily. Repeated confiscations throughout the sixteenth and seventeenth centuries had afforded many chances to acquire rebels' lands. Sometimes, with the next throw of the dice, rebels became rulers. Frequently beneficiaries of the redistributions were made to disgorge part of their booty. Uncertainty persisted well into the eighteenth century, increased by the willingness of the English parliament in the 1730s to listen to a principal casualty of the Williamite Wars, Lord Clancarty.[167] Sovereigns and sovereign parliaments exercised their powers with such seeming arbitrariness that the recent victors suspected that all too easily they might turn into losers. As a result, some lands, or the titles to them, were little valued because they were insecure foundations for fortunes. No one was criticized when they grabbed what was emptied by the state from its bulging store. But some remained wary about allying with families whose principal properties might easily be resumed by the authorities. Such apprehensions diminished, but never wholly disappeared. In time, sharp practice and negligence lowered the reputations of the apparently magnificent. Transgressors, far from living in an entirely unregulated culture of acquisition, were watched and censured. In 1660, the cavalier, Richard Lane, vilified the St Georges and Cootes, calling Captain Oliver St George the 'greediest man, advancing unjust use on unjust use, keen to wrestle poor gentlemen out of their estates'.[168] Such judgements did not arrest the advance of the St Georges and Cootes into the peerage. Ironically, by the 1720s, the then head of the St Georges, now a peer and relaxing in his western fiefdom, shared the Lanes' doctrines. St George opposed his own *noblesse oblige*, not harrying tenants during grim times, to his brother's cupidity.[169] The first earl of Anglesey, irritated by the whispering campaign

which lowered his standing at Charles II's court, piously explained
to his son-in-law how he 'came honestly and dearly' by his Irish lands.
He even claimed to have refused the parcels dangled by the Cromwellians
throughout the 1650s.[170] Similar niceties exercised two settlers in 1690. Sir
Richard Bulkeley from Old Bawn in County Dublin gloated over an
inheritance in his family for four generations. In addition, he boasted that
the property had been acquired neither through perjury nor 'indirect
courses'. 'Honest industry and good husbandry' had increased its value.
Bulkeley's adversary, Sir St John Brodrick from Ballyanen in County Cork,
conceded that his estate had been bought only recently.[171] In the same
mode, a wealthy clergyman in Country Antrim during the 1720s vetoed
a possible partner for a daughter because 'most of his estate is very unjustly
got'.[172]

What was done with land as well as how it had been gained affected
the reputation of the owner. The path between neglect and greed was
hard to walk. Attentiveness and residence were approved; their opposites,
not. An owner was expected to ensure that an inheritance was transmitted to the next generation intact if not improved. 'A family is an edifice
always in building, but never builded.'[173] In County Louth, Sir John
Bellew was reviled in the 1670s for his severity. So, too, in the following
decade was Sir Matthew Deane in County Cork.[174] In County Donegal,
Henry Conyngham acted as agent of the Murrays, absent in Scotland
throughout the 1690s. In 1704, Conyngham protested against the severity
proposed by Murray. 'For my part, I can have no hand in sending hun-
dreds of families a begging and, abstracted from the charitable part, I am
sure it would not be common prudence'. Conyngham added rhetorically,
'I would rather live on bread and cheese all my life than do it'. Secure
on his salary as an army officer, there was little danger that he would have
to.[175] In the equally harsh 1720s, Lord St George joined others in criti-
cizing landlords who, indifferent to the welfare of tenants, racked rents
regardless of the impact on tenants.[176]

Feelings about a moral economy, strongly held, loudly voiced but often
contradictory, complicated the social stratigraphy of eighteenth-century
Ireland.[177] Absenteeism, although sometimes extenuated and even represented as a benefit, was widely condemned.[178] Presence could result in
greater problems. The proper care of an inheritance meant more than
maximizing its revenues: it was widely agreed that the current possessor
had obligations as a custodian both to those who occupied the land and
to heirs. Aspirations to benevolence were more freely expressed in the
eighteenth century than in the seventeenth. By explicitly inserting a moral
element in formulations of landownership, commentators were influenced
by pervasive and novel notions of gentility, civility and refinement.[179]

Christian teaching united with humanist beliefs to recommend benevolence to the propertied. Prudence seconded these injunctions. Especially during the severe conditions of the early and late 1720s and 1740–41, when famine struck, proprietors who harried a starving tenantry were lashed verbally.[180] In the north of County Cork, one observer despised the actions of Colonel St Leger at Doneraile and predicted, 'sure a country will not suffer by losing such a tyrant'. Another who hoarded potatoes during the famine in order to sell them profitably was also arraigned.[181] The humane and generous were praised. After 1730, the lordly bishop of Ossory, Sir Thomas Vesey, was remembered affectionately for his generosity towards tenants.[182] At the same time, a starchy cleric, basking in the riches which his father – Dublin's most fashionable doctor – had bequeathed him, contrasted the reputable manner in which he had bought the Shelton Abbey estate in County Wicklow with the disreputable methods by which the Wentworths had earlier gained theirs at nearby Shillelagh. Bishop Robert Howard hoped that his acquisition of 'a great, continuing and as good an estate in that county as Mr Wentworth . . . [would] show the world that industry and slow honest care can make as good a fortune as the rapine and oppression of the great earl of Strafford'.[183]

The cultivated Howard invested his own custodianship of Irish lands with a moral worth lacking in the Wentworths. He represented the tendency among the consciously active and public-spirited to comment caustically on those who fell short of their high ideals. Yet, from another perspective, the Hibernian Howards were themselves ridiculed. The bishop's painter brother, Hugh Howard, had done well in England: through marriage rather than his brush. His pretensions were scorned. 'By means of name and affecting to be [a] Norfolk Howard', together with 'a small estate of a gentleman, a solemn air and slow discourse, with a very moderate smattering of polite knowledge . . . he easily passed for a leading virtuoso with the nobility'.[184] This scoffing recalls another hazard to which the quality of Ireland were exposed. Those who ventured further afield found that what entitled them to deference in their own constricted society was mocked in London, Bath and Bristol (or Brussels, Paris, Rome and Vienna). Remoteness and generally lower incomes led to *gaucheries*.[185] Among the social and cultural leaders of Dublin, the position of Hugh Howard and his brothers (one, the bishop; a second, a prominent barrister and member of parliament) was unassailable. Their father had flourished as a fashionable physician. The Howards' problems began when they travelled beyond Ireland. Careful schooling in the ways of that wider world best protected against humiliation. Increasingly, for those who counted themselves as members of the quality in Hanoverian Ireland, education became vital. The traveller had to prepare to avoid gaffes; travel then familiarized the rambler with the conduct and conventions of the quality.[186]

As with many fashions embraced by modish Irish Protestants, this route to refinement elicited contradictory responses. One parent, a Fermanagh squire, forbade his heir to indulge in educational tours. In 1728 a Dublin lady noted, ' 'tis become a great fashion with us for our ladies to travel, and do everything that is expensive'.[187] Stay-at-homes classified travel as another extravagance which increased the tendency of the wealthy to abandon Ireland. Archbishop King, a monotonous critic of all who betrayed the interests of Ireland as defined by himself, expressed the inconsistencies in attitude. He had recommended the cultural benefits of foreign tours, yet railed against the Irish who stampeded to London. King knew the city well. However, he warned the visitors that, far from enjoying themselves, they would be 'entire strangers to the pleasures of London, live as it were out of the world there, and converse only with one another, without making any figure or having any interest, and a nobleman that would appear with credit, reputation and splendour in his own country, sinketh there below the ordinary rate of gentleman. They are despised, ridiculed and hated . . . treated with reserve and contempt'.[188] Despite these warnings, England and continental Europe beckoned alluringly to the quality from Ireland.

One who had succumbed, the first Lord Molesworth, insisted on the benefits of travel. It introduced wider perspectives, which separated the cultivated minority (like himself and his sons) from the generality. He despised gentlemen with 'a cramped and low education, helped by little or no reading'. Needing to oversee their farms and meeting only 'mean company at fairs and markets', they lacked any stimulus to improve, and so 'grow narrow spirited, covetous, ungenteel'.[189] Some, passing as quality in their own baronies, made a pitiful impression in the county town, let alone in Dublin or London. Divergences in upbringings and habits told usually of variations in income. Those with meagre incomes travelled little and lived among peasants and beasts, as a result taking on the local coloration: 'a country gentlemen is a compound of much pride, and little merit, a sultan in a small parish, a tyrant in busto, and a clown'.[190] In 1743 it was reported that 'most of the first gentlemen' of Cork and Limerick were away in Dublin.[191] This lucky group, familiar with metropolitan and perhaps cosmopolitan standards, corresponded with 'gentlemen of estates and quality', and was distinguished from the unregenerate provincials who rode no further than the market town. In 1757 a prosperous landowner from County Cork was regarded as 'a plain country gentleman', because disorientated by the complexities of fashionable Dublin.[192]

Awareness of these internal stratifications within the gentry and quality expressed itself when a pamphleteer of the 1750s apostrophized separately 'our polite gentry', 'men of mode', and unadorned 'gentlemen'.[193] These divisions, often originating in financial inequalities, also reflected differences in attitude and behaviour. Irony prompted the owner of Shelton Abbey, Ralph Howard, the son of Bishop Howard and later to be ennobled, to enumerate the several peers or heirs to peerages whose company he was keeping in Rome. He ended, 'the rest are simple squires, like your humble servant'.[194] Squire Cosby classified some of his neighbours as plain country gentlemen, a term which seems to have denoted habits innocent of the sophistication of Dublin, London, Paris or Rome. Cosby, Janus-visaged, gazed admiringly backwards to the old-fashioned ways of some neighbours and forebears and outwards to the novel and stylish. In 1748, a refugee from France thought that Ireland did not abound in gentlemen 'of figure'. Provincial rust was precisely the trait against which the Crosbies of Ardfert, Kerry baronets and future peers, wished to protect their heir. It was hoped that a spell at Trinity College, Dublin and perhaps another abroad would advance him beyond 'the qualifications of a country squire'.[195] In 1717, Anne Chetwood mocked 'two of our country gentlemen', who appeared at Cootehill in County Cavan. Observing their bizarre dress, she concluded 'one is like numps [a silly person] and tother would serve in Dublin for somebody's butler'.[196] Later in the century, a poet satirized the squire's habitation. It served as an emblem for 'the goodly family . . . neither by fashions nor by seasons changed'. Dirt and decay invested the old-fashioned mansion. Each backwoodsman was liable to be dismissed as a 'fox-hunting sot', but preserved habits of expansive hospitality that were still admired.[197]

The unadorned epithet of 'country gentlemen' was not always pejorative. 'This person', an apologist reminded readers in 1726, 'is one who having had a liberal education, and looked into most scenes of life, has now determined to sit down and observe the manners of other people'. An ideal country gentleman was distinguished by 'the simplicity of his manners, the disinterestedness of his views and the firmness of his principles'. He was expected to serve the public as a magistrate and perhaps as a member of parliament.[198] In Queen Anne's reign, Colonel William Ponsonby was praised as 'a country gent. of good credit' in the House of Commons. His political stance, preserving independence and refusing offices from the administration, earned the praise and the description. Ponsonby also exemplified the ideals of residence and activism. In his neighbourhood he was reckoned 'a gentleman of good estate and consideration and who has the most English improvements of planting gardens, &c. of any in this part of the country'.[199] Ponsonby personified another characteristic of the public spirited: a willingness to accept a military commission and the affectation of continuing to use it. The quality in Ireland were mocked for their fondness for such titles.[200] The style of the no-nonsense country gentleman was deliberately adopted by the two most successful politicians in early Hanoverian Ireland, Conolly and Boyle. They, too, were happy enough to be described as 'Squire', although Boyle also liked his rank of colonel. Much of this fustian garb was assumed. Conolly and Boyle were sophisticated both in their political arts and their domestic arrangements. Colonel Ponsonby, with his taste for the latest in gardening, was not sunk in the cultural backwoods. These were not the bucolics at whom Molesworth had sneered.

Even in the supposedly intimate and relaxed society of Protestant Ireland, rankings mattered and were maintained. A chasm in fortune and experience yawned between, on the one hand an Ormonde and Cork and Burlington, and their impoverished kinsmen among the peerage, let alone their professionals and tenants accounted gentlemen. The grand veered between *bonhomie* and *hauteur*. In 1680 William Molyneux, the cultivated son of a long-established and respected family at the heart of official Dublin, shrank from importuning the lord chancellor, Archbishop Michael Boyle of Dublin, because 'he is a great person, and I have no acquaintance with him'. Boyle held in plurality two of the highest offices in the kingdom: the primacy and the lord chancellorship. His wealth had also led to the recent ennoblement of his son. Molyneux might have retorted that his family had been established longer in Ireland than the Boyles.[201] In the 1740s, Edmund Spencer as an impoverished squire lacked the money to frequent the smartest club in north Cork. Although the boon companion of gentlemen, he was disabled from appearing at Castlelyons because Lord Barrymore 'has such a run of grand company . . . as I do not know how one in my way may be liked among so many of the best fortunes'.[202]

III

Attitudes

Deference was accorded to acknowledged superiors. In return, the elevated were expected to prove themselves worthy of respect. Ties of reciprocity united the several degrees in society. Preachers in reminding people of this delicate structure, divine in origin, sought to check the insubordination which regularly threatened the social fabric. At the same time, they reminded notables of their obligations to underlings.[203] Failure to render the expected courtesies revealed gaps between self and others' assessments, and caused anger. Early in George I's reign, an aggrieved Welshman wrote from County Kerry to his absent landlord, 'Your agent to lessen me calls me ensign in his rent roll and calls Mr Herbert, esq[uire]. I was lieutenant when he was a scoundrel. Sir', Ensign Robert Lloyd continued, 'I was born a gent and always behaved myself as such, and my father had 20 tenants and paid more rent each than Edward Herbert was or is worth'.[204] Touchiness about style shaded into sensitivity over treatment. Mingling of the quality sometimes led to quarrels. The actor Tate Wilkinson had been reared with the Midlands magnifico Lord Forbes, future earl of Granard. During a dinner in the 1750s, Forbes contrived to insult Wilkinson before 'several persons of quality'. As the humiliated Wilkinson stated, he did not 'think it excusable in any rank whatsoever, by any speech or look, to lessen the guest invited in the presence of others'. He concluded, 'from such honour, from such behaviour, heaven defend me'.[205] Reactions like Wilkinson's echoed the impatience with 'a boasted lineage' expressed in 1761. 'The worth of dignified ancestors', it was noted, 'too often serves only to reproach the degeneracy of their descendants'.[206]

Behaviour appropriate to station was expected. Henry Osborne from Meath, enquiring after a relative, worried lest he be 'a clown' incapable of carrying himself 'as a gentleman'.[207] Increasingly, at least a semblance of gentility was expected of those who mingled regularly with the quality. Servants, in particular, had to pass muster. Even would-be gamekeepers, if they were to reflect credit on their masters, had to 'to look more genteel', not like a butcher or ploughboy. No huntsman should intrude himself into the company of gentlemen.[208] Among the worst conundrums for both the directors and directed in polite society was how to popularize polite and civil ways without erasing the demarcations between the distinct social orders. One method among the quality was to cultivate restraint instead of ostentation. However, this reticence was not always easily understood, and might be mistaken for niggardliness. Furthermore, the availability of cheaper versions of the commodities with which the genteel surrounded themselves meant that only those with the most acute antennae could distinguish the true alloy from the base metals. All, nevertheless, agreed that these possessions helped to define the quality. Women were discerning judges in these matters. During the 1740s, Lady Theodosia Crosbie, the daughter of an earl, journeying to Kerry, paused in the city of Limerick. She regaled her sister with an account of the droll entertainment to which she had been treated by a leading citizen, a vintner, and his wife. Lady Theodosia sketched a comedy of manners, in which her maladroit hosts afforded much merriment. She hooted at the blunders of the well-meaning Limerick pair. The utensils of polite hospitality, a cause of increasing expense and anxiety to those who wished to succeed in society, excited particular hilarity. A domestic, it was noted, 'brought in the cups, wrapped up very nicely in a dish clout that had been wiping the dripping pan, I am sure, the minute before. Then there was a pewter teapot, but I believe it was designed for silver, and pewter dish for bread and butter.' On the verge of laughing in the face of her hostess, Lady Theodosia confessed, 'I had like to have shamed myself indeed, but with much pain to myself kept it in'. In the end, perhaps, she had behaved as her station and her hosts demanded. Furthermore, sensing the generosity that had inspired the excess, she adjudged the wine merchant's wife 'a good woman'.[209]

Lady Theodosia Crosbie might mock what her inferiors essayed, but her equals found fault with her manners. Conventions among the quality altered rapidly. Women policing the table of ranks found much to condemn. In 1731 Lady Midleton decried the rise of card-playing and the decline of conversation among 'all the fashion' in Dublin.[210] By 1747 Lady Arbella Denny acknowledged how meetings of the quality at public assemblies, drums, concerts and routs had reduced the frequency and importance of private visits. Nevertheless, she refused to overlook a slight offered by her niece, Lady Theodosia Crosbie, and her new husband, the heir of Ardfert. Indeed, so enraged was Lady Arbella that she vowed to strike the Crosbies from the list of her acquaintances. Ironically, young Crosbie was delighted with his reception in the city, where he had been entertained (not by Lady Theodosia) 'very genteely'.[211] Here, two notions of proper behaviour diverged strikingly. The Crosbies' failure when in Dublin to contact their imperious kinswoman led Lady Arbella to pronounce, 'I take for granted a slight so public could be designed for no other purpose than to drop all correspondence, for, tho I confess I am not of much consequence in the world, yet I can't have quite so insignificant an opinion of myself as to think because Lady Theodosia Crosbie did not take leave of all the girls which in her unmarried state she honoured with her acquaintance, that was a sufficient reason to take no notice of me'. A more crowded calendar aggravated the difficulties of negotiating society. Further hazards appeared as some clung to older modes while others embraced the new. Lady Arbella Denny knew of the innovations 'among well bred people'. Even so, she insisted that, 'I know no other way of dropping an acquaintance than that of not returning visits'.[212]

Lady Arbella Denny was not impervious to evolving fashion. She herself adjusted by holding her own weekly assembly. She also allowed visitors to tramp around her seaside gardens at Blackrock. She blended social punctiliousness with civic duty. She busied herself about a variety of charities. Yet, on occasion, even she was felt to have erred in her judgement of genteel proprieties.[213] Signifiers of the politeness and civility so prized by the quality proliferated. Houses, such as those of Lady Arbella, were contrived for both sociability and intimacy. Simultaneously they accommodated public and private needs. Even in the mid-eighteenth century, there were few indications of women being banished to the purely domestic sphere. Indeed, by the 1760s, women dined alongside men at the table of the lord-lieutenant in Dublin Castle. Lady Arbella Denny was one of those bidden to these dinners.[214] The growth of occasions on which male members of the quality could meet, in guild and Masonic conviviality or the earnest tasks of collective betterment through the Dublin Society and boards of hospitals, was matched by a busy calendar of charitable concerts and assemblies. Private houses or lodgings continued as vital settings for the entertainments of the quality.[215] Promiscuous resort was not approved. Visitors, once admitted, were further honoured by the rooms into which they were ushered. Visiting – as Lady Arbella disclosed – was regulated, but by rules which were never universally agreed. One courtesy generally recognized was to call on a mother after a successful accouchement. In 1760, the wife of an army officer having given birth, it was noted who presented their compliments at the Dublin house, either in person or through a servant. Gratifyingly, the roll was headed by the dowager countess of Kildare. She was followed by courteous professionals and squires.[216] However, these pleasures were open only to those of means. An impoverished visitor from Mayo reported home, 'you know how people in Dublin can't make visits without money in their pockets and tolerable clothes to appear in'.[217] Another from the west had detected the shifts by which the ingenious overcame this want of cash. Dublin ladies, bent on entrapping their beaux, 'put on good clothes by tick' to hide the fact that most were 'dowdies'.[218]

Lady Theodosia Crosbie's oversights and Lady Arbella Denny's edicts introduce a factor vital in social classification: the impact of women. Most wives took their ranking from their husbands. Exceptionally, thanks to their own higher standing or their wealth, they lifted their husbands higher. Speaker Conolly owed much to his bride, the daughter of Sir Albert Conyngham from Donegal, his superior in wealth and status. It was Lady Blayney rather than her indigent husband who bought a copy of Crossly's *Peerage*: a sign perhaps of her greater consciousness of status.[219] Since most within the aristocracy and gentry in Ireland married the like-circumstanced, the scope for advancement through marriage was limited. What marriage conferred, in the eyes of one widow, was 'an *éclat* and elasticity which has not of late years belonged to her'. At the same time, and seemingly contradicting this enthusiasm, there was a recognition that many women, without large portions, lacked the freedom to 'pick out one that [they] can live easy and comfortable with'.[220] Startling disparities in the social locations of partners were rare enough to be remarked. A clergyman in Ulster refuted the calumny that his first wife was of lowly background. He insisted that she came of 'a family of figure and consideration in this country'. Her family, he continued, 'have always made a handsome figure and lived with reputation'. The same cleric was equally touchy about his second wife, the daughter of linen trader at Dromore. The bride had been raised by a rich uncle and his wife, 'a virtuous gentlewoman, who keep as handsome a table as any person whatsoever in the country where they live'.[221] Differences in the geographical backgrounds of spouses introduced other strains. Brides from distant parts of Ireland or from further afield could be disconcerted by the backwardness of the regions in which they were deposited.[222] A Welsh woman removed to Castlereagh (County Roscommon) complained, 'not a creature do I see when out of this house that I can converse with'. She had visited only one other house, 'the second best' in the town.[223] Isolation could afflict those high on the social scale. The English wife of the second duke of Ormonde repined at being immured over the winter at Kilkenny Castle, with only a single female companion.[224] Another English woman who had married into the Irish peerage, Lady Shelburne, craved news of the outside world while at Conyngham Hall.[225] Unease frequently reflected strange and remote habitations, but it also arose from the more restricted circuits travelled by women of the quality. Especially in the Irish provinces, the number of those who shared their social position and cultural values was small.

By way of consolation, disoriented women might introduce and spread the unfamiliar. Such innovations extended beyond styles of housing, decoration, dress, deportment and diet to opinion. Women shaped and modified the hierarchies of regard by which the quality were ordered. They might popularize decorous gatherings, practical piety and domestic virtues, promote uxoriousness, and redefine true nobility or gentility. Katherine Conolly not only set her own standards in public entertainments and philanthropic endeavour, but judged those around her. In her estimation, public spirit, particularly when directed to the good of Protestant Ireland, raised repute. Political and personal failings – drunkenness or sexual infidelity – depressed it. [226]

Women, sensitive to the nuances which determined membership of and position within the quality, struggled hard to preserve their rankings. In the 1690s, it was noted that 'all the daughters of families are of the same rank, but not all the sons'. The latter were sorted socially according to the careers that they followed; the former, on the basis of parentage.[227] The term 'gentlewoman' was much used, but, no less than the counterpart 'gentleman', inexactly and idiosyncratically.[228] Customarily it implied merit, whether inherited or acquired. The remarkable views of the Giant's

Causeway taken by Susannah Drury and engraved in 1741 were recommended to subscribers because the artist is 'a young gentlewoman'.[229] In addition she was praised, not just for her skill as artist, but as 'a modest and well behaved young woman'. In 1750, when the archbishop of Tuam fussed about a deranged fugitive from Bedlam, Susannah Hasset, daughter of a Kerry notable, he reported that her 'behaviour plainly shows that she has had a gentlewoman's education'.[230] In the 1770s, Catherine Royse fulminated about how she had been maltreated by her husband's family. She protested, 'my family are people of figure in both England and Ireland. I had a genteel education and am not allowed [considered] to be either ignorant or ordinary'.[231] Earlier, Frances Bellew, scheming to escape from the clutches of her brother-in-law, wanted only 'to live like a private gentlewoman'. It irked her to see her tormentor 'flying about like a man of quality, who my mama, my sister and myself made so great, and we to be reduced to beg to enrich his relations'. In these straitened conditions, Frances Bellew intended to remove from Dublin to Chester, where, she believed, she could live more cheaply without compromising her gentility.[232]

The concept of a 'gentlewoman', invoked by women threatened with the loss of individual identity, could be turned against them by despotic spouses. Elizabeth Cooke, estranged from her husband, a Kilkenny squire, was told of the conditions for a reconciliation. She was to treat her partner, on his instructions, as 'her husband, adviser and governor: that I expect an absolute and cheerful compliance to every request I make and command I give her, provided I require nothing from her inconsistent with the Christian and the gentlewoman'.[233] The final caveat hardly protected a harassed wife when her own and her husband's ideas of a gentlewoman's entitlements collided.

The sensitive sympathized with women of superior rank and breeding whose *mésalliances* tumbled them downwards. In 1749, Bishop Edward Synge of Elphin lamented the fate of a 'young lady of family and fortune' who had married into the Conroys of Elphin. She was 'environed with all the canaille of Conroys . . . and probably condemned to pass her days among them in a cabin'. Similar indices measured another social descent in George II's Roscommon. A girl of good birth, although allied with the thoroughly respectable St Georges, a family which included a peer, squires and professionals, was housed in a cabin intended only for summer holidays and without female friends. Her dissolute husband attracted pot companions unfitting for any gentlewoman to know.[234] If some women were pitied, others were blamed. Problems with a tenant in County Down in the 1740s were traced to his having married a Scottish gentlewoman. She was portrayed as both too proud to work and 'a drinker of tea'. The latter affectation involved expense and pretensions beyond the husband's means.[235] The accessories of the quality, always increasing in number and price, were hard to come by for the unmarried or widowed. Women, fearful of being expelled from the order into which they had been born or married, were more constrained in earning than men. Economies included moving into smaller towns where reduced circumstances would go unremarked. Drogheda, Enniscorthy, New Ross, Derry, Mountmellick, Portarlington and even Chester sheltered indigent gentlewomen.[236]

Women needed patrons as much as men. Accordingly, they traded on kinship. The first duke of Ormond was solicited by a woman of his name, granddaughter of James Butler of Crahanagh in County Waterford. While her mother lived, she had kept a school in Dublin. On her mother's death, Anne Butler had had to give up teaching and enter domestic service. Then she fell ill, lost her position and was forced to sell or pawn her clothes to survive. Left without decent dress, she could not seek a fresh post. Her plight contrasted with the better fortune of a brother, recommended already by Ormond to James Butler, a lawyer in London, and is a warning of the limited employment available to women.[237] The desperate appealed to kinship. Roger Power, a wealthy squire in County Waterford, was told of a woman who had arrived at the door of a friend in London and claimed kinship with the distant Power. The Londoner, on the strength of her claims, had lent her money. Then, suspecting an imposture, he checked the details of her story with Power. He had indeed been gulled.[238]

Teaching was a popular method by which women could survive without plunging too far down the social ladder.[239] In the 1720s, the head of a branch of the Crofton tribe, the best of them a baronet and established squires, counselled his widowed mother and unmarried sisters to move to Dublin where, in addition to running a school, 'their own work would help it out a little, whereas in the country they will have nothing to employ themselves upon'. The absentee brother, prospering as an army officer overseas, had chances denied his sisters. The Dublin project foundered. Soon, Mary Crofton, the sister who had taken charge of her mother, tried farming. She hinted at the resulting privations. 'I have lived before now in a barn upon a mountain and without a chimney, tho indeed I would not choose the latter'. By 1737 she was disillusioned with the hard life of a farmer and contemplated a return to schooling. To this end, she had brushed up her French by reading Corneille's plays over the winter. By the 1740s, when her elder brother had more than £6,000 to sink into an estate in the Irish midlands, she was shifting as best she could on £10 p.a.[240] Betty Dennis, Mary Crofton's contemporary from Waterford, was thought a fitting recruit to teach at a school run by her sisters in Chelsea because she at least knew French.[241]

How valiantly women might fight the forces dragging them from the company of the quality is illustrated by the Misses Povey, Eliza Hewetson and Jane Crosse. The Poveys came of a family whose fortune in Ireland had been made by a judge. A whiff of scandal from a marriage that never happened clung to these independent and doughty sisters. By the later 1740s their lives had degenerated into endless quests for suitable lodgings and servants in provincial towns like Enniscorthy and New Ross. Simultaneously, they schemed for ways to make some money. A favourite was to sell the last of the carriage horses for which the family had once been famed. The sisters, hearing that the best prices were commanded at Mullingar fair, inveigled a cousin in the midlands to organize the sale. Next they fussed the cousin – a squire – over what should or should not be arranged. Predictably the outcome disappointed, leaving them to rage against the drunkenness of the ostler and the carelessness of their kinsman. Querulous and snobbish, the Povey sisters hugged the tatters of their gentility tightly to warm them against the chill of indigence. By dint of ingenuity and importunity, they still mingled on occasion with the quality. Their greatest treat was to come to Dublin. More often they mouldered in provincial dinginess.[242]

In 1756, Mrs Hewetson set out – and perhaps embroidered – her woes in an appeal for aid. Nevertheless, the essentials of her predicament are unlikely to have been invented. She insisted that she had been born to 'a gentleman of considerable fortune'. Her father bequeathed her £600, but the income from this legacy was 'too small to support the way I had been bred'. Marriage to Hewetson, possessed of an income of £600 p.a., had promised a return to her accustomed gentility. Disasters intervened. The cumulative result was to force her to live obscurely and in 'extreme poverty'. Her husband's death worsened her plight as she struggled to place her son suitably. At first she had tried to apprentice him to a wine merchant, a branch of trade compatible with gentility. When this failed, she turned to the army as the solution. She feared that 'Irish interest' alone, all she commanded, would not succeed, so she approached her landlord in England, Lord Digby of Geashill, claiming that 'a word of yours would give him instant bread'.[243] Jane Crosse descended from a family, originally from Lancashire, which had flourished under the Ormondes. A grandfather, Silvester Crosse, had sat in the Irish parliament. By 1770, the embarrassed woman looked to Lord Wandesford to deliver her from want. Wandesford allowed her £10 yearly.[244] Others, plagued with entreaties of this kind, faced down 'genteel beggars'. The stories of those who lived 'formerly in a genteel way, but by crosses and losses were brought to their present distresses' had become so common that they had to be ignored.[245] Contemporaries might harden their hearts, but not all harrowing stories of women brought to dire straits were fabricated.

Gentlefolk fallen on hard times not only taxed patience and resources, they destroyed any easy equation of the quality with the well-to-do. Inner attributes might be the key, but outward appearances were all that could guide – and often fool – onlookers. Bishop Edward Synge had to apologize shamefacedly after dismissing a respectable if penurious visitor as the 'errantest Irish trull', adding even so, 'her appearance is just as I described it'.[246] Others in Dublin were taken in by a new arrival who set up in style. Having passed as a German prince, he was discovered to be a nobody from the Irish provinces.[247] Feints of this sort were not uniquely the work of aspirants to the quality. Shopkeepers put empty packages on shelves to give the illusion of substance, and banks simulated large deposits to instil confidence.[248] Artifice was also the stock in trade of the actor. Yet not all those who appeared on stage had to assume the persona of a gentleman, for that was what they already were. In the mid-eighteenth century, an actor-manager reassured one of his thespians, 'there is not a man in the company who is not a gentleman by birth and education'. The player, John Carteret Pilkington, the son of a clergyman and grandson of a Dublin doctor, had toyed with medicine, the Church, Grub Street, genteel Dublin society and the landed community. Beset with misfortunes, he was mortified not to be accepted as a gentleman, or into an occupation where he would be accepted as one. At last, in the theatre, he was acknowledged as what he aspired to be.[249]

Money, as well as birth and upbringing, was required to live as one of the quality. What constituted a competence was the subject of wildly discrepant notions. Between £5 and £6 might suffice for a year to sustain a labourer in County Sligo, when £40 would scarcely pay the expenses of any hoping to pass as quality. Acting and dressing for a part were what many of – and aspiring to – the quality did. Indeed they were necessities in the higher reaches of respectable society. During the 1750s, Godwin Swift, exiled to the south-western tip of Munster, wrote of the environs of Crookhaven, 'nor is the living it affords fit for any man that was bred or born a gentleman'. Those of gentle ancestry, like Swift, balked at living in a cabin and off potatoes.[250] Having moved thirty miles east, he announced contentedly that the metropolis of Skibbereen is 'a place for a gentleman'.[251]

There remained an elasticity about concepts, such as nobility, gentility and quality, which allowed in a motley crew. Professionals who serviced the polite and affluent in turn set up as property-owners. Others, thanks to the nature of their callings, were admitted to the members' enclosure. As noteworthy and less contentious than the actor Pilkington was Laurence Delamain in the city of Cork. When he died (in 1763), he lived close to the Protestant cathedral. He had amassed many of the appurtenances of genteel life, and was styled a 'gentleman'. His prosperity rested on his popularity as the instructor of the smart of town and countryside in the mysteries of dancing.[252] The actor and the dancing master were as much a part of the quality of Protestant Ireland as the squire and magistrate whom they entertained and informed.

Chapter 4

Clergy

I

In 1736, Bishop Robert Howard of Elphin complained of 'the too great power of professions against the general good of the country'. He instanced the army, the law and (perhaps more surprisingly) the Church.[1] Both the financial exactions and the arbitrariness of these groups had long furnished themes for critics and reformers. Others took a friendlier view. A recently disembarked judge, William Yorke, wrote complaisantly in 1743, 'the station which I am in admits me freely into the best company in the nation, which . . . is chiefly compounded of the professions of the law and divinity'. A visiting cleric in the 1750s viewed the higher clergy as the leaders of polite Protestant society in Dublin and Limerick.[2] This consciously cultivated society can be glimpsed in the 'belle assembly' to which Laetitia Pilkington, daughter of a physician and wife of a thrusting curate, was admitted or in the gatherings assembled by Bishop Thomas Rundle in his central Dublin mansion.[3] The bishop congratulated himself on the motley which thronged his library. 'Gentlemen and ladies, old and young, rich and poor, soldiers and bishops' brought 'learning into chit-chat'.[4]

The clergy, lawyers, military and naval officers, patentee officers and other professionals inflated the quality of Protestant Ireland. Convention accorded the style of gentleman to each within these callings. Contemporaries might argue whether the honour was always merited, and whether it did not counterfeit true gentility. Although some used their profits from these occupations to set up as landed gentlemen, few except the clergy practised their professions in the countryside, so that these were seen as primarily urban – and indeed Dublin – avocations. Such genteel occupations enabled some to remain within its pale and allowed more to enter it. Yet concern was expressed lest either the military or the religious trespass into areas not properly theirs.[5]

Incumbents of the Church of Ireland had long been in the vanguard of the campaign to conquer Ireland for England. The task provided a living for between 800 and 1,200 by the early eighteenth century.[6] As with their counterparts in the army, revenue and law, the clergy varied from affluence to indigence and from the well-born, including peers and sons of peers, to the socially dim. All by virtue of the sacerdotal office were accounted gentlemen. They were expected to perform an exemplary role: simultaneously apologists of the established political order, 'almoners of providence' and promoters of civility.[7]

Long and costly preparation became the norm for clerics, physicians and barristers. However, would-be ordinands of the Church of Ireland differed from the lawyers and doctors.[8] Aspiring clerics had no need to travel outside Ireland. Trinity College in Dublin sufficed to train them. By the 1740s, in dioceses such as Ossory or Raphoe, the incumbents were overwhelmingly (90 per cent) Dublin graduates.[9] Preparing for the ministry – in Ireland as in England – might cost less than for the law or medicine.[10] Nevertheless, the costs deterred the humble, and closed the vocation to the talented poor. In the 1730s, one aggrieved ecclesiastic quantified how much it cost to make a minister. Seven years at school required in all £91; then another seven years at Dublin University consumed £280. Once travelling expenses and sundries were included, the total neared £400.[11] Expenditure of this order debarred sons of the poor from entering the Church, unless they had been heavily subsidized by well-wishers. Even in the dissenting denominations, expenses, although lower, were beyond the purses of the humble. Three Baptists, whose preparation for the ministry was financed by an educational trust, cost an average of £74 to train. At Glasgow University in the 1770s, basic expenses for a year amounted to thirty-three guineas.[12] Looked at simply as an investment, better returns were to be had elsewhere. Moreover, hardship could continue long after ordination. In 1729 a frustrated applicant wailed, 'they that have the best estates are the best provided in the church'.[13] This echoed the view aired during the 1690s: 'in the law, talk and acquaintance carry it; and in divinity, interest'.[14]

The inadequacy of provision and the disparities in value between benefices were readily acknowledged. Remembering, too, that requirements for ordination had become more onerous, it is puzzling why so many nevertheless chose to enter the established Church.[15] In 1738, it was alleged that too many curates were being licensed. Again, in 1758, an observer stated resignedly, 'old curates. Alas! They are and ever must be too numerous'.[16] Not just money, but often a patron, was needed to put a foot on the first rung of the ladder. Given these material discouragements, a wish to save souls motivated some to labour for a pittance in the Lord's vineyard.[17] Social standing was confirmed or improved. The Ulster parson, Skelton, disliked the convention which styled him and his kind 'gentlemen', but it was accepted happily enough by his brethren. However, this courtesy title added to expectations inherent in the sacred office that the clergy would live and dress for the part. Increasingly, bishops at their visitations pressed their clergy to do so. In addition, between 1695 and 1721, acts of parliament gave financial incentives to incumbents to reside on their cures and to build more commodious dwellings.[18] Such obligations overstretched the attenuated resources of curates living on £20 to £40 annually. A curate's long service, if meritorious, might be rewarded. But other curates were despised. Archbishop King – a cranky bachelor – fulminated against poor clerics who married and begat children, 'all which prove beggars and commonly their wives are poor contemptible creatures, a disgrace to themselves and their function'.[19]

In the straggling diocese of Meath in the later seventeenth century, 47.2 per cent of benefices were worth less than £30 annually.[20] By 1758, a yearly stipend of £60 – or less – constituted a small living, as defined by statute. This contrasted with the £50 p.a. established earlier by the administrators of Queen Anne's bounty as the threshold below which incumbents in England could be assisted financially.[21] The bald figures masked a more complicated reality. Because it cost so much to create each cleric, many came from families of at least modest substance. Most enjoyed supplements to their purely ecclesiastical emoluments which raised them above the notional £20 to £40 p.a. Then, too, opportunities existed – even for drudging curates – to increase earnings. At one extreme lay the dues from officiating at clandestine marriages as a 'couple-beggar'. At worst, this illegal trade could bring a poor cleric to the scaffold, as it did the Dublin graduate, Edward Sewell, in 1740.[22] More orthodox were activities such as delivering a funeral sermon. For this a Dublin incumbent was paid an additional two guineas in the 1660s.[23] More regular were the payments collected by Francis Houston. In 1731 he was appointed to the curacy of Templemore, which included the city of Derry. Houston lodged comfortably in the deanery. With a second curate, he shared the fees from funerals: a valuable perquisite although it brought him into demeaning disputes with his colleague.[24] Exactions for performing the essential rites of the Church hardly ingratiated either it or its personnel with the laity. It provoked accusations that the spiritual shepherds minded the fleece more than the flock.[25] Nevertheless, they did enable the likes of Houston to live in greater comfort than his nominal stipend at first suggested. Houston, the son of an attorney, after long apprenticeship, gained a parish of his own. As a graduate and a beneficed clergyman he had improved on the standing of his father.[26] How much he improved the standing of the Church of Ireland among the communicants and other inhabitants of his parishes is less clear.

The rising expectations about the proper behaviour of the clergy brought them under increased pressure. During the 1720s, a Dublin curate, Valentine Needham, aspired to mix with 'people of quality and fortune' in the parish of St Michan's. Needham's ambitions irritated his rector, who itemized the curate's failings. In church, Needham's affectations were thought to have detracted from his office and distracted from worship. He lolled at his reading desk, fiddled with bands and wig, pared his nails and stretched out his hands to display a ring. He gazed around and bowed to acquaintances. At the altar, he leant against the pillars. In climbing into the pulpit, he provoked titters 'by an uncouth way of crawling up the stairs and peeping over the rail on either side'.[27] This caricature of refinement was perhaps occasioned by the special demands of Dublin. It offended against what spiritual directors recommended.[28] In remoter locales impoverished clergymen lamented that they were unable to fulfil the scriptural precepts of hospitality and charity. The wish to do so was sometimes used to second requests for removal to less remote and better paid cures. William Hansard pleaded to be removed from his westerly living in the diocese of Ardagh. Much of the profit was detained by the lay impropriator, Lord Westmeath. Hansard alleged that he was unable 'to carry on my building nor to use that hospitality and charity that become me'. Further, his shabbiness brought him into contempt with the local laity.[29] In 1710, the Reverend Alexander Young from Glencolumbkille in County Donegal pleaded to be shifted to a more accessible and rewarding spot.[30] The Reverend Richard Vaughan depicted himself as a 'mountaineer' among the lakes and drumlins of the Cavan–Monaghan border. He warned the vicar-general of his diocese, Ardagh, that this environment stunted refinement, so that he could not 'pretend to that degree of politeness or nicety of good manners' of urban colleagues.[31] About the same time, the Reverend John Leathes schemed to escape from his parish on the magnificent but bleak Londonderry coast. In this backward spot, Leathes argued, he attended to the 'business and amusements of a country life', and was 'in a manner a stranger to the arts and niceties of polite conversation'. Eventually, by removing to the more populous settlement of Hillsborough in County Down, Leathes re-entered the pale of the polite.[32]

The poorer clergy, lifted by education, job and culture above the generality of laypeople, wanted the means to blend easily into the gentry or squirearchy. Those lacking extra revenues longed only to be advanced in the Church. The kind of living that they craved was described by Archbishop Hoadley of Dublin: 'a very pretty preferment in my church, of near £200 and a good fine, ready money, as it were in hand, fit for any gentleman as it is a perfect sine cure'.[33] Preferment of this sort tended to go to the sons of gentlemen attracted into the Church, rather than to the obscure hoping to be levered into the clerical gentry. The hopeful watched for vacancies. They courted potential patrons and intermediaries. Those who could, posted to Dublin or London to make interest when a better living was to be filled. Bishops, whether from England, like Nicolson and Rundle at Derry, or those of Irish origin such as the Veseys, father and son, of Tuam and Ossory, looked after their own. Already in 1692 Archbishop John Vesey was nicknamed 'il nepotismo'.[34] Sir Thomas Vesey was so relaxed as to be accused of making 'priests . . . of debauchees and troopers'.[35] A brother, the Reverend Muschamp Vesey, was collated to a prebend in the diocese worth a yearly £260. Living in the family home at Abbey Leix and happy to spend an annual £30 on claret, he deputed the duties to a curate.[36] Nepotism of their superiors frustrated the would-be nepotists below. Archdeacon James Smythe complained of his diocesan in Meath, 'I do all I can for my friends and relations, but there is no opposing the bishop's nephews and nieces or grandchildren. It is happy when we [the Irish-born] get one man in ten'.[37] Hopes rose when a windfall dropped in the night. In 1757 one curate cheered to hear that 'there are two or three old men, and the fattest deer in our herd, just dropping into their graves'. A few years earlier, when the incumbent at Mullingar sought a curate, he was able to choose between three candidates.[38] Similarly, in 1759, two competitors squared up to one another to succeed to the Wexford living of Clonegal, said to be worth an annual £300.[39]

How a comfortably circumstanced incumbent discharged his several functions was shown in the Ulster of Charles II's time. The Reverend Andrew Rowan served as rector of Dunaghy in County Antrim. He lived in a house with four hearths: a scale unknown to most of his parishioners.[40] He filled it with goods bought sometimes in Coleraine, Carrickfergus, Derry or Belfast, from the fair at Clough or nearer to hand from local artificers. These possessions again marked him off from almost all his flock. So, too, did his books, often procured from London, Dublin and Scotland.[41] Rowan's standing was acknowledged when he was added to the commission of the peace, a distinction which few incumbents enjoyed. The resultant duties obliged him to mix with the important of the county, joining fellow magistrates over their bottles of wine.[42] This he was doing already, independent of any secular office. Lady Margaret O'Neill of the family of the marquess of Antrim came to the christening of one of Rowan's sons, who was named Neil in honour of the noble house.[43] However, the rector did not consort solely with the grandees. Engaged in farming on his own account, he went regularly to the nearby markets and fairs. He offered his flock loans and other practical aid, as well as spiritual salves. Relations with parishioners were not always untroubled, especially with the spread of Presbyterianism in the area.[44] In the end, what distinguished Rowan from his neighbours was his capacity to spend. Between 1674 and 1680, his annual expenditure was £185.[45]

Rowan's sense of belonging to a distinct caste was strengthened not only by the services which he uniquely offered to others, but by the regular meetings with fellow clergy. Summoned to the bishop's visitation, usually every year, this was a command increasingly difficult to defy.[46] These sociable occasions did not always unite the clerical estate. Bishops and their adjutants lectured and hectored. Their austere ideals could grate against the preferences and circumstances of subordinates. Customarily, the gathering ended with dinner. Sometimes the bishop paid for all, but – with increasing frequency – each diner had to pay his own bill.[47] The engineered fun of the economic and cultural gulf between the fortunates habituated to these pleasures and the penurious who enjoyed such elegant plenty only on this single day in their year.[48] Common concern to defend the rights of the established Church and its clergy might be underpinned by shared education and theology. Rowan, like others in Ulster, beneficed in the Church of Ireland, had studied in Scotland.

Clerics, keen to give a lead in their localities, were not just impeded by inadequate stipends. The Reverend William Preston exemplified the frustrations of the ardent missionaries for 'English' civility, Protestantism and (increasingly) respectability. Preston, an Englishman, was delighted to be inducted into a living in County Carlow in 1738. The parish was said to yield a yearly £200.[49] He owed this happy turn of events to a patron, Edward Southwell, whose family Preston had tutored. Southwell in turn had recommended the cleric to Lord Arran, the absent patron of the living. At first, Tullow and its environs had the charm of novelty. Indeed, the town had 'a good neighbourhood', thanks largely to the presence there of other clergymen from the vicinity. Soon enough Preston was disillusioned to discover 'a ruinous, tottering church and a very licentious, dissolute parish'.[50] Some of his disappointments were physical; others financial. Under the laws to encourage incumbents to build glebe houses, Preston had to pay his predecessor £300 for his improvements. He calculated that he would be left with an annual income of only £78. For others of the laity, this sum more than sufficed to live respectably. Preston, mindful of what was expected of a man of the cloth, expostulated that the total 'will never allow me to furnish my house, keep table, servants, horses and put things in proper order'. Much of Preston's dissatisfaction focused on being surrounded by the uncouth and mainly Catholic. He confided, 'men of independent fortunes may overlook the low vulgar company and amusements may divert the thoughts, but hard it is on me that I must depend on such bloody vermin'.[51] He considered establishing himself in Kilkenny, where more of the *beau monde* was to be encountered. But in the event he sought the permission of the bishop to put in a curate and return to England.

Preston's was an extreme case of the cultural dislocation of living in a largely Catholic countryside. His eagerness to confront 'a strolling, degraded Catholic priest' hardly endeared him to locals.[52] Others, more familiar with the realities of the provinces, jogged along amicably. Even so, incumbents, if dedicated to implanting a basic Christianity, were often disheartened. Philip Skelton, a strenuous curate, battled against ignorance and indifference in Counties Fermanagh and Donegal. Once habituated to life in the cultivated household at Manor Waterhouse, he still visited Dublin and London. He made money by writing and, in order to help starving parishioners, from selling his own library of books. Impatient of the vanities which obsessed too many clerics, he nevertheless knew that an incumbent should educate parishioners by way of living. He sensed the derogation when he lodged in Pettigo (County Donegal) with a 'low farmer'. In a farm with an earth floor, barely divided and sparsely furnished spaces, Skelton could scarcely lecture his parishioners on the physical decencies of the Christian life. More seemly were the rooms taken subsequently and successively with a physician in Enniskillen, a shopkeeper in Fintona, a bookseller and tobacco merchant in Dublin or a nephew at Drogheda.[53] As so often, a town with its bigger Protestant population suited the cultivated better.

Most of the beneficed had modest private resources to eke out their stipends. Fond parents may have spent their all if, as was calculated, about £400 was needed to put a youth into holy orders. However, inheritance and marriage brought additions. Around 1760, the Reverend Samuel Span gave his five children portions worth £5,900, and distributed another £2,047 in legacies. The retiring Ulster cleric, John Leathes, leased two farms from an absent brother. He also accumulated a good stock of silver.[54] The relative proportions of these elements are suggested by the circumstances of the Reverend John Cliffe late in the eighteenth century. Of an expected annual income of £392, 55 per cent derived from his clerical livings.[55]

Income of the Reverend John Cliffe, 1780

Curacy in diocese of Ferns and Leighlin	£50
Living in diocese of Elphin	£130
Living in diocese of Cork	£30
Estate in city of Dublin	£80
Interest on wife's fortune	£72
'Mrs Wilson'	£30
Total	**£392**

II

By the early eighteenth century, although the prelates and dignitaries shipped over from England attracted unfavourable and disproportionate notice, the bulk – as much as 90 per cent – of the beneficed clergy had been educated in Ireland. Almost all had also been born there. These ties carried advantages and hazards. Members of Irish Protestant society by inheritance and upbringing, they had been put into or put themselves into the Church of Ireland as a means of support. The living to be derived from it, especially for the drones and novices, did not always answer what had been spent on the preparations. In the longer term, however, there were chances of profit. Throughout the sixteenth and seventeenth centuries, the well-placed and avaricious stripped many of the assets. In particular, lay impropriation of tithes and ownership of advowsons redirected church wealth into lay pockets. In the 1680s, two-thirds of the tithes of livings in the bishopric of Clonfert had passed to Lord Clanricarde. By 1693, so much of the wealth of the diocese of Killaloe had been engrossed by Lord Thomond that 'he is in a manner the bishop of the diocese'.[56] Bishops, deans and their cathedral chapters and even parish incumbents, as well as laypeople, leased ecclesiastical property on long and beneficial terms. Belatedly, efforts were made to stop these destructive practices, but by then much had been permanently alienated, enriching clerical dynasties, patrons, clients and neighbours.[57]

Detrimental as these habits were to the economic well-being of the Church of Ireland, they entrenched it and its incumbents more securely in the affections of Irish Protestants. The Church resembled branches of the civil and military establishment in being annexed to the system of benefits available to the lucky or pushy. The austere who sought to end these practices risked alienating the influential among the laity. Particularly with efforts in the 1730s to extract more by way of tithes, clerical and lay interests collided. In the event, an embattled clergy were poorly placed to insist on legal entitlements. At the height of the controversies, a pert child was thought 'quite genteel' because 'she hates the clergy and tells them that she does not like the colour of their cloth, which is a new word much in vogue'.[58] Reformers, who disturbed these cosy arrangements, threatened to rupture the always fragile relationship between laypeople and their spiritual directors. Easygoing, even lax practices embedded some clergymen even deeper in a society to which they – and their kinsfolk – belonged. Such accommodations, dismissed by precisians as triumphs of the carnal, did not necessarily debar the worldly from spiritual leadership in Protestant Ireland. Four successful dignitaries reveal something of these ambiguities.

William Jephson came of a family prominent among the Tudor and early Stuart settlers in County Cork. He accumulated choice livings in three separate dioceses and, in 1692, was made dean of Lismore. The economy which supported the cathedral at Lismore in County Waterford had been picked virtually to the bone to gratify the local potentate in Lismore Castle, Lord Cork. Jephson doubled as chaplain to a regiment: pluralism which excused his frequent absences from Ireland. Jephson's metropolitan, Archbishop William Palliser of Cashel, pleaded to have him recalled to his Irish duties and to stop any further preferment. Jephson's behaviour provoked some of his diocesan's denunciations of the worldliness of his subordinates. Bishop Foy of Waterford railed unavailingly against the negligence which Jephson personified.[59] The dean was immune from discipline, thanks to his connections with powerful laymen, including the lord justice, Lord Romney, and Lord Inchiquin.[60] Jephson's standing among the laity was publicly announced when, in 1698, he was invited by the House of Commons to preach before it on the red-letter day of 5 November. Since his address was subsequently printed, its message presumably pleased. Conventionally but no doubt sincerely, Dean Jephson enthused over the Church of England, with which he equated the Church of Ireland, as 'the graceful, ancient and enduring oak, the prince of the wood . . . the best established, both in its doctrine and discipline for the salvation of souls, of any other in the world besides'. This encomium contrasted with warnings about the continuing danger from Catholicism, especially from the Jesuits, fittingly recalled on 5 November. Jephson also subscribed to the growing cult of William III, as saviour of the Protestant interest. Protestants in Ireland owed their deliverance and Jephson his own elevation to the Dutchman.[61]

Jephson's contemporary, Rowland Davies, successively dean of Ross (1679–1710) and of Cork (1710–22), was equally enmeshed in local landed society. His immediate forebears in south Munster had taken tenancies from the predominant proprietor there, Lord Cork.[62] Through further leases, the dean consolidated his position in the area. These tenancies made him dependent on laymen; they also gave him the same concerns as other members of landed society. Direct involvement in farming offered energetic clergymen the chance to show neighbours how best to improve holdings and yield. It also made them practically as well as theoretically interested in the projects of improvement. Davies, in return for forbearance from his landlords and their agents, steered some of the remaining resources of the church towards them.[63] Meanwhile he exploited the Church for his own and his sons' benefit. When he died he was accused of having stripped his parishes.[64] Having been made vicar-general of the Cork diocese, Davies turned the office to his own profit. As a result, like

Jephson, he enraged superiors.[65] He also shouldered secular responsibilities. He and his clerical sons after him served as justices of the peace. The dean combined the magistracy with the duties of registrar of the Vice-admiralty Court of Munster.[66] A shortage of suitable candidates may at first have sanctioned the employment of clergy in local government. By Davies's time, the supply of potential functionaries in south Munster was more than adequate, so that Davies's appointment owed most to his own self-seeking dynasticism. Bishops, horrified at what they saw as his misconduct, were powerless to bring him to heel.

In County Cork, Davies spoke effectively for the Irish Protestant cause. He shared the preoccupations and anxieties of his neighbours; he – like many prosperous laypeople – had removed himself to England during the Jacobite episode of 1688–90. These experiences were remembered when he preached to Cork congregations. 'The calamities' under James II were blamed on the 'over-heated zeal' of the Romanists.[67] He repeated the usual Protestant objections to the Catholic doctrine of transubstantiation, and the practices of confession and absolutism. Superstition and idolatry were ascribed to the Catholics. Instead, he hymned the superiority of the Church of England, again synonymous with the Church of Ireland. It, not the Church of Rome, was the direct descendant of the primitive Christians. In constructing a lustrous lineage for his Church, Davies included Berengarius, Wycliffe, Hus and Jerome of Prague. However, his learning was tinged with Irish patriotism and so he incorporated Saints Patrick and Columbkille as progenitors of Hibernian Protestantism.[68] Davies upheld the civil government. In 1716, on the anniversary of Charles I's execution, 30 January, he reminded Corkonians of the need for obedience. With rumours rife about the Old Pretender's intentions, he spent less time on the heinousness of regicide than on the 'abdication' of James II and the legitimacy of the present government, resting on a variant of the Lockean contract between ruled and ruler.[69] In addition to the external threats to a Protestant Ireland, the dean warned of internal weaknesses which, if not quickly checked, might prove fatal. Critics, especially among his clerical combatants, might have argued that misconduct such as Davies's as vicar-general split and enfeebled the Protestant interest. However, rather than amending his own behaviour, Davies exhorted auditors to attend to their failings. He took up a topical issue, felt by many to offer the best prospect of fortifying Protestantism in Ireland. Across the river from Davies's cathedral in Cork, the incumbent of Shandon, Henry Maule, had set up an educational charity. Davies urged his listeners to support the hopeful initiative. Thereby the impressionable young would be weaned from vice and idleness, Catholics might be converted and the benevolent would earn celestial benisons.[70] Earlier, Maule, the stooge of earnest bishops, had clashed with Davies. At least in this matter of practical piety, they were at one, and – furthermore – united with concerned worthies in the city of Cork.[71]

The established Church enabled Davies to consolidate his position among the quality in south Munster. One of the sons who followed him into the ministry was Boyle Davies, his Christian name recalling the source of some of Davies's affluence: his leases from the earls of Cork. Boyle Davies succeeded to one of his father's benefices, reputed by 1743 to be worth £400 p.a.[72] In itself this income would situate the cleric comfortably among the middling ranks of landed gentlemen. The son also succeeded the dean as registrar in the vice-admiralty and as a county magistrate.[73] Like his father, Boyle Davies defended the Protestant interest from his pulpit. He remained implacably opposed to the Catholics among whom he lived. In 1719 he warned, 'while we have papists among us, we never shall want an enemy, nor an executioner fitted to our destruction'. So long as vivid memories of the Catholic *revanche* of 1688–90 persisted, Cork Protestants would be on their guard. However, it was not only the political danger to 'our safety and liberties' that he dreaded. 'Popish errors', he contended, 'are really in themselves monstrous and dissonant to all sound principles, both of reason and religion'.[74] How best to contain the threat divided the Irish Protestants. Some strategists counselled prosecution; others favoured more constructive measures, such as Maule's at Shandon. In general, the uncompromising like Boyle Davies disagreed with the apparently compassionate Maule more in emphasis and timing than in fundamental aim, which for both was the extirpation of Catholicism from Ireland.

The characteristics of Jephson and the Davies family reappear in another cadet from the countryside who secured a deanery. Charles Massy, maturing in the 1720s, subscribed still to a rampant anti-Catholicism. Living near his cures in Counties Clare and Limerick, he deployed spiritual and secular weapons. In 1739 he was agitated by evidence that soldiers from the region were deserting to serve in the Spanish army. A rumoured plan to invade the west coast, near which he lived, stimulated defensive measures. Massy wanted the Protestants armed as a militia, which would be 'a glorious thing'. If authorized by the current lord-lieutenant, Devonshire, it would remind of the services of the duke's grandfather in inviting William of Orange to England. Massy regarded the Glorious Revolution as the foundation of the Irish Protestants' good fortune. He feared that, as recollections of those events faded and as the years of peace lengthened, the Protestants of Ireland were being lulled into false security. He rounded on local justices of the peace for failing to check Catholic insolence.[75]

Massy shared an approach common among his colleagues which would unite coercion and persuasion. The numerous laws against Catholics should be strictly enforced. True to the mood of the 1730s, Massy moved beyond providing basic education to sponsoring rural industry with the subsidized cultivation of flax and manufacture of linen. He conceded that his wholehearted involvement in these matters might seem odd in a parson. In 1740, he revealed that he had for the last twelve years been 'endeavouring to reform this stiff-necked people by gentle methods'. Disappointed, he now urged severity.[76] The old tensions between sword and word had reappeared. Massy's value to the government, with his exertions in Clare, was formally recognized by his addition to the commission of the peace.[77] Massy's vision of Ireland as Protestant, prosperous and 'civilized' justified a variety of endeavours, many of which went beyond what might be thought the usual remit of a cleric. Although eager to transform the customary worlds of Catholic and Gaelic Ireland, he was not insensitive to traditional culture.[78] From his vantage point as dean of Limerick, he watched and eventually contributed to the squabbles within the Protestant municipality and between its oligarchs and the gentry of the neighbouring countryside.[79] He was devoted alike to the safety of Protestant Ireland and the prosperity of his own extensive kindred. If, during the scare of 1740, he addressed the Catholic menace, he also identified and attacked enemies within the Protestant community. He organized resistance to the tyranny which a few had established over the corporate life and assets of Limerick corporation and belaboured those Protestants whom he judged to be corrupt. This brought him into such ill odour with the ruling aldermanic clique in the city that he was forced to flee for fear of arrest. His horsemanship – he had supposedly galloped from Dublin to Naas in half an hour – suggested how well he could defend physically as well as spiritually the interests of Protestant Ireland.[80] He linked the urban politics of Limerick with those of Dublin in 1749, and hinted at a connection with the fomenter of the latter contest, an apothecary originally from County Clare, Charles Lucas.[81] Dean Massy, like Jephson of Lismore and Davies at Cork, exposed the dangerously fissiparous and factious nature of Irish Protestant communities. But he also revealed how concerned clergy could bestride their own professional world and that of the laity.

Ulster reproduced this pattern noted in Munster. Families planted early in the seventeenth century, by the eighteenth had ramified. Cadets colonized the Church. Between about 1740 and 1780, of 118 beneficed ministers in County Down it is reckoned that 68 sprang from or married into landed society.[82] The Hamiltons, whose properties included Castle Hamilton and Caledon in County Tyrone, again revealed the overlap of squires and ecclesiastical dignitaries. The family, through ancestry, marriage and neighbourhood, was part of the thick and increasingly tough mesh of

Ulster notables, such as the Conynghams, Leslies and – in time – Conollys, the heads of which had gravitated towards Dublin and the Pale by the early eighteenth century. Two brothers, born into the settler society of north-west Ulster and educated at Trinity College, Dublin, both became archdeacons: Andrew, of Raphoe; and William, of Armagh.[83] Andrew Hamilton's sense of Irish Protestant sufferings was intensified, as were Dean Davies's and Dean Jephson's, by having to uproot himself in 1688 from Dublin, where he was training at Trinity College, and complete his education at Oxford.[84] As well as this brush with assertive Catholics, the Hamiltons, like others in the north, feared the aggression of Protestant dissenters. Relations with the latter varied. In some matters, notably the campaign of the 1690s to reform Protestant manners, the different churches made common cause. At the same time, the new strength and assertiveness of the Presbyterians in Ulster alarmed churchmen. Longer than most within the established Church, William Hamilton tried to preserve the Protestants' popular front against vice. It was work appropriate to 'the most useful member of the commonwealth, the best patriot of his country'.[85] In the face of lay indifference, Hamilton burnished the image of James Bonnell. Bonnell, the former accountant-general and a connection through marriage of the Hamiltons, had promoted godly reformation. Hamilton's bid to elevate him into a Protestant saint failed in the factious atmosphere of Queen Anne's reign, and by the time that George I came to the throne the sights of reformers had shifted to other targets.[86]

Hamilton was a political parson. He unashamedly handled public questions. His connections, which included the Speaker of the Commons, Conolly, allowed him platforms.[87] On 5 November 1723 he preached in the cathedral at Armagh. The published sermon was dedicated to Conolly, whose forwardness in the revolution of 1688–90 was praised. Archdeacon Hamilton, looking back to that event, usually celebrated as inaugurating the modern Ireland controlled by Protestants, agreed that William III had not been perfect, but still deserved thanks as a deliverer. Thirty years later, the political benefits – 'limited monarchy, good laws and liberty' – were coupled with material gains. Approvingly, Hamilton eyed improved lands and growing wealth, but he cautioned his Protestant auditors lest they forget the Catholic threat. Catholicism was unequivocally written off as 'a lunacy of the soul'.[88] Hamilton and his views were acceptable enough to Conolly and his group for the archdeacon to be invited to preach before the House of Commons on 5 November 1725. Once more, he reminded his audience of the Catholic danger. Recent events in France and Hungary, as well as the more familiar history of Catholic schemes in England, prefaced a call for vigilance in Ireland. Hamilton, however, derided the methods so far adopted. Persecution, he concluded, was not working. Few, under duress, converted; most proved insincere. Because coercion was seen as the Catholics' tactic, Hamilton wanted fellow Protestants to proceed 'with reason and argument, with meekness and charity'. In this spirit, Hamilton would allow the Catholics in Ireland 'the common privileges of mankind; and their consciences should not be forced any more than ours'. But he stopped short of arguing that the Catholics' legal disabilities be removed. They remained a threat to the state, and were rightly debarred from 'honours and employments'. Accordingly, the archdeacon endorsed the nascent Protestant Ascendancy, in which 'those of his own persuasion enjoy the greatest share of his trust and favour'. In the longer term, these privileges must be used properly. Failure to do so might bring down on the Protestants of Ireland the divine wrath, as in 1641 and 1685–90. Hamilton argued that, since 1690, the authorities in Church and state had trusted too much 'to laws, armies and power', rather than to spiritual weapons.

Unfashionably, the archdeacon wanted to evangelize among the Irish in their own language. This method had been tried fitfully, and was contentious. Earlier, in 1712, he had mused on the obstacles to converting the natives in western counties, like Mayo, Galway, Kerry, Leitrim and Clare, 'when ministers and people are barbarians to each other'. The small number of resident clergy was one problem; their ignorance of Irish was another. Hamilton liked the project of John Richardson, the rector of Belturbet in County Cavan, to promote Protestant preaching and instruction in Irish. But, as Hamilton conceded, 'too many of those whose great business is to take of them and instruct them do oppose those methods'. Moreover, factionalism within the Church of Ireland meant 'that whatsoever one party proposes, tho never so good, will be sure to be opposed by another party, so that I doubt God will punish our ingratitude for our past deliverances by suffering us to neglect those from whom our dangers humanly speaking only can arise'.[89] Hamilton made little headway against the inertia and introspection of those who directed the state Church and government.

The disillusionment to which the archdeacon of Armagh was prone in time enveloped his brother, Andrew Hamilton, the archdeacon of Raphoe. By 1737, having ministered in parishes for forty-six years, he lamented how he was crossed both by the Presbyterians and by conformist landowners reluctant to pay tithes.[90] Like his clerical brother, Archdeacon Andrew Hamilton had a comfortable temporal estate. A property acquired through his wife, Castle Conyngham, was made over to his heir. By the 1750s his livings yielded between £500 and £600. Part of the year was spent in his parish of Doneheady in County Tyrone, 'where he takes great pleasure in a fine congregation, lives retired and easy', with a glebe house and three servants. Winters were passed in the city of Derry, of whose cathedral he was chancellor.[91] He was one of several whose expectations of a bishopric had been dashed by the sudden death of Queen Anne. These setbacks doomed him to remain 'a drudging man' throughout a ministry of more than half a century. When he died in 1753, he had retired from his isolated glebe house to the Tyrone town of Strabane. Like other clerics, he was attracted by the greater amenities for the genteel and elderly.[92] Archdeacon Andrew Hamilton personified qualities in vogue by the 1750s. One memorialist eulogized him as 'a most polite, agreeable, well-bred and charitable gentleman'.[93] Civic and social virtues, as much as evangelical fervour, were demanded of the clergy. Archdeacon Hamilton of Raphoe had exhibited them in both town and country. In his cure, he erected a parsonage. The thatched and single-storey dwelling – 'a long and large cabin' – was later adjudged fit for a bachelor. Fronted by six 'magnificent' sashed windows, it contained a twenty-foot-square parlour, two bedrooms, a kitchen open to the roof and two servants' rooms. It remained of one storey, despite Hamilton's scheme for something grander, because 'in this country, they have not the art of building a staircase'. Just as the standards of behaviour and instruction expected from incumbents altered over the decades, so too did expectations about housing. What had looked a welcome improvement when Hamilton first arrived in the parish, by the 1750s fell victim to modern tastes.[94]

In print, the Hamiltons warned of the continuing Catholic danger. But by the 1730s, the archdeacon of Raphoe was locked in a bitter dispute over his tithes with local Presbyterians. By then the dissenters had spread into the more westerly regions of Ulster and so forced themselves on Hamilton's attention. In an effort to collect his tithe of barley, he was reported to have descended on the crops of defiant parishioners with a posse of sixty-two men and horses. The crops were badly damaged.[95] Incumbents might justify such aggression as necessary to maintain the rights of the established Church and their successors. Whatever principles were at stake, there were also more pressing concerns over their own livelihoods. In common with others in Protestant Ireland with a position to safeguard, the clergy worried over provision for their children. The Hamiltons, like Davies and Jephson, used their control over some ecclesiastical assets to assist offspring. Recalling the erenachs – the families of priests – in the earlier Irish Church, the clergy of the post-Reformation Church of Ireland could be likened to a hereditary caste.[96] This characteristic was not unique to Ireland: it paralleled a clerical tribalism in the Church of England throughout the seventeenth and eighteenth centuries.[97] Yet the Church could not accommodate all the sons of the fecund clerics. Andrew Hamilton had six to place. The wish to find respectable vocations came up against the costs of doing so. Also, parents scrupled about forcing children into careers for which they were clearly unsuited or unenthusiastic.[98] The Hamiltons, like others in their circle, put promising sons into Trinity College: an option likely to cost a minimum of £40 yearly. Trade, medicine and soldiering were alternatives. The clerical Hamiltons, in order to start sons on the right courses, used tenuous contacts in London, the United Provinces and Bordeaux. All involved trouble and expense; each indicates the wider worlds in which they routinely participated.[99]

Parsons who set themselves up in the countryside as squarsons were both applauded and condemned. In doing so, the diligent clerics aimed to show agreeable hospitality, philanthropy and refinement to neighbours, and so simultaneously recommend improvement and Protestantism. Scripture exhorted physical improvements. Richard Barton, ministering at Lurgan, commended another clergyman situated near Lough Neagh who employed himself usefully in 'religion and husbandry'.[100] The industrious proprietor was distinguished from the hedonists who 'like grasshoppers glut themselves with the luscious juices of spring and summer'.[101] Most clerics depended directly on the harvest for their revenues. Stipends did not appear as bank drafts or monthly credits, but had to be garnered from often refractory or penurious parishioners. By setting an example of innovative husbandry, these pioneers hoped to prosper. Just how evangelism and agriculture interlocked was shown on the south Wicklow and north Wexford estates of the Wentworths, which were taken in hand by a new owner early in the eighteenth century. This zealot, Thomas Watson Wentworth, intended to create what had frequently been essayed but seldom achieved before: a Protestant colony. In an effort to speed the process, he sent from his home in England portraits of himself and his wife, catechisms and seeds.[102] These offerings frequently fell on stony ground. However, among the Wentworths' flourishing Protestant tenants around Arklow, Carnew and Shillelagh, a clergyman, Michael Symes, shared the philosophy of his absent landlord. Admirers held up Symes as a model of the active improver. He was said to love his spring wood as much as his Bible.[103] Others liked him and his works less. Symes's devotion to his holding was dismissed as self-interested indulgence, not disinterested activism: he calculated that he would be recompensed by Wentworth. Instead the latter's agent advised a careful survey of Symes's property, 'to take him down and not to give him too great liberty to boast his improvements'.[104] A nearby proprietor was equally unimpressed and believed that Symes was disturbing the district.[105] Wentworth's agent saw Symes's outlook as symptomatic of the pretensions of different tenants, among whom the clergy were conspicuous, damaging alike to the landlord and to the heirs of the squarsons. Yet, others praised Symes and his well-wooded lands as worthy of imitation. Public acclaim in the shape of a gold medal from the Dublin Society rewarded Symes's successor.[106] Symes's display of how the works of nature could be improved may have sharpened his poorer parishioners' awareness of the beneficent deity who had created the marvels. Clearer are the gains for Symes. From the solid foundation of the estate, members of the family assisted philanthropic initiatives in Arklow. They also advanced themselves through further service in the Church, the professions, bureaucracy and armies of the Hanoverians.[107]

Careerism and materialism, perhaps inevitably, bulk largest in the correspondence of the clergy, who had their way to make in the Church and children to assist. Vacancies were not formally advertised; requirements for ordination still varied from diocese to diocese; no pensions cushioned retirement. Accordingly, even the unambitious had to prod and probe. These preoccupations did not exclude the spiritual. The apparently indolent or venal, such as the irascible and hard-drinking Archdeacon James Smythe of Kells, the artistic Bishop Simon Digby of Elphin, the obsessive bibliophile, Bishop John Stearne of Clogher, or the lax and lordly Sir Thomas Vesey at Abbey Leix, won plaudits from contemporaries for their charity and efficiency. Bishops and deans seem often to have assumed the public functions neglected by the absent or indifferent laity. They, and subordinate clergy familiar with the island, initiated ventures which might achieve the long-standing promises to transform Ireland under English rule. In their sermons they set out the justifications for conquest, dispossession and discrimination. In the localities, vigorous clergymen demonstrated the merits of English and Protestant overlordship. Clerics were disproportionately important in ventures to help the poor and ignorant. They pushed hard for a more systematic approach to educating the deprived. The Incorporated Society crowned these efforts. The Society, granted a royal charter in 1733, drew together the diffuse initiatives of the previous thirty years. The earlier experiments had originated with clergymen, such as Maule in Cork, Richardson in Belturbet and Edward Nicholson in Sligo. Episcopal and clerical interest remained high. Of 115 who originally subscribed to the Society, seventy-five were clergymen.[108] Once the Society was established, differences of approach divided the directors. Some recalled the divergences in outlook and priorities between laypeople and clergy which often bedevilled and weakened the Protestant interest. Attempts to protect the professional interests of the clergy were usually resisted as sacerdotalism and theocracy.

Any sense of cohesiveness within the clerical army was undermined by diversity in origins and circumstance. Income most obviously divided its personnel. The adjutants, sometimes subsisting on £20 a year, inhabited a different world from an Edward Synge at Elphin, reputedly with a fortune

of £100,000, and annual emoluments from his diocese approaching
£3,500.[109] Between the extremes of the spiritual lords and the scruffy
curates, rectors and vicars usually lived in greater affluence than the generality of farmers. More often remarked – and regretted – was the difference
between imported leaders, born and trained in England, and the bulk of
the parish clergy, of Irish upbringing. The policy of reserving the best
appointments for strangers affected the episcopate. The rationale was the
shortage of the suitably qualified within Ireland – an argument difficult to
sustain by the end of the seventeenth century – and the need to conform
Irish institutions more closely to their English prototypes. The same
approach was adopted with the judiciary, bureaucracy and armed forces.
The resentments which resulted, far from integrating the Church better
into a pan-Britannic system, accentuated differences between the lucky
English minority and the less fortunate clergy of Irish birth and education.

The number of prelates brought over from Britain was frequently
exaggerated. In 1738 an aggrieved laywoman, observing the shortcomings
of Bishop Rundle of Derry, wrote, 'God forgive them [the government],
and send us a better set' of bishops, 'for the present has no thought of
their charge'.[110] Derry, one of the richest prizes in the Church of Ireland,
attracted a succession of English intruders, few of whom attended closely
to its needs. However, not all dispatched from England neglected their
charges. Some, such as Hugh Boulter at Armagh, Josiah Hort and John
Ryder successively at Tuam, identified strongly with their adopted country
and spent heavily on its behalf.[111] Furthermore, although strangers
undoubtedly obtained some of the most important positions, like the arch-
bishoprics of Armagh and Dublin or the bishopric of Derry, they never
predominated, even on the episcopal bench of the Irish House of Lords.
Between 1707 and 1716, of thirty-one appointed to Irish sees, only seven
were imported. The need thereafter to ensure an episcopate loyal to the
Hanoverians brought an increase in outsiders. By 1760, the twenty-two
bishops divided exactly between locals and strangers. A more exhaustive
analysis of the later eighteenth-century consecrations found sixty-seven
sent from England and fifty-six supplied from Ireland.[112] Below the rank
of bishops, few dignities in the Church of Ireland tempted clerics from
England to emigrate.[113] On average, stipends in lowland England, although
not necessarily in remoter districts, surpassed those in Irish parishes.[114]
Church of England incumbents might face the difficulties of anti-
clericalism and dissent, but not the sort of tensions experienced by Preston
at Tullow in upholding the state Church in the face of indifference or
hostility from the majority in the vicinity. Whereas in the first century
after the Reformation, lack of livings in England and missionary fervour
propelled many Protestant clergymen to Ireland, by the eighteenth

century, both forces had weakened. Moreover, the indigenous Protestant community was better able to staff its own institutions. As the examples of Jephson, Massy, the Davies and Hamiltons indicate, there were good livings from 'lazy deaneries' and other incumbencies for those who knew where to look and to whom to apply.

Whatever the statistical reality, the perception that the Church in Ireland, like other institutions there, was being stripped to feed the greedy from Britain militated against any easy acceptance of the leadership of these immigrants. Archbishop King was to the fore in inveighing against this policy, which he saw as an aspect of constitutional and cultural subordination to Britain.[115] The newcomers, arriving with differences in background, schooling and approach, added to the tensions within an already discordant body. Moreover, the apparent ease with which Britons were preferred in Ireland contrasted with the absence of movement in the opposite direction. Between the translations of William Fuller from Limerick to Lincoln in 1666 and Edward Jones from Cloyne to St Asaph in 1692 — neither man was born in Ireland — it was not until 1868 that an Irishman, William Connor Magee, was consecrated bishop of Peterborough and then advanced to the archbishopric of York. Below the bishops, cathedral and parish clergy increasingly shared similar backgrounds. By the early eighteenth century, as much as 90 per cent of the beneficed ministry had been educated at Dublin University. However, this common formation did not result in uniform products. Tutors changed. So, too, did the prevailing divinity and politics.[116] Clerical graduates maintained and developed their cerebral and utilitarian interests through correspondence, reading and travel. But these contacts spoke more of personal alliances than of a strong professional identity. Briefly, during the reign of Queen Anne, Convocation supplied a forum in which grievances could be ventilated and a combined front cemented. In practice, its meetings revealed and widened disagreements, both between the upper house (of bishops) and the lower (mostly the parochial clergy), and between high-flyers and the more latitudinarian.[117] After 1713, Convocation was suspended, and so the national forum vanished. It was left to the bishops in Parliament to promote the welfare of all clergy. Attempts to do so, particularly by insisting on and extending the right to tithes in the 1730s, rekindled lay animosities. Just as the indiscretions of Tory churchmen in the later years of Queen Anne's reign aroused Whig ire, so after 1714 robust Erastianism and suspicion of priestcraft increased. These sentiments sometimes coalesced with a crude anti-clericalism, or even freethinking and libertinism.[118]

Individual clergymen incurred unpopularity through their exactions, attitudes or ethnicity. Some failed spectacularly, owing to oddities or poverty, to discharge their proper duties or to keep their appropriate

station in local society. Lapses and non-residence persisted. Indeed, by
1769, with the superstructure top heavy with English dignitaries, four
bishops, including Primate Robinson of Armagh, were listed in the
shameful catalogue of absentees.[119] In 1735, Archbishop Theophilus Bolton
of Cashel caricatured 'a good bishop' with 'nothing more to do than to
eat, drink, grow fat, rich and die'.[120] A few conformed to this unkind portrait; more contradicted it. Diocesans, like Hutchinson of Down and
Connor, Howard and Synge at Elphin, Berkeley in Cloyne, and Maule,
first at Cloyne, then at Dromore and finally in Meath, may not have followed the apostolic models of Titus and Timothy, but they did advance
collaborative projects of improvement.[121] Whether at the boards of the
societies, from their seats in the Lords, their pulpits or at their dinner
tables, they promoted worthy causes.

Middle-ranking clerics – usually but not invariably from Ireland – also
figured conspicuously in the constructive schemes beloved by the public-
spirited. The Dublin Society and the five hospitals opened in Dublin
between 1717 and 1758 catered to some of these impulses. Bishops, with
numerous commitments and their need to reside more regularly in their
dioceses, could seldom spare much time to run the charities and societies
of Dublin. Their names, like those of the titled laity, lent tone to organizations competing for attention and funds.[122] But, from the beginning,
these organizations relied on others less encumbered with weighty public
offices. Typically these men lived in Dublin and followed a profession;
often, they were clerics. Samuel Madden, an incumbent in County
Fermanagh and squire of Manor Waterhouse, revived the drooping Dublin
Society.[123] Later, another restlessly inventive clergyman, William Henry,
dean of Killaloe, lavished his time on it. Henry saw the Society as a collective means of strengthening Protestant Ireland. Concurrently, he was
working towards the same end with his settlement at Ballymote in
Connacht. There, he intended to give to each male settler 'a bible and
backsword to defend it, and to every woman a prayer book and spinning
wheel'.[124] Madden and Henry, although frequently in Dublin and
enthusiastic about the work of the Society, were tied to Ulster by their
properties and cures. Much then devolved on those permanently in the
capital: deans, prebends and rectors. During the first decade of the Dublin
Society, among the most assiduous in attendance were Dean Richard
Daniel, the Reverend William Jackson, the Reverend Daniel Jackson, the
Reverend John Jebb, the Reverend John Kearney, the Reverend Edward
Molloy, Dean William Perceval, Dean Robert Taylor, the Reverend John
Whetcombe and the Reverend John Wynne.[125]

On the board of Mercer's Hospital between 1737 and 1757, a similar
pattern can be discerned.[126] Diligent clergymen were joined by office-

holders, lawyers, merchants and doctors. This pioneering institution was sustained by urban professionals rather than by the country grandees. This was true of the medical charities of mid-eighteenth-century London.[127] In Dublin, instead of bishops, it was Dean Samuel Hutchinson, the Reverend John Wynne and the Reverend John Owen who laboured longest for the hospital. Each was connected to one or other of the two Protestant cathedrals of the capital.[128] Wynne showed how busy fingers could dabble in many pies. In addition to his duties at Christ Church, he acted as keeper of Archbishop Marsh's Library from 1730 to 1762. He was a trustee of the benefaction which would create Wilson's Hospital (a Protestant school) at Multyfarnham in Westmeath. Personal interest in physical improvements combined with hopes of personal profit when he joined a partnership to mine at Tigrony in County Wicklow.[129] Owen similarly united ideological and practical concerns. In the 1720s, while a curate in Dublin, he worked for a group trying to instruct 'poor natives'. He undertook such chores as correcting the proofs of the cheap edition of the Bible which was to be distributed to humble householders.[130] These labours were combined with polemic and scholarship. He edited controversial 'Cases against Popery', as a warning to the insouciant not to forget 'the distant dangers of popery, nor think of proper measures to prevent its growth'. He also assisted Bishop Nicolson of Derry with his *Irish historical writers* (1724).

III

The disproportionate impact of the clergy, especially in Dublin, on literary and intellectual life was thought proper by one. Richard Barton observed, speculated and wrote. He believed that it was 'highly becoming a clergyman, to interest himself in the phenomena of the natural world, which is the handy work of God, whose minister he is, and whose works are the objects of study'.[131] These activities enabled the clergy to retain a ranking in Protestant Ireland which neither income alone nor the neglects of some among them, justified. In numbers – perhaps 800 to 1,200 – the order probably equalled those practising law and almost certainly surpassed qualified medical practitioners. As in the law and medicine, so in the Church, a tripartite division existed. Below the beneficed, curates subsisted as best they could. Some simply marked time until they would be advanced; others drudged throughout their lives. Lower still in the pecking order were the parish schoolteachers. The clergy shaded into the teaching profession, as the recently graduated and newly ordained made shift as instructors. Moreover, bishops – at least in theory –

appointed and oversaw schoolmasters. In practice, many more than they approved officiated. But the system of licensing stressed the position of the authorized as servitors of the established Church.[132] Few Protestants maintained resident chaplains, but tutors were more common. The tutors were typically young graduates studying for ordination or deacons awaiting preferment. By the mid-eighteenth century, they were paid between £15 and £30 annually.[133]

Just as Church livings varied in value, so too did posts in schools. The hierarchy was headed – notionally – by schools in each of the twenty-two Church of Ireland dioceses. Progress towards the foundation of all had been slow, but by the eighteenth century, most if not all dioceses had their academies.[134] They were supplemented by the initiatives of the crown in Ulster, and of corporations and benevolent individuals. Endowed institutions fluctuated in reputation and enrolments, in accordance with their masters' skills. However, each was a permanency. Most concerned with book learning were grammar schools, where masterships carried stipends and status. Alongside the fixtures, numerous private establishments opened: by 1788, an enquiry recorded 348 private schools in Ireland. Many reflected opportunism or desperation on the part of their creators, hopeful of cashing in on the demand for education. The creative hoped to find a profitable niche in a crowded market by using new methods or teaching unfamiliar and vocational subjects.[135] A few prospered; others were derided. In 1749, a don at Dublin University scoffed at the tuition of a Dublin master, whose very name was disparaged as 'a very Irish one'.[136] These establishments gave work to perhaps a thousand. Wives usually helped husbands in schools where pupils boarded. Ushers assisted. Other assistants on occasion used the subordinate positions to train and then tried to set up on their own account.[137]

By the mid-eighteenth century, a former fellow of Trinity reported an abundance of excellent schools in the capital.[138] Yet, if Dublin contained the most, provincial schools had their admirers. Reputation again depended on the aptitude and attentiveness of the staff. Archdeacon William Perceval, an erstwhile Oxford don, professed himself happy to board his sons at a school in Mullingar run by another cleric.[139] Similarly, Richard Edgeworth removed his heir from the prestigious school at Drogheda, thinking that the boy was bullied. Instead, his schooling was finished at Longford town with a cleric, Thomas Hynes. This episode was marred by the relationship between the Edgeworth heir and a daughter of the master. It ended in a suit for jactitation of marriage in the diocesan court of Ardagh and Kilmore. The social distance between the Edgeworths and the country cleric and master was indicated by the sneer that the publicity over the case did no harm to Miss Hynes since 'it brought her into notice among persons with whom she might not otherwise have been acquainted'.[140]

The different diocesan academies rose and declined in esteem, as did schools established by landowners at Athlone, Carrickmacross, Charleville, Clonmel, Kilkenny, Lismore and Youghal.[141] Teachers were supported at assorted but rarely elevated levels. During the Cromwellian interregnum, the authorities decreed standard payments for approved preachers and schoolteachers. Annual pay for male teachers ranged from £20 to £40, and for women from £5 to £10 p.a.[142] After this brief interlude, education was financed by the churches, corporations, private benefactors and parents. This fragmented provision allowed wide variations in the pay, and so in the standing of the masters and mistresses. A few could be assured of admission to the respectable, even to the quality. Moreover, teachers in the grander establishments imparted civility and gentility. Familiar – at least in theory – with these qualities, some pedagogues claimed to possess them. Elevated customers, such as Squire Edgeworth, clearly contested this claim: he did not want a son to marry into such a family. Cultured masters, loaded with book-learning and perhaps university graduates, contrasted with the teachers in charity and petty schools. There, vocational training, such as spinning and husbandry, was offered, usually by laypeople without degrees. The instructors, sometimes former soldiers, more closely resembled tradespeople and craftworkers than the quality. Intermediate, even indeterminate, stations were occupied by teachers of mathematics, in demand from would-be sailors, surveyors and merchants. William Starrat presided over such a school at Strabane.[143]

Some teachers received fixed salaries; others depended entirely on the fees of the pupils. Rarely did the rewards equal those of the best ecclesiastical livings. As with indigent incumbents, so with masters, pluralism could raise their incomes. In Athlone, the curate received an extra £20 yearly for teaching in the free school.[144] At St Michan's in Dublin, the vestry clerk doubled as parish schoolmaster.[145] The Dublin parish of St Catherine's allowed its charity schoolmaster, Samuel Suffolk, an annual £14 during the reign of George II.[146] Elsewhere in the provinces, as at Athlone or Navan in County Meath, stipends varied from £20 to £35 p.a.[147] Lord Cork and Burlington allowed the master in Youghal a yearly £30; the peer's brother, Orrery, with more grandiose ambitions, had earmarked £50 p.a. for the head of his establishment at Charleville.[148] Bishop Foy stipulated that the director of his institution in Waterford should receive an annual £40.[149] More generous was the allowance from Viscount Weymouth for his school in Carrickmacross. In 1711 the first master, John Carver, would be paid £70 p.a. Out of this, he had to maintain both an usher and the school buildings. The post was clearly intended to be full-time, since the occupant was permitted only five weeks of absence in each year.[150] Carver was lured to Carrickmacross from the diocesan school in Meath. His successor, a Cambridge graduate, William Folds, after more than thirty years as master was preferred to the vicarage of Ardee in County Louth. In turn he was succeeded by a son, who combined teaching with acting as the Weymouths' agent.[151]

Municipalities also employed schoolmasters. In Dublin during the 1650s, the master received a yearly £60, and an usher £20.[152] In Waterford, the corporation was persuaded to double the Latin schoolmaster's salary in 1727, from £20 to £40.[153] At Kinsale, the borough accepted the need for a Latin master, but at first contributed only £6 p.a. Gradually this was raised to £10. It sufficed to attract Ferdinand Bowler, son of a merchant from the port. After schooling at the diocesan establishment at Rosscarbery, he graduated at Trinity in 1705.[154] A successor shared the pittance equally with an usher.[155] Only in 1745 did the corporation propose enhancing the salary to £20 p.a.[156] These wages did not necessarily represent total earnings. The council provided the teacher with a house; he may also have collected small fees from some pupils. Despite the decline in the roll – by 1750, the Latin school had only four pupils – the municipality continued to support the academy.[157] The town council distinguished this more prestigious post from a second which it funded, to teach gratis the fatherless and impoverished. Between 1724 and 1733, Luke Roche was paid £2 10s. for this service.[158]

A few teaching posts offered emoluments generous enough to attract the academically well qualified and place their holders unquestionably among the pseudo-gentry. Weymouth's statutes for his school at Carrickmacross stipulated that the master be a graduate in holy orders, 'loyal, orthodox and conformable to the present Church of Ireland'. He must teach 'religion, virtue and learning in Latin, Greek and Hebrew; also oratory, poetry, antiquities, arithmetic, geography, surveying and other parts of practical mathematics'.[159] Those who met such onerous obligations could prosper, socially as well as materially. Richard Norris at Drogheda or the Chinnerys, successive heads of Midleton College, achieved this respectability.[160] Several desirable postings lay in Ulster. There, thanks to the plantation during James I's reign, royal schools had been well endowed.[161] Sion Hill regretted that he had declined the mastership of the Royal School in Raphoe for a post at Lismore, a foundation of the Boyles. The former was worth £100 annually; the latter, only £40. However, Hill united the Lismore mastership with a curacy in the town.[162]

Another of the Jacobean royal schools in Ulster, Portora at Enniskillen, attracted in succession a former fellow of Trinity College Dublin (Charles Grattan) and the master of St Patrick's School in Dublin. By the end of the eighteenth century, this billet was equated – implausibly – with a bishopric and alleged to be worth £2,000 p.a.[163] In Limerick, Jacques Ingram, having had difficulty securing ordination, was made master of the diocesan school. It boomed. By 1737 Ingram had enrolled eighty-six scholars and eleven boarders. Each of the last paid annually £16. Ingram enjoyed an income with which, so he boasted, he might support a wife in genteel style.[164] The buoyant demand emboldened others to set up as teachers. During the 1750s it was even suggested that schoolteachers in Ireland were too well paid and had too little to do.[165] Some entered the profession by circuitous routes. At Ballyhack in County Wexford, the local lady of the manor persuaded a corporal to open a school.[166] Earlier, during the 1720s, a lieutenant had run the school in Kinsale.[167] In Downpatrick, it was decided to install a former sergeant and clerk to a regiment as the schoolmaster.[168] Oliver Goldsmith was taught in the Irish midlands by a one-time regimental quartermaster.[169] Some appointed to teach in the establishments of the Incorporated Society, the educational charity founded in 1733, as at Sligo and Ballycastle, had previously served in the forces.[170] James Fontaine, a Huguenot refugee, disillusioned by a spell as magistrate and farmer in south-west Cork, opened an academy for the fashionable in central Dublin.[171]

Necessity drove many – women as well as men – into teaching. In so far as there was a recognized progression in the clerical profession, tutoring could be a first stage, succeeded perhaps by doubling as curate and parish schoolmaster. Other teachers were unashamed opportunists. Some detected a demand; others drifted into it as a change from different work, including – as has been seen – soldiering. The results could disappoint expectations. The Reverend William Owen supplemented his clerical stipend by undergoing 'the slavery' of teaching the boys of Wexford town.[172] Miles Higgins, discouraged in his efforts to teach at Arklow, entreated an appointment in Wexford. Failing to secure it, he removed to County Mayo. Both at Arklow and in Mayo, he complained of competition from 'popish schools'. Higgins alleged that at Ballinrobe, he could not walk in the street without the Catholics' 'taunts, cracks and scoffings and scurrilous domineering crew. They raise hue and cry after me. They bawl out and call me many names. At last they sing "Calvin, Calvin" after me, thinking I abhor that name.' Assailed with sticks and stones, the beleaguered Higgins depended on hand-outs from the local bishop and squire. At Arklow he had only six poor country boys to instruct once the son of a notable had gone elsewhere to learn his Greek.[173] Higgins, like others licensed to teach by the Church of Ireland, may have been a convert from Catholicism.[174] The ecclesiastical authorities seem often to have been reluctant to entrust these recruits with cures of souls. Higgins's recent defection may explain much of the hostility which he excited in over-whelmingly Catholic communities. Early in the 1690s, John McCollin was engaged to teach the children of the owner of an estate near Clones in County Monaghan. McCollin complained that he went unpaid when the proprietor returned to England, and could find no other pupils in the vicinity.[175]

Good pay occasionally attracted masters from England. Elisha Coles, compiler of a famous dictionary, was tempted by the salary of £66 13s. 4d. to take charge of Smith's academy in Galway.[176] The first head of Orrery's swish establishment in County Cork was a deprived minister from England, Daniel Burgess.[177] But as with clerical posts, by the later seventeenth century, there were enough Protestants born in Ireland to fill vacancies. In the diocese of Limerick, the total of approved teachers rose from three in 1698 to twenty-one by 1714.[178] The northern diocese of Clogher recorded thirty-five licensed masters in 1719, forty-four in 1725 and thirty-seven in 1747.[179] Qualifications but not always income entitled the dominies to respect. As with the beneficed clergy, so with the masters, incompetence, the result of age, illness and drink, could forfeit the respect intrinsic to their calling. At Downpatrick the dean complained in 1712 that the local master, formerly a man of learning, by 'his language, stammering and unpoliteness make[s] many gentlemen send their children to other places'.[180] The next master so enraged the dean that the latter chastised him physically, and urged his replacement.[181] In the corporation of Kinsale, a kindlier view was taken of the decline in the Latin school. The port also assisted an aged schoolmaster who had lived in the town for twenty-six years. By 1714, aged sixty-six, he subsisted by teaching the children of a few neighbours. The town council accepted his petition that he lived 'by nature of a pilgrim being by age and crosses reduced to extreme poverty', and paid the rent on a room in which he could instruct his charges.[182] At Lifford, the free school had declined as the 'sorry' master concentrated on running an inn. However, a rival jumped into the gap and set up another, which attracted 213 boys.[183]

IV

At the summit of the official educational system in Protestant Ireland was Trinity College, the university of Dublin. Its fellows presided over the intellectual and cultural formation of many clergymen of the established Church and of a growing number of those soon to be important in the larger Irish Protestant community. Most fellows of the College were themselves clergymen, and spanned the spheres of teaching and preaching.

Some climbed high in the Church of Ireland; most were accepted as denizens of the quality. The college, from its creation by Queen Elizabeth I in 1592, was conceived as a seminary for the Protestant and English interests. Trinity, like the Church and schools, from which it was inseparable, remained an object of official interest. Occasionally this made it the recipient of government largesse. More often, the authorities intervened to ensure (or restore) good government. In practice, this meant choosing its provost and other leading functionaries.

The need to make it responsive to the vagaries of English policy – as in the 1650s, under James II or with the rapid reversal of Tory high churchmanship after 1714 – justified meddling. For some, the docility with which the institution – necessarily, given its constitution and role – followed government directives lessened its attractions. So, too, did its annexation to a spoils system which reserved the better paid posts – notably the provostship, worth £200 p.a. in the 1650s – for outsiders.[184] However, after a sequence of Englishmen – Bedell, Temple, Chappell, Winter, Lingard, Marsh and Huntington – from the 1690s it was possible to appoint sons of Protestant Ireland. George Browne, St George Ashe and Peter Browne, all alumni of the university, now presided over it. They were succeeded by others – Benjamin Pratt and Richard Baldwin – with similar local provenances. Their appointments confirmed Trinity's centrality in the life of the Irish Protestant élite, which its location in Dublin already proclaimed.[185]

The college, with its discipline, focused Irish Protestant pride. Cheaper and seemingly better governed than its rivals in Oxford and Cambridge, it was particularly popular among those of modest but respectable circumstances, notably among the clergy.[186] In addition, as bishops insisted that those whom they ordained should be graduates, most would-be ministers in Ireland repaired to the university. Its head in 1692 hoped that, with 200 scholars in residence, the college would 'be able to furnish the church with able ministers, which are at present extremely wanted'. However, the recent warfare had disrupted the education of many, 'so that a great part of the tutor's time is employed in furnishing them with sufficient grammar learning, and finishing the schoolmaster's work'. As more peaceful conditions returned, the 'extreme backwardness and rawness' of most entrants were reduced.[187] Tutors – the fellows – varied, not just in politics and theology, but in status. Most, especially the junior fellows, were transients, for whom the berth was a temporary one while they awaited more lucrative preferment. The emoluments of junior fellowships – a mere £15 p.a. – did not conduce to long tenure. However, both junior and senior fellows (the stipend of the latter was an annual £48 6s. 8d.) supplemented their earnings by fees from tuition.[188] A few, holders of

established professorships and senior fellowships, proved permanent fixtures. On them depended the reputation of the institution. Members of
the college were active in several schemes of improvement. In 1683 and
again in the 1690s the Dublin Philosophical Society owed much to the
support of dons. Even critical English administrators allowed that the
college harboured 'several very learned and ingenious men' and that
Provost Ashe was 'polite, learned and ingenious'.[189] It was not by chance
that the first gathering out of which the Dublin Society developed
occurred in Trinity.[190] Early in the eighteenth century, the composer
Johann Cousser looked to the fellows, both senior and junior, to support
his activities. Eighteen of their number were noted as potential patrons.[191]
This donnish activism solidified the sometimes tenuous links between the
declared patriots and the sole Irish university. Samuel Madden, graduate
and benefactor of the college, included its reform in a plan which also
encompassed the faltering Dublin Society and the Irish economy.[192]
During the 1730s, fellows like Edward Molloy and John Whittingham
pushed the craze for betterment in polite Dublin.[193] Other campaigners
for material and ethical improvements, such as William Maple, George
Berkeley and Robert Howard, although former fellows, hardly derived a
common approach to the problems of Ireland from their time there.[194]
Fellows, like Patrick Delany and his colleague, Richard Helsham, set a
pattern of suburban refinement in their bachelor establishment at Delville,
to the north of Dublin.[195] But their cultivated retirement was as much
from Trinity as from the hurly-burly of the city. Other dons, like John
Lawson and Henry Dabzac, as well as undergraduates, were to be encountered at the smart dinner tables and drums of the city. In their turn,
residents and visitors were entertained in the college. At once tourist
attraction and seat of intense sociability, its physical appearance increasingly reflected its importance in the formation of Protestant Ireland.[196]

   The college, the better to function as an engine of Protestant and English
interests, received official support. In the early 1660s, with a new land settlement on the anvil, the college might either lose or gain. The provost was
delighted when Robert Southwell, 'wonderful civil', offered his help.[197]
Southwell, although not a Dublin graduate, professed a disinterested
affection for the college. Another Irishman who knew his way around
Whitehall, William Temple, son of a pre-war provost, also espoused the
college's claims.[198] These services were continued into the eighteenth
century by another from a family high among the clerisy and office-holders
of Protestant Ireland. Dr Samuel Molyneux, strategically situated as
secretary to the Prince of Wales, intervened to minimize the potential
embarrassment when the chancellor of Dublin University, Ormonde, flitted
across to the continent. In England, the college was rumoured to be 'a

garrison holding out for the Pretender'. Molyneux eased the coup by which the prince, his master, succeeded the Jacobite duke. Thereby, the institution was restored 'to the good opinion of the gentlemen of Ireland'.[199] Later, in 1731, official favour was again exhibited when the current lord-lieutenant, Dorset, had one of his sons, Lord George Sackville, study there.[200] This was intended to reverse the habit of shipping the impressionable young from Ireland to Oxford. Indeed, in the seventeenth century, the first duke of Ormond – and others – distinguished between a few grandees, like his grandson and eventual heir, needing to equip themselves to act in both England and Ireland, and lesser fry who would swim only in Irish waters. He was keen to encourage members of the first group to matriculate at Oxford, of which – in addition to Trinity College – he was chancellor. Dorset's gestures neither stopped the flow of the wealthiest and smartest from Ireland to be educated outside their own kingdom nor brought numerous Britons into Trinity. Always more convenient for the inhabitants of North Wales and north-western England than Oxford and Cambridge, the college drew few from elsewhere.[201]

Fears that Trinity might be colonized and controlled by predators from Britain, 'who will rule with a rod of iron', revived in the 1730s, perhaps as part of the worry over absentees and English incursions into Irish places.[202] In the context of the university, these forebodings proved unnecessarily alarmist. It remained the domain of the Irish Protestants. In 1747, when candidates for the provostship were considered, the government interested itself closely, 'as it concerns the education and government of the youth amongst the nobility and gentry'. But the choice lay between locals.[203] More ominous was an apparent decline in the popularity of the university. In its heyday early in the eighteenth century, on average seventy-eight matriculated each year, and so the college had a total complement of between 340 and 440. Economic difficulties early in the 1740s reduced annual admissions. Education there, at a minimum of £50 p.a. probably a third or a quarter of the price of the English alternatives, strained the resources of parents on the fringes of gentility, who had an annual income of maybe £200 to £300.[204] By the 1750s, the Irish economy was recovering, and with it the fortunes of the college. At all levels, from election to scholarships to selection of fellows and appointment of provost, it resembled the other established institutions of Protestant Ireland. Interest had to be mobilized; adequate means were vital.[205] Only the naïve supposed that scholarships and fellowships were awarded entirely on merit. The university was included in the manoeuvres of the *bons bourgeois*. The extended circle of the Conollys was only one of the affinities who had kindred and acquaintances among the fellows. The dons were caressed and cajoled on behalf of the well-connected youths whom they oversaw.[206] Speaker Boyle was asked to intercede with the college authorities on behalf of the sons of dependants.[207] Scholarships and fellowships, distinctions carrying emoluments, enabled their holders to edge ahead in the competitive society of Protestant Ireland. By 1750, the university accommodated twenty-eight senior members in agreeable style.[208]

Representative of those who used the university to advance financially and socially was Patrick Delany. Popular as a tutor and preacher, by the 1720s he was envied for earning perhaps £700 or £800 yearly from his pupils.[209] In the end, Delany, disliked by the ardent Whigs for his Tory leanings, was prised out of his fellowship. Yet, after he had become a dignitary of the established Church, he, in common with other distinguished alumni among the bishops and deans, retained a close interest in the college.[210] Others cherished their links. A quondam fellow, William Palliser, archbishop of Cashel from 1694 to 1727, lodged in the college when in Dublin. His affection led him to bequeath part of his library to the old place.[211] Benefits flowed from those who identified with their *alma mater*. So, too, did embarrassments. Unlike Oxford and Cambridge at the time, the college was physically as well as ideologically at the centre of the predominant caste. In 1734, after riots in which a fellow had been killed, pamphleteers ruminated. Reforms were proposed to promote 'manly politeness', rather than the fashionable but 'false notions of politeness'. The spartan despaired of 'the luxuriousness, softness and nicety of persons', which sapped the institution.[212]

Changed standards of polite hospitality obliged the college to hire china for the entertainment which accompanied the installation of a new chancellor in 1768.[213] Before this, heirs to substantial fortunes, such as Ralph Howard, son of Robert Howard, a former fellow and bishop, spent lavishly to reorder their rooms in the latest vogue. Howard already displayed that enthusiasm for paintings which would later turn him into a dedicated collector. His requirements from a Dublin cabinet-maker included twelve picture frames and another two of pear wood, gilded and carved.[214] In 1760, Richard Lovell Edgeworth, heir to Edgeworthstown, ran up numerous bills in addition to those for tuition. His chamber was taken over from alumni also from the midlands, at a cost of more than £60. Nearly twenty years earlier, it had cost Patience Howard £55 to buy for her son the interest in Simon Davenport's rooms at Trinity.[215] In the cases of both Howard and Edgeworth, more was spent buying old furniture left in the sets and then equipping them according to the sons' exacting tastes. In 1760 a carpenter fashioned a frame over the chimneypiece and paper was hung on the walls of Edgeworth's room. Then expenses such as coal, linen and laundry inflated costs further. The young Edgeworth, like others of his position, was accompanied by a servant and frequently had food and drink sent in from the town. In retrospect, Edgeworth commended his tutor as 'a gentlemanlike and worthy man'. Not unduly troubled with academic exercises, he admitted to passing his time in dissipation, and was soon removed to Oxford.[216] Others of similar background, such as Billy Smythe, eventual owner of Barbavilla in County Westmeath, took their studies more seriously. The modest, including Smythe, economized by lodging outside the college or, as in the case of Edmund Burke, by living at home.[217]

Smythe, the heir to Barbavilla, indicates strengths and weaknesses in the institution. Contrary to some impressions, he was earnest – even too earnest – about his studies. He thought his mentors were the same. He enjoyed the communal rituals of the place. Yet, living out and returning to Westmeath often, his attachments to the college were selective and (perhaps) transitory. Even in the city, he relaxed in the company of kindred and connections as much as in the rooms of the few grandees among the undergraduates. Once gone, there were few opportunities in days before corporate fund-raising to reunite with college contemporaries. Smythe, waiting to take his place as a notable in his county, had no need of the university to promote himself, either socially or occupationally. Equipped already with an extensive affinity, at best he added a few from his college circle to it. Whether this is typical of the members of the establishment has yet to be discerned. In one way, Smythe did personify the prevailing tone. He was well rooted in Protestant Ireland. By the 1760s, the university enticed few from outside Ireland into fellowships or scholarships. Here was one Irish field which had not been invaded. Yet, the optimistic interpretation of the place as an avenue where Protestants of divergent means mingled and then advanced has to be verified. For the same reasons that those bent on the professions needed to be backed by parents or guardians who could spare at least £40 p.a., the entrants to the university were recruited from a minority within the Protestant population. Once entered, the high spenders – the likes of Ralph Howard and Richard Lovell Edgeworth – frequented distinct societies. How much they sensed a shared culture and loyalty with the studious and poor may be questioned, and with it the degree to which the college instilled a common outlook.

In practice, for the college to retain its hold over its local constituencies it had at once to reflect and to implant the changing notions of gentility. Critics decried these pretensions. The attributes of a 'fine' or 'pretty' gentleman were acquired only at 'monstrous expense'. In the longer term, it was alleged, these qualifications earned only 'a bare livelihood'.[218] Nevertheless, wholehearted participation in these wider worlds, lamented by a few purists, guaranteed the college's continuing importance to Protestant Ireland. For this reason, even apparent embarrassments could be glossed more favourably. In 1767, the provost, Francis Andrews, appeared in the updated catalogue of absentees from the kingdom. This confirmed Andrews's low reputation among some over whom he ruled. One undergraduate confided to his father that the provost was 'so base a man that I would blush were I to tell you'.[219] Even more scabrous was an epitaph

> *Incontinence was his supreme delight,*
> *In bestial pleasures, he consumed the night*
> *Wallowed in vice, as swine repose in mud*
> *Deep 'mersed in whoredom, drunkenness and blood*
> *Oh! Rare director of untainted youth*
> *A scourge of honour, probity and truth.*[220]

A depressed standing among those who saw the provost in action (or inaction) could not exclude him – any more than it could avaricious landowners or indolent clerics – from the standing to which position and stipend entitled him. Andrews was away touring the continent, refining his connoisseurship. By undertaking an ambitious building campaign on behalf of the college (and himself) and sitting in parliament, Andrews may have done more for the esteem of the university among contemporaries than by assiduous attendance to the minutiae of the provostship.[221] Worse still in the eyes of conscious patriots was the appointment of the egregious John Hely Hutchinson as provost in 1774. To idealists, Hutchinson as a married layman contravened the statutes and signified the spread of venality into education. Yet Hely Hutchinson, of Irish – indeed Gaelic – stock was a reminder of the extent to which the Protestants of Ireland had commandeered and now ran the ecclesiastical and scholastic establishments.[222]

V

Alongside the ministers and educators of the established Church were their Catholic and dissenting equivalents. All occupied a shadowy zone. Catholic priests and religious remained in Ireland in defiance of the law, and risked arrest, imprisonment and even execution. These penalties did not clear the kingdom of Catholic competitors. Indeed, in 1731 there were thought to be at least 1,445 in Ireland.[223] In addition, 549 Catholic schools were identified.[224] Other than at moments of panic, few of these pastors concealed themselves. On occasion they were invited into the homes of Protestant notables, suggesting that they could pass muster in polite society.[225] A few joined in scholarly as well as polemical exchanges with the educated of the ruling caste.[226] The clandestine presence of functionaries of the rival denominations not only challenged the authority of the clergy of the established Church, but complicated the social description of Ireland. Some Catholic priests and most dissenting pastors possessed qualities, notably training for a lettered calling, which commanded social respect. However, in the same way that the regulators of the Church of Ireland disagreed over whether or not to cooperate with Presbyterian colleagues, laypeople were uncertain whether these dissenters should be admitted into the palladium of respectability. Few with unequivocally dissenting credentials survived in the higher reaches of rural society.[227] However, in Dublin, some of the larger towns and throughout Ulster, dissent had adherents of substance and civility.

By the simple test of income, dissenting ministers were edging towards the 'quality'. In 1674, the Synod of Antrim set £30 as the minimum annual competence. By the 1690s, stipends averaged £33 9s. 3d.[228] In 1753, the General Synod of Ulster established a minimum of £40 p.a., raised in 1770 to £50.[229] This aim was not universally realized. In 1767, there were at least thirteen meetings unable to pay their pastors even £30 yearly.[230] Matters had hardly improved by the 1790s. Then, a wide-ranging enquiry showed that only two ministers – both in Belfast – were receiving more than an annual £150; 131 (or 70 per cent) of all Presbyterian ministers in Ulster had stipends of less than £60, which was now proposed as the minimum.[231] In the smaller dissenting denominations, such as the English Presbyterians, ministers in large towns could expect similar salaries. At Cork, pay crept up from £70, with a house, in 1757, to £120 twenty years later, and £150 in 1796.[232] In comparison, the withered remnant of the Baptist congregation in Cork city could offer a putative pastor only £60 p.a.[233] Nonconformist ministers, like their Church of Ireland counterparts, received benefits in kind: housing, fuel, grain and labour in their fields. These gifts were sometimes begrudged and – no less than with the dues of the established Church – might occasion contention.[234] Forty pounds was often taken as the threshold above which one could live politely. Thanks to their private resources, many nonconformist ministers passed as 'pseudo-gentry' in their small towns. In addition, conscious of a role as exemplars, the active could exercise an influence out of proportion to their incomes. They were not numerous. The largest group – the Presbyterian ministers of the Synod of Ulster – totalled 185 in the 1790s.[235] In all, perhaps 250 dissenting preachers can be added to the total of Protestant clergy in mid-eighteenth-century Ireland.

All ordained clerics, regardless of denomination, possessed some of the attributes which entitled them to be counted among the quality. Many, thanks to training and culture, enjoyed a respect not justified by income alone. Indeed, meagre salaries meant that they could buy few of the conventional accoutrements of gentility. Benefits in kind, especially housing, eased difficulties. Nevertheless, with obligations from book-learning through seemly dress to philanthropy, many had to supplement their incomes.[236] Teaching and medicine were thought the most fitting, but not the only, methods.[237] All churches expected high qualifications of their priests. Increasingly these could be met only by university education: for Presbyterians, often in Scotland; for the Catholics, in continental Europe.[238] Such preparation outside Ireland separated them from the clergy of the Church of Ireland, mostly educated in Dublin; and also from the majority of laypeople. In means, these clergy resembled the craftworkers and farmers among whom they dwelt. However, like their equivalents in the established Church, the teachers of the other churches aimed by example to demonstrate civility and cultivation. Thereby they strengthened their claims to be accounted of the quality. The ambiguities in the position of the Catholic priests was a reminder of the possibilitiy that Catholics, even when debarred legally and by meagre income from so many of the opportunities to act genteelly, might nevertheless do so.

Chapter 5

Professions

I

The bishop who bewailed 'the too great power of the professions' in 1736 itemized the clergy, army officers and lawyers.[1] Each group became a beneficiary of the system which in 1704 aimed to turn these occupations into Church of Ireland monopolies. Each then had a strong incentive to defend the emergent Irish Protestant ascendancy in Ireland. The clerics fabricated and expounded an ideology; barristers interpreted and applied the laws which created the system of privilege; the soldiery, when necessary, would fight to maintain it. They had rivals. Other denominations maintained sacred ministries. Catholics followed the flags of foreign powers, and might return to seize what they had recently forfeited. It was suspected, too, that Catholics survived as lawyers, evading the ban on their practising by nominal conversion.[2] At the same time, Irish Protestants were – as a matter of policy – excluded from some of the most attractive posts in the three callings. Instead, the jobs were reserved for the trustworthy from Britain. Irish Protestants resented, and sometimes feared, these competitors. Chances for reasonable livings in the professions existed, but never as many as were desired. The established Church and its ancillaries of teaching may have supported 1,200. Those practising in the three branches of the law – as barristers, solicitors and attorneys – whether in Dublin or the provinces, probably numbered between 800 and 1,000. The officer corps of the army in Ireland amounted to about 800. In addition, numerous Irish-born soldiers and sailors served in Britain and its empire. Although there was some overlap with the 3,000 to 5,000 freeholders seen as the core of the Protestant élite, these professions, predominantly urban in their orientation, considerably inflated that total.

The high costs and sometimes disappointing rewards of entering the Church might suggest that it is inappropriately likened to other, more venal professions, and is better regarded as a vocation. However, training for the bar, apprenticeship to an attorney or solicitor or the purchase of a military commission, entailed considerable expense not quickly recouped. Those who wished to practise in the Dublin Four Courts had first to study at the London Inns of Court. This increased cost of preparation deterred those of modest means. The experience exposed future Irish barristers to a world outside Ireland. The same was true of the physicians who worked in Ireland. Of necessity, with no medical faculty in the kingdom, they travelled overseas in order to learn. In many instances, indeed, they went further even than the lawyers: to continental Europe. Army officers from Protestant Ireland were technically prohibited from serving in their own country, so they too were compelled to see more distant parts of the Hanoverians' empire. These requirements to train beyond Ireland made lawyers, doctors and military officers promising agents through which greater integration of Ireland into Britain might be accomplished.

Confessional tests opened up a prospect for the Protestants of Ireland that they would soon be fattened in lush pastures. In England, lawyers had proliferated since the late fifteenth century as both the crown and other property-owners used law to regulate relationships and settle contests. By the later seventeenth century, a more general increase in governance and overseas expansion led to what has been called 'the rise of the professions'.[3] An enlarged machine, responsive to the needs of a 'fiscal-military' state, accounted for some of the growth. In addition, a larger and prospering population, especially in the towns, bought the help of experts. The functionaries groped towards disinterested and impersonal ideals of state service rather than unabashed profiteering or fealty to an overlord.[4] These groups, advancing in step and venerating education and cultivation, soon considered themselves educated and cultivated. In these guises, they inspired and were themselves influenced by the 'urban renaissance', which saw towns spawn unprecedented services and forms of recreation.[5] They powered the associations and charities which proliferated throughout the eighteenth century.[6]

Land at bargain prices ceased to be the readiest route to fortune and fame. Instead, the hard graft of office, profession or fighting away from Ireland enabled the embarrassed and ambitious to subsist, and even prosper. The shrewd – or merely desperate – equipped themselves to enter these openings. Two peculiarities marked the professional and official worlds of Ireland. As in England, so in Ireland from 1704, a sacramental test legally debarred all but certified communicants of the state Church from office and the learned professions, other than medicine.[7] At the same time, the presence of more Protestants in Ireland ensured that they could staff the posts. Indeed, the proliferating Protestants needed all these employments. Otherwise they might be forced into work which involved social derogation. Accordingly, the aspiring were dismayed when so much of what they coveted was reserved for interlopers from Britain. Others were aggrieved by the confessional exclusions. Conspicuous among the victims were the lawyers. The import and application of English law throughout Ireland had always bulked large in English plans for the island.[8] By the late seventeenth century, even the remotest counties had seemingly been subjected to the imported system. Relationships and property were increasingly defined and regulated by law. Purchases, tenancies, marriages and inheritances all required legal practitioners. Framing, interpreting and enforcing the laws made ample work. The requirement of study at one of the English Inns of Court[9] added to the expense of legal training, but did not deter the fortunate from the landed families of Catholic Ireland.[10] Doubts persisted about the reliability of the law as an instrument to subject Ireland to England and English habits so long as Catholics remained prominent in the Irish courts. In consequence, efforts were intensified to turn first the judiciary, then legal practice in the courts and finally the trade of the attorney into Protestant monopolies.[11] The process continued into the 1730s. Even then it was suspected that Catholics had not been totally debarred. Some advised in chambers; others underwent only nominal conversion.[12]

Until 1641, and even between 1660 and 1689, Catholics had filled government offices and flourished in the higher reaches of the law.[13] Thereafter, Irish Protestant enjoyment of their new monopoly was marred by suspicions that Catholics were evading the bans. But even more distressing to the new incumbents was the practice of reserving many of the highest and best places for immigrants. At first the excuse for appointing strangers to the bishops' and judges' benches was the lack of adequate locals. But it was also designed to speed the assimilation of Ireland to English ways. This remained a motive throughout the eighteenth century. Then, the viceroyalty itself was added to the list of offices reserved for biddable Englishmen. Such a policy might promise to integrate Ireland into a pan-Britannic system. In practice, it treated the Hanoverians' territories individually. Scotland lacked any equivalent of the lord-lieutenant, never saw the transfer of larger tracts of its surface to outsiders and retained its own forms of ecclesiastical government and law. In Scotland, unlike Ireland, strangers were not intruded into the most attractive places in the civil and ecclesiastical establishments. Nevertheless, less antagonistic devices were strengthening the feeling among officers and professionals that they were part of something other than Ireland. Spells at the London Inns of Court heightened awareness of a legal culture essentially English in origin and application. Novice barristers, sampling the costly delights of Hanoverian London, responded ambivalently.[14] The expense of residing far from home for several years ensured that this course could be followed only by the prosperous. Training could consume £1,000 to £1,500. However, the financially embarrassed from Ireland, if they passed only three years at the London Inns, presumably spent less.[15]

On returning to Ireland, work awaited the well-connected and proficient. More laws and a propensity to resort to litigation or legal process to deal with family and property – all part of the English design for Ireland – meant more briefs and fees. At the end of the seventeenth century and into the eighteenth, the four central courts in Dublin gave employment to perhaps 200 qualified barristers.[16] In 1734, 190 barristers qualified by taking the oaths required to continue in practice. Below them a larger group of attorneys and solicitors operated, sometimes in the central courts, but also in chambers or subsidiary and provincial courts. Eighty-seven solicitors and 573 attorneys swore the oaths in 1734.[17] Regular assizes and quarter sessions, and a multiplicity of borough and local jurisdictions, drew some votaries from the capital, but also kept others more precariously as 'hackney' attorneys.[18]

Before the seventeenth century ended, Catholics spotted loopholes. In manorial courts, such as that at Finavarra in County Clare, the O'Davorens, previously proficient in the brehon laws, were active during Charles II's reign.[19] In this manner, they preserved their traditional trade under the inauspicious conditions of Protestant Ireland. However, remunerative legal business was increasingly engrossed by the (nominal) adherents of the state Church. For practitioners, the rewards remained uncertain and uneven. A few enriched themselves sensationally, and were popularly mistaken for the entire profession. In Charles II's reign, the younger Sir John Temple steadily pushed his yearly income up from about £500 in 1656 to nearly £1,800 in the early 1670s. Earnings of this magnitude easily surpassed those of country squires and equalled those of some solvent peers. Temple's appointment as solicitor-general crowned a lucrative and prestigious career. However, he – in common with most successful lawyers and office-holders – had scarcely arrived at this eminence from nowhere. His father had served as Master of the Rolls and a grandfather as provost of Trinity College in Dublin.[20] Another from the seventeenth-century settler community who thrived on the law was Alan Brodrick. From his first year of practice in the 1680s, he grossed £120; in the second, he expected £200. By the next decade, he was hoping to earn £1,000. Later he became lord chancellor. A third success story was that of William Howard. When he died prematurely in 1728, he was said to make £1,500 p.a. He, too, had been launched on this successful career from a secure background in the academic, clerical and administrative establishment of Dublin.[21]

Howard sat briefly in parliament, for the city of Dublin. Successful lawyers often went into parliament. Their skills, whether oratorical or of draftsmanship, were valued. Legal skills and office united to lift William Conolly up the crucial first rungs of the social and economic ladder, until by the 1720s he was probably the richest commoner in Ireland. Conolly practised as an attorney in the 1680s.[22] In common with others following the trade, he had probably equipped himself through a clerkship or formal apprenticeship in another attorney's office. During the confusion after 1690, he acted for Londonderry corporation in its legal business.[23] He also took on the office of deputy alnager. The latter brief, the statutory regulation of the wool trade, afforded modest but useful patronage across the country.[24] In both capacities, he familiarized himself with official Dublin. He retained and enlarged this base, compounded of law and revenue administration, and eventually presided as a commissioner over the Revenue Board in Dublin.[25] In 1694 he acquired a wife, a daughter of the Donegal notable Sir Albert Conyngham, higher in social standing than himself. Through Katherine Conyngham he gained not only her portion of £2,400, but a brother-in-law, James Bonnell, strategically placed as accountant-general and secretary to the commissioners overseeing the latest confiscation of rebels' estates. Conolly's earnings from the law and office were shrewdly invested in some of this forfeited property.[26] After 1700, the future was unlikely to bring fresh windfalls. By the 1720s, if Conolly and his kind wished to add to their holdings, they must buy in the usual way.

Sandy Nesbitt, in 1735 eager to enter parliament for the Conolly borough of Limavady, had trained as a barrister at a London Inn. Of him, it was said, 'he never read a word of law for pleasure, and politics took up his whole time'.[27] Once in the Irish Commons, reputation and consequently the likelihood of further preferment might be enhanced by performance in the chamber. But lawyers were also credited with less pleasing traits. At the English Inns of Court, they sometimes acquired fashionable tastes and disturbing opinions. In 1703, Archbishop Palliser of Cashel traced anti-clerical rumours in Dublin to John Ormsby, 'a young-Inn-a-court gentleman that came lately from London'.[28]

Recruits were tempted into the legal profession by the vision of a comfortable livelihood. Sometimes it proved a mirage. One sceptic suggested that no more than forty lawyers in any generation thrived.[29] Also attractive was the lawyers' larger role in the public and cultural life of Protestant communities. Because of the length, cost and tedium of tuition, it was not a course to be undertaken lightly. These high barriers meant that novices were generally recruited from the already landed, such as Brodrick, or the prospering professionals like Temple and Howard. Heirs to estates, such as Michael Ward from County Down and Francis Bernard in County Cork, qualified, practised and eventually gained judicial office. By following a profession and occupying office, they supplemented static or inadequate revenues from their lands.[30] Other squires with legal qualifications – Richard Edgeworth and Robert French – on inheriting soon shut their legal chambers.[31] Their protracted training for the bar was not wasted: knowledge of legal processes and terminology was deemed useful to running an estate. However, they were no substitute for professional competence. Even landlords who had once studied at the London Inns had still to fee attorneys and barristers for their complicated affairs.[32] On the magistrates' bench, too, justices conversant with the law not only reached for the handy vade-mecums compiled for their instruction but whispered to the clerks of the peace to request guidance.[33] Yet the allure of a legal education, with its applications to the practicalities of estate management and its potential profits, commended it to shrewd parents when they considered what to do with their sons. Richard Edgeworth enjoined his heir to 'apply himself to some useful profession or employment that if he doth not add much to his estate he may not however lessen it, and I wish that profession may be the study and practice of the law above all others'. Earlier, Sir Robert Southwell proposed legal training for the young as 'a necessary stake in the hedge'. His experience of affairs caused him to conclude, 'I know not a better method for his preferment in the world'.[34] Richard Cox, a lawyer himself, wanted his son to follow that calling rather than to soldier.[35] Similarly, Archbishop King urged his charge, the young Samuel Foley, to attend seriously to his studies at the London Inns. In the event, Foley was delivered from this drudgery by the opportunities to soldier afforded by the War of the Spanish Succession.[36]

Not all were enthusiastic. Cox conceded that 'the crabbed study of the law' might disgust the young.[37] In the 1740s, the leading Belfast merchant, Daniel Mussenden, mocked his heir's wish to qualify as a barrister, seeing it as an instance of undesirable social climbing.[38] Parents had long worried about the temptations which beset sons dispatched to the Inns of Court. The violent death there of a son of the Percevals from County Cork in the 1670s hardly allayed these anxieties. Sir Robert Southwell worried about the indolence of his cousin from County Limerick, Sir Thomas Southwell, who had been entered at the Inns of Court.[39] In 1732 the Dublin notable, Sir William Fownes, lectured his errant grandson on the extravagances and indulgences into which he had fallen while ostensibly studying the law.[40] Despite these misgivings, the profession appealed and so enticed many from Ireland to London. John Prendergast confessed that legal training alone would equip him for 'some other good, genteel employment, whereby I may honestly live in the world'.[41] So brisk was the traffic that of those enrolling at the London Inns between 1688 and 1714, 9.3 per cent came from Ireland. The Middle Temple was particularly favoured by the Irish-born: 15 per cent of its entrants in the same period hailed from the western kingdom.[42] Cox reckoned the Inner Temple the cheaper option. The essentials of a chamber and diet could be had for an annual £34. Other expenses quickly increased this total. William Howard, admitted to the Middle Temple in 1708, was allowed £80 annually while studying there. This was probably in addition to the basic expenses. Howard's father further assisted by dispatching a large parcel of law books from Dublin, where they were to be had more cheaply. If, as has been argued, the costs of making a barrister could amount to £1,500, then this far exceeded apprenticeship for a prestigious trade or preparation for the Protestant priesthood.[43] In comparison, securing a place to train as an attorney was expected to cost between 80 and 100 guineas, to which living expenses had to be added.[44]

The propertied, although happy to have sons at the bar, remained at best ambivalent and at worst hostile to lawyers. One within the profession asserted that the law was 'the most insipid and dull of all professions'.[45] More typical of the protests were those of the first Viscount Shannon. In 1691 he complained that innocents were inveigled into needless or reckless litigation; cases were unashamedly dragged out; fees for routine and even non-existent services multiplied; offices and agencies were undertaken. Like others with land, Shannon was obliged to use the courts and their practitioners to protect it. Also, in common with those disappointed by unfavourable verdicts and financial losses, he blamed the lawyers.[46] The processes of the courts were felt to favour their own personnel, not litigants. Fees for formalities multiplied and rose. Regular bids to control or reduce them as regularly failed.[47]

Lawyers as a group were sometimes disliked. By the 1730s, their numbers in the Irish parliament were criticized.[48] Most earned less than was popularly supposed. Outsiders – notably from England – disparaged their abilities. In 1695 the new attorney- and solicitor-general were said to be 'two terrible bawling lawyers, which is the way of practice' in Dublin.[49] For the practitioners themselves there were consolations. One was social. The occupation automatically entitled to the suffix 'esquire', a courtesy which hinted that only those of creditable standing could complete the costly preparation. It also acknowledged the learned nature of the profession. As a result, the 190 barristers who formally qualified themselves to continue to plead at the bar in 1734 swelled the squirearchy.[50] Many, by virtue of lands inherited or recently acquired, enjoyed this honorific independent of their profession. Without a full prosopography, it is impossible to gauge how many were elevated, thanks to the convention, into the ranks of the squires, probably as a predominantly urban – indeed metropolitan – component which purists might dismiss as a pseudo-squirearchy. Those of the lower branch of the legal trade, the attorneys, were by custom in Ireland, as in England, designated 'gentlemen'.[51] In general, thanks to cheaper training, the work of the attorney was open to those of lower social status than the barristers' profession. Yet, once licensed as an attorney, an individual was guaranteed social promotion into the gentry. In 1734, 573 attorneys and 87 solicitors qualified in Dublin by swearing the necessary oath.[52]

Dublin, with the business of the four central courts and of its own municipal jurisdictions, supported the most attorneys. Limits were set to those who were licensed to practise in the civic courts: first, six; then eight; next a dozen, and finally two dozen. The intrusion of the poorly qualified was thought to have led to the failure of just causes owing to the incompetence of some attorneys.[53] These seem to have been only notional ceilings. The lucky, authorized to plead as attorneys, probably traded the right to deputize. Between 1696 and 1715, seventy-nine attorneys were licensed to practise in the Dublin Tholsel Courts (the jurisdictions of the lord mayor and sheriffs of the city).[54] Two of these fortunates, Jacob Peppard and Francis Skiddy, received the passport to civic office as, respectively, town clerk and deputy town clerk.[55] Others had worked their way towards this safe plateau. Hugh Kelly in 1671 sought an attorneyship in the Dublin Tholsel with the claim that he was 'a person well-skilled and knowing in clerkship, having had his education that way'.[56] More to the point, attorneys were charged for the right to work in the municipal court. Those already serving as clerks there paid an entry fee of £20; others were required to pay £50.[57] Attorneys, like Thomas Dalrymple in the mid-eighteenth century, cared enough about their tasks to compile precedent books for their own guidance.[58] Only occasionally did incompetence or corruption bring dismissal.[59]

Smaller knots of attorneys were licensed to plead in the courts of boroughs such as Askeaton, Belturbet, Cavan, Cork and Limerick.[60] Critics contended that the usage of 'gentleman' when applied to these hacks debased the term. Unlike the barristers, attorneys were not obliged to train in London. Instead they were prepared through apprenticeship. Some admitted into the Dublin Tholsel had qualified through mastering the routines of an office.[61] Attorneys, perhaps even more than lawyers, varied in what they earned and how they lived. In Dublin, a successful barrister routinely commanded a fee of £2 6s.; an attorney, 6s. 8d.[62] The constricted horizons of hackney attorneys, especially in the provinces, were felt to demean the order of gentlemen.[63] Yet, even if the attorneys exhaled only a bogus gentility, they swelled the numbers who could legitimately claim places among the quality.

The lower branch of the law was more crowded than the bar. Of necessity, attorneys were flexible in what they did. James Morley was tempted from Yorkshire to work in Restoration Ireland. Over ten years he thought he had earned £1,180 from one particular group of clients.[64] Morley's contemporary, Nicholas Jones, admitted as an attorney in Common Pleas, acted on behalf of the absent Legges. The rewards, eclipsed by that of a few 'toppers', nevertheless eased practitioners from pinching want. Of course, offices had to be rented, furnished, lit and (sometimes) cleaned. Clerks must be paid, and stocks of parchment, vellum, paper, quills, ink, sand and wax laid in. Jones, in common with others, grumbled about tardy payment. He also insisted that, in order to serve clients more effectively, he had to maintain a proper port and to keep an assistant.[65] Routine legal tasks led easily into other work. The industrious or ambitious garnered patentee offices, agencies, collectorships and *seneschausées* (seneschalships). William Conolly's start as an attorney in the 1680s has been noted. Gorges Edmond Howard, also an attorney, in time bitingly catalogued the failings of too many of his colleagues. Howard had served an apprenticeship with an attorney of the Dublin Court of Exchequer. He cannily accumulated patentee offices, in the Quit Rent Office and the Revenue Commission. By 1743 he was solicitor for the king's rents in Ireland. He was also appointed registrar to the trustees for the creditors of the failed Burton's bank and registrar and treasurer of an act (which he had helped to promote) to improve thoroughfares in central Dublin. Facile with his pen, Howard defended the Dublin Castle administration, composed manuals on bureaucratic and legal procedures, and unsuccessful plays. Howard valued his legal practice at £1,600 p.a. in 1765, when he retired.[66] Professional and financial success had enabled him to exchange the honorific of gentleman for that of esquire.

Robert Roberts was another attorney who heaved himself up the bureaucratic ladder from the remembrancer's office in the Court of Exchequer into parliament and the squirearchy. Roberts, trained by an uncle, graduated from a clerk's desk to the sonorous dignity of the deputy chief remembrancership.[67] Close relations already in the law may have drawn him into it. More distant kinship brought him into the ambit of the Temples who – from 1715 – controlled the chief remembrancer's office. In the course of this progress, Roberts lived first on fashionable St Stephen's Green, then joined the smart exodus to seaside Monkstown and finally bought a country estate south of the capital.[68] He assembled a large library, attended meetings of the Dublin Society and sent his heir to Dublin University and the English Inns of Court. His family intermarried with others, such as the Helshams and Putlands, who had prospered in the capital thanks to trade, office and the professions. His heir's bride, Bridget Putland, brought (it was said) £10,000 with her.[69] Roberts's distant superior, the chief remembrancer, Henry Temple, Lord Palmerston, might josh him on his new grandeur: 'auditing accounts and hearing references brings in money, or it would not enable you to bring up your family as you say it does'.[70] But none could doubt that Roberts, the erstwhile attorney, had joined the quality. In 1737, when he subscribed to the Dublin edition of Harington's *Oceana*, he was already ornamented with a doctorate of laws. As a subscriber to another legal publication two years later, he was also styled 'esquire'.[71]

Essential to Roberts's transmutation from the dubious gentility of an attorney to assured gentility as a squire with a country place was the acquisition of a patentee office on the civil establishment. Offices, such as that of the chief remembrancer, expanded in Hanoverian Dublin, and offered work to attorneys. Much of it was routine and unglamorous. But, as in the case of Roberts, it could lead to better. Successful attorneys can be glimpsed only occasionally. Robert Nelson, overseeing a bill to put Mercer's Hospital on a more secure foundation, was addressed as esquire in 1749.[72] So, too, was Barry Colles, an Exchequer attorney, who handled the complicated affairs of his entrepreneurial relations in Kilkenny.[73] Samuel Martin, originally from Belfast, had transferred from trade to the law with the help of Sir Audley Mervyn, prime sergeant and Speaker of the Irish House of Commons. Martin, once an attorney in Dublin, was hired by many still in Ulster. On the profits, he put his own sons into medicine and the army.[74] Francis Anderson also levered himself into the quality as an esquire and into wealth thanks to his long practice as an attorney.[75] His status was, like that of Roberts, enhanced by appointment to an established office in the Court of Exchequer.[76] Anderson's reputation also owed much to his diligence and probity; he was remembered as 'a very honest man and a careful, good officer'.[77] Another attorney known to have amassed considerable wealth was William Crookshank. In 1739 he served as churchwarden of the Dublin parish of St Bride. Ten years later, he gave a daughter a portion of £3,000: more than many squires could afford. He, in common with the successful, was in demand for multifarious tasks.[78] Many arose from the tribulations of landowners, to whom some attorneys acted as agents and collectors on annual retainers or salaries, and who in turn disparaged attorneys for exploiting and increasing their problems.[79] But there was a multiplicity of business for those willing to oblige. The aptly named Thomas Vice was used by the Dublin parish of St Michan's to prosecute brothels. For this service he received £1 4s.[80] Richard Morgan started as an attorney in King's Bench. Coming to the notice of Archbishop Lindsay of Armagh, he became registrar of the archdiocese, practised in its prerogative court and served Lindsay and his successor as secretary and agent.[81]

Most of those who come briefly into view were using the law to climb. Others resorted to it, seemingly, in desperation. One within Roberts's and Anderson's orbit in the Exchequer was William Yarner, whose immediate forebears had used the army, medicine, church and office to thrive in seventeenth-century Ireland.[82] Yarner wormed his way into practice at the Exchequer in part thanks to kinship with the Temples.[83] Henry Temple, in particular as chief remembrancer, shielded Yarner from the consequences of his negligence and (perhaps) dishonesty.[84] Temple felt some obligation towards his indigent Yarner kinsfolk, whom the attorney supported, but family sentiment did not extend to entrusting Yarner with delicate commissions.[85] Despite a spotted reputation, Yarner lived comfortably on the outskirts of Dublin, and never lost his social acceptance.[86] Not for him the humiliation of Picket, an attorney in Common Pleas, who, in 1726, having forged a bond, was publicly stripped of his gown and made to wear a wooden ruff.[87]

Provincial practitioners of the law were regularly sneered at. 'Counsellor' Robert Cooke, while his practice languished, farmed in County Galway. This activity, coupled with Cooke's education as a barrister, told of comfortable circumstances if not lofty social standing.[88] The country attorney usually originated and dwelt in greater obscurity. Alex Harper, in County Down early in George I's reign, leased property for £6 p.a. and worked as 'a little attorney in the manor courts'.[89] Manorial and borough courts were outlets for the attorneys. More generally, both rural and urban communities needed defences which these legal mercenaries willingly supplied. Totals outside Dublin are not easily gauged. During the 1730s, it was regretted that there were only two attorneys practising in the Tholsel Court of Kinsale.[90] In 1769 the city of Limerick advertised twenty-two attorneys, three public notaries and six commissioners for taking affidavits, alongside five barristers at law. By 1788, the county town of Clare contained at least eighteen attorneys and notaries.[91] Haphazardly trained, these provincials did not always behave as befitted their honorific of gentleman. An extreme example of misconduct troubled Counties Limerick, Clare and Cork in the mid-1740s. An heiress, under the guardianship of a judge and immured in a country rectory, was abducted. The principal malefactor described himself as an attorney. So, too, did a chief accomplice. In the case of the first, Hugh Massy, a precarious future as a younger son in a cadet branch of landed dynasty may have propelled him into the more menial side of the law. It could be that attorney was an assumed designation, since it protected against the full weight of the law. The already poor reputation of attorneys could only be depressed by such well-publicized escapades.[92] Yet they were offset by the solidity of others in the provinces. John and Daniel Crone, based in the north Cork town of Mallow, looked after the interests of the respectable and prosperous of the area, and by so doing joined them.[93]

Contemporaries did not always distinguish precisely between barristers, solicitors and attorneys. The last term, sometimes applied to those who had been trained and practised as lawyers, may have separated those who pleaded in court from those who laboured constantly in chambers. The unfriendly belittled unpopular professionals by assigning them to the humbler trade. Prosperous 'attorneys', not lawyers, were noted in the provinces.[94] Astonishingly, a survey of the straggling diocese of Elphin in 1749, with its busy towns of Athlone and Sligo, recorded neither lawyers nor attorneys. Practitioners, sensitive to the unpopularity of some of their kind, may have sheltered behind the generalities of 'esquire' or 'gentleman'.[95] Notwith-standing the disfavour with which the calling was frequently regarded, legal experts were wanted for a variety of offices. Most lustrous but not always most remunerative were those in the gift of the government. Seats on the judicial bench proclaimed pre-eminence. Locals competed against the English for them. Judges repeatedly complained that the salaries – between £600 and £800 in 1715 – were less than they had earned from their practices. In 1729, Francis Bernard acted on this belief when he proposed to quit the bench and return to his chambers.[96] In fact, being a judge did not prevent a lawyer from receiving fees for delivering opinions. Law offi-cers of the government advised its members about private as well as public business. For the personal – and perhaps political – favours they could be generously rewarded. In 1742, the solicitor-general and prime sergeant were each given 100 guineas for drawing up the admittedly complex marriage settlement for the lord-lieutenant's son and his intending bride.[97] Practi-tioners competed for the few distinctions – attorney- and solicitor-general, first and second sergeant, and king's (or queen's) counsel – which marked them off from colleagues.[98] In 1686, Sir Thomas Longueville was made a king's counsel, in order to allow him, at his advanced age, to sit within the bar of the court and to be heard first. Longueville's principal recommen-dation was being 'an old cavalier and decayed in his fortune'.[99] In contrast, younger lawyers, such as William Howard in the 1720s, rather than being eased in old age, hoped to be propelled forward more rapidly if they received this particular mark of government favour. Howard discovered to his cost that the lord chancellor had his own favourites – mainly kindred – for these limited promotions.[100]

In the provinces, gownsmen congregated during the assizes and sessions. Sittings of the more mundane manor and town courts brought together those who practised law. In general, they were too few or their stays too brief to create a distinctive legal society or culture. Lawyers, familiar with the constitutional histories of Ireland and England, might resent the subordination of the former to the latter. In the seventeenth century, the legally trained, first Patrick Darcy and then William Domville and his son-in-law, William Molyneux, led the attacks.[101] Resentment might move up a register into political disaffection. Barristers entered parliament, where their forensic and rhetorical skills guaranteed a hearing. Some used these vantage points to harass governors in Dublin Castle deemed too servile to British rather than Irish concerns. Others, such as Gorges Howard, used their legal acumen to defend unpopular administrations.[102]

The judges, barristers and attorneys riding the circuit tended to keep the company of the squires and gentry who acted as sheriff, grand jurors and magistrates.[103] Legal practitioners living permanently outside Dublin joined in the conviviality of freemen, burgesses, Masons and private houses. The capital afforded better prospects of gatherings out of which professional solidarity might grow. Commensality was required of men of law from their early years at the Inns; students from Ireland, accustomed to eating together, sometimes shared lodgings.[104] The habit of communal meals persisted after they had qualified. Business was often conducted in taverns, so that the demarcations between work and pleasure blurred.[105] In the absence of a cohesive political stance, legal practitioners gravitated towards contemporaries and colleagues.[106] The established attorneys of Dublin developed companionable rituals, often modelled on those of the gregarious barristers who assembled regularly at the taverns in the town. In the mid-eighteenth century, Thomas Dalrymple immersed himself in the recreational round of other professionals and the respectable from the middling orders. He was in the habit of gathering with colleagues at the Black Lion in Queen Street. In the summer of 1757, the group, perhaps an unofficial club, jaunted into the country to Chapelizod.[107] Richard Edgeworth, although retired from the bar, when in Dublin joined his former colleagues, 'the gentlemen of the law', for dinners at the Rose.[108]

Smaller groups, centred on legal offices, met socially.[109] Jocelyn Pickard, a lawyer temporarily in Dublin during the 1730s, followed an orbit centred on other professionals and office-holders. At long bouts over the punchbowl and pipes, with absent comrades toasted, talk no doubt reverted to briefs, pleadings, fees and verdicts. However, this company merged into that of doctors, divines, war veterans, solid merchants, *rentiers* and squires temporarily in the city, so that chat ranged widely. It assumed conversance with a literate if not literary culture. As in eighteenth-century Paris, so in Dublin during the same century, fewer libraries were collected by rural notables than by the urban. Of 175 collections of books known to have been auctioned in Ireland between 1741 and 1760, twenty-two or 12.6 per cent were owned by peers or squires. In contrast, those who can be classified as professionals constituted about 70 per cent of sellers. Thirty of these libraries (17.1 per cent) had been assembled by lawyers. Members of the lettered professions depended on books. What they collected helped them in their work, but some volumes revealed a wider culture.[110]

Through these and other interests, men of the law made good the claims to gentility inherent in their learned calling.[111] Familiar with London, often still in touch with benchers there, the notions and adjuncts of genteel living moved along these channels. Sets of the latest Hogarth engravings or the most modish wigs were as likely to be exchanged as legal opinions. Especially in Dublin, communal entertainments drew in a larger group of the polite and modestly prosperous. In lodgings, private residences and even taverns, these gatherings were attended with new refinements of silver, imported porcelain, delft, local napery and painted or carved decorations. Gustatory novelties were dispensed, often requiring an unwonted elaboration in their presentation and consumption.[112] All catered to the politeness and gentility proper to those styled as esquires and gentlemen. By such methods, the urban office-holders and professionals proved their right to be ranked among the quality. Indeed, some Dublin sophisticates, confident that they best recognized and practised civility and gentility, disputed the cultural leadership of the country squires and gentry. For the latter, this worsened the offence of the pretenders, who had grown fat by battening on them.

II

Catholics lacked all but covert chances to profit from the law, a profession which they had dominated a century earlier.[113] If, as was contended, the aim of English policy in Ireland was to advance the Irish to a different level of civilization, denying them office and professional livelihoods cut them off from an agreed instrument of improvement. Alone of the professions in Ireland, medicine remained without explicit confessional tests. The technical requirement survived that physicians, along with schoolmasters, should be licensed by the bishops of the Church of Ireland. In 1683, the bishop of Ossory made use of his power to prosecute an apothecary in Kilkenny for practising physick. Since the alleged offender was prominent in civic life, the bishop's motive may have been more political than medical.[114] In the main, however, entry was curtailed – as in the established Church and law – by the costs of preparation, and by institutional restrictions. The government had few posts to offer doctors, so they seldom looked to the state or powerful intermediaries to succeed. The comparative freedom attracted Catholics and Protestant dissenters to doctoring. A few flourished as physicians. During the interregnum, Dr Thomas Arthur, originally from Limerick, attended the family of the lord deputy, Henry Cromwell.[115] A century later, Lord Trimlestown, returned from France, drew the smart to his house in County Meath by his unconventional therapies.[116] Edmund Burke's father-in-law, Christopher Nugent, built up a fashionable practice in Bath.[117] In Dublin, a prominent dissenter, the egregious Duncan Cumyng, ministered to the important, including the dying William Conolly, and grew rich.[118] In Ulster, one of the leading medical men, Victor Ferguson, was deep in the counsels of the Presbyterians.[119] Particularly in the dissenting communities, clerics doubled as doctors. The Reverend John Kennedy, Presbyterian minister of Benburb in County Tyrone, personified this habit.[120]

Protestant conformists had to compete for patients. Potentially, doctors ought to have outnumbered clergy and lawyers. All craved health. Rather fewer could pay the fees of the expert and smart, and resorted instead to alternative therapists. Just as the Church had its curates and schoolmasters and the law, attorneys and solicitors, so medicine sustained auxiliaries.[121] Surgeons, apothecaries and midwives underwent apprenticeship, not university degrees, which lowered them to the status of adept craftsmen. Beneath these traders in sickness opened a cavernous world of neighbourly nursing and traditional cures. Admission to the upper sector of the medical profession, in common with the priesthood and law, required time, application and – above all – money. In 1723, Charles Ward was reluctant to allow a son to study physic, 'because he will not probably be able to live by his practice for some years after he commences doctor in that faculty'.[122] Regulatory bodies but no medical faculty existed in Ireland. Aspirant medics were obliged to go overseas: to Britain or, most popularly, continental Europe. By the later seventeenth century, the United Provinces were the favourite destination.[123] Cheaper alternatives did exist. The Scottish universities offered a frugal regime to some, especially from nonconformist backgrounds.[124] For those wanting to become surgeons, apprenticeships were available. Often this meant arranging for provincials to train in Dublin or London.[125] Ferguson recommended a succession of hopefuls who had had preliminary induction in Belfast to the Ulster physician who had triumphed in London, Sir Hans Sloane. It was hoped that Sloane would assist the ephebes to find masters in London.[126] Sloane himself had learnt the rudiments from apothecaries in London before continuing his medical education in Paris and Montpellier.[127] Those who underwent only practical instruction from surgeons and apothecaries entered occupations still reckoned as trades rather than, as with the

university-educated physicians, a profession. This sharp stratification of
those working with the sick was perpetuated in supervisory bodies. From
1667, an exclusive College of Physicians contained and overlooked the
upper branch of the profession.[128] Humbler adepts were corralled into the
Dublin Guild of Barber Surgeons. The enforced union of apothecaries and
surgeons with barbers and periwig-makers was increasingly strained, until,
in 1747, it was sundered when the apothecaries broke loose and set up
their own association. The surgeons, unyoked from the barbers and wig-
makers, escaped minute oversight.[129]

The success of a few doctors dazzled. Dr John Stearne, first president of
the College of Physicians, was succeeded by Charles Willoughby, John
Madden, Thomas Molyneux, Sir Patrick Dun, Ralph Howard and Edward
Worth, several of whom also held office in the college.[130] In each generation, fashionable practice was engrossed by a handful. In 1732 it was alleged
that Dr Edward Worth, 'a physician of great merit and generosity', had
dominated the profession in Dublin for the previous twenty years.[131]
Institutional controls, through the College of Physicians, aimed to keep it
that way. At its foundation, it had only fourteen fellows. In 1762, a
directory listed forty-nine medical practitioners in Dublin, a city of perhaps
140,000. Of these, at least twelve have been identified as Catholics.[132] Rare
practitioners were knighted or even – in Molyneux's case – created a
baronet. Success was generally measured by the number and rank of patients
and the resultant fees, not by government appointments. The army offered
a few salaried positions, which increased in times of war. Petty had first
been tempted to Ireland in 1652 as physician to the English army of
occupation.[133] The opening of the Royal Hospital at Kilmainham brought
further opportunities for a few. At first, however, it was proposed to seek
surgeons from England.[134] In the main, service in the army and navy – especially once foreign wars became common after the 1690s – afforded better
(and cheaper) opportunities for medical training. The grandson of the
Belfast Presbyterian minister, John McBride, was one example of a novice
who trained under a naval surgeon, on the *Argyle*.[135]

The Dublin government, lacking patronage, could not turn the upper
reaches of the profession into a preserve of the Scots, Welsh and English,
as the Church, law and bureaucracy allegedly had become. The office of
state physician represented the formal peak of the profession. In turn,
Petty, Charles Willoughby, Patrick Dun, Thomas Molyneux and Robert
Robinson occupied it.[136] The absence of much else at the disposal of the
state to tempt doctors separated the medical profession from churchmen,
lawyers, soldiers and sailors, all of whom badgered the government for
preferment. A few were tempted from Wales to practise in Dublin. Owen
Lewis served as surgeon to Steevens' Hospital. Later, John Nicholls, a native

of Chester, became surgeon-general in Ireland.[137] But, as Lewis's position hinted, it was the size and value of private practice in Dublin which acted as a magnet. Furthermore, the opening of privately funded hospitals created salaried posts for doctors and surgeons.

The situation in the capital contrasted with that in the provinces, where the supply of those with formal medical qualifications was meagre. In provincial towns, medical practitioners who might pass as gentlemen or pseudo-gentry were rare: rarer than clergymen, office-holders or lawyers. In Queen Anne's reign, the Church of Ireland bishop of Limerick licensed three physicians and three surgeons, all but one located in the city. By 1769, ten physicians and seven surgeons were advertised in Limerick.[138] One who lived in considerable style, his portrait painted by a Frenchman, and with a nephew in Bordeaux, was John Martin. Designated an esquire, he was a Catholic trained on the continent. Martin reminds us of the importance of this calling as a means by which Catholics could achieve status and wealth.[139] In mid-eighteenth-century Cork, a dozen doctors were noted.[140] Populous towns such as Waterford, Derry and Belfast could be expected to support a few. In the Waterford of 1773, Dr Semphill, member of an Ulster family, was 'in much practice and esteem here'.[141] The Connacht side of Athlone had its practitioner: Thomas Bell. In 1749, Sligo contained a Protestant doctor and surgeon.[142] Affluent and educated Protestants living in the provinces, such as successive bishops of Elphin, nevertheless worried about the absence of competent doctors, which particularly endangered wives and children. In 1717 the bishop of Killala complained that there was no physician and scarce an apothecary within thirty miles of his Mayo seat. Clerics and their families at Clogher had to send to Armagh for medical aid. In the County Antrim of 1716, it was thought that there were no competent physicians closer than Dublin. But soon Derry supplied the want.[143] By 1749, the archdeacon of Kells in County Meath sent to a surgeon in Drogheda to perform the newly fashionable inoculation on his children.[144] In the absence of professionals, the more lowly apothecaries were used. Thomas Vero, the apothecary at Loughreagh in County Galway, serviced families not just in his own county but in Mayo as well. In addition to medicaments, he traded in rat poison and garden seeds.[145]

In its upper reaches, medicine had become overwhelmingly an urban practice. Members of the quality sent to the nearby town or, if they could, to Dublin, where (it was assumed) the best advice was to be had. In 1744 Dr Robert Robinson, the state physician, dispatched a subordinate to a sick friend (a squire) in the midlands. Robinson's aide, Nicholls, would charge fifteen guineas for the journey in his own chariot and four or five guineas for each day's attendance. Nicholls's assistant would be paid at a daily rate of a guinea. Robinson reported these terms as a favour to his provincial acquaintance. He himself willingly (and freely) advised by letter.[146] Correspondence could overcome the isolation of those remote in the countryside, but it introduced delays and increased the likelihood (already great) of erroneous diagnoses and futile prescriptions. The eminent Sir Patrick Dun in Dublin consulted Hans Sloane in London on behalf of his important patients, the Southwells.[147] Independently, Lady Betty Southwell also sought Sloane's advice by letter, without disclosing to Dun that she had done so.[148] Others, such as the Hamiltons of Killyleagh, Tollymore and Bangor who had known Sloane before he removed to England or his father, agent to the Lord Clandeboye, presumed on these links to seek the adept's advice.[149] From County Cavan, Bishop Joseph Story asked another famed London practitioner, Richard Mead, about his symptoms.[150] The valetudinarian first Lord Molesworth, contemplating retirement to Ireland, enquired after surgeons there. Worried about their competence to cut for the stone and fistulas and to probe with catheters, he feared that he and his ageing wife might have to trek to Paris.[151] Lord Mountrath also confided, late in the seventeenth century, 'I have very little opinion of the skill' of the Dublin doctors. This repeated the dismissal in 1674 of the physicians and surgeons in the capital as 'but bunglers'.[152] Sir Richard Bulkeley, a landowner in Counties Dublin and Wicklow, resorted to Ralph Howard and Thomas Molyneux, the most prominent practitioners of the capital. But he also reported in detail his own symptoms to medical friends in England, like Martin Lister. Moreover, the public-spirited if eccentric and deformed Bulkeley practised surgery and therapies on his poor tenants.[153] The younger John Evelyn, in Dublin as a revenue commissioner, considered himself lucky to have as his doctor Thomas Molyneux, 'a very learned, careful and judicious man'.[154]

In a countryside starved of recognized physicians, Catholic practitioners and apothecaries could fill the gap. In the diocese of Elphin, at least eight Catholic doctors and a couple of surgeons were recorded in 1749.[155] Comparable to them may have been Dr John McKeogh, who worked in the neighbouring diocese of Killaloe. His 'oak chest for the anatomy' hinted at his operations and (perhaps) tuition of novices. Judged by his possessions, McKeogh lived comfortably.[156] In Kerry, Anthony Mulshenoge was described as 'an old practitioner in physic and surgery . . . who has been very useful and serviceable' to the tenantry around Castleisland. In turn, Mulshenoge was succeeded by his son.[157] The lower repute of the surgeons and apothecaries was reflected both in their more modest remuneration and in the tendency for the quality to hire them primarily (but not exclusively) for servants and dependants. In 1741, when Archbishop Boulter directed relief to the poor, it was through apothecaries in Armagh and Drogheda.[158] Whereas fellows of the Dublin College of Physicians matched high fees to elevated social rank, surgeons and apothecaries usually enjoyed a standing akin to that of tradesmen. In the Youghal of George I, one surgeon, Charles Ray, was illiterate.[159] The different scale of charges was shown when a son of Richard Edgeworth was inoculated against smallpox. Kingsbury the physician was paid thirteen guineas; Mills, the surgeon, received £1 2s. 9d.[160] Edgeworth was prepared to fee three doctors during the last illness of a daughter, yet the corpse of a son was opened for an autopsy by the surgeon's mate from a regiment of the army in Ireland. The last job cost £2. The physicians, in contrast, were paid between £8 and £10.[161]

The wealth of a few spectacularly successful doctors was widely known. Petty's notable fortune owed less to his medical prowess than to his involvement in the land settlement of the 1650s. Sir Patrick Dun was alleged to be worth £5,936 16s. 08½d. at his death.[162] Thomas Molyneux was paid an annual retainer of £23 by Archbishop King. Nominally it was to attend the archbishop's household in Dublin, but to earn this wage Molyneux may have been required to minister to the poor as well.[163] Thomas Kingsbury, a popular Dublin physician, received a fee of £120 and all his expenses for attending Lord Charlemont at Kilkenny over twelve days in 1743.[164] Kingsbury, unsurprisingly, lived well in Dublin. He kept a coach and a carriage and was a discerning judge of what was modish in architecture and interior design.[165] Even the rich like Katherine Conolly, faced with such charges, moaned that sickness soon ran away with money. The terminal illness of her favourite, Frank Burton, had cost three or four guineas daily for his two nurses and totalled about £500.[166] The widow of Castletown invited agreeable physicians like James Grattan to her mansion, since she enjoyed their society as much as their ministrations. Earlier, Archbishop King had happily played cards with Sir Patrick Dun and his wife.[167] By 1744, Grattan was described by Mrs Conolly as her 'good doctor and kind friend'. He visited the rich but sickly widow twice daily, 'all this without fee or reward, except true love and friendship'.[168] Since Grattan, according to Swift, 'kills or cures half the city', he could afford to flatter Katherine Conolly.[169] Grattan's insinuating bedside manner may partly have explained his popularity. Mrs Conolly liked other medical attendants less. Having consulted a surgeon about her swollen legs, she exclaimed against 'his cookery'.[170] Her disfavour may have had a social dimension, telling – consciously or involuntarily – of the lower esteem of the mechanic surgeons. It was long remembered among the Hamiltons of County Down how a surgeon had 'missed his aim' when operating on a son of the house.[171]

Grattan, three times president of the Dublin College of Physicians, personified not just success but the background from which most of his prominent colleagues had come. His father had been a fellow of Trinity College before accepting a prebendal stall in St Patrick's Cathedral. The senior Grattan built himself an innovative house at Belcamp outside the city. The eldest of the doctor's brothers had lands in Cavan, which linked him with the notables from the north-west, of whom the Conollys were leaders. Other of Grattan's brothers entered the Church, rose to be lord mayor of Dublin and held the valuable mastership of Portora Royal School at Enniskillen. A kinsman acted as recorder of Dublin.[172] Grattan had been able to train as a physician at Leiden thanks to the evident prosperity of his family. Born (like Thomas Molyneux) into the purple of Protestant Ireland, he had retained and indeed strengthened his position within it.[173] Thomas Kingsbury also studied with Boerhaave at Leiden.[174] Kingsbury, practising in George II's Dublin, typified the style and habits of a prosperous practitioner.[175] He assembled a library, ran a spanking new equipage, and adopted the latest in dress, wigs, books and furnishings.[176] Not indifferent to the plight of the poor in the harsh conditions early in the 1740s, he watched balefully the antics of 'the mob'.[177] As one of the prosperous and consciously cultivated, he defined himself, at least partly, in opposition to them. His world, essentially urban, was of the educated and genteel. The companions with whom he relaxed worked like him in the professions and administration of the capital. Yet Kingsbury, in common with many city-dwellers of his rank, was not ignorant of the rural hinterlands. He represented an acquaintance, now removed to North Wales, as agent for interests concentrated in County Cork,[178] and also journeyed into the provinces to treat important patients. In return, some of his country clients, such as Squire Edgeworth of Edgeworthstown, were admitted to his polite circle when in Dublin.[179]

Kingsbury's cultivation was shared by another successful Dublin physician and midwife, John van Leuwen. He too was used by Edgeworth when in Dublin.[180] During the 1720s, the van Leuwens 'lived after so elegant a manner' that it was assumed they were rich.[181] The family had adopted the manners of the genteel and were part of the polite society of the town. The fragile foundations of the van Leuwens' show were exposed when the doctor died. Immediately the sheriff's men were in the house to grab goods as security for the debts. In the event, the contents had to be sold and the house relinquished. The widow was put to board in the country with a clergyman's widow: the acme of respectability. This *bouleversement* meant that a grandson, intended for medicine after study in Leiden, chose the less expensive option of the army. Soon Dr van Leuwen's grandson was fretting over social derogation and his failure to be accounted a gentleman.[182] In a similar manner, Kingsbury's death uncovered the sandy foundations of his impressive establishment. First his library was dispersed, and then his widow was badly embarrassed by the Dublin bank failures in the mid-1750s.[183] Ralph Howard, quondam president of the College of Physicians, also faced financial difficulties after illness had disabled him from doctoring. When he died in 1710, so little ready money remained in the house that he had to be buried 'very private' for a mere £25 or £30. However, Howard had invested in land in County Wicklow. In the longer term, especially when leases were renewed, this ensured generous maintenance for his widow and children. The former was bequeathed an annual £100; a younger son in the Church received £750; another, training for the bar in London, £550, together with an annuity of £80 so long as he remained at the Inns of Court.[184] None of these families faced the distress of the relict of Dr Cudmore: by 1725 she depended on her Church of Ireland parish for doles.[185]

The licentiates of the Dublin College of Physicians were respected (and rewarded) as the gatekeepers of life and death. They had also travelled further than most of their patients. Indeed, this characteristic set them apart even from other professionals. By the early eighteenth century, most incumbents in the Church of Ireland had been born and educated in the island. The barristers who worked in Dublin or the provincial circuits had been obliged to pass some time in London at the Inns of Court. This might – but did not always – widen horizons beyond the year-books, precedents and digests. Qualified doctors had usually ventured overseas. The adepts, on their return to Ireland, commanded a respect based on more than simple mastery of Galenic or Hippocratic mysteries. The leading practitioners were welcomed into, and gave a distinctive colour to, the polite society of Dublin and the bigger towns. Part of the reason was their strong contribution to learning, enquiry and charity. Medics were prominent in the groups – Hartlib's friends in the 1650s, the Dublin Philosophical Society of the 1680s and 1690s, and the Dublin Society after 1731 – which aimed to collect, increase and spread useful knowledge.[186] John Stearne, the founding president of the College of Physicians, bridged the gulf between philosophy and theology on the one side, and physick on the other. His teaching at Trinity College as much as his medical cures influenced a later generation of clergymen, as well as of doctors.[187] Dr John Madden, from a family in which medicine was established as a career, exemplified how wider scholarly and antiquarian interests could be united with renown as a physician.[188] In County Down, Victor Ferguson bewailed his lot: 'I want converse and improvement'. He consoled himself in part with 'a small library, well picked', which contained 'the marrow of all ancient and modern authors'.[189] Only the clergy, a larger group than the doctors, did more to enquire into the natural and supernatural worlds.

Intellectual and antiquarian interests were not monopolized by the polished physicians. In Dublin, Charles Smith became ubiquitous in the associations which mixed utilitarian with philosophical interests. Smith continued to describe himself as an apothecary from the Waterford port of Dungarvan.[190] By the late 1750s, he channelled his curiosity into a small coterie in which at least one other physician, Dr John Rutty, was active. Rutty had trained in Leiden.[191] Meanwhile, in Limerick, the Catholic Sylvester O'Halloran, described as a surgeon, enquired into Irish history and antiquities. For O'Halloran, as for other of his co-religionists, medicine gave him money and status from which he could launch into other spheres.[192] He published medical tracts – on cataracts and gangrene – but these failed to win him official recognition. However, he believed that 'the respectability of a gentleman' could be displayed by forwarding the work of learned societies, as he did.[193] Such leanings towards experiment and observation were perhaps strengthened by the nature of the training which some doctors and apothecaries had undergone.

The sense of belonging to a community larger than Ireland persisted among some doctors. Kingsbury, back in Dublin, remained in touch with his master, Boerhaave, in Leiden.[194] Hans Sloane, as he climbed to eminence in early eighteenth-century London, maintained his Irish connections in good repair. Through these channels, he offered medical assessments of cases to his cronies still in Ireland, such as Ferguson, Dun and Molyneux. He also supplied them with recent publications, notably prized copies of the *Philosophical Transactions* of the Royal Society in London.[195] Sloane's correspondents in Ireland were not confined to fellow doctors. Helena Rawdon received a microscope thanks to his good offices. He also guided the Rawdons in their hunt for exotic plants.[196] In another of his guises, as an avid and discriminating collector of prints, he may have assisted the interested in Ireland. Archbishop King was gratified with a portrait, and sent his own in exchange.[197] Furthermore, Sloane, in his private capacity as a collector and in his public post as secretary of the Royal Society, was the focus for the curious in Ireland, as across much of the rest of Europe.[198] Another medical luminary in London, Richard Mead, may have had Irish kindred, the Meades of Ballintobber near Kinsale. At all events, Mead welcomed the curious to his London house, where he showed off his famous collections of art, *objets de vertu* and *seraglio*. The Howards, themselves sons of a Dublin physician, were encouraged in their collecting by Mead. His own collections included curiosities found around Lough Neagh.[199] In addition, he advised Irish correspondents about ailments and treatments.[200]

The wider impact and higher repute of some doctors, especially in Dublin, came from their interest in providing better for the poor and sick.

Practicality and humanity impressed the sensitive with the need to act. Collective responses resulted. Notable among them was the foundation of six hospitals in Dublin between 1718 and 1757.[201] Another was opened in Cork, but the remainder of the kingdom lagged behind.[202] Some municipalities paid for medical services within their jurisdictions. In 1709, Waterford gave a surgeon £10 annually to attend the poor free. Early in the eighteenth century, the corporation of Drogheda allowed a 'town physician' £20 p.a.[203] Not until 1765 were county infirmaries statutorily authorized.[204] Doctors were directly involved in the Dublin ventures as benefactors: Dr Richard Steevens, Dr Edward Worth and Sir Patrick Dun. The doctors' bequests suggested how much they had made and (perhaps) qualms about how they had done so. The hospitals generated, and were funded by, assemblies and concerts, which implanted fashionable sociability deeply in Hanoverian Dublin.[205] The doctors were seldom the impresarios, but the hospitals did modestly add to the stipendiary posts for the medical fraternity.[206] John Whiteway, having acted as assistant surgeon to Steevens' Hospital, in 1756 was chosen as surgeon at the newly opened foundation of Dean Swift. His remuneration was modest: a yearly £10, and another £10 for diet. Nevertheless, from this modest security he rose to preside over the College of Surgeons in 1786.[207] Important also for social station was the fact that the physicians and surgeons – John Anderson, Hannibal Hall, George Daunt, Rice Gibbins and William Stephens at Mercer's Hospital – sat beside civic worthies on the panels which governed these foundations. They were included primarily because of their expertise. Stephens, for example, was both a Leiden graduate and a fellow of the Royal Society of London. Thrice president of the Dublin College of Physicians, he also acted as physician to Steevens' Hospital. Similarly Anderson, having spent time at Trinity College Dublin, studied with Boerhaave in the Low Countries. Returning to professional distinction in Dublin, he too presided over the College of Physicians.[208] The places of the doctors and surgeons on the hospital boards denoted their easy admission into company of the public-spirited. Doctors mingled with urban activists elsewhere – masonic lodges, meetings of the Dublin Society and Physico-Historical Society – so that board meetings of the hospitals merely added to these occasions.[209] Another active in overseeing the Dublin hospitals, Francis Le Hunt, retired to an estate in the country. There he was praised both for his cultivation and public spirit.[210] Medical practitioners at this level belonged unequivocally to the quality.

Surgeons attached to the Dublin hospitals avoided the social exclusion which, as mere tradesmen, they might otherwise suffer. The skilled, such as Hamilton, who served the household of Archbishop William King, were let loose not just on servants but on the ailing prelate himself.[211] Thomas

Proby was praised for his skills as surgeon and achieved social eminence.[212] In contrast, Lewis, surgeon at Steevens' Hospital, by failing to satisfy convention, lost his job, 'besides his reputation and business', and was obliged to remove to Waterford. His principal offence had been to contract a Catholic marriage.[213] The altogether rougher services offered by surgeons were hinted at by comments about 'Surgeon' Redmond Boate, proprietor of two madhouses in Dublin. Boate was remembered as 'a rough brutal fellow'. This was not only because he extracted teeth. Some of his prosperity could be traced to his marriage with a suicidal patient, the daughter of a Church of Ireland dean. Yet he was not a social pariah to all: he was accepted into the highly respectable fraternity of Friendly Brothers in County Kildare.[214]

Some surgeons had travelled. In 1746, Alexander Crommelin, a 'sober youth', had trained first in Lisburn and then Edinburgh. He hoped next to purchase a place as a surgeon's mate so that he might rise to be an army surgeon.[215] Yet those outside the charmed circle of the Dublin College of Physicians were ranked uncertainly. John van Leuwen's brother, George, plied for hire as a doctor, but in Cork. Apparently without formal qualifications, this provincial showed a versatility probably common among his similarly situated colleagues. George van Leuwen embalmed corpses skilfully. He also slipped easily enough into the society of professionals and merchants in the city, as is clear from his place in a Masonic lodge there.[216] Local prominence was further revealed when he served as master of the Cork Guild of Barber Surgeons.[217] 'Dr' George van Leuwen occupied a lower place on the professional scale, and seemingly in the economic and social hierarchies, than his brother in Dublin. In his turn, the Cork van Leuwen ranked above a near-contemporary in the city, the apothecary John Bentley. But Bentley was far from a nonentity. He had surrounded himself with the 'old books' and dispensaries from which to concoct his remedies. These, accessories or necessities, invested him with an arcane aura which may have inspired confidence among his numerous customers in the city. His other possessions implied more conventional habits. A formidable battery of porcelain, glass and silver dispensed the hospitality which either his work or leisure demanded. In addition, Bentley had acquired houses across the city. These may represent his considerable profits from selling cures, but they also meant that he no longer lived wholly – or even primarily – on professional earnings.[218]

Bentley revealed the respectable circumstances which an apothecary could attain. Another – Robert Higgins – became sheriff of the city of Limerick during Charles II's reign.[219] In Dublin, Bishop Synge of Elphin entrusted multifarious business to the apothecary, Ned Curtis. Also in the capital, the Wilsons, apothecaries established in Bride Street, over two generations enjoyed a respected place in the civic order.[220] The paucity and high fees of licensed physicians obliged the sick to turn to the cheaper surgeons, apothecaries and 'quacks'.[221] Some of these alternative practitioners belonged to the guilds which strove to oversee their training and activities. As late as 1746, periwig-makers were united with surgeons and apothecaries in a guild at Kinsale.[222] More practised unconstrained by any supervisory body. Acquiring their skills on the job rather than overseas, they used assorted therapies. Some helped, more harmed. But they can scarcely have inflicted more pain, and charged less, than the leaders of the profession. The pervasiveness of disease guaranteed a demand for placebos, potions and prophylactics which would never be satiated.[223] In the three weeks before Grace Waring died in Dublin in 1722, one apothecary supplied forty-seven separate concoctions, costing £7 3s. 5d. Another 'druggist' provided both palliatives like hartshorn and almond milk and beverages such as chocolate, coffee and tea.[224] The endless quest for cures inspired the invention of Waltho van Claturbank, High German doctor, the seventh son of a seventh son, an 'unborn doctor', whose *Pharmacopola Circumforaneus* catered to these cravings. The Dublin newspapers by the 1730s were dotted with advertisements for medical services and cures scarcely less improbable.[225] In the face of these supposed charlatans, the privileged custodians of medical knowledge strove to keep their monopoly. Most extreme among the signs of hostility towards interlopers who undercut their fees was the notion of castrating quacks. It picked up on, or perhaps parodied, the recent suggestion (of 1719) that Catholic priests should be emasculated.[226] A public parade of the freemen of the Dublin Apothecaries' Guild in 1767 prompted a tirade against those

> *Who most by fraud and impositions thrive,*
> *Whose monstrous bills immoderate wealth procure*
> *For drugs that kill as many as they cure.*
> *Well are they placed, the last of all the rout,*
> *For they're the men we best can live without.*[227]

In 1761, concern about adulterated medicines and other impostures prompted legislation against frauds.[228]

In the penumbra around the Dublin College of Physicians a multiplicity of health workers and charlatans thrived. Dublin apothecaries, through their guild, resembled other solid freemen of the city. Moreover, their communal life, although sometimes fractious and factious, introduced them to the rituals beloved of the urbane.[229] In provincial towns, apothecaries enjoyed a repute which rested on more than their facility as pharmacists. Robert Ormsby, one of three apothecaries in Sligo, achieved a respectable station there. He involved himself in, and probably benefited from, the nearby charity school.[230] In 1745 the inquisitive curate of Lurgan, Richard

Barton, shared with the Dublin Physico-Historical Society his discoveries relating to Lough Neagh. These were attested by a group which consisted of five linen drapers, three apothecaries, a surgeon, the gauger in the Revenue Service and a Presbyterian minister. This suggested powerfully the respectable sort who might dominate the intellectual life of a provincial town.[231]

In the provinces, sharper distinctions were maintained. In the Burlingtons' establishments, their agents were tended by physicians, but an apothecary, Philip Gould, dealt with a housemaid sick with smallpox.[232] The Flowers of Castle Durrow patronized several apothecaries, mostly in Dublin. Their lotions and potions were applied to the Flowers' servants.[233] These suppliers left it to the customer's discretion to add to the bill, 'what you please' for attendance and care. By this device, Henry O'Hara had his account of £3 12s. 9d. rounded up to £10.[234] In the light of this stratagem, the prosperity of a Bentley becomes more readily explicable. In the country, apothecaries outnumbered qualified doctors. Twelve are noted in the diocese of Elphin in 1749; all but three were Catholics. In Limerick city, by contrast, seventeen physicians and surgeons were advertised in 1769, but only seven apothecaries. The prosperous and Protestant were concentrated in the largest towns, and it was they who could most readily afford the highest grade of medical help.[235] A surveyor, Joshua Wight, unwell in Newcastle West (County Limerick), sent about twenty miles to Charleville for an apothecary, but he hedged his bets by resorting to a 'knowing person' nearer to hand.[236]

Uncertainty about where to locate apothecaries on the social scale may have arisen from the fact that many were Catholic. This ethnic characteristic could hardly be separated from the status of the occupation as a trade. Moreover, its repute was further depressed by its failure to care enough about training and standards. Charles Lucas, scourge of oligarchy in the Dublin municipality and himself an apothecary, addressed these issues. He argued that his craft had been discredited by the peddlers of bogus medicines and that only proper professional supervision would restore the collective reputation of the apothecaries. In 1735, Lucas asked the Irish parliament to empower the College of Physicians and Dublin University to step in as regulators. In 1741, the physicians assumed oversight in an effort to restore the arts of surgery and pharmacy 'to their natural dignity and pristine utility to the public'.[237] Lucas bewailed two simultaneous processes. Apothecaries craved 'the dress and mien of a physician, well knowing that esteem is oftener gained by artifice and outward appearance than by real worth or merit'. In order to build up a lucrative practice, there were few subterfuges to which the cunning apothecary would not stoop.[238] At the same time, the ignorant and dishonest took up the work.

All too easily, a footman, porter or 'ignorant women' could trade as apothecaries. Lucas fulminated against one particular establishment opened by 'a journeyman of a certain mean, mechanic trade who knew not the alphabet'. Not entirely consistently Lucas blamed some of the troubles on the lowlier status of pharmacy in contrast to the liberal study of physic. Yet to master an increasingly diversified pharmacopoeia took time and effort. This tedium, coupled with the uncertain social standing once qualified, apparently discouraged all 'but the meaner sort' from setting their children to become apothecaries. Again, this left room for the mountebanks. Lucas hoped that by reviving strict apprenticeship, standards would improve, and with them the standing of his calling.[239] The apothecaries, once gathered into their own guild in 1747, sought to monitor medicines and therapies.[240]

Worry continued that the medical authorities had failed to control the unscrupulous. In 1759, doctors were strikingly missing from a panegyric to the élites in Ireland. Simply, they were culpable for not curbing those who traded on the credulity and desperation of the sick.[241] William Stephens, a prominent Dublin physician, published a tract on gout. This was designed to check the pernicious practice of people 'quacking with themselves upon a presumption of understanding such books of physick . . . which, whether hurtful to the physicians, have I am sure been so to the patients'.[242] Soon parliament acted against these abuses. The physicians might condemn quacks and their remedies; MPs legislated. Yet they could not stop resort to them. In the end, the cordial of bilberries, a quack salve of country people, administered to Mary Brock in County Donegal, harmed less than the expensive attentions of the registered.[243]

Apothecaries, like surgeons and physicians, were recruited from all the confessions in eighteenth-century Ireland. Medicine offered both Catholics and Protestant dissenters the best chance to marry financial comfort to social esteem in a system otherwise tilted towards the members of the Church of Ireland. Medicine resembled the law in giving livelihoods to auxiliaries who, thanks to different training and functions, enjoyed lower fees and social ranking. Indeed the same tripartite division was found in both the Church and the law. In addition, medical practitioners like barristers were obliged to travel in order to qualify themselves. Even after they had returned to practise in Ireland, they kept in repair friendships made overseas. Isolation was diminished and the awareness of belonging to a larger intellectual and professional community, confined neither to Ireland nor to Britain, was fortified. Naturally, those most keen to correspond with acquaintances elsewhere have left the clearest record. Ministering to the body, they rivalled the guardians of spiritual health in diagnosing social ills and promoting cultural renovation or innovation.

Thereby they raised the repute of their calling: higher sometimes than conventional social stratification decreed. In contrast, the incurious, content simply to enjoy the material comforts that professional success delivered, remain anonymous.

The Church, law and medicine added to the character and numbers of the prominent in Protestant Ireland. The beneficed clergy totalled perhaps 800, with the unbeneficed curates and schoolmasters adding – possibly – another 400. The different legal advocates, including those in the provinces, numbered between 800 and 1,000; and the doctors and surgeons (the most difficult to spot) 200–250, with the apothecaries supplying many more. Direct comparisons of their earnings are hazardous. Within each group, circumstances varied greatly. Also, if some depended entirely on what they could earn, others collected rents or salaries from public and private offices. Even the fees charged to clients are hardly a secure basis for comparisons. In the 1680s, a prominent Dublin lawyer could command a fee of £2 6s. An attorney might be paid only 6s. 8d. However, particular proficiency or favours could attract bonuses.[244] A physician in the 1730s was paid a standard fee of £1 3s. Again, special services, occasioned by serious illnesses, childbirth, inoculation or death, attracted higher pay.[245] Beneficed clergymen, unlike the lawyers and doctors, could expect an annual stipend, even if it was often hard to extort from parsimonious lay patrons and resistant parishioners. They were additionally entitled to dues for officiating at rites of passage. In the 1660s, Convocation promulgated a uniform table of fees, but within thirty years Dublin parishes had departed from this uniformity. These payments were not always easily collected. Nevertheless, the frequency with which curates christened, married and buried laypeople makes the minimum stipend of an annual £20 enjoyed by some unsafe as a guide to their income.[246] Furthermore, notional annual revenues did not come as monthly cheques or credit transfers. Some clergymen delegated the irksome task of collecting tithes to others (tithe farmers), who simply paid the incumbent an annual sum. Others chased late or non-payers. Income fluctuated with the vagaries of the agricultural seasons, and gave most incumbents a direct monetary interest in the land and its yields, either as farmers in their own right or dependants on farmers for their tithes. Contemporary comments make it clear that some, especially in the lower echelons of these professions, received less than the yearly £40 deemed necessary to live with any pretension to gentility. This confirmed the place of many attorneys, curates and apothecaries among the middling ranks of tradespeople. Others insisted on and were accorded the courtesy of assignment to the quality.

Chapter 6

Offices and Office-holders

I

In the reign of George I, one Lambert succeeded to an office 'of some honour and profit' in the port of Dublin. A rival besmirched Lambert for keeping a mistress and fathering several bastards. Equally damaging, the official was said to be infamous in character and 'very atheistical in his ordinary converse with his acquaintance'.[1] Whether or not these dirty tricks dislodged Lambert from a job worth £300 p.a. matters less than the situation revealed by the accusations. Established posts on the civil list – in the revenue there were about 350 of consequence by the 1760s – were avidly sought.[2] Competitors used unscrupulous tactics, knowing that, because office-holders were in the public eye, they were vulnerable to personal attacks. In the same decade, an acquaintance of Speaker Conolly asked his help to start a son on his career. Francis Alen, himself a revenue collector, hoped that the youth might be placed as a clerk in the Secretary's Office at Dublin Castle. Alen professed less interest in the profit – reckoned to be an annual £50 – than in the training for business. The boy's qualification, other than his father's interest with the main political boss of the day, was to write a fair hand.[3] Similar skills were credited to the grandson of an Ulster acquaintance of the Sloanes. The hopeful boy, son of a dissenting minister, 'is a good clerk, well skilled in most of the hands used in writing, bred a merchant and would be employed by some considerable trader either at home or abroad'. Alternatively, he might go into the Revenue Service, 'could he make friends to assist him'. As the grandparent schemed on the boy's behalf, he invoked shared schooling in Killyleagh with Sir Hans Sloane and acquaintanceship with another grandee, Sir Wilfred Lawson, who could vouch for the candidate's merits.[4]

More modest than Lambert's job in the port of Dublin was that of Thomas Rutledge, the sentry at the gate of Primrose Grange school in Sligo. Rutledge was issued with cloak, laced hat and brass-headed stave, and had a sentry box for shelter. This outfit and subsidized diet as much as his stipend of £1 distinguished him from his neighbours.[5] Rutledge was not appointed by the state, but by one of the numerous local bodies which were proliferating across the island. Even to secure his humble place, he had made interest with the governors of the Sligo school. Just as the government debarred religious nonconformists, especially when Catholic, from offices in its gift, so the institutions which flourished in Ascendancy Ireland reserved their best jobs for communicants of the Church of Ireland. Offices could involve irksome, repetitive or hazardous work, but conferred rank. Sometimes status was proclaimed by distinctive attire. The eminent as well as the likes of Rutledge were not impervious to the glamour of projecting the 'grand figure'.

In Ireland, although the reach and complexity of the state increased, bureaucracy grew slowly. The secretariat in Dublin Castle was – and would remain – minuscule.[6] Other departments did expand. An office like that maintained by the chief remembrancer of the Exchequer in the heart of the capital employed well-paid and socially elevated deputies as well as humbler clerks.[7] Most spectacularly, the revenue and the army grew. In the 1720s, the first gave work to perhaps 1,100 throughout the kingdom, and by the 1750s, maybe 1,600.[8] By the eighteenth century, the Irish parliament was allocating money to improvements. These were overseen by boards, such as the trustees for the linen manufacture, inland navigation and the numerous turnpike roads. Appointment to these quangos was sought because it brought chances of patronage and profit, and of furthering the public good.[9] Seats on the boards tended to reward the already elevated. From their vantage points they redirected funds towards their dependants and localities. For the trustees, gains were indirect, even surreptitious, and sometimes more in the shape of an enhanced reputation for public spirit than financial. The official agencies employed a few salaried officers.[10] Beadles, doorkeepers, clerks and inspectors might be doubtful additions to the quality. Nevertheless, all benefited from the doctrine of exclusion which underlay office and much professional activity in Protestant Ireland. In 1732, a porter working for the linen trustees in Dublin was about to be sacked, but was saved when it was discovered that he had converted to Protestantism.[11] Moreover, the sometimes laughable dignities carried a degree of financial security and status denied to most contemporaries. The secretary to the linen trustees was paid £80 p.a. in 1711. The messenger and doorkeeper each enjoyed a yearly £10. By 1728, not only was the porter at the gate of the Dublin Linen Hall paid £18 annually, he was provided with gown, cap and staff.[12] Unusually, a few women had salaried posts at the Linen Hall as clerks and office-keepers.[13]

Permanent and salaried posts proliferated outside government and its agencies. In modest ways, counties, baronies and parishes, as they were burdened with more tasks, required treasurers, clerks and strong-arm men.[14] These usefully supplemented the influence and wages of locals. Best-documented were the offices in the gift of the functioning boroughs and trading guilds. Some – mace and sword-bearers, water bailiffs and bellmen – confirmed local respect and flattered vanities. Others, such as clerk of the market or weigh-master, brought the likelihood of more substantial gratuities. A few – the recorder and town clerk – needed professional qualifications, but in return offered extra prestige and profits.[15] In the late seventeenth century, the manner in which the hitherto obscure, like the lawyer Cox or the Singletons of Drogheda, emerged from the urban shadows into professional and political eminence varied a strategy used earlier by other office-holders. In addition to the municipal posts, parishes, as they developed the administrative unit of the vestry, baronies and manors required modest establishments of permanent functionaries. Some were sinecures; others, although exacting, could be combined with other occupations.

Office could be seen to have assisted the ascent of those situated near the summit of Irish Protestant society in the later seventeenth and eighteenth centuries – the Boyles, Pettys, Parsons, Edgeworths and Wares.[16] It was a base camp from which they had assaulted the peaks that their descendants confidently commanded. Fables such as the rise of Cork and Petty circulated. Origins were sometimes played down to make the subsequent rise yet more dramatic. Successors, seeking to emulate them, looked around for chances. War and the consequential confiscations of land still offered the best likelihood. However, the aftermath of 1685–91 warned that the stock of Catholic-held property and offices had been so depleted by the earlier redistributions that soon it would be exhausted.[17] Talents more appropriate to peace were developed. In Queen Anne's time, Sir William Robinson, surveyor-general and accountant-general, was rumoured to have been rescued from the heat of a kitchen where he slaved as a scullion. He himself attested that by 1682 he held a small office in the Ordnance, worth £68, with the 'convenience of a small hole to lodge in'. This polymath – architect, surveyor and accountant – gained riches, estates in Ireland and England and was knighted. Success bred an arrogance which tempted Robinson to overreach himself. His career in Ireland ended in 1703 when he was disabled from ever again holding office there.[18]

There were not enough offices to satisfy the Protestants in Ireland. Too many were kept – unofficially – for outsiders. Chief of these was the lord-lieutenancy. After 1713 it was not to go to any born in Ireland. Other attractive positions in Church and state were earmarked for reliable Britons. This policy was doubly insulting. It implied that the Protestants of Ireland were still not trusted to run their own affairs. It also deprived them of employments with which they might eke out inadequate inheritances. Accordingly the introduction of immigrants into some of the best Irish offices constituted a grievance about which the aggrieved huffed and puffed. The magpies on the eastern margin of the Irish Sea spotted some of the sinecures and patents.[19] In 1732, the death of Charles Delafaye freed posts on the Irish establishment, which an Englishman eyed greedily. These sinecures in Ireland had allowed Delafaye to live comfortably in England. One post, his wife's as housekeeper in Dublin Castle, he had sold for £3,000; another, of king's wine-taster in Ireland, was judged to be worth £300 p.a.[20] Yet some of the grievances of the Irish Protestants were more imagined than actual. Below the eye-catching dignities, much remained for locals. But, as so often, perceptions that those born in Ireland were denied their deserts mattered more than statistics which showed otherwise. Connected with the complaints was the sense that whereas Ireland lay open to strangers, the Irish Protestants were unlikely to storm the heights in England. Neither the English bench of bishops nor that of judges accommodated Protestants from Ireland. Medicine and the armed forces, on the other hand, erected less intimidating hurdles. The bureaucracy too was penetrated by the determined from Ireland, as the public careers of Sir Robert Southwell, Lord Molesworth, William Leathes and Samuel Molyneux demonstrated.

Patentee offices, like military commissions, were investments. They brought a degree of financial security and social standing. If cashed in on retirement, the seller received welcome capital on which to live in style. The British government combated the trend to venality of office in Ireland. For these reasons, the freedom of the patentees to make the offices hereditary in their family or to sell to others had to be checked. It took time to eradicate practices which treated important posts as private property. The glee with which, in 1683, the lord deputy announced that the monarch had vowed to grant no more reversions to offices in Ireland proved grotesquely premature.[21] The government, in restricting the disposal of these posts, did not always act consistently. Frustrated suitors were convinced that interest decided not only who received offices, but which were then entailed on the sons or nominees of the patentee and the terms on which incumbencies could be relinquished.

Inconsistencies in approach and the treatment of individual officeholders were sometimes irritating. In 1749, the Master of the Rolls, Thomas Carter, a powerful politician, asked that a son succeed him. He justified the demand by reminding the lord-lieutenant that he, Carter, a self-made man, had earlier paid £11,000 for the mastership. Piqued at the refusal of what he thought a reasonable request, he redoubled his political opposition.[22] Earlier, Carter had scrambled upwards by purchasing profitable and prestigious places. It was rumoured that his father had been a footman. In 1717, the future Master of the Rolls had negotiated with Edward Southwell to buy the clerkship of the crown in Ireland, offering £4,000 for it.[23] In 1725, Carter fell foul of the authorities when he wanted to dispose of his post of second sergeant at law. The king objected, 'this having the appearance of a bargain or resignation for a sum of money'.[24] However he had come by his positions and notwithstanding disappointments about trading them in, Carter exploited his offices fruitfully. One perquisite of the mastership of the Rolls was the right to dispose of each of the six clerks' places. Formal consent from the Master was needed before any of the six clerks could resign or sell his office. Carter charged £100 or 100 guineas for his approval.[25]

Like many others who had once sued for a place, Carter, when established, was courted by others. In 1732, Boyle Browne, claiming kinship with the rising politician Henry Boyle, entreated an employment in one of the numerous offices maintained by Carter, a political crony of Boyle. Browne had been trained in clerking, but concluded that this preparation was 'no use without friends, and clients I cannot have without money to carry on causes'. He believed that the only way to launch himself was to be 'introduced into employment' as a 'hackney clerk', ideally under Carter.[26] Too experienced to act solely on sentiment, Carter checked with Boyle that Browne's claims of kinship were true.[27] The extent to which Carter exploited the trainees in his office is also suggested by the complaint of a civic worthy from Kinsale. James Dennis had placed a son with Carter for three years, during which time the novice's support had cost his father £70. Carter, it seemed, allowed young Dennis none of the fees for the business which he transacted.[28]

The prosperous and high-ranking, like Carter and the Southwells, owed much to their offices. Precisely how much is harder to decide. The elder Robert Southwell, settled in the port of Kinsale before 1641, had used a post in the Customs to gain control of much property and power within the borough. His son, the younger Robert Southwell, personable, well travelled and ambitious, thought office in Ireland would not allow full scope to his abilities, and so switched his career to England. There, in 1664, he bought a clerkship of the Privy Council for £1,600 to £2,000. The vendor was another from Ireland, Sir George Lane. In 1679, the clerkship was sold: at a reasonable profit of £2,500.[29] It had been part of a strategy encompassing the cultivation of the important and marriage into a landed and office-holding Kentish family, which, by the close of the 1670s, had established Southwell as a grandee in Gloucestershire. Sir William Petty held up Southwell for admiration in this astute use of office.

An original investment of £2,000 was said to yield him £1,000 annually.[30] The Southwells did not relinquish their interests in Ireland. The strategic importance of Kinsale was effectively promoted with the naval and commercial authorities in England.[31] Also, from the 1690s, they took over the office of secretary in Ireland. As factotums to successive governors, Southwell and his heirs continued to interest themselves in and influence Irish affairs.[32] In addition, the Southwells, like their kinsfolk among the Percevals and Derings, appreciated the utility of patentee offices independent of the politics of the viceroyalty and the secretariat. The clerkship of the crown, which eventually passed to the Carters in 1752, was one of their shrewdest investments. At the close of Queen Anne's reign its annual value was estimated at £800.[33]

The eminent cherished the offices which shrewd ancestors had acquired. In 1661, the second earl of Cork plumed himself proudly when he was installed as successor to his father – belatedly, owing to the civil wars – as lord treasurer of Ireland. It gave him precedence above other Irish peers and carried a daily allowance of £1. The pay, although eclipsed by his rentals yielding yearly between £25,000 and £30,000, was not something that Cork would willingly forgo. However, more than money and prestige attached to the lord treasurership. It controlled subsidiary posts in the revenue administration with which Cork could gratify allies and rivals in Ireland and England. The disposal of sinecures in remote Irish ports also brought cash payments which gave the earl welcome spending money at a moment of heavy expenses.[34] Cork, touchy about his role in the Irish government of the 1660s, hoped that the high office would involve him closely in the making of policy. In this he was disappointed. Indeed, control of fiscal affairs was passing from Dublin to London, while much of the patronage, profitably disbursed by Cork, would soon be controlled by a panel of revenue commissioners in Dublin.[35] The Corks (after 1665 also English earls of Burlington) retained the post. In the mid-eighteenth century, Speaker Boyle held it in trust for his kinsman, the earl, who was habitually absent in England. It continued to attract its daily allowance and to confer precedence. Otherwise, like so many of the other sonorous dignities in the civil list, it had become entirely a sinecure. Holders sometimes resembled the Southwells and Boyles in being direct descendants of those who had with foresight secured patents, or reversions to them, in the seventeenth century. By this device they had calculated that possibly transitory standing and perquisites might continue in their family. Seen as an investment, it often paralleled purchases of scattered or distant properties. Sir William Domville, attorney-general in Charles II's Ireland, although balked of the lord chancellorship, gained the clerkship of the hanaper, a branch of the Court of Chancery. Already, in the 1680s, his heirs derived a useful income from the post, discharged by deputies. By the early eighteenth century, the stated salary of £60 10s. was reckoned in reality to be ten times that amount.[36]

An equally long game had been played by another family prominent in the public life of Charles II's reign. The Temples had first occupied the provostship of Trinity College Dublin. In successive generations, they served as Master of the Rolls and attorney-general. While the younger Sir John Temple prospered through legal office in Dublin, a brother, Sir William Temple, emulated Sir Robert Southwell and went to continental Europe on diplomatic missions for the king.[37] In 1680 Sir John Temple purchased the reversion to the chief remembrancership in the Irish Exchequer. Only in 1715 did this investment mature. Sir John Temple had died, the family had returned permanently to England and a son, Henry Temple, soon to be ennobled as Viscount Palmerston, benefited from his parent's farsightedness. The Temples, although living outside Ireland since 1688, depended on it for the bulk of their remittances. In 1712, 79 per cent of Henry Temple's recorded annual income of £2,939 came from Ireland. Located chiefly in Dublin and Sligo, the holdings made work for several.[38]

Henry Temple acted quickly once the Irish post was his. Even before the previous holder had expired, Temple moved to smooth his own succession. The lord-lieutenant and barons of the Exchequer in Dublin were apprised of the situation.[39] The lord-lieutenant, conveniently in London, promptly introduced Temple into George I's presence. He kissed hands and formally assumed the dignity.[40] A partner in the original patent was bought out for a meagre £100. In his place, Temple, as insurance for the future, had his own son's name inserted.[41] In 1740, when the heir died, he strove to have a second son substituted. He backed his suit with a reminder to Sir Robert Walpole, 'I hope my uniform behaviour may deserve some notice'.[42] But, no matter what Palmerston (as Temple became in 1723) deserved, in 1742 the chief remembrancership was given instead to Viscount Limerick for his son. In consequence, when Palmerston died in 1757, the post returned to Ireland.

Palmerston, although across the water, always took seriously the discharge of the post. At his entry, he was inundated with requests for posts. He vowed not to sell any of the subsidiary offices,[43] but facing pleas from kinsfolk, he enunciated a philosophy: 'I would do for a relation that is fit, but not put an unfit person in because he is my relation'.[44] He was, therefore, unmoved by the suit of a cousin in Ireland, even when seconded by the barons of the Exchequer.[45] A remote kinsman, Abraham Hill, was given a junior clerkship from kindness. He was recommended by 'his poor mother and aunts', who, Palmerston suspected, 'put a greater value on his ability in business than the perquisites of that branch will recompense'.[46]

From afar, the imperious Palmerston let the youth know what was demanded. 'Be civil and obliging to all. Despatch them in their turns. Don't be easily affronted. Get the good will of all. Behave well: diligent, just, impartial, or I shall turn you out.'[47] Hill, whose relations had thought of sending him to sea, evidently satisfied his exigent master. Thirty years after first entering the office, he was still there, promoted within it.[48] Undeserving kinsmen, such as William Yarner, already in post when Temple inherited, found their ascent within the bureaucratic hierarchy halted. Yarner's moral and professional failings combined to displease Temple.[49] Politics – 'people's principles' – had also to be taken into account in appointments. Especially in 1715, Tories were *personae non gratae*.[50]

The business of the office of the chief remembrancer was parcelled out between a deputy and five 'secondaries'.[51] The conventional qualification for each of these functionaries was legal, either as barrister or attorney. Temple believed that the reputation and profitability of the office depended on the right choice of secondaries. Eager to select the promising, he canvassed opinion among acquaintances and kinsmen in Ireland.[52] In the main, he then left to the five principals whom they employed under them. Sometimes, he pressed them to accept his own dependants and relations as apprentices or clerks.[53] He also laid down certain basics: the secondaries were to attend in person to the work of their divisions, and not leave all to subordinates. He also forbade the use of inexperienced attorneys and the unqualified.[54] Not everyone selected by Temple accepted a place in the office. Richard Michelburne, an incumbent inherited by Temple in 1715, declined promotion, 'being a single man and not intending to marry, and having one of the sweetest seats in the kingdom'. Having been in the chief remembrancer's office for thirty years, he preferred to relax at Ballyarthur in County Wicklow rather than taking on more work which would necessitate attendance in the city during vacations.[55] Daniel Reading, a distant kinsman of the Temples, lawyer, squire and member of parliament, was too elevated for such humdrum work as the office required.[56] In 1715, he was granted a termly retainer of £25 to handle the Temples' legal affairs in Ireland. By 1717, this fee had been raised to £40.[57] A decade later, he hoped that he might be made an Irish judge.[58] He deputized for Temple as chief remembrancer, and discharged the duties punctiliously. For this he received an annual £160, and an additional £40 for helping to collect the Temples' Dublin rents.[59] At the same time, Reading worked for others, including the Wentworths in County Wicklow.[60] He held a second established post: as examinator of decrees in Chancery. On Reading's death in 1726, £1,500 was offered – unsuccessfully – for the place.[61]

With the post of chief remembrancer, Temple gained extra revenue and a useful source of patronage. Mindful of public responsibilities and highly conscious of his own profit, he nevertheless drew on a loose group allied by cousinage and familiarity with the Dublin law courts, with which his own family had been associated since the mid-seventeenth century.[62] Furthermore, those employed about the Temples' Sligo and Dublin estates kept an eye on the running of the remembrancer's department. At the same time, its officers might be dispatched into the west about the Temples' private concerns.[63] Temple, as chief remembrancer, headed a government department. The auxiliaries who ran it also dealt with his personal affairs. This confusion of public and private functions typified government at the time. Temple may have been more alert than many to the notion that both his own and the collective interest could be advanced simultaneously by careful management. His office recorded and made accessible records of judgments in the Court of Exchequer.[64] The security of much property throughout the island depended on the safe custody of these documents. Anxiety was expressed in criticism of the haphazard way in which such materials were kept. The muddled and poor condition of the records, together with exorbitant fees charged for access to them, irritated many. Temple was alive to these criticisms. Aghast at stories of how dirty and untidy were the records in the remembrancer's care, he acted. At a time when even the viceroy was housed in cramped and makeshift quarters, subsidiary departments squatted in decrepit premises. Office-holders themselves made whatever arrangements they could to lodge staff and the necessary papers. Some roosted like cranes on dishevelled nests throughout the alleys and tenements of central Dublin. Daniel Reading, accustomed to greater comfort, begged to remove his office from above an alehouse where he was either choked by smoke from below or perished by the cold outside.[65] Temple decreed that a new office be taken, and premises in the centre of Dublin were rented from the ubiquitous Thomas Carter, at an annual £42.[66] Immediately £80 was laid out in fitting them up. Temple fussed that a caretaker live on the premises and that fires be lit to dry the newly plastered walls. Three clerks were requisitioned to clean and sort the documents alphabetically.[67]

As soon as the improved office was open, the pernickety Temple enquired, 'why not a table of fees [to] be affixed in my office so as all shall know what they pay'. This proposal, in advance of a general edict, was an astute move to calm public resentments at overcharging. Tidiness announced good order in the running of the department, and soon attracted more business.[68] However, the chief remembrancer continued to worry about the safety of the numerous memorials in his and other offices' care. Often former officers incorporated state papers into their own archives so that they vanished from public view.[69] The processes on penal statutes and forfeitures were registered and stored in the chief remembrancer's section. On this mass of parchment and vellum rested the Protestants' predominance, especially over land. Chewed by rats, obliterated by damp, misplaced by the incompetent or removed by the malicious, and all vulnerable to the flames which regularly licked around the area, the papers caused Temple to be justifiably worried. This anxiety was shared by parliament. In 1727, when a capacious new parliament was under construction, Palmerston urged the lord-lieutenant, the Speaker, the lord chief baron of the Exchequer and the two architects, Burgh and Pearce, to make spaces to store the state papers.[70] In 1740, a committee proposed better protection of records, 'on the preservation of which the peace and safety of this kingdom does in a great measure depend'.[71] That the problems had not been solved was shown in 1755 when George Robinson was rewarded by parliament for having saved the Exchequer Office in Castle Street from fire, as earlier he had the Common Pleas Office.[72]

Palmerston's anxiety on this score, reasonable for any functionary whose office rested on generating and retrieving information, stemmed too from how his ancestors in Ireland had contributed to the Protestant interest there. In the 1640s, his great-grandfather, the elder Sir John Temple, publicized what the Protestants had allegedly endured by way of massacre and torture in his *History of the Irish Rebellion*. Temple's message was the more readily believed because he wrote as Master of the Rolls. He appended to his chronicle copious and apparently authentic evidence in the form of legal depositions as to what Protestant victims had suffered and lost. Since the history of the Irish Protestants as a chosen people, no less than their future security, was bound up in the voluminous records, it was understandable that Temple's descendant should plead for their better care.

Temple's eagerness to reorder his department enhanced its reputation and his revenues. Business boomed. Between 1715 and 1726, the net annual profit to Temple of the chief remembrancer's place averaged £1,275. This added between 33 per cent and 40 per cent to his disposable income in England. However, these remittances, although welcome, did not alone transform Temple from wealthy Anglo-Irish landowner and office-holder into an absent holder of an Irish peerage with a London house in smart St James's Square and an impressive Hampshire estate.[73] Marriage to the daughter of a governor of the Bank of England materially improved his fortune. In 1735 she bequeathed him over £22,000, mainly in stocks and annuities.[74] Because of this access of money, while receipts from Ireland as remembrancer rose steadily, they declined as a proportion of his total revenues. However, in the income which Palmerston drew from Ireland, the remitted fees eventually overtook the rents from his property there.

Henry Temple, 1st Viscount Palmerston's Irish revenues, 1712–38[75]

Year	Irish rents	Dublin rents	Sligo rents	Chief remembrancer's office	Total receipts
1712	2,311	1,810	501		2,939
1713	2,319	1,817	502		2,905
1714	2,319	1,817	502		2,942
1715	2,433	1,832	601		3,071
1716	2,527	1,834	693	1,014	3,230
1717	2,556	1,849	707	985	3,057
1718	2,709	1,967	742	1,227	3,609
1719	2,709	1,967	742	1,253	3,609
1720	2,694	1,949	745	1,171	3,280
1721	2,694	1,949	747	1,199	
1722	2,694	1,950	747	1,295	3,280
1723	2,694	1,950	747	1,380	3,280
1724		1,950	747	1,463	
1725		1,954	747	1,372	
1726		1,954	747	1,673	
1727		1,955	747	1,777	
1728		1,955	747	1,988	
1729		1,955	747	1,885	5,620
1730		1,958	772	1,943	6,905
1731		1,998	772	2,260	6,155
1732		1,999	772	2,262	6,489
1733		1,999	773	1,915	6,923
1734		2,015	773	2,304	6,888
1735		2,013	773	2,656	9,652
1736			773	2,711	29,433
1737			773	3,802	8,985
1738			773	3,745	17,480

Cynics might account for this rise as resulting from the notorious preference of Ireland's inhabitants to go to law rather than to farm their lands. Palmerston more prosaically acknowledged that the diligence of adjutants attracted custom. His thanks took solid form. Deputies were presented with showy silver cups.[76] The absent Palmerston might benefit most from the greater volume of work in his office, but others prospered as a result. Some, as has been seen, were kinsmen; others, attorneys. Notable among the latter was the Roberts family, whose ascent shadowed that of the Temples. The Robertses were at the heart of the official and social worlds. Their success depended heavily on professional talents and the urban, indeed metropolitan, environment of Dublin. Unlike those who had used office in the seventeenth century – the Boyles, earls of Cork and Burlington and of Orrery, Petty, the Percevals, Southwells or the Temples themselves – to lift themselves high in England, the Robertses opted for an agreeable Irish existence. The family had arrived in Ireland from Anglesey, probably only in the late seventeenth century.[77] They joined other migrants who came from North Wales, so handy for Dublin and Ireland's eastern seaboard, to run the Church and state of Ireland. By 1671 there were enough of these expatriates in and around Dublin to celebrate 'a great feast' on St David's Day. One of the numerous Welsh dignitaries in the Church of Ireland would deliver the sermon. Grandees with Welsh links were asked to donate a joint of venison, in return for which they and St David would be toasted.[78]

The Robertses allied with the Cambrian tribes which proliferated in south-eastern Ireland and Dublin.[79] In 1726, Lewis Roberts was appointed to succeed Reading as Palmerston's deputy in the remembrancer's office.[80] This set the seal on a long career in the Exchequer. As early as 1697 Roberts rented property close to the office of the second remembrancer. In 1704, Roberts, trained as an attorney, was granted the pompous dignities of transcriptor and foreign opposer in the Exchequer.[81] These titles acknowledged a mastery of procedure which would subsequently impress Palmerston. They also accorded Roberts the security, more social than monetary, of a place in the civil establishment. For the ascendant Whigs after 1714, Roberts well deserved this distinction. He had defied Tory judges during the acrimonious struggles of 1712–14. Later, it was remembered that Roberts had warned the judges that their orders 'were contrary to law'. In 1714 a Whig annotated the names of Lewis Roberts and his son, William, 'both good men'.[82] Cases in the Exchequer – with the Tory attempts at the end of Queen Anne's reign to impose their nominee as lord mayor of Dublin and then the clash of jurisdictions between England and Ireland – had serious political connotations. These would continue into the 1730s, with the bishops' struggle to collect the tithe of agistment.[83] Officers of the court, therefore, had to be steadfast against blandishments and threats, and their conduct might attract favourable or unfavourable publicity.

Lewis Roberts hoped to put his professional and social ranking on a surer footing by securing the reversion to his patentee posts for his son, William Roberts. The young Roberts, 'bred to business and well instructed' in the arcana of the Exchequer, was poached by the lord chief baron to be his own secretary.[84] When Lewis Roberts died in 1727, it was a nephew, Robert Roberts, not the son, who took over as the working deputy for Palmerston. Roberts had already been trained by his uncle in office routines. Robert Roberts had also allied himself with the affinity of the Temples through marriage into the Yarner family.[85] In characteristic mode, the latter dinned into Roberts what was required. 'Follow precedent. Let no man, tho' never so great make you do wrong'. He and his assistants were to take only the permitted and advertised fees.[86]

Quickly Roberts's industry and probity earned Palmerston's trust. It also hitched Roberts higher. By 1742, his master could rib him on the style of living which he had adopted.[87] Evidently Roberts saw no need to conceal the assets that money honestly gotten had bought. He had graduated from the rank of gentlemen, to which he and his uncle had been entitled automatically as attorneys, into an assured esquire. The social move was mirrored by physical relocation: first on St Stephen's Green; then at the newly desirable seaside suburb of Monkstown.[88] A country property at Old Conna in County Wicklow, convenient for the city, was acquired. In 1743 one of his cows grazing in another suburb, Donnybrook, was rustled.[89] His children's marriages bound him more tightly to the prospering families from which he hailed in County Wexford – Edwards, Maddocks and Nunn – and to the successful mercantile and office-holding dynasties of Dublin, such as Putland, Riall, Helsham and Dawson.[90] One hint of broader interests than the minutiae of the law is given by Roberts's library.[91] Another was his membership of first the Dublin Society, to which he had been elected in 1732, and then, in the 1740s, of the Physico-Historical Society. In time, his son, Lewis Roberts, would also be elected to the Dublin Society. Robert Roberts's acuity was exploited by the Society, which included him in the governing committee of twenty-one throughout most of the 1730s.[92] This cultivation could be explained either by utility or fashion. *Par excellence*, the bookish were concentrated among the professionals of the towns: families indeed, like the Ridgates and Putlands, into which the Robertses married.[93] Another sign that Robert Roberts was quitting the undifferentiated company of attorneys was his decision to put his heir, a second Lewis Roberts, through Dublin University and then into the London Inns of Court. As a further guarantee of future respectability and earnings, a patentee office in the Exchequer was purchased for him. The father had also jobbed his son into one of the secondaries' positions. Absent at the London Inns, deputies did his work.[94] Just how far the Roberts family had travelled from devilling attorneys is hinted by the fortune of £10,000 secured by the younger Lewis Roberts with his bride, Biddy Putland, in 1746.[95] The match endorsed the Robertses' position among affluent and educated Dubliners.

Roberts was cried up as the coming man in the 1730s. He was much in demand: so much so, indeed, that Palmerston feared that he would be enticed away from the Exchequer. Lord Cork and Burlington invited

Roberts to supervise his declining Irish empire.[96] A trial soon convinced Roberts (and others) that he belonged not to the country but the town.[97] Returned to Dublin, Roberts retained one souvenir: a seat in parliament for the Burlingtons' borough of Dungarvan. A not altogether convincing picture of Roberts careering through Dungarvan, 'feasting, revelling, receiving homages and worship', in the mode of a Gaelic chief, was painted by a competitor.[98] In parliament, he was marked out as, but never turned into, a government manager. By 1753–54, he aligned himself with the 'patriots' against the government.[99] Palmerston tried to bring Roberts back to the government's side. After 1755, he was among those members wooed by Hartington, the lord-lieutenant, with invitations to dinner at the Castle.[100] But Roberts never dominated parliament. His forte was accounting, drafting and the tedium of committees. Such skills made him an obvious choice to be chief agent of the creditors of Burton's bank, which had failed in 1733. In this guise he promoted bills intended to recompense the losers.[101] As Roberts stepped more boldly into the public arena, so he was sometimes attacked. Disgruntled employees of Burlington rounded on him, and it seemed that he was slow to settle his accounts with Burlington.[102] Some hurt by the collapse of Burton's bank impugned Roberts's stewardship on behalf of the creditors. Those in other legal departments, jealous of the business in the remembrancer's office, whispered against Roberts. Palmerston's trust was not shaken. He exhorted Roberts, 'honesty, integrity, truth, flourish by detraction. Go on and triumph.'[103] Occasionally he was irritated by Roberts's refusal to depute to others,[104] but in general the absentee was well pleased by swelling remittances, even in the difficult early 1740s. He agreed with Roberts's assessment that 'moderate fees, no extorting despatch money, due attend-ance and skill in executing' attracted business.[105] Yet, towards the end of his life, for whatever reasons, Roberts's meticulous habits slipped. Caught up in the fresh banking collapses of the 1755, Palmerston's death in 1757 obliged Roberts unexpectedly to account to the executors. They discov-ered that Roberts had used a judgment in favour of Burtons' creditors as security against a loan of his own. Roberts's creditors pressed him for payment and the whole edifice raised on his long career seemed about to topple. His own properties, valued as £7,927, might have to be sold.[106] These pressures apparently turned the ageing Roberts's mind, but he died before he was publicly disgraced. Moreover, Roberts, glimpsing possible hazards ahead, conveyed much of his most valuable property through collusive trusts to associates.[107]

Of the several employees of Palmerston who prospered, Roberts comes momentarily into focus. Another, Henry Hatch, said to have originated as a grazier in the Irish midlands, rose even more spectacularly. But Hatch, in contrast to Roberts, was essentially a land agent.[108] In time he – in common with Roberts – put his son through Trinity College, secured him a patentee office and a seat in parliament.[109] Other attorneys in the remembrancer's employ thrived. Francis Anderson attained the desk of a 'secondary'. As early as 1711, he was preparing briefs and having 'some toppers feed'. By 1726 his practice was buoyant enough for him to accept apprentices.[110] Anderson inspired unusual confidence among clients, one of whom, in 1737, went so far as to call him, exceptionally, an 'honest' attorney. Like Roberts, Anderson moved in formal rank, and probably in wealth and culture, from the despised hackney attorneys into the squirearchy.[111] Office helped to promote a few, such as Roberts and Anderson, from the ranks of the 573 licensed attorneys and solicitors.[112]

Palmerston's death delivered his valuable Irish office to Lord Limerick. Just as Palmerston had been besieged for places in 1715, so in 1757 Limerick was pestered. Richard White, for example, craved 'a place of honour and profit' from him. White had spotted the mastership of references under the chief remembrancer, worth, conservatively, £400 annually. White appreciated that the office would not usher in a life of ease. Nevertheless, he made interest for the post. First, he persuaded the lord chancellor to write on his behalf to Lord Limerick. He also cultivated those with whom he would have to work in the Exchequer. He arranged a dinner for nine of the principal attorneys of the court. In rotation, he would entertain the officers of the courts and two or three more sets of the attorneys. White perhaps went further than was strictly necessary to gain appointment,[113] yet it seemed that a degree of fraternity bound together those associated with a particular Dublin department. Earlier, this community had been underpinned by extended kinship. Increasingly there were signs, too, of shared values, especially the convivial civilities which distinguished the respectable and genteel from lesser mortals.

II

As the business of the government and the law courts grew in the early eighteenth century, so did the hitherto attenuated bureaucracy. Nevertheless, in Dublin, the supply fell woefully short of demand. Hopefuls crowded around the narrow entrances. One of these, the Admiralty Court, sitting occasionally in St Patrick's Cathedral, had dwindled into a seemingly anomalous survival by the 1740s. The decay was attributed to the lethargy of the judge, John Hawkshaw. Under him, the business of the court 'had sunk to nothing and came to be in great disrepute and but little used'. Emoluments may have dwindled to a yearly £10 or even £5.[114]

For Judge Hawkshaw, the place retained some value. He had his son, Richard, act as his legal amanuensis.[115] This work served as the youth's apprenticeship as an attorney.[116] When the registrarship became vacant, there was a flurry of activity to secure it. Judge Hawkshaw pushed his own son, but unsuccessfully. The merits of a functionary in the six clerks' office in Chancery, Joseph Bayly, were also canvassed. Bayly knew the 'minute proceedings' of Chancery, which were felt to be more relevant in Ireland than in England to the business of the civil law. He had been trained by one of the six clerks, his uncle, Thomas Towers, 'who is the most eminent in the country and has £1500 p.a. estate in land'.[117]

John Hawkshaw belonged to a family which had arrived in seventeenth-century Dublin from Cheshire. The Hawkshaws, inserting themselves into the ecclesiastical and bureaucratic establishments of the capital, bound themselves through marriage to similar families, some from North Wales and Cheshire.[118] The judge, although indolent, frequented sociable circles of similarly circumstanced professionals in Dublin.[119] The respectability of his family was further demonstrated by two sons, who may have followed him into the law, and a third preferred in the Church. What Hawkshaw had neglected, it was said, 'may be worth the while of a man who is in other business to accept'.[120] Ideally, if the jurisdiction was to revive, 'a knowing man', indeed 'a gentleman of figure and character', must be appointed.[121] Hugh Baillie fitted the bill. Baillie's qualifications included extended travel in Europe and a consequent familiarity with foreign languages. This facility perhaps helped him to revive the popularity of the court among traders. Increased work meant more fees for functionaries, so suddenly subordinate posts in the Admiralty were desired. Baillie, despite his success in the office, was superseded in 1757 by a political follower of the now ascendant Ponsonbys.[122]

Offices in the administration, like preferments in the Church, law and army, were battled over. Edward King, grandson of a former bishop of Elphin and a Roscommon squire, recounted how he had acted as clerk in Chancery. However, his father had failed to buy him an established office before he died in the 1680s. Despite devoting himself to 'court concernments', the untimely death of his parent and the upheavals of James II's reign had left King to fend for himself.[123] In 1706 the wife of an army officer in Dublin begged for help to secure 'any sort of civil employ that was fit for a gentleman'. Although he was a skilled accountant and a sober man, he would be satisfied with a 'small' post rather than return to the army.[124] The desire for very modestly remunerated offices was further illustrated by Richard Moore, a kinsman of the currently powerful Dublin revenue official, Nathanael Clements. In 1756, Moore secured the clerkship of the wool accounts through Clements's intercession. Moore's predecessor had paid a deputy £12 yearly to do most of the work. Moore, however, could not afford to continue this arrangement, and discharged the job in person.[125] Office-holders, especially when astute pluralists, made money from their patentee posts. But the salaries, both nominal and actual, varied so widely that these employments, which elevated some to wealth and into the quality, conferred on others a precarious or even spurious gentility. In 1735 Dr Marmaduke Coghill, universal man of affairs, son and brother of prominent office-holders, wished to vacate his onerous but powerful seat at the Revenue Board in Dublin. He sought the chancellor-ship of the Exchequer, 'a place of honour and dignity, and very little to do, so that I have now reason to hope for ease and comfort in the latter end of my life'.[126] At the same time, a functionary in the Pells Office, John Bayly, was soliciting his patrons whenever alluring vacancies occurred. One, for which Bayly bid £150, was thought by him, 'an office of very genteel appearance and must necessarily add to my expense in living'.[127] If Bayly were to prosper, he proposed uniting the hard graft as deputy to an established officer with 'a patent place without business to help me out in the other'. So he considered becoming searcher in the port of Limerick. Once he had provided a deputy, it would yield yearly £20 or £25.[128] Only through ingenious pluralism of this kind could those wishing to hitch themselves and their families into the genteel or the quality earn enough to do so. But as Bayly disclosed, servants of the crown, clergymen and army officers had to live and act in a manner which did not demean them.

These genteel habits catered primarily to their own sense of impor-tance. Coghill, having recently entered into the chancellorship, fussed that a portrait must depict him in the appropriate robes. Similarly, the son of the Irish lord chancellor, Robert Jocelyn, worried lest his father be portrayed in incorrect dress and posture.[129] Surviving images of the suc-cessive speakers, Conolly, Boyle and Ponsonby, portray them in their robes of office. Also in the mid-eighteenth century, the recorder of Dublin, Eaton Stannard, having had his salary trebled, was to be painted 'by the most eminent hand' in Ireland. In this way, Stannard was thanked for 'his unwearied and frequent attendance' to the city's affairs.[130] Through these images, descendants and clients would be impressed.

Less clear is the extent to which pride in serving the monarch trans-lated into impartiality or public-spiritedness. Palmerston enjoined high standards on his subordinates in the chief remembrancer's office. But much of this concern could be traced to his justified belief that the good reputation of the department increased his profits. Furthermore, he did not distinguish precisely between the public and private work done by these employees, the most important of whom drew salaries from the state, fees from the public and wages from himself. An inchoate striving towards the concept of serving the state was heard in the Irish Secretary's Office in 1746. 'Officers', it was argued, 'were the servants of the public, and not of particular people'.[131] In late seventeenth- and early eighteenth-century Ireland, state servants were felt to serve themselves more than their clients. Their exaction of fees, often for formulaic services, was frequently criticized, but efforts at regulation failed.[132]

Office-holders attracted dislike because, having solicited jobs from the administration, they were supposed to be too indebted to it to preserve political independence. Place-men, in Ireland no less than in England, were regarded as stooges of unpopular ministries. Already in 1720, 72 were listed among the 300 members of the Dublin parliament.[133] In practice, in Ireland successive governments despaired of buying political tractability through the award of offices. Office-holders, invariably failing to support the administration, were occasionally disciplined by dismissal, as in 1711 and 1753.[134] However, the habits of independence went too deep to be eradicated by such gestures. A correspondent from England in writing ironically to Dublin in 1736, 'yours is a free country indeed where men in place and pension are under no restraint and pursue and speak their opinion without control', disclosed the differing attitudes in the two kingdoms.[135] Part of the problem, perhaps, came from the variety of intermediaries from which appointments had come. The local brokers, the undertakers and the heads of offices, were more immediate presences, and therefore had to be cultivated. On occasion, as in the remembrancer's office, this calculation induced a kind of departmental *esprit de corps*. An apparently deferential deputy, such as Robert Roberts, looked to more than one master. Furthermore, he had to calculate how best to advance his own and his family's interests.

In the event, the uprightness of Roberts was compromised by the imbroglio at the end of his life. If nothing else, the uncertainties over whether he had treated what he held in trust for others as his own highlighted the unclear conventions. A second model of public probity, Edward Synge, bishop of Elphin, was embarrassingly caught in a comparable position, using money of which he was a trustee as his own.[136] Spectacular, too, was the entanglement of three prominent office-holders, Anthony Malone, John Gore and Nathanael Clements, in a bank which collapsed in 1759. The trio had been trusted because they were 'gentlemen of the highest station amongst us'.[137] More to the point in creating confidence among depositors were the facts that Malone was chancellor of the Exchequer, Clements deputy vice-treasurer and as such working head of the Irish Treasury, and Gore a revenue commissioner. The failure resulted in a statute which cordoned off private banking from government finances

by forbidding the involvement of office-holders in banks.[138] Until this prohibition, public and private moneys often seemed irretrievably confused.
Yet the reputations of Malone, Clements and Gore were not seriously
blemished. Public office, especially in the treasury and other departments
handling large receipts of cash, offered temptations. Temporary use of
deposits until they had to be accounted for gave officials irresistible
chances.

In 1703, Sir William Robinson came unstuck. Robinson's polymathic
skills had lifted him out of the smoky kitchen where supposedly he had
toiled as a scullion into the posts of surveyor-general and receiver-general.
Arrogance and political partisanship as much as malpractice made him the
target of angry MPs. In 1703, he was accused of falsifying the state of the
Irish finances and disabled from holding public office in Ireland. In 1706
he was charged with fraud in supplying clothing for the army in Ireland
and extortion in relation to some suppliers. Robinson fled to England
where – in addition to his substantial holdings in Ireland – he had acquired
property. He severed his links with Ireland.[139] But others implicated in this
scandal retained strong Irish interests. In particular, Thomas Putland, an
associate of Robinson, strengthened his mercantile dynasty through office-
holding: he became a freeman of the city of Dublin in 1671 via the Smiths'
Guild.[140] Putland diversified by importing and exporting. Commercial
success enabled him to buy more property and invest in joint-stock
companies by the 1690s. Further respectability was conferred with his
acquisition of a patentee post in the Treasury. There, he acted under
Robinson, whom he probably knew already. Putland, like other prosperous merchants, functioned as a banker.[141] Robinson used him as his
cashier. As such, he was implicated in Robinson's frauds which parliament
later investigated. Putland, it was suggested, knew more about leather-
selling than banking. He himself acknowledged that the accounts had
failed to distinguish clearly between transactions with the state's creditors
and his own business.[142] Putland, censured by the Irish Commons and
debarred from holding office in Ireland,[143] retired to England. However,
he still itched to make money. In his capacity as an executor of Robinson's will, he was accused of detaining revenues owed to the estate of the
dead man. Whatever chicanery Putland had practised, it did not prevent
his son and grandson from consolidating the wealth and reputation of the
family. The younger Thomas Putland continued his father's activities as a
banker in Dublin and was remembered for his philanthropy. In turn, his
son, John Putland, became the quintessential urbane and civic-minded
Protestant Dubliner.[144] By this stage, neither the younger Thomas Putland
nor John Putland needed the income from or adornment of office. Maybe
they were chary about reviving memories of their recent forebear's

shame; or perhaps they simply grew so wealthy that they did not have to bother.

Robinson and Putland were tarnished by their financial malpractices while holding public places. Their pursuit by an indignant parliament contrasted with the greater leniency to another whose tenure of a financial office ended in disaster. In 1725, official Dublin was rocked by the spectacular fall of the deputy vice-treasurer of the Exchequer, 'the honourable' John Pratt. An unexpected inspection of his books uncovered a deficiency at first said to total £70,000 or £75,000. Pratt, long in the post, was reckoned 'a nice accountant and a wary manager of the public money as [of] his own private estate'.[145] This high esteem, together with attractive rates of interest, had encouraged private investors to entrust him with their money. When Pratt and his clerk were hustled away to the Dublin Marshalsea, wild stories spread through the capital. His assets in real and personal estate were valued at £43,320.[146] Hitherto, the grandeur in which he lived had been traced to a fortunate marriage to an English heiress and his clever investments. It was well known, too, that the nominal salary of the deputy vice-treasurership – of £50 – might in reality exceed £8,000.[147] Opinions changed. Pratt had sustained his luxury by speculating with the funds of the state as well as of his customers. His clerk, Marcus Dowley, like Putland before him, was said to have profited to the tune of £50,000.[148] The Pratt débâcle was used for political ends. Some criticized the lord chancellor and the barons of the Exchequer for not being more vigilant.[149] Those ill disposed to the Speaker, Conolly, whispered that he had borrowed £25,000 of public revenue from Pratt. Conolly replied by declaring that he was still owed £5,000, which he had advanced to the Exchequer during the emergency of 1715.[150] Pratt, foreseeing trouble, had spirited valuables away from his Dublin house.

Pratt, after the initial shock, resumed a place in respectable Dublin life. He joined and attended the Dublin Society.[151] The episode happened during a time of heightened political consciousness over Wood's Halfpence. Patriots resented fiscal control from England, and blamed it for economic damage. Criticism was easily extended to the management of the Treasury. Pratt was hardly an innocent, but he was a member of the Protestant community. His people had settled in Drogheda and County Meath during the seventeenth century. While 'Captain' Pratt insinuated himself into the Treasury, a brother, Benjamin Pratt, presided over Trinity College as provost. John Pratt invested a part of his new wealth in developing a Protestant colony on the desolate coast of Mayo. This settlement, Newport Pratt, had been acquired from a fellow government functionary, the revenue commissioner, Thomas Medlycott, and would be passed to another.[152] Pratt's Lucifer-like fall alarmed contemporaries, particularly if they had invested with him. However, extenuation was offered. The titular vice-treasurers, two absentee Englishmen, the future Lord Mount Edgcumbe and Lord Falmouth, were castigated for not attending more to their responsibilities in Ireland. Even the lord-lieutenant was culpable in not insisting on more regular accounting. Few could deny that Pratt had 'been very negligent in his management'; but those who knew Pratt's circumstances traced his failures to the accidental drowning of his son. Archbishop King, a scourge of those in public places whose conduct did not reach his exacting standards, sympathized with Pratt, observing that his 'head and heart has failed him'.[153] As with the failures of private banks, so with the money outstanding from Pratt, the state tried to recover the debt. The total owing, stated variously as £94,000 and £125,254, was gradually reduced. Nevertheless, in 1767, Pratt's executors had yet to repay £17,994.[154]

The deputy vice-treasurership passed in turn to Luke Gardiner and Nathanael Clements, both of whose names became bywords for wealth conspicuously displayed. Clements's part in the bank which collapsed in 1759 suggested that the proper spheres of public and private finance were still uncertainly demarcated. To concentrate on officials whose tenure of their places ended in scandal ignores the majority whose behaviour attracted no hostility. More onerous requirements – of attendance and probity – felled a few. As early as 1693, one official in the revenue at Dublin was pained that 'there is not a farthing to be got beyond salary, with honour or safety'.[155] After 1715, some office-holders were removed because they were Tory partisans.[156] Thereafter, if political partisanship led still to appointments, prominent casualties, such as Sir John Eccles, nominal head as customer of the revenue in the port of Dublin, or Henry Cust, tax collector in Armagh, were punished for neglecting their duties.[157]

III

The panel of seven revenue commissioners in Dublin presided over one of the most important institutions in the kingdom. The commission resulted from a bid by the English Treasury during Charles II's reign to control Irish finances more stringently. It was designed to subordinate Ireland, and was always manned by some from England (but never any from Scotland). By the eighteenth century, Irish Protestants skilfully gained effective control over it. A place as a commissioner – by Queen Anne's time, paid £1,000 annually – was one of the best posts in Ireland to be had from the ministry. Lucky Englishmen were appointed: John Evelyn, a son of the diarist; Francis Robartes, a Cornish member of parliament, fellow of the Royal Society, and kinsman of Lord Kildare; and Thomas Medlycott, another English MP, whose service with the Ormondes recommended him.[158] While in Dublin, each enjoyed and added something to Irish Protestant society.[159] However, as strangers, especially if they failed regularly to appear in Ireland, the English revenue commissioners fuelled anti-English feelings.[160] Englishmen, reviled as interlopers who denied the Irish-born their deserts, by their absence delivered control to the Irish Protestants. This, as Evelyn remarked, was 'called putting the geese into the fox's keeping'.[161] First William Conolly after 1714, then John Ponsonby, used their mastery over the commission to strengthen their political dominance. From this capacious cornucopia, Conolly and Ponsonby fed their associates. The ultimate prize was a seat at the board. Allies of Conolly, such as Sir Thomas Southwell (a local hero of 1689–90) and Dr Marmaduke Coghill, and later the idiosyncratic patriot from County Cork, the younger Sir Richard Cox, were appointed.[162] The salary of £1,000 could double the income of even a parliamentary squire. Coghill frankly totted up his assets: an annual £1,500 from his offices and another £1,500 from lands. He had, additionally, amassed £5,000 in money.[163] However, he relished the opportunities for patronage less than some of his colleagues in the commission. 'The obloquy of some disappointed, complaints, backbiting, etc.' wearied him.[164]

The commissioners controlled more than 1,000 provincial posts. Many in Protestant Ireland wanted to be collectors, receivers, searchers and supernumeraries – despite yearly salaries of only £20 or £40. Conolly, during his primacy, was deluged with requests. Some came from the important (or self-important); more originated with those whose situation in the north-west of Ulster made them turn automatically to its most eminent son.[165] A collectorship based at Ballinrobe in County Mayo satisfied one of the Crofton brothers in the 1730s. In 1759, the newly named surveyor of the port of Derry, Joseph Mortimer, owed his place to Ponsonby. Mortimer was entitled to an annual £50, but Ponsonby predicted that he 'will make his fortune in the cruising barge'.[166] The six boatmen under Mortimer, technically employees of the Hanoverian state and undoubtedly profiteers from the Protestants' ascendancy in Ireland, can scarcely have reached Mortimer's level of wealth. The unfortunate squire of Renny, Edmund Spencer, had also looked to a job with the revenue as his financial salvation. He waited more than sixteen years before this deliverance came, thanks to the interest made by his friends with Ponsonby.[167] Spencer, like others reduced to this strait, saw the employment as a form of slavery.[168] His employers in Dublin imposed exacting conditions. Even so, by paying a deputy, Spencer was freed to work in a private capacity as an agent for landowners. Furthermore, if office on the civil establishment did not automatically confer gentility in the way that the practice of a profession or the county shrievalty did, a patentee post in the provinces bestowed status.

The revenue commissioners in Dublin stressed – sometimes inconsistently – minimum qualifications. In 1716, they demanded of their collectors that they had 'been brought up in the knowledge and practice of our revenue'.[169] This tactic shut out most strangers from Britain. By 1760, horror greeted the information that the gauger at Dingle, John Spring, was ignorant of the work and of 'keeping books'. Rather than dismiss Spring, the commissioners in Dublin ordered that he be properly instructed.[170] Attention to duties was required, and the negligent were eventually sacked. Bysse Molesworth, son of a peer, well travelled and prominent in Dublin society, was taken to task by local merchants when he failed as clerk of the land permits to attend at his office in the afternoons. He insisted that he was on duty between the hours of ten and three, and then again from four until six. Much of the routine was handled by clerks, and in 1739 the revenue commissioners agreed to maintain one at a salary of £30 p.a. from the civil list.[171]

In 1718, the commissioners in Dublin repeated the prohibition on incumbents selling their offices. The collector at Youghal for forty years, Briscoe, had hoped to dispose of his position for 300 guineas, but was prevented.[172] Ways round such bans could be devised. Those resigning their places might be paid 'pensions' by their successors. These were not always subterfuges since, other than exceptionally, the commission itself did not pension the aged and superannuated. Joseph Sotheby, for forty-six years a revenue officer at Drogheda, was lucky in being put on the short charity list maintained by the commission.[173] For many, adequate provision in old age and infirmity was a constant worry, raising prospects of a reduction in both circumstances and social standing. An established officer might make money through the disposal of junior posts within his purview.[174] The profits were not solely monetary, but could take the form of gratifying and fortifying a clientele. The activities of Brettridge Badham exemplify this.

Badham emerged from the settler community of south Munster as a supporter of the Tories during the reign of Queen Anne. A landowner, he secured the collectorship of Youghal, and was soon meddling in its politics. Badham, in addition to his local supporters, had friends in higher places. He was a brother-in-law of Henry Boyle, the future Speaker. Another Boyle, the absent earl of Orrery, recommended him for a more lucrative post in the revenue at Cork.[175] Badham was important enough himself to be elected to the 1713 parliament. However, he fell heavily from grace in the following year. Not just his politics, but also his unconcealed dishonesty condemned him. In 1715, the revenue commissioners denounced him 'as obnoxious as any in the revenue of all Ireland'.[176] Sunderland, lord-lieutenant of Ireland, intervened from England to save him from ejection. Furthermore, he survived as agent of the absent Orrery until incontrovertible evidence of his dishonesty brought dismissal. Despite these misdemeanours, Badham remained a powerful figure in County Cork, and was again returned to parliament in 1743. Unloved by contemporaries, he showed how serving state, superiors and self could be combined.[177]

Badham's strength in his locality depended on his ability to gratify dependants there, and link them with the powerful elsewhere. His property was one means of doing so; his position within the revenue, another. One who benefited was Cornelius Buckley, added to the revenue as a supernumerary and paid £6 yearly as a boatman. Badham's protégé was an incongruous state servant. Originally known as Mulpatrick, he had been a labourer in Badham's neighbourhood, supplementing his income with petty thieving. With the proceeds, he bought new clothes and pumps, on to which he fixed sparkling buckles. He was immediately renamed in Irish, 'Connor of the buckles', or in English, 'Cornelius Buckley'. In court, Buckley was acquitted. Badham promptly took him on as a footman. Unsuited to that potentially genteel occupation, he was jobbed into the revenue.[178] Buckley personified the authority of the British state in Ireland. How conscious he was of this responsibility and what his presence did for the acceptance of English rule in provincial Ireland can only be guessed.

Badham's flagrant misuse of the opportunities afforded by state and private service hardly typified the generality of his contemporaries. His activities were widely censured, although his spotted reputation did not exclude him from recognition as one of the élite either formally through return to parliament or informally by his acceptance by the local squires. More characteristic of the social and economic leverage afforded by office are the examples of the Custs and Wahabs. In 1697, Henry Cust was appointed tidewaiter and coast officer in remote creeks of County Sligo. He had sufficient interest to be transferred first to the revenue and then to an outpost of the Derry port district. Meanwhile, a son, Jones Cust, embarked on the same career. He began promisingly in a clerkship for the port of Dublin, with a stated salary of £40 p.a. Soon Dublin was exchanged for the Donegal harbour of Killybegs. There, as collector of the customs, he was paid an annual £100. In a little more than a year, he removed to Armagh, still on the same stipend, but now as collector of the excise. In 1738 he surrendered this office to his son, Henry Cust. Old Cust had not abandoned office-holding. He moved to a newer branch of the bureaucracy, becoming a local barrack-master. These moves had been aided by patrons, notably the archbishop of Armagh, whose tenants the Custs had become. Public employment ended abruptly in 1758 when Henry Cust failed to account for his excise receipts. The Dublin revenue commissioners suspended him as collector, and in 1761 he resigned. This irregularity brought no lasting shame to the Custs. Henry Cust still lived well, served on the grand jury and (in 1769) as high sheriff of County Armagh, and was accepted as an esquire.[179] The Wahabs similarly exploited the revenue service. In the late seventeenth century, they collected dues on the shore of Carlingford Lough. Meanwhile, a relation in England pressed their claims to promotion at court.[180] By 1705, William Wahab had been made boatman for the customs at Skerries to the north of Dublin. Possessed of effective patrons and attentive to duty, the Wahabs steadily improved their standing. Over the next two generations they continued to work in the revenue. Concurrently, they established themselves among the workhorses of their Church of Ireland parish. They married into the Church of Ireland clergy and local gentry, and, serving in the British army, advanced higher on the social scale.[181]

Those named in the civil establishment had made interest, often long and hard and sometimes deviously, to achieve inclusion. In some ways, being employees of the state did set the lucky few apart from their neighbours. In common with the clergy, they had access to ready money, at least temporarily and under increasingly strict accountancy. With this asset, a rarity in the provinces where small coin was sparse, they lent money and traded.[182] In the parish church of Kinsale in 1715, fifteen functionaries from the customs house there qualified themselves by publicly taking communion.[183] In another busy port, Sligo, a census of 1749 identified the officers of the revenue, as of the parish, by their positions. At Drogheda in the recently rebuilt parish church, two seats were reserved for the revenue officers of the town.[184] These officials might be noted as a distinct group in more controversial circumstances. In hotly contested elections – at Dungarvan in 1703 and Charleville in 1713 – candidates like Badham, able to mobilize their adjutants in the customs and revenue, were accused of intimidating electors. Badham was alleged to have brought thirty-six supernumeraries from the customs house at Dungarvan to vote for him at Charleville.[185] More than Cornelius Buckley were indebted to Badham for their posts. However, the personal dependence of functionaries of the revenue on superiors and patrons coexisted with obligations to the state. What separated the office-holders in the revenue from the bulk of the population was the duty of enforcing laws, often unpopular ones. Officers, when impounding contraband and destroying illicit stills, sometimes encountered violence, and as regularly returned it. Jonas

Griffith, excise officer at Tralee in Kerry, had his horse stabbed under him by an angry crowd.[186] As enforcers of the laws, they were allied with the magistrates, constables and garrisons throughout the island. But revenue officers and their working deputies could not always rely on these supports. In 1754, Squire Puxley, a revenue collector, was shot while trying to enforce the law against smugglers in the remote Beara peninsula. Agents of the Hanoverian order in Ireland were vividly reminded of the hazards that could attend privilege. Puxley had gained from his official employment, but ultimately forfeited his life because of it.[187]

His was an extreme example of the risks faced by officials. More common were the obstacles which impeded the employees of the revenue when they policed their walks and inlets. The value of smuggling to the economy of maritime regions meant that the locally important, including magistrates, connived at and profited from the activity.[188] On occasion, revenue officers collaborated with the malefactors. At Sligo in 1747, it was proposed that the entire establishment of tide-waiters and revenue boatmen in the port should be changed, 'they having been long employed in that place and contracted such acquaintance and interest with the inhabitants as renders them incapable of serving in their several stations'. Fifteen years later, a similar purge was suggested of all except two excise surveyors and gaugers at Cork, and for the same reasons.[189] A lack of interest in pursuing those guilty of regulatory offences sometimes combined with contempt for British statutes which inhibited Irish trade. The otherwise respectable happily broke laws which they regarded as 'oppressive and unjust'.[190] At the same time, hostility towards the revenue officers might be increased by the suspicion that they acted arbitrarily and vindictively.[191]

State service did not always create solidarity among the servants. Resentment sometimes prevented cooperation between civilians and the military. Regular soldiers worked uneasily with the officers of the local militias. Revenue officials occupied an awkward position between the civil power and the army.[192] The resulting tensions fragmented the Protestant interest in Ireland. Superiors resented attempts by underlings to enforce the law. The surveyor at Carlingford, Benjamin Span, provoked a local notable, Lambart Brabazon, when he boarded the latter's pleasure boat. Span's wife was intimidated and his horses maimed, so that he planned to retreat to the safety of Dublin.[193] Orders from Dublin were muted and even muddled by the time they reached the provinces; decrees of the imperial government were neither easily nor precisely enforced when they reached Ireland. In the same way as the harshness of official diktats was moderated by local governors in England and Wales, substituting their own priorities for those of the centre, so in Ireland, much control rested with the locals. The machinery of the state in Ireland, bit by bit becoming more complicated, appeared to be supervised by lords-lieutenant, judges, bishops and commanders shipped over from Britain. This impression created by a few at the top misrepresented a situation in which institutions were mostly staffed by the Protestant – and predominantly conformist – people of Ireland. Nowhere was this better shown than in the Dublin parliament. Its members, nominally constrained by irksome procedures upholding English overlordship, successfully resisted proposals whereby Irish taxes might have been spent outside Ireland.[194]

Yet more impressive as an exercise in self-interest was the blocking, after 1698, of a land tax. Repeatedly, it was rumoured that the English ministry might revive the impost.[195] But the threat was averted. Landowners were lightly taxed, so lessening the disparity between their own and their English counterparts' spending power. In addition, through offices – in the revenue and on the state-subsidized trusts – the adroit controlled the revenues collected on behalf of the state. Some of this money was returned to the propertied through schemes funded by the government: the building of canals and roads, the promotion of flax-growing and linen manufacture, and the siting of barracks across the kingdom.[196] One observer wrote of how 'the public money passed fluent as water through so many sieves, though we may with reason presume that each vessel was sufficiently wet by the way'.[197]

IV

Salaried employments expanded, albeit modestly. Turnpike trusts or barrack, linen and inland navigation boards did not exhaust the stock. Boroughs, guilds, parishes and voluntary foundations needed more staff. From the 1690s, most of these jobs resembled those in the gift of the state in being part of the apparatus of a confessional system. The bigger boroughs appointed recorders and town clerks and licensed attorneys to practise in their jurisdictions. They supplemented the stipends of incumbents, paid for special sermons, lectures and chaplains, and hired schoolmasters.[198] Lesser jobs – mace- or sword-bearer, water-bailiff, beadle and bellman – brought arresting attire, modest emoluments and an afflatus of self-importance.[199] Already in early Stuart Dublin there were ten officers of the mace. To be sword-bearer in late Stuart Dublin was to enjoy an annual salary of £25. The beadles, by the 1690s obliged to swear the Oaths of Supremacy and Allegiance, received a yearly £6.[200] These posts were eagerly sought.[201] The attractions extended beyond the nominal salaries: anciently £4 p.a., but in some cases increased to £10. Holders wore special gowns, which might be supplied as part of the perquisites of the place.[202]

No legal expertise was needed, as the appointments as a sword-bearer in 1650 of a cutler and – in 1715 – of first a weaver and then a baker showed.[203] The main motive for advancing William Barlow in 1654 to be one of the Dublin water-bailiffs was that he had worked steadfastly for the corporation for forty years.[204] Whatever formal duties accompanied the office could be performed by deputies, with the bulk of the fees going to the patentee. Appointment to these places indicated a degree of favour; further favours came in the awarding of leases on municipal property on advantageous terms.

In the provinces, the equivalent posts were fewer and generally paid less generously. In Cork, Drogheda, Kilkenny and Waterford, the wages of the sword-bearer to the corporation varied from £5 to £15. Most were also robed splendidly.[205] At Limerick, the municipal establishment during Charles II's reign consisted of a sword-bearer, paid a yearly £15; four sergeants of the mace, receiving £3; two beadles, at £3 each; a sexton to keep the public clock, also paid £3; the keeper of the common clocks, more generously remunerated with £8, and a water-bailiff allowed an annual £2.[206] The work of these functionaries was not always easy. In eighteenth-century Ennis, as in Dublin, the officers of the mace had to enforce the judgments of the borough court. In the Dublin parish of St Michan's, the beadle and his wife were required to seek out the parents of foundlings.[207]

Towns required of some functionaries more than physical might or alertness. The larger and wealthier, such as Derry and Kinsale, appointed treasurers or chamberlains.[208] Clerkships of markets and weigh-masterships, also in the gift of corporations, promised profits.[209] Kinsale took advantage of potential competition by auctioning the post of water-bailiff to the highest bidder in 1731. Indeed, at Kinsale, even the gaoler, given a yearly wage of £6, was required to provide a surety of £100. Only someone of modest substance could do so; in return, as the terms indicated, profits were to be made.[210] Technically more demanding, potentially lucrative and prestigious were the positions of town clerk and recorder. In the later seventeenth century, the annual remuneration, although not derisory, mattered less than the introductions to the locally important and to the official and legal worlds of Dublin. At Drogheda soon after Charles II was restored, the town clerk received £10, but was given a special payment of £6 13s. 4d. – perhaps as recompense for particularly onerous duties when charters and civic property had to be confirmed. In Kinsale, the town clerk was paid only £6 p.a, but at Waterford, £20.[211] In the small Cork town of Clonakilty, this official's salary was a modest £3. However, he was permitted to levy a fee from all burgesses and freemen. Also, by 1703, he deputized for the recorder. As so often, the stated wage bore little relation to total earnings. Nor were many of these duties the sole occupation of the holder, but simply one in a quiver full of miscellaneous arrows.

Civic positions were attractive enough to become venal, in the same way as patentee places. In 1664, Owen Silver rented the town clerkship of Youghal for ten shillings yearly. He united this job with the recordership of the borough. Silver was well qualified, and met the legal needs of the town at a busy moment. As legal luminary, he dealt with the government in Dublin. Silver flourished, and soon his family sparkled as country squires.[212] In Drogheda, Alderman Edward Singleton, having obtained the town clerkship of his borough, bequeathed it to a son. The latter, Henry Singleton, reached the chief justiceship.[213] Although Singleton lorded it over the grandest Dublin society, he did not abandon his house in Drogheda, which remained a noteworthy sight in the 1750s, and he was buried in the parish church there.[214] In 1690, a busy Corkonian enquired how he could purchase the town clerkship of Cork, hoping thereby to provide for his son. Plans for the eighteen-year-old had been wrecked by the Jacobite interlude. The family had hopped over to Minehead, and the promising lad had been put into the 'great school' at Tiverton. Owing to losses in the upheaval, he felt unable to place the son at Trinity College, but still hoped that he might study law. The father offered to pay an honest deputy to do the work, but the deal was never done.[215] At Waterford in 1712 it was possible for the town clerk to be succeeded by a brother whose training had been an apprenticeship with the retiring sibling.[216] However, the affairs of towns like Cork and Waterford demanded the full time of its officials, and mastery of legal processes.

The practices of treating municipal posts as private property and protracted absence, winked at when the supply of Protestant functionaries was inadequate, were no longer acceptable to the bigger boroughs by the eighteenth century. They had to extort a higher price, in terms of service, from those whom they appointed. This changing situation made anachronistic one of the final acts of Ormonde as lord-lieutenant. In 1713, he granted in trust to the son of Alderman Robert Dent the offices of town clerk and clerk of the peace in the corporation of Londonderry. These were intended to support Dent's widowed mother and her nine children.[217] Even in Dublin during George II's reign, Henry Gonne secured the succession to his father as town clerk. The son, like the father and earlier town clerks, was an attorney working in the Exchequer Court, and had served his apprenticeship with his parent. In return for the dignity, he was to pay the city an annual rent of £100. Presumably he recouped this – and more – through the fees that he collected, especially in the Tholsel Court of the city. On the city's side, because the town clerk's duties (unlike the recorder's) had become essentially formulaic, it no longer needed to keep strict control over the selection of this functionary.[218]

Towns and parishes, in handing out their limited offices, conferred and received honour. Once confessional exclusions strengthened in the 1650s, and again in the 1690s, towns recently ruled by Catholics struggled to find suitable officers. At Galway, Colonel Theodore Russell acted as mayor for ten years of Charles II's reign. Russell, often away in England, asked to be reimbursed at the startling rate of £200 p.a. In the end, the borough compromised with yearly pay of £100.[219] Galway during the early 1680s also suffered from a titular recorder, William Sprigg, who was seldom available. Thomas Yeeden, the deputy, did most of the work.[220] In 1716, when Counsellor Farren deputized for the recorder of Kinsale, the corporation resolved to dock from the absent recorder's salary the fee paid to Farren.[221] Waterford corporation sacked its recorder of ten years' standing, Robert Marshall, in 1736. Among other neglects, Marshall was said to have put in as his deputy a grocer, 'never bred to a learned profession'. This rebuff did not stop Marshall's ascent into the judiciary.[222]

For young barristers like Richard Cox, Alan Brodrick, Francis Bernard and Henry Singleton, recorderships in their local towns – Kinsale, Clonakilty, Cork and Drogheda – served as base camps from which to scale the legal peaks of the Dublin Four Courts.[223] Others, whether contentedly or not, vegetated in municipal offices. At Atherdee, in Louth, a qualified barrister, Thomas Burton, accepted the recordership in 1662. Burton and his counterpart in restoration Youghal were paid £10 yearly. Richard Hungerford was chosen as deputy recorder of Clonakilty in 1715, although he apparently lacked formal legal qualifications. Clonakilty, although a parliamentary borough, did not generate enough litigation to force its deputy recorder into frequent attendance in Dublin.[224]

As the supply of potential Protestant officials increased, so rivals competed for the town clerkships and recorderships, just as others sought church livings, military commissions and patentee posts. This helped boroughs to choose those likely to further local concerns. In Galway, the re-election of the town clerk, Robert Shaw, was opposed in 1681. Shaw, a pluralist who practised as an attorney in the Tholsel Court and held the clerkship of the peace and staple, had been superseded by 1682.[225] At Waterford in 1701, Richard Cox, a judge and soon to be lord chancellor, promoted his young neighbour and political ally, Francis Bernard, as its next recorder. The corporation ignored Cox's advocacy, and instead elected Minard Christian, a candidate with much stronger local links.[226] Christian took his duties seriously enough to travel to England and there harry those believed to be enemies of Waterford.[227] In 1746, the borough of Athy in County Kildare replaced the incumbent recorder, Nicholas Aylward, with Robert Downes.

Aylward may have offended through neglect or his politics.[228] In Dublin during the 1760s, four candidates appeared for the vacant recordership. The salary attached to the office fluctuated with the occupant's and the municipality's political allegiances. In 1734, Eaton Stannard saw his salary increased from £35 to £150. His successor, Thomas Morgan, started at a modest £50, but was soon granted £150 p.a.[229]

At a lower level, parishes and their vestries, loaded with administrative chores, hired permanent and salaried clerks.[230] The parish clerk, assisting at religious services, was a canonical requirement; the vestry clerk, merely an administrative convenience.[231] At St John's in Dublin in 1691, one brother succeeded another as parish clerk.[232] In the Cork parish of Bandon – part urban, part rural – the clerk was recompensed by dues paid by parishioners for his services. When, in 1729, these were withheld, he was guaranteed a minimum of thirty shillings yearly. The County Meath parish of Agher paid its clerk an annual £5. In another Meath parish, Kells, the clerk, was paid partly in kind. This engendered disputes, as did his bringing vexatious suits against parishioners in the bishop's court. During the 1750s, the wage of this functionary rose from an annual £10 to £15 p.a, probably reflecting the difficulty in this predominantly Catholic area around Kells of finding a suitable candidate. So much is suggested by the inducements of £10 offered to Fairfax Ennis to take the job, and a further £10 if he converted.[233] In the 1720s, the vestry clerk of the Dublin parish of St Catherine's saw his yearly pay double to £8. His counterpart at St Bride's received £10. At St Michan's, the stipend crept up from £14 13s. 4d. to £20 in 1761. The vestry clerk there also taught in the parochial school.[234] Clearly, the skills needed as clerk (or organist) differed from those commanded by beadles. For the last, as with the uniformed attendants of the corporations, a striking rig – cloak, hat and a profusion of gold lace – was an important element in the remuneration.[235] Other benefits came the way of these functionaries. At Carlow in 1724, the parish bore the costs – modest – of burying its beadle. At Castle Durrow, the local landowner donated ten shillings for a winter coat to the parish clerk during the hard winter of 1740.[236]

The chartered trading companies, capitular and charitable foundations also supported small permanent staffs. Dublin, again, set a standard in numbers and remuneration not surpassed elsewhere. During the 1690s, the Weavers' Guild paid its clerk £4 10s.[237] By the 1720s, the Barber Surgeons' Company allowed its clerk £6 p.a. This functionary was styled 'gentleman', and would later be pensioned off with a yearly £6.[238] The Merchants' Guild of the capital, the most prestigious, allowed its clerk £10 in the 1660s. By 1709, the Guild of St Anne's gave its clerk and receiver £14 yearly.[239] The clerkship of the Dublin Goldsmiths' Company was attractive enough to generate competition in the 1690s.[240] Skills of accountancy and penmanship, as well as literacy, were needed, and perhaps explained why the courtesy of 'gent' was extended to these hirelings. Often duties were readily combined with other work. In 1747, the beadle of the Apothecaries' Guild doubled as a victualler. Paid an annual £6, he cut a striking figure in orange cloak with purple cape and hat with silver lace.[241] Through pragmatic pluralism an adequate income might be earned.

Office-holders, whether of the state, the revenue, the municipality, the trading incorporations, the parishes or the voluntary associations, were most densely concentrated in Dublin. Outside the larger towns, a permanent bureaucracy was slower to develop and remained smaller. Clerkships of the peace and crown and county treasurerships, potentially onerous and contentious, were sought. [242] Edmund Walpole, a prominent lawyer in Athlone, engrossed the places of clerk of the peace and coroner for Roscommon.[243] By 1746, Paul Whichcote, clerk of the crown in Leinster, living outside London, lamented that the post yielded him no profit. Moreover, his hopes of disposing of it to another had been dashed by a recent resolution of the Irish parliament.[244] Whichcote had gained the clerkship from George I in 1724.[245] His powers under it, and with them the profits, had soon been questioned. The deputies whom he nominated to officiate in the separate counties of Leinster (no doubt for a handsome consideration) were obstructed by others named by local notables, such as Lords Drogheda and Meath, by virtue of their commissions as *Custodes Rotulorum*.[246] Whichcote, in common with the clerks for Munster and Ulster, resided outside Ireland, and became unpopular for that reason. Contrary to what he asserted, the post was thought to yield him a useful £250 p. a.[247]

Those grubbing about for offices resorted to some grubby tricks. Just as the offices could confer prestige on the holders, intermediaries who had promised but then failed to procure places for clients lost face. The remuneration and even the standing of these offices hardly seemed commensurate with the intrigue to secure them. Intangibles, the sense of authority and local precedence or the opportunity to name underlings, contributed to the demand. But in the end, the driving force remained a need to supplement inheritances, no matter how modestly. A commentator in 1728 sympathized with the lot of younger sons, 'either above or unacquainted with trades'. 'Howsoever well affected and qualified', they were for the 'most part out of the road of employments or preferments, either ecclesiastical, civil or military'.[248] Eldest sons also needed to add to the often paltry revenues from property. Spencer, the north Cork squire, in his protracted quest for civil employment, exemplified this. Office, like a fortunate marriage, beckoned more in prospect than in actuality. It was elusive, and those whom it eluded cursed both the system and their luckier rivals. Fewer than the envious supposed gained either an heiress or an office. Yet, the officers and officials were important presences. No less than the rural freeholders and urban freemen, they benefited from the Protestant monopolies created after 1649. Even for the relatively humble tasks associated with vestries or chartered companies, the officials were typically Protestants serving Protestant organizations. The holders of an office which carried a regular salary and conferred precedence, once the lesser functionaries were counted, numbered 2,000 to 3,000. Some, by virtue of inheritance, professional qualifications or other occupation, were already enumerated among the quality. So what proportion used the extra leverage of an established office to prise open the narrow aperture into gentility and respectability can only be guessed.

Office-holders hardly united behind either the ruling dynasty or impersonal British state in its Irish manifestation. They did not obviously hasten the incorporation of Ireland into a British or imperial system.[249] In part this was because the continued appointment of English and Welsh to prestigious posts, and then their absence from them, opened a gulf between nominal holders and those who discharged the essential duties. The active office-holders tended to be those reared in Ireland. They might pride themselves on being local agents of the monarch, and therefore identified with a transnational monarchy. However, there is little sign of bureaucrats in Ireland feeling solidarity with their counterparts in other of the Stuarts' or Hanoverians' possessions. Indeed, there was little solidarity and much rivalry between employees of separate departments and institutions in Dublin. In some instances, they competed against each other for the same business and fees.[250] In addition, these officials varied in their origins, the routes by which they had arrived at their stations and their remuneration. By the eighteenth century, relevant training and personal attendance were demanded. Fees were more closely monitored and sales of places discouraged. However, this greater rigour did not instil a common philosophy of public service. Nor, to the fury of ministers, did the grant of office to Irish Protestants hobble them. Important office-holders, oblivious apparently to any debt of gratitude, strayed regularly into political opposition.[251]

Atomized departments engendered their own local loyalties. The distant – the king – and the abstract – the Protestant interest, the empire or the state – exerted less power. By the 1690s, minor worthies in small towns were required to swear oaths to a monarch distant in England (or Holland or Hanover).[252] Images – heads on coins or coats of arms in churches and courtrooms – and words – proclamations and prayers – might call to mind the ultimate spring in the machine of which the functionary was a cog.[253] Yet, in the provinces, the servants of the state were not always

strongly aware of even the local representative of that monarch, the lord-
lieutenant in Dublin. The viceroy alighted briefly like a bird of passage,
and, by the eighteenth century, rarely toured the hinterlands. In the
localities, rituals in which the officers joined – parading in gowns and
preceded by regalia to church or court – mimicked the choreography
of state days in Dublin and even in London. At New Ross, the chief
magistrate (or sovereign) walking to Protestant worship with other corporation notables belonged to a chain of command which stretched from
the Wexford town through Dublin to the British monarchy. How conscious of this either the sovereign or the townspeople were may be
doubted. Armed with a rod, 'by way of distinction', he personified a more
local jurisdiction.[254] In Youghal, the civic sword-bearer rested his symbol
of authority in a purpose-carpentered holder during services in the parish
church. In doing so, he followed rituals observed on other shores of the
Hanoverians' territories.[255] But whether any in the Youghal congregation
made that connection rather than noting the local officials from whom
wages, pensions, uniforms and leases flowed may again be questioned.

Service as a paid – and sometimes unpaid – official fostered feelings of
importance.[256] It differentiated a fortunate minority from the bulk of their
co-religionists. In Ireland, privilege, enjoyed by all office-holders, although
usually modest, in some measure also rested on confessional exclusions.
These prohibitions, increased after 1649 and completed with the Test Act
of 1704, defined the small worlds of the law courts, revenue offices, Church
of Ireland parishes, municipal and trading corporations and many voluntary associations. Membership of this confessional community, not any
shared education or philosophy, united the lucky few in established offices.

Chapter 7

Soldiers and Sailors

I

In 1745, a squire down on his luck considered how best to subsist. Becoming a merchant was swiftly rejected, as he had not been 'educated in a way of understanding trade'. The options reduced themselves to two: a commission in the army, 'the genteelest'; or a patentee office on the Irish civil establishment, thought 'the easiest'. After a long wait and much lobbying, the erstwhile squire was appointed to a post in the revenue, worth – on paper – £40.[1] Back in Queen Anne's reign, the son of a Church of Ireland bishop was undecided between soldiering and ordination.[2] In the event, the black coat of the cleric was preferred to the red of the officer. At the same time, Archbishop William King in his table talk contended, 'that when gentlemen could not prevail upon their sons to study either divinity, law or physick, they generally purchased for them a commission in the army as the last refuge'.[3] For some, serving in the forces was opportunistic, even impromptu. Others, in contrast, single-mindedly pursued the career. In 1690 Richard Waring, the younger son of an Ulster squire, wanted a captaincy of grenadiers. For an outlay of £100 or £150 on the commission, he would soon enjoy a yearly £500. The purchase was, additionally, an investment which might in time be sold for £1,200 or £1,400. Equally important for Waring was his belief that the captaincy constituted a 'genteel, pretty post, fit for any private gentleman in England'.[4]

Military and naval service attracted the sons of Irish Protestant settlers, as it did the Catholics whom the newcomers had supplanted. Whereas the Catholics usually enlisted under continental and Catholic monarchs, Protestants from Ireland generally – but not always – served under the British colours.[5] They were beguiled by the prospect of a salary, although it was often paid irregularly. A life removed from the placid Irish provinces was also exciting, at least in anticipation. It was, moreover, an occupation which did not diminish the officers' own or their contemporaries' sense of gentility. Soldiering also fitted well with the military traditions on which settler society was founded and to which it still subscribed.[6]

Fighting had first brought the founders of landed dynasties to Ireland. Paid partly or wholly in land, some of these servitors had stayed. During the century after the 1690s, Ireland ceased to be an important theatre of war. Even before that, the material rewards for victorious commanders dwindled. William III's wish to gratify intimates from his campaigns was frustrated by the Irish parliament and instead his adjutants were decorated with magnificent Irish titles: Schomberg, as duke of Leinster; Ruvigny, earl of Galway. However, William's involvement in European warfare drew in England and Protestant Ireland. From 1699, a force of 12,000 was to be stationed in and paid by Ireland.[7] In 1752, the army was dispersed in fifty-two locations in Ireland.[8] Those born in Ireland were formally excluded. Even before the prohibition was surreptitiously breached, the army afforded Irish Protestants chances of prestigious and lucrative employment.[9] Indeed, the opportunities reconciled many of the disgruntled Irish Protestants to their country's increasing constitutional subordination to England. The cynical, indeed, predicted that the troublesome patriots would quickly forget their opposition to an enlargement of the military establishment supported by Ireland as they realized that any increase would add to the number of commissions available for their sons (and even for themselves).[10] The officer corps numbered between 650 and 700 during George I's reign, while non-regimental posts and those in the artillery train supported another 167. If present in the island, these army officers were more or less equal in numbers to the beneficed clergy and the various legal practitioners.[11] In addition, the construction of barracks across the kingdom added twenty-five places as barrack-masters to those in the revenue.[12] Building and supplying these quarters benefited many more civilians.

Irish Protestants seemingly equalled their Scottish contemporaries in their ability to colonize the profession of arms. In the first half of the eighteenth century, a quarter of all regimental officers and about a fifth of all colonels in the British army were Scots.[13] If, as has been asserted, between one quarter and one third of the officers around 1760 were from Ireland, then as many as a thousand Irish Protestants were thus employed.[14] Thereby – in theory at least – they were removed temporarily from Ireland. Absence reduced the officers' impact on the structure and culture of Irish Protestant communities. However, even when absent their remittances, gifts and letters had some influence over the society from which they hailed. On furlough and in retirement, they were a formidable component. Contemporaries argued about the benefits and drawbacks. Swift and Sheridan disliked the pretensions of the veterans thronging

Dublin after the War of the Spanish Succession, who aspired to be 'dictators of behaviour, dress and politeness'.[15] Some serving in the army agreed that the garrisons preserved a 'Gothic barbarism' long banished from polite civilian society.[16] Late in the 1760s, a thoughtful member of the Irish parliament worried lest gratitude to the soldiery make civilians too fond of their presence. Robert French was alarmed to see the sons of peers and the gentry 'running under military discipline who may be future guardians of our liberties'. Mindful of the tyranny introduced by victorious generals, French favoured 'a well regulated militia' rather than a standing army.[17] Others credited the army officers with a civilizing effect on Protestant Ireland. In 1759, they were publicly praised for introducing into the kingdom 'such manifest degrees of politeness in behaviour, regularity of conduct, affability of manners, punctuality in dealing and generous but prudently governed domestic economy'.[18]

Those who disputed how the soldiery affected Irish Protestant society tended to conflate two discrete groups: those born in Ireland and so notionally obliged to serve elsewhere; and soldiers from other parts of the Hanoverians' empire quartered temporarily in Ireland. The two contingents need first to be considered separately in order then to evaluate their rather different contributions to Irish Protestant society. The issues of the impact and influence of military and naval officers invite reflections on their potential to serve as agents through which Ireland could be better integrated, both politically and culturally, into a 'British' system.[19]

How to secure military commissions, whether on the Irish or British establishment, preoccupied generations of hopefuls. As in the judiciary, Church and civil administration, the English government tended to reserve the highest prizes for its own. As a result, many from Ireland were denied what they regarded as their due. In the 1670s and 1680s, as London asserted greater control over the Treasury, army and navy, so the power of the important in Ireland to distribute largesse diminished. Lords-lieutenant in Dublin protested. Without the means to reward supporters, their standing was whittled away.[20] In 1703, Queen Anne reassured the new lord-lieutenant, Ormonde, that she would not weaken his authority by acceding to requests for appointment made in London.[21] Nevertheless, the fear of governors in Dublin that they were being bypassed and so reduced to political nullities recurred.[22] By 1727, it has been estimated that no more than 150 offices remained in the viceroy's gift. The right to name the lowest ranks of commissioned officers – ensigns and cornets – was removed.[23] Governors in Dublin, when distributing their depleted stock of goodies, had to balance demands from patrons, allies, rivals and clients in England and Ireland. These numerous suitors, if disappointed, aspersed the incumbent viceroy, and the aspersions carried a dangerous political charge.[24]

Often the stock was too meagre to satisfy all the clamant. In military matters, lords-lieutenant had to endure growing interference from monarchs keen both to introduce greater efficiency and to please favourites. English commanders-in-chief, the War Office, the Board of General Officers and lords of the Admiralty by interfering reduced further the powers of the nominal ruler in Dublin.[25] Throughout the sixteenth century and much of the seventeenth, the principal function of the viceroy had been military. In the later seventeenth century, more settled conditions, together with the greater integration of the Irish administration into the British system, reduced this work. For a time, under the dukes of Ormonde, this trend was masked.[26] The second duke, by virtue of his high rank in the army (in 1712 he became commander-in-chief), the martial traditions of his family and his own temperament, attended minutely to military matters.[27] More to the point, thanks to his post within the British army, he helped others from Ireland into army commissions. Once Ormonde had departed, the consequences of the lord-lieutenancy being uncoupled from the command of the army in Ireland showed more clearly. Some governors still strutted in their gaudy regimentals, but others paraded their civilian status.[28] Lords-lieutenant were sometimes caught in the crossfire as the commander-in-chief skirmished with his counterpart and the Board of General Officers in London. As in the similar tussles over civil appointments between the Revenue commissioners in Dublin and the lords of the Treasury at Whitehall, the lord lieutenant seemed little better than a bystander.

Once the viceroy ceased to be a sure route to military preferment, would-be officers were bewildered as to whom they should approach. During the 1680s, some officers cashiered by James II were assisted by early contact with the Prince of Orange.[29] These ties tightened when William himself campaigned in Ireland. As early as 1690, Frederick Hamilton from County Londonderry, a victim of James II's and Tyrconnell's remodellings, bragged of his power as a broker at court.[30] The subsequent recruitment of armies to fight first William III's continental wars and then the War of the Spanish Succession afforded chances for Protestants in Ireland which may never have recurred on the same scale.[31] The prominence of a few Irish Protestants within the army, headed by the second duke of Ormonde, helped others into junior posts.[32] Highly placed officers from Ireland – Peter Echlin, Richard Gorges, Frederick and Hans Hamilton, Richard Ingoldsby, Nathaniel Kane, William and Moses Leathes, James Macartney, Charles Otway, Robert Stearne, Richard Waring and Owen Wynne – offered possibilities.[33] The well-connected mobilized the interest of acquaintances or kindred in the ministry or high command in Britain. The more obscure depended on intermediaries. Since demand exceeded the supply of commissions, competition could be fierce. Livelihoods were at stake. Cash was a prerequisite, but alone did not ensure entry into the army (or navy). Being permitted to buy a commission depended on making interest powerfully. In 1691, the Ulsterman Richard Waring had first to prise from reluctant parents his portion of cash with which to pay for the desired post. Next he needed the approval of Ormonde. In catching the eye of the latter he was helped by a family connection, through his elder brother, with the duke's younger brother. Others in Ormonde's entourage, as neighbours of the Warings in Ulster, seconded the aspirant's request.

Personal qualities were not irrelevant. Waring's conduct in the recent campaign assisted his claims. He also possessed a zest for the military life. Studying at Trinity College in Dublin, Waring had seized on the renewed conflict during 1689–90 as the chance for profiteering on the scale of the 1640s and 1650s, from which his own father had benefited.[34] A similar opportunism took him to campaign with William III in the Low Countries. Earlier, William's presence in Ulster may have fostered a personal allegiance among some notables like the Warings. That interest as well as money still had to be deployed to join the officer corps was shown in 1717 when Richard Waring, now a general, sailed back to Dublin. His errand was to secure a cornetcy in his own regiment for his heir. To this end, the father entreated the backing of his former comrade and senior, General Frederick Hamilton.[35] At the same time, another from Ireland travelled in the opposite direction. Amateur Bouhéreau, the son of a Huguenot who had settled in Dublin and become first keeper of Archbishop Marsh's library, had soldiered for ten years. In 1715, he went to England to solicit for a commission in one of the new regiments being raised. By 1716 he had succeeded, and returned with his troop to Ireland. Fresh disbandment in 1717 again propelled Amateur Bouhéreau to England. He was pleased to be instated as major of the garrison in Dublin, and even more so to be given a command of a company of the old corps by the lord-lieutenant, Bolton.[36]

Bouhéreau's success contrasted with the frustrations of another family of Huguenots in Ireland. Jacques Fontaine first settled in the wild Beara peninsula of west Cork and then moved to Dublin to run a school. He was aggrieved at the way superiors treated his son. Backing from Sir Richard Ingoldsby, a governor of Ireland and leading commander under Queen Anne, had secured the son's initial advancement to be an ensign. Fontaine *père* recalled that he had not had to buy the commission but only equip the young officer. Fitting him out cost £70. Thereafter, the boy's career languished. Sent to fight in Spain under the commander, Lord Slane, 'an unfair and greedy man as well as a drunkard and debauched', the victimized Fontaine because a protégé of Ingoldsby.[37] The senior Fontaine, although a Huguenot among whom military traditions were powerful, was reluctant to let young John Fontaine be exposed to soldiering. The father rejoiced when the son returned: 'he has not killed anybody or acquired any bad habit, for which I praise the infinite bounty of the Almighty'.[38] Happier was the experience of James Dougherty, son of an attorney. The war of 1689–91 obliged Dougherty to abandon trade. He purchased a commission as an ensign for £75. This led to a captaincy and service in England, Spain, America and Barbados. Captain Dougherty was remembered as 'the properest son', 'the best accomplished' of his siblings, who kept good company and was much respected.[39] Arthur Ussher, from the borders of west Waterford and east Cork, became captain of a company in 1708. In 1727 he was still in the army. He had served in the Low Countries, but in 1719 was stationed in the more familiar setting of Waterford.[40] The profits of soldiering enabled Ussher to consolidate his and his family's position among the squirearchy of the area.[41]

As with vacancies in the Church and civil administration, so in the forces early application was regarded as vital. This explained an otherwise morbid obsession with the health of existing incumbents and an unseemly haste in acting before the dead were buried. One junior officer, eager for promotion, begged a patron in London not to spread the news that a captain had died, since 'no body hardly knows of it but I and another'. In particular the colonel was not yet to be told of the event, 'by reason he hath so many hangers about him, it would spoil all'.[42] Hopes of placements rose in Ireland when war was rumoured. Early in the 1740s, talk of fresh fighting heartened hopefuls. New regiments would be raised, and the old recruited. Even so, those remote in Ireland often thought themselves at a disadvantage, being so distant from the fresh allocation of favours. In 1740, the distressed squire of Renny in the north of County Cork chose this seemingly propitious moment to sue for a commission. A name (Spencer) shared with the commander-in-chief, the duke of Marlborough, was an asset on which he traded. He, and his supporters, rehearsed the services of ancestors in Ireland. Renny's grandfather had shown William III the terrain before the battle of Aughrim in 1691: earlier, Edmund Spenser, the poet, had served Queen Elizabeth I in Ireland. Spencer's suit for employment was supported by officials and politicians in Ireland.[43] Yet they failed to unlock the door to preferment. Spencer himself wavered between concentrating all his efforts in Dublin and transferring his campaign to England. Without intimacy with the powerful in either capital, he was at a loss as to how best to proceed.[44] In consequence, an episodic campaign for an army commission failed. After a long pursuit – upwards of fifteen years – he finally bagged a more modest quarry: a post in the revenue.[45] Meanwhile, his brother Nathaniel had been more readily accepted as an army recruit, only to be rejected after a week of arduous training as too short. Nathaniel Spencer was immediately compensated with a place in the revenue.[46]

In 1705, a disappointed applicant railed that 'merit is not preferred'.[47] Nor were sentiment and connections invariably successful. In 1742 Richard Edwards recited his many relations who had already served in the British army, in order to second his entreaty for a commission.[48] Earlier, a supplicant for a colonelcy catalogued service which had taken him from Ireland to North America, Spain and Flanders.[49] Patrons received more requests for assistance than they could satisfy. The important to whom the optimists and desperate looked were caught in reciprocal relationships which could cause inconvenience. One disappointed suitor for promotion taxed his patron that his rivals had succeeded because 'their friends are sincere friends'.[50] Not just the lord-lieutenant, but others high in Protestant Ireland, risked humiliation if they failed to win places for followers. In 1707, the archbishop of Dublin, when trying to put a nephew into the army, pleaded with Edward Southwell, an official familiar with government in both Ireland and England, 'I am at a loss how or who to ask it and I beg the favour of you to help me in this, as you have done in many cases'.[51] Even the grand were beset both by uncertainty and anxiety lest they be repulsed. Archbishop King solicited on behalf of his brother-in-law, Charles Irvine, who aspired to a lieutenant-colonelcy. In 1709 and 1710, the archbishop wrote to Ormonde and his predecessor as lord-lieutenant, Rochester, but confessed disarmingly that he had no faith in such appeals.[52] Later, King in his capacity as lord justice hoped he might appoint his kinsman as his own aide-de-camp. However, the lord-lieutenant foisted another on him.[53] In 1718, King approached Lord Cadogan, a commander with vestigial Irish links. The archbishop confided, 'it can't but be a great mortification to have my recommendation so much slighted as not to succeed in any one instance'.[54] This sentiment had been voiced earlier in 1690, when William Jephson had admitted, 'I am really more concerned . . . for the discredit of being baffled in so modest a pretension . . . than for the profit of it'.[55] Katherine Conolly, the widow of the Speaker, was equally discomposed that her applications on behalf of others might be ignored, so lowering her reputation.[56]

Rebuffs convinced many in Ireland that they were at a disadvantage when patronage was disbursed. The humble simply did not 'know where to apply'.[57] Another disappointed of a military commission concluded in 1741, 'recommendations from persons of ever so great weight and dignity do it seems but faintly operate in matters where *aurum potabile* has been the predominant ingredient to influence all before it'.[58] It was a commonplace that 'the person who best solicits is the soonest provided for'.[59] Merit, it was felt, counted for little.[60] Others added that 'an Irish interest' seldom triumphed, particularly when competing against those backed by the powerful in England.[61] This again spoke of the practical impediments in the way of the modest from Ireland picking their way through the mazes of Whitehall, St James's and Westminster. Not just favour, but disfavour could also show the relative standing of suitors and patrons. The Ormondes, formidable in their control of army posts, were identified with particular groups of partisans: the first duke with the returned royalists; the second with the emergent Tories. Those belonging to opposed groupings traced any slights and disappointments to the dukes.[62] Dudley Cosby, the squire of Stradbally, and Henry Conyngham, son and heir of the Donegal hero, Sir Albert Conyngham and brother-in-law of the future Speaker Conolly, blamed Ormonde's vindictiveness when they were posted to the Iberian peninsula during the War of the Spanish Succession.[63] Political alignment or social obscurity continued to arrest progress. Nicholas Delacherois, son of a Huguenot family involved in the linen trade around Lisburn, secured a lieutenancy in the 9th Regiment in 1756. Thereafter, he marked time. Without the right connections, only money would advance him quickly. But he lacked the £1,200 to £1,500 needed for a captaincy. Only the death of a wealthy relative, Lady Mountalexander, gave him the necessary in 1771.[64] By then, too, he was recommended by long service.

Efforts to limit or end purchase, favoured by English sovereigns and commanders, never eradicated venality. Under assorted guises – the money paid was represented as a pension for the retiring officer – sales continued.[65] The practice sometimes excused the powerlessness of patrons. In 1758, the lord-lieutenant Bedford explained how 'by the pernicious custom of buying and selling, I have very few opportunities of promoting those who by long service in the corps have a just pretence to expect a rise'. In this way, Bedford, although eager to promote veterans in Ireland, was unable to stop the advance of strangers.[66] The caprices of the system – and of those running it – baffled the uninitiated or unconnected. It remained clear that money and patrons were required, but the relative importance of these two ingredients varied. An increasing professionalism in the forces also meant that requests had to be backed by some evidence of aptitude or experience.[67]

The cost of commissions rose steadily. Prices varied according to the type and allure of the regiment. A commission in the cavalry was more expensive than one in the infantry. Supply contracted during intermittent periods of peace and prices increased accordingly. In 1691, Richard Waring spent £100 to £150 on his commission as captain. The true costs were greater, owing to the need to equip himself with uniform, weapons and horse. He expected to make £500 p.a., in line with the pay of a captain in 1740.[68] Waring flourished. Within seven years, he had £1,000 to invest.[69] This happy situation arose partly from the trade of war, but also through a good marriage.[70] In 1721, Waring, by then a general, sold his colonelcy to another from Ireland, Viscount Shannon, for £7,500. Not only did this look a reasonable return on the initial, modest investment, it allowed General Waring to set himself up in style, first with a house in Westminster and then a country estate in Berkshire.[71] Waring had been favoured both by the special opportunities offered by the War of the Spanish Succession and by his marriage. Jack Sotheby from Drogheda profited less sensationally from the captaincy which he had acquired during the same war. In 1727, it was reported that he had 'handsomely quitted his redcoat', and was £1,000 in pocket.[72] Not all seized the chance of a military occupation so enthusiastically. Will Close, a nephew of Richard Waring, unfitted for Trinity College Dublin, was sent to soldier. The youth would have preferred to become a merchant. His severe grandfather, William Waring, decreed that Close could not serve as a private and must have a commission. His uncle advised a lieutenancy, not an ensigncy.[73] Others in the army were enlisted to help, notably the future lieutenant-general Frederick Hamilton and his brother, Colonel Hans Hamilton.[74] Close's commission was duly purchased: for £160.[75] It proved a less satisfactory investment than Richard Waring's. Close served in the Netherlands, but without conspicuous success.[76]

There was a danger that the rising prices of military commissions would put them beyond the reach of most in Ireland. Archbishop King took seriously his responsibilities as executor to his erstwhile colleague on the bench, Samuel Foley, bishop of Down and Connor. But in 1710, the archbishop jibbed at paying £2,400 for a captaincy in the dragoons for the young Foley. King argued that the post, commanding an annual salary of £200, was worth only £1,400. The archbishop, like other trustees and parents, compared this investment with alternatives. In effect, the price represented seven years' purchase, but it differed from the purchase of land, office or an apprenticeship. Wartime commissions carried no security of tenure, and could be terminated abruptly.[77] This uncertainty was one factor in the hostility of some elders to the army as an occupation. By 1720, a tariff attempted to regulate the prices for which commissions would be sold. They ranged from £9,000 for a colonelcy of dragoons to £170 for an ensigncy in a foot regiment on foreign duty. By the 1760s, the lowest commission in the infantry could be bought for £400.[78] These charges surpassed those of apprenticeships. They were closer to what it cost to train a cleric, medic or lawyer, but the expenses of preparing for the professions were spread over several years rather than having to be met at once. In 1742 an officer in Dublin, although confident of the lord-lieutenant's support, feared he would have to spend £1,200 to obtain a captaincy.[79] The previous year the archdeacon of Meath had spent £800 on a cornetcy for a son. To this expenditure had to be added another £150 for horse and uniform.[80] In 1750, a second lieutenancy, without pay, was being touted for 200 guineas. In 1752, an ensign's commission, the first rung on the ladder, was priced at £450.[81]

Boys destined for the army had often been schooled in the same establishments as those intended for the Church and the law. Even if they then avoided the expense of the university, they had to be prepared for military service either at an academy or by undertaking practical instruction. Nathaniel Clements, an affluent officer of the Dublin Treasury, had subsidized the upbringing of a brother's family. The brother, Colonel Harry Clements, was killed at Fontenoy in 1745. When a son, Lieutenant Robert Clements, died in battle in Flanders two years later, the uncle calculated brutally that he had lost £1,000: apparently the costs of the youth's education and commission.[82] Before joining his regiment, the lieutenant had been entered in an academy in Brussels.[83] Earlier, General Waring had proposed to prepare his own heir by putting him into an academy in Angers.[84] A cheaper, though not inexpensive, option, was to enrol a son in the academy at Portsmouth which equipped the young for the navy.[85]

The difficulty of raising such sums, often greater than the annual revenues of an Irish squire, deterred some and involved many in credit transactions which left them indebted. Philip Rawson, a landowner in King's County, continued to importune his patron, Lord Gowran, even when serving in England. Unexpected expenses combined with irregular pay to embarrass this officer. He was dogged by the debt entailed by borrowing to buy his commission on the security of his lands.[86] The hopeful or desperate strained to find the necessary funds. They were beguiled by the regular pay and the notion that in time they would sell the commission for a good profit. Wages stretched from £748 5s. for a colonel in a smart regiment, through £438 for a colonel of foot to £66 18s. 4d. for an ensign.[87] In 1759, the average earnings of an army officer in England were put at only £100. In 1768, this was the total that an officer from Ulster had to live on in his foreign quarters.[88] Many junior officers were disappointed by these modest returns. An officer from Ireland serving in the Scottish campaign of 1745–46 complained that he, like all military men, was 'very poor'. In 1749 the would-be officer, Edmund Spencer, conceded that an army commission offered only 'poor bread'.[89] Samuel Bagshawe, a colonel stationed in Ireland for much of the 1740s and 1750s, sought unavailingly to limit his spending. Economies, such as living in barracks or during part of the year in a provincial town rather than Dublin, were contemplated. Once married, to a bride from the landowning hierarchy of Fermanagh, he sought to retrench. In 1750, Bagshawe needed to cut £104 from his annual spending if he were to subsist on his pay as a colonel of almost £230.[90]

Officers were embarrassed by debts incurred to enter the army corps. They were also plunged into emulative and competitive spending in the mess and on campaign. In 1757, the recently commissioned Nicholas Delacherois found Dublin life more expensive than Limerick. The requirement to trim his new regimental frock coat with silver or gold lace set him back nine guineas. Eating with 'strange officers' from other regiments he admitted 'costs me my pay'. To a stern parent who had to finance him, the novice wrote ingenuously 'I can't account for it [the money] how it is gone'.[91] Rawdon Hautenville, on becoming a lieutenant in 1770, immediately pestered relations in Dublin for subs to cover unlooked-for expenses. Again the right rig, inseparable from the impression to be made on comrades and civilians, was vital. He bought some items from a fellow officer who had run up debts through gambling, but the epaulettes and silver or gold lace for his uniform were to be had only from one supplier in Dublin. Hautenville also complained of the high costs of living in Kinsale and Cork. As an officer, he was conscious of having to 'live in a public manner'. Hautenville was remarkably prone to accidents which justified fresh demands for money. A burglar purloined kit; a careless servant dropped his sword overboard. When Hautenville embarked for England and Minorca, custom demanded that soldiers of the regiment remaining in Ireland should be tipped.[92] Comparable pressures made Henry Brown, a cornet in the 1770s, beseech his father, a squire in County Limerick and agent of the absent Lord Southwell, for further advances. Without them, Brown alleged, life as an officer would be rendered unsupportable, since it was vital to 'live in it like a gentleman'. To support the requisite style would take an extra £100 p.a. Otherwise, he might have opted for the less prestigious and apparently less costly naval service.[93] The wise or modest shunned the company of high-spending bloods, and lodged privately.[94] Yet, even when living outside barracks, officers had to maintain an appropriate look. Admiration of the soldiery as innovators and engines of refinement occurred because of their high spending. Officers were welcomed by and into the quality of Protestant Ireland. However, on an annual income usually between £100 and £200 these exemplars struggled not to be eclipsed by squires with £800 to £1,500 a year.

Given these problems, the popularity of the army (and navy) as a livelihood for young Protestants from Ireland (as elsewhere) owed as much to the lack of alternatives as to the allure of a red coat or shouldering a musket. Parents and guardians were often unenthusiastic about the trade of arms. The doting feared the physical hazards; the nervous, the moral ones. Richard Waring had had to conquer parental opposition. In turn, his own wife was reluctant to allow their son to follow the father into the army.[95] In many cases, placement in the forces was a last resort. The Herberts in Kerry had too many youths unprovided with gainful careers. In the 1760s, a new war might accommodate at least some.[96] The decision of a nephew of Speaker Henry Boyle to soldier was described simply as a 'misfortune'.[97] Similarly, Katherine Conolly viewed the army as a *pis aller* for the least promising members of her extensive affinity. This disenchantment was the more striking in a family, like hers (the Conynghams), with a strong military tradition.[98] Katherine Howard was dismayed by rumours that a son, installed in the Middle Temple, might enlist during the War of the Spanish Succession.[99] In 1695 Richard Cox, the lawyer, mustered even less enthusiasm when told that a son wished to be commissioned in the army. Cox preferred that the boy should become 'an honest country gentleman of £200 p.a.' rather than 'the best colonel in Europe', because – simply – Cox did not 'like the trade'.[100] In the end, in common with many other of these parents, he relented and, albeit reluctantly, funded his son's military career.

The army, seen as a seminary of extravagance, violence and vice, was likely to infect precious progeny. It threatened as well as protected. Its officers channelled novel notions, commodities and habits into the Irish hinterlands. Politeness and sociability were displayed; so, too, was a libertinism which scandalized the staid.[101] Whiggish officers in large garrisons such as Limerick, Waterford and Kilkenny teased and tormented morose Tory bishops. Later they meddled in municipal affairs. Commanders pursued political ambitions in Ireland. Thomas Pearce in Limerick and Henry Hawley at Kinsale disturbed the already turbulent civic scenes.[102] Overbearing soldiers, giving themselves airs and graces, sneered at civilians. In the 1770s, Lieutenant Henry Brown from County Limerick was disconcerted by Tramore, on the Waterford coast: 'a most shocking place, not a single gentleman to speak to'. Society improved in Tipperary, which was well stocked with hospitable and sporting gentlemen.[103] Lieutenant Delacherois similarly appreciated the welcome extended to him, and his fellows, by the gentry of County Cork. He noted admiringly that some hosts were worth £2,000 and £3,000. Had he not held the king's commission it was unlikely that he would have had the entrée to their houses.[104] Gratitude towards his hosts did not entirely disarm Delacherois. In common with other officers who had used the ample time at their disposal to reflect on their surroundings, he, having already analysed the defects of Bermudan society, caustically commented on what he encountered in County Cork. He warned his industrious brother in County Down, 'you'll never see the poverty, distress of their kingdom till you visit this part of the country. The poor are poor indeed, and the higher class of people only distress their vassals or slaves to support their luxury and extravagance'.[105]

One reason why officers exerted considerable influence in Ireland outside the purely military sphere came from this capacity to view sights and experiences from fresh — and sometimes critical — perspectives. Virtually all had travelled beyond Ireland and Britain, and so had grounds for comparison denied even to the majority of clergy and lawyers. For a Delacherois, this widened angle of approach did not lessen his regard for Ireland. He enjoyed the liveliness of Bristol and Bath, but dismissed the cathedral city of Wells as a 'retired town inhabited by parsons, super-annuated coachmen and postboys'. Kidderminster was thought even worse, with 'no sociability amongst the inhabitants'. Worst of all was Bridgnorth. There the townspeople were entirely unacquainted with con-versation and politeness. 'Their principal object' was 'who can bluster for their own interest'. The discerning soldier dismissed them: 'calloused and without the least sensibility or feeling for the misfortunes of others, they exult in all public computations of their wealth, tales and conduct in getting money'. Unpardonable was the neglect there of wives.[106] Even London, visited by Delacherois after his long tour of duty in the Caribbean, failed to match the splendours of Dublin in 1770.[107] This officer's quirky opinions were communicated to his civilian kindred in County Down. Delacherois cherished vivid but perhaps distorted memo-ries of what he had left in Ulster.[108] But, just as the personable and opinionated British officers in Irish garrisons amused hostesses and hosts with their exotic experiences and notions, and in doing so modified atti-tudes, so those from Ireland quartered in the Mediterranean, the Orient or the Occident continued to shape the way that Ireland was evolving.

II

Officers, whether the English and Scots of the garrisons throughout Ireland or the Irish Protestants on leave or retired from service overseas, were courted. They were customers, shields, possible husbands and novelties. In the Sligo of the 1730s, it was reckoned that most of the £7,000 p.a. from the pay of the two companies quartered there was spent in the town.[109] The army sheltered many of meagre and some with multiple talents. They enlivened and extended the respectable society of Protestant Ireland.

Galleries had to be inserted into some churches to accommodate them. The rank and file swelled sparse congregations. They married the women and fathered the infants whose names are inscribed in the Church of Ireland registers of military bases such as Athlone, Kinsale, Waterford and Youghal.[110] They varied and sustained much of the social and associational life of these provincial centres. They were useful to philanthropic ventures, such as the charter schools.[111] The Hibernian Society, an educational charity, was established to cope with the children abandoned by their soldier fathers.[112] By their presence, perhaps 800 officers strengthened the Protestant interest in Ireland. Yet ambivalence persisted. Some of the same chauvinism directed against the immigrant bishops, administrators and judges enveloped the commandants sent from Britain. There was also ambivalence about the authority on which the military acted. One commander who suffered these inconveniences railed against the profiteering and obstructiveness of the local civilians: 'we have not met with that kind of usage we might expect in a Protestant town like Bandon'.[113]

Well-groomed officers ingratiated themselves with useful locals; the unruly antagonized them. The Protestants of Ireland, despite prohibitions, found themselves serving in Ireland. Humphrey Thomson, originally from Monaghan, was stationed in Dublin, Kilkenny and the midlands. Unable to match high spenders among the mettlesome officers of the horse, he separated himself. In Kilkenny, Thomson fell in with congenial civilians; at Donoughmore, he passed his days in fishing, shooting and setting with dogs and kept the company of prosperous farmers, 'living well and hospitably'. Thomson, liking these relaxed modes, 'was invited to every wedding and merry meeting in that neighbourhood'.[114] Yet, if Thomson abstained from the excesses of his English comrades, he still wanted to 'support the character of a gentleman'. Pleased, he reported revisiting his home town of Monaghan, 'as genteely . . . as when I left it'.[115] Lieutenant Delacherois also dreaded the competitive display of mess-mates in the Dublin of the 1750s.[116] In most respects, Limerick, with its affable civilians, suited him better. Yet he shared the desire to act – and be seen as acting – as 'an officer and a gentleman'.[117] In 1769 Delacherois was followed into the army by a younger brother. The latter, Samuel, was commissioned into a smarter regiment, 'particularly distinguished for their regularity, good order and genteel behaviour'. Soon enough, the impressionable subaltern learnt the extravagance of his seniors.[118] Another from Ireland, George Boles (or Bowles) was struck by the visible variations in culture between different regiments. Boles, from Tallow in County Waterford, benefited from the help of relations already in the army in London and of a peer from County Waterford, Grandison, also in London. Having secured a commission as an ensign, Boles was posted to York. Most of the officers in the regiment were Scots, 'agreeable men', but 'in general excessively proud'. Soon he exchanged his ensigncy for a commission in the 7th Dragoons. Boles was delighted. 'I find the great difference of this service from the foot, and am now sure of standing, this regiment being one of the oldest in the king's service'.[119]

Officers born in Ireland posted throughout the later Stuarts' and Hanoverians' empire may have discerned how Ireland fitted into it. These experiences did not dissolve the sense of a distinctive Irish Protestant identity. By the same token, those from Britain whose careers brought them to Ireland, although welcomed, were seldom permanently incorporated into the Protestant communities. Adolphus Oughton knew Ireland from studying at Dublin University. Soon he returned as a junior officer.[120] Later, when he reminisced, Oughton criticized the customs of the 'military gentry'. In the isolated barracks of the midlands and west, bored officers were tempted to drink. Once in drink, comrades quarrelled. Duels could result. Oughton condemned this practice as a relic of 'Gothic barbarism'. It had long disquieted the rulers of Ireland. In 1710, Queen Anne had commanded Ormonde as her lord-lieutenant to curb duelling among military officers. However, shortly after he landed in Dublin, he was faced with a fight between two high-ranking commanders, Echlin and Gorges. They may have imported what they had learnt in Britain and during postings to the war-racked Low Countries.[121] With difficulty, Oughton resisted the pressure to participate. In doing so he prefigured the anti-duelling societies, the knots of Friendly Brothers of St Patrick, which – from the 1750s – were sustained by officers in Dublin and provincial towns.[122] Oughton remembered how, at Gort, one officer went mad and tried to detonate the barracks and occupants, but killed only himself and his dog. Oughton was inventive in his strategies to stave off boredom. He responded with an appreciation unusual at that time to the wild landscape of the west. He made pets of various animals, including an otter, with whom he shared his bed. He read and inspected nearby curiosities. His responsiveness to what he saw endeared him to locals and he was entertained by hospitable bishops at their rural retreats. In Ballyshannon, County Donegal, he was taken up by a local proprietor, John Foliot, a man 'of worth, sense and learning'. Indeed, in each of his postings Oughton cultivated or was cultivated by people of local consequence. At Castle Caldwell, it was Sir James Caldwell; at Sligo, Michelbourne Knox, an active merchant; in nearby Annaghmore, the cosmopolitan squire, O'Hara. At Castlebar in County Mayo, he was fêted by Sir John Bingham, whose town Castlebar was; in Roscommon, by the Gunnings.[123] Despite these many invitations, Oughton did not entirely eschew the companionship of congenial officers with similar interests.

Comparable problems and solutions marked the Irish career of Samuel Bagshawe. An officer brought to Dublin originally in the train of the lord-lieutenant Devonshire, Bagshawe quickly slotted into the routines and society of the capital. A little diversion came from the tired rituals of the Castle, attendance at levees or eating meals with other officials; more, in the populous city and its environs.[124] Like Oughton, he vowed not to depend solely on the regiment, the Castle, the garrison or the town to divert him. He not only read manuals on drill and discipline, but books in French and Italian.[125] Tours of duty in the provinces introduced him to the pleasures of Limerick and Bandon.[126] Bagshawe, a Derbyshire connection of the Devonshires, stayed in Ireland longer than he had expected or wanted. Married to an Irish Protestant and elected to the Irish Commons in 1761, he looked a fixture in Ireland. However, he had not set himself up as a property-owner in Ireland. Indeed, he struggled to cut the right figure in Dublin society, and died before founding a dynasty in Protestant Ireland.

These awkwardnesses complicate any assessment of where the 650 to 700 British officers belonged in any social taxonomy of Protestant Ireland. Although numerous, many, when they could, absented themselves. Some who stayed – Oughton or Bagshawe – took to their billet. Yet almost all passed like shooting stars across the Irish sky only to embed themselves in British soil.[127] One such was Cuthbert Ellison during the 1730s. Ellison, inheriting an encumbered estate in County Durham, joined the army in 1723 in the hope of paying off his debts. Soon he discovered that the obligations of life as an officer added to the problems.[128] Financial burdens increased once he was ordered to Ireland, in part because he had the mistaken reputation 'of having a fortune independent of my post'.[129] The honour of being named as an aide-de-camp to the lord-lieutenant ran him further into debt: he calculated that his annual pay amounted to £130, that he owed his regimental agent £150 and was saddled with repayments to creditors at home in northern England.[130] The expenses of attending the viceroy, the magnificent Dorset, dressing and mounting himself for the part, together with the tedium of much of the service, had to be balanced against the chance to ingratiate himself with the important. A sign of the high style which Ellison thought necessary was a request to have a silver monteith, engraved with his armorials, sent to him.[131] The waiting game was a costly one. However, it was a conscious calculation. As Ellison expressed it, 'people in our trade should always look forwards'.[132] True to this philosophy, while lamenting the costs of duty in Dublin Castle, he eagerly solicited to continue as an aide-de-camp to Dorset's successor.[133] Much as he might complain, Ellison interspersed the uncongenial service in Dublin with lengthy spells at Bath. He was also stationed in the provinces: at Longford, Loughreagh, Philipstown and Sligo.[134] In common with colleagues, he appreciated the welcome extended by local squires.[135] Otherwise, he was singularly incurious about his surroundings. Nor did Dublin excite him much more. In the dog days of 1739 he dismissed it as 'neither a scene of business, action or politics'.[136] He waited desperately for tidings from England. Keeping the company of other officers, he interested himself chiefly in horseflesh, election gossip from northern England and how to exchange his Irish station for a more attractive one.

Ellison, treating Ireland as no more than an unwelcome but protracted episode in his soldiering, left the kingdom for good in 1739. He retained few links and little affection for the place. This contrasted with the veterans of the Tudor and early Stuart campaigns who founded dynasties in Ireland. Their penurious descendants sought relief by enlisting in the British armies of the eighteenth century. A few, such as the Caldwells in County Fermanagh, even joined the forces of continental monarchs.[137] At the same time, as Ellison's case suggests, intimacies achieved in Ireland, notably with the lords-lieutenant Dorset and Devonshire, furthered careers.[138] Ellison would end as a lieutenant-general, not only restored to profitable enjoyment of the County Durham inheritance but possessed of a fashionable London establishment.[139] In practice, as Ellison himself recognized, patrons acquired while in Ireland, counted less in his promotion than those whom he knew already in England.[140] Moreover, he was helped upwards – like most of his comrades – by dogged service and the opportunities afforded by renewed warfare after 1739.[141] In only one way did General Ellison revert in later life to his Irish apprenticeship. In 1761, a nephew contemplated how best to prepare for the future. The possibility of attaching himself to the entourage of the Irish viceroy was mooted. The general advised against the youth adopting the course which he himself had earlier followed. The main reason was not the irksomeness of the duties but the meagre patronage at the lord-lieutenant's disposal: reduced even since the 1730s.[142]

III

Difficult to evaluate, other than through the history of individuals, is how upwards of a thousand Protestants from Ireland were affected by serving outside the kingdom in the British army and navy. For General Richard Waring, it built a bridge from his native Ulster into the landed society of the English home counties. In the same fashion, Waring's contemporaries and neighbours, the Leathes brothers – Moses and William – used their profits from European warfare to storm English society. Yet neither the

Leathes nor Waring detached themselves wholly from property and
kindred still in Ulster.[143] Others enriched by fighting – Frederick and
Hans Hamilton, Henry Conyngham and Henry Crofton – retired to
Ireland. For the heirs and inheritors of substantial estates, the pay of a
senior officer bailed out waterlogged estates. Just as the legal fees and back-
handers collected by Francis Bernard and Michael Ward underwrote Castle
Mahon (later Castle Bernard) in County Cork and Castle Ward in County
Down, so the pay of high-ranking officers sustained their Irish ventures.[144]
The Wynnes, settled at Hazelwood outside Sligo, achieved high rank in
the British army in three successive generations. The rewards enabled them
to turn Hazelwood into the model of a modern estate. So important had
military service become to the Wynnes' operations that in 1752 the current
head proposed spending £4,000 on a lieutenant-colonelcy.[145]

The Wynnes visibly thrived. Other Irish Protestant landowners kept
afloat more precariously thanks to the extra buoyancy from army wages.
The finances of a Henry Conyngham resist penetration. Already by 1690,
a large if not especially wealthy landowner in County Donegal, he came
of a family well used to exploiting offices. His father, Sir Albert
Conyngham, had been muster-master-general.[146] Henry Conyngham had
several strings to his bow. Agent, landowner and soldier, the relative importance of each of these callings to his revenues cannot yet be determined.[147]
At the start of the eighteenth century, Conyngham moved from Donegal
to Slane in County Meath, where he began to erect a new mansion.[148]
Conyngham Hall proclaimed the prosperity and importance of its owner.
Military service combined with landownership to support this display.
General Conyngham's death in Spain in 1706 cut off revenues essential
if the family was to continue in this splendour.[149] A wastrel heir, Williams
Conyngham, brought fortunes to a low ebb. Inheritance in 1738 by a
younger brother, Henry Conyngham, saved the Slane estate. Marriage to
a London heiress helped; so, too, did the younger Henry Conyngham's
career as a colonel in the British army.[150]

A second family, the Croftons, found the army useful. The Croftons
arrived in Ireland to fight in the Elizabethan wars, and settled. The senior
branches joined the squires and titled of the midlands.[151] The death early
in 1720s of the head of a junior branch living at Baskin outside Dublin
embarrassed his dependants. The father, Theophilus Crofton, had
bequeathed 'only his good character and Providence to support them'.[152]
However, the fatherless Croftons adroitly exploited their kindred and connections. In 1716 the heir, Henry Crofton, was commissioned as an ensign
in the foot regiment of Lieutenant-General Richard Gorges, also from
Ireland. By 1718, Crofton was posted to Minorca.[153] His yearly pay was
£79 13s. 06d. He secured a station there for his younger brother, Thomas,

who in 1723 bought a lieutenancy of foot for £450. On the island, the brothers shared the office of secretary and then registrar to the governor.[154] Minorca, with its remoteness, torrid climate and tedium, repelled the fashionable and active.[155] Yet the posting evidently suited Henry Crofton, who was promoted to major. By 1736, he had £5,000 to invest in an estate in the Irish midlands.[156] The lands alone were unlikely to yield more than £300 or £400 p.a.[157] As a supplement to regular military pay and as a base on which to live as a squire, the property meant more. Crofton, when on leave in London or Ireland, mingled easily with the quality.[158] But dying on active service in Minorca, he himself – like General Henry Conyngham – never set up permanently as a landed grandee in his native country. Others who sank their military earnings into Irish property lived to enjoy it. Lieutenant-General Frederick Hamilton added a house in Dublin's most luxurious quarter, St Stephen's Green, to his Londonderry estate of Walworth. As a privy councillor, the retired Hamilton was prominent in the public life of the capital during George I's reign.[159] Major-General Gustavus Hamilton, another veteran of the Williamite and later campaigns, ennobled as Viscount Boyne, built a substantial mansion at Stackallen in County Meath.[160] Richard Kane, who had governed Minorca and ended as a brigadier-general, bought an estate north of Drogheda for £12,700.[161] Bland, retired from the army, became a neighbour of Cosby in Queen's County.[162]

The Croftons of Baskin used their connections to secure posts consonant with their quality. Not only had a younger brother followed the major into the army, a third, Perkins Crofton, studied at Dublin University and then, thanks to the backing of Lord Forbes, heir of Lord Granard and a midlands potentate, became a naval chaplain.[163] Soon he wearied of life afloat and, with the patronage of the bishop, was beneficed in Cork. There he accumulated livings, made an advantageous marriage and bought an attractive estate.[164] A fourth brother, Robin Crofton, pushed by his eldest brother and the latter's friends, secured a patentee post. In 1734, he was made revenue collector for the Ballinrobe walk in County Mayo.[165] In a classic configuration, the youngest brother, John Crofton, intended for trade, was apprenticed to the leading ironmonger in Dublin. The plan failed, and Jack Crofton dabbled with several occupations. His increasingly shabby condition and uncertain status, ending as a 'builder' in the stews of Roscommon town, contrasted with the substance of his elders.[166] Jack Crofton's precarious economic and social footing resembled that of his widowed mother and unfortunate sister, shifting as best they could on little more than £10 p.a.[167]

For the active officer like Henry Crofton or Nicholas Delacherois, the gains from army service were financial and social. Through long overseas

service Henry Crofton amassed savings which were then used to shore up
and improve his position in Ireland. Lieutenant Delacherois adopted a
similar strategy. Throughout much of the 1760s he was exiled in the West
Indies. Eventually, and with the help of Lady Mountalexander's legacy, he
acquired an estate near Comber in County Down. In retirement, he took
his place among the quality.[168] Families, with a son, husband or father
soldiering outside Ireland, felt other effects. Minorcan specialities – Sièges
and Canary wine, melon seeds and carpets – deluged Croftons in Ireland.
In return, they sent parcels of potatoes and neats' tongues.[169] Delacherois
treated his kindred active in the linen trade around Lisburn to observations on the topography and customs of the Caribbean, in addition to
exotic presents.[170] By such devices, the worlds of the more sedentary in
Ireland were enlarged, at least vicariously. The role of the army and naval
officers as cultural innovators is illustrated by Henry Conyngham and
William Leathes. On campaign in foreign parts, they lived with an amplitude greater than that of their homes in Ireland. Conyngham travelled
through Iberia with a heavy weight of silver consecrated to conviviality.
He had evidently adopted the novel beverages of tea and chocolate. Few
of his effects were shipped home to grace Conyngham Hall. Instead they
were dispersed among junior officers of the regiment.[171]

William Leathes did not die abroad. A member of a family prominent
in and around Belfast, he served the forfeiture commissioners in Dublin
as secretary and surveyor between 1700 and 1703.[172] Already a lieutenant
in the army in 1698, he soon channelled his skills into the commissariat.[173]
His talents found fullest expression as paymaster and agent of the Royal
Irish Regiment. After the War of the Spanish Succession, he retained his
contacts with a group of officers mainly from Ireland, including Robert
Parker, Robert Stearne, Richard Kane and Henry Ingoldsby. Leathes
remained in the Low Countries, where he had links in the commercial,
banking and artistic purlieus. He could also thread his way around the
Treasury and War Office in London. The task of clothing the troops
thickened the mesh which bound textile traders from Ulster to their
counterparts (and rivals) in the Low Countries. Leathes, used to handling
large sums of money on behalf of fellow officers, continued to offer financial services in peacetime. He and several others from the regiment
invested heavily in South Sea stock.[174] The state used Leathes's expertise,
with George I appointing him as his emissary in Brussels. Throughout the
1710s and 1720s, William Leathes was obviously a useful person for any
Irish Protestant to know. He could arrange the itineraries and education
of visitors to Flanders. He bespoke goods on behalf of his friends and
kinsfolk back in Ireland. For a sister in Dublin he procured engravings;
for others, he commissioned portraits and supplied other paintings. For a

superior, General Frederick Hamilton, back in Ireland, he ordered a suite of Brussels tapestries. Soon Lord Kildare, having seen and admired them, craved a second set.[175] Leathes bought a London house and a country estate on the borders of Suffolk and Norfolk. These, not any Irish residence, were stuffed with the artistic loot from the Low Countries.[176] Leathes, like General Waring, loosened but did not break his Irish links. As his absence from Ireland lengthened, his impact on the society and culture of Ireland was indirect. To friends and acquaintances in Ulster and Dublin, he offered a foothold from which they might clamber into a regiment. But he also offered glimpses into and artefacts from more distant places.

A few from Ireland made fortunes from the War of the Spanish Succession; more made careers. Thereafter, the likelihood of valuable plunder from warfare lessened.[177] Instead, profits derived chiefly from selling a commission well.[178] Pay, as has been suggested, compared poorly with the income of a landowner in lowland England. The disparities between landed revenues and military wages lessened in the westerly and hilly regions of Britain and throughout much of Ireland. Yet even there, only the rare colonelcies matched what a substantial squire could reasonably expect by the mid-eighteenth century.[179] However, such earnings were not to be derided. Carefully husbanded, especially by sharp bachelors, they bought a genteel life. But caution and parsimony were despised as inimical to the image of a high-spending and ebullient officer. A culture of excess permeated many regiments and weakened the economic benefits of a commission. The sight of profligates dissipating their pay did not deter optimists from entering the army. Low and static rents in early eighteenth-century Ireland drove the penurious to scavenge for supplements. Moreover, as the population of Protestants rose, so cadets proliferated. Demographic pressures, reinforced by the working of primogeniture, made military wages especially attractive to younger sons unlikely to inherit more than a single farm. Nor were heirs, like Owen Wynne or Henry Crofton, indifferent to additions to scrawny patrimonies. Comparable pressures impelled apparently disproportionate numbers from the uplands and poorer peripheries of Britain into the army.[180] Except during the War of the Spanish Succession, when several from Protestant Ireland achieved spectacular promotion, military service consolidated the position of those already precariously situated among the quality, and advanced others from the middling ranks into it. Of perhaps 800 officers stationed in Ireland and another 1,000 from the kingdom soldiering elsewhere, the proportions lifted thereby into the 'military gentry' are currently unknown.

Some hopefuls, like Edmund Spencer and Richard Edwards, eager to be commissioned, never were. The lucky, commissioned in a regiment, were subjected to mortifications. The frustrations and attractions were summarized by Nicholas Delacherois. Languishing in Bermuda, seemingly forgotten, he reflected on the causes. During the years of peace, when vacancies were rare and costly, 'powerful interest or purchase' were the sole routes to advancement. He lacked both. He longed for a lieutenancy because (he thought) it would 'remove me from this tiresome rank, and, tho' it would be only nominal, it would screen me from many of those laborious and disagreeable duties with which we are so constantly harassed'.[181] The money spent on an exchange to achieve a higher rank, Delacherois reckoned a sounder investment than stock. Himself unable to find the cash to become a captain-lieutenant, he moped. 'I am spending the noon of my life in the solitude of a hermit, but a military life is a state of slavery, and in the course of my reading I remember certain authors remark that as soon as a man embarks into a military life he exchanges his liberty for a hat and feather'.[182] Delacherois protected himself against *longueurs* and loneliness though intellectual and physical exercise. Inevitably, among soldiers, the reflections of the thoughtful – Oughton, Thomson and Delacherois – not of the duellers and sots, survive. Delacherois diverted himself with music, drawing, observing indigenous and settler society, and by reading.[183] Back in Dublin in 1769, an abundance of smart company reminded him more sharply than the isolation of Bermuda of his 'present inferior and servile rank'.[184] In this mood, he jumped at a transfer to the remote north-west of County Cork. With three others, he lived near Inchigeela in 'freedom, concord and friendship'. 'Freedom and liberty' in this wild spot were infinitely to be preferred to confinement to garrison or a subaltern's duties.[185] Despite numerous disappointments, Delacherois confessed to being 'enthusiastically fond' of a soldier's life. He enjoyed the society of County Cork, and insisted, 'a good deal of hunting, shooting, freedom of conversation, a little variety of company, good eating and drinking alleviates all misfortunes'.[186] He did not, as he had sometimes threatened, resign. Belatedly he secured the lieutenancy for which he had schemed. This satisfaction led him to conclude, 'the little checks on our liberty are the chief disagreements of a soldier. Otherwise, it's the most rational and social life that I know of . . .'[187]

IV

Most turned to the army in the expectation of regular 'bread'. In weighing up other advantages, social *éclat* counted for more than the rationality of the officer's existence valued by Delacherois. The same was true of those who contemplated seafaring. Ireland, despite its being an island, has not been regarded as a nursery of mariners. Its function in supplying the scarce knee-timbers from its oak woods, essential to construct men-of-war, not the crew of those men-of-war, has more often been noticed.[188] The navy, less prestigious than the army, for that very reason beckoned to Protestants who lived in Ireland, especially close to its long coasts. Places on ships were cheaper than those in regiments. Nevertheless, interest had to be made if Irish provincials were to procure naval postings. As in the army, recruitment was also affected by efforts to monitor and improve the calibre of entrants.[189]

The Southwells, owners of much of the busy port of Kinsale, had long been linked with the Customs and naval administrations in England and Ireland. Knowing their way around the relevant departments which awarded naval appointments and contracts, they were often approached to help the promising into the navy and merchant marine.[190] The Southwells in their turn were unabashed in 'teasing' their connections on the Board of Admiralty on behalf of clients from Ireland.[191] In 1712 Edward Southwell sought a naval place for Anthony Hyde, a kinsman from County Cork. The youth had served already for eight years as a lieutenant. Southwell confided, 'this favour being a matter I have so much at heart to see a relation preferred in the world, who has full service to back his pretensions withal'.[192] The Southwells' backing probably explained how Henry Tom, son of the Kinsale parson, served in the navy as a surgeon for at least twenty years. The younger Edward Southwell supported Tom's pleas to be posted back to Kinsale. Yet, Southwell drew the line at supporting Surgeon Tom's nephew, as he had six or seven others with better claims to his intercession.[193] Southwell also helped a son of his County Down agent, John Trotter, first into the navy and then into East India service.[194] At lower levels than the commissioned officers, the Southwells proved their worth to clients and dependants on their Irish estates. The superannuated were steered into Greenwich or Chelsea Hospital. The son of another Kinsale incumbent, the Reverend Peter Hewett, served as a gunner on the *Panther*, a grandson worked as a joiner in the docks at Portsmouth.[195] In 1718, the son of a Church of Ireland minister in County Down had been at sea for thirteen years since the age of seventeen, in the royal fleet. The sailor had served in the Straits, the West Indies and off the African coast.[196]

In Queen Anne's time, Sir Richard Cox, also from maritime Cork, pressed to have a kinsman promoted to a naval lieutenancy.[197] Another secretary at Dublin Castle, Joshua Dawson, bombarded the Admiralty commissioners in London on behalf of one of the numerous sons of Robert Travers, a well-affected County Cork clergyman. Travers, with eight or nine offspring to send into the world, needed all the support he could muster. One young Travers had been a volunteer on a man-of-war since the age of fourteen. The arrival of a new commander threatened the novice with removal. Sea service, it was said, had 'turned his head to that way of life'. The most that the Admiralty could do was to urge the seaman himself to identify a vacancy among the vessels in Irish waters. Then Travers would be given the requisite warrant.[198] Archbishop King managed to send a stubborn and wayward nephew to sea. After fourteen or fifteen years before the mast, William King had redeemed himself. Under the tutelage of a benevolent captain, he flourished. By 1717, his uncle was prepared to spend perhaps £100 or £200 on a commission for him. King was soon told that it would cost £300. The price was modest when set beside the £2,500 for a captaincy of dragoons sought by another of King's charges.[199] The young King gained his lieutenancy and later served in the Mediterranean. The mariner had progressed largely thanks to his captain, not through the interest among grandees mobilized by his uncle, the archbishop.[200]

Familial networks were used by those seeking maritime careers. As in the army, so in the marine, aspirants were helped by the established. Particularly useful were two from Ireland. Matthew Aylmer, later Lord Aylmer of Balrath, and John Norris rose to be admirals by the end of the seventeenth century.[201] Aylmer came from the titled Old English of the Pale. Despite the conversion of his line to Protestantism, Aylmer's circumstances remained shaky. Perhaps this caused him, when an irascible lieutenant, to bluster at his captain that 'he was a better gent than any of the Roydens'.[202] Aylmer had been aided by Ormond and George Legge, earl of Dartmouth: he in turn helped his son-in-law, Norris. However, with the official insistence on aptitude and experience, unbridled nepotism was restrained. Instead, the example of the successful, such as Aylmer and Norris, emboldened others from Ireland.[203] The constant arrival of ships and their officers in the ports of Ireland offered further stimulus and opportunity. Relations, at their wits' ends as to how to provide for their young, snatched at the expanding navy. In 1684 Alan Brodrick, a rising young barrister in County Cork, urged that a brother be sent to sea, because 'he may make a good tarpaulin and nothing good else'.[204] This attitude recurred in numerous families. In 1731, James O'Brien requested the support of the Munster politician Henry Boyle to place a kinsman in a ship.[205] One of Boyle's own sons was subsequently found serving on a warship.[206] Ten years later, a son of Lord Dunalley was commissioned as sixth lieutenant on the *Royal Sovereign*.[207] A Tyrone squire was delighted when a son, together with the nephew of Lord Blayney, was favoured by Admiral Knowles and both were placed as midshipmen on his boat.[208]

These openings appeared only after solicitation. In 1763, Thomas Colley sought promotion for his nephew, John Biddulph. The latter had served with Admiral Saunders for three years and risen to a lieutenancy. Now the uncle appealed to his employer, the absentee Lord Digby, lamenting that as the youth 'had no interest, [he] has got no preferment, tho several under him has'.[209] To interest, money had to be added. Higher standards for entrants obliged parents to put them through costly training. Richard Purcell of Kanturk, in northern Cork, had seven sons to launch into the world. The expense made him beg for the agency in County Limerick to add to that which he already occupied. The post, rumoured to yield a yearly £500, would enable him 'to make a genteel provision for my large family'.[210] Purcell's heir was studying at Trinity College; the second son was already a midshipman on a warship. The father was dithering over his third son: whether to buy him an ensign's commission (for £200 to £300) in an Irish or English regiment or send him into the marines. If he opted for the latter, he would have first to be trained at the academy in Portsmouth. Purcell gained no extra agency and his ambitious project was dropped.[211] At much the same moment, a cleric from County Cork was arranging that a son be educated at a suitable English school 'for the king's sea service'.[212] Throughout maritime Ireland, the call of the sea was not to be denied. The tribe of Herberts sent its young into the navy, although perhaps not in such quantities as into the army.[213] In 1768, the *Solebay* was commanded by Captain O'Brien and crewed by 104 men. At least thirty-two came from O'Brien's home county of Cork and another seven from Kerry.[214]

Adventuring into the unknown might bewitch the young. Elders, apprehensive of what the army might do to the tender, equally dreaded the sea. William Peard, another agent from County Cork, consulted his employer about how best to provide for his son. Seafaring was an option. Peard, having lost several small children and with his wife in deep depression, confided that, were the boy to go into the navy, their hearts 'would never be at ease'. In the end, the parents gave up the idea so that they would not be 'in a perpetual state of inquietude and fear as to make our lives a burden to us, as he is the only child left us'. A better plan would be to apprentice the lad to a Liverpool merchant: a course which the patron – living in North Wales – might organize. If this apprenticeship cost too much, then he could begin in a small way as a trader in the city of Cork. In time, perhaps, and with luck (that vital additive), he might prosper, especially if the patron's English network were to be activated on the youth's behalf.[215]

The growth of the Hanoverians' empire created work for soldiers and sailors. Distant territories had to be administered as well as defended. Priv-ileged corporations rather than the government frequently handled these tasks. Already in the first half of the eighteenth century, Irish Protestants made careers in running these possessions. Arthur Dobbs, renowned as a patriotic commentator on and improver of Ireland, governed North Carolina.[216] Yet it was the east which bedazzled. In 1737, a survey of north-eastern Ulster noted three nabobs, Macrea, Macky and Cowan, all from Derry, who had risen to rule the East India Company.[217] Cowan was reputed to have returned with £100,000 from the Orient.[218] In 1761 it was reported that a 'Mr Maguire', originally from Ireland but then resident in London, was in a fair way to acquiring a fortune from a trading venture to Patna. Later James Alexander (also from Derry) amassed a nabob fortune and, sinking it into Irish property in 1776, was subsequently made earl of Caledon.[219] More modest but nevertheless admired was the £1,000 p.a. with which James Echlin, another Ulsterman, returned from the Indies about 1739.[220]

Sometimes the gaze of the youthful turned east thanks to particular Irish connections. The Herberts in Kerry thought that their namesakes and landlords on the Welsh borders, being neighbours of Clive in Shropshire, could procure Indian appointments for their kindred. In the event, the Herberts' supplications were drowned because of 'so many gentlemen of rank and distinction being ambitious to go with Lord Clive'.[221] Alternative routes to employment by the East India Company were offered by Luke Sullivan (a rival of Clive) and Sullivan's ally, Lord Shelburne, an absentee with extensive property in Kerry. At least one candidate – John Sullivan – was helped to become a writer in the Company by sharing a name with Sullivan. Yet John Sullivan, originally from Cork but more recently educated at Thomas Bracken's academy in Greenwich, had the standard qualifications to be sent to toil at Fort St George. He had not been appointed simply on the basis of a tenuous kinship.[222] Earlier, a medical acquaintance of Sir Hans Sloane had turned to the notable in London because 'I am told your interest is good in all the trading companies'. The hope was that a nephew of the Belfast physician, Magnus Prince, having sailed with ships of the East India Company might be promoted to third mate.[223]

South-west Munster had its routes east. Sir William Hedges, an early profiteer from the oriental trade, came from Youghal, Around 1700, a son of the Kilkenny Hewetsons ventured to Surat. There he doubled as soldier and painter. He boasted to his mother in Ireland of being 'in favour with his Excellency in those parts, who had sent for him to paint their pictures'. The climate soon killed John Hewetson.[224] In 1741, Archdeacon James Smythe in Meath, having sent sons into farming and the Church, dispatched another with a commission from the East India Company.[225] One of Edmund Burke's closest friends at school in Ballitore, Newcomen Herbert, chose service with the Company. To prepare himself, Herbert had

had to supplement the conventional curriculum with lessons in French and mathematics.[226] In 1768, a tenant on Abercorn's north-western property sought a loan from the landlord to fit out a son to serve in the East Indies.[227]

So far as the civil administration of India was concerned, more from Scotland than from Ireland applied to work there. Yet the Orient enticed Irish Protestants.[228] By the 1730s, those from Ulster in particular seemed advantageously placed to serve the East India Company. The extensive estates of the London chartered trading companies, especially in County Londonderry, smoothed the movement of tenants, or their dynamic sons, into the commercial worlds of the capital. Dynasties from the north of Ireland, such as the Cairnes or Nesbitts, had members high in banking and overseas trade. They may have levered others into pole positions. More generally, after 1690 the balance of advantage was felt to have tilted in favour of the Protestants of Ulster. A small part was played by the earliest contacts of these fortunates (such as the Warings) with William of Orange, newly disembarked at Carrickfergus. Ulster familes, like the Hamiltons, Leslies, Clements, Conynghams, Gores, Cairnes, Nesbitts, Pratts and Conollys, did well as confiscated land was redistributed.[229] This group also amassed offices, moving first into the administration and then into the government of Dublin. Through parliament, it redirected benefits financed by taxation into the province, via the Linen and Inland Navigation Boards. Members from this group – Clements, Conolly, Gore and Pratt – ran the Irish Treasury and Revenue Commission, and in doing so necessarily knew their counterparts in London well. Since the barriers between public and private finance were easily permeable, money washed around without its being clear whether it properly belonged to the personal or the official accounts of Irish government functionaries. In this hazy world, Ulstermen enjoyed unusual opportunities to thrive. Success in the officer corps of the British army and in overseas territories may have been an aspect of that good fortune.

V

Nabobs were rarities in eighteenth-century Ireland. More numerous were the veterans roughened and toughened under the harsh southern sun. Service outside Ireland enabled them to maintain or improve their standing within the kingdom. Working for the East India Company or in the government of north American colonies simply varied the more familiar option of entering the British army or navy. The hazards and separation dismayed parents and wives.[230] The processes which persuaded a

Hewetson from Kilkenny to voyage to Surat – financial need, adventure, parental tyranny or a patron – are hidden. Pulses quickened as resplendent soldiers paraded or brave vessels were espied from headlands. Oughton recalled how children and their parents rushed from their cabins to watch his regiment on its march through rural Ireland. [231] In 1744, one woman in Dublin noted 'a noble sight, very well looking men in regimentals'. [232] A rendezvous of the army at Bennetsbridge near Kilkenny in 1746 was expected to attract throngs of civilian spectators. [233] These sights may have kindled youthful ambitions to join those troops, described in Cork in 1756 as 'clever, sightly men, very civil in their behaviour'. [234]

Civilians who alternated between delight and horror at the conduct of the military showed something of the ambivalence with which swaggering officers were regarded. The drunken Captain Wade, who terrorized Derry and Belfast in 1703, did little for the reputation of the service. Wade, 'in his fits of extravagancy', tried to run through his own men with his sword. Merchants from the Ulster ports refused to go in the convoy nominally under Wade's protection. Although superseded as commander of the *Arundell*, he reappeared as a captain in Irish waters. [235] Press-gangs further reduced the popularity of the navy. In 1708, the mayor of Cork clashed with the captain of a press gang in the city. The mayor – like his counterparts in England – was upholding civic and civilian authority against what he saw as illegal invasions. He was happy enough that 'young idle fellows' and experienced mariners should be pressed. But the press had worked indiscriminately. Its depredations, at night, with entry forced into private houses, had enraged the city. The mayor with a sheriff acted to restore order. [236] There were suspicions that the leader of the Cork party was taking bribes to let off some threatened with service. In the light of these troubles, it was prudent, when – during the 1750s – fresh levies were required, to enjoin officers to cooperate carefully with the magistrates of Cork. [237]

Civilians continued to be affronted by the arbitrariness of the forces. In Dublin, commanders were warned not to interrupt the cargoes of Whitehaven coal bound for the city. In an excess of zeal, one recruiting party grabbed an innocuous Bremen merchant from his Dublin lodgings. [238] This offended less than the seizure in 1742, once more from a Dublin house, of the newly arrived gardener for the owner of Powerscourt, Richard Wingfield. [239] Such incidents outraged the influential, and cooled the ardour of civilians for the uniformed. Naval officers obtruded less than the soldiery, who repeatedly misbehaved. Lady Anne Conolly, new to official Dublin, was horrified to witness, as she left the Castle, a drunken soldier run through a peer's footman. [240] In Cork city, some of its garrison were accused during 1755 of acting 'very rude and vile in knock-

e Remportée par LE ROY GUILLAUME III. sur les Irlandoise a la Ruuere de Boyne en Irlande le 1 Juillet se

Desiqné apres la Nature et paint pour le Roy, et Gravé par Theodor Maas

1. D. Maas, *The Battle of the Boyne*, 1690.

2. *The Royall Orange Tree*, engraving of Williamite victories in Ireland, 1689–91.

3. After A. Van Dyke, *Richard Boyle, second earl of Cork and first earl of Burlington* (1612–98).

4. I. Fuller, *Sir William Petty* (1623–87), painted before he went to Ireland in 1652.

5. P. Hussey, *Richard Edgeworth* (1701–70), painted in 1757.

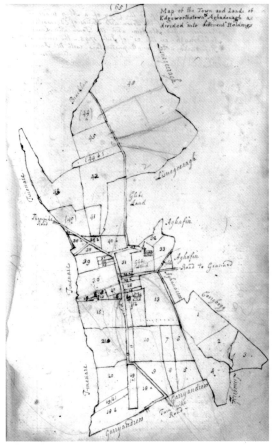

6. Map of Edgeworthstown in the mid-eighteenth century.

7. H. D. Hamilton, *Lady Arbella Denny* (1707–92).

8. Ralph Holland, *Archbishop William King of Dublin* (1650–1729).

9. Thomas Hickey, *The Reverend Samuel Madden* (1686–1765).

10. James Latham, *Eaton Stannard* (1685–1755), recorder of Dublin.

11. (*above*) J.-F. Roubiliac,
funeral monument to Sir Thomas
Molyneux (1661–1733), in
Armagh Church of Ireland
cathedral.

12. H. van der Myn, *William
Leathes* (died 1727).

A Prospect of the Barracks of DUBLIN from S.t James's Church Yard.   Les Point de Veux des Corps de Caserum de DUBLIN de l'eglise de S.t Jaque de la cour

13. (*above*) J. Tudor, *The Royal Barracks, Dublin*, engraved by A. Walker, 1753.

14. N. Hone, *Captain Walsingham Boyle, RN*, 1760.

15. William van der Hagen, *View of Waterford, c. 1737.*

16. Anonymous, *View of Ballyshannon, Co. Donegal,* late eighteenth century.

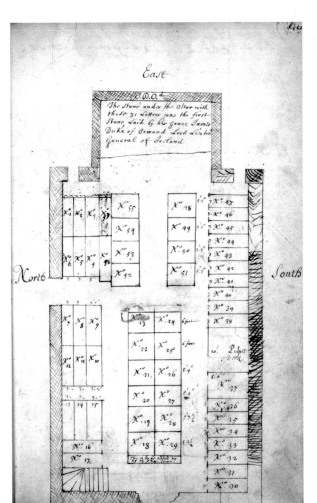

17. (*left*) Plan of pews in St Peter's Church, Dublin, 1693.

18. Mayoral sword-rest, St Mary's, Church of Ireland, Youghal.

19. The Exchange, Cork.

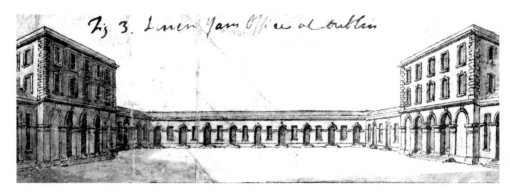

20. The Linen Yarn Office, Dublin, after 1732.

21. J. Tudor, *The Custom House, Dublin*, engraving published by 1753.

w of the LAKE OF KILLARNEY from the Park of ... the Right Honourable LORD VISCOUNT KENMAR ... To whom this Plate is INSCRIBED ... BY HIS Lordship's most humble Servant ...

22. After J. Tudor, *Prospect of Lord Kenmare's park and Lake of Killarney, Co. Kerry*, engraving published in 1770.

23. William Pars, *A view of Hazelwood, Co. Sligo, c.* 1771.

CALDWELL CASTLE, the Beautiful Seat of S.ʳ James Caldwell, in IRELAND.

24. Caldwell Castle, Co. Fermanagh, the seat of Sir James Caldwell.

25. John Nixon, *The surroundings of St Patrick's Cathedral, Dublin.*

ing down the people and abusing them several ways'.[241] In the aftermath of the festivities when a new mayor and sheriffs were installed, violence erupted in a poor district. 'Abundance of people' were 'cut and wounded', but the only death was that of a grenadier.[242] In County Kerry in 1762, an affray at a fair was traced to the aggression of drunken officers. Intent on recruiting, four identifiable officers – a captain, a lieutenant and two ensigns – had egged on thirty of their 'insulting men'. In the resulting mayhem, 'they spared no one, young or old, but hacked and cut everyone they could come at'. It was averred that 'more blood spilled at that fair than was in any fair or quarrel in Kerry since the last wars', presumably of 1689–91.[243] Sometimes these violent confrontations expressed rituals. Thomson, while serving in Queen's County, witnessed battles at patterns and popular festivals. He observed that the 'commonalty value themselves highly on it if they are able to flog the army out of the field'. Any in the distinctive red coats of the regiment became targets of the infuriated civilians.[244] Such contests, fought chiefly with stones, hardly touched the respectable of Protestant Ireland: they involved unruly and presumably Catholic rustics. The soldiers could be pardoned because they upheld the authority of the British state in Ireland.

In other episodes, substantial Protestant inhabitants found themselves ranged against officers (and men) of the occupying army. These occasions recurred. Limerick, location of a garrison of about 1,000, reverberated to trouble. Early in the eighteenth century, the politics of garrison officers and prominent townspeople often diverged. In Limerick, as in other towns with sizeable military presences such as Kinsale, Derry, Youghal and Waterford, interfering commanders were resisted.[245] In 1706, the prosecution of a grenadier for shooting a civilian in a Limerick shop may have had no wide implications.[246] However, in 1725, when the town clerk was charged with riotous conduct and cursing the governor and 'all arbitrary powers', it signalled renewed hostilities between political partisans.[247] In the controversy, the commander, Colonel Thomas Pearce, was not passive. The use of the military to try to swing townspeople behind particular candidates in municipal or parliamentary elections inevitably made it unpopular with opponents. In Limerick this dislike may have been worsened by the indiscipline for which the garrison was notorious throughout the first half of the eighteenth century.[248] Yet this tradition of turbulence did not stop new officers from being welcomed fulsomely. Also, the municipality might ask the guards for help in keeping order. Behind these outward courtesies and collaborations there survived more critical views about the conduct of the officers. At Bandon, Colonel Bagshawe was aggrieved that such a famously Protestant enclave should obstruct and abuse his soldiers.[249]

The government in Dublin, regularly told of officers overstepping the mark, responded brusquely. The history and present condition of the kingdom required rougher methods than would be tolerated in England. This had been the opinion of the lord-lieutenant in 1674 and was repeated by a successor in the middle of the next century. The latter felt that the aggrieved civilians in Ireland should be reminded that they had 'no pretensions to any property they may enjoy but what they received from military power'. The viceroy thought that 'the army is the only method of dealing with those gentry'.[250] In actuality, the regular army was seldom turned against restive Protestants. Indeed, its officers were punctilious about not trespassing into areas which properly belonged to the civil authorities. This reluctance sometimes created greater problems than forwardness would have done. Revenue officials frequently appealed to the army for help against smugglers and illegal distillers. Sometimes, they asked in vain. These two arms of the British state in Ireland did not always act in unison. On occasion, the soldiery were accused of abetting lawbreakers.[251]

Tensions from time to time marred peacetime administration. They worsened during alerts, and threatened to pit regulars against irregulars. When invaders were feared in 1715–16 and 1745–46 and actually appeared in 1760, the county militias were mustered. These volunteers were to join the professionals to protect the island. The latter, often from Britain, mocked the incompetence and vanity of the militia bands composed of and commanded by local Protestants. The latter, fond – even over-fond – of their military titles conferred through militia duty, and of the convivial rituals, resented these jeers.[252] The propertied of Protestant Ireland used service in the militia to emphasize the heroism of their ancestors and their own attachment to the classical ideal of active citizenship. They happily sent their sons to soldier. However, when they themselves were ridiculed for their martial awkwardness, they reverted to worries about standing armies. In this atmosphere, regular officers were vilified as – at least potentially – disturbers of the peace, champions of arbitrary rule and the cat's-paws of an intrusive Britain.[253]

These reservations weakened the armed forces as agents unifying the Hanoverians' territories. The frequent shuffling of the pack of soldiers dealt some from Ireland to Scotland, Minorca or the Americas, and Scots or English to Ireland. More than the import of lawyers, ecclesiastics and administrators into Ireland, or the training of would-be professionals from Ireland in England and Scotland, this regular movement of the military promised to dissolve localism and even fierce Irish particularism. In theory, officers had loyalties beyond the immediate locale and *patrie*. In actuality, soldiers and sailors from Protestant Ireland, like its civilians, remained

taciturn about the questions of identity which have come to obsess rootless moderns. Soldiers and mariners, moving within and beyond Ireland
and Britain, readily assumed identities appropriate to setting and audience.
An officer within a regiment or a vessel could balance a continuing
attachment to now-distant family and neighbourhood with the abstractions of the Protestant interest, the Hanoverian succession, 'the glorious
memory', 'liberty' and 'honour'. Moreover, the troop or ship itself – and
those serving in it – focused devotion. Great Britain, its empire and rulers
were not always uncritically revered. Success in army or navy helped some
Protestants from Ireland to turn English. Richard Waring, Moses and
William Leathes, buying property in England and living on it, personify
that process. It paralleled the entry of Catholics exiled from Ireland into
the élites of continental Europe. Other veterans returned with their earnings to respected rankings in Protestant Ireland. They remained silent as
to whether, after fighting for the Hanoverian monarchy, they were now
'English', 'British' or 'Irish'.[254] Nor did such issues decide how they were
regarded by their contemporaries. The latter were chiefly impressed by
how much the victorious officers had amassed. Possessions – the elegant
residences of Frederick Hamilton and Owen Wynne – were admired. In
addition, these veterans had acquired objects, manners and ideas during
their travels, which commanded attention. Seasoned officers frequently
returned to a station in Irish Protestant society higher than that into which
they had been born.

Chapter 8

Agents

I

In 1691, Lord Massareene sought 'some sturdy, trusty, robust, clownish fellow', living either in Cavan town or nearby Virginia, 'to ride to and fro to see how the lands are planted and come home a night and see what stock is going and coming on the premises'.[1] The duties demanded by the largely absent Massareene were less onerous than those expected of agents on the huge enterprises of his contemporaries such as Ormonde or Cork and Burlington. Their scattered holdings were run like government departments, and employed teams of commissioners, collectors, lawyers, surveyors, seneschals, bailiffs and sergeants of woods. The absence from Ireland of owners, decried from the 1680s (if not earlier), gave chances to the resident.[2] Moreover, a proprietor, even when present, might divide his or her time between widely separated estates, or between them and Dublin.[3] Economic prudence encouraged landlords to oversee their own farms; so too did patriotism.[4] Yet grandees who played the ploughman or shepherd usually required practical assistants. The irksome and even risky tasks of setting or gathering rents were often delegated to the hardy. Also, there was a growing awareness that specialist tasks, such as framing leases and mapping properties, demanded experts. Indeed, so great was the demand that by 1733 a porter at the Dublin Tholsel advertised a choice of 'agents, stewards, clerks, book keepers and servants' for 'lords, gentlemen and others'.[5] Where landowners engaged in proto-industrial ventures, such as ironworks, collieries or linen manufacture, they turned to knowledgeable overseers and managers.[6] However, many owners drawing no more than £50 or £100 yearly from their holdings could barely support their own families, let alone a train of subordinates. Farming themselves, they hired the necessary services – of surveyors and attorneys – only when unavoidable.

What proportion of the 3,000 to 5,000 freeholders in late seventeenth-century Ireland used agents is hard to gauge. The few with teams of assistants were outnumbered by the resident farmers able to attend in person to their concerns. Agents, in any case, readily served more than a single master. The repute of the successful, such as Dr Jeremy Hall or the Hatches, brought them numerous potential clients, and retainers from more than one. Many agents inherited or amassed property of their own. Those not born into the quality were sometimes enabled to enter it thanks to their agencies. A few went on to enter parliament. Other agents doubled as lawyers or – more rarely – as clergymen and physicians. Just as those lower in society adopted an opportunist attitude towards profitable jobs, trying several simultaneously or seriatim, so agents pocketed retainers for supervising the affairs of others. This labour was not demeaning. Some, especially when they followed another calling in Dublin, deputed work to drones on the spot. Even the assiduous, precise as accountants and punctual as collectors, relied on specialists. Agency was not, therefore, invariably a full-time or exclusive calling. Agents shaded from reputable squires and urban professionals into the despised middlemen. Hostility towards them, understandable when agents initiated onerous policies and ostentatiously paraded their own good fortune, ignored the utility of much that they did. In their localities, they served as magistrates, grand jurors and militia officers. In the provincial towns, fairs and markets, they were valued customers. Their importance as cultural innovators, growing novel crops, testing unfamiliar techniques or living with unwonted refinement, was great: greater, arguably, than that of their absent superiors. The habitually non-resident, such as a Palmerston or Egmont, could advance the interests of tenants through exertions in Westminster and Whitehall. But agents as well as – or instead of – proprietors mediated with the trustees of the Linen, Barrack and Inland Navigation Boards to direct bounty towards their district. They lobbied at the assizes and sessions and agitated in the grand jury for the same ends.

No standard training prepared for an agency. Jeremy Hall impressed families like the Wentworths and Boyles when he tutored their sons and conducted them around Europe. Hall also possessed a medical degree and in 1667 was a founding fellow of the Dublin College of Physicians. His versatility turned him into the indispensable factotum of the aristocracy. Something of his resulting status and wealth showed in his bequest of illustrated guides and maps of the antiquities of Rome to Dublin University and moneys to found a school in Limerick.[7] In the 1720s, John and Henry Hatch emerged from very different backgrounds. Where Hall migrated from Yorkshire to Ireland, Hatch was said to have started as a grazier in the Irish midlands. Once in Dublin, the Hatches attracted approving notice, and were soon in demand as estate managers.[8] At the time when the Hatches flourished, Thomas Kingsbury combined fashionable practice as a Dublin physician with loose oversight of the Irish interests of an old acquaintance, Frank Price, from the 1730s living in North Wales. The Price portfolio then passed to Kingsbury's widow and on to her son, a barrister. The latter acted for family friends resident in Ireland itself, such as the Edgeworths.[9] Samuel Waring, frequently in Dublin, deputed care of his County Down property to a younger brother, Thomas. Francis Bernard, successful lawyer, judge and member of parliament, similarly entrusted his interests in County Cork to a brother. Thomas Waring was enabled by his duties to take a place in his own right as a squire in the county. Arthur Bernard enriched himself at his brother's expense. He too scrambled into the squirearchy.[10] William Eustace sued for a place as steward in County Kildare on the basis of tenuous kinship with the owner.[11] Consanguinity explained why Lord Digby of Geashill chose John Digby, a substantial squire in County Kildare and member of parliament, to look after his Irish holdings. Squire Digby, benevolent, even enlightened in the management of his own properties, resented any attempt to curb his independence when handling the absentee's concerns. Lord Digby's lands also gave a living – at least temporarily – to two of John Digby's sons.[12] The squire haughtily denied that he helped his distant kinsman other than from the sense of affinity, and angrily refused to compromise his political principles.[13] The Kingsburys were similarly touchy about imagined slights or imputations about their conduct. They thought they conferred a favour rather than gained an employment by supervising the Prices' Irish properties.[14]

Agencies were desired on account of both legitimate and illicit rewards. Competition for the employment could be fierce. Patrons put forward candidates when a vacancy occurred, as they might for a church living or a patentee office. Henry Temple, living in England, was inundated with suggestions as to whom he should appoint to succeed a recently dead agent. Temple, anxious not to antagonize the important in Ireland, thanked his informants politely, kept his own counsel and made his own selection. He suspected that those hoping to snap up parts of his Irish patrimony were trying to insert their own Trojan horses into his confidential affairs.[15] Supplicants for agencies inevitably reported (and sometimes fabricated) what incumbents like John Digby did wrong. This time-honoured tactic to supplant a sitting agent magnified transgressions. Outsiders, dispatched either from other regions of Ireland or from Britain to overhaul a holding, disparaged what others had or had not done. On the Digby estates, for example, a new representative was bewildered by what he discovered on a frustrating trip to the midlands in 1715.[16] Robert Lloyd arrived in County Kerry at much the same time. He was campaigning to take over the agency of the Herberts of Cherbury (also absentees). Immediately locals ganged up against Lloyd. He – the presumptuous interloper – was baffled by a formidable league compounded of kinship, neighbourhood and collusive profiteering.[17] The proprietors, living on the border of Wales and England, persisted in using as managers their kindred settled in County Kerry. Try as Lloyd might to show how family sentiment had masked systematic fraud, he could not dislodge the Kerry Herberts. The two principals, Arthur and Edward Herbert, unblushingly invoked the tie of blood by begging their employer to remember 'that a branch of your name has been planted here [in Kerry] by your ancestors'. They saw off the challenge from Lloyd. He retreated from Kerry, 'a hellish country', lamenting that 'it's impossible for me, a single person, to give battle to a united country'.[18] Lloyd felt that he 'had as good be in Tartary'.[19] Meanwhile, the victorious Herberts of Kerry, undisturbed by what had been rumoured of their malpractices, dug deeper into the wealth of the county.

Another owner of vast tracts in Kerry, Sir William Petty, had earlier struggled to enjoy his estate. Contrary to his intentions, he and his wife had had regularly to travel to the remote region.[20] In addition to these personal inspections, permanent staff had to be placed on the spot. Would-be agents competed for what they suspected could be a profitable post.[21] Petty, in the heady days of first coming into possession, repudiated any compromises with the displaced Catholic owners. As a result, he found proprietorship dispiriting. Soon he repined, 'our estates here are mere visions and delusions, and require more attendance than a retail shop'.[22] No new owner approached his property with more ingenious ideas of how it might be improved, and few were so roughly disabused. Despite Petty's command of theory and a passionate belief that it should be applied to the common good, his schemes for his Irish estates were conventional. Both in the projects to exploit resources, such as timber, iron ore and fish, and in his deployment of personnel, he diverged little from neighbours or predecessors. However, the value and nature of his acquisitions justified a long train of overseers. A rental approaching £6,000 p.a. from at least five counties gave varied work. Those thus sustained encompassed a kinsman of Lady Petty, James Waller, who sat in parliament, relations of Petty himself and others lifted from obscurity. Among the last, Richard Orpen, a likely lad plucked from school by Petty, heaved himself into the local squirearchy through his Kerry agency.[23]

Scattered and intractable holdings like those of Petty hint why management in Ireland generally consumed a larger percentage of income than in England.[24] However, these difficulties hardly explain the tendency of agents in Ireland to be drawn from and to occupy higher social stations.[25] Absenteeism, although often described as a peculiarly Irish curse, afflicted large parts of Britain. With it came the chance for agents to undertake more than just the management disdained by their employers. In Ireland, those born on the land had limited opportunities to supplement often exiguous incomes. Agencies accordingly offered an attractive prospect. The work could be combined with both continued residence in the country-side and care of one's own plot. Furthermore, although recondite legal, actuarial and agricultural abilities were increasingly wanted, there was a perception that the clever townsperson lacked some qualities vital to evaluating farms and tenants. Robert Roberts, exemplary in running his department in the Dublin Court of Exchequer, came to grief when he ventured into south Munster as Cork and Burlington's man. As a successor commented sardonically, 'Roberts was a likely fellow to be sure to do my lord service, who was not master of one faculty sufficient to clear off the incumbrances of one farm'.[26] This feeling that the urban expert might miss a trick or two may account for the longer survival in Ireland of the apparent amateur recruited from the landed community.

The amateurism was often more apparent than real. The calling of agent, unlike others on the margins of respectability and in acknowledged professions, lacked any agreed qualifications.[27] Whereas clergy were almost all graduates and quizzed thoroughly before ordination, lawyers veterans of the London and Dublin Inns of Court, and physicians quondam students of the medical schools and fellows of the Dublin College, agents belonged to no professional body and had undergone no uniform prepa-ration. This haphazardness allowed Catholics to be recruited. Indeed, by the mid-eighteenth century, worries about the ease with which Catholics had moved into this work brought calls for a statutory ban on their employment as agents.[28] The absence of formal instruction did not mean that agents were ill-equipped for their duties. However, they had come by their proficiency variously, and little in the process is well documented. Assisting a father, whether Digby of Landenstown or Dick Bagge around Lismore, was one device. By the mid-seventeenth century printed texts and the circulars of well-meaning groups such as Hartlib's friends (a group interested in practical and religious reforms) and the Dublin Philosophi-cal Society reached the interested. Agricultural evangelism was redoubled in the eighteenth century, sometimes as a part of Protestant proselytism. During the 1720s, famines shocked the hitherto complaisant or indif-ferent, warning of the apparent backwardness of Irish agriculture.[29] First, the Dublin Society and then the Physico-Historical Society diffused infor-mation about new equipment and crops. The Dublin parliament modestly subsidized some of these innovations. Much of this activity was directed by metropolitan sophisticates, such as James Ware, John Putland and the Reverend John Wynne. Living usually as *rentiers*, they seldom or never rambled – so far as we can judge – around the remoter reaches of their scattered properties. At the same time, the voluntary societies galvanized others in the provinces. The enthusiasts, among whom the clergy were disproportionately well represented, sometimes themselves owned farms or superintended them on behalf of others. They had ample chances to test what they had learnt in the committee rooms and clubs of Dublin.[30]

It may be doubted just how much could be learnt from manuals, no matter how simply and clearly written. Moreover, the relevance of broccoli, mulberries and silkworms to raising Irish rents could reasonably be questioned.[31] The intellectual and fashionable were too easily diverted from the dull but reliable staples by the crazes of the moment. In order to run an estate satisfactorily little surpassed intimacy with its physical and human geography. Unfortunately this was an education which rarely left clear traces. Some agricultural experts were autodidacts. Nicholas Peacock, moving daily around the fertile barony south of the Shannon in County Limerick, knew the peculiarities of each townland. This knowledge informed what he did on behalf of his employers, the Hartstonges and Widenhams, and for himself.[32] Bit by bit, Peacock's proficiency assisted his own advance.

Landlords naturally expected agents to collect rents in full and remit them punctually.[33] Yet the size and regularity of receipts were not the only measures by which agents were assessed. Lords Burlington and Orrery or Judge Bernard, far from their lands and with other preoccupations, craved freedom from importunate tenants. Accordingly they left their deputies, Brettridge Badham, Andrew Crotty and Arthur Bernard, largely to their own devices. The paymasters called these cheats to account, but too late to recoup losses. Employers seemingly tolerated 'shuffling' stewards whose honesty might be suspect because they fended off other irritations. Among those keen to be spared the chore of minute oversight of their inheritance were the first and second dukes of Ormonde. The Ormondes, rivalled only by the earls of Cork (after 1665 of Cork and Burlington) in their income from Irish lands, contrast with the Cork and Burlingtons both in attitude towards and practice on their estates. After 1698 when the Cork and Burlingtons lived permanently in England, the cases of these two greatest estates came more closely to resemble one another. Each, whether in its heyday or in decline, offered generous pickings to others. With an annual yield in the later seventeenth century of £25,000 to £30,000 both needed a phalanx of managers.

The Ormonde enterprise, apparently similar to that of the Cork and Burlingtons, differed in several details. Both the first and second duke shrugged off estate management as a wearisome distraction from public duties as viceroy and army commander. Nor did such drudgery sit comfortably with the Ormondes' notion of the aristocrat. A lofty detachment from some of the detailed administration marked their government of their duchy and the kingdom of Ireland. After 1641, the Ormondes relied on a council. This management may have resurrected a system used earlier on their estates. It paralleled how Ireland was governed. The first duke's half-brother, George Mathew, dealt with the routines of an extensive estate – choosing and chasing tenants and gathering and remitting rents. Mathew, already of consequence, used this occupation to raise a dynasty which would dominate Tipperary.[34] Above the familiar tiers of collectors and stewards were placed committees. The remit of the latter was to reduce – or at least manage – the massive debts of the Ormondes. By the 1690s, the committee-men, having failed to persuade the duke to economize, schemed to cash in some of his assets. They promoted bills in the Irish and English parliaments which authorized sales of land, and then arranged the sales. These responsibilities differed from the usual ones of agents and required different qualifications. A grasp of finance helped; so too did expertise in the law, parliamentary procedures and political lobbying. Committee members included Lord Longford, connected by marriage with the Ormondes and also experienced although not necessarily competent as a financial administrator. Others were Richard Warburton, lawyer and member of parliament; William Worth, an Exchequer judge; Richard Cox, a future lord chancellor; the surveyor-general, Sir William Robinson; and Edward Corker, another member of the Irish parliament.[35] They put their talents at the disposal of the Ormondes. In return, they may have looked for further preferment from their patrons. Whether by design or chance, these aides were ideally placed to profit from the dismantling of the estate over which they presided. Sales early in Queen Anne's reign were followed by yet more after the English attainder of the exiled second duke as a Jacobite after 1715. Agents, servants and officers who had once deferred to the Ormondes now flourished on the ruins of their empire.[36] The Ormondes' lost territories set up several as substantial proprietors, soon to be adorned with peerages. What was said of the Boyles' fiefdom, that if divided it would suffice for several earldoms, was true of the Butlers' possessions.[37] After the duchy had been dismembered, later eighteenth-century Tipperary and Kilkenny supported an unusual number of the wealthy and titled.[38]

Early in the seventeenth century, the first earl of Cork had carved a great apanage from south Munster and guarded it vigilantly. He dinned the same obsessive attentiveness into his heir.[39] The second earl made it his life's work to pass on this patrimony, enhanced not diminished. Contemporaries praised him as the ideal of the careful custodian.[40] Hapless underlings may have rejoiced less. No detail of their accounts and behaviour escaped their exigent master. The second earl questioned spending

on cakes of rat poison when Youghal had to be rid of an infestation associated with the Williamite garrison. Angrier were his objections to what
had been spent when James II slept at Lismore, the earl's chief seat, in
1689. 'For one supper and a breakfast, and in Lent, when there were very
few but papists there, and neither the king nor any of them did eat a bit
of flesh, yet for the expenses, I say, of two meals, there was disbursed
of my money, £171 8s 6d'.[41] Interests in Dublin and – increasingly – in
England took the earls from south Munster more often and for longer.
Even when in Ireland, a band of subordinates handled the routines. From
1690, with successive earls always away, these subordinates increased in
power.

A team of four ran Irish operations. Under them flourished a larger
tribe of collectors, bailiffs and seneschals. Each in the quartet was designed
to check the shortcomings of his colleagues. Any gains were offset by the
personal animosities which arose from being spied on. Nor, in the end,
did the arrangement prevent corruption. Partly fortuitously, but also by
plan, a balance was struck between locals well versed in the ecology of
the district and supposedly disinterested outsiders. In addition, the talents
of the four complemented rather than duplicated one another: legal
acumen, accountancy, expert appraisal of the worth of lands and peoples,
and easy access to the powerful. Management of the Burlington estate was
evolving in response to the changing circumstances and priorities of the
owner. A change of approach with the succession in 1698 of the second
Lord Burlington was announced in a letter to his main Irish managers: 'I
have discoursed with several people about the lands of Ireland and am
informed that an old rental is not a sure mark to go by: that some lands
may never come up to it, and others far exceed the old rent, the course
of trade may alter it, the humour of the people in particular trades, and
the manner of living or peopling of a country.' Faced with these impon-
derables, he departed from the philosophy of his ancestors, the first and
second earls of Cork, and concluded that 'you that live upon the place
are the best judges of those accidents and will decide accordingly'.[42]

The Burlingtons did not detach themselves as completely as the declaration of 1698 promised. Periodically they threatened to descend on
Ireland, sending agents into a frenzy to repair their own depredations
and physical dilapidations. Moreover, the Burlingtons and their English
advisers pestered the Irish managers about irregular and disappointing
payments.[43] Irish operations were expected to underwrite the family's
life elsewhere. When remittances failed to keep pace with the third earl
of Burlington's spending, Ireland was raided. Sales in the 1720s and 1730s
reduced the acreage and the rental. After this contraction, and in response
to its notorious failings, the unwieldy machine was overhauled. Fewer but

better-paid agents resulted. During the 1690s, their salaries had never exceeded £100. By the later 1720s, Andrew Crotty acknowledged being paid at a daily rate of £1.[44] Crotty's work for Burlington took him to England and the continent. John Ussher, himself a member of a family long established in Ireland but not in south Munster, was appointed agent at Lismore in 1739. He received a yearly £400.[45] In the next decade, the chief agent of the Courtenays' County Limerick estate, reputed to yield a yearly £9,000, received £500 or £600 p.a.[46] In Ulster, the chief representative of one of the greatest proprietors, William Conolly, was handsomely rewarded.[47] At Lismore, Ussher's installation marked a stage in which control was transferred from those enmeshed in local alliances to supposedly more impartial strangers. Belatedly the Burlingtons were learning the lesson which had been impressed on other Irish proprietors: no agent would serve his employer wholeheartedly so long as he was a tenant of lands in the district which he oversaw.[48] Strategic guidance was removed to an auditor and lawyer either in Dublin or – ultimately – London. But the fashion for disengagement could go too far. No estate could be run properly with agents totally detached from it. In the Burlington concern, Lismore remained the administrative as well as symbolic centre. An agent there, more generously remunerated and more minutely supervised, was aided by subalterns in the main towns of the earldom: Bandon, Dungarvan and Youghal.[49] These dispositions, reflecting the geography of the holding, modified rather than overturned what had traditionally been the administrative divisions. Numerous trials and many errors occurred before structures of control were finalized. Nor was the system proof against the crook. In 1792, the agents at Lismore were discovered to have tricked their employer.[50]

The annual receipts from the Butler and Boyle enterprises surpassed those of many departments of the Irish government and allowed an administration similar to that in the Dublin offices. In some cases, the mechanisms for overseeing a large estate suggested how the state in Ireland might be administered. The Ormondes, as frequent lords-lieutenant, and Cork and Burlington, as lord treasurer and an Irish privy councillor, sometimes blurred the demarcation between national and family affairs. These were never completely sealed off from each other. Few believed that they should be. Occasionally too flagrant misuse of public places for personal gain was censured. The Ormondes, it has been suggested, benefited from the advice about their personal troubles of several high in the Irish government. Worth and Cox as judges had the ability to favour the Ormondes. More visible was the way in which the Ormondes swapped staff and goods between their own and the state's houses. Given the attenuated budget on which the viceroyalty had to be run, this practice eased the state's embarrassments. Without the ducal servants and furnishings, Dublin Castle, official residence of the sovereign's deputy in Ireland, would not have dazzled. However, the Ormondes extorted their price. They stuffed employees and dependants into whatever openings appeared in army, Church and government. Many of these appointments were no more than customary patronage. Unless clients, kindred and allies were gratified, the dukes' following might melt away, and with it their authority. Understandable, too, was the temptation to install functionaries from Kilkenny into salaried positions on the civil and military establishments. Some of these rewards – like inclusion in the commission of the peace – brought no salary and considerable inconvenience, but they did increase power and status. On the Cork and Burlington estate, the earl routinely had agents added to the county commission of the peace.[51] In 1691, he reassured one, reluctant to undergo the labour, that being a magistrate will 'add to your interest and credit in the county'.[52] What was unspoken but understood was how such a post also advanced the interests of the proprietor.[53] The reluctance of another Burlington employee to become a magistrate in Queen Anne's reign considerably annoyed his employer.[54] By becoming justices of the peace, agents consolidated their local standing. They also assumed responsibilities shirked by their missing or indifferent masters.[55]

More obviously profitable to employers and employed alike was the ability of the powerful to appoint agents – or have them appointed – to salaried offices. Military commissions were a favourite way in which the Ormondes pleased followers. The staffing of their palatine court at Clonmel was another. But there were further sinecures in Dublin and the localities which might accommodate employees, reduce what the Ormondes had to pay them and increase the dependants' gratitude. Thomas Page, secretary to the first duke of Ormond, was elected to a fellowship of King's College, Cambridge, as well as to a seat in the Irish Commons. He also secured the clerkship of pleas in the Irish Exchequer. He eventually relinquished his post with Ormond, but not his sinecures on the Irish establishment on becoming provost of King's and vice-chancellor of Cambridge University.[56] Henry Gascoigne, successor to Page, accumulated even more established offices on the Irish civil list through serving the Ormondes.[57] The second Lord Cork had access to fewer sources of public bounty. Nevertheless, entering on to the lord treasurership in 1660, he rapidly grasped the chance to award collectorships in Irish ports. In bestowing these sinecures he astutely flattered the important in England and Ireland, from the monarch downwards. Few posts went to his own dependants.[58] However, as *Custos Rotulorum* and governor of Counties Waterford and Cork, he could distribute attractive local positions. He appreciated the importance of hanging on to these posts in the new reign of William and Mary, not just for the precedence and prestige but for the patronage.[59] Beneficiaries included his own employee, Leonard Gosteloe, and his brother's, Lionel Beecher. Gosteloe was described as the earl's secretary during the interregnum.[60] Subsequently he dealt with a multiplicity of matters, including some which took him to Dublin on his master's behalf.[61] The better to protect Cork and Burlington's interests, he was added to the commission of the peace. The expenses were met by the estate.[62] Gosteloe clashed with the agents of the Dublin government, and specifically the alnager, when he took to licensing woollens manufactured around Tallow and Lismore, and extracting fees for the licences. Gosteloe, secure in his master's confidence, was not easily checked.[63] Beecher served Orrery as seneschal of his manors at Askeaton and Charleville, but also acted in the Customs at Youghal.[64] Later, Burlington's cousin Orrery approached the government to move his agent, Badham, from the collectorship of Youghal to the better remunerated one at Cork.[65]

Magnates like the Ormondes, the Cork and Burlingtons and Orrery were essential to the English regime in Ireland. Without the local authority of these peers behind it, the government would have struggled to make its writ run into the remoter provinces. Grandees extorted their price, sometimes openly, often covertly. Just as they ensured that much of the revenue collected from taxes paid for better roads and waterways or subsidized flax, hemp and grain, so national and local bureaucracies were stuffed with their auxiliaries. Agents gained precedence and power from such appointments. They served their employers well by exploiting public positions – in the magistracy, grand jury, urban council or even parliament – to favour the estates for which they worked. Representatives of the usually absent regularly approached the important in Dublin, and so, as in the cases of Henry and John Hatch, acquired greater confidence when they frequented the society of the grand.

II

The sort of people who served as agents can first be illustrated from the undertakings of the Boyles in south Munster. The estates, because so large, hardly typified the generality. However, the employees do reveal the diversity of backgrounds from which agents came. Two distinct portions – the western centred on Bandon, the eastern on Youghal and Lismore – had long had separate collectors.[66] The quartet which assumed effective control during the 1690s was a mixed bag: Digby Foulke, Colonel William Congreve, Roger Power and Richard Bagge. Foulke, from a family of long-standing but poor-paying tenants of the Boyles, first entered their service in the 1660s. In 1684, he had been appointed a justice of the peace; in 1695 he served as high sheriff.[67] He had risen from a captaincy to a colonelcy in the recent Williamite campaigns.[68] These distinctions indicated that he was 'a person of credit', independent of his employment with, but not of his tenancy from, the Boyles. He started at a salary of £50 p.a., supplemented by a riding fee of five shillings for every day that he was away from home on Burlington business. The obsessive old earl expected Foulke to account weekly.[69] By 1704, Foulke was too aged and infirm to stray much beyond Youghal.[70] Sentiment best explained both his retention and the approval (in 1711) of an arrangement whereby he divided the work with his son-in-law.[71] Others of his family made a living from the Boyles. 'Mrs' Foulke, presumably the colonel's wife, received £10 yearly to tend the college gardens at Youghal, 'she obliging herself to keep them in good order and also the kitchen garden walled about'. Another of the colonel's kinswomen was inserted as housekeeper there: she was paid an annual £5. Not without reason, the earl grumbled about Foulke's numerous family.[72]

Of the four, Richard Bagge was at first the junior in terms of pay and standing. His salary, starting at only £20, was raised to £40 in 1697.[73] Still he remained lowest in esteem. His colleagues, Congreve, Power and Foulke, in common with peers like Lord Barrymore, were each to be presented with a buck from Burlington's deer-park. Dick Bagge, however, was allowed only half a beast: an honour certainly, but one which could too readily be measured against the greater courtesy accorded his fellows.[74] In 1696 he took on the collection of rents in Clare, Clonmel and Ormond. This brought him an extra £20 p.a., but he had been obliged to enter into security of £1,000.[75] In the same year, and with his employer's permission, he married.[76] Bagge took time to persuade the always suspicious earl of his talents. In 1694, the tetchy octogenarian expostulated about the inexperienced Bagge being 'so selfish, so negligent and so partial' in collecting rents and finding tenants.[77] Comrades played on these doubts.[78] Bagge was granted lodgings in Lismore Castle, where Power and Congreve were also accommodated. However, relations between the agents had deteriorated so far that the other two communicated with Bagge only by letter. In 1698, the new earl urged these subordinates to put aside their animosities.[79] So far from doing so, the chill deepened. Bagge's relative inferiority put him at risk from his better-established colleagues. In the atmosphere of mutual recrimination which enveloped the estate during the absences of the second and third earls of Burlington, Bagge was accused of corruption and dismissed.[80] The veracity of the allegations cannot now be proved or disproved. It is true that, by 1700, four of Bagge's name were Burlington tenants in Dungarvan.[81] But this dynasticism was not uncommon in an area where potential English and Protestant tenants were scarce. The unhappy episode of Bagge's employment dragged on long after he had been sacked, when the Burlingtons' representatives went to law to recover arrears owed by Bagge. He retaliated by suing for unpaid salary.[82] In doing so, he asserted that he had advanced the Burlingtons' rentals by £8,000: an unlikely claim, for which there is no corroboration.[83] Bagge briefly flourished under the Burlingtons. His salary had eventually climbed to £100 p.a. A sign of his solid worth was his ability to put two sons into Trinity College in Dublin.[84] The father claimed that two other sons had assisted him on estate business.[85] After their father's removal, they were cast adrift. However, the training may have fitted them for a variety of occupations. In 1757, a Richard Baggs was appointed a land-waiter in the revenue, suggesting that one member of the dynasty had turned to a familiar source of sustenance. Others were to be found in the Church.[86]

The third of the four agents, Roger Power of Mount Eglantine, came of an Old English family long settled on the borders of Waterford and Cork. Of the quartet, he was the most solidly based in the region and almost certainly the richest. When he died in 1707 he was said to be worth £6,000.[87] Burlington gained much from his help; perhaps more than Power derived from serving the earl. This made for an uneasy relationship between the two. Burlington was quick to imagine that Power had neglected his concerns and slighted his privileges. He peremptorily reminded the wayward Power, that he was 'a person that owes me duty being employed in my service'. Burlington also contended that he owed his appointment as a justice of the peace to his recommendation: 'you had not been elevated to that degree to which you are now arrived'.[88] The proud Power was unlikely to be humbled. Bagge later averred that 'it's notoriously known' that Power 'made his fortune the few years he was employed' by the Burlingtons.[89] The second earl himself gave some credence to this view when, in 1692, he claimed that Power's neglect had lost him £10,000.[90] Power, as seneschal of the manor of Dungarvan and manager of the jointure estate of Burlington's heir, Lord Dungarvan and Clifford (who predeceased his father in 1694), had the possibility of surreptitious profits.[91] Attending the assizes at Cork and Waterford and the sessions at Dungarvan, he charged his expenses to Burlington. As a magistrate, he might have been expected to act impartially, but the bills suggested he saw himself as the champion of the Burlingtons.[92] In the end, following the second earl's death in 1698, this was how the Burlingtons viewed Power. In 1703, he was elected to parliament for Dungarvan in the Burlington interest. His professions of 'so much zeal for the service and interest of this noble family [of Boyle]' were evidently believed. When he died, he was venerated as 'so long a servant to the family'.[93] Power's instinct for survival made him attach himself to those who had arrived more recently and threatened to eclipse dynasties like his. This same pliancy showed in his choice of a husband for his daughter: Arthur Bernard, whose defrauding of his elder brother would become the talk of the province.[94]

The final actor in Burlington's troupe in the 1690s was another colonel: William Congreve. His connection with Burlington had begun in Yorkshire probably during the 1660s.[95] One advantage of owning lands on either side of the Irish Sea was the possibility of shifting stock, goods and personnel between them. Congreve never broke his English links. Burlington reminded Congreve, as he did other agents, how much his ascent owed to him. When Congreve puffed himself up as a colonel, the earl punctured this pretension by recalling how recently he had ranked as a lieutenant.[96] Nevertheless, Congreve was the agent for whom Burlington showed most respect (or fewest misgivings) and even a hint of affection. The pernickety earl commanded the ageing Congreve to keep a clerk who could write and account weekly when Congreve was indisposed.[97] Congreve was the first of the agents to be permitted to lodge in Lismore Castle; he was to have his honourable complement of venison.[98] The first Lord Burlington was intimate enough with him both to advise on ailments and to enthuse over the success in London of Congreve's son with his play, *The Old Bachelour*. The earl's grandson, when in England, executed errands for Congreve's wife.[99] By the next decade, with the Congreves in England, the colonel begged to be accommodated in the Burlingtons' suburban seat of Chiswick. Moreover, the old faithful merited a pension of £50 p.a. when, ripe in years, he retired.[100] Meanwhile in Ireland, Congreve had become a model of gentility. He was able to put his son through the smart college at Kilkenny. He himself frequented the spa at Castle Connell in County Limerick.[101] The Congreves were on book-lending terms with their grander neighbours, the Villiers at Dromana.[102] Congreve, more clearly than his three colleagues, turned his agency into a springboard from which to launch himself into Irish Protestant society. He already had kindred there, tempted to Munster in an earlier phase of the plantation.[103] In contrast to Congreve, the Powers were long and the Foulkes more lately settled as squires when they were placed on Burlington's payroll. Bagge was dropped and had to make his own way.

The agents of the 1690s, despite friction, possessed complementary attributes. Whether this balance was planned by the earl is unclear. The chances which brought each into the Burlingtons' service are hidden. Subsequent promotion spoke more clearly of trust gradually created. Congreve transferred to Munster the talents which he had first shown in the north of England. Power and Foulke were plucked from a press of supplicants on the Irish lands. Bagge's background proves more elusive, although it too probably lay among the Protestant settlers of south Munster. Bagge was expected to bring a dogged dedication to his arduous brief. The others brought to their agencies familiarity with local and national politics and the law. When these originals had to be replaced, a less adventitious approach prevailed. The first two earls had been shrewd judges of those reared on their properties, and groomed the promising. Thereafter, this personal interest weakened, and would-be agents had to make interest to persuade the absent proprietors to employ them. Formal qualifications possibly counted more. Yet personal recommendations still swayed fickle masters, especially the third earl of Burlington, who came of age in 1715.

Of the new agents of the early eighteenth century, one, Richard Musgrave, resembled Congreve in having originated on the English side of the water. Musgrave uprooted himself from the north-west and founded a house of squires beside the River Blackwater. Within a generation, his son was also serving Lord Grandison, a neighbour and rival of the Burlingtons.[104] While Musgrave stepped into the vacancy left by Congreve, Thomas Baker took Bagge's place. Baker, it was said, trained as a book-keeper in Ostend. Whether this apprenticeship had come about through working with the army commissariat during the War of the Spanish Succession or through a foray into trade is unknown. In bringing the dis-cipline of the accountant to the Burlingtons' affairs, Baker disturbed other agents whose accountancy was laxer. The third spot was taken by Jeremy Coughlan. His expertise was primarily legal, and was being applied to the Burlingtons' affairs in the early 1690s.[105] It took time for him to meet the exacting tests of the first Burlington. In particular, the earl was displeased with a proposal of 1697 that the Irish Catholics be allowed to rent prop-erties in and around Lismore. Burlington intended this town to remain a model Protestant settlement.[106] Coughlan, once secure, prospered. Already in 1694 he was able to advance money to the earl on a mortgage.[107] Added to the agents in the reign of Queen Anne, he proved indispensable. When, on Power's death in 1707, the seneschalship of Dungarvan was vacated, Coughlan was preferred on account of his legal expertise.[108] By then he was esteemed 'a very honest gentleman'.[109] This reputation recommended him to Burlington's uncle, Henry Boyle, the future Lord Carleton, whose Munster properties Coughlan subsequently managed. Boyle flattered Coughlan by telling him 'you are under a very good character of ability and integrity'.[110]

Any large estate generated much legal business. The Burlingtons paid practising barristers termly retainers.[111] Coughlan, as an attorney, both instructed superiors and dispatched much business himself. Leases and other legal instruments needed to be drafted carefully. The law might be used to discipline or remove errant tenants and to repulse any external threats. He attended the local courts, but also consulted judges and politicians in Dublin.[112] Coughlan, of Old Irish stock, had conformed to the established Church. At what point the family had taken this momentous step is unknown. Coughlan may have done so to qualify himself to practise at the bar. These timely conversions have sometimes been seen as no more than nominal. Furthermore, they endangered the Protestant interest by planting within it a fifth-column for the Irish Catholics.[113] The date and motive for Coughlan's switch escape us, but there seems little doubt about his enthusiasm for his new confession. Between 1694 and 1713, fourteen of Coughlan's children were baptized in the Church of Ireland cathedral at Lismore.[114] Three sons later entered Trinity College and one was ordained.[115] Coughlan, partly because of his local and Catholic links, was denounced by disgruntled rivals.[116] Coming to his work with existing alliances in the region undoubtedly increased his value to Burlington; in its turn, Coughlan's affinity may have been helped by his employment with Burlington. At his death, his payments to Burlington were in arrears, and these took years for his sons to settle.[117] The agent Coughlan had married a son into the episcopal and official Maules, and through them connected with the local aristocracy in the persons of the Barrymores. The Coughlans established themselves in splendour on their coastal eminence of Ardo, but also fanned out into the lands of County Meath.[118] Working for the Burlingtons raised the Coughlans higher. What else they gained, perhaps covertly, from their employers is harder to ascertain.

The Old Irish Coughlans had joined the established Church. Other agents, despite the preference of their employers for Protestants, remained Catholic. An example was Andrew Crotty, the fourth member of the quartet which acted in Ireland during the architect earl of Burlington's minority. A William Crotty, perhaps the father of Andrew, served as bailiff or sergeant of the manor of Lismore in 1694.[119] Andrew Crotty, 'as zealous a Roman Catholic then as now', having entered security of £500, in 1712 was empowered to collect rents on the Burlington lands.[120] By the 1720s, Crotty had so charmed Lord Burlington that he was assigned a room in the earl's London house.[121] His employer exploited Crotty's numerous Irish Catholic contacts by dispatching him to continental Europe. Crotty was generously reimbursed at an annual £365.[122] His intimacy with the earl, together with the evident profits, were envied, but as a Catholic, he was vulnerable.[123] In 1715, with the Pretender in the offing, he was apparently indicted as a Jacobite conspirator. The escapologist easily freed himself from this charge. What eventually brought him down was his deception of Burlington. The earl was blamed for failing over ten years to call his agent to account. It was said that 'his [Burlington's] confidence in Mr Crotty at that time was such that he was careless what deeds he executed provided they were prepared by him'. In the mid-1730s, Burlington realized Crotty's neglect, if not outright chicanery, and threatened to prosecute him.[124]

The over-confident Crotty was constantly 'seeking too far'.[125] Relations received leases on generous terms.[126] Crotty himself abused his position on the estate with a land transaction which would be described in 1756 as 'a very dark affair, which I never could discover though I have taken a good deal of pains for that purpose'.[127] Either in 1726 or 1731, he had been granted a preferential lease of forty-one years – technically illegal since he was a Catholic – 'in consideration for great services done'. This had been assigned promptly to two London tradesmen, Nathanael Gould and Albert Nesbitt, to cover debts of £4,000. Gould and Nesbitt had then leased the property back to Crotty at a peppercorn rent, or alternatively for £500, for the maximum term of thirty-one years which, as a Catholic, he could enjoy. However, in 1734 he had mortgaged it to Elizabeth Mutlow of Waterford as security for a loan of £1,000. In 1739 Crotty, dismissed from Burlington's service, was threatened as a Catholic with a bill of discovery. Despite these challenges, Crotty and his heirs retained the desirable property, within sight of Lismore Castle.[128]

Crotty, like other admired agents, was in demand. He acted for the Inchiquins, some of whose lands marched with Burlington's. By 1726 he was involved in the affairs of the Hills from County Down.[129] During the 1740s, Crotty worked for Lord Barrymore, another non-resident, who was related to the Boyles and had estates in County Cork. Crotty was thought to be at his old, shady tricks, trying to recoup some of his losses at Barrymore's expense.[130] Before this fall from grace, Crotty insinuated himself into the confidence of the cultured Burlington and dealt on easy terms with Lord Grandison and Henry Boyle of Castlemartyr.[131] He affected the high style of his master, Burlington. Near the end of his life, it was noted that he had behaved 'very genteel' by treating neighbours in County Cork to 'a merry bottle'.[132] Something of Crotty's florid elegance, evident in his elaborate handwriting, is conveyed by the order he sent to Bruges for linen. He requested a cambric handkerchief for himself, 'of middling price', 'for I always carry such for tenderlies'.[133] His overblown courtliness toppled into foppishness. Sycophancy may have inhibited him, when in Paris in 1731, from 'pretending to describe buildings or improvements' which Burlington was 'perfect master of'.[134] However, on his own account he was introducing cultural novelties into south Munster. In 1727, for example, he sent designs from the architect William Kent, another

Burlington employee, to Henry Boyle.[135] Crotty's own seat at Modeligo was said to excel, at least in size, the residences of the Villiers at Dromana and Henry Boyle at Castlemartyr.[136] Nothing is known of Modeligo, and whether it reflected the Palladian preferences of Burlington. Its fashionable contents are suggested by Crotty's receipt of a set of engravings from England.[137] As an intermediary, he also pleased local sportsmen. For Squire Boyle, he procured a couple of hounds. One dog, Crotty affirmed, still had 'his castanets'. The other, having been gelded, was 'qualified only for the seraglio or opera'.[138]

Crotty moved backwards and forwards across the vague frontier between the gentry and squirearchy. Often he was styled 'esquire'. However, in 1742, having been dismissed by Burlington, he was demoted to 'gent'.[139] The newspaper reports of his death restored him to the dignity of a squire.[140] Uncertainty about how exactly to classify Crotty, a reflection of the indeterminate position of the agent, was increased by his confessional and ethnic background.[141] Coughlan, his comrade, having thrown off his cultural and religious inheritance, was welcomed more wholeheartedly into the ranks of Protestant Ireland. Some contemporaries, however, hardly differentiated the cases of the convert Coughlan and the Catholic Crotty. An aggrieved victim of their regime on the Burlington estate detected the essential bond of ethnicity and religion, and accused the pair of conspiring to overthrow the Protestant plantation in south Munster.[142] Agents were routinely abused. To those aspersions were now added others arising from Catholicism and Irishness. In practice, whatever Coughlan and Crotty had done arose from confederacies with kinsfolk, neighbours and allies, not from enmity towards the Protestant interest.

Fear of Catholic (or crypto-Catholic) agents led to the 1750 bid to outlaw them. Alarmists thought that 'the whole weight of many Protestant estates is employed against the Protestant religion', and that former Protestant settlements had been depopulated.[143] The proposal failed, but those who called for a ban had spotted a gap in the hedge with encircled Protestant Ireland. Catholics succeeded as agents. Adjoining the Burlingtons' estate, the holding of the Villiers (Earls Grandison) by the 1730s was overseen by a Catholic.[144] Outside Munster, too, Catholics gained employment, as the Corkrans in Sligo showed. There, the absent owner, Henry Temple, first Viscount Palmerston, shared the dream of the Boyles of creating a wholly Protestant community. The project failed even more abjectly than the Boyles'. The Temples had agents in Dublin, but the Sligo property remained important: it contributed about £750, or 38 per cent, of their annual rents from Ireland. A surrogate in the town was essential. Thomas Corkran, a merchant in Sligo, fitted the brief, except, as Temple expostulated in 1719, 'I know you are a Roman Catholic'.[145] At first, Corkran was paid a modest £20 or £25 annually. But this changed to a commission of a shilling on every £1 collected.[146] Corkran's Roman Catholicism reduced his usefulness to Temple in only one obvious way: he could not be made a justice of the peace. Although debarred from the legal side of an agency, Corkran brought to Temple's concerns in Sligo what the proprietor otherwise lacked: local connections and experience as a successful trader. Members of his family were established in Dublin, London and North America.[147] So, notwithstanding misgivings about the Corkrans' faith, the father was succeeded in the Temple agency by two sons, Edward and Francis.[148] In 1733 it was reported that Francis Corkran carried on a 'very pretty trade of his own'. When he died in Dublin in 1748, he could be described as an 'eminent merchant of Sligo'.[149]

The Corkrans were not given total freedom to direct the Temples' Sligo interests. Temple in England decided how tenancies should be framed and awarded, how the other Protestant landlords of the town were to be handled and how the recurrent economic crises might be surmounted. He instructed the Corkrans about corporation affairs and elections. Nor did Temple rely exclusively on the Corkrans for information about Sligo; they competed with Henry Hatch for his ear. Their prime advantage was residence in the port. On occasion, their schemes for its improvement diverged from Temple's. The Corkrans were credited with the demolition of the ancient abbey in order to construct a new street which bore their name. In contrast, in the 1720s Temple had ordered that the monument should not be desecrated by removing its stones for building elsewhere. So far as Corkran was concerned, the relics of the past could be swept away. The most that Temple would allow was for the fabric to be raided for materials for a new Protestant church.[150]

III

The example of the Corkrans suggests that stated salary alone hardly explained the eagerness to act as agent. Except on a few of the largest holdings, annual salaries usually ranged from £20 to £40. Humphrey Owen, representing the Herberts in Kerry during the 1690s, was paid a yearly £40, as was his successor.[151] Lord Anglesey had scattered Irish estates which, early in George I's reign, yielded an average of about £6,000. A superintending agent, a Clements, was paid £100. Three subordinates each oversaw a discrete area. Salaries were graduated according to the rental of the three districts, and stretched from £51 12s. 8d. to £30. Anglesey's staff was completed by two bailiffs, both paid £10, and a wood ranger, given £8. These salaries constituted about 4 per cent of the gross receipts.[152] At the same time, Lord Digby of Geashill's holding, mainly in King's County, produced scarcely more than £800 p.a. There the agent was paid only £30 p.a.[153] Lord Abercorn, the often non-resident owner of estates concentrated in north-west Ulster, by 1767 drew a reputed £7,000 annually from them. In 1757 he had proposed installing either two or four agents to oversee his manors in Counties Donegal and Tyrone: each would be paid £60 p.a.[154] These were not derisory salaries. In themselves they supported the possessor on the margins of gentility. If, as often happened, a single agency rarely monopolized the agent's time, when added to pay from other work, it was worth undertaking.

Pluralism was openly practised. Richard Purcell, attentive agent of the Percevals, asked his masters in England to recommend him for the vacant post with the Courtenays, rumoured to be worth £500 p.a. (By 1759 it was valued at £700 p.a., and occupied by a member of the Irish parliament.)[155] Purcell clearly expected no problem about combining the two since the Percevals' and Courtenays' holdings marched together.[156] Many agents were themselves landed proprietors or substantial tenants, and so had concerns of their own to direct. The ease with which these interests could be fitted together encouraged the resident to undertake duties for the absent. Remuneration, although welcomed, was seldom the prime consideration. Agencies enlarged opportunities for patronage, and so enhanced authority in the locality. William Waring ascended in County Down society thanks to his own lands and the offices which he occupied. Also, from the late 1650s, he looked after Ulster holdings recently acquired by others: Colonel Richard Lawrence, who lived in Dublin, and the Smiths, remote in Essex. Serving the Smiths added no more than an extra £20 yearly (maybe an additional 3 or 4 per cent) to Waring's income.[157] This return hardly matched the effort. Neither Lawrence nor the Smiths understood the local conditions which depressed and delayed receipts. Waring was pressed to report in detail why returns were slow and low. His explanations – heavy mortality among animals, bad weather and the depredations of armies in 1689–90 – although real enough, may sometimes have been exaggerated.[158] Waring perhaps calculated that his monotonous reports of poverty and privations would persuade the distant owners to sell. If so, he succeeded, and himself bought – probably at bargain prices – what he had long known as agent.[159] In Kerry, the Herberts and their confederates hoped that the absent Herberts of Oakley Park would do the same. In 1730, Edward Herbert and a kinsman offered to rent the entire Herbert holding for £2,000 p.a. By 1733, much of the seignory granted to the Herberts in the sixteenth century had been leased to a syndicate which included Edward Herbert of Kilmacow and Muckross.[160] On the Burlingtons' estates, former agents, as well as cadets of the Boyles and erstwhile tenants, were prominent among those who bought at the sales in the late 1720s. Bernards, Conners, Longfields and Beechers added handsomely to their holdings.[161]

Even when lands were not sold outright, it was possible for agents to install themselves, relations, clients and allies on farms with long leases at low rents. The agents enjoyed much discretion over arrears and renewals, and could favour kindred and confederates. The prohibition of such cosy arrangements urged by reformers like Hatch was seldom practicable.

Agency was one of several avenues along which the enterprising advanced. A kinsman of the Essex Smiths, Alderman Erasmus Smith, had also acquired Irish lands during the interregnum. He, too, as an absentee from Ireland deputed the management of his ample portfolio to others. Joseph Damer, arriving in Ireland about 1670, was soon entrusted with Erasmus Smith's affairs. Damer brought political and legal prowess to these tricky tasks, which included educational benefactions. By the early eighteenth century he had emerged as a rich man, in part from serving Smith. He was allowed 1s. 3d. in the £ commission on a rental worth £631 in 1678, and £1,110 by 1709.[162] He rented farms from Smith, which formed the nucleus of the Damers' County Tipperary estate.[163] He also tried Waring's tactic. In the depressed aftermath of the Williamite warfare, Damer offered a generous £1,500 p.a. for a lease on the entire Smith empire in Ireland, but in vain.[164] In unusually acute form, he faced the dilemma of the servant of an absentee. He interpreted his duty as remitting to England as large a proportion of the Irish receipts as possible. As early as 1685, embryonic patriots were angered by 'taking away any part of the revenue . . . out of the kingdom'.[165] The tension between the trustees in Dublin, anxious to retain Smith's Irish revenues for his schools in Ireland, and Damer's divergent priority led in 1709 to his dismissal.[166] Earlier, he had written plaintively but misleadingly of how little he had gained from the agency. He thought less of his regular commission and more of marks of honour. His English employers took the hint and gratified him with an engraved silver cup.[167] Solid testimonials to their employers' regard were valued, especially when they came as silver utensils which might be converted into cash.[168] But Damer hardly wanted material recompense for his labours: he was reputed to be one of the wealthiest commoners in early eighteenth-century Ireland. A mansion at Roscrea announced this. Agency had assisted Damer, as more modestly Waring, to this eminence. But, like Waring, he had worked for others besides Erasmus Smith.[169]

Defaulters and frauds leave more evidence than the unblemished. Agents, intermediaries between recalcitrant and impecunious tenants and importunate landlords, were often awkwardly placed. Late and low remittances might tell of negligence or corruption, but real crises hampered their activities. Until bills of exchange and banking developed, large sums collected in rents were not always easily transferred from the provinces either to Dublin or Britain.[170] Unavoidable delays increased the temptations to hang on to and use cash collected for others. The regularity with which even the respected had to be chased for their balances indicates – at the very least – a reluctance quickly to pay over balances. Damer was dunned in Chancery for what he owed to the trustees of the Erasmus Smith schools; Robert Roberts was pursued by the Burlington estate for what was outstanding after his short term as agent; Coughlan's heirs were slow in settling with the Burlington creditors on behalf of their dead parent.[171] In 1710, Thomas Forster was replaced as collector of Henry Boyle's rents in West Cork, having been detected slipping 'fictitious sums' into the accounts.[172] The reforming Conners who had succeeded Coughlan in County Cork were eventually exposed for their tricks. Arundell Best, agent to Viscount Shannon, professed an ambition only 'to propagate your [Shannon's] interest' or 'merely to gain the esteem of your [Shannon's] family' while endeavouring to 'preserve a good character'. This echoed Crotty's insistence that he was interested only in Burlington's 'honour, ease and interest'.[173] Crotty's relationship with the earl had ended acrimoniously. Best's devotion to the Shannons had to be reconciled with his work for Viscounts Allen of Stillorgan and the bishop of Kilmore.[174] The Shannons eventually saw through Best, and sent him packing. By then, however, it hardly troubled Best, snug in his Carlow nest of Bestville, styled 'esquire' and indulging his wife's penchant for spas.[175] The Hatches had wormed their way into the confidence of Palmerston, Blundell and Abercorn, and transformed themselves from ranchers into squires, Dublin graduates, qualified barristers and members of parliament. Yet, in retrospect, their reputations were tarnished. Early in the nineteenth century, Lord Blundell surmised that his ancestors had been tricked by the all too plausible Hatches. Their 'accounts . . . were confused, and as a man of business, full of professions and bustle, dishonest. He [John Hatch] died very rich, much of his wealth having been accumulated out of the estates of absentee proprietors.'[176]

Astute agents who amassed wealth were vilified by both tenants and employers. Incoming or aspirant agents repeatedly criticized the cosy arrangements through which incumbents enriched themselves and their chums. Any newcomer who abstained from these confederacies was liable to be intimidated. Robert Lloyd retired from Kerry beaten by the Herberts. Even the dynamic Henry Hatch faced guerrilla warfare in and around Edenderry from the supporters of his displaced predecessor.[177] In south Munster, Josias Bateman broke his lance tilting against the combination of Coughlan and Crotty. About 1732, Bateman, a tenant and for fourteen years also an agent and surveyor on the Burlington estate, was so angry that he published a history. Plausibly enough, he traced much of the disorder to the absence of the previously vigilant earls. According to his – no doubt partial – story he had entered the Boyles' service after an apprenticeship (costing £50) and trading on his own account. A native of Youghal, like so many in the port he was linked by commerce and kinship to Bristol.[178] When fire destroyed his warehouse, with its contents valued at £250, he was forced to work for the Burlingtons. His aptitude lay in accountancy, but he also made surveys.[179] He gained a minor corporation post as weigh-master of the butter sold in Tallow.[180] Troubles soon crowded in. His surveys and valuations conflicted, he believed, with the designs of the Crotty–Coughlan faction. Bateman was harassed, denied the tenancy of farms and had his livestock impounded. He and his deranged wife were cast into Tallow gaol. Two sons engaged in nailing and cutling had their tools seized. The Batemans' maid was assaulted in the street. Many household furnishings were impounded, including a map of the world and a looking-glass. Some were grabbed by Mrs Crotty.[181]

Bateman elevated his personal tragedy into the epitome of what the likes of Crotty would visit on all Protestants in Ireland. Bateman may not have been altogether an innocent, but others remarked on the ferocious feuding which enveloped the district once the lynx-eyed owner had departed.[182] Elsewhere, the self-interest of agents was noted. In south Wicklow, the Wentworths' representatives were said to tyrannize the poor. These functionaries, tied to the squires and would-be squires who leased the best properties, were supposedly incapable of the disinterested lordship practised by those born to abundant acres. Protesters were given short shrift. While the prosperous tenants settled matters with the agent over a bottle or two of wine, 'the poor undertenant standeth without in the cold and rain and dare not come in to justify his complaint'.[183] If magnates like Ormonde and Cork and Burlington were revered, their substitutes were reviled for rapacity. These attacks failed to distinguish middlemen, aspirant and 'half-mounted' gentlemen, and agents.[184] Just as the reforming pamphleteers fused these figures into a composite villain, so in actuality the separate callings were often combined.

Critics either ignored or disparaged the wider cultural role of active agents. In south Wicklow, they were accused of a brashness to which the newly prosperous were notoriously prone. Agents were not commended for diffusing polite and polished ways and so fortifying the civility thought to be inseparable from the English Protestant interest, but condemned for vainglory. Crotty was mocked for building Modeligo; Coughlan, for Ardo. They were given no credit for improving architecture. In similar fashion, Wentworths' agents and head tenants were reproved for waste and vanity. Obvious targets for the attacks of the austere were the likes of the Nicksons, simultaneously agents and tenants. During the Wentworths' protracted absences, they had thrived. In 1709 'Captain' Abraham Nickson was paid £100 annually as the chief agent. The captain had also taken advantage of leases granted on long and generous terms in the dislocated 1690s.[185] The Nicksons' local stature grew as members of the clan amassed other positions. Joseph Nickson, a cousin of the captain, worked for the Wentworths, mainly on legal matters; a brother-in-law, Joseph Waterhouse, acted as an accountant.[186] In 1717, when the proprietor, Thomas Wentworth, was planning to build a house at Coollatin for his own occasional use, he was prepared to lease it to Abraham Nickson's daughter for twenty-one years.[187]

The Nicksons lived like gentlemen. Substantial houses were erected, gardens were laid out 'very beautifully and pleasant', paddocks enclosed and avenues and hedges planted. In 1728 Abraham's successor, John Nickson, was said 'to take a particular pleasure in planting and improving, and to have a genius for it'.[188] The outsider Hume, eager for reform, disliked the Nicksons and what they personified. Residences were built 'so prodigiously large that the income of the farms will not support the great houses', and they would prove 'an incumbrance to posterity'.[189] Hume ignored what the Nicksons had achieved for the Wentworths. The agents had energetically marketed the timber and bark from the woods which remained the greatest asset of the estate. They had sold to tanners, shipbuilders in Arklow and Whitehaven in Cumberland, furniture-makers in Dublin and private customers. The wood went to church-builders in Wicklow town and Limerick as well as to the new library at Trinity College in Dublin. The Nicksons struck deals at assizes and sessions or over drinks in taverns.[190] At the same time, Captain Nickson had forwarded the schemes of local improvement, especially in the township of Carnew, where amenities such as church and inn were to be erected. Hume was disquieted by methods which he thought dangerously casual. Arguably, they conduced to the quiet of the district better than Hume's aggression.

Propagandists for the English Protestant interest treated material life as important in itself and as a mirror of inner merit. They had an ideal of civility which the zealous strove to implant in the rural hinterlands. Some steps towards this objective seemed to have been taken on the Wentworths' estate by the 1730s. Hume, although a staunch proponent of this English Ireland, failed to applaud the transformations. Hume could not, or maybe would not, agree that a more desirable society resulted when commodities proliferated and diversified and when genteel recreations, such as tea parties or dancing, took hold. He did not concede, nor probably did he conceive, that refined modes assisted the integration of Ireland into the rest of the Hanoverian empire, not least by separating the civil from the supposedly uncouth Irish Catholics. Other evidence contradicted Hume's assessment by suggesting instead that the Wentworths' agents and tenants adopted novelties too slowly. The contents of one of the Nickson houses in 1730 hardly disclosed the ostentation belittled by Hume. The Nicksons farmed. They kept cattle and horses. The household made its own cheese, brewed beer and owned admittedly 'old' flax and wheels to spin worsted. Ten stones of wool and another two of lamb's wool in the house suggested domestic production. The house, with separate spaces named as 'parlour', 'nursery' or 'women servants' room', accommodated various functions. Elegance was sparse. Neither the names nor the furnishings of the rooms betrayed great sophistication. In an alcove of the parlour, probably with lockable wooden doors, were stored the valued utensils for gentlemanly life: six silver spoons, six more teaspoons, china and earthenware.[191]

Hume, fresh from Yorkshire, disliked these frivolities, and those who affected them. Agents, short of admirers, had to defend themselves. The Herberts in Kerry, attacked for many of the same indulgences catalogued in south Wicklow, listed the numerous improvements which they had contrived. Skilled craftsmen, such as dyers, weavers, hatters, nailers and shoemakers, had been introduced into Castleisland, the main town on the estate. An innkeeper, 'which was very much wanting', had been settled there. Roads had been constructed or repaired.[192] Arthur Herbert, so far from living extravagantly, defended his 'decent and creditable living'. Moreover, it was adopted, he protested disingenuously, primarily to uphold the standing of his employer.[193] To the unfriendly, the Herberts looked rather different. As earlier, with overmighty subjects, whom these agents recalled, a distant overlord endeavoured to have his delegated powers exercised on his own rather than solely on their terms. Arthur Herbert's wife was said to pull rank at the Castleisland markets by insisting that she buy produce first.[194] Her husband was accused of developing his own settlement at Currens as a rival to Castleisland, and schemed to divert the road to Cork from the latter to the former.[195] At Castleisland, the parson had been suborned by the agents.[196] The Herberts' associates were regularly jobbed into the shrievalty and grand jury. Edward Herbert's professed willingness to aid tenants in trouble with the law could be seen in a more sinister guise: disdain for the regular operations of the common law.[197] The powerful Herbert brothers were thought to be 'for military execution if things do not square with their sentiments and desires'.[198] Of all the sinister practices of the Herberts in Kerry, the one which most damaged the interest of their absent kinsman was the stifling of competitive bidding for farms. They tolerated – or perhaps encouraged – 'confederacies to keep the estate in their hands at the lowest rate they can by overawing their neighbours, and by practices peculiar to that country, deterring strangers dealing in it so as to interfere with their interests'.[199] Innovators, such as Lloyd in Kerry or Burward at Lismore, tried to engender competitive bidding for farms.[200] Hatch, finding 'an idle, slothful set of people' on the Temples' Sligo holdings, proposed stimulating them 'with a pretty smart rent and then it may make them apply themselves to industry'.[201]

Agents, near absolute in their localities, resented any curb on their independence. Those who were squires in their own right were difficult if not impossible to discipline. Colonel – soon to be General – Henry Conyngham lectured the Murrays of Broughton about policy towards the impoverished tenants on the Murrays' Donegal estate.[202] The Conynghams, acting for the Murrays who lived in Scotland, reasonably claimed to know conditions better.[203] The Conynghams despised the harshness proposed by the absentees. This propensity to see themselves as the proper custodians of lands on which they were merely tenants and agents was shared – vehemently – by Conyngham's wife, Lady Shelburne. Socially and financially stronger than the laird of Broughton, she rounded on the unfortunate Scot, telling him 'you are a young landlord'. 'Tho' Mr Conyngham farms your estate, he is neither your vassal nor servant, but were he the meanest of both you could not treat him with more severity'.[204] Agents, living among the tenantry, could sympathize with its predicament and restrain absentee owners from raising rents. Often, these calls for restraint were self-interested, since the agents themselves benefited from the relaxed regime. In contrast, agents new to a region and unencumbered by familial and sentimental ties with the tenants, often favoured dramatic increases. On the Herberts' lands in Kerry, Humphrey Owen took a jaundiced view of the incumbent agent in 1686, and eventually replaced him. Later, Lloyd bragged that the Herbert lands could yield £1,088 instead of the £828 for which they were currently let.[205] He would lease the mountain farms in Kerry 'to the middle rank of the Irishry, who by their frugality and ordinary way of living can outbid the better sort of Irish and English by 30 per cent'.[206] Agents with such views were guilty of some of the contemporary charges against them. For example, they advocated the introduction of large numbers of Catholics, on the simple grounds that they would pay more rent. Thereby the Protestant interest was enfeebled and an already straitened peasantry further impoverished.

Agents were trapped between several, often irreconcilable loyalties. Those living among tenants whom they were to control differed from the supervisors who dwelt at a distance and visited periodically. The residents, moreover, might be proprietors on their own account or tenants to the same landlords by whom they were employed. The simple farmer made

good as agent to a grandee brought to the task a different outlook from
that of the accountant, lawyer, surveyor or agronomist, imported from
outside. Even those seemingly professional agents who appeared in the
mid-eighteenth century – such as the Hatches – did not find all parts of
their brief equally congenial. The Hatches built up an enviable reputation
for taking a firm grip of an estate. But what suited the environs of Sligo
and Edenderry did not necessarily fit the towns themselves. Dublin, where
the Temples owned much, offered special prospects quickly spotted by the
Hatches. Premises used as a brothel, like 'The Cherry Tree', might be supplemented with developments of suburban 'villas'.[207] Further north, John
Trotter, agent of the Southwells, dealt confidently with Downpatrick. He
lived there and knew the place intimately. He was less sure-footed when
he intervened in the Southwells' second borough, Kinsale. Trotter's
activity during the 1750s worsened some townspeople's resentment of the
absentee owners.[208]

Trotter, although he did not handle all commissions with equal dex-
terity, nevertheless personified the standing that an agent could achieve,
both with his employer and in his locality. He worked for the Southwells
from about 1725 until he died in 1771. In Downpatrick he lived in style,
as the addition of a library to his house suggests.[209] He even passed muster
with the exacting Delanys, resident in the neighbourhood once Patrick
Delany had been appointed dean of Down.[210] Trotter's apparent devotion
to the Southwells fostered a reciprocal relationship repeated with other
successful agents and their employers. One sign was Edward Southwell
staying in the Trotter house when in Down. Another was the naming of
a son Southwell Trotter. Often a master or mistress was requested to stand
as godparent to the offspring of an agent.[211] Flattery united with
calculation. Trotter later consulted Edward Southwell about careers for his
offspring. Not just advice but practical assistance was solicited. Southwell
may have helped Savage Trotter first into the navy and then into the East
Indian service. Other Trotters, however, cantered into the world without
such spurs. Southwell Trotter went into 'a Roman trade', conceivably
linked with the traffic in antiquities and tourist mementoes. John Trotter
was taken up by the Dublin Society and travelled as an artist to Rome.[212]

The mutuality was repeated with other agents. Richard Purcell from
Kanturk in northern County Cork consulted his masters in England, the
earl of Egmont and Viscount Perceval, about his own and his sons' futures.
Purcell had impressed the Percevals with his strenuous promotion of their
interests.[213] In partial recompense, he wanted them to further the careers
of his boys, especially those in England. Lord Perceval was asked to keep
his eye on a Purcell in London. The youth was to be obliged to buy the
Spectator or another improving volume and transcribe a portion weekly.

Purcell, magistrate and esquire, was a figure of consequence in the north of County Cork, as is demonstrated by his ability to put his most promising sons into Trinity College in Dublin. But, like others in the landed interest, he struggled to preserve his gentility and to transmit it to all his progeny.[214] In common with Coughlan, Purcell placed at least one son in the established Church. There he flourished, securing one of the most valuable livings in Munster. To the yearly £766 from this cure, the Reverend Richard Purcell added another £160 from cures in the diocese of Ardfert. Nor did these responsibilities prevent him from spending time in Bath.[215]

Richard Orpen similarly used his employment by the absent Pettys to plant his progeny deep in the Protestant society of the south-west. Marriage to a daughter of the local parson assisted. Sons went into the Church, trade, surgery on a merchant ship and landownership. One, Abraham Orpen, combined the port surveyorship of the local town of Kenmare with profitable trading in Jamaica. In the next generation, the army as well as land, trade, medicine and the Church absorbed the prolific Orpens.[216] Henry Hatch showed most vividly how agencies might advance the trusted. In 1728 he had become a freeman of Dublin, as a member of the Carpenters' Company. By 1746, celebrated now as a top agent, he was recommended to Lord Blundell as 'a man of fortune and character'.[217] Transformed from a gentleman into a squire, Hatch, although still patronized by superiors, was becoming a patron in his own right.[218] Success permitted Hatch to give his son a university education in Dublin and legal training both in London and Dublin. John Hatch, the heir, his family's shadowy origins obscured, joined the Dublin Society and entered parliament, yet continued some of his father's agencies. Perhaps the most revealing indicator of how far and how quickly the Hatches had travelled from the plains of the midlands was the honour accorded them by Lord Palmerston. The last, entitled through descent from a provost of Trinity College to a chamber in the college, allowed the undergraduate John Hatch to use it.[219]

Agency allowed some Catholics to prosper. The work, without agreed qualifications, was also open to women. Usually they succeeded husbands or fathers. At Kinsale during the 1690s, Barbara Banfield took over from her dead husband some of the Southwells' business.[220] Esther Kingsbury attended to the Prices' affairs when her husband, Dr Thomas Kingsbury, died in 1747. Embarrassed by the bank failures of 1755, she was less easy in dealings with the Prices in Flintshire. Elizabeth Fagan followed her husband, Bryan (a brewer), as Dublin representative of the Fitzwilliams. Reckoned 'most adroit and clever', she handled the Fitzwilliams' extensive property in and around Dublin.[221] Eventually, in the 1780s, her daughter, who became Barbara Verschoyle, moved into the agency.[222] Female participation was rare: rarer even than the direction of an estate by a woman owner. More commonly the wives or kinswomen of agents assisted in a subordinate but distinct capacity. The female Foulkes at Youghal have been encountered already. The daughter of Sir Boyle Maynard was happy to act as paid housekeeper to the Burlingtons.[223] Earlier, the wife of another employee, Gosteloe, filled a similar position.[224] As housekeeper or overseer of gardens, women ruled particular provinces. Their services could complement what their husbands did as agents. In Dublin during the 1720s, the wives of Gallagher and Wilson, agents of Oliver and Mary St George, grandees who had removed to London, profited from the connection. Sarah Wilson and Mrs Gallagher flourished as dressmakers in Dublin. A smart clientele clamoured for their creations, knowing that they copied the latest at court in London. Although sheltering behind their husbands, these deft and literate seamstresses were able to communicate directly with their patrons.[225] Agents' wives were seemingly flattered to be asked to run errands: procuring bolts of Irish linen, preserved fish and meat or whiskey, or hunting for Dublin lodgings.[226] Agents, in performing a larger cultural role, were assisted – either directly or unobtrusively – by their wives. As the jaundiced Hume suspected, women, whether among the tenantry or agents, were precocious innovators. They first adopted novel housing, diet, dress and entertainments.[227] Strong female preferences could determine the pace and depth of social, economic and cultural changes.

The ideal landlord attended assiduously to his concerns. But even these paragons required assistants. Specialists in the law, accountancy, surveying and the linen trades were guaranteed work. As with other servants, personal recommendations and observation identified the likely candidates. It may be, as has been argued, that a growing professionalism can be detected among agents from the 1740s.[228] Yet a century earlier, on the largest holdings, factotums designated curtly as steward or bailiff acted in essence as agents. Moreover, these massive concerns employed a variety of skills. Prudence counselled proprietors to employ those unencumbered with local links. But amity and an easy life frequently meant the retention of agents who belonged to the local landowning orders. Agencies afforded a good livelihood and evident social advance to an Orpen, Coughlan or Hatch. With others like the Herberts, Conynghams and Nicksons, the work consolidated rather than created wealth and position. Edward Kenney, agent at Castleisland in 1686, was reputed to be worth £1,000 p.a., beside which his salary of £40 from the Herberts paled into insignificance. Kenney's kinship with a leading merchant in Cork city helped the Herberts' interests in the remote location. But they also involved Kenney in the recession of the mid-1680s. Indeed, it was alleged that he owed £2,000 and had been arrested for debt in Cork. At the same time, active as a magistrate and as seneschal of the manor court, he lived in state. He kept a coach with six horses, 'and hath a good show of plate on his table'.[229]

Occasionally, those with substantial English holdings, notably the Boyles, moved agents between the kingdoms of Ireland and England. But before the end of the eighteenth century it was rare to procure overseers from Britain. Bishop Edward Synge tempted the Yorkshire agronomist, Charles Varley, to Elphin in the 1750s; Lord Kingston enticed Arthur Young to Mitchelstown in 1777. Varley was already settled in Ireland before involving himself with Synge.[230] Young toured Ireland before his brief encounter with Kingston.[231] Neither employment encouraged English (or Scottish or Welsh) reformers to transplant themselves into inhospitable Hibernian environments. Strangers brought fresh perspectives to Irish problems, but these were neither easily nor successfully applied to local needs. Agents who dreamt of transforming sour and wet lands into blossoming Edens, like earlier projectors, were disappointed. More successful, both for their employers and their own advancement, were those who settled for the customary crops, tenures and tenants, and merely tightened or varied what traditionally had been required. Yet, in so far as these agents proceeded through written leases, measures, maps and legal processes, they disturbed earlier, sometimes informal agreements. As mediators between proprietors, many of them installed as a result of the forfeitures of the seventeenth century, and a tenantry, the bulk of which was drawn still from the Irish Catholics, agents faced unenviable and ultimately irreconcilable demands. From all quarters they were condemned. The rigorous and innovative were accused of implanting wasteful and pretentious habits. The lax were enervated by the pervasive torpor of the Irish countryside. Almost all, with modest salaries but considerable authority, were believed to have insinuated themselves into unjustifiably high stations in their neighbourhoods. This unpopularity was not unique to Ireland; it has been noted, for example, in rural Wales.[232]

Ardent champions of the English interest in Ireland aimed to dethrone the petty tyrants who had ruled Gaelic society. Too often, it seemed, the upheavals of the seventeenth century had substituted new dictators for the old. How agents might slip into the places vacated by the former sept chiefs was suggested in Kerry early in the 1690s. This remote county, regarded as a kingdom on its own, resolutely resisted complete assimilation to the new order. Landowners, such as Petty and the Herberts, if they were to prosper, had to accommodate themselves to the tenacious locals. Captain Robert Topham, intriguing for the lucrative Petty agency, adopted what he believed to be indigenous modes even more wholeheartedly.

Favoured by Petty's widow, Lady Shelburne, Topham repaired to Kerry. There he parodied a Gaelic chief's progress. Display mattered. Topham arrayed himself gorgeously, with gold and silver lace glittering at neck and cuffs. He dazzled onlookers with his 'state and glory'. Indeed, travelling sometimes by night, accompanied by pipers 'for several miles together', he so amazed the locals, 'that many of the superstitious Irish ran out of their beds to meet him, believing him to be the old Messias McFinn [McFinin, the head of the local sept], who was buried with a piper, and that he had risen from the dead and brought his own piper along with him out of the grave'. If the cavalcade impressed, so too did Topham's courtship of the Kerry people. He was said to have sat drinking with them for nights on end, and even to converse with them in Irish. Topham's courtesies were reciprocated with gifts of horses, cows, fish, golden guineas and butter such as a Gaelic chieftain might once have commanded.[233] Detractors no doubt exaggerated this would-be agent's relapse into Gaelic primitivism. Yet it was true that some agents, thanks to the powers they wielded, lorded it over their neighbourhoods.

Chapter 9

The Middle Station

I

On Sundays, in the parish churches throughout Dublin the Protestant population displayed itself. In Cork, too, it was decreed (in 1681) 'that all the parishioners of the said parish [Christ Church] should be seated in seats suitable to their qualities'.[1] In the town of Wicklow, the incumbent announced that he was 'settling the parishioners in their respective seats, and fixing the rate of each seat agreeable to the rank and ability of each parishioner'.[2] Presbyterian congregations were similarly differentiated. In north Antrim in 1701 it was ordained that 'each man in his own proportion should have the choice of his seats according to his payment'.[3] These practices resembled those in contemporary England.[4]

The Protestants were indeed ranked in the Dublin churches. At St Peter's on the south side of the city, the earl of Longford, in whose speculative development the church was the centrepiece, graced the pew in the middle of the gallery. Around or below him were seated Lord Abercorn and the marchioness of Antrim. Other titled members of the congregation owned pews: Ladies Cuffe, Clonally and Ponsonby. The seventy-seven pewholders also numbered a couple of baronets, a judge, a brace of clergymen, an alderman, three with military ranks and ten squires. They rubbed shoulders with an affluent brewer and an undifferentiated group of residents prosperous and respectable enough to own pews.[5] A similar mixture characterized nearby St Paul's. In the gallery sat (at least notionally) three peers – Charlemont, Drogheda and Lady Shelburne – and their households. In the thirty-three pews in the body of the church were listed a single knight, an alderman and one 'Mr'. The remainder can be presumed to have been tradespeople, craftsmen and shopkeepers: in short, the middling orders of the parish.[6] By 1717, fifty-two pews belonged to two peers, a bishop, a baronet, a judge, nine esquires and two plain 'Mr's. Thirty-five pews were occupied by families without honorific prefixes or suffixes.[7]

This pattern recurred on the north bank of the River Liffey. At the newly established St Mary's, two pews were reserved for Lord Moore, heir of the former owner of the quarter, the earl of Drogheda. The district had been cleverly developed as a smart residential area, and something of that modishness could be seen within the parish church.[8] Those who, early in the eighteenth century, had bought seating included a second peer, Lord Mountalexander, four judges, the attorney-general and Speaker of the House of Commons, together with other prominent barristers and government functionaries. Among these worshippers were Ulster King of Arms, William Hawkins, 'esquire'; the lord-lieutenant's secretary, Edward Southwell, a squire who possessed much of Kinsale; and his kinsman, Sir John Perceval, a baronet. Four civic dignitaries had pews. This impression of the Protestant faithful in St Mary's as socially and politically important is conveyed by the courtesy extended to the remaining seat-holders. All without any higher style were designated 'Mr'. In addition, three pews were kept for servants.[9] In St Catherine's, a church built to accommodate the workers of the Liberties, the disposition of pews again told something of the stratification of the Protestant population. For the earl of Meath, owner of much of the liberty and contributor to the new church, a pew prominent in the centre of the gallery was reserved. Dr William Molyneux also had a seat at the front of the gallery. Molyneux, belonging to a family eminent in Protestant Dublin for a century, a lawyer and member of parliament, would soon champion the interests of his co-religionists against what he saw as English vindictiveness.[10]

Parish clerks, like other scribes, probably erred on the side of generosity when they assigned parishioners to social categories. Nevertheless, their lists remind us that in some Church of Ireland parishes the majority of pewholders were not obviously of the quality. Nowhere was this clearer than in St Werburgh's church. Huddled around Dublin Castle, the parish had long been the domicile of the weighty.[11] The lord-lieutenant himself had once worshipped in the parish church. However, by the eighteenth century the building had fallen victim to altered residential patterns. The wealthy and elegant were deserting the cramped alleys and courts of the ancient centre for more spacious suburbs. This receding tide left only one peer, Lord Molesworth, with a pew. This was a courtesy, for he owned the ground on which the building had been erected. By the 1720s, because the holder of the title was generally absent from Ireland, the pew was unused by the family. The lord-lieutenant also prayed elsewhere. Only in 1828 did he resume regular devotions at St Werburgh's.[12] Of 114 named in 1725 as pew-holders, a mere five were listed as 'esquires'. Four aldermen, a former lord mayor and ten women had pews, together with an assortment of grocers, goldsmiths, printers and shopkeepers.[13] These findings back the assertion in 1716 that St Werburgh's parishioners were 'mostly shopkeepers and tradesmen'.[14] It was still the situation when the pew-holders were surveyed afresh in 1760.[15]

Possession of a pew came only after a donation, purchase, or the payment of rent. Even the most modest charges for this convenience, around £2 10s., were not to be contemplated by those of meagre means. Indeed, they were higher than those that prevailed in the English countryside a century earlier.[16] Yet, if the price shut out the poor from Church of Ireland worship, those prosperous and respectable enough to have their own pews were seldom assuredly of the quality. The middling station of the majority active in the Dublin parishes is again evident in St Michan's, across the river from St Werburgh's. Of the ninety-two parishioners known to have bought their seats between 1725 and 1761, four were described as 'esquires', and eleven either as gentlemen or plain 'Mr'. They were outnumbered by eighteen 'merchants', twelve concerned with the drink and food trades, another twelve involved in building, eight working with metal, another eight dealing with textiles and seven who can loosely be called professionals.[17] The rating records of St Michan's reinforce the impression of social and occupational diversity. In 1711, of the 851 householders who were assessed, only thirty-three were awarded an honorific. Three bishops, two judges, eleven with military ranks and five baronets, knights or their ladies were joined by nine esquires. In 1724, the appearance of Viscount Blayney as a resident attested, as had the presence of three Ulster bishops, to the popularity of the parish among grandees from the north.[18] Like more modest immigrants, they stopped in the first district which they hit on arriving in Dublin. Telling, too, as an index of the dominant social colour of the parish are the identities of those who supervised the parish watch. In the 1720s this strategic committee contained two 'gentlemen', one 'merchant' and six tradesmen.[19]

The social profiles of Dublin's Church of Ireland parishes were not altogether uniform. The tendency of the well-to-do to crowd together rendered some areas more attractive than others. New building, which included the construction of places for worship, tempted the smart into different districts.[20] By the 1690s, concerned commentators alleged that the conformist communities were polarized into the undoubted grandees and the poor. Dissenters, it seemed, claimed a disproportionate share of the middling kind.[21] Even so, throughout most parish churches in Dublin, Sunday by Sunday, squires and gentlemen were outnumbered by their social inferiors. The worshippers ranged in their pews amounted to perhaps a quarter of the conformist population of the capital. In 1733, it was thought that no more than 11,000 from a total of 45,000 adherents of the Church of Ireland could be seated in the Dublin churches.[22]

Champions of the Protestant interest, like Archbishop King, sought to rectify the want.[23] The church building was the focus of the communities which ruled the kingdom of Ireland. In it was staged the act which qualified the actor for full citizenship: taking the sacrament according to the rites of the Church of Ireland once a year. The importance of churches as physical and symbolic centres of the emergent Protestant Ascendancy provoked attacks in the 1640s and 1688–89. If the parish in Ireland had not developed as an administrative unit to the same extent as in England and Wales, it was nevertheless loaded with regulatory tasks by the authorities. It shared oversight of the localities with the manor, barony and municipality. Running parochial affairs stimulated the appearance of a committee, the vestry, to assist and sometimes to correct the incumbent. Soon these meetings, to which potentially the heads of all rate-paying households could come, proved too cumbersome for the efficient dispatch of business. An inner group of the civic-minded and active emerged as the select vestry. In the 1660s and 1670s, the vestry of St Bride's in Dublin was attended by between twelve and twenty-one parishioners.[24] Similarly, a vestry meeting at St John's in Dublin in 1719 attracted twenty laymen and the curate. This continued the practice evident for almost a century of an inner circle of parishioners arrogating to itself much of the regular business.[25] At Lurgan, it was those in the middling bands of rate-payers who officiated in the vestry.[26] The solid worth of those shouldering parochial burdens is conveyed by the need in the Cork parish of St Mary, Shandon to postpone a vestry meeting in 1724 owing to the absence of its members at the assizes in the city. The same individuals were involved in a multiplicity of local affairs.[27]

As in England, so in Protestant Ireland, a willingness regularly to assume the burdens of parochial office may have helped the middling sort to define and so distinguish themselves from the lower ranks. In assessing and collecting levies and deciding how they should be spent, parish officers exercised power over neighbours. In particular, the functionaries could decide between the deserving and undeserving when doles were to be distributed.[28] But even in the range of jobs to be done within the parish, some, although onerous, conferred dignity and precedence – notably being churchwarden – whereas others (watchman or constable) were merely troublesome. In Dublin, and elsewhere, the titled and undisputed members of the quality did not jib at these jobs. Both Lord Meath and William Molyneux attended vestries in their parish of St Catherine, but not habitually.[29] Similarly, if important work had to be done, involving contacts with the government and parliament, as when the church of St Mary was rebuilt after 1713, a committee of the grandest parishioners was established.[30] In the same parish, it also fell to the eminent to audit the accounts.[31] Yet, it was seldom possible even in the most fashionable Dublin parishes to rely exclusively on those already high in local society. Some from the middling ranks served their turn even as churchwardens. St Paul's in Dublin had as its churchwardens in 1698 Thomas Keightley, one of the revenue commissioners, a one-time lord justice and through his wife related to the royal family, and an esquire and member of parliament, Edward Corker. At St Michan's in 1726, a goldsmith and a brewer served in the office. They were succeeded by a linen draper and an apothecary.[32]

Occupational and social diversification in urban parishes was displayed in the seating and offices of the established Church. In much of the countryside, the sparseness of the Protestant population stunted the growth of a respectable middling order which could display itself on Sundays and undertake parochial duties. In 1749, in the rural parishes of the diocese of Elphin, Protestants were both fewer and harder to spot than in the towns of Athlone and Sligo. In one rural parish, Kiltoom and Cam, in southwestern Roscommon close to the River Shannon, 472 households were enumerated. No more than 2.35 per cent were returned as Protestants. They were mostly grouped at the upper economic and social levels.[33] Kiltoom and Cam, perhaps, were extreme examples of how top-heavy the Protestant community could be. Roscommon, never the focus of assisted projects to settle Protestants and away from the southern and eastern seaboards where subsistence and betterment immigrants first disembarked, had little to entice laborious Protestants. Athlone, a military and marketing centre, with its higher proportion of Protestant inhabitants, scarcely touched these parishes. Remote Roscommon a few years later resembled County Sligo. There, an analyst, Charles O'Hara, himself a substantial landowner, bewailed a community polarized into 'gentlemen farmers and the cottage tenants who were the lowest species of slaves'. What was wanted, and which was appearing belatedly (or so O'Hara contended), was the mediating and modernizing order of a yeomanry.[34] Yeomen were also associated with the defence of the Protestant order in Ireland. Notionally they would be the backbone of the militia which would defend the island against invaders, as in 1715 and 1745–46. A contemporary of O'Hara, George Stacpoole, was saddened by the want of 'a substantial tenantry' or 'a proper middle state of people'.[35]

The weakness or absence of vigorous yeomen dismayed more than just O'Hara and Stacpoole. Government policy in the seventeenth century had tried to create this element. The designation 'yeoman' quickly entered the vocabulary of the social classifiers. For them, indeed, it was a godsend, since it expanded the otherwise limited repertoire of designations.[36] By the 1660s the authorities sanctioned its use as a synonym for farmer or husbandman. Such interchangeability hardly encouraged its precise application.

In consequence, the name appeared before the actuality. Ironically, some 'yeomen' confounded expectations by subverting the order they were designed to uphold. In the 1740s the notorious highwayman, Freney, was denominated a yeoman.[37] But tacitly, and explicitly, it was conceded that a yeomanry vital alike to agriculture, the Protestant state and English interest scarcely existed. Some blamed the greed of landlords. By the 1750s, parliament was pressed to act against grazing and animal husbandry and instead to sponsor tillage. Only then would a yeomanry flourish.[38]

Before this campaign, other schemes of social engineering had been tried. They would pacify the kingdom, enrich its owners, sedate the unruly and swell the middling ranks. Urban development produced the best results. But much attention focused on creating rural industries, which were designed to supplement rather than to replace existing agricultural employments. The prime purpose was to enable tenants more easily to pay – and in time to increase – their rents.[39] Landowners like Sir William Petty clutched at rural industries as a means to improve remote holdings. Petty viewed fishing and ironmaking as the two most promising for his Kerry properties.[40] In interesting himself in these ventures, he exemplified the tendency of investors and entrepreneurs in projects to make cloth, iron or glass to be drawn from stations already higher than the middling strata.[41] Landowners, urban professionals and office-holders, retired soldiers and shrewd merchants forwarded these schemes, few of which in seventeenth-century Ireland permanently altered the economy. Nor did they bring about great social changes. The industries employed a few managers and specialists, whose functions and yearly salaries lifted them above the labourers whom they oversaw. One manager of the ironmaking enterprise outside Enniscorthy during Charles II's reign was paid a generous £240. More usually these superintendents received a yearly £40.[42] It edged them into the middling ranks of attorneys, curates, schoolmasters and minor bureaucrats, and even towards the quality, yet it did not buy much in the way of education for offspring, and certainly not terms at Trinity College. Furthermore, the enterprises, at least until linen manufacture developed on a large scale in the early eighteenth century, were more often sites of disorder than of the sober industry that had been envisaged.

The numerous disappointments over often chimerical and usually unprofitable ventures of the late seventeenth century gave way to a greater optimism. Prospects brightened with the rapid progress of linen manufacture. Travellers, especially in Ulster and its environs, delighted in what they saw. Flax was being grown, yarn spun and linen woven.[43] Even before these visible changes, textiles had been an important manufacture. Domestic production of cloth and clothing is difficult to quantify. Petty speculated on how many people were needed in each of the chief manufactures and trades.

Tailoring required 45,000; textiles, 30,000. The elder Sir Richard Cox disputed Petty's estimate, wanting to multiply Petty's figures by a dramatic (and improbable) ten.[44] In England at the time, it was reckoned that on average as much as a quarter of annual budgets went on clothing.[45] In Ireland, notwithstanding the poverty of more of its people, the proportion was scarcely less. If the craze of the smart to wear imported textiles reduced home demand, periodically the fad of dressing Irish compensated.[46] Small-scale, indeed often domestic, production offered work to country-dwellers, including women and children. Yet the benefits to a scattered tenantry were less frequently noted than to the inhabitants of towns. Textile-making, after agriculture and perhaps domestic service, was the largest employer. About 1686, Dublin had 300 master clothiers. By 1707, the Weavers' Company in the city had 209 brethren.[47] The majority of these master craftsmen as freemen, either of the Trinity (Merchants') or Weavers' Guild, employed journeymen, apprentices and other operatives, and were counted among either the middling sort or quality.[48] But such entrepreneurs possessed of capital and respectability were only a tiny proportion of those working in crafts and industry. The economic interests of the few with resources clashed with those of their employees resentful of depressed pay or of customers angered by price-fixing. Producers, especially when gathered into chartered guilds, retaliated. Their collective defences encouraged a greater consciousness of standing which marked them off from the less fortunate. This paralleled the ways in which vestrymen distinguished themselves from the generality of parishioners. Each constituted a hierarchy: the one of the parish; the other of a craft or trade.

Artificers worked; the master craftsmen, traders and entrepreneurs profited. The former were often denied a place among the respectable middling sort; the latter aspired to and might enjoy a higher ranking. The clothing trades established around Mountrath and Mountmellick (both in County Offaly) before 1641 owed much to the initiative of the principal proprietor, Sir Charles Coote.[49] In south Munster, a similar situation has been observed in towns where textiles were made.[50] In Carlow, late in Charles II's reign, profitable undertakings, such as the manufacture of frieze, could be traced to two projectors: Thomas Spaight and William Crutchley. Both benefited from their relationship with the absent owner, Lord Thomond. Spaight acted as seneschal and steward on his County Clare estates. Crutchley, responsible for physical improvements in Carlow, may have started among the middling, as a small tenant to Thomond and a miller. However, once named as a justice of the peace and high sheriff of the county, he had clearly risen above that level.[51] Nearer Dublin, the textile mill at Chapelizod was expected to enrich its director, a former Cromwellian army officer, Richard Lawrence. Despite contracts to clothe

the army and the importation of workers and techniques from Flanders in the later 1660s, this enterprise did not answer expectations. Lawrence had to revert to a series of opportunist and not altogether successful trading projects.[52] Chapelizod failed, as did fifteen other hopeful ventures begun at the same time, mostly by landed proprietors.[53]

In Lord Cork's bailiwick, manufactures continued or revived. The undertaking at Bandon lasted longer than many. Again a couple of entrepreneurs were behind the manufacture. Links with customers and artificers in the Low Countries and England assisted.[54] One – John Langton – was important enough to serve as sovereign (or mayor) in 1684.[55] He may also have had connections with the pre-war industry in the town.[56] Responses to the impact of the industry were ambivalent. The Bandonians could be congratulated as 'industrious and given to manu-factory', but were 'naturally of a stubborn disposition'.[57] Part of their obstinacy could be traced to an attempt by the proprietors to fix pay so 'that they may not give weavers, spinners, etc. the opportunity to raise prices'.[58] Despite setbacks in the late 1690s, a domestic trade survived. By the 1740s, the textile industry in and around Bandon supported Armiger Sealy, reputedly worth £6,000.[59] Sealy belonged to an urban dynasty of the sort to be found in most towns of the size of Bandon. Since the seventeenth century, the Sealys had amassed both urban and rural prop-erty by lease, mortgage and purchase. One brother of Armiger Sealy served as chief magistrate of Bandon; a second, trained at Leiden, practised medicine. The Sealys moved erratically between the styles of esquire, gentleman and merchant. In the north Cork town of Kanturk during the 1730s, the promoter of textile-making, Richard Purcell, worked for a distant proprietor, the earl of Egmont. Purcell as agent and entrepreneur might seem – like the Sealys – to merit a middling station.[60] But Purcell was accounted an esquire, became a justice of the peace and, with some strain, lived up to a more lofty position.[61]

Profits from these undertakings frequently disappointed; so, too, did the extent of social change and the arrival of unexpected problems, such as lawlessness among the workers. Outside Dublin and Ulster, it is difficult to identify many who were brought permanently into the middle ranks thanks to this manufacture. Projectors, investors and beneficiaries were as often landlords as urban and international merchants. This impression may be distorted by a contemporary belief which credited most useful innovations to nobles and gentlemen, and by the distribution of surviv-ing documentation.[62] Irish landowners, struggling to increase revenues, developed urban interests and rural industries, but meagre capital and limited mercantile contacts restricted what they achieved. Access to capital, credit and markets outside Ireland – in London, Amsterdam, Rotterdam,

Hamburg and other north Atlantic ports – brought success to a few traders in the Irish ports.

In Ulster, linen gradually diffused modest prosperity. The province, thanks to the immigration and resettlement of the seventeenth century, had a more diversified Protestant population than in most other areas of the island. The industry, where it flourished, strengthened this already complex Protestant society. A middling order, rural as well as urban, was more visible than elsewhere.[63] This situation did not always yield the expected dividends. In Ulster, the modestly successful, often tenaciously Presbyterian, invigorated dissenting congregations. These nurtured traditions of independence and criticized the legal ascendancy enjoyed by the adherents of the established Church.[64] The industrious manifested a sturdiness which, for long the objective of the engineers tinkering with Ireland, by the 1760s alarmed by its awkwardness if not dissidence.[65] Elsewhere, from Dungarvan, Tallow and Youghal to Mountmellick and Edenderry in the Pale, unrest throughout the 1750s and 1760s was traced to wool combers and textile workers. Literate, politically aware and electors, they constituted a middling stratum. Yet, instead of their independence being welcomed, the unfriendly, especially among the landed, lashed 'the inconsiderable'. In 1748, a pamphleteer imagined the politicization of the middling kind of Dublin. 'They now read newspapers, drink porter, smoke tobacco, and talk as freely of religion and politics as the Londoners.' These traits were not universally applauded. Indeed, those who displayed them were relegated to the lower ranks by unfriendly commentators.[66]

Despite worries about how textile and other industrial workers behaved, the industries continued to be encouraged. The value of linen in enabling poor tenants to pay rents was widely appreciated. The culture spread beyond Ulster, assisted by state subsidies. In 1736, Sir Maurice Crosbie planned to establish 'a colony of northerners' in Kerry.[67] Lord Malton, absent in Yorkshire during the same decade, was advised that the existing inhabitants in his township of Carnew, straddling the Wexford–Wicklow border, 'a lazy, sluggish people', should be entirely replaced with 'a new colony of industrious people . . . who understand manufactory business'.[68] At Sligo, the Temples' agents appreciated the value of importing the industry; so, too, did the Smythes in Westmeath, where at Collinstown they tried to create a manufacturing centre. The Smythes hoped to attract the skilled from Ulster, with the promise of a loom, spinning wheel and cow, 'which is a beginning several are content with . . . honest Protestants who, getting looms to hire, will take apprentices in the country till their children grow up'. However, those used to eastern Ulster were scared by the 'popery' of the midlands.[69] Nevertheless, Smythe managed to nurture the industry, until by 1754 his tenants had two dozen looms at work and he benefited from a brisk market for yarn.[70] From Tullamore at the same time, it was reported that all 'the middling sort' were bred to the linen business.[71] Two other resident proprietors, converted to linen as the cure for the problems on their estates, were held up as admirable models. The younger Sir Richard Cox, grandson of Queen Anne's Irish lord chancellor, an obsessive self-publicist, cast linen as the reviver of his wilting plant at Dunmanway in West Cork. He popularized the industry through competitions, prizes and treats. He even aimed to remake the cycle of the year. He culled the still abundant holy days in the Church of Ireland calendar, and substituted a festival at the start of May, sacred to linen. Confessional transformation was more noticeable than social. In 1749, Cox breathlessly announced the news, hot from the press, that for the first time Protestants had overtaken Catholics as the majority in the town. In addition, 'the lowest class' was being weaned away from idleness and debased ways. But how many of this 'class' were then propelled into the middling orders, Cox never specified.[72] Clearer was the addition to the stock of sturdy Protestants capable of bearing arms in an emergency. Dunmanway was returned in 1757 as containing 119 who might serve in the militia. This was approaching the total in longer-established settlements such as Mallow (142) and already surpassed Doneraile and Newmarket, with, respectively, 51 and 73. However, Cox's fledgling could not rival the strengths of Kinsale (314), Youghal (378), or Bandon with 688.[73]

A second persuaded that linen-making would improve his patrimony was Robert French. 'Boggy, melancholy Monivae' in east Galway, inherited by French in 1744, during the 1770s was celebrated as an example of what active stewardship could accomplish.[74] French spent heavily – by 1755, an estimated £1,147 – and created a cluster of 276 houses, with 96 looms and 370 spinning wheels. Proficient bleachers, spinners and weavers were procured from elsewhere. Deliberately French had allowed only small plots of land to the workmen, so that they remained 'mere cottagers in a town, without any land except a cabbage garden'. Unable to double as farmers, the weavers had to buy food and other basics at market. Such arrangements worked satisfactorily until a slump in 1770 reduced demand for linen and raised agricultural prices. With this setback, French reviewed his strategy. He now decided that 'the only manufacture which can never be carried too far' is 'the cultivation and improvement of the earth'. Accordingly, he pledged that henceforth he would rely on 'plough and manure' rather than 'on population and necessary manufacture'. French's modernization of Monivea gave it the classic configuration of parish church and manor where he resided. But, as in so many settlements, the confessional balance and social structure of the village remain uncertain.

The community had diversified as agents, overseers, teachers and bleachers placed a buffer between owner and cottagers or labourers. A few in this intermediate group were called 'esquires'. But the middling sections of the Protestant population were at best modestly recruited.[75]

As an instrument of social change, rural industry, even linen-making, did less than predicted. Yeomen were desired, but few appeared. Instead, another group – 'middlemen' – arrived unbidden. Middlemen could fit snugly into the largely vacant station in rural society between the quality and the labourers. To them might reasonably fall tasks of cultural mediation, commercial innovation, agricultural improvement and local leadership neglected by non-resident squires or non-existent yeomen. However, few publicly rejoiced when middlemen were noted in the 1720s. At times of dearth and distress they were reviled in much the same terms as hoarders, forestallers and regrators. They racked rents; they abandoned tillage, turned grazier and speculated in leases. Middlemen, dissatisfied with a median position in rural communities, aimed higher. They mimicked the manners of squires and gentlemen. Adopting gentility, so far from being lauded, they were often derided as maladroit and comical.[76] Descriptions of the middlemen were suffused with moral indignation, and could degenerate into rants. Characteristic of the tone, albeit at the close of the eighteenth century, was a diatribe against 'agents, middlemen and upstarts who had acquired property by having been tax-collectors, tithe-jobbers, petty-foggers, attorneys, &c., all of whom thought themselves of sufficient importance to tack the title of esquire to their names'.[77]

This attack continued a long tradition of pillorying middlemen. It spoke of unease about several developments in rural areas. Many middlemen, it was agreed, were leaseholders, usually on secure and easy terms from which they benefited handsomely. Some were Catholics. Ousted from their hereditary possessions, they adapted by becoming tenants or even squatters on the properties which once they had owned. Others were Protestants, who assembled large and scattered holdings. In the absence of the lord of the soil, they performed many of the social and administrative functions which the owner had abdicated. In this respect, they resembled agents. Moreover, both middlemen and agents linked the elevated with the humble, and the locality with more distant worlds. Often, indeed, middlemen worked as agents to their distant landlord. As residents, these subordinates enjoyed formidable local powers: more in practice than the nominal proprietor. By the 1750s, as the value of land rose sharply, the head tenants were joined by speculators in leases, some of whom were bustling townsmen.[78] Where, earlier in the century, Catholic middlemen were *revenants*, their Protestant and Catholic successors were now mocked as squireens and *arrivistes*.

Accounts of middlemen, in the eighteenth century and since, frequently conflated the separate phenomena of those on their way into and those falling from the landed gentry. 'Middlemen' they might be by name and function, but being assigned to the middling station displeased them. Their inclusion among the gentry was grudging and qualified, as one description, 'half-mounted gentry', signalled. The gentility which they affected could be questioned. The negative was constantly stressed. Middlemen served as scapegoats for every sort of social and economic ill in the Irish countryside. They racked rents, driving poor tenants off the land and sometimes to America, so hurting the Protestant interest. The talk grew louder that their avarice created shortages, raised prices and exploited others. In unkind accounts, these villains retarded improvements. They neglected civic duties in favour of private revels. They broke laws which as magistrates and agents of the state they were sworn to protect. Through their habits they levelled the fences, not just between true and counterfeit gentlemen, but between Irish and English, Catholic and Protestant, and thereby were thought to endanger the very survival of the Protestant Ascendancy. Not just patriotic pamphleteers, but concerned landowners and their agents declared war on the group, announcing that they would let only to tenants who resided on their farms and so end the profiteering.[79] Such pledges were rarely honoured, since most proprietors were keen to collect the highest possible rents. Moreover, the distaste for the profiteers and racketeers ignored the technicality that many grandees, leasing parcels of their lands, were themselves middlemen. So, too, were numerous agents, guilty of that same rapacity which they condemned in others.

'Middleman' was a loose term, applied inconsistently. It inserted a useful if often confusing contour into the map of rural Ireland. 'Middleman' might vary the terminology of leaseholder and farmer. Many lumped in this category had heaved themselves through aspiration and exertion to a loftier station. They expected to be, and were reluctantly, accounted as 'of quality'. Unadorned farmers might more confidently be situated in the middling ranks. In 1753, a considerable 'farmer' died near Newcastle in County Limerick. He was remembered as 'a friendly neighbour to rich and poor but by over fast living shortened his days'. Another, Tom Burgess of Labacolly in the north of County Cork was regarded by a contemporary as 'a hearty, honest farmer'. Burgess was 'noted for keeping a good house and drinking a vast quantity of spirits'. This 'good-natured, honest old bachelor' was also much mourned in the locality.[80] Farmers who discharged neighbourly obligations were admired. But, as with the peerage and gentry, the criteria by which they were judged might suddenly alter. The virtues of hospitality were turned into the vices of extravagance and waste. It is not altogether clear whether expansiveness or parsimony was the better regarded.[81] What is conveyed is again the importance of behaviour and attitudes in creating reputations, which in turn influenced ideas of status and social positioning.

II

These speculations can be pinned to something more solid. Farmers, prospering tenants and busy agents might be on course to enter the gentry. For the present, modest income and a need to watch over the seasonal cycles of cultivation grounded them among the middling. Two from this group are Lucas and Nicholas Peacock. Both farmed in the environs of Limerick city in the 1740s. Lucas's Christian name has not come down to us: an indication of how spectral most at his level are. He lived with his parents on their farm at Drumcavan, three miles from Corofin in County Clare. The Lucases paid an annual rent of £51 0s. 2d., and attended closely to the cultivation of their lands. They engaged in mixed husbandry, growing cereals, pulses, flax and cattle. The routines of dunging, planting and driving livestock to markets and fairs were interspersed with conviviality. Drink, meals and talk were shared with kinsfolk and neighbours. Much produce was sold at Ennis, the county town. There, too, Lucas had relations. It was the place to shop. Only in the autumn, with harvest home and money in his pocket from sales of beasts (a total of £78 12s. 6d. is recorded in 1741), did Lucas relax. He followed a jolly circuit which encompassed a grander kinsman, 'Squire Lucas', and the Bindons, a powerful family from Ennis who had joined the parliamentary gentry and who retained links with commerce and the law. Lucas once or twice betrayed the traits for which subsequent middlemen would be lambasted. In a summer binge, he roistered all night in the company of others, like the Bloods of Craganbouy, of comparable background and standing. At home he entertained the family of the local incumbent, Ambrose Upton. Lucas coursed hares – a pursuit which would have been illegal if he or his father were worth less than £40 p.a. – and bought fencing lessons. His mother ordered modest improvements to the farmhouse; his father went as a medical pilgrim to a local spa. In the single year during which Lucas emerges from the historical deep, he ventured no further than Limerick, thirty miles and seven hours away.

In general, Lucas, apart from the odd indulgence, was constrained by modest resources and the imperatives of the farming year. He performed his religious observances dutifully. He valued amity within his intimate community. He tried to adjudicate between villagers at loggerheads over boundaries. He aimed 'not [to] be troublesome', declaring that 'we must be good neighbours'. Indeed, reciprocity was vital if this fragile economy was to work. The potato garden was dug in return for a fat sheep delivered before Christmas; a neighbour spun stockings from a sheepskin; the colt of another serviced the Lucases' mare; meals were shared after church on Sunday. Yet the Lucases had settled where Protestants of their means and standing were almost as sparse as in Kiltoom and Cam. The cultural and economic gulf that yawned between them and the generality of the locals showed most obviously in the diarist's ability to record his doings: a skill denied to most in the district. Also, this act may have betokened an urge to distinguish himself from the commonalty.[82] Notwithstanding a degree of physical and cultural isolation, the Lucases did not want for company, including that of superiors charged with the governance of Protestant Ireland. Otherwise, the Hanoverian state seemed remote. No Lucases rose to the commission of the peace or the grand jury. Only the more local institutions – parish church and manor court – gave structure to Lucas's year. In the parish, Lucas discharged the tiresome and contentious – but profitable – function of tithe farmer. It could be, although we do not know, that he served his turn in jobs generated by the established Church and manor court, such as juror, churchwarden, overseer of the poor, surveyor of highways and applotter or collector of church rates.[83]

While Lucas was working his farm, Nicholas Peacock supervised a variety of rural activities close to the parish of Kildimo, near Adare, a few miles south-west of Limerick city. Peacock's condition, superficially akin to Lucas's, differed subtly from it. Peacock acted for two local landowners, the Hartstonges and Widenhams. The Hartstonges, originally legal baronets, ran into financial difficulties during the decade. These arose from the premature death of Price Hartstonge, heir to the baronetcy and Peacock's employer.[84] The Widenhams, to whom Peacock was related, were also cadets of a ramifying tribe and had intermarried with the Hartstonges.[85] Routine dealings with the gentry familiarized Peacock with ideas, expectations and commodities apparently outside Lucas's ken. Peacock rode often into Limerick city, sometimes for business; frequently to relax in its crowded and congenial spaces. He had relations in the vicinity. Once he served as a juror there.[86] Twice during the decade he journeyed to Dublin about his employers' affairs.[87] He was more evidently touched by the operations of the distant Hanoverian state than Lucas had been. A brother, an occasional visitor, worked for the Revenue. During the alert in 1745, Peacock joined the local militia raised by Southwell and travelled to a muster in Kilmallock.[88] Newspapers, as well as the gossip in Limerick, kept him abreast of British and international happenings.

Peacock is known to us only because he wrote a terse diary.[89] As with Lucas, this introversion distinguishes him. Where he belongs on the social scale remains elusive. Indeed, his placement may have changed over the decade. Agent, tenant farmer, middleman, half-mounted gentleman: each and all may describe the multiple functions he performed. Equipped with some of the props of gentility – ample supplies of linen, books and newspapers – he acquired more, especially under the tutelage of a wife after 1746. While still a bachelor, his small household of servants constituted his 'family'.[90] But he also passed much time with his aunt and employer, Alice Widenham, at the grander establishment of Court at Kildimo. Court had ten hearths; Peacock's dwelling, of a single storey and perhaps thatched, two.[91] Peacock's servants (indoor and outdoor) were separated from him by confession and (probably) by language. They walked to the regular patterns and festivals of the Catholic Church, especially at nearby Patrickswell. Peacock instead went, if less regularly than Lucas, to Church of Ireland worship. He also read in solitude. Becoming a husband and a father expanded the occasions for, and complicated the nature of, sociability. He hunted with his social betters, drank (once or twice to excess) with equals, talked with all and sundry. Both as an agent and as a farmer on his own account, he rubbed along with his neighbours. He welcomed the parish priest into his house: once at Christmas; later to spend a night during the summer of 1751. He assisted in the frequent rites of passage which punctuated life in the vicinity. He also picked up administrative tasks on behalf of the Church of Ireland vestry. Thanks to retailers and craftsmen in Limerick, the wares sold at fairs and the auctions of the contents of local gentlemen's houses, he added to his rudimentary possessions. His wife introduced him to new refinements and comforts. The elaboration of the interior of his house (and perhaps of his mind through reading) spoke of respectability, perhaps even gentility. Mrs Hartstonge was on friendly enough terms to assist at the lying-in of Peacock's wife in 1748; Hartstonges also dined *chez* Peacock.[92] The terms on which Peacock joined the squires and their families escape us, but certainly he was invited to hunt with the young squire. Only once did Peacock record distancing himself from an encounter. Arriving at the Hartstonges' manor to mark the birthday of its absent owner, he ran into 'a company of rag, tag and bobtail that came to celebrate the day'. Invited to join them, he declined.[93]

Where to place Peacock, among perhaps 400,000 co-religionists in Ireland in the 1740s, is baffling. His family, arriving in Ireland in the previous century, had sent out numerous offshoots. Some thrived, others withered. Peacock's literacy, his kinship with minor functionaries of the state as well as the prosperous in town and country, all place him higher than the commonalty, but suggest he was outside the gentry into which some kinsfolk would soon be admitted. This uncertainty captures the haziness of the frontiers in eighteenth-century Irish society. Peacock's striving to match the cracking pace set by grander neighbours – the Widenhams, Hartstonges, Burys, Hunts and Quins – may have made him the butt of their jokes. Marriage into the Chapmans, minor gentry and middlemen from north Cork, most obviously altered Peacock's habits. He bought more, including goods which betokened greater refinement. He and his wife intended to live more comfortably, indeed genteelly. Peacock was assisted into these polite habits not just by the prodding of his wife and her people, but by the new availability of commodities in the shopping mecca of Limerick.

The behaviour of the obscure like Peacock, whether in town or country, is too readily portrayed as uncritical imitation of social and economic superiors. *De haut en bas*, Lady Theodosia Crosbie guffawed at the maladroit tradespeople of Limerick. Yet the subordinate, while they spoke deferentially, did not invariably admire those on whom they attended. Peacock undoubtedly picked up notions and articles from the Widenhams and Hartstonges. Although ultimately limited by income and what he could procure locally, he selected which material novelties he should acquire. He expressed impatience with Dublin and its ways after one of his two recorded visits during the decade. The squires and gentlemen encountered by Lucas and Peacock have a substance lacking in their humbler neighbours whose names alone survive. Lucas's and Peacock's meetings and dealings with the ordinary were not free of strains, but they seem also to have brought pleasures. The barriers of language and confession reinforced those of money, leisure and literacy. In Peacock's diary a faint echo of his northern English ancestry can be heard. Otherwise, he indulged his 'small family' of servants by giving them money for 'Patrick's pots' and to enjoy themselves at the local festival. Although he rode weekly to fairs and markets, he abstained from these essentially Catholic observances. Even his ability to take horse to these neighbouring spots distinguished him from most who, through lack of money and through Catholicism, were debarred from owning a nag. The likes of Lucas and Peacock defined themselves as much by reference to inferiors as superiors.

Protestants dependent on land struggled to keep a reputable position in society. Heirs discovered that their inheritances, encumbered with jointures, annuities and mortgages, yielded disappointingly. By the eighteenth century it was difficult to acquire more, other than by marriage, costly purchase or lease. Cadets, even more than their lucky elders, had to discover alternative avenues into the quality. Otherwise they risked slipping into the anonymity of the middling. The Limerick cadet, Hugh Massy, mentioned already, illustrates how ruthlessly the desperate fought to avoid social derogation. His designation as an attorney may have been more fictive than actual. It did at least entitle him to retain the crucial appellation of 'gentleman'. Rather than applying himself to the humdrum business of the law, he roamed the countryside of Clare and Limerick, and with other ne'er-do-wells disturbed it. By snatching the Ingoldsby heiress, he electrified the locals. The action also exposed a rift between those who thought that it should degrade the perpetrators from the company of the quality and those less disturbed by Massy's offence. One contemporary reported that Massy 'has the misfortune of not being liked or regarded by any person of figure or character in this country'.[94] Be that as it may, the local power of his family helped to secure his acquittal in court. Once his daring marriage was legalized, he gained access to his wife's money. The extra £800 a year set up Massy as a squire on his own account in the wilder uplands of the county and promoted him swiftly from gentleman to esquire. By 1769 his son was pricked as high sheriff, flagging entry into the innermost sanctum of Limerick society. By any visible measure, Massy had lived down the *brouhaha* of the 1740s. An unsavoury reputation may have hung about him, but he had avoided being submerged among the nameless of the middle rank.

The misdeeds of cadets, half-mounted squires, would-be gentlemen and ruthless *rentiers* could be elaborated. Their relevance to attempts at social classification is that they showed how groups that might have swelled the middling ranks of Protestant Ireland deliberately flouted the values of order and civility professed by the champions of the Protestant interest. Indeed, middlemen were censured for acting in fashions which made them unworthy of respect. Yet, in the end, they had to be placed somewhere. Reputation might push them down, but income and manner of living entitled them to higher placements. Purists dismissed the show of a Massy as bogus. But much of it was tangible, tied up in land, possessions and even office, so that he – and his kind – could not be denied an elevated position. Agents were also intermediaries, the pivot on which much of the rural world turned. They aspired and often unequivocally belonged to the quality. The ambiguities in the ranking of both middlemen and agents compound the difficulties caused by the small Protestant presence throughout much of the countryside in spotting many undeniably in the middle bands.

III

Towns were more promising nurseries for the middling sort and their values. They housed more Protestants than dwelt in the countryside. By the 1730s, perhaps 75,000 Protestants lived in Dublin. Elsewhere, it has been estimated that between a third and 40 per cent in Cork, 29.4 per cent in Limerick, 26.5 per cent in Drogheda, about a quarter in greater Athlone and a fifth in Kilkenny but no more than one-eighth of the total in Galway were Protestant.[95] Towns were not cordoned off from their rural hinterlands. Even when enclosed by walls and with gates securely locked between dusk and dawn, they enticed the gentry and the lower orders from the countryside. The former often owned property in towns. Some, reliant on their urban remittances, fostered improvements designed to increase the custom of the places. Counties were administered from towns. Around the regular assizes and sessions there developed sociable rituals. Above all, squires and their tenants came regularly into the towns in order to buy and sell. Boroughs, complex in their occupational structures and vital to the English project in Ireland, were congenial habitats for Protestants of the middling kind.[96] In addition, through their corporations, vestries, guilds and voluntary associations they offered many outlets for public activism and sociability. In time, they sponsored races and assemblies. Through these activities, the respectable distanced themselves from those below.

In the mid-eighteenth century, the few Protestants in the remote rural parishes of the straggling diocese of Elphin contrasted with the situation in the westerly town of Sligo.[97] The squires who owned much of it – Wynnes, Irwins and Gores – lived nearby. Another proprietor, Temple (Lord Palmerston from 1723), was habitually absent, but watchful from afar. On the edges of the borough dwelt a lawyer, Ormsby, member of a prolific local clan, and Mrs Booth, an affluent gentlewoman, who lived with two nieces and thirteen servants. The separate households of another half-dozen gentlemen and six gentlewomen were sprinkled over the extensive parish. Some, although nominally social leaders, lived obscurely, striving perhaps to preserve status against erosion through penury. Others, enriched through trade and manufacture, were crossing the frontier between the merchants and the gentry. The resident and adjacent gentry did not explain the brisk traffic of Sligo. Rather its several functions as port, corporate and parliamentary borough, market, county town and garrison supported gaoler, barrack-master, tide-waiter, gauger, customs collector, vestry clerk, weigh-master, bailiff, postmaster and surveyor. Sligo also contained a surgeon, doctor, three apothecaries, schoolmasters and mistresses, cabinet- and watch-makers, a cutler and confectioner, as well as more humdrum trades and services. Much, though not all, of this élite was Protestant. Some of the callings with their grandiloquent titles, stated stipends and – on occasion – uniforms enjoyed a status which immediately pushed their holders upwards. Others had an agreed superiority in skill and reputation, which again elicited respect. Trade earned some the wherewithal to live with the refinements that connoted gentility and respectability.[98] As a proportion of the total population of the town, or even of its much smaller Protestant community, this intermediate group was small: smaller than in an English or Welsh town of the same size. One resident in 1739 doubted if Sligo contained twenty 'men of business' able to spend £50 p.a.[99]

A similar diversity was found in a second borough in the diocese of Elphin. Athlone straddled the River Shannon and commanded the border between Connacht and Leinster. In the shadow of a sizeable and sometimes troublesome garrison, a degree of occupational and social variegation developed. A few professionals supplied a leaven of the urban or 'pseudo' gentry. More were active as merchants and in providing services, as innkeepers, apothecaries, teachers, writing masters and musicians. These were callings in which confessional frontiers were easily traversed and in which boundaries between the genteel, middling and mere mechanics were often unclear. Although well-to-do townspeople bought up property in the hinterlands of Athlone, few extricated themselves entirely from the borough to live as country gentlemen. Again, the town was more occupationally and economically diversified than its surroundings.[100] This greater diversification was replicated in boroughs across the island, from Limavady to Carlow.[101] As had been intended, towns in Ireland were gradually introducing the variety of crafts and trades found in the buoyant English boroughs.[102] However, into the eighteenth century, the more appropriate comparison was with the towns of Scotland and Wales.[103]

Urban traders prospered by serving their locality. Few outside Dublin specialized before the end of the eighteenth century. Opportunists, the merchants handled whatever was available and promised profit. They stimulated and sometimes created demand for imported novelties. Increasingly through advertisement and display, canny retailers implanted the desire to own what they sold. The titled and unequivocally genteel did not disdain the services of these provincials. However, the glamour of wares and expertise from Dublin or further away commanded a premium among those who could pay. Provincial merchants did supply the locally important; but such accounts, although individually valuable, could not match, when aggregated, those of the middling and humble.[104] Merchants, outwardly civil, did not fawn on their social superiors. The traders necessarily subscribed to notions of credit and reputation essential to the well-being of their fragile business. Often these values were at variance with those of the landed.[105] Indebted squires needed the help of the solvent townspeople more than the latter required their orders. Even the government in 1690 acknowledged that the traders of Dublin alone among Ireland's inhabitants had reserves of specie.[106] This realization flattered mercantile self-esteem, increased confidence and swelled balances. Furthermore, these traders, like other urban residents, notably in the ports, were advantageously placed to adopt the new. They were important to, and may sometimes have been the originators of, a civic culture characterized by public service and sociable pleasures set in increasingly sophisticated spaces.

From the 1650s, the larger towns were turned deliberately into Protestant strongholds. This policy was moderated after 1660 and briefly reversed in the 1680s. Expelling or disenfranchising Catholics at first depressed urban economies, because Protestant newcomers lacked the resources and contacts of their predecessors.[107] Yet, especially in the ports and – by the eighteenth century – inland centres such as Athlone, Birr, Edenderry, Kilkenny and Roscrea, trade enriched a happy few and offered employment to more. Occasional glimpses are caught of the successful. In the Youghal of Charles II, Samuel Hayman traded in numerous commodities, including varieties of cloth. He also gained civic office and leases, both urban and rural. Through partnerships, marriages and deals he wove an intricate net in which were enmeshed many of note in the vicinity and beyond. In his solid house in the town, he adopted some of the comforts which he was purveying to the local peers and gentry. Content himself to be classed either as alderman or merchant, he had built the base from which over the next century descendants would move into the gentry, the professions and membership of the Irish parliament.[108] Equivalents included George Macartney in Belfast, William Hovell in Cork, Michelbourne Knox of Sligo and William Colles in Kilkenny.[109]

Important in the affairs of their parish and municipality, these wholesalers subscribed to a philosophy sometimes impatient and even contemptuous of the seemingly feckless or backward country people. Vital to the mercantile credo were notions of credit and reputation. These, not always consistently, went beyond crude monetary considerations. They paralleled, in the urban and commercial contexts, the concern with nobility, gentility and honour among the landed. The preoccupations of the landed and the merchant sometimes overlapped. Both the second Lord Cork and William Waring prided themselves on straightforwardness in much the same way as their urban counterparts. In 1694 Lord Cork and Burlington proclaimed, 'I am a very plain and punctual dealer and can not forbear telling truth, let it offend whom it will'.[110] Those running rural concerns knew the importance of reputation. Nevertheless, the livelihoods of urban traders, entangled in dealings of debt and credit and with distant strangers, depended on probity and punctiliousness. Thanks to financial interdependence, the failure of one could topple many more like so many skittles. In 1740, a merchant, 'in great business' and sober in habits, failed, and by doing so ruined a hundred others. James Arbuckle of Belfast went bankrupt. He valued his warehouse and cellars at £1,500; his shares in ships at £800; tobacco to be sold in Glasgow at £300. He had lent £600 at interest. In addition, he was owed £7,000 in Ireland. The non-payment of much of this money probably explained his predicament.[111]

The letters of George Macartney, a leading merchant in Restoration Belfast, afford insights into these attitudes. Macartney fretted lest he forfeit his 'credit', as well as damage his trade, by selling bad wine in Belfast.[112] He tried, whenever possible, to deal only with 'honest and able men' and the 'punctual'. He asserted 'I do not care what people say, I shall do the thing that's just and shall expect the like'.[113] Those who fell short of his standards were variously described: as 'very simple', 'a simple, foolish boy', 'a cunning man' or 'scrambling men'.[114] On his side, Macartney was praised as 'a very honest man', but one capable of dealing 'hardly' with others.[115] William Waring, a kinsman of Macartney, thought alike. Waring had been trained in the same competitive school as Macartney, but had moved from the town into the countryside. There, in acting as agent for absentee owners, Waring stiffly rebutted any imputation that he behaved other than honestly and openly with his distant clients. The same concepts of credit were invoked, and – as in the case of Macartney – revolved around strict accountancy and the punctual remittance of rents. Towards the end of his life, Squire Waring was pleased to have had 'the good hap hitherto to meet with honest and fair dealing' from those with whom he had transacted financial business.[116] A similar ethic underpinned the activities of the Cork trader, William Hovell. Like others in his position, he was keen to impart his standards to apprentices and novices. Hovell minutely instructed a cousin embarking on his first voyage about proper accounting and correspondence. The neophyte was admonished, 'your acquitting yourself handsomely this first essay will impress an esteem and credit for you in most men which will endure long . . . While you act justly and diligently, God will prosper you.' In particular, the youth was told that incurring bad debts must be avoided, 'for to lose the goods is not worse than that'.[117]

These criteria offered alternative rankings by which to judge and sort contemporaries. They were not uniquely urban. Nor were they necessarily born of the pressures of trading with strangers in remote ports, with trust essential to the satisfactory functioning of the system. Just as the rural world shaded imperceptibly into the urban, so the importance of credit, reputation and honesty was appreciated by all striving to make a living. Religious precepts on the necessity of trust also entered into these attitudes. Quakers involved in business explicitly applied biblical teaching to their everyday dealings. The Friends were enjoined to cultivate restraint.[118] In several towns – Edenderry, Cork, Lisburn and Limerick – Quakers were thought to be disproportionately well represented among the affluent tradespeople. A Dublin Friend, Joseph Gill, early in the eighteenth century resolutely shunned 'riches, family, greatness, &c., commonly sought after'. He, too, wanted only to emerge from 'business with reputation'.[119] In the same spirit, Elijah Chamberlain in the Dublin of 1733 scorned selling shoddy handkerchiefs, because 'I shall get no credit in selling them at any rate'.[120] By the mid-eighteenth century, an exacting Quaker approved the head of a mercantile dynasty in Cork city, Edward Hoare, as 'much reputed for his honest dealing'.[121] Yet, even the most austere did not wholly renounce principalities and powers in the carnal world. In 1708, Gill delighted in a wedding attended by 'some [of] the greatest rank'. Nor could he resist the temptation, despite frequent Quaker lectures, to sink part of his profits in fine furnishings. The desire to do so introduced tensions into the lives of the puritanical.[122]

Macartney, Hovell and Waring might not obtrude their religious beliefs, but often they lay behind their approach to the market place.[123] The withering gaze sometimes turned on associates and contacts who fell short, and seared landowners. Resourceful traders provided the propertied with loans, mortgages, bills of exchange and letters of credit. They also collected and remitted rents from Ireland to England. It was essential, in these circumstances, to judge the creditworthiness of local dignitaries. Macartney in Belfast approved some, such as Lady Antrim, 'a very careful woman in her credit'.[124] Others, like the earl of Ardglass, Sir Maurice Eustace or Sir Robert Colvill, were eyed narrowly.[125] In Cork, Hovell was wary of 'a worthy, ingenious gentleman' with £300 p.a. in the district, because he had several 'chargeable' daughters and was 'somewhat bare of money'.[126] He also disapproved of Sir Matthew Deane, whom he considered guilty of numerous sharp practices. Equally, he distanced himself from the buccaneering of the raffish gentry. In 1686, it would prove difficult to secure execution of a judgment against Squire Tynte of Kilcredan, who seldom rode about the county 'unattended by persons (as phrase) husses and bravos of honour and gallantry'.[127] Even fellow merchants in Cork were not spared. Hovell was, for example, irritated in 1685 when he was prevented from concluding a deal because the other parties were revelling at a 'church feasting' on the anniversary of Charles II's restoration.[128]

Merchants worried about reputation. For them it held the same importance as honour did for the landed gentleman. From it flowed 'all the comforts, nay, the necessaries of life'.[129] Daniel Mussenden in the middle of the eighteenth century showed the preoccupation. By his own boast the most prominent and wealthy merchant in the port of Belfast, he needed to preserve his good standing. Accordingly, when, in the 1750s it was impugned, he referred the entire controversy to colleagues in the town. Similar worries among Dublin worthies created a fraternity – the

Ousel Galley – to umpire disputes. Members, in 1769 limited to forty, were recruited from a social and economic élite rather than from the generality of Dublin traders. Solidarity was further revealed when, in 1753, a group portrait was painted.[130] In Belfast, Mussenden successfully vindicated 'his integrity, and the uprightness of the part he acted'. Testimony to this effect came from one of the local gentry, Arthur Hill of Belvoir, with whom he had long dealt. Hill, having known Mussenden for thirty or forty years, reassured the trader, 'I never saw anything by you but honesty, plain dealing, sincere good will and perfect respect towards me'. Mussenden, although suspicious of the habits and pretensions of the landed, gravitated towards their company and ways. His Presbyterian affiliation may have restrained him from full-blooded enjoyment of what his wealth might command.[131]

Objects – their ownership and use – denoted both wealth and cultivation. Even the ascetic were not altogether immune from these feelings. But sophisticates either in Dublin or among the landed laughed at the urban and middling who were bewitched by goods. Some contended that true refinement or gentility was conveyed through restraint, not show. In following such self-denying ordinances, whether on religious or cultural grounds, it was difficult to steer between the rocks of penny-pinching and ostentation. Furthermore, many articles had practical uses and an intrinsic value. To have them fashioned out of costly hardwoods – oak and elm rather than deal – or exotic imports – like walnut and mahogany – could be justified as these were more durable and the objects were more likely to retain value when resold. Pewter, silver and gold made better investments as well as bringing more *éclat* than treen or base metal wares. Daniel Mussenden, notwithstanding contempt for an heir who might end at the tail of the country gentry, eased himself into the squirearchy of County Down. This transition was accompanied by and partly achieved through the embrace of material delights. For his estate at Larchfield he bespoke silver and furnishings in Dublin and Lancashire. Chairs shipped through Liverpool were made 'in the very newest fashion'. From Bath via Bristol were dispatched a pair of 'Marlborough [stone] urns' intended to surmount the gate piers at the entrance to the *cour d'honneur* at Larchfield. Mussenden's surrender to a conventional gentility appeared most strikingly in the purchase – from Dublin – of a post-chaise for £75. Immediately, he had to agonize whether to have its doors emblazoned with a monogram or full armorials.[132] He himself stimulated and then gained from the craze for novel objects, since he invested in potteries in Scotland and the north of Ireland.[133] An Ulster contemporary of Mussenden, himself serving in the British army, advised (perhaps jokingly) a brother still in the linen trade to extricate himself, build a handsome house and lay down a fine cellar.[134] Traders who followed such advice were not necessarily enslaved to the country gentry and their values. In Cork, the prominent merchant and banker, Edward Hoare, set up on an estate outside the city, but did not abandon trade. His seat at Dunkettle was one of several along the banks of the River Lee admired by visitors as evidence of the riches and refinement of the local merchants.[135] Similarly, Daniel Mussenden, even when possessed of Larchfield, did not abandon Belfast or deny his attachments there.[136]

The pretensions of merchants were mocked. Targets for abuse seem most commonly to have been those who chafed against their modest ranking in the middling sort and craved a higher station. Just as the Irish were felt to be over-generous in whom they accounted gentlemen, so 'who ever is a shop-keeper is amongst most of them a merchant'.[137] Richard Lawrence agreed. In Ireland, he complained, 'every peddling shopkeeper and pettifogger is styled a merchant; that Ireland breeds merchants as beggars do lice, from its poverty and idleness: for turning merchant is the last shift of a lazy mechanic or a beggarly citizen . . .'[138] To be a merchant satisfied some, as an apparent escape from a lowlier condition. William Waring probably drew on his own youthful experiences to disabuse a grandson of his dreams of quickly becoming a wealthy merchant adventurer: 'a fine name if he know how to accomplish what he might project'. Training meant being 'apprentice seven years. For the first two or three years to stand in a cellar or warehouse, retailing goods as iron, sugar, fruit, dyeing stuffs, etc. and to wear a frock above his clothes, to keep the dirt off them, to be company for porters and such kind of people'. Liberty was exchanged for a condition 'in the nature of a slavish servant to master, mistress and it may be children and other elder servants'.[139] Such privations deterred the faint-hearted; others admitted that the mysteries of accountancy and bookkeeping were closed to them.[140] Snobs, being 'too high minded or proud for any trade or calling', ruled out such livelihoods.[141] Realists knew that the preparations could be costly and arduous, and therefore did not suit all sons. Seven years of apprenticeship, obedience to a master, and inscribing and totalling columns of figures lacked the glamour of soldiering and seafaring.

Provincial towns rarely harboured the spectacularly rich. The smaller the town, the less likelihood there was of making much money. In the unofficial league, the port of Cork overtopped Kinsale. In the 1680s, it was said that £1,000 'makes more noise' in torpid Kinsale than £10,000 would in Cork.[142] In Dublin specialisms abounded which were unthought of in the provinces. More than 50 per cent of the total tonnage of Irish shipping was registered in the capital. Similar proportions of the most lucrative export trades were channelled through its harbour.[143] The majority of traders handling valuable imports and exports were based there. Yet even in the capital, those in the same craft or trade, from 'merchant' *tout court* to mercer, tailor, goldsmith, tanner, grocer and chandler, could differ greatly in skills and incomes. The same variety marked the brethren in the trading companies. Entrepreneurs and artificers were sometimes jumbled into a single guild. In early eighteenth-century Dublin, wig-makers, barber surgeons and apothecaries coexisted uneasily in one institution.[144] These *mésalliances* recurred in many provincial boroughs. In the Limerick Masons' Guild, a local landowner, Henry Ievers of Mount Ievers in County Clare, rubbed shoulders with the craftsmen of the town. Indeed, outside the metropolis, the existence of fewer guilds created incongruous and sometimes acrimonious partnerships, in which fraternity threatened to degenerate into fratricide.[145]

Some callings entranced the ambitious with bright prospects of eventual wealth and social eminence. The costs of apprenticeship reflected these evaluations. Fees stretched from £2 or £3 for charity school children put to tailors, weavers, seamstresses and stay-makers to £100 or £200 to be trained by the owners of substantial businesses and offices.[146] In Charles II's time, 'an ordinary gentleman' happily apprenticed a relation as a goldsmith, but despised the surveyor's calling as a 'beggarly undertaking'.[147] Surveyors, possessed of technical and literate skills, soon took their places among the respectable. By the early eighteenth century they were on the margins and sometimes within the lettered professions.[148] Wine merchants were another group felt to be worthy of respect.[149] As with the goldsmiths, so with the vintners, the capital that was needed to start, the overseas contacts and the intimate relationship with genteel customers enhanced standing. Merchant adventurers, involved in overseas commerce, followed 'a very genteel employment', which was not to be confused with that of a 'scrub draper'.[150] Acceptable, too, was entry into a foreign trading house. In the 1750s a brother of Sir James Caldwell from Fermanagh, Henry Caldwell, revolved rival schemes. The Church had first been considered, but was vetoed by his formidable mother. In the end, he joined Barton, originally from the Caldwells' neighbourhood but now a merchant in Bordeaux.[151] His elder brother, James, opposed the choice, but Henry Caldwell declared, 'I like it very well myself'.[152] He planned to conduct himself 'with honour and becoming a gentleman'. This was not easy while he served Barton as little better than an apprentice. Nevertheless, Caldwell defended trade against detractors, insisting that honourable merchants were benefactors to society.[153] In the event, although Caldwell prospered under Barton, his career as a merchant was truncated by the War of the Austrian Succession. Warfare gave him, like many of his countrymen, a fresh start. Favoured by General Wolfe, he rose to be governor of Fort Augusta in the West Indies in 1764, then returned to Canada where he acquired lands, grew wealthy and became treasurer-general of the colony.[154]

Opportunists seized whatever careers were on offer. The ease with which individuals followed several callings either seriatim or simultaneously contrasted with the seemingly more rigid occupational patterns described by London apprentices.[155] An enforced versatility among industrious and ingenious Dubliners told of the smaller markets there. Within Ireland itself, Dublin possessed a unique concentration of offices, trades and crafts. The hopeful young congregated there, in the expectation that they might be trained to take their places among the middling and quality. By the middle of the eighteenth century, the solid burgesses of Dublin were organized in twenty-five guilds.[156] These oversaw the system of formal apprenticeship. The pattern was replicated on a smaller scale throughout the provincial boroughs. The brethren, both in Dublin and the provincial boroughs, took seriously their responsibilities to associates, factors, correspondents, customers and apprentices. These ideals were expressed in the preamble to the charters which had incorporated the bakers and butchers of Kinsale during the Cromwellian interregnum. Thanks to the trading corporations, the 'well ordering and good government', together with the 'prosperity and safety' of the municipality were advanced. The experienced transmitted skills to their juniors.[157] In addition, it was usually through membership of a guild that inhabitants became freemen of their towns, a privilege that carried the right to vote in parliamentary elections. The political implications diluted the membership of the corporations. Freemen were admitted who no longer worked at the crafts or trades to which the guilds ostensibly were dedicated. Honorific admissions increased in the eighteenth century. This brought friction between those resident and active in their boroughs and the non-residents who rode in only for elections.[158]

The exact relationships between freemen and their community became more complicated than that of simply trading and living there. The numbers possessed of this status were considerable. In Dublin, nearly 3,500 freemen and freeholders voted in the parliamentary election of 1749. They formed a contingent almost equal in size to the landed throughout the entire kingdom.[159] Protestant citizens also abounded outside the capital. Fifty-four boroughs functioned as something more than mechanisms to send members to parliament. Enthusiasts for this participatory fraternity contended that 'corporations were in their institution the best school for the vulgar to learn and to practise virtue and public spirit'. The enfranchised were able 'to enjoy liberty, power, pre-eminence, and distinction'.[160] Administering their towns may have involved more than 5,000 Protestant men in humdrum but not derisory tasks. In Waterford, while spoils of office and property were distributed, the well-being of the borough was advanced. A physician was retained to treat the poor; money was spent to pilot vessels up the river into the port; the nearby oyster beds were restocked. Even the physical attractions of the place were increased.[161] What has usually been seen as their most important task, to choose between rival candidates for parliament, happened unpredictably and rarely. More frequently, the freemen selected local officials, allocated leases, pensions and charity, and tackled problems. These chores, the staples of corporation and guild meetings, trained the participants. Assemblies often proved boisterous, but more refined rituals aimed to calm the antagonists and teach cultural as well as political lessons.[162]

Among the guilds themselves, hierarchies survived based upon antiquity of incorporation. In processions, precedence was accorded on this basis. The separate companies vied to outdo one another. Within the individual guilds, differences were uneasily contained. Each sheltered operators of divergent circumstances. In 1656 the Dublin Carpenters' Company enrolled 119 freemen, all nominally Protestants. These were divided into the specialists needed in a city already expanding and rebuilding. Twenty-nine carpenters, twenty-three coopers, sixteen joiners, thirteen bricklayers, eleven plasterers, seven heliers involved in roofing, five masons, four distillers, three millers, two turners and one each of box-makers, plumbers and trunk-makers were recorded.[163] The capital's occupational richness was regularly revealed: in a list of 'principal inhabitants' in 1684; the callings of sureties in the municipal court during the 1690s; the range of crafts into which the pupils from the King's Hospital were apprenticed throughout the eighteenth century; and the advertisements which filled the newspapers.[164]

In Dublin, the Merchants' guild was both the oldest and the largest incorporation. Almost 500 brethren were noted in 1749.[165] By then some members had abandoned trading, but for reasons of ancestral sentiment or convenience kept the link. The Merchants' Company included brethren who, by virtue of wealth and ancestry, were assured of places among the quality. The Merchants' Company, like other Dublin guilds unwieldy in size, entrusted much to an inner cabal. It sought to limit the number who regularly attended halls. In 1664, a gerontocracy of forty-eight was introduced. By 1679, the guild was said to have 400 brethren. Again inconvenience to the younger members was given as the reason for setting a quorum of thirty at the quarterly meetings.[166] Meanwhile, the freemen of the Weavers' Company formally separated into two groups, the elders and the younger freemen.[167] Among the Barber Surgeons, a clique dominated the offices of master and wardens and the standing committee, and so

controlled decisions. In 1734, irritation at the ploys of the few led to a
ban on the officers incurring expenses 'in taverns or alehouses on pretence of council business'.[168]

In the populous trading companies, just as in the urban parishes, smaller
knots of the energetic and ambitious emerged. Despite this trend towards
oligarchy, traditions of participation did not vanish. However, as earlier
in London, it is often hard to assess whether these organizations served to
integrate and placate those of divergent backgrounds and circumstances,
or to aggravate their differences.[169] On occasion, guild meetings drew large
numbers. During the agitations of the 1740s, when a prominent member
of the Weavers' Company, James Digges La Touche, joined Charles Lucas to
challenge the aldermanic control of the city corporation, his guild brethren
were galvanized. In 1749, 105 brethren came to a hall at which a vote
censuring the Dublin civic hierarchy was passed.[170] Members, occasionally
excited – and split – by political controversies more commonly united to
defend privileges and profits. The Weavers and Barber Surgeons conducted
long campaigns against competitors and interlopers. In Limerick during the
1750s, the Masons' Company still strove to police the craft, and inspected
defective workmanship.[171] Within each guild, established masters shared an
interest in preserving monopolies, prices and standards. This separated them
from the unfree artificers, journeymen, quarter-brothers and their own
apprentices.[172] There was a tendency – paralleling that in the vestry and
borough council – for small and self-perpetuating groups of office-holders
to engross power. At the same time, solidarity among the substantial
employers might be threatened by their different specialisms. In Dublin,
until 1747, an incongruous institutional marriage brought strife between
the surgeons, periwig-makers and apothecaries. In the textile trades of the
capital, a basic division separated those who made broad and narrow cloths.
To these were added the discords between the makers of common poplins,
worsted, forest cloths, beaver, druggets, half silks, German serges, velvets and
many qualities of handkerchief.[173] These operatives were frequently competing for the same customers. However, local manufacturers and their
operatives shared a desire to prevent a flood of imported commodities.

Journeymen – the wage labourers – dwelt in the penumbra around the
established corporations. It is not clear what proportion boarded with their
employers, as was often the practice in Tudor London. The journeymen
improvised their own organizations (again consciously or unconsciously
copying their counterparts in London). These societies, imitating the guilds,
united vocational aid with commensality.[174] From time to time, journeymen
and 'undertakers' combined to ask for better pay and shorter hours from
their masters. Their combinations were resolutely resisted. As early as 1683,
investors and directors of the Bandon manufactures devised a cartel to check

truculent weavers.[175] Later – in the 1740s – the Dublin Weavers' Company promoted an act of parliament which would outlaw such workers' protests.[176] Periodically the aggrieved took direct action against rivals, notably those who sold or wore imported fabrics. In doing so they terrified shopkeepers and respectable customers, and were denounced. In 1753, the master of the Weavers' Company had his own clothes cut to tatters.[177] Whether it was always the poorest operatives who staged these demonstrations may be doubted. The journeymen aspired to and periodically achieved a degree of solidarity of their own which mimicked that of the masters in the chartered guild. The hostile, including the established within the Weavers' Company, looked down on the workers, whose wages they were so eager to reduce, and readily demonized them as 'the idlest of men' or simply 'rabble'.[178] On occasion, fraternal relations recalled those of Cain and Abel.

Freedom of a guild or corporation implied at least modest substance and differentiated the fortunates from the commonalty. However, where on the social scale these thousands of townsmen were to be situated, and whether (and how many) among the 'middling', are not easily decided. The simple description 'weaver', like that of 'merchant', masked extremes of wealth and standing. Within the textile trades, a few belonged to the quality; more to the lower ranks. Weavers seldom owned pews or ran vestries. In 1725 John Dwyer, a clothier of Pimlico in the city, had a seat in St Catherine's transferred to his use. A sheerman was allotted a place in the gallery in the same church.[179] But the textile workers were more likely to feature in the ratings of Church of Ireland parishes as recipients of relief. It was the functionaries of the guilds, bestirring themselves to preserve privileges and profits, who enjoyed elevated status. Their sense of importance was fostered by regular consultations in taverns and the company's hall.[180] These activists tended to be the masters.

The prosperity awaiting some master 'weavers' is suggested by Anthony Sharp. Originally from Gloucestershire, Sharp settled in Dublin about 1669. Soon deep in the affairs of the Weavers' Company, he was rumoured to employ 500.[181] Other master weavers were said to have 1,000 working for them.[182] Sharp was a Quaker, and as such possessed widely spread contacts, which assisted his success.[183] His creed inhibited him from full-blooded indulgence in all that his wealth might buy. Others among the successful in late Stuart Dublin were less abstemious. During the 1660s and 1670s, David Johnson, free of the Merchants' Guild, dealt in cloth, skins and metalware. He also supplied provincial squires with novelties. He used his profits to amass table and personal linen and imported glass and silver utensils similar to those accumulated by his grandest customers.[184] Other of Johnson's and Sharp's contemporaries in the city surrendered to similar impulses. John Barlow in 1689 was happy to be remembered as a bricklayer and George Craford a year later as 'gunsmith'. Like many urban traders, they dabbled in several businesses. Barlow's interests extended into brewing; Craford traded in textiles. Barlow was able to bequeath to his wife £400 and another £100 in gold, as well as silver and plate. He set aside between £20 and £30 annually to maintain each of his sons until they reached the age of eighteen.[185] Owning a valuable portfolio of properties in Dublin, he counted William King, future bishop and arch-bishop, among his friends. Barlow had equipped himself with some of the valued adjuncts of the respectable, notably silver. He also kept more than £315 in gold and silver coin on his premises.[186] Possessions of the kind and value amassed by the likes of Johnson the merchant, Craford the gun-smith and Barlow the bricklayer, raised them above many who shared the same occupational designation. Where precisely it deposited them on the social scale is less easily determined. They had not dropped their vocational titles in favour of 'gentleman' or 'esquire'. The processes of gen-trifying the urban, evident in the transformation of provincial merchants such as the Haymans, Hoares and Mussendens, were certainly occurring in Dublin, but are hard to trace in any detail.

In 1725, the newly dead Dublin alderman, Ford, was remembered as 'placed . . . in the middle state' thanks to his fortune.[187] Whether this place-ment equated with 'the middling sort' is unclear. The aldermanic rank of itself conferred distinction, and avoided the conundrum of more conven-tional social classification. Aldermen had by definition reached the upper slopes of the civic establishment. This eminence was usually matched by prosperity, which in turn might purchase the styles denoting gentility. Alderman William Stowell ran an ironmonger's emporium during the 1690s. Its vast stock met Dubliners' wants: more than 500 of assorted social designations, from peers to other tradespeople, dealt with him.[188] In a similar and equally profitable way of business was John Molyneux. Having been instructed in England in the skills of making 'the finest sorts of smith's work and gun work', he settled in Dublin. There, he claimed, his operations had not only brought specialists from England to assist, but supported twenty English families, two 'blue boys' at the King's Hospital, apprentices and workmen. Molyneux astutely stimulated and then cashed in on the Dubliners' taste for the basics and extras of elegant living.[189] His standing led to, and was increased by, appointment as the city water engineer. He took on duties in his parish as churchwarden and profited from its needs by supplying ironmongery.[190] Younger Molyneuxs contin-ued the business.[191] Application earned Molyneux repute and wealth. Successes encouraged imitators, and gave trade allure – at least in its Dublin manifestations. One bedazzled was Will Close, the wayward grand-son of William Waring. The grandfather rudely disabused Close of his misconceptions about the easy riches that awaited the merchant adventurer. Another entranced by the possibilities, late in the 1720s, was Jack Crofton. His brothers had opted for well-trodden paths to respectability: the army, the Church and the Revenue service. In contrast, Jack Crofton was apprenticed to Molyneux. With this grounding, Crofton planned to cash in on the consumerism which was infatuating so many around him. He set up as an interior decorator. But the project was wrecked by Crofton's airy notions.[192] By 1749, he had seemingly slid down the social ladder: from scion of a gentry family to being a 'builder' in a midlands town. Those who pursued their skilled callings exclusively in the provinces are hard to disinter. Baldwin Potter was respected as a clockmaker in the Cavan town of Belturbet, where he was entrusted with care of the town's public clock, at an annual salary of £4 10s. in 1704. His skills were also applied to engraving a silver plate to be given by the corporation as a prize in the local races. In 1739, a Barnaby Potter appeared in the county town of Mullingar as a watchmaker. Probably he was a son who had followed his parent's craft.[193]

On the way up while Jack Crofton was descending was John Putland. A Putland first appeared in Dublin in 1649, as a member of the Blacksmiths' Company. By the 1680s, the head of the second generation, Thomas Putland, also free of the Blacksmiths, radiated the admired qualities of a merchant, being accounted 'cautious, just and ingenious'.[194] His contacts included the Cork merchant Hovell and the Dublin office-holder and virtuoso, William Robinson. Putland dabbled in banking. Detractors thought he would have done better to stick to selling leather, about which he knew more. Within three generations, office, education, increased wealth and marriages into the clerisy of Dublin transformed the Putlands into *rentiers* and urban squires. By 1749, John Putland, the quintessential civic activist, had so far outgrown the commercial roots of his family that he voted in Dublin simply as a freeholder, not as a member of any guild. However, his sons resumed the family tradition of acquiring freedom of the city via the Merchants' Guild. By then, however, the Putlands, acknowledged as esquires, had left the middling station far behind.[195]

Enthusiasts praised urban life for its numerous opportunities to learn and show civility. The guilds – like the vestries – were schools for these refinements. The hostile saw the organizations as dedicated primarily to restrictive practices or indulgent conviviality. The guilds bulked large in the public life of their boroughs. In Dublin, they elected annually representatives for the common council. There, and in the provinces, they assisted in ceremonies and yearly perambulations of the boundaries.[196] These civic and craft festivities had confessional elements. By the 1690s, those not Protestant were excluded from citizenship and full membership of the trading companies.[197] The latter fobbed off Catholics with a second-class status as quarter-brothers, for which they paid dearly. Church of Ireland chaplains were retained to preach after the brethren or freemen had paraded through the streets and before they marched to their feasting.[198] On these days, harmonies might suddenly modulate into discords. Furthermore, if an essential brotherhood of those free of the corporation or guild was displayed, so too were the hierarchies within those sodalities. Gowns formally and deportment unofficially registered gradations in standing.[199] Communal rituals accentuated the exclusions. In 1750, the Dublin Weavers' Company resolved to celebrate the anniversary of the battle of the Boyne. As a permanent reminder of the events sixty years earlier which had led to their present privileged position, they proposed erecting a statue of William III outside their hall, 'as a mark of their sincere loyalty and affection to him and his illustrious family'.[200] Other organizations in the city adopted the emblems of the Protestant deliverer.[201] Notable in these acts was the emphasis on William of Orange as source of their happy condition rather than love of the Hanoverians. Other political icons were exhibited, such as portraits of reigning monarchs or coats of arms.[202] Nevertheless, encouragements to think of these trading bodies as elements within a British system were few. Indeed, townspeople were more likely to question the connection, which damaged Ireland's trade. Occasionally, the trading companies made common cause with groups in other Irish towns, such as Cork or Limerick, to protest against recent discriminatory English laws.[203] It was also possible, as in the 1670s, to liaise with the discontented in London, and copy metropolitan tactics.[204] But these contacts across the later Stuarts' and Hanoverians' territories did not weaken the essentially cellular structure of Protestant Ireland.

Traders in the towns were hard to place socially, in part because they varied so greatly in financial strength. But ranking was further complicated, especially in Dublin, by the presence and success of dissenters and Catholics. The latter were legally excluded from full participation in the corporate life of the guilds. By-laws circumscribed their trade and crafts in the provinces. However, barriers raised in the late seventeenth century were being dismantled or lowered by George II's reign.[205] It was feared that Catholics, prevented from buying freeholds, unable to rent land for more than thirty-one years and excluded from office and most professions, were infiltrating commerce. These fears were probably exaggerated, but the odd conspicuous example kept them alive.[206] At the start of the eighteenth century, William Conran, a grocer in Bridge Street and a member of a long-established commercial and civic dynasty in Dublin, thrived. Conran, apparently a Catholic, used profits of £7,000 or £8,000 from his grocery to buy back a lost estate in County Meath, which yielded £500 p.a.[207]

Clearer than these, probably exceptional, Catholic triumphs are those of the dissenters. After 1704, the Test Act drove scrupulous Protestant non-conformists from civic office.[208] In the capital, the latter readily circumvented obstacles and became full members of the guilds. The Quakers and Presbyterians were the largest of these denominational groups, and crowded into particular trades, such as textiles, tanning and tallow chandlery. They were assisted in their businesses by networks of Quakers and Presbyterians in other parts of Ireland, Britain and beyond.[209] However, the dissenters were also numerous in the snooty Merchants' Guild: 22 per cent of its known brethren in 1749 were Protestant nonconformists.[210]

Proportions of Protestant dissenters in the Dublin guilds, 1749

Guild	Dissenters	Conformists	Percentage of dissenters
Merchants	107	380	22.0
Tailors	28	113	19.9
Smiths	9	157	5.4
Butchers	3	105	2.8
Carpenters	27	150	15.3
Shoemakers	9	68	11.7
Saddlers	3	102	2.9
Cooks	1	27	3.7
Tanners	20	24	45.5
Tallow chandlers	28	58	32.6
Glovers	10	34	22.7
Weavers	79	180	30.5
Sheermen	7	27	20.6
Goldsmiths	3	63	4.5
Coopers	6	51	10.5
Feltmakers	6	46	11.5
Cutlers	9	62	12.7
Hosiers	8	41	16.3
Curriers	3	9	25.0
Brewers	0	11	00.0
Joiners	3	39	7.1
Apothecaries	5	15	25.0
Bricklayers	4	67	5.6
Barber surgeons	9	78	10.3
Bakers	1	16	5.9
Total	**388**	**1,923**	**16.8%★**

★ Average percentage of dissenters.

'Dissent' may have described at best residual attachment to the habits of ancestors rather than exclusive membership of a dissenting congregation. In addition, the term may have been applied to those who held particular (dissident) political opinions or who pointedly did not display their wealth. Also, the practice of occasional conformity, revealed when Quaker merchants of Edenderry bought pews in the reordered parish church there, meant that nonconformity shaded into conformity.[211] Only in some of the buoyant towns of Ulster did distinct but parallel Protestant hierarchies – one of Church of Ireland members; the other of dissenters – evolve.

IV

The larger towns perplexed commentators. One response was to pass quickly over their complex social and occupational structures; another was to belittle them. The result was to ignore ingredients vital to the Protestant interest. The sophisticated, such as Lady Theodosia Crosbie, looking down on the town-dwellers assumed that they wanted nothing more than to ape their betters. The middling sort, it was supposed, longed to scramble upwards. In 1691, a commentator had noted the tendency of merchants to 'turn purchasers as soon as they have gotten as much as will maintain their families'.[212] However, if they invested enthusiastically in land (as in urban properties), these traders did not always extricate themselves from the town. Their efforts were derided as provincial, pushy, uncouth or malapert. In like manner, the ineffably superior Mary Delany wrote off Samuel Cooke, a knight, member of parliament for the city of Dublin and patriot hero. Political differences coloured her assessment, but it took the form of disparaging the Cookes for *arriviste* pretensions, glaringly manifest in their out-of-town house and garden, 'as formal as bad taste could make it'.[213] Cooke's aesthetic ignorance might be linked to the source of his wealth: brewing. The less exacting admired Cooke and his country place near Leixlip.[214] To rebut the snobbish Mrs Delany, it might have been remarked that her own husband, Patrick Delany, dean of Down, was newly rich. However, Delany's fortune derived from a good marriage and the emoluments of the Church. Further, his background, while obscure, lay in the countryside. Others appreciated mercantile wealth. A Londonderry patriarch, Thomas Ash, contentedly traced his clan which had colonized not only the law, ministry (both Church of Ireland and Presbyterian) and army, but also trade and manufacturing crafts such as textiles, tanning, watchmaking and iron-founding. Ash approved of his relations because they had made money or for the manner in which they lived.[215]

Katherine Conolly admired those who flourished in commerce. Indeed, to be 'of note in the way of business' was high praise.[216] Cosby, the squire of Stradbally, and Synge, bishop of Elphin, happily acknowledged less socially elevated relations. Kinship was not denied, but direct contact was limited.[217]

Praise or condemnation did little to define who exactly occupied the middle ranks. In the abstract, those of middling condition were approved since they avoided the extremes of wealth and poverty. Indeed, one who did so was Dean Delany.[218] Often the dread of being sucked down, not the enticements of gentry and squires, drove the seekers after respectability and gentility. Classical theory, emanating from Aristotle, commended sufficiency, not excess or want. Civic virtues were more likely to be developed by those of modest rather than of great wealth. One pamphleteer asserted that 'it is among such people that virtue and patriotism are more generally to be found'.[219] Furthermore, this middling order took most seriously religious observances, schemes of material and moral improvement and public responsibilities. Those in 'the middle state' sustained the voluntary and associational initiatives and much of the cultural life of eighteenth-century Dublin. Yet these activists, including John Putland, Patrick Delany himself, Thomas Kingsbury and Robert Roberts, came from the professions and urban gentry, and are not appropriately located in 'the middle station'. Towns treated the obviously eminent, peers and esquires, to precedence and with politeness. But the boroughs cherished their own hierarchies, embodied in the corporation, the chartered companies and voluntary associations, and their own values.[220] On to the familiar veneration of towns as the most comfortable seats of civility and – in the Irish context – English and Protestant ways were grafted newer notions. Politeness, respectability and sociability were better practised in the towns than in the countryside. Implicit in this thinking was dissent from the arrogant assumption of the landed that they alone set the standards of honour, reputation, nobility, gentility and civility. A description of Belfast in 1738 lingered over the town house which, on its upper floor, incorporated an assembly room. Fortnightly gatherings proved that 'trade don't always spoil politeness'.[221]

The callings and meetings of the larger boroughs, if not on the scale of London or Hamburg, nevertheless afforded unique outlets for qualities such as brotherhood, community, urbanity, industry and public spirit.[222] This pride was evident in 1727 when a candidate in the parliamentary election for Dublin city asked rhetorically whether 'none are noble but country gentlemen, nor is there respect due but to such as, like some of the old Egyptian deities, grew in the fields'? It was reiterated, more satirically, during Lucas's struggle in 1749 against assorted tyrannies.[223]

Dublin freemen, affecting a language of deference, were capable of reject-
ing the arrogance of the rural squires who set themselves up as the arbiters
of the correct. Credos of fraternity and cooperation also approved hierarchies and competition. Critiques questioned who were the true patriots
in the kingdom. No longer were the landed unthinkingly accorded ethical
pre-eminence. Absent or indolent peers and bucolic squires gave a less
pleasing tone to Protestant Ireland than the cultivated and active townspeople. Wealth, associational life, physical and cultural improvements were
uniquely concentrated in Dublin, making it the dynamo of Protestant
Ireland.

By the 1760s, one optimist discerned a growth in 'the middle class of
people'.[224] It was seen as an urban, and predominantly Dublin, achievement. However, this 'middle class' was not to be equated with 'the middle
station'. Its members – professionals, office-holders and civic worthies –
promoted social, economic and cultural changes. They and those beneath
them – the freemen, vestrymen and jurors – sustained and bulked out an
otherwise puny Protestant interest. Some in the middle class shaded into
the quality. Where the boundary lay was constantly altering according to
individual and collective perceptions. Some conventionally permitted the
honorific of 'gent', such as attorneys or curates, because of their lettered
calling, belonged through income and manner of living to the middle
ranks. Similarly, in the lower branches of medicine, surgeons, apothecaries
and midwives varied as to whether they were most appropriately placed
among the quality or the middling. Evaluations of decorum, respectability and politeness coalesced into the baggy concept of gentility.
Possession of this last attribute, it has been argued, divided the middling
sort: those thrusting upwards were thereby differentiated from a rude
mass.[225] But, by the eighteenth century, ideas of civility and gentility, never
entirely the monopoly of gentlefolk, were complicated by talk of credit,
reputation, politeness and respectability. Sometimes these ideas were merely
synonyms. On other occasions, the separate concepts, and those who
claimed them, were antonyms. Towns, especially Dublin, offered the most
promising incubators and outlets for these refined attributes, notably
through forms of collective activity in the guilds, vestries, voluntary and
recreational associations and in the municipal corporation itself. But towns
also added to the stresses of achieving a modicum of gentility. If action
mattered, so too did appearance. The figure projected could crucially
determine ranking. This, in turn, depended on attire, deportment, housing
and furnishing, all of which consumed not only money but time in which
to learn their correct uses.

For women, the likelihood of achieving the respectability of the middling orders usually depended on a husband or relations. On occasion, they

did take over the businesses of their spouses when widowed. The relict of William Scriven supplied rich customers with high quality furniture in Queen Anne's reign after her husband had died. Jane Sampson ran the family wine importers, but was soon in partnership with her daughter Angel Sampson.[226] In the print trade, a few succeeded husbands or fathers.[227] In the provinces, too, an occasional widow, such as Edward Lawndy's in Youghal, stayed in commerce.[228] However, these women remained exceptional. More abundant were the opportunities for women as shopkeepers and artificers, especially in millinery, dressmaking and haberdashery. These operators took girls as apprentices, usually for small premiums. By this device, no doubt, they gained cheap labour.[229] At this level, it is hard to identify those in sufficient business and esteem to be counted among the middling and those who were conventionally located in the lowest ranks.[230]

Economic uncertainty awaited women who had to earn their own livelihoods. Even those with adequate wages or the assured standing of marriage lacked – or were debarred from – much that differentiated the middling from the lowly. Low levels of female literacy prevented full enjoyment of the increasingly diversified cultures of print. Women were denied parish office, other than as nurses to foundlings, and most pleasures of public and associational life. The routines of the guilds, corporation, Masonic lodges and voluntary boards, no less than those of vestries, were reserved for men. Only in the Dublin Guild of St Anne were sisters given a vestigial role alongside the brethren.[231] Processions and feasts lacked defined places for women: they were relegated to the same obscurity as the labouring and dependent poor and religious non-conformists, whether Protestant or Catholic. Even inside the church, office-holders and other worthies may have been separated physically from their womenfolk.[232] Yet some newer forms of polite conviviality catered for women. Assemblies and concerts welcomed them. But the requirements of tickets and fitting dress put these events beyond the reach of most.

The removal of male supports caused some women to slide into indigence. The widow of Jonathan Butterton, formerly active as a pewterer, was admitted into the privileged company of the twelve female pensioners of Dublin corporation in 1691. This attested to her and her husband's good standing within the city. Widowhood may have pushed Mrs Butterton into a new economic dependence, but it did not necessarily depress her local status.[233] The daughter of William Snow, an agent in Munster, who in his prime had earned £180 yearly, was left 'in indifferent circumstances'. Her brother was praised as 'a frugal, diligent man', but she, denied her brother's assets, had no option but to try her luck in London.[234] Her shaky situation highlighted the greater resources of women higher on the social and economic ladders. Daughters of the

Corrys, prominent landowners in eighteenth-century Fermanagh, were allowed between £20 and £60 p.a. (depending on age) while they were unmarried. Portions would then assist them to find partners.[235] Snow's daughter, in contrast, not only drifted downwards in the society of Protestant Ireland, but might well leave it.

Unmarried women schemed to earn a livelihood. Established posts that guaranteed gentility were few. The corporation of Dublin had in its gift the job of caretaker of the Tholsel. Open to a woman, from the 1690s, in accord with the tighter confessional tests she had to be a Protestant. The occupant, Mary Seamour, had her annual stipend of £4 raised to £6 in 1702 and £10 in 1714.[236] In 1713, the duke of Ormonde supported Mrs Sternfield for the place of washerwoman at Kilmainham Hospital as 'a gentlewoman, well-born but now much reduced, and will carefully execute the place'.[237] The position of caretaker and gardener at Chapelizod, the viceroy's retreat on the river outside Dublin, was held in the 1740s by Margaret Humphreys. Whether or not a gentlewoman, she was capable of writing to the lord-lieutenant about the sorry state of the gardens.[238] Housekeepers wielded authority and enjoyed status. At the college in Youghal, the daughter of a knight was entrusted with its care during the absence of the owner, Lord Cork and Burlington.[239] The overseer of the bishop's palace in Kilkenny saw to it that the goods to be sold from the residence fetched their proper price. Margaret Stephenson, managing the household of Richard Edgeworth, was one of her calling rewarded by a grateful employer in his will.[240]

The rarity of posts with fixed stipends and status destined most women to other strategies. Typically they were expected to marry and then undertake the running of the household. Archbishop King revealed these conventions when he directed the upbringing of the daughter of a former colleague, Samuel Foley, once bishop of Down and Connor. Betty Foley had been educated at a boarding school, but at the age of seventeen was dispatched to an aunt in Sligo. There she would both avoid the distractions of the city and learn the rudiments of domestic economy, 'the managing of a family or the business of a kitchen and the provisions and offices that belong to a house'.[241] The archbishop urged the girl to practise her reading, writing and casting up accounts. He also impressed on her the need to care for her clothes. Above all, in order to understand the 'management of a kitchen or family which is a woman's chief business', the novice should 'put your hand to everything ... for there is no learning these things without practice and it is a great shame to be ignorant of them'.[242] Only when this practical preparation was completed would it be time for the young woman to return to the capital where she could adjust herself 'to all persons and stations'.[243]

Church of Ireland parishes took some responsibility for necessitous women (and men). The amount of their alms varied according to rank. During the 1720s, St Michan's in Dublin was more generous to a distressed gentlewoman and the widow of a physician than to the generality of its female pensioners.[244] Women preponderated among the deserving whom the parish relieved. In 1724, thirty-five of its forty-three pensioners were female.[245] Special attention was paid to others, such as three disordered in their understanding whom the parish authorities tried to have admitted into the city workhouse. Failing to do this, the parish paid another woman 1s. 6d. weekly to feed and lodge the unfortunate Jane Welsh, who had become 'burdensome' to her neighbours. It also gave £1 0s. 1d. to reclothe her.[246] A few others, born to gentility but sliding into distress, were helped by Lady Arbella Denny. In 1767 she opened a refuge for prostitutes. There, in the Magdalen Asylum in Dublin, she and the matron tried – in the manner of the recently opened refuge in London – to give these unfortunates new identities.[247] Inmates were renamed 'Miss One', 'Miss Two' sequentially until 'Miss Hundred' was reached in 1776. The reformed were returned to the world, but in fresh guises: for example, as Martha Fairly or Sophia Godley. What had brought the magdalens to these straits can only be guessed. Some had been born to a perhaps precarious gentility. Jane King, *alias* Purcell, *alias* Gallagher, an early entrant, was a daughter of a widow 'of good character' from Sligo. Able to read and write, she eventually returned to nurse her aged parent. Of Alice Scott it was specified that she had had a very good education and was a gentlewoman by birth. Similarly, Catherine Robison was noted as being of good family. The parents of Mary Daly, from Drogheda, had supposed she was staying with that acme of respectability, the widow of a clergyman, not exploring the twilit zones of the capital. Harriet Reubery arrived at the Asylum in 1774 with many possessions. These included clothing, jewellery, silver and thirteen books. It is impossible to know whether her belongings attested to genteel birth or a gentility assumed as part of her trade. If some sojourners at the Asylum had once belonged to the quality, the most that they could expect on leaving was respectability. The tractable made a livelihood through needlework or domestic service.[248]

Others, not brought to such a dismal pass, also achieved or retained respect. Margaret Purdon, when widowed, adjusted to her changed condition. Her husband had acted as seneschal to the manor of Askeaton in Limerick. During the year in which a brother served as high sheriff of the county, John Purdon was his deputy and clerk. Next he made a living through a shop in the city of Limerick, where he sold wines and groceries. This was then exchanged for a public house back in Askeaton. After his death, Margaret Purdon, who had earlier trained as a maidservant, survived through needlework and as a companion to local ladies. She was pleased to live 'decently and reputably with a fair character in the neighbourhood'. In similar fashion, Margaret Smith at Castlelyons (County Cork) exclaimed, 'I thank God, I owe little and live on my credit'. With a child to maintain, she too kept a shop and worked, and so 'keep ourselves from want'.[249] These epitomized the respectability of the middling.

Chapter 10

The Lower People

I

Attitudes

At the bottom of the social and occupational pyramid in Ireland were 'hewers of wood and drawers of water'.[1] Likening the lowly and laborious to the Gibeonites in the Old Testament was intended to reassure both employers and employed. Similar in attitude, if not in language, were the ruminations of a well-to-do Ulsterman, James Traill. Secure on more than £100 p.a. in County Down, Traill from time to time caught himself valuing agricultural profits before his and his family's spiritual health. Musing about the landless poor, he quickly reassured himself that, 'being accustomed to labour and care from infancy and from their constant attendance on their business, having got a mastery of it, and from their low manner of life having no extraordinary stock of anything to provide but what they can either procure or bring home themselves or at most a few neighbours assisting one another occasionally', they 'appear to live very comfortably and seem to have a true enjoyment of life'. Unusually, in eastern Ulster, those inured to hard labour were predominantly Protestant. In this countryside, Traill met poor Protestants who, elsewhere in Ireland, were more often seen in the towns.[2] The poor also intrigued Bishop Edward Synge, marooned among his social and economic inferiors at Elphin. Few Protestants lived around him. The bishop reassured himself that the monotony of the lives of the laborious numbed their reactions. They might enjoy fewer pleasures, but they suffered less intense grief.[3]

The ecology of the island produced local variations in wealth and occupation which, *mutatis mutandis*, could be found in any country. Two features of the Irish social landscape were, however, thought distinctive and unwelcome. The base of the human pyramid was wider and deeper than in neighbouring Britain, owing to the supposed backwardness of Ireland. Moreover, those on whom the edifice rested were – for the most part – 'Irish' and Catholic. This had been the intention of English policy since the island had first been conquered. It did not preclude, although it seldom encouraged, the possibility that the indigenes should be drawn upwards into prosperity and civility. However, the legal barriers erected throughout the seventeenth and early eighteenth centuries impeded the advance of all but Protestants.

Protestant prescription and practice never made altogether clear whether an order of helots composed of the Irish Catholics had been planned or whether it occurred by chance. Schemes to banish all from the island, or – as was briefly proposed in the 1650s – west of the River Shannon soon foundered.[4] Too few Protestant immigrants ever arrived for them to be substituted everywhere for the indigenous. Making the best of the inevitable, realists conceded that the sturdy Catholics possessed skills invaluable in the tricky terrain of Ireland.[5] Even those less appreciative of the locals' skills calculated that if habits of industry and the truths of the Gospels were to be diffused, then the obstinate Catholics had to be retained alongside the Protestant newcomers.

By the later seventeenth century, the Protestant presence had grown. It was strongest still in Dublin, the larger towns and the recently settled areas of Ulster and south Munster. As it grew, it diversified. Despite the monopolies enjoyed by the Protestants over freehold property, office and the lettered callings other than medicine, the Protestant interest was bulked out by its middle and lower ranks. Peers, the quality, professionals, officers, officials, freeholders and freemen, considered above, probably totalled no more than 20,000. Craftworkers added considerably to this number. In 1672, Petty assigned 48,400 to 'trades of fancy and ornament'; 45,000 to tailoring; 30,000 to the making of textiles. He thought – on rather slender grounds – that 25,000 worked as smiths, 20,000 in shoemaking, 10,000 each in building and carpentry, and tanning. Another 2,000 were involved in the manufacture of iron and 1,600 were millers. Each total included wives, but divided in unknown proportions between the separate confessions, and between the substantial and humbler workers.[6] In each trade, a minority – the masters – counted as quality. More, 'useful tradesmen and artificers', edged into the middling order and away from the poor day labourers whom they employed.[7] Yet labourers were the largest group. Both Catholics and Protestants laboured. The further down the social and economic scale, the more Catholics – whether absolutely or as a proportion of the work force – were encountered. In 1745, worries were expressed in Munster about the declining number of Protestants in 'the inferior rank of men'. This repeated the anxiety of Ormond in 1678 about the 'want of the drudging sort of English' in the larger towns. In this situation, even champions of the Protestant interest had to admit that 'the papists, though they are bad members in this society, are yet better than none'.[8] Nevertheless, as much as 90 per cent of the Protestant population competed (or cooperated) with Catholics to hew wood and draw water, or – more realistically – to till the land, serve in houses, run messages and carry packs. Irish Protestant society had at last succeeded in one of its objectives: it reproduced the full range of income and ranks to be found in contemporary Britain.

Totals of Protestant households, county by county in the 1730s, revealed that many more lay outside than within the office- and property-holding élites, which seldom amounted to more than a couple of hundred.[9] In Dublin, too, the politically active – freemen and freeholders – formed at most a quarter of the adult male Protestants. These mostly hidden Protestants disconcerted observers. Penurious Protestants were unexpected and unwelcome presences in the kingdom. The worried offered explanations. What caused Catholic indigence – laziness and vice – also accounted for Protestant failings. Equally alarming was the evidence noticed in the eighteenth century of industrious and frugal Irish Catholics, whose thrift rebuked the fecklessness of all too many Protestants.[10] Awareness of the scale of Protestant pauperization and belief that it had ethical as well as material causes and ramifications accentuated the tendency of Irish Protestants towards introspection. In this mood, thinking on poverty current in England and continental Europe was applied to Ireland. The immiseration of many was routinely ascribed to their own failings. The charitable offered extenuations: famines, epidemics and recessions claimed numerous victims. Others were vulnerable because young, aged or ill. Populous Protestant communities soon had their dependent orphans, invalids, widows and old. Arguments over the reasons and ideal solutions persisted, but the plight of impoverished Protestants stimulated charity. The benevolent, especially in the larger towns where hospitals opened, showed ingenuity and compassion. But philanthropy conferred a type of power, both moral and practical. Under any scheme, beneficiaries had to be chosen. Choosing further divided Protestant communities. The prosperous and respectable, in dispensing parish and private doles, giving menial employment or scarce beds in hospitals, engaged in acts of patronage.

The vogue for counting heads, hearths and houses revealed – at least in outline – the extent of the problem. Accommodation was the readiest reckoner of the poor. However, the relationship between house size, income and status, reasonably clear at the elevated levels, became hazier the lower the scale is descended. In the later seventeenth century, it was thought that the overwhelming majority in Ireland (87 per cent) dwelt in houses with one hearth or chimney.[11] Observers familiar with more sophisticated and commodious housing in England were aghast. In Ireland, seemingly low quality housing did not necessarily betoken a low standing, let alone indigence. The proportion of householders exempted from tax-paying because they lived on alms, usually as widows, was small: 6 per cent of all noticed in one barony of Wicklow in 1668, 9.4 per cent in the Dublin of 1695. The national total was 3.5 per cent in 1725.[12]

Analysts wrote less about how the labouring population subsisted, or about the gradations within it. In the 1760s, the inquisitive Sligo landlord, Charles O'Hara, chronicled how the remoter west had been tugged into a more commercialized and interdependent economy. The transformations over the last half-century had further stratified the industrious poor. They gained from the greater chances of regular work. Even modest cottagers were pulled into the markets, sometimes as buyers as well as sellers. O'Hara argued that it required £5 8s. 6½d. to support a humble householder for a year. The same household, he calculated, might earn £13 by its members' labour.[13] These figures, if a household of between four and five is assumed, are close to those for the similarly circumstanced in Wales. There, a cottager's family needed from £21 to £27. Other information about Irish earnings suggests – unsurprisingly – differences in wages between Dublin and the countryside.[14] The labourers may have been predominantly Catholic, but Protestants delved and spun. Few Protestants were observed by O'Hara in County Sligo, which was said to contain 1,166 Protestant families in the 1730s. A rural proletariat dominated by Catholics was revealed by the diocesan census of Elphin in 1749.[15] In the Roscommon parishes of Kiltoom and Cam, barely 3 per cent of the inhabitants were Protestant. They congregated in the upper levels of the social order. This corner of rural Roscommon supported a variety of activities: thirty-three tenants, twenty-six carmen, a dozen each of shepherds and weavers, ten cottiers, eight widows, seven smiths, three millers, three hatters, two wig-makers, two tailors, two managers, two feathermongers and singletons engaged in dancing, malting, tiling, masonry or as a tinker. The lowliest were cottiers and labourers, although even they were not entirely uniform in their circumstances.[16]

O'Hara approached the lowest elements compassionately. Familiar with later seventeenth-century theories, he saw them as an asset, which, belatedly, was being used constructively. Projectors in Ireland had long disagreed as to whether it contained too many or too few people. A debate which had raged in sixteenth- and early seventeenth-century England was picked up in Ireland.[17] By the mid-seventeenth century, the poor, hitherto a threat, were regarded as a potential resource.[18] With population at best growing slowly, anxiety mounted that there were not enough people. In Ireland, apologists of the Protestant interest gave these ideas a distinctive twist. Ireland, they felt, contained too many Catholics and too few Protestants. Worse still, the Catholics were known to 'breed very fast'.[19]

Massive mortality followed the Confederate War of the 1640s. Despite these debilitating losses, Petty, having quantified them, contended that there were many idle awaiting employment. During the 1670s, he dreamt of finding profitable activities for 340,000 (about a third of Ireland's inhabitants).[20] His schemes would benefit the commonweal and the individual entrepreneur alike.

Petty's practical philosophy was shared by many who, like him, owned Irish property. Throughout the seventeenth century and into the eighteenth, projects multiplied to put tenants to work. Experiments in extracting iron, silver, lead and coal, timber- and charcoal-working and fishing were trumpeted. The earthenware pottery established with loud fanfares in the Dublin of the 1750s employed twenty to fifty rather than the projected 200 or 300.[21] The familiar staple of textiles employed more. Early in the eighteenth century, it has been suggested that they gave work to at least 10,000 in and around the capital.[22] Linen, promoted because it threatened English industries less than woollen manufacture, attracted most publicity. At first associated with the Protestants (often Presbyterian) of Ulster, the fashion soon spread beyond the north-east. Growing and dressing flax, spinning yarn and weaving involved Catholics. By utilizing the labour of all, the virtues of order, application and civility, prized components in anglicization, were expected to be implanted throughout the kingdom. The poor would be disciplined through regular and arduous work.[23]

These hopes were not always fulfilled. The unemployed or underemployed continued to frighten property owners. So, too, did the dense congregations of workers, particularly in the clothing industries.[24] As early as the 1660s, when a state manufactory of textiles was opened at Chapelizod near Dublin, there were worries about how best to discipline the artisans.[25] These anxieties persisted as the consciously respectable were confronted by uppity journeymen, migratory workers and others who were masterless. The industry, valued because of the large numbers which it employed, by the same token was disquieting. At moments of recession, usually precipitated by English embargoes, the numbers engaged in making fabrics were estimated and (no doubt) exaggerated. In the late 1690s, when the English ban on importing Irish woollens came into force, 'thousands' in south Munster were reported to have been thrown out of work. It was predicted that some might abandon Ireland for good, so enfeebling the already puny Protestant interest. Eight hundred were said to have quit the city of Cork, Bandon, Midleton, Tallow and Youghal. Many had sailed to Holland, 'so that there are no common English left in this county at all, which was the only place like an English plantation in Ireland'.[26]

As a source of work, textiles continued to matter. In the Cork region alone, it has been estimated that in 1710 as many as 12,000 females were spinning. During the 1740s the specialized sailcloth factory at Douglas outside Cork needed 250 hands on the premises, and another 500 outside. In this same Cork area it is thought that by the 1760s, 15,000–20,000 were producing yarn for export.[27] In the 1750s, Bishop Richard Pococke linked the 'very great' manufacture of serges in Limerick with the abundance of working people there.[28] The thriving condition of Clonmel at the same time was ascribed to its textile industry. In the same decade, 'many thousands' of woollen weavers and wool-combers were alleged to have invaded Cork to protest against the manufacture of stamped linens and cottons.[29] Later in the century, another Tipperary town, Carrick-on-Suir, specialized in the making of fashionable rateen. More than a fifth of the town's male inhabitants were thus employed. An unknown, but probably larger proportion of Carrick's women worked in the industry and its ancillaries. At best, these kinds of work allowed the humble to subsist.[30] But, vulnerable to collapses in demand, the workers proved worryingly volatile. In Carrick-on-Suir, the dependence of so many on the manufacture may explain why by 1741 it was 'famous for popish rioters'.[31]

Towns were the favourite locations for these industries. As in so much else, Dublin predominated. The resulting dependence could be dangerous. The recession of 1720–21 threw 7,000 out of work in the Dublin Liberties. One Church of Ireland parish in the district – St Catherine's – had 1,300 in dire straits, 'besides wives and children, out of employment, having sold everything to get bread'.[32] The parish had a long history of providing for its poor. Already in the 1680s, annual rates of £100 were collected.[33] These levies, even if fully paid, hardly sufficed for the numbers of destitute in 1720–21 or 1740–41. Institutional help was directed primarily towards the Protestant parishioners; Catholic weavers had to look elsewhere for relief. The humane sympathized with the starving. Some even blamed the masters in the trade for aggravating distress by fixing prices for piece-work.[34] However, workers who tried to remedy their predicament forfeited sympathy. Militant journeymen and artificers, aiming to better conditions, were resisted by the employers.

Weavers regularly remonstrated and demonstrated.[35] Attacks on shops and people impolitic enough to sport foreign fabrics unnerved the respectable. In 1711, it was reported from Dublin that the weavers 'have been up two or three days'. Protesting against the wearing and sale of imported calicoes, they processed to the gallows which they then hung with calico.[36] In 1752 a crowd gathered in Weavers' Square. Forty or fifty, armed with sticks and short swords, marched to the New Market in Dublin where they then ritually burnt a length of – presumably –

imported cloth.[37] In Cork, too, disciplined protests were staged. Often these embroidered and parodied the pageants devised by entrepreneurs to advertise local manufactures. On 23 July 1754, about 400 journeymen weavers of Cork processed to the gallows, parading a ragged fleece. The demonstrators, some arrayed in mourning, had dressed an effigy in imported chintz and 'foreign cotton' before hanging and burning it.[38] By the end of the same year, the families of many Cork weavers and wool-combers were said to be perishing. This situation was partly attributed to the import of banned textiles.[39] More ominous still were the forms taken by some of the rural protests which disturbed Tipperary and Cork in 1762–63. Hedges and enclosures were levelled; the townspeople in the Protestant settlements of Tallow, Lismore and Dungarvan were intimidated. But the demonstrators, presumably rural and Catholic, also displayed the same patriotic enthusiasm as townspeople for local manufactures.[40]

The spontaneity of some of these manifestations may be questioned. Masters and functionaries of the trading guilds, as well as journeymen, protested at official – usually English – policies that damaged their liveli-hoods. Collaboration in or collusion with the protesters was risky. Masters who employed large numbers of weavers and marketed their wares gen-erally differed in interests and outlook from the operatives themselves. The privations of 1740–41, which resulted in severe mortality, may have reduced the number of the skilled workers and so increased their bargaining power. In the aftermath, combinations were formed.[41] The Weavers' Company retaliated by promoting an act of parliament to outlaw such combinations among the journeymen.[42] Thereafter it exerted itself to have the law enforced. It exploited its long-standing contacts in corporation, parliament and Dublin Castle. It financed the prosecution of offenders. It also intervened to set the prices to be paid for various kinds of work.[43]

Textile workers faced a gruelling regimen. During the 1750s, journey-men and sheermen in Dublin were to work from five in the morning to seven at night throughout the summer. For this they were paid nine shillings weekly. They agitated to have the wages increased to a daily two shillings.[44] Such a rate would have been double the average earned by the unskilled in Dublin at the time. Craftsmen could expect a shilling daily; general labourers, tenpence.[45] Journeymen peruke-makers laboured from seven in the morning until nine at night throughout the winter, and from six to eight in the summer.[46] Onlookers defended the long hours as likely to inculcate industry. In the countryside, too, it was supposed that labour-ers could earn enough not just to subsist but sometimes to buy more than the basics. It was stated confidently that the poorest labourer could earn sixpence daily. In mid-eighteenth-century Fermanagh, unskilled agricul-tural workers were paid fivepence for a day's toil.[47] Ulster linen weavers of the 1740s were credited with the ability to save sixpence weekly. Too often, the alehouse, not thrift, attracted them.[48] Women, too, could earn reasonable sums. In 1775 it was calculated that a deft needlewoman might earn a weekly 4s. 6d. One exemplar surpassed this target, and for nine weeks secured an average of 5s. 11d. per week.[49] The problem for the industrious and accomplished was that good times seldom lasted. Notional earnings based on daily or weekly rates are not an accurate guide to annual income. Too often work dried up, or incapacity disabled the worker. These uncertainties made life for the majority precarious, just as they render any calculation of annual incomes among the poor entirely speculative.

Faced with the poor, the propertied sympathized with individuals. In 1683, Matthew Deane, who would go on to head the guild of wholesale merchants in Cork city, combated the Youghal Tailors' Guild. Deane took up the cudgels on behalf of one of 'a mean profession', the tailor Cornelius Cany, and his wife. The couple had been driven from Youghal. Deane declared that 'this sort of combination amongst tradesmen' was 'common to hunt better workmen out of a town than themselves'. 'Indirect means' removed an interloper whose principal offences were probably Irish ancestry and Catholicism.[50] Pamphleteers loved to lecture artisans on how best to improve their situation. Late in the 1750s, after riots which had alienated the respectable, textile workers in the capital were advised to display loyalty and restraint. A journeyman weaver might efface recent, hostile impressions by working six days of the week, maintain wife and children in 'a clean and decent manner', and so live in 'credit'. This paragon was told not to subscribe to any society of journeymen, since the money simply underwrote boozing. Meetings of such groups, it was alleged, degenerated into raucous binges at which it was impossible to know what was being debated.[51]

Sympathy with larger groups was stifled by fears about their incendiarism – potential and actual. In exceptional instances, as in 1721 or 1740–41, self-protection as much as compassion inspired the giving of relief. Even in these crises, some felt that the workers had brought the problems on themselves. Katherine Conolly, generous in relieving the poor in Dublin and County Kildare in 1740, soon complained that the unfortunates had quickly learnt the habit of begging. By the summer of 1741 she had withdrawn much of her charity.[52] At the same time, the Church of Ireland parish of Kells, in County Meath, felt it worth raising £4 12s. to be rid of four foundlings who did not belong there. The following year Kells decided to employ a suitable person to expel the poor and beggars who did not come from the parish. Christopher McGuire was being paid a yearly £2 as 'whip beggar' in 1747.[53] These exclusions allowed the Protestants of Kells to aid their own.[54]

The churches, although they arranged special collections in 1720–21, were liable to be overwhelmed by the sudden increases in those needing help. They limited regular relief to specific groups and numbers. The Dublin parish of St Catherine's, for example, sheltered a large population vulnerable to the fluctuations of trade. During the 1720s, it devoted between 31 and 38 per cent of its annual budget to philanthropy.[55] Increasingly, the doles were directed towards those considered most deserving rather than to all the able-bodied. A limited list of the aged received pensions. Parochial nursing saved foundling and impoverished children, who were then instructed by a schoolmaster. A few were helped into modest apprenticeships. Beggars were licensed and badged; in 1724, eighty-six badges were needed.[56] Increasingly, the parish sought to rid itself of superfluous burdens imposed by 'strangers' unconnected with the quarter of St Catherine's. Responsibility was also willingly transferred from the parish to the municipality as the city workhouse, the King's Hospital, the soldiers' infirmary at Kilmainham, and medical hospitals came into use. By the 1740s, the rate-payers of St Catherine's no longer paid to nurse the indigent infants, but only for coffins in which to bury them. In the harsh year of 1740, the parish provided 121 coffins. Throughout the rest of the decade, the yearly tally varied from 57 (in 1743) to 98 (in 1749). A few years earlier, the number of houses in the parish had been estimated at 1,361, and the conforming population at 5,444. Later, between 1754 and 1757, the parish found itself disbursing more on coffins. However, the sums were considerably smaller than those paid for nursing in the 1720s.[57] A similar change in methods of relief occurred in another inner-city parish, St John's, during the same period.[58]

At best, a minority of the labouring population, deemed deserving, was assisted. In default of more support, the poor resorted to mutual aid and self-help. Often these initiatives, especially the combinations of journeymen, were thought sinister. The craftworkers professed peaceful aims. The societies of journeymen, modelled on the corporations of the masters and freemen, united economic, eleemosynary and sociable objectives. In 1728 the 'poor societies belonging to the clothing trade' in Dublin claimed to have 1,500 members. Separate groups represented different specialities: broadcloth weavers, stocking-knitters, and silk and worsted operatives. Meeting in the hall of the Weavers' Company, they relieved widows and children as well as colleagues fallen on hard times. Subscriptions, albeit modest, were levied.[59] In Cork, the 'society of wool combers' expected each of its members in 1722 to subscribe one penny weekly.[60] The hope of mutual benefits drew in the artisans. In addition, there was an element of commensality. Activists stressed the essential respectability of these efforts. These journeymen, casting themselves as aristocrats of labour, hovered uncertainly between the middling and lower orders. In adopting habits associated with the polite, they raised themselves above the uncouth mass. Furthermore, through intermittent sallies into public arenas, they exhibited confidence and developed a collective consciousness. Whether or not they simply tagged along behind their superiors in the Weavers' Company, the journeymen aired more than narrowly vocational grievances. They demanded an economy in which local products should be preferred before the British and foreign, a creed that echoed the patriotism professed by some much higher on the social gauge. Aggrieved workers protested their constructive and conservative aims, but may not always have been believed. In Ulster, too, by the 1740s, the weavers of south Down were suspected of combining and raising money through subscriptions to resist Church of Ireland incumbents' claims to tithes.[61]

This restless body of artificers, its confessional composition and ultimate intentions impenetrable, posed a conceptual problem for the celebrants of the Protestant and English Ireland. Evidence of industry delighted the improvers; the corollary, denser concentrations of workers, less.[62] Sites of manufacturing, whether at Chapelizod or near Enniscorthy, were soon linked with unruliness. The weavers brought this restiveness into the closely packed quarters of larger towns such as Cork and – most conspicuously – Dublin. These difficulties resembled those arising from potentially disruptive elements in Britain. The dispersed and smaller communities of linen workers in Ireland were more regularly praised. Yet they, when they combined a sturdy self-reliance with dissent from the established Church and its exactions, might be frowned upon.[63] Larger and largely urban colonies of workers came to worry employers and observers. These labourers could be labelled 'the rascal multitude', 'the mob', the 'scurf', 'cattle', even 'vermin'.[64] The propertied and privileged watched the lower orders warily, both in the abstract and in the mass. Pejorative phrases originally reserved for the Irish and Catholics were extended to indolent and insolent Protestants. The vocabulary of abuse and fear was applied to any who ruffled Protestant Ireland, whether in town or country. The traditionalism of much of the invective frequently hid Protestant miscreants among the larger body of property-less Catholics. Worried investigators identified failures specific to the Protestants, but routine accounts of poverty and unrest failed to separate the confessional components. This undiscriminating approach assumed that trouble was habitually caused by discontented Catholics. Within rural society, Catholics preponderated in numbers, and seem to have dominated the sporadic protests – such as the houghers in 1711–12 or the Rightboys of the 1760s.[65] Yet the lawbreakers on the Wentworth estate in south Wicklow, indicted in the early eighteenth century for wasting woods, bore names which often suggested English origins and Protestant affiliations.[66]

Two processes were at work among the lower sorts. The long established, both indigenous Irish and earlier immigrants from Britain, found gainful employment. Concurrently, more recent arrivals fell into the lazy ways of pastoralism. An unsympathetic grandee in later Stuart Munster favoured rigour 'to take the people from that lazy, sleepy, easy way of getting so much money as will just buy them brogues and sneezing [snuff] and strong beer'. This reformer expected trades and manufactures to 'improve and enrich and beautify the kingdom'.[67] As earlier across Britain, so in Ireland tillage was invested with moral as well as economic value. It was added to the armoury of seeds (flax and hemp) and catechisms with which ignorance and idleness were to be combated. Rural fastnesses, once the seats of trouble, were vanishing. To clear them, the redoubts of rebels, rapparees, tories and buccaneers, was approved as 'commonwealth work'.[68] The imperatives to clear trees, drain bogs, reclaim marshes and wastes or to enclose and improve were primarily financial. However, energetic improvers congratulated themselves on forwarding the divine scheme of creating a prosperous and Protestant kingdom of Ireland.

The very rootlessness of the humble, itself a moral as well as practical failing, horrified enumerators. A frantic agent in Donegal complained in 1665 that he and his fellow Protestants 'have estates and are easily found', whereas the Catholic tenantry, 'snail-like, carry their houses on their heads, and will easily so abscond themselves as never more to be seen by us'.[69] These traits were customarily traced to the Gaelic practice of seasonal migration from summer to winter pastures (or transhumance).[70] Later commentators updated these observations. It was asserted that poor cottagers, now dependent on potatoes, having planted them, travelled as far afield as Britain for seasonal work or to beg.[71] Yet more unsettling was what was reported from early eighteenth-century Kerry. Locals, once they had sown their corn in the spring, 'take vagary of going into Spain and there spend the summer in begging, and wander up and down among the places on the north side of that kingdom, not returning home till their corn is fit to reap'.[72] In the 1720s, there were tales of 'marching gangs of women, children and youth, who sally out from their own homes, set their cabins, gardens, cows or goats for some months'. They then travelled to arable areas to assist with the harvest.[73] Landlords also decried the tendency of Catholic tenants to flit shortly before their leases expired, having exhausted the soil and cut timber, leaving behind debts. Yet Protestant proprietors continued to let their lands to Catholics, notwithstanding their supposed shortcomings. With relatively few Protestants, landlords had little choice. Furthermore, it was widely remarked that Catholics outbid Protestants when farms were to be leased.[74]

Reports on the Irish hinterlands often contradicted one another. Irish Catholics, pushed to the barren margins and stony uplands, were berated for incivility. Remote, scattered and impermanent dwellings went with a dissociability, which in an age when the polite esteemed the cultural benefits of association, was reproved.[75] More viscerally, self-preservation recommended to nervy Protestants an 'unsocial sociability', in order to tame the otherwise restless.[76] However, in the absence of Protestant tenants and labourers, the aboriginal Irish lived cheek by jowl with the newcomers. In the past, numerous blueprints had recommended such arrangements as likely to implant passivity and industry. Optimists announced that this was indeed happening. From County Armagh in 1682, William Brooke claimed 'those few Irish we have amongst us are very much reclaimed of their barbarous customs'. They had abandoned the Irish language and embraced English farming. But, as Brooke stressed, the Irish were outnumbered by the newer settlers: a situation which seldom recurred outside eastern Ulster.[77] In most places, the Catholics predominated. Commentators could never decide definitively whether they were an unrealized asset, 'civil, hospitable and ingenious' and 'very hardy, laborious and industrious', or a liability.[78] The Irish Catholics' strength rekindled fears that the habits of the majority would corrupt the Protestant minority. The poor and young were thought to be especially open to Irish Catholic influence, and so needed particular protection.

Protestants isolated in remote districts shuddered. Shortly after Charles II's restoration, Bishop Synge of Cork bewailed his lot, cast in 'a kernish country'.[79] Nearly a century later, Godwin Smith, at the south-western extremity of Crookhaven, bewailed a situation unfit for either a Christian or a gentleman.[80] Throughout the seventeenth century, the isolated rightly feared physical danger.[81] In distant locations, these worries persisted. In 1762, Thomas Hutchins planned to seek refuge with his family and Protestant neighbours in the small West Cork town of Bantry rather than risk continuing in the country.[82] For the exacting it was the absence of services and comforts which condemned the provinces. A gloomy Quaker found much to complain of in the towns of Limerick, Newcastle West and Mallow, and mourned 'poor slovenly Ireland, overrunned with sloth and idleness'.[83] The politeness and sociability without which the respectable wilted were missing from these rustic locations. Nevertheless, travellers were pleased by signs of change in the hinterlands. Industries were noted approvingly. Better roads linked the towns, a few of which looked urbane. Barracks, garrisons, tidy farms, canals: all reassured them. Maps and histories celebrated what human intervention had lately accomplished.[84]

Conversely, unimproved landscapes either scared or offended. They spoke to the attentive of how the new proprietors of Ireland were neglecting the God-given duty of tapping natural resources. In the mid-eighteenth century, the Reverend Richard Barton and his kind, active in the Dublin Society and Physico-Historical Society, believed that all the works of nature and man contained a moral charge. Barton enthused over the orchards, farms, bleach greens and flax fields of Armagh, 'which has made a great part of the county like a garden'. These improvements confirmed his credo that 'paradise may be recovered in any country where people are made truly moral and industrious, and the surface of the globe has always been emblematical of the morals of the people upon it'.[85] Advances were not attributed to untouched nature but to the exertions of local gentlemen, such as Lord Kenmare and the Herberts. In patriotic guise, Barton begged that artists paint these rather than foreign scenes, and so encourage local instead of overseas tourism. He took the distinctive plant of the region – the arbutus or strawberry tree – as an 'excellent moral emblem'.[86]

Religious duty coincided with humoral theory to implant the view that physical appearances reflected moral states. A landowner from County Cork applauded the reclamation of the last large bog in his area. What had served in 1656 as 'the harbour of wolves and tories', by 1730 had been 'drained and civilized'. This transformation came with the political changes which uprooted a Catholic owner, Clancarty, and planted Protestants. It offered a model by which 'even the most barbarous parts, yet not amenable to the law and civil law [might be] rendered habitable'.[87] In 1756, another relentless improver, William Henry, ascribed underdevelopment to the political and social systems of the Gaels. While their rule prevailed, the terrain was covered 'with thickets of woods and briars, and those vast extended bogs, which are not natural but only the excrescences of the body'.[88] Neither Henry nor Barton, although each preferred what humans had achieved, was impervious to the majesty of mountains.[89] The natural and solitude started to be appreciated.[90]

This shift in attitude away from censure to applause reflected a stronger Protestant presence and the general passivity of the Catholics. By the later 1730s, the Wicklow Mountains could be admired because they 'give the traveller a pleasing idea of the infinite power, greatness, majesty and goodness of the omnipotent creator'.[91] In the next decade, Robert Clayton, having been transplanted as bishop from tame Cork to Clogher, enthused over a 'beautifully wild' country. He rejoiced at 'an opportunity of seeing nature in almost its original state'.[92] The natural was also promoted as the physical equivalent of the uncorrupted institutions to which patriots and reformers wished to return. In 1749 Charles Lucas's periodical, *The Censor*, fulminated against landscapes and gardens which strove 'not to follow or improve but to hide or restrain the innumerable and inimitable beauties of nature'.[93] Changing tastes slowly opened the eyes of a few to the attractions of the primitive. This craze directed the gaze of the curious towards crags, cliffs and customs. In the late seventeenth century, the elder Richard Cox, surveying the sights of County Waterford, extolled 'the romantic'.[94] From the same area, the Catholic agent Crotty praised his locale as 'very near as romantic' as that around Bristol, and 'capable of diverting as well as exercising a good genius'.[95] In 1770, an officer quartered at Inchigeela in the rugged extremity of County Cork appreciated 'this fanciful and romantic place'.[96]

By the eighteenth century, the intrepid returned from the Irish peripheries with tales of natural savages innocent of modern corruption. These reporters varied an old theme in English responses to the Irish. The commonalty was viewed as material which, if only freed from its current overlords, would prove malleable. In previous centuries, the tyranny of priests, chiefs and the hereditary castes had stunted this potential.[97] Now new landlords – mostly Protestant – riveted the manacles. In place of the view that the locals were dangers or wasted assets, they were treated as victims. Molyneux, touring Kerry in Queen Anne's reign, admired existence on the island of Valentia. 'No people in the world live more free from troubles and anxieties of this life than the inhabitants of this place. They have little to do but put their corn in the ground and with patience expect a plentiful crop.' Seldom disappointed of their expectations, 'they sit down and eat it with temperance and frugality, luxury and variety of food (those enemies to the health and happiness of mankind) being never known in this place'. These lotus eaters hardly had to stir.[98] Others, able to 'earn their bread by walking about a fair and watching bargains', were disinclined to follow more arduous callings.[99]

In the middle of the seventeenth century, the west coast and its islands were conceived as an Alcatraz where Catholic subversives might be marooned. A century later, these places offered refuges from the speeding commercialization of agriculture.[100] In the 1730s, John Digby, the suave squire of Landenstown in County Kildare, acquired the Aran Islands.[101] Digby contrasted his own approach to the oppression of his predecessors, who had enslaved the islanders. On his Kildare holdings he was a vigorous improver, but he led the people of Aran with a looser rein, since he believed that they practised the husbandry best suited to the terrain. Dairying had been fostered thanks to an imported breed of larger cattle. Barley and rye were grown. Only the islanders' unwillingness to fish upset Digby.[102] As a distant and detached owner, he preserved the apparent idyll of the Aran islands into the 1740s. A similar freedom had also prevailed on the more northerly island of Inishmurray until the 1760s. There, an unstinted hospitality greeted visitors. A Sligo squire admired the 'innocent simplicity of their lives'.[103] The islanders attended church each Sunday, although the priest came only once a year and then to collect his oblations. The locals were 'very decently dressed', lived industriously, paid their rents promptly and looked content. All changed when the absent proprietor, Lord Palmerston, leased Inishmurray to the Wynnes, resident at Hazelwood near Sligo town. Wynne's rent was rendered in fish. The islanders, lacking the incentive to farm, grew 'dispirited and lazy'. They were corrupted by goods shipped over from the mainland. The gifts from an anglicized and commercial world included alcohol. Addiction and enervation were said to have resulted.[104]

The poor encountered and were drawn into the market. The results, once universally approved, were regarded more ambivalently by the middle of the eighteenth century. These doubts seized the English army officer, Adolphus Oughton. He saw much of the west. On quitting Ireland in 1741, he pointed to the gap between potential and achievement. 'Both the country and inhabitants appeared to me much more indebted to nature than art, and, in general, capable of much higher improvement.'[105] However, he admitted to being stirred by the drama of mountains and the dismal beauty of bogs. Near Sligo, the landscape was more readily comprehended by being likened to Cervantes's descriptions. Locals with similar tastes invited Oughton to explore. One, John Foliot, was so enraptured by the sea-eagles which haunted the cliffs around his estate on the Leitrim and Donegal frontier, that he forbade tenants to kill them. With unaffected wonder Foliot and Oughton watched an adult teach the eaglets to hunt: no matter that the quarry included the tenants' stock. An openness towards the untamed went beyond the fauna and flora to the indigenes. Oughton, while climbing in the mountains behind Sligo, met an inhabitant who had 'never been in any town in his life'. Once a month, this countryman worshipped at a distant church. Neutrally, rather than censoriously, Oughton reported that this innocent derived his knowledge of the world entirely from the priest and religious services. Where earlier reporters would have inserted a sermon on popish ignorance and superstition, Oughton relished the simplicity.[106]

A taste for the wild slowly spread. Vicariously, through rambles and picnics, the adventurous sampled the simple life. Medical faddism enticed the fashionable up steep hillsides to quaff goat's whey or into the chilling sea.[107] On 'innocent frolics', the smart derived amusement from the untamed.[108] They sought both living and inert relics of the older worlds.[109] These excursions showed how hostility towards Irish customs had moderated, and served further to moderate it. But it had not been banished altogether. The noble savages chanced upon when on the tourist trail in the west were not equated with those met daily at home, such as slatternly servants and mutinous artificers. Nor did the encounters across cultural and social frontiers prompt any careful discussion of the occupations, incomes or numbers of the lowly. The poor, *en masse*, whether Catholic or Protestant, perturbed and perplexed their economic and social superiors. Disasters produced commiseration born of a shared humanity: most obviously the episodic famines. Local contretemps – scores drowned when forced by an agent across the Shannon in flood in order to attend a fair, servants poisoned by a stirabout made with oatmeal laced with rat poison, or kegs of gunpowder detonated on the quays at Limerick and Athlone – also horrified.[110] Those whose possessions were destroyed by fire were relieved by the prosperous.[111] So long as the large and undifferentiated mass of the lowly could be broken into smaller units, its members might then be helped. In the process, the fortunate judged their subordinates either as unlucky but meritorious or as unworthy and dangerous.

The lower people were easily conflated with the poor. Poverty was relative, and often temporary. Also, the lowliness of a station depended on the altitude from which it was viewed. It implied subjection, but – as with indigence – this might be short-lived. Dependence frequently marked a particular stage in life. The aged and stricken had earlier ranked higher; apprentices, orphans and the pupils of the charity schools hoped in time to rise. Servants frequently moved in and out of their jobs. Not all were permanently in service. Three groups regularly impinged on substantial Protestants: domestic servants, apprentices, and the deserving poor. None could be regarded as typifying those who hovered around, and sometimes plummeted below, subsistence; none was composed exclusively of Protestants. The elevated, in so far as they encountered the lowly, met Catholics. Thereby, beliefs were strengthened that the poor and servile were Catholics and, because Catholic, were destined for poverty and servitude. At the same time, many terrors conjured by fables of the Catholics in the mass were allayed by quotidian dealings.

II
Servants

Outside north-eastern Ulster, only in the grandest houses were servants exclusively Protestants. At Boyle (County Roscommon), Lord Kingsborough surpassed all others in the mid-eighteenth-century diocese of Elphin with the grandeur of his establishment. His thirty-one servants divided between seventeen Protestants and fourteen Catholics. The females included two Protestants and seven Catholics.[112] At Hazelwood outside

Sligo, held up as a model of a modern mansion, the Wynnes were served by twelve Protestant men and ten Catholic women. Clergy in the same diocese, other than the bishop, could not avoid employing Catholics. Bishop Synge's palace at Elphin was unique in housing seventeen, all nominal Protestants.[113]

In eighteenth-century England, five to seven was thought to be the requisite number of servants. Grandees, naturally, employed more. The staff of large houses in South Wales ranged from twenty-eight at Llantrythid to forty-six at Tredegar.[114] Bishop William Nicolson when in his Derry diocese maintained twelve servants, but in the capital made do with seven.[115] Near the end of his life in the 1760s, Richard Edgeworth, now a widower, kept eleven.[116] At first glance, it seemed, as contemporaries asserted, that the affluent in Ireland maintained unnecessarily large retinues. Some critics saw this as a survival from times, whether in late medieval England or Gaelic Ireland, when status had been connected with the complement of followers. Others linked the prodigality with the Irish Protestants' love of superfluity.[117] The situation can be explained more prosaically. Totals of servants seldom distinguished between those working indoors and outdoors. Since most country houses also functioned as farms, much of the staff consisted of servants in husbandry rather than domestics.[118]

How much, in total and as a proportion of outgoings, went on servants varied considerably, not just from individual to individual, but during different phases of a family's life. In Charles II's Ireland, Sir William Petty reckoned that servants' wages and liveries would consume 9 per cent of his annual budget. The expenses of the stables, with the pay and clothing of the coachmen and ostlers, pushed it higher. Actual spending in 1685 revealed that 14 per cent of outgoings went on the servants, or – when the stables were included – 17.5 per cent.[119] These high percentages told both of time divided between Ireland and England, and of a Dublin rather than provincial establishment. William King, while bishop of Derry, devoted a smaller proportion of his annual expenditure in 1693–94 to his servants: approximately 5 per cent, or, with the stables, 7.6 per cent. As a bachelor in the provinces, he existed modestly.[120] Once translated to Dublin, his rank obliged a greater show. By 1706, in addition to a steward and factotum paid £40 yearly, he had eighteen servants. These ranged from cook, coachman and housekeeper through postilion, pantry, kitchen and stable boys to chamber and kitchen maids. In 1706–7, 8 per cent of his spending went on the indoor servants. A further 8 per cent was spent on the stables. In total, King had disbursed £291 on this establishment: far in excess of what most of his contemporaries lived on.[121] Moreover, the proportion of King's income devoted to servants grew. By 1708–9, the total spent on stables and servants had risen to about £387. The servants' costs now consumed 8.3 per cent of his annual disbursements; the stables, 12.8 per cent. Lordliness, especially in his equipage, may have been demanded by his regular inclusion among the lords justice, the deputies of the lord-lieutenant. And, King, longer in England and having preached before the Queen, may also have adopted metropolitan habits.[122]

Public place excused ample attendants. The first earl of Orrery, determined to meet his own if not public expectations of the state in which he should appear as lord president of Munster, reckoned that between 16.7 per cent and 20 per cent of his spending would go on servants. To these disbursements would be added between 6 per cent and 12 per cent for stables and liveries. Those unencumbered by such a consciousness of dignity, and the need to express it through retinues, faced smaller bills. The Flowers, established in their new mansion at Castledurrow, between 1726 and 1749 found that the servants' wages consumed no more than 2.4 per cent to 6.1 per cent of their yearly expenditure.[123] There is no reason to suppose that the Flowers, with annual receipts nearing £3,000, stinted on their staff; different methods of accountancy may have removed outdoor servants from the reckoning. Fluctuating totals reflected pregnancies, illnesses, the number of children at home and the intermittent but sometimes prolonged absences of the owner. In 1756 Ralph Howard, inheritor of Shelton Abbey and former sheriff of County Wicklow, devoted about 7.7 per cent of his annual budget to his servants.[124] These lower totals were not necessarily the result of the cheaper regimes possible in the country. James Ware, living on St Stephen's Green in the 1740s, spent about 10 per cent of his budget on servants The sum involved was a paltry £11 08s. 2½d.[125]

Estimates of the number of servants in Ireland disagreed. Petty suggested a total in the 1670s of 32,400, or hardly more than 3 per cent of the entire population.[126] Petty, as so often, approached the problem schematically. He believed that the number of servants was related directly to – and so could be deduced from – the size of a house. House size, so far as Petty and his followers were concerned, was measured by the number of hearths: the basis of taxation. Certainly, size of dwelling and number of staff were loosely related. But other factors, including the ostentation which purists decried, and even *noblesse oblige*, governed how many were kept. Magnificence need not exclude munificence. After 1729, Katherine Conolly retained the forty who had served her husband, lately dead, and herself. As a widow she was said still to be attended by fourteen servants.[127] This compared with the modest *équipe* of her widowed sister. The latter, living in Dublin lodgings which she took by the year, had dismissed her maid, kept a manservant, hired a nurse when ill, and had a former servant wash her linen. In her turn, Katherine Conolly wondered at the extravagance of a nephew, the squire of Slane, Williams Conyngham. Returning to his County Meath seat with a bride, he was accompanied by a groom and two running footmen. Never before had a brace been seen in attendance.[128] Contrary to what Petty rationally averred, size of house alone did not tell how many servants were kept. Gender, age and temperament all came into play.

Analysts after Petty classified a larger segment of the population as servants. In 1696, it was suggested that Dublin had 7,000 servants, constituting about 17 per cent of the total population. A few years later, servants were said to make up approximately 16 per cent of adult males in Dublin.[129] Towards the end of the eighteenth century, the percentage of servants among the inhabitants of the capital had dropped to little more than ten. However, more were concentrated in the smartest parishes: 27.7 per cent in St Anne's and 33.4 per cent in St George's.[130] Servants amounted to about 15 per cent of the later eighteenth-century populations in the towns of Armagh and Carrick-on-Suir.[131] Across the straggling diocese of Elphin in 1749, around 10 per cent of the people were recorded as 'servants', but without separating the many agricultural labourers from domestics. Towns, such as Athlone or Strokestown, again returned more servants. Indeed, in Athlone, of the 415 recorded as in work, 44 per cent were 'servants' and 13 per cent labourers. In these returns, indoor and outdoor workers were conflated.[132]

How properly to handle domestic servants preoccupied the thoughtful. Dean Patrick Delany, benevolent towards his own, treated the genus warily. Because humans were born 'nearly equal', those of limited capacities were fitted for repetitive tasks. At the same time, Delany hoped that service would discipline the insolent and unruly.[133] Fear lest the bold challenge their betters made the dean counsel masters and mistresses to praise menials sparingly. Underlings had ideally to strike a balance between being 'low and creeping to a fault' and 'imperious and proud beyond bearing'.[134] To model a harmonious household demanded time. Delany admitted that the human materials with which he, and other employers, had to work were flawed. A contemporary, also a clergyman, concurred. 'Prudence' demanded that servants be treated strictly. 'Harshness, irksome to my self, I find necessary to keep them in order.'[135] In the end, clerics could only reiterate the Christian injunction to servants, 'to be content with that low condition of life in which it has pleased God to place you'. The aggrieved had to console themselves with the scriptural reminder that 'the title of good and faithful servant shall be the highest and noblest distinction'.[136] The Irish history cherished by Protestants afforded one striking personification of this fidelity. The plot to seize

Dublin Castle in October 1641 had been betrayed by Owen Connolly, often characterized as a servant. His name was still venerated in the eighteenth century. Indeed, in the Protestant drive to convert the Irish Catholics, he exemplified what instruction could effect in a 'mere Irishman', and so could hearten the Protestants striving to win over the Irish Catholics.[137]

Conscientious householders treated their employees responsibly. They created domestic hierarchies up which the assiduous might climb. In this way, Robert French of Monivea held on to satisfactory servants whom he had trained rather than having them poached by richer neighbours.[138] The astute, such as French, schooled the inexpert so that, bit by bit, they graduated to greater responsibilities and a higher place on the table of domestic ranks. Charles Macarthy served Charles O'Hara as his 'own man' for almost ten years, and was entrusted with substantial sums of money.[139] At Edgeworthstown, Margaret Stephenson, first employed as a lady's maid for Mrs Edgeworth, advanced until as housekeeper she was effective controller of the establishment. Over nearly thirty years, her wages increased from an annual £4 to £10.[140] Winifrid Higgins, admitted to Monivea in a similar capacity to Margaret Stephenson, not only ended by running the establishment but in the widowed Robert French's bed.[141]

Squire Edgeworth was one of many who paid the costs of medicines, nursing, the wake and burial of favoured employees, such as his coachman Higgins in 1756.[142] In Dublin, the Reverend Henry Ware, although he quickly gave the inadequate their *congé*, also cushioned the old age of some no longer able to work. Rachel Winterbourne, first employed by Ware's father in 1740, was noted as an employee at an annual wage of £4 in 1766. Ten years later, Ware 'parted with her, being in a dying way and had a great loss in her, but will allow her wages during life'. Mrs Rebecca Kelly, like Mrs Winterbourne, had been taken over with the house on St Stephen's Green. Originally she entered service as a housemaid in 1755 with James Ware, the Reverend Henry Ware's elder brother. She left in 1776, 'being quite worn out'. Again Ware undertook to support her for the remainder of her life. Another whose departure he regretted was Mrs Alicia Lewis, considered 'thoroughly careful and honest'.[143] Ware helped Catherine Byrne, also in his employ, with the expenses of burying a sister and brother.[144] In 1748, John Hall, then working for James Ware, was allowed to visit a sick wife in Kerry. Hall's son, enlisted in the navy, was aided by Ware. Twenty-two years after he was first recorded in the Wares' house, Hall was granted an annual pension of four guineas. In addition, the Reverend Henry Ware paid the rent on his lodgings.[145] Earlier, in Dublin, Archbishop King had paid to bury the widow of his former postilion and then supported the orphaned daughter.[146] Edgeworth subsidized the education of his gardener's son and daughter, and administered a trust which supported the son of another former servant.[147]

Superannuated nursemaids for children attracted special generosity.[148] Just as their neglect could kill, so their care saved the tender.[149] An aged Nurse Ward, revered in the Conolly circle, received a weekly sixpence and lived rent-free, admittedly in a dilapidated house.[150] Lord Blessington had a nurse of his family buried in style. Indeed, his largesse to her in death, if not perhaps in life, worryingly elided the distinctions between the quality and their inferiors.[151] It was common for the long-serving to be remembered in the wills of their masters and mistresses. What retainers were left varied between a year's wages or a parcel of their employer's clothes to substantial lumps of money. Some set up in shops or crafts thanks to legacies; others were bought apprenticeships.[152] This belated recognition hardly compensated for a life of drudgery. The reciprocity inherent in the relationship between employer and employed caused the negligent to be censured. Katherine Conolly was admonished – posthumously – when she failed adequately to reward her long-serving attendants from her ample fortune. The servant who had broken the mistress's fall as the stout widow tumbled down the grand staircase at Castletown might well feel mortified. The ideal of mutuality was difficult to sustain in such an unequal relationship.[153]

Relations between employers and their staff in theory were regulated by contract and, in the last resort, by law. In most cases, it was the master or mistress who set and noted down the terms, adjudicated on violations, and decided the penalties. Other than to abscond with pilfered articles, individual domestics had little chance of satisfaction against arbitrary superiors. Especially in small establishments with no more than a couple of servants, the multiplicity of tasks weighed down all but the toughest. Yet there were unexpected signs that employees enjoyed leeway. This latitude may have told of the problem of finding better. The habitual cheek of footmen was overlooked; the drunken japes of retainers did not bring invariable dismissal but instead a weary forbearance.[154] Habituated to each other's foibles, householder and servant overlooked provocations. Katherine Conolly was resigned to the fact that footmen were almost universally 'saucy'.[155] In the end, the wise heeded the advice given by Bishop Synge to his daughter: 'look out for such servants as will make you easy'.[156] Cultural and confessional differences hindered but did not necessarily prevent the development of affinities. Servants lived alongside Protestant householders in an intimacy unmatched by any other Catholics, chiefly tenants and shopkeepers, whom the employers routinely met. Except in the most splendid houses, it was impossible to segregate servants from those whom they served.

Domestic service defined by an agreement, no matter how sketchy and one-sided, involved a loss of freedom. However, it was not altogether incompatible with a measure of gentility. The pretensions of upper servants who mimicked the ways of their masters and mistresses were repeatedly derided or rebuked. Yet those in intimate contact with or on public exhibition to their social superiors had to comport themselves appropriately. Standards of demeanour became more exacting as the lives of the quality and middling sort were permeated with notions of politeness and gentility. Servants were expected, indeed required, to conform to these changing manners. But, by doing so, they simultaneously reassured their employers by becoming more pleasing as servants and alarmed them by feigning the attributes of those whom they served. The ease with which the deportment of the quality could be learnt was a warning not to rank according to external rather than inner qualities. Butlers and housekeepers, sometimes valets and ladies' maids, scorned to be lumped among the lower orders, and claimed a place among the respectable. In general, they were better regarded and paid than postilions, footmen, gossoons and maidservants. The untrained seldom received more than £3 or £4 p.a. In time, the more experienced, like the Flowers' Cupid Gallop, could earn £8 or £10 p.a.[157] The hierarchies of regard and reward were not uniform throughout all houses which kept a staff. Aristocratic (or would-be aristocratic) households, such as those of the Ormondes at Kilkenny, Dublin Castle or in England, or the Kildares' at Carton and Kildare (from 1766, Leinster) House, rewarded the specialists essential to their elaborate operations.[158] Elsewhere, repute as cook, coachman or gardener commanded a better wage than a mere valet or maid. Edgeworth, for example, gave his gardener, George Kelly, £8 p.a.; his coachman, £6.[159] At Beaulieu (County Louth) during the 1750s, the butler and gardener each received an annual £8.[160] The St Legers of Doneraile allowed coachman and butler £8 apiece.[161] Culinary feats impressed guests indoors; horticultural virtuosity was acclaimed outside. In the 1740s, the O'Haras were paying their cook a yearly £10.[162] The proficient were lured to Ireland from Scotland, England and even continental Europe.[163] In the 1770s, it was rumoured that Lord Clanbrassil's cook was paid £50 annually.[164] Henry Ingoldsby, feckless owner of Carton, in the 1720s procured a gardener in England, as later did the proprietor of Powerscourt.[165] Lord Drogheda's came from Scotland.[166] William Stewart, gardener at Waringstown from 1712, although paid only £5 p.a., in common with numerous other gardeners received the profits from the fruit and vegetables which he was allowed to market.[167] Archbishop King had different priorities. John Nelson the cook was paid £20 p.a., the butler £10; the coachman, £8; his gardener, Elias Roberts, only £4 p.a., suggesting a purely mechanical function.

Among King's servants all were eclipsed by the steward, on an annual salary of £40. Henry Green, the steward, was married to Jane Green, the housekeeper, herself paid £20 yearly: an arrangement duplicated in other households. Both by stipend and accomplishments they were positioned among the respectable, even in the quality.[168] The same could be said of the butler to Bishop Stearne of Clogher. This factotum, Francis Kelly, was related to the bishop, who remembered him generously in his will. Stearne bequeathed £100 each to Kelly, his wife and their three children. The Kellys were also left the furnishings from their apartment and a goodly stock of linen.[169] The employment of kinsfolk complicated the social stratigraphy within the house. These followers sometimes smacked of the retinues of the toppled Gaelic chiefs, and were to be discouraged.[170] Less menacing were the unpaid companions, customarily women, who amused by their accomplishments. Lady Echlin, in her retreat at Rock Hermitage on the coast of north County Dublin, enjoyed the company of a cousin who was an expert needlewoman: 'she works, I read'.[171] In comparable mode, Mary Mathew, living comfortably off her rents in suburban Dublin, shared her house with a cousin. She evoked a predominantly feminine domesticity. Having played cards with Lady Westmeath, she returned home at nine, 'read to Miss Mathew till supper which is at ten, we retired before eleven, dine at four, breakfast at nine . . . this need not be repeated as we are very regular in our hours'.[172] Laetitia Bushe, daughter of an office-holding gentleman, shuttled between the residences of sympathetic women, admirers of her pluck, her drawing and her conversation. But she dwelt in an ill-defined category in which her dependence usually cancelled her inherited rank.[173]

For women, the salaried post of a housekeeper conferred clearer status than the often awkward role of companion. The job of housekeeper was one of the few reserved for women in the civil establishment.[174] By 1727, Archbishop Boulter of Armagh allowed his housekeeper at Drogheda £14 p.a. This compared unfavourably with the £20 that King paid Mrs Green. Working for King in Dublin may have carried a premium.[175] Particularly in houses of bachelors or widowers, housekeepers enjoyed great power, as the example of Margaret Stephenson at Edgeworthstown in the 1760s demonstrated. A vignette of the housekeeper in the bishop's palace at Kilkenny, extorting high prices for the goods of the previous occupant, indicates the majesty of this position, far above that of the lower people.[176] But few scaled those heights.

Despite the law and Christian doctrines which stressed the mutuality of the relationship between householder and domestic, the latter were easily dismissed, whether as an economy or for real or imagined failings.[177] Wages were withheld for long periods, and sometimes reduced by seemingly arbitrary deductions. The value of breakages and losses (always calculated by employers) was docked from pay.[178] The Reverend Henry Ware, appreciative of diligence among those who skivvied in his central Dublin house, was impatient of failings. Grounds for summary dismissal included 'intolerable sullenness, obstinacy and rudeness', carelessness, stupidity, being 'a little inclined to whoring', bigamy, drunkenness, laziness, ill management of the horses, imperfect care of linen, pertness and being a scold. Thomas Slattery survived with Ware for nearly five years before being sent packing for 'getting constantly drunk in the morning'. Female servants gave children scabies or 'the itch'. One was reputed 'a vile woman by whose mismanagement I almost lost my child'.[179] They were frequently pursued for alleged damage or thefts. Fires also were often traced to their carelessness.[180] Particularly sinister could be their malign influence, sowing dissension within a family, turning spouses against one another, or corrupting the weak. Williams Conyngham's sprint down the primrose path was thought to have been assisted by a former butler or footman.[181] Captain John Meagher, notorious as a tory, was reputed to have been a gentleman's servant for five years.[182] So, too, was the highwayman, Freney.[183]

The rapid turnover of employees reflected not just, or always primarily, the dissatisfaction of masters and mistresses but of the servants themselves. A berth within a comfortable house was to be preferred before many more precarious situations. Indeed, an unfriendly commentator stigmatized the 10,000 who 'squeeze into houses for an easy and indolent life where they may feed and lie well'.[184] Another Protestant reformer railed against youths 'skulking about gentlemen's stables and houses', often abetted by their relations who worked as servants in the place. Petty thieving supplemented earnings, as did selling newspapers, blacking shoes and running errands from taverns.[185] In 1767, John Conner was dismissed from the St Legers' employ for stealing two guineas from a guest in the house.[186] A high proportion of those indicted for infanticide were maidservants. Often they had been impregnated by master, master's son or a higher servant.[187]

The servant problem agitated Protestants in the 1720s. The concerned schemed to find enough 'honest, conscientious and laborious Protestant servants' to replace the unsatisfactory Catholics.[188] Part of the problem was a supposed unwillingness among Protestants to wear livery; they saw it presumably as a badge of servitude rather than as a source of pride.[189] The dearth of Protestants in many districts added to the already considerable difficulty of procuring competent and trustworthy servants. In Athlone, 29 per cent of male servants on the west bank of the town were Protestants, but only 9 per cent of the female domestics. Throughout the whole diocese of Elphin, of those classified as 'servants' (including servants in husbandry) 13.3 per cent of the men and 6.7 per cent of the women were Protestant.[190] These figures remind us that towns still constituted Protestant citadels. They were magnets for the obscure hunting for work. The boroughs, notably Dublin, contained the largest number of prosperous Protestant households, into which Protestant servants were disproportionately recruited. Yet, even in these strongholds, it was seldom possible to insist that all profess the same religion as the master and mistress. The majority of Protestant families, although uneasy about entrusting the impressionable young to those of another confession, resigned themselves to being served by Catholics. In 1725 a pamphleteer railed against 'the idleness, the wickedness or corrupt religion of such as are admitted into the service of most families'. Another, in 1750, proposed to tax foreign servants.[191] Only exceptionally did the keeping of Catholic servants provoke public reproof, as with the already unpopular tory bishop of Waterford, Thomas Milles in 1713.[192] Unhelpfully, the expatriate Irish Protestants in London suggested (in 1740) that 'Protestants of condition' in Ireland should set an example by employing only Protestants as servants. The meddlers conceded that this was unlikely since Catholics supposedly were prepared to work for lower wages, sometimes 'for meat, drink and clothing only'. Also, it was thought that employers could exercise 'a more despotic power' over them than over Protestants.[193]

By the mid-eighteenth century, it was said to be impossible to find either coachmen or cooks who were Protestants. In 1760 one Westmeath squire expostulated, 'I have had at least 50 coachmen and not one worth a farthing, and not a single Protestant to be got'. However, he engaged Terence Carroll at eight guineas per annum. Carroll seemed 'sober, diligent and honest', understood horses and, although a Catholic, was willing to attend family prayers and church if required.[194] Less happy was the experience of Lord Cavan with his coachman, James Butler, who tried to kill his employer on a country road, and promptly fled.[195] One of the most common failings in otherwise competent domestics was not creed but alcohol. French sacked a coachman for drunken driving. Elsewhere, a cook could be described as a 'very honest, quiet woman, but loves drink'. Indeed, just as it was hard to find cooks other than Catholics, so there were reputed to be few who did not drink.[196] Employers, desperate or indulgent, forbore always to expel the delinquent. Richard Allen agreed that his cook, Dan Flanagan, would not do for the grander Henry Boyle of Castlemartyr. Allen was happy enough with Flanagan, who 'behaved himself well, honestly and civilly, in my family except when he got drunk which was too often'. Furthermore, the cook could never be kept fit to be seen, since he either sold or pawned his linen and clothes.[197] Squire Smythe of Barbavilla tolerated a series of drunken japes by his servants.

Those discharging messages or on the way to fairs might mysteriously be
robbed of money; others were more candid about spending money on
drink, with resulting loss or damage to employers' property.[198] In general,
less effort was expended on converting menials into Protestants than on
training them as competent servants: better Catholic servants than none,
or indeed than cack-handed Protestants.

Earnest Protestants worried that servants were foreign, Irish, Catholic,
dirty, diseased, dishonest, dilatory or dim. Efforts were made to improve
the local supply. The charter schools and Lady Arbella's Asylum specialized in training reliable and Protestant domestics. In 1721, one charitable
institution promised to banish the prevalent 'ignorance, negligence and dishonesty of servants'.[199] Star pupils were sent into 'good service'.[200] Some
girls were apprenticed into housewifery.[201] Skills learnt in the schools, such
as numeracy and literacy, were esteemed by employers. In 1693, Bishop
King wanted to replace a manservant who had left to be married with
another 'to tend me in my chamber', and to act as an amanuensis.[202] Yet
it was feared that clever servants would chafe against their subjection.
In 1749 Bishop Synge, looking for a new butler, told his daughter, 'I
should be glad of a right good one, genteel, honest, and clever, tho no
fine gent[leman], and one that can write and understands figures'.[203] More
usual was concern over honesty and competence in driving the coach,
handling the horses, nailing up espaliers, dressing meat, baking bread,
shaving the master or washing lace and laundering 'small linen' for his
lady. George Mathew, at Thomastown in County Kilkenny, hesitated
about engaging a gardener because he was Catholic, but acknowledged
that his being a good nurseryman and kitchen gardener outweighed his
confession.[204]

Specialists of high repute were prized. They, in common with their
masters and mistresses, were bothered about standing. Personal recommendation of the reliable was much valued among friends. Mary Drew,
lately with Major Nunn in County Wexford, was praised for her skill in
keeping 'small linen' fresh and her ability to dress a lady. In addition, this
nonpareil could make pastry and prepare meat. But the converse, passing
on the idle or dishonest and faking references, was much resented.[205]
Within larger establishments, servants, differing in qualifications and pay,
demarcated – and sometimes enlarged – their territories. The O'Haras in
Sligo rid themselves of a housekeeper because she proved 'very uneasy' to
the other servants.[206] Mary Drew, with her culinary prowess, quarrelled
with the 'man cook', who regarded this prestigious duty as his domain.[207]
Similarly, in the Elphin establishment of Bishop Synge, the male cook and
housekeeper circled suspiciously around one another and occasionally
sparred over the boundaries of their respective territories.[208] Anne

Langford, newly arrived at Castlereagh in County Roscommon, reported a battle for ascendancy over the cook, 'that gets drunk almost every day, and is the best scold I ever met with'. Gleefully, Mrs. Langford announced, 'we had a fair trial who should be mistress and I carried the day'.[209]

In smaller households, versatility was essential. In County Leitrim, John McCaine was hired as a post-chaise boy. Related to another servant already working in the place, McCaine was required to 'put his hand to anything about the house [and] stables'. A girl trained by the housekeeper at Sonnagh, the Tuites' seat in County Westmeath, cleaned rooms, made beds, cared for linen and, if requested, cooked a dinner of up to six dishes. All this was available for a mere £3 yearly.[210] Others, despite careful tuition, never progressed beyond 'a farmer's business', or such basics as bed-making and scouring utensils.[211] Domestics might suffer from the oddities of employers. In the Kinsale of the 1680s, a female servant acquired on a voyage to Antigua performed unusual acts for her deranged master. She was locked into a shed, forced to sit on hens' eggs, and fed with bran until the chicks hatched.[212]

Even some carefully trained in the charter schools and the Magdalen Asylum disappointed. Jane Farrell, an eighteen-year-old Protestant, left Lady Arbella Denny's institution to work as a children's maid in a smart Dublin house. It was acknowledged that being short-sighted she might not please. Sure enough, she soon quit her first post. However, she was taken into the household of the clergyman who had recommended her originally as an object of charity.[213] Less creditable was the record of another from the Asylum. The Protestant Margaret Hill, also engaged as a children's maid, stayed out at night without leave and was discovered drunk at Blackrock. She was immediately dismissed.[214] Jane Burnford, another magdalen, was recommended as a children's maid in 1768. She had been born to 'rich and opulent people', but the extravagance of her father had reduced her to a menial.[215] Often service was a temporary posting, supplying bed and board while the opportunist reviewed alternatives. The speed with which servants came and went in many establishments did not always signify imperious and unreasonable masters and mistresses.

The constant turnover of hirelings unsettled households. In other ways, servants might disturb as much as ease the lives of prosperous Protestants. The domestics, because so often Catholic and Old Irish, introduced an alien element into their employers' houses. Worried clerics adverted to the risks of entrusting children to servants whose religion and education were thought defective.[216] Masters and mistresses, as 'governors and rulers in their own houses', were enjoined to look to the spiritual as well as physical welfare of all under their roofs.[217] In reality, the underlings were more

likely to be clothed, fed and sheltered than drilled in the rudiments of
Protestantism. Seats were sometimes reserved in the local parish church
for the households of the grand. In 1735, Lord Inchiquin's servants from
Rostellan were to be accommodated in a special pew at Cloyne
cathedral.[218] In Dublin, at St Peter's, a pew was reserved for the servants
of Lord Longford; in St Bride's, the servants of the physician, Ralph
Howard, had a pew for which their master had paid £2 10s. In the new
church of St Mary's, on the north bank of the Liffey, six of seventy-nine
seats were for servants.[219] In the 1680s, the readiness of a householder to
sit with servants in church was commended.[220] Otherwise, there was not
enough room, were domestics to decide to worship in Protestant churches.
The ideal of ensuring that every household, if not every member of it,
possess a copy of the Bible, Book of Common Prayer and *Whole Duty of
Man* proved equally elusive.[221] Zealous clerics strove to provide for the
ignorant and vulnerable.[222] Many employers resigned themselves to the
inevitable, and accepted that their servants would adhere to a different
confession. Peacock outside Limerick lived with a small 'family' of
Catholic domestics. He let them follow their own observances. Indeed,
he, like Edgeworth in County Longford and Bishop Francis Hutchinson
in County Down, acknowledged their industry with 'Patrick's pots' and
cash to visit nearby patterns.[223]

The presence of servants in 'the family' muddled otherwise simple units,
composed of elements drawn from a common ethnic, social and confessional pool. Protestants shared this, the most intimate of spaces with some
who diverged in culture and creed. The notion that the grandees secluded
themselves from possible pollution runs counter to the ways in which all
but the most magnificent of houses were organized and in which personal servants worked. Simply, the majority of residences were too small
to allow any strict segregation. The relationship, inevitably unequal, in the
Irish context crackled with more than the usual social and economic
differences. In dealings with servants, as with other underlings or the
refractory, there was a tendency to fuse and confuse social and economic
inequalities with confessional and racial divergences. If servants seemed
slatternly, mulish, idle, dishonest or bold, the failings were traced back to
their being Irish Catholics.

III

Apprentices

Some servants moved in and out of the occupation; others passed their
working lives in strangers' houses. Apprentices differed. Their servitude

usually lasted seven years, customarily during late adolescence and early adulthood.[224] At least three different types of apprenticeship can be discerned: individual compacts on behalf of children or wards; parochial provision for the poor; and other charitable assistance. Private compacts probably prevailed in callings which verged on the professions: the import and export trades, surgery, surveying, and painting. An attorney within the orbit of the Temples and Robertses in the Dublin Court of Exchequer was persuaded to take a distant kinsman as a trainee.[225] The Warings of Waringstown used kindred in Belfast, Dublin and London to help them into their careers, including trade. The Perys, established at Clonmel and Limerick, as well as London, Glasgow and (eventually) North America, again exploited this family network.[226] The Ulsterman William Stannus was pleased to apprentice a son to a French merchant in Dublin. The youth was prepared by spells at a mathematical school.[227] Charles Donnell, son of an Antrim squire and brother of two clergymen, failed to apply himself at Dublin University so instead was apprenticed to a merchant in the city. In this capacity he voyaged to Virginia. But Donnell's promising career ended when his master suddenly died. He would end on the gallows.[228]

Parents or guardians arranged privately for their charges to be trained, as earlier they had vetted schools and tutors. The likes of Vesey, Brabazon and Owen sought trades which brought respectability, even gentility, as well as a livelihood. In 1674, Thomas Batty in Clonmel sought guidance from a grander friend in London about a suitable master for his second son, who wished to become a merchant.[229] Archdeacon Hamilton of Raphoe apprenticed one of his sons to a surgeon in London.[230] An Ulster landowner worried over the spending of a son bound to a leading Dublin attorney. The trainee, Matthew Brett, was eventually sent packing in the last year of his term for 'repeated misbehaviour' by his master, Francis Anderson, clerk in the chief remembrancer's office.[231] Watt Plunkett had been apprenticed by a kinsman to a leading London silversmith shortly after Charles II's restoration. To the dismay of his patron, Plunkett quit his trade, 'in which he was most perfect of any in London', and instead adopted 'that beggarly undertaking of a surveyor'.[232] Apprenticeship was not confined to towns and their trades. Joseph Lloyd in Tipperary contracted in 1684 to accept Patrick Meagher as an apprentice farmer. The training was to last five years. When it ended, Meagher would be given a cow, calf, six lambs and a suit of clothing. With no corporation or guild to oversee the arrangement, any infringement was not easily detected or corrected.[233]

The standing of the trade or craft for which the neophyte was to be prepared was shown in the fee required of the apprentice. It took

premiums of £200 or £100 to apprentice sons of Archbishop Vesey of
Tuam and an erstwhile high sheriff of Mayo, Anthony Brabazon.[234]
Michael Stritch, active in the overseas trade of Limerick, paid 200 guineas
to have a son apprenticed to a wine merchant in Bordeaux.[235] In 1723,
Mrs Grace Kempston left £100 to apprentice a grandson.[236] Walter
Burton, powerful in Dublin as an officer in Chancery, accepted a lad from
North Wales as a trainee in 1719. The price was £100 'in hand'; the term,
four years. The novice, John Owen, was to eat at Burton's table, obey him
and be treated as a son. The regimen worked so that, by 1725, the former
apprentice deputized during the master's absence, sometimes working
fourteen hours daily.[237] Owen, born into the squirearchy, would be trained
for an equally respectable situation. At a more modest price, Andrew
Johnston, the son of a clergyman and 'willing to be bound anything', was
put to a master in Belfast in 1764 for £48 9s. 10½d. An attorney colleague of Anderson also took apprentices. In 1724, the entrance fee was
£30.[238] Terms had to be negotiated and interest had sometimes to be made
to persuade a successful practitioner to accept a trainee.[239] Josias Bateman
revealed that he had spent £50 to be apprenticed to a merchant, only to
have his promising start as a trader ruined by a fire.[240] The sum of £200
or £100 might not compare with the larger investment required to put
a son through university, the Inns of Court or a continental academy, but
it was beyond the purses of the majority.

Many crafts and trades were more conventionally entered through
formalized apprenticeship. This system was policed either by the municipality or urban guilds. It was intended to guarantee minimum standards
of workmanship while regulating the supply of adepts.[241] These included
the trades overseen by the Dublin Guild of St Luke, which incorporated
stationers, printers, painter-stainers and cutlers. The guild enrolled 430
apprentices between 1740 and 1799. An analysis suggests both the laxity
with which the laws relating to apprenticeship were treated and the allure
of careers in Dublin. Of the 142 boys whose parentage is noted, a
majority came from families of some standing and means: a seven-year
term with an established freeman of Dublin was not purchased cheaply.
Nearly two-thirds of the St Luke's apprentices for whom a place of origin
is known hailed from Dublin and its environs. A few came from as far
afield as Clare or Galway, but the magnetism was exerted most strongly
over the larger Dublin region, not least because this was the area with an
abundance of Protestants able to afford admission.[242] Apprenticeship of this
type, once completed, brought freedom of the guild, and with it membership of the municipality itself.[243] Since it was an obvious route to full
citizenship, admission was monitored. The wayward and inept were to be
rejected. Increasingly from the mid-seventeenth century, as in other aspects

of citizenship, the main criterion was not aptitude but confession. Guild brethren were sometimes debarred from or otherwise rigorously restricted in taking Catholics as apprentices.[244] Those privileged Catholics, if they survived their seven-year novitiate, could hope only for second-class membership, as quarter-brothers.[245]

These organizations sought through their rules to preserve standards. A system which elsewhere disciplined potentially headstrong youths, in Ireland had the further purpose of bridling Catholics. During the term of apprenticeship, the novices were subject to master or mistress. But the controls were not easily enforced. Advertisements, new regulations or the repetition of old all suggested that apprentices absconded before they had served their full seven years or that the untrained set up on their own account.[246] On occasion, too, seniors failed to keep their side of the bargain. Simon Griffith, a butcher's son from Dolgellau in Merionethshire, travelled to Dublin. There, another butcher, James Reynolds, contracted to instruct him for £4 p.a. Griffith complained that the agreement had been disregarded and that he had nearly starved.[247] He sought legal redress. Formal apprenticeships were, indeed, regulated, and sometimes enforced, by municipal or trading corporations.[248] In the hope of protection against a brutal master, James Brenan appealed in 1695 to the Dublin Goldsmiths' Company. The master, David Swan, had not taught Brenan his craft, had failed to allow him any decent clothes, and 'used him most barbarously'. The guild ordered Swan to repay Brenan's £10 fee and furnish him with new apparel.[249]

The discipline of apprenticeship which so irked the young appealed to elders at their wits' ends to provide for them. The device, a continuation of education, attracted the proponents of a Protestant Ireland. Masters and mistresses, surrogates for parents, were required to watch over the spiritual as well as physical well-being of their apprentices. The training instilled habits of industry, and so would protect against the idleness which too often spawned vice. It could also enlarge the numbers fit for skilled and specialized crafts, to the general benefit of the community. Further, it offered the hope that the poor, potential parasites, might acquire the means of independence. At the same time, the impressionable – some doubtfully Protestant; many stubborn Catholics – would be brought to knowledge of evangelical religion. Patrons and proprietors assisted a lucky few by finding masters and mistresses and feeing them. Just as parishes and voluntary societies assumed more of the burden of the poor and aged previously shouldered by individuals, aided apprenticeship became an important part of the work of educational charities for the young.

The way in which assisted apprenticeship fitted into philanthropy in Protestant Ireland is illustrated by several initiatives in the main towns. A notable pioneer was the King's Hospital, a municipal school in Dublin, which opened during Charles II's reign. Financed by the corporation and the worthies of the capital, it was unusually well supported by the Protestant community.[250] Its intention – to equip its pupils to contribute usefully to the local Protestant interest – largely succeeded. An entrant had to be nominated by either a parish or a freeman of the city. To achieve this, as in so many other spheres, interest was needed.[251] The boys, marked out by recommendation, clearly had deserts which included not just need but the merit of now dead parents. Once set on this track, the hospitallers basked in favour. The same respectable traders, craftworkers and shopkeepers who had donated money took the alumni as apprentices. Protestant Dublin contained a unique mixture of respectable and potentially profitable callings in which the young could be placed. As a result, the King's Hospital succeeded unusually well in finding work for its quondams. Entrants to the school formed an élite among the impoverished Protestant young of the capital. What it cost to maintain each pupil for a year – £5 6s. 5½d. – almost equalled what a cottier needed to subsist for a year in County Sligo.[252]

Of nearly 3,400 pupils of the King's Hospital recorded between 1669 and 1800, 80 per cent secured apprenticeships. Since 9.5 per cent died while at the school, this represented remarkable success. In contrast to pupils from schools elsewhere, few of these Dublin boys were sent into the world as servants, agricultural labourers or workers in the linen industry. Few institutions in Dublin approached the triumphs of the King's Hospital. In 1731, it was announced that thirty-four boys and twenty-two girls were educated by St Andrew's parish. Since 1717, one hundred had been apprenticed. In the nearby parish of St John's, a school was set up in the 1690s. It was one of several in the capital to offer the twin benefits of tuition and eventual apprenticeships. Pupils were bound to masters and mistresses for fees of £3 or £4. They gravitated towards the humbler crafts – shoemaking, patten-drawing, button-making, hosiery and weaving.[253] In contrast, the products of the King's Hospital entered prestigious crafts and luxury trades.[254]

Other towns attacked the poverty and ignorance of the young. In early eighteenth-century Kilkenny, the bishop, Sir Thomas Vesey, paid – usually £4 for each – to apprentice children of the town.[255] In Shandon, a northern suburb of Cork, the initiative was taken by the Church of Ireland incumbent, Henry Maule. A complex of hospital, old folks' home, library and school exploited the fears and self-interest of a populous and prospering Protestant community in the second city. Maule intended his foundation as a prototype for what might be erected elsewhere. He loudly publicized what had been done. In the heady years between 1718 and

1722, seventy pupils were placed as apprentices. By 1735, 170 had been apprenticed; by 1790, the total was 407.[256] Once the exhaustingly dynamic Maule left the city, the enterprise was becalmed. Nevertheless, it still benefited from the occupational variegation of a sizeable Protestant population. In addition to the staples of 'housewifery', mantua-making, shoemaking and weaving, some fortunates had the chance to train with goldsmiths, book-binders, stationers, printers, a writing master and a surgeon. The young were also in demand as servants in the households of the respectable whose donations financed the school.[257]

The same approach and similar results were found in eighteenth-century Waterford. There, thanks to the beneficence of a bishop, Nathaniel Foy, who died in 1707, a school for boys was opened. By 1745, 29 per cent of its pupils had been found apprenticeships. This was a lower rate than at the King's Hospital and Maule's Cork academy. Nevertheless, remembering that some went on to more advanced schooling and others died or deserted, it alleviated even if it did not cure the problems of the penurious young. The Waterford establishment was hampered by a smaller and perhaps less affluent Protestant community than existed in Cork or Dublin. In order to secure apprenticeships for the Foy scholars before 1745, employers as far away as Carrick-on-Suir, Dungarvan, Kilkenny and Youghal were used. In 1745, it was minuted that 'no sufficient proper masters appeared to whom the rest of the boys might be bound'. If accurate, this comment hinted at the depleted Protestant community in the borough. The custodians of Foy's foundation searched Dublin for suitable masters, particularly in the trades lacking in Waterford.[258] From the middle of the century, policy towards entrants altered. Thereafter the school accepted only the sons of Protestants, usually endowed with basic literacy. The proportion of pupils bound as apprentices increased. Annual admissions had settled at about eighteen. Never less than 60 per cent, and often 80 per cent, of the youths were now apprenticed, and into a wider range of trades and crafts. In the second half of the eighteenth century the economy of Waterford was diversifying. There appeared paper-stainers and hairdressers as well as periwig-makers who could take apprentices. Despite these novelties, the bulk of the boys went into manufacturing, most commonly shoemaking and textiles. Few went into the food trades, perhaps because they were dominated by Catholics. None of the alumni of Foy's foundation, unlike the products of the charter schools, is recorded as entering domestic or agricultural service.[259] Greater selectivity may have brought this success. The Waterford boys, like their counterparts from the King's Hospital in Dublin, were qualified by their literate skills for something more mentally taxing. In Waterford and Dublin, the educationally accomplished had floated towards the top thanks to the oxygenizing effects of the teaching available in their neighbourhoods. They replenished the stock from which they had generally come: *menu peuple*. They were returned to their familiar quarters literate and numerate, and with the essence of Protestantism derived from the Bible, catechisms and *The Whole Duty of Man*. Privilege of a sort had been accorded them, as they were snatched from the heap and helped upwards.

Establishments in Dublin, Cork, Waterford and Sligo set a pattern for the kingdom.[260] The Incorporated Society, chartered by the king in 1733, aimed to train the idle and ignorant so that they would become productive members of the commonweal. Conventional thinking averred that only industry would inure them to the wiles of popery and render them useful. Members of the Society alternated between treating the Catholic poor as ripe for conversion and leaving them to the attentions of their own.[261] Regularly the Society stressed what it had done. In 1757, with 1,600 pupils on its books, it claimed to have apprenticed 1,500 since 1733.[262] Most of its schools were outside the large towns. One consequence was to worsen the difficulty of finding reliable Protestant employers. Quantities of the charter school children entered domestic service or became labourers. So far from repining, the Society turned a necessity into an article of faith. It stated a preference for placing its pupils in agriculture and linen manufacture rather than in 'mechanical trades'.[263] In 1769, the directors of the charity turned from 'sedentary and effeminate occupations' for boys, such as spinning, towards 'masculine labour', which would be more marketable in adulthood.[264]

Earlier, during the heady days of the charity, its products were advertised in the Dublin press. There, the secretary of the Incorporated Society offered a supply of apprentice linen weavers.[265] At Sligo around 1760, a deal was struck with a local linen manufacturer who agreed to accept as apprentices several from the local charity school. Others from the same institution frequently became servants, sometimes in the houses of members of the committee which ran the school.[266] The charter school at Ardbraccan owed its existence to the furious energy of Maule, now, as bishop of Meath, resident nearby. Maule badgered local notables to support the venture.[267] Dublin was close enough to take some former Ardbraccan scholars. Even so, between 1753 and 1784 only 84 of a recorded 256 pupils (about 33 per cent) were apprenticed. The majority went to local houses (including Bishop Maule's) as servants. The cambric factory at Dundalk also accepted some. A few secured placements with farmers, shoemakers and the local washerwoman, and as gardeners.[268] The Dundalk enterprise also received a handful from the more distant charter school at Arklow in County Wicklow. Arklow was well placed to find alumni apprenticeships in the capital. It succeeded best in its first years. Again, as at Shandon and

Ardbraccan, this may be attributed to the dynamism of its original patrons. Of its seventy-three pupils at Arklow in the years from 1748 to 1753, fifty-five (75 per cent) were apprenticed. In contrast, among 175 enrolled between 1762 and 1786, 59 (34 per cent) were noted as becoming apprentices. Over the entire period from 1748 to 1786, 46 per cent secured apprenticeships. Destinations split fairly evenly between domestic work, farming, textiles and other urban crafts.[269] Prospects around Dublin differed from the situation of the charter school of Ballycastle, in northern County Antrim. The local landowners, the Boyds, had developed the area and supported the school. Between 1748 and 1782, 90 of 174 leavers (52 per cent) secured apprenticeships. Helped by the availability of work in the linen industry, fewer became household menials.[270]

Great, and maybe extravagant, hopes of what sponsored Protestant education could do declined. So, too, did the effectiveness and reputation of many of the charity schools. By 1765, difficulties about placing their pupils led to their qualifications being posted on church doors and market houses.[271] Moreover, factions among the directors squabbled about priorities. Schools had usually prospered where the Protestant worthies of the neighbourhood were involved. The Society, in danger of knocking aside these props, failed to find new ones. Towns, notably Dublin, offered the brightest prospects, but also the worst problems of indigence and idleness. Collective schemes, under the auspices of the Incorporated Society after 1733, built on but never entirely superseded parochial and personal schemes. Dublin parishes, such as St John's and St Catherine's, employed teachers and bought apprenticeships for the deserving.[272] In 1686, Elinor Jordan, an orphan, was apprenticed to William and Margaret Friend. She was to learn the art of periwig-making. The term would be six years and the fee, £4. The action was taken and the money provided by the churchwardens and overseers of the poor in the Dublin parish of St Werburgh.[273] In the nearby parish of St Catherine's, early in the eighteenth century, yet more modest sums – as little as £1 – could buy an apprenticeship.[274] Those accepted at such low rates were probably treated as drudges, and given scanty instruction. Parish officials, like relations, friends or benefactors who also bought apprenticeship indentures, intended them as a mechanism to lift children from the untrained poor. In 1668 two youths from Charleville in County Cork bound themselves to the countess of Orrery. One undertook to serve her for eight years; the other, for nine. In return, she would eventually put them to whatever trades she thought appropriate.[275] Esther Sweetman, living in County Dublin, arranged that each of her three sons should receive £10 from the profits of her farm in order that they might then be apprenticed.[276]

The wealthy interested themselves in some children of their meritorious tenants and dependants. Archbishop King bound a youth as an apprentice to a smith for a fee of £4. He also bought a suit of clothes and three shirts for the boy, so adding £2 13s. 6d. to the expense.[277] In comparison with what he had spent on a nephew destined for the navy or other kinsfolk, this was a modest outlay: meagre when set – for example – against spending on the archbishop's library. Pole Cosby arranged for the niece of a local clergyman to be apprenticed to the 'top' mantua-maker in Dublin. Cosby was chagrined when the girl failed to show enough gratitude.[278] The Flowers of Castle Durrow, Katherine Conolly and the Kildares all financed apprenticeships for their favourites. The fees, at £3 or £7, hardly burdened the benefactors.[279] They were negligible sums besides those spent by Mrs Conolly on nieces or Flower on his children's education. But the beneficiaries were thereby marked out, and set on the way to greater independence and standing as master craftsmen.

As with other efforts at improvement, those being bettered – the apprentices – did not always rejoice. Some of independent means and lofty rank were temporarily condemned to servitude. Worse awaited two novice seamen whose master sent them on a north American voyage with his nephew. The latter sold the apprentices into slavery.[280] Usually apprenticeship lasted seven years. Sometimes, the sentence was shorter still. Francis Anderson ejected young Brett from his office because the latter proved recalcitrant. A Plunkett abandoned his master, a goldsmith. James Traill threw up his training with a Dublin trader, toyed with entering the university, then the army or navy, before returning to run his Ulster estate.[281] William Waring probably spoke from his memories of mid-seventeenth-century Belfast when he warned of the privations that awaited an aspirant merchant adventurer. A novice, especially if educated at college, would resent donning the demeaning attire and 'to be in the nature of a slavish servant to master and mistress, and, it maybe, children and other elder servants'.[282]

Apprenticeship agreements varied considerably. There were fears that masters took on more apprentices than they could properly instruct, seeing them as cheap labour.[283] In 1745 it was disclosed that Cork city boasted only three competent plumbers. They were too busy to attend to the concerns of Lord Grandison, distant on the Waterford–Cork border. However, one offered to send an apprentice, who would expect to be paid at a daily rate of 2s. 6d. as well as being boarded and fed.[284] Henry Delamain sought to ingratiate himself among the important, and secure parliamentary subsidies, by promising to take charity school pupils into his Dublin pottery. They would be paid on a sliding scale: from a weekly two shillings in the first year to 4s. 6d. each week during the last three-years of the seven-year term.[285] *Ad hoc* arrangements with putative employers, in which the length and cost of the training were adjusted to individual wants, were hard to police. But, free of the restrictive by-laws of the municipalities and chartered companies, these agreements opened apprenticeship to Catholics, who were otherwise debarred from the professions and the most lucrative trades.[286]

Liberty was not lost permanently. Hopefuls might endure the humiliations buoyed up by visions of eventual independence and prosperity. Obscure apprentices from Ireland sometimes made good, like Mordecai Abbott, who rose to eminence within the City of London. These exemplary biographies, in which apprentices won the favour and in the end took over the businesses (and even the widows) of their one-time masters, resembled the publicity around the *nouveaux riches* like Cork, Petty and Conolly. At a more modest level, a one-time pupil, John Owen, ingratiated himself with the exacting Walter Burton. Owen speculated whether or not, when his former master died, he might succeed to his offices.[287] Humbler, but still useful, was the preference given by an apothecary in Mallow to his apprentice to buy his shop after his own death.[288] More commonly, the advantage of good training came from a proficiency which could then be exercised and advertised on one's own account. The dressmaker, Mrs Gallagher, was inconvenienced when her apprentice departed to set up on her own.[289] When John Sparks established himself on College Green in Dublin he could announce that he had been apprenticed to a 'famous gown-maker'.[290] In time, novices rivalled in skill and business those from whom they had learnt.

Apprentices were sometimes maltreated. To seize upon the occasional instances may distort the horrors which beset the young. The tyrannical master was probably less common than the oppressive parent or guardian. It was expected that masters and mistresses would discipline their charges, otherwise they failed in their duties. Apprenticeships registered by guild or municipality were most likely to be enforced. Especially with a craft keen to uphold its reputation for good work, such as the Dublin goldsmiths, infringements of apprenticeship compacts were investigated.[291] Hazards existed, but the term with a master did equip the hopeful for gainful work: 36 per cent of those apprenticed to stationers in Dublin between 1741 and 1800 took up their freedom of the Company so that they could trade.[292] This lengthy progression did not lead irresistibly to financial security and social esteem. Yet freemen of a Dublin trading guild, although some might remain poor, hardly ranked among the lowliest. However, in a sample of apprentice stationers, a majority failed to become free of the Company. Rare details of individuals' lives reveal sudden changes of course, with seven year terms not finished and switches into alternative callings.[293]

Apprenticeship was not for the poor, unless subsidized by charities. Yet apprentices as a group were endowed with some attributes of the poor.

Young and lusty, they might disturb good order. 'Idle and loose apprentices', along with journeymen and workmen, were conjured as menaces.[294]
Affrays in Dublin were traced to bands such as the Liberty Boys. In this
context, 'boys' tended to be a generic term applied to males regardless of
age.[295] Riots in 1671 against a new bridge across the Liffey were traced
specifically to apprentices.[296] In practice, they rarely coordinated activities.
Masters and mistresses chosen by Protestant institutions were required to
oversee the continuing religious education of their charges. Their failure
always to do so stimulated fresh schemes to channel the energies of
apprentices into acceptable activities. In the 1690s, the religious societies
intensified the Protestant instruction of apprentices.[297] Nearly a century
later, the Incorporated Society had to reiterate the value of reading,
writing and simple mathematics to those 'in the lowest stations of life',
not so much to fit them for employment, but to prevent any 'relapse into
popery'.[298] Notwithstanding these anxieties, apprentices lacked opportunities and occasions in which to act collectively. Any sense of fraternity was
weakened by the essentially fissiparous and often competitive nature of
their callings. The distinctive contribution of apprentices to culture and
protest, observed in sixteenth- and seventeenth-century London, is hard
to spot in Ireland.[299] More characteristic of the transgressions of the
apprentice in Ireland were those of one, led on by a salt and coal meas-
urer in Kinsale, to desert and rob his master, a collier.[300] Apprenticeship,
and particularly abandoning it prematurely, featured in the cautionary
stories of those who ended up swinging from the gallows.[301] Otherwise,
when the alleys and squares of eighteenth-century Ireland resounded to
the boisterous, the violence was easily explained. Traditional hostilities
between Protestants and Catholics, soldiers and civilians, journeymen and
masters, country people and town-dwellers, or English and Irish sufficed.[302]
The lack of comment on any specific role of exuberant adolescents need
not mean that they were absent from these gatherings, but they were not
seen as prime movers of 'the mob'.

IV
The Poor

Not all who had served their time as apprentices became masters on their
own account. But the problems of the able-bodied young paled into
insignificance beside those of the infirm and elderly. In 1672, Petty stated
that in Ireland there were only 2,000 incurably disabled, although he took
no account of the aged. This contrasted with a grotesquely inflated reckoning of 220,000 'cosherers and fait-neants': the able-bodied who declined

to work regularly.[303] Petty wholeheartedly endorsed the contemporary belief that the deserving poor had to be distinguished from sturdy beggars. His high figure of the wilfully indolent tallied with the Protestant belief that poverty often resulted from deliberate choice by the Old Irish and Catholics. The large bands of poor were supposed to have opted for an easy pastoralism. If the Protestant incurables were as few as Petty assumed, then philanthropy, coupled with church rates, could deal with them. But, as the total of Protestants in Ireland steadily increased, so too did that of the destitute, making Petty seem complacent.

Ireland lacked the statutory mechanisms for relief across the country which had been put in place in England by 1601. Irish systems, although discretionary, otherwise resembled those in England and Wales in using the parish and borough as their basis.[304] Parishioners limited what they would give, considering their own purses rather than the extent of the problem. They discriminated even more than their English counterparts. The poor were classified according to merits. In the Dublin parish of St John's, one of the first to minister systematically to its poor, the dozen entitled to relief were to be aided only 'during their good behaviour'.[305] In this claustrophobic atmosphere, when the seventy-one-year-old Jane Vickhurst appealed to her Dublin parish for help in the 1680s, she proffered testimonials from four local notables. Now 'reduced to extreme poverty', she was well known in the parish, having lived next to the church for twenty years and 'been a good housekeeper'.[306] Candidates for doles queued. Those seeking admission to hospitals, schools and almshouses engaged the interest of subscribers to and governors of these institutions. The prosperous accepted that they had duties to assist the helpless, but, as in exercising other patronage, they adjudicated between competing claimants. In Youghal and Lismore, the absent owner, Lord Cork and Burlington, maintained almshouses. Billets in these shelters were eagerly sought: an almshouse was a convenient home for superannuated servants, such as a warrener and gardener.[307] An unfortunate was urged on the peer in 1712 because she was the daughter of one of his agents, the widow of a government employee at Youghal, 'a real object of charity', 'a constant church woman' and 'an aged gentlewoman and widow'. On occasion, the political supremo of Munster, Henry Boyle, was asked to intercede, not least because of his kinship with Burlington. In 1753 Boyle recommended Widow Knight for a vacancy in the refuge because 'in times of old, with others of the neighbourhood', he himself had 'fared well' at her and her husband's table.[308]

Founders of charities often loaded them with conditions. Most commonly Protestantism was the *sine qua non*, as at the Orrerys' almshouses in Castlemartyr or Denny Muschamp's at Maryborough.[309] James Knight, a gentleman of the city of Dublin, was caught up in the renovative and innovative atmosphere of Protestant activism during the 1690s. Knight, interested in schools and hospitals, endowed a poorhouse in his parish of St Peter.[310] He also arranged that after he died (in 1726), 200 poor Protestant families should be relieved. The day on which the annual doles were distributed – 4 November – underlined the denominationalism of the gesture. On the birthday of the Irish Protestants' deliverer, William III, the unfortunate would be given money. In addition, each week a dozen four penny loaves, placed 'on the shelf put up for that purpose by my dear wife in St Peter's church', would feed the hungry of the parish.[311]

Bequests such as Knight's supplemented what the Church of Ireland parish routinely disbursed. At Delgany in County Wicklow, seven, including three widows, were on the list of the poor aided by the parishioners.[312] In 1697, the thriving Protestant borough of Bandon was directing its efforts towards 'the English poor'. However, by 1712, the vestry specified that only 'the Protestant poor' should be helped.[313] Individual benefactors had already imposed such restrictions. In 1693, the absentee owner of Buttevant (County Cork) stipulated that the poor Protestants of the place should have treble the gift of corn allowed to their Catholic neighbours.[314] Such selectivity may indicate how the favoured community of the kingdom of Ireland was being defined more through confession than ethnicity. The simple test of names – apparently Old Irish, Old English or New English – was all too fallible owing to intermarriage and acculturation. Instead religious tests, embodied after 1704 in a sacramental requirement, sorted the population. Not only was it applied to those allowed over the threshold of privilege, but – increasingly – to those who begged charity.[315]

The emergencies of the 1720s or 1740–41 stretched parochial resources. Dearth and destitution moved the humane.[316] How far confessional exclusions could be maintained during the crises is unclear. In Bandon, as elsewhere, the famine of 1740 increased the numbers helped: twenty-three were added to the list of recipients of bread, including old Doctor Ree and 'the counsellor'.[317] Within Dublin, where the scale of the problem was greatest, inter-denominational relief continued.[318] However, the types of poor were more sharply distinguished. In St Michan's the amount given weekly varied, as much according to ideas of merit as of want. A 'Mr' Coughran was favoured with 5s. 5d., a distressed gentlewoman received 2s. 2d., whereas the humbler were given weekly either 1s. 4d. or 8d. In 1723, the parish assisted forty of the indigent; by 1730, the number had doubled. During 1730 the parish dispensed charity to three distinct groups: reduced housekeepers; the 'accidental' poor and sick; and the 'stated poor'. The first two categories grew during economic crises. In the spring of

1730, the parishioners relieved thirty-three reduced housekeepers, thirty accidental poor and ill, and nineteen stated poor.[319] St Michan's also took responsibility for foundling children. Nurses were paid to care for them. Then, in 1725, the parish orphans were obliged to wear strings around their necks fastened with lead clasps, so that they were visibly distinguished from others.[320]

By the early eighteenth century Protestant parishes expended considerable labour and a significant proportion of their annual budgets in helping the deserving in their midst. Mechanisms to tackle the problem tapped Christian and humanist impulses. Committees oversaw the levies and disbursements and in some places the aged were secluded in special accommodation. In the 1680s, St Bride's in Dublin built a poorhouse with money bequeathed by a parishioner.[321] Similarly, at St Michan's during the 1720s, eight poor widows were accommodated in the parochial poorhouse. However, the parish was reckoned to have a Church of Ireland population of almost 5,000.[322] From 1682, the corporation of Dublin authorized licensed beggars to be identified by special badges, issued by each parish. This renewed and refined the periodic drives against the beggars and vagabonds who thronged the capital.[323] Until a city workhouse was opened early in the eighteenth century, the corporation returned the problems of poverty to the separate parishes. St Catherine's, a labouring quarter with acute problems, distributed twelve badges in 1681, and 86 in 1724.[324] Here, and in other parishes, nurses were paid to rear foundlings. Parish funds bought coffins and burials for the destitute. Penurious youths were educated, sometimes in a parochial school or recommended to and funded at nearby establishments, such as the King's Hospital, Maule's Greencoat School at Cork and Bishop Foy's School in Waterford. Masters and mistresses were reimbursed for taking adolescents as apprentices. These practical remedies had created and now satisfied the expectation of dutiful churchgoers that their church should function as a friendly society. Other denominations offered similar help.[325] Dublin practices spread only slowly into the provinces. In 1725, the Cork parish of Shandon decided to end complete reliance on church collections and instead levy a rate for the maintenance of foundlings and the aged. The innovation, urged by the indefatigable Dean Maule, was lifted directly from the Dublin parish of St Michan.[326] Badging was also adopted in Cork, but belatedly in the eighteenth century and then somewhat hesitantly.[327]

In Kinsale, the corporation continued to dispense charity to those it thought meritorious. Some of its alms were channelled through the parish church, which, in 1713, was allowed £35 for its poor.[328] But aid was also dispensed directly by the corporation itself. Typical of the objects of its generosity was a freeman of the town, David Howe, who suffered, 'not owing to any idleness or profaneness', but through sluggish trade and a large family.[329] Kinsale had its weekly pensioners, and Howe was added to the twelve. In 1733, the pensioners, divided equally between men and women, were paid anything from sixpence to two shillings weekly. In exceptional cases the corporation acted to save a widow from abandoning her husband's trade, or to procure an apprenticeship, as with a weaver in the nearby town of Bandon. Like most communities, the port wished to rid itself of strangers. 'Mad Bobby' was to be transported to Blarney, in order 'to prevent his being troublesome to the inhabitants' of Kinsale. Vagrants were whipped out of town. Mary Kirk, pregnant with the child of her soldier husband but abandoned, was to be paid to return to Derry. Its own were more generously treated. Essential to each case was knowledge of the individual. Eleanor Macey, a native of the town, was an orphan denied her share of an estate near Plymouth. Prone to fits of 'lunatism', she could not fend for herself. A widow, Eleanor Tolby, had languished in bed for months. A cooper, another native of the place, had been ill for a year. Unable to work, he and his family had been reduced 'to the last degree of poverty'. Denis Donovan, also known as Tugg Mutton, was approved because, despite his Irish-sounding name, he had been educated among the English and had helped to build the Charles Fort close to the town. He was granted 2s. 6d. to buy a new coat for the winter.[330]

Craft guilds also eased the hardship of members. Brethren no longer able to work were pensioned. In Dublin, the Guild of St Audeon's was particularly solicitous towards Michael Chamberlain, its former master, when he fell on hard times. Widows and orphans were also helped.[331] Again, the numbers of pensioners were small, and to be eligible for such assistance in the first place implied a previously respectable standing. In addition, Masonic lodges functioned as friendly societies. Brethren in difficulties were given cash; funeral expenses were occasionally paid.[332] The lucky enjoyed a benevolence which was strictly rationed; those down on their luck were obvious beneficiaries. The lists of those assisted were short. They were limited to the well-known. Yet, in the face of widespread distress, the principle that charity began with and was confined to their own could be relaxed. The Coleraine Freemasons in 1757, 'in which year there was a very great scarcity of the necessaries of life', helped the famished.[333]

There were signs of a more concerted attack on the problem of endemic poverty. In addition to creating work and wealth, permanent mechanisms for relief were constructed. By the 1770s, the united parishes of Coleraine and Killowen in County Londonderry maintained a poorhouse, provided flax to be dressed, and gave money. Rather than rely on the uncertainties of church collections, parishioners subscribed on an annual basis. In this way it was possible to depend on an income of at least £190. The parish could then plan disbursements to seventy-six individuals.[334] It took time for these schemes, seemingly more impersonal, to be accepted. In Sligo, townspeople were unhappy about helping 'a parcel of beggars' brats'.[335] Archbishop King wrote of the reluctance of Dublin Protestants to support the city workhouse. In part this was because it removed responsibility from the individual vestries to a more centralized body. This loss of control was perhaps more imagined than real, since each parish in return for its payments to the workhouse had the right to nominate inmates. Another complaint was the bad management of the enterprise.[336]

The Dublin workhouse was one of the alternatives to care within the parish. Hospitals opened in Dublin thanks to the generosity of individuals, such as Sir Patrick Dun, Edward Worth, Richard and Grizel Steevens, and Dean Swift. This provision spread into the provinces slowly.[337] The Dublin workhouse had a chequered history. Intended to house 310, by 1725 it had 222 inmates.[338] Of those helped, 56 per cent were female; 44 per cent male. Forty-two per cent of beneficiaries were children. Among the adults, only thirty, or 13.5 per cent of all, were listed as too old to work.[339] Even if the workhouse was well run, it was incapable either financially or physically of coping with the multiplying numbers of Protestant poor. In default of a more comprehensive assault on poverty and incapacity, the disabled still relied on the charity of the few. The benevolent, although stirred by compassion, could be imperious towards supplicants. The 'good behaviour' expected of the pensioners in St John's parish was demanded – with individual variations – of others granted alms. Katherine Conolly accepted that her wealth brought special responsibilities. After her husband died, she retained a larger staff of servants than was essential. Christian charity and *noblesse oblige* inspired her gifts to the starving during 1740–41. In January 1740 she was sending eighty loaves of bread each evening from Dublin to be handed to the poor at Castletown. She was also feeding 100 daily at her Dublin house.[340] She contributed to public collections, financed works around her Castletown estate, so that the poor might be employed and paid, and nagged acquaintances to buy tickets for a performance of Handel's *Messiah*, staged to raise funds for a Dublin hospital. Yet, in the autumn of 1741, she repented of her largesse. Better weather and a more abundant harvest ought, she believed, to have ended the crisis. Yet beggars still swarmed. Uncomprehending of the continuing dearth, she railed, 'they have got such a custom of begging . . . They will not work, tho they can get it'.[341] This attitude recurred. A censorious Quaker in Cork acknowledged the genuine distress of the poor in the summer of 1756 when scarce bread, flour and meal were sent to neighbouring counties. Human failings were also blamed. Greed led to grazing of cattle, especially to meet the demand for butter and barrelled beef, rather than to growing corn.[342]

The danger of being gulled by reprobates was relentlessly dinned into the prosperous.[343] Charity was a Christian duty, but to be practised carefully. Katherine Conolly heeded such injunctions. Even in her private giving, she was wary. A Mrs Hamilton, probably a kinswoman, to whom she had given money and clothing, was exposed as 'a poor, worthless creature'. The donations had, so Katherine Conolly learnt, been 'pawned for drams as fast as she got them'. They instantly ceased.[344] Becoming behaviour, including thanks, was expected by donors. Nevertheless, obligations to faithful servants as part of the householders' 'family' were widely acknowledged. Mrs Conolly, like others, appreciated the care of skilled nurses, and eased their retirement.[345] James Ware pensioned off aged servants when they could no longer work in his Dublin house. He paid for their lodgings and discreet funerals, as earlier he had advised on and subsidized the servants' provision for their own dependants. An awareness of personal misfortunes also inspired the Incorporated Society. Twice, in 1744 and 1750, it purchased wooden legs for maimed pupils. The costs were not constant: perhaps the types of wood and the lengths differed.[346]

The numerous voluntary associations and parochial innovations did not substitute an altogether impersonal approach to relief. Personal knowledge and evaluations continued to decide how sparse resources were allocated. Parishioners, especially the active vestrymen, retained great discretion. Most Protestant communities remained small enough for it to be easy for them to ascertain the condition and worth of any who applied for aid. In order to be admitted into the few hospitals or almshouses, cases had to be made.[347] Just as those who craved advancement in the Church, army and Revenue needed patrons, so too did the seekers after charity. Subscribers to and trustees of hospitals and the charter schools expected to place tenants and dependants in these institutions. The women entering the Magdalen Asylum came recommended by the clergymen and charitable whom Lady Arbella Denny had badgered on its behalf. Furthermore, householders still faced begging in the streets and at the doors of church and home. This resembled the situation that prevailed in mid-Wales during the eighteenth century.[348] Again the givers, resistant to intimidation, gauged merit.[349] Any retreat into impersonal charity, detected in other Protestant societies, is hard to document in eighteenth-century Ireland. Responsibility for unfortunate kinsfolk continued to be acknowledged and discharged. Pole Cosby allowed a second cousin, Jane Rotherham, 'a sad, idle wandering sort of woman', a weekly fivepence. In time, he raised it to thirteen pence. He had constructed a small house for her near the Protestant church at Stradbally, but then hit on a strategy which united fashion and philanthropy. He installed her in his newly built hermitage, where she was to tend the fires.[350]

The bulk of the population, Protestant no less than Catholic, probably missed these forms of help. Labour, skilled and unskilled, was the common fate. Despite the availability of figures for weekly wages, both in town and country, and for the specialist and casual, yearly earnings are impossible to ascertain.[351] Much work was irregular, dependent on the seasons and weather. Prospects of employment improved, especially in growing towns. But grim conditions pushed many overseas. Protestants from Ulster sailed to new worlds in North America. Maybe 7,000 left for this destination between 1717 and 1720.[352] Others escaped by joining the British forces. Just as the financially embarrassed among the quality – or aspirant quality – soldiered and sailed in the armed services, so too did the poor. In 1691, the attractions of military service meant that workmen were scarce in eastern Ulster.[353] Recruiting drives recurred. It was thought that the marines were depopulating coastal areas of Connacht in 1760.[354] At this time, the lack of soldiers to defend the Hanoverians' empire was to be overcome – in part – by raiding Ireland. In 1758, 327 of the troopers in the Enniskillen Dragoons were from Ireland. Landowners in Ulster were permitted to raise forces, in the belief that the northern province was best furnished with sturdy Protestants. Volunteers came forward, but not in the numbers predicted. Winter was most propitious, as the weather suspended agricultural and other outdoor occupations.[355] But alternative civilian employments competed against the uncertain appeal of the army. Freeholders, at whom the campaign was directed, were less interested than the unskilled.[356] As with the sailors, so with the land forces, Connacht yielded more recruits than the now thriving Ulster.

Time in the army and navy delivered some in Ireland from desperate want, but the military themselves were not immune from poverty. Also, by jettisoning wives and children and fathering litters of pups, soldiers, then posted elsewhere, added to the numbers of paupers. When regiments were suddenly withdrawn from Ireland in 1762, a single Dublin parish was left with 392 destitute children whose fathers were soldiers.[357] At Waterford, the garrison had a comparable impact.[358] The Incorporated Society struggled with the resulting problem, and the Hibernian Society was founded specifically to tackle it. In easier times, fecund soldiers populated Protestant Ireland. At Kinsale, the children of soldiers made up 44 per cent of the 311 baptized between 1730 and 1732. In the harsh years from 1740 to 1743, the hundred offspring of the military amounted to 53 per cent of the total born in this urban parish.[359] In numerous communities of this sort, the army alone through the exertions of individuals arrested an otherwise steady decline in Protestant numbers.

Returning veterans, likely to increase the stock of poor, received particular care.[360] In advance of the Dublin hospitals which nursed civilians, from the 1680s the Royal Hospital at Kilmainham cared for old soldiers. Others of the superannuated troops were designated as Chelsea Pensioners. The recipients of this assistance once more signalled how a minority could secure favours. In order to be admitted to Kilmainham or to become a pensionary of Chelsea, a backer was vital. The locations whence the veterans came to Kilmainham reveal more about the distribution of the governors than about the geographical origins of the inmates. In contrast, the Chelsea pensioners, some still fit for garrison duties, were concentrated around military bases, such as Limerick, Athlone (the Roscommon contingent) and Sligo, not otherwise notable for large Protestant populations.[361]

Last recorded domiciles of inmates of the Royal Hospital, Kilmainham, *c.*1741, and locations of Chelsea pensioners, *c.*1748[362]

County	Inmates at Kilmainham	Chelsea pensioners
Antrim	28	78
Armagh	17	48
Carlow	2	9
Cavan	9	25
Clare	1	4
Cork	98	109
Donegal	9	17
Down	38	108
Dublin City	169	{303
Dublin County	10	
Fermanagh	11	15
Galway	5	29
Kerry	4	8
Kildare	5	8
Kilkenny	17	27
King's County	2	13
Leitrim	1	19
Limerick	19	57
Londonderry	19	29
Longford	8	15
Louth	5	10
Mayo	3	12
Meath	0	7
Monaghan	6	23
Queen's County	4	23

Last recorded domiciles of inmates of the Royal Hospital, Kilmainham, *c.*1741, and locations of Chelsea pensioners, *c.*1748
(*continued*)

County	Inmates at Kilmainham	Chelsea pensioners
Roscommon	12	20
Sligo	8	27
Tipperary	11	28
Tyrone	12	47
Waterford	29	49
Westmeath	4	10
Wexford	4	22
Wicklow	4	14

Popularly linked with the large contingent of soldiers were prostitutes, an occupation that revealed another strategy for the poor and the problems of women. Fewer trades beckoned to them. A reformer pleaded that they might be instructed in 'painting, music, dancing, reading, French, writing, arithmetic, hair-dressing, stay-making, shoe-making, &c, &c.', to equip them to earn creditable livelihoods.[363] Charities embraced these aims. They also tried to rescue those who had strayed into alternative occupations. Lady Arbella Denny's Magdalen Asylum in Dublin hoped to divert the poor, both Protestant and Catholic, from prostitution.[364] Entry required a recommendation. Within the refuge, as has been seen, the magdalens took on new identities. Most were released back into the world after eighteen months. Habits of industry were to be inculcated as a defence against any fresh descent into vice. Those who meekly applied themselves to needlework – sewing Dresden ruffles or at the tambour – won the approval of the exigent founder. Daily supervision was delegated to a female superintendent, but Lady Arbella Denny knew the details of each charge. Those admitted into the home, as into the charity schools, voluntary hospitals and almshouses, enjoyed a type of privilege which separated them from most poor women. Their circumstances and inclination to repent made them fit objects of charity. Some had undoubtedly sunk into miserable conditions, borrowing clothes in order to appear decent enough to be taken in. Others arrived in filthy rags which were immediately burnt. A few evidently came from genteel families, had been educated and retained an air of respectability in their dress and possessions. After their rehabilitation, only those adjudged penitent were recommended to employers, and then usually in lowly capacities as domestics or seamstresses.[365]

The hostile dismissed the poor, unless docile and grateful, as potential or actual criminals. In the seventeenth century, 'the rascal multitude' was said to have been guilty of rebellion.[366] By the eighteenth century, at least until its last decade, the rootless and shifty did not rebel, but engaged in petty theft, trespassed on property and flouted regulatory laws. Schemes were devised to wean the young and vulnerable from these vices.[367] Of the Protestant (and Catholic) poor in seventeenth- and eighteenth-century Ireland, only the exceptional – notorious law-breakers and objects of compassion – emerge from anonymity. Notwithstanding the inclination to demonize them, levels of indictment and conviction hardly prove that the poor typically supported themselves through crime.[368] Their passivity in the face of adversity is more striking. If, as seems probable, as many as 400,000 Protestants inhabited mid-eighteenth-century Ireland, the circumstances of over 90 per cent are hidden. Day labourers, journeymen and domestics are espied only when they haul themselves higher or engage in religious introspection hardly characteristic of all. Those clambering from the undifferentiated and unskilled poor occasionally deposited traces. Others, identifiable as the recipients of help, had been picked out because of special merit or demerit.

The lower sort may all have been poor, but what it meant to be poor varied. Not all were universally or permanently doomed to griping want. Nor were they indifferent to questions of virtue, credit and repute. Some were drawn into the commercial and respectable worlds of goods, markets and fairs, both as producers and vendors, and – increasingly – as buyers.[369] Superiors were capable of sympathy towards the poor. They singled out some to be charity school children, and assisted apprentices, servants, soldiers and sailors. Yet there was a nervousness about advancing too many into better stations too quickly. By doing so, the social order might be subverted or even inverted. These unspoken anxieties slowed the drive to turn all in Ireland into civil Protestants. Slow transformations were best accommodated in structures – parishes, manors, baronies, boroughs, schools and guilds – which could simultaneously educate and restrain. Hierarchies, because part of the divine plan, should and would survive. [370] In the face of manifest inequalities in personal circumstances, resignation not indignation was urged. Archbishop Synge, in soliciting donations in Dublin during the recession of 1721, reassured his auditors, 'God has in his providence decreed many different degrees of men in the world'. Warming to his theme, the archbishop insisted that political and social harmony required that 'the distinction that is between them should several ways outwardly appear'. He did not argue that a greater propensity to destitution, dearth and premature death was among the divinely approved denominators of the lowly. However, he did approve differences of 'apparel and furniture . . . with respect to the cost and charge of them'. By doing so, Synge reminds us of how outward appearances – 'the grand figure' – bewitched and defined Irish Protestants.[371]

This worry about externals affected the practice of charity. The Dublin parish of St Michan's furnished the eight inmates of its poorhouse with two sets of shifts, caps and aprons, 'to render their presence more sweet, clean and decent'.[372] It was widely held that outward markers reflected inner worth. All could use these, the handiest of reckoners. Another preacher during Queen Anne's reign had decried those who distanced themselves from humbler neighbours, 'affecting to distinguish themselves from 'em by the luxury of their garb, of their houses and furniture, of their table and expenses'.[373] The ascetics might lament, but they could not stop Protestants in Ireland from running after novelties. Education, bearing, accent, dress, house, furnishings, diet and recreations increasingly demarcated the quality, the genteel and polite from the boors. Realists knew that these attributes could be bought and even faked. Accordingly, they worried about sifting the genuine from the counterfeit. In answer to this puzzle, restraint, not excess, came to be prized as the mark of the truly elevated. Rank was best displayed through conduct. But inner worth was less readily assessed than outward manifestations. Even the austere, such as Archbishop Synge, agreed that appearances should match moral worth. In his own expansive manner of living he acted on this philosophy.[374]

The inhabitants of Hanoverian Ireland were most conveniently and convincingly ordered, not on the basis of ancestry and innate attributes, but according to how they lived. This realization obliged many to scuttle after extra employments and earnings, many of which have now been detailed. These supplements enabled the privileged Protestants to buy what was essential to denote civility and respectability. The ease with which these adjuncts could be acquired instead of being a cause of celebration, is a reminder that the distinctions between social orders, and between Catholics and Protestants or English and Irish, might easily be erased. Among the poor, both Catholics and Protestants lacked goods, making it impossible on the simple basis of externals to differentiate the separate confessions. Few Catholics or Protestant dissenters had the means to be recruited into the cantonment of the polite. All too many Protestant conformists – probably 90 per cent – because they were poor, could do little to escape being lumped with their Catholic and dissenting neighbours as the lower people.

Chapter 11

Conclusion: Ranks and Rankings

This bumpy tour has pointed out some obvious features of late Stuart and early Hanoverian Ireland. Few are surprising, since most, with variations, could be found in Wales and England. Here was an island in longitude and latitude close to Britain. Climate and geology varied from what was to be found in its eastern neighbours, but not greatly. Its history, like theirs, was of conquest and colonization. Only in the more recent date of these experiences of defeat and resettlement did Ireland differ.

Odd figures, John Putland, Robert Roberts, Hugh Massy, Sarah Povey, Jane Vickhurst and Cupid Gallop, momentarily take form. Yet most within and almost all outside the quality obstinately elude historical resuscitation. An effort has been made to gauge the contours of the social landscape. The majority of Protestants dwelt at the middling and lowest altitudes. Neither income nor ancestry, alone or in tandem, always determined these rankings. Reputation, credit, and style of living all counted towards contemporary evaluations. So far as the distant governments in Dublin and London were concerned, Ireland, whether a kingdom, wayward province or precocious colony, needed the same array of paid and unpaid functionaries as did England and Wales. Where Protestants and administrative tasks were most densely concentrated, notably in Dublin, a few larger towns and eastern Ulster, it was practicable to erect the overlapping systems of vestries, municipal corporations and chartered guilds. In manning these bodies, Protestants of all denominations often cooperated. Only in the Presbyterian redoubts of Ulster did the dissenters scruple about qualifying themselves through occasional conformity for full participation in this work. Catholics, for the most part, did not compromise in this way, and accordingly were debarred from civic routines.

Tenure of what might be dismissed as risible offices mattered. It could consolidate or improve social ranking. Conventionally, it was seen as a training in citizenship. For aspirants and occupants, the places could bring money. In the Dublin parish of St Catherine, it was objected that the small group which held the chief offices had burdened poor parishioners by proposing to add a spire to the church. The contractor and officers benefited.[1] Much of the kingdom, as has been stressed, lacked enough Protestants of assorted ranks to run it as had been planned. In consequence, the state in Ireland rested on a precariously narrow foundation. If it was to work, it had either to burden a few with numerous jobs or to abandon many of the regulations and responsibilities undertaken throughout Britain. Another solution was to waive or ignore the bans, and employ not only dissenters, as in the north, but also Catholics. These accommodations appeared in the freedom to trade extended early in the eighteenth century by boroughs such as Waterford and Youghal, or in the use of Catholics as parish constables in Connacht.[2] However, these relaxations resembled the connivance at Catholic worship. They might be rescinded at will and on whims. In any case, the breaches in the armature of conformist Protestant ascendancy before the 1770s were too narrow to satisfy Catholics or resolute dissenters.

Much of rural Ireland lacked Protestants. Because of this situation, the few substantial residents were saddled with numerous duties. Exactly who ran the localities as county magistrates, grand jurors, seneschals of manors and constables of baronies and parishes still requires more thorough investigation. Preliminary findings suggest a small cadre of the busy landowners in rural districts.[3] Equally important to the government of the kingdom were the incorporated boroughs, garrisons and the revenue system. This account has considered such institutions chiefly as devices for individual betterment rather than as agencies of the English state in Ireland. The thrust of recent work on English parochial, municipal and voluntary associations has been to insist on the high proportions and modest circumstances of many who participated. Even so, analysts disagree as to whether communitarian cooperation or social and economic exclusivity was uppermost. The magistracy and militia groomed for citizenship, and then gratified active citizens. Through these tasks, it was believed, and not just in an Irish context, vital lessons about fraternity and hierarchy, civility and moderation, were to be learnt. Increasingly in the eighteenth century, desirable accomplishments of politeness, refinement, sociability and gentility could be acquired and perfected through these public duties. Moreover, while the senate, corporation and guild offered arenas in which to display the appropriate cultivation, the council boards of charities and the convivial tables of clubs and lodges supplemented the outlets. More frequent chances to display political and social skills delighted a lucky minority. For the many, exclusion was accentuated. Women and the dependent poor were customarily absent; the middling enjoyed uncertain roles in official institutions.

In these limitations, Ireland resembled Britain. In each country, confession was added to gender and income as a determinant of complete or incomplete membership of the state. Whereas perhaps 5 per cent of the population of England was debarred from the higher offices because Catholic, 75 per cent was in Ireland. This statistic was at once the foundation and the nemesis of the Irish Protestant Ascendancy. Despite the size of the excluded majority, few from it have appeared in the preceding pages. This invisibility reflects the sources, and so, it could be argued, a bias of the Protestants whose writings constitute so much of the surviving evidence. Almost everywhere before the nineteenth century, written history was controlled and composed by the victors, the literate and the leisured. At best, the poorer sorts appear as an aggregation or stereotype. In Ireland, this was as true of the Protestant as of the Catholic poor. The majority of poor Protestants found there was no room in the churches for them if they could not afford either seats or decent clothes. Left to drift outside the net of officialdom, they were hard to distinguish from the shoals of Catholics. Indeed, since the notion persisted that poverty was a peculiarly Catholic failing, it was all too easy to assume that all the poor were either already, or on the way to being, Catholic. Those who wrestled with the resulting problems urged severity in the abstract. When faced with sorry individuals, the severe could act more kindly. Comprehensive bans on Catholics as teachers, landowners, town-dwellers and members of borough and trading corporations were enacted. Similarly, the stern inveighed against entertaining them as tenants or even as servants. In practice, each of these prohibitions was breached – casually and often. The result was regular encounters with Catholics: at closest quarters as domestic servants. In virtually all the situations, the Catholics were in dependent, indeed subservient positions. The occasional exceptions – gentlemen able obviously to live as such, affluent traders, officers in foreign armies home on leave, wily chamber counsel, industrious and frugal craftsmen – unnerved Protestant observers.

The originals of the Protestant society imported from England, Wales and Scotland were never uniform. Little wonder, then, that hybrids and sports abounded across Ireland. These certainly merit comparison with what developed in British America and India, as well as with what survived in different regions of Britain. The modest aim of this study has been to be more precise, if not concise, about the briefly dominant Protestant population of Ireland. Above all, it has examined how they made an English Ireland work and how they worked to make money. As yet, how they made sense of their situation, at once precarious and precious, has not been addressed explicitly. In the past, nimble craft have busily explored Irish waters, their able pilots returning with authoritative charts. Too often, it seems, they neither disembarked to tread the terrain nor quizzed the inhabitants. The next instalment of this report will look more closely at the habitats and habits of the settlers. It will also consider how they schemed to improve Ireland, and what physical imprints they made, evanescent as most proved. In short, the skeleton will be fleshed out and be seen to move.

Notes

1. The Problems of Orders

1. Sir R. Cox to W. Harris, 6 March 1740[1], Armagh Public Library, Physico-Historical Society Mss.

2. Abp. W. King to H. Maule, 8 and 26 May 1722, TCD, Ms. 750/7, pp. 104–5, 117–18.

3. W. King, *The state of the protestants of Ireland under the late King James's government* (London, 1691); R. Cox, *Hibernia Anglicana*, 2 parts (London, 1689–90).

4. C. S. King, *A great archbishop of Dublin: William King. D.D., 1650–1729* (London, 1906), pp. 1–42; P. O'Regan, *Archbishop William King of Dublin (1650–1729) and the constitution of church and state* (Dublin, 2000).

5. For the Coxes, T. C. Barnard, 'The political, material and mental culture of the Cork settlers, 1649–1700', in P. O'Flanagan and N. G. Buttimer (eds), *Cork: history and society* (Dublin, 1993), pp. 343–4; R. Caulfield (ed.), *Autobiography of Sir Richard Cox, Bart.* (London, 1860); D. W. Hayton, 'Dependence, clientage and affinity: the political following of the second duke of Ormonde', in T. Barnard and J. Fenlon (eds), *The dukes of Ormonde* (Woodbridge, 2000), pp. 215–17, 220, 235, 237; E. Magennis, *The Irish political system, 1740–1765* (Dublin, 2000), pp. 34–7; J. Ware, *The history and antiquities of Ireland*, ed. W. Harris, 2 vols (Dublin, 1764), ii, pp. 207–51.

6. Barnard, 'Cork settlers', pp. 309–65; M. MacCarthy-Morrogh, *The Munster Plantation: English migration to southern Ireland, 1583–1641* (Oxford, 1985), p. 260.

7. *An abstract of the number of protestant and popish families in the several counties and provinces of Ireland* (Dublin, 1736), p. 6.

8. Census of the diocese of Elphin, 1749, NA, M. 2466, pp. 396–421; J. Cuffe, account of Co. Mayo, *c.* 1738, p. 5, Armagh Public Library, Physico-Historical Society Mss; J. P. McDermott, 'An examination of the accounts of James Moore, esq., land agent and collector of fees at Newport Pratt, Co. Mayo, 1742–1765', unpublished MA thesis, St Patrick's College, Maynooth (1994).

9. Bp. J. Evans to Abp. W. Wake, 30 April 1717, Christ Church, Wake Ms. 12, f. 149v; W. Macafee and V. Morgan, 'Population in Ulster, 1660–1760', in P. Roebuck (ed.), *Plantation to partition: essays in Ulster history in honour of J. L. McCracken* (Belfast, 1981), p. 58; T. C. Smout, N. C. Landsman and T. M. Devine, 'Scottish emigration in the seventeenth and eighteenth centuries', in N. Canny (ed.), *Europeans on the move: studies on European migration, 1500–1800* (Oxford, 1994), p. 88.

10. R. J. Dickson, *Ulster emigration to colonial America, 1718–1775* (London, 1966); Patrick Griffin, *The people with no name: Ireland's Ulster Scots, America's Scots Irish, and the creation of a British Atlantic world, 1689–1764* (Princeton and London, 2001); G. Kirkham, 'Ulster emigration to North America, 1680–1720', in H. T. Blethen and C. T. Wood (eds), *Ulster and North America: transatlantic perspectives on the Scotch-Irish* (Tuscaloosa, AL, 1997), pp. 76–117.

11. *Abstract of the number of protestant and popish families*, pp. 1–6; S. J. Connolly, *Religion, law and power: the making of Protestant Ireland 1660–1760* (Oxford, 1992), p. 146. The average family (or household) size was put at five, but it was allowed that this figure varied considerably. It was thought to be larger in the prospering towns, rising to ten in Dublin. *Abstract of the number of protestant and popish families*, p. 8.

12. D. Dickson, 'The demographic implications of Dublin's growth', in R. Lawton and R. Lee (eds), *Urban population development in western Europe from the late-eighteenth to the early twentieth century* (Liverpool, 1989), p. 180; P. Fagan, *Catholics in a protestant country: the papist constituency in eighteenth-century Dublin* (Dublin, 1998), pp. 9–52.

13. Dickson, 'Economic history of the Cork region', i, p. 180; ii, pp. 419–21; D. Dickson, '"Centres of motion": Irish cities and popular politics', in L. Bergeron and L. M. Cullen (eds), *Culture et pratiques politiques en France et en Irlande XVIe–XVIIIe siècle* (Paris, 1991), p. 106.

14. Dickson, '"Centres of motion"', p. 106.

15. Abp. W. King to Sir H. Sloane, 27 Nov. 1725, BL, Sloane Ms. 4049, f. 66v.

16. B. Connor, *The history of Poland, in several letters to persons of quality*, 2 vols (London, 1698); R. Molesworth, *An account of Denmark, as it was in the year 1692* (London, 1694); W. Temple, *Observations upon the United Provinces of the Netherlands*, ed. G. N. Clark (Oxford, 1972). Also, on Connor, R. H. Dalitz and G. C. Stone, 'Dr Bernard Connor: physician to King Jan III Sobieski', *Oxford Slavonic Papers*, new series, 14 (1981), pp. 14–35.

17. R. Molesworth, *Some considerations for the promoting of agriculture, and employing the poor* (Dublin, 1723); W. Temple, 'An essay on the advancement of trade in Ireland (written to Lord Essex), 22 July 1673', in W. Temple, *Miscellanea* (London, 1680), pp. 97–145.

18. [H. Brooke?], *An essay on the antient and modern state of Ireland* (Dublin, 1759), sig. A2.

19. Abp. W. King to Sir H. Sloane, 27 Nov. 1727, BL, Sloane Ms. 4049, f. 66v; K. C. Balderston (ed.), *The collected letters of Oliver Goldsmith* (Cambridge, 1928), pp. 21–2.

20. *The present state of Ireland* (London, 1673), pp. 33–40; J. Davies, *A discoverie of the true causes why Ireland was never entirely subdued* (London, 1612), pp. 156–69.

21. R. Lawrence, *The interest of England in the Irish transplantation stated* (London, 1655); R. Lawrence, *England's great interest in the well planting of Ireland with English people discussed* (Dublin, 1656).

22. S. R. Gardiner, 'The transplantation to Connaught', *EHR*, 14 (1899), pp. 700–34; T. C. Barnard, 'Planters and policies in Cromwellian Ireland', *P & P*, 61 (1973), pp. 31–69.

23. R. Lawrence, *The interest of Ireland in its trade and wealth stated* (Dublin, 1682), 2 vols; T. C. Barnard, 'Crises of identity among Irish Protestants, 1641–1685', *P & P*, 127 (1990), pp. 58–68; T. C. Barnard, 'The "fanatic zeal and irregular ambition" of

Richard Lawrence', in C. Brady and J. Ohlmeyer (eds), *Argument and power in early modern Ireland* (Cambridge, forthcoming).

24. Barnard, 'Crises of identity', pp. 56–68; T. C. Barnard, 'The uses of 23 October 1641 and Irish Protestant celebrations', *EHR*, 106 (1991), pp. 889–920.

25. Barnard, 'Uses of 23 October 1641', pp. 889–920.

26. For example: Molesworth, *Some considerations for the promoting of agriculture*; [George Rye], *Considerations on agriculture* (Dublin, 1730).

27. [Brooke], *An essay on the antient and modern state of Ireland*.

28. Ibid., p. 95.

29. Lawrence, *Interest of Ireland*, ii, p. 51. The same sentiment had been voiced by a parliamentary committee at Westminster in 1654. T. C. Barnard, *Cromwellian Ireland: English government and reform in Ireland, 1649–1660*, pbk edn (Oxford, 2000), p. xxi, n. 37. Cf. D. Armitage, 'The political economy of Britain and Ireland after the Glorious Revolution', in J. Ohlmeyer (ed.), *Political thought in seventeenth-century Ireland* (Cambridge, 2000), pp. 227–8.

30. As is argued by or can be deduced from: Connolly, *Religion, law and power*; D. W. Hayton, 'The beginnings of the "undertaker system"', in T. Bartlett and D. W. Hayton (eds), *Penal era and golden age: essays in Irish history, 1690–1800* (Belfast, 1979), pp. 32–54; D. W. Hayton, 'Walpole and Ireland', in J. Black (ed.), *Britain in the age of Walpole* (Basingstoke, 1984), pp. 95–119; Magennis, *The Irish political system, 1740–1765*; C. I. McGrath, *The making of the eighteenth-century Irish constitution* (Dublin, 2000); P. McNally, *Parties, patriots and undertakers: parliamentary politics in early Hanoverian Ireland* (Dublin, 1997).

31. J. Kelly (ed.), *The letters of Lord Chief Baron Edward Willes to the earl of Warwick, 1757–62* (Aberystwyth, 1990), pp. 53–4; J. McVeagh (ed.), *Pococke's Irish tours* (Dublin, 1995), p. 98; J. Loveday, *Diary of a tour in 1732 through parts of England, Wales, Ireland and Scotland* (Edinburgh, 1890), p. 40; C. Massy, *A collection of resolutions, queries, &c.* (Limerick, 1769), p. 48.

32. [R. Cox], 'Irish politicks or an historical record of proceedings of the House of Commons of Ireland in the year, 1737', TCD, Ms. 586, p. 4.

33. *Ireland's case being the most deplorable of any in the Christian world* (London and Dublin, 1737).

34. J. H. Andrews, *Shapes of Ireland: maps and their makers 1564-1839* (Dublin, 1997).

35. S. Pender (ed.), *A 'Census' of Ireland, c. 1659* (Dublin, 1939); R. C. Simington (ed.), *The Civil Survey, 1654–56*, 10 vols (Dublin, 1931–61); R. C. Simington (ed.), *The transplantation to Connacht, 1654–58* (Dublin, 1970).

36. *Abstract of the number of protestant and popish families*; 'Report on the state of popery in Ireland, 1731', *Archivium Hibernicum*, 1–4 (1912–15); Census of Elphin, 1749, NA, M. 2466; T. P. Cunningham, 'The 1766 religious census, Kilmore and Ardagh', *Breifne*, 1 (1961), pp. 357–62.

37. Pender (ed.), *A 'Census'*; J. C. Walton (ed.), 'The subsidy roll of County Waterford, 1662', *Analecta Hibernica*, 30 (1982), pp. 50–92; D. Dickson, C. Ó Gráda and S. Daultrey, 'Hearth tax, household size and Irish population change, 1672–1821', *PRIA*, 82, sect. C (1982), pp. 125–81; *Statutes*, ii, pp. 504–6.

38. Dickson et al., 'Hearth tax', pp. 125–81; *Writings of Petty*, i, pp. 142–4; ii, pp. 496–8; below, pp. 35–71.

39. G. S. Holmes, 'Gregory King and the social structure of pre-industrial England', *TRHS*, 5th series, 27 (1977), pp. 41–68; P. Mathias, 'The social structure in the

eighteenth century: a calculation by Joseph Massie', *Economic History Review*, 2nd series, 10 (1957–8), pp. 34–45.

40. Sir R. Southwell, memoranda, BL, Egerton Ms. 1633, ff. 94–94v; H. W. E. Petty-Fitzmaurice, marquess of Lansdowne (ed.), *The Petty–Southwell correspondence, 1676–1687* (London, 1928), pp. 51, 96–7, 259–60, 298, 322.

41. His most extended reflections are printed in *Writings of Petty*. Other, more fragmentary pieces are now in BL, Add. Mss 72,865–72,899. For a guide to the latter: F. Harris, 'Ireland as a laboratory: the archive of Sir William Petty', in M. C. W. Hunter (ed.), *Archives of the scientific revolution: the formation and exchange of ideas in seventeenth-century Europe* (Woodbridge, 1998). On Petty's approach: L. G. Sharp, 'Sir William Petty and some aspects of seventeenth-century natural philosophy', unpublished D.Phil. thesis, Oxford University (1977); T. Aspromourgos, 'The mind of the oeconomist: an overview of the "Petty Papers" archive', *History of Economic Ideas*, 9 (2001), pp. 39–101.

42. H. Piers, 'A chorographical description of the County of Westmeath', in C. Vallancey (ed.), *Collectanea de rebus Hibernicis* (Dublin, 1770), i, p. 115.

43. N. Taaffe, *Observations on affairs in Ireland from the settlement in 1691 to the present time* (Dublin, 1766), p. 13.

44. Cf. J. Campbell, 'Bede's names for places', in P. H. Sawyer (ed.), *Names, words and graves: early medieval settlement* (Leeds, 1979), pp. 34–54; P. Lindert, 'English occupations, 1670–1811', *Journal of Economic History*, 40 (1980), pp. 690–5.

45. M. Campbell, *The English yeoman under Elizabeth and the early Stuarts* (New Haven, 1942); R. C. Allen, *Enclosure and the yeoman: the agricultural development of the south Midlands, 1450–1850* (Oxford, 1992).

46. C. O'Hara, observations on Co. Sligo, s.d. 1757/8, NLI, Ms. 20,397; diary of Nathanael Ryder, s.d. 25 July 1753, PRONI, T 3228/2/1; N. Garnham, *The courts, crime and the criminal law in Ireland, 1692–1760* (Dublin, 1996), p. 276; G. E. Howard, *Some hints for the better promoting of the laws in this kingdom* (Dublin, 1766), p. 11; *An inquiry into some of the causes of the ill situation of Ireland* (Dublin, 1731), p. 12; Kelly (ed.), *Letters of Lord Chief Baron Willes*, pp. 76, 96; *A letter from Sir Richard Cox, Bart. to Thomas Prior, Esq: shewing, from experience, a sure method to establish the linen-manufacture* (Dublin, 1749), p. 43; *A letter to a member of the Irish parliament relative to the present state of Ireland* (London, [1755]), p. 9; S. Madden, *Reflections and resolutions proper for the gentlemen of Ireland* (Dublin, 1738), p. 16; T. Rundle, *A sermon preach'd in Christ-Church, Dublin, on the 25th day of March 1736* (Dublin, 1736), p. 23; M. Whyte, *An inquiry into the causes of our want of tillage in Ireland: with some hints for establishing a yeomanry* (Dublin, 1755).

47. Rental of Lord Massareene, Co. Cavan [1691], Warwickshire CRO, Newdegate Mss, CR 136/B 2701; deposition of J. Moore, after 5 May 1719, Flintshire RO, Ruthin, DD/BK/1/510; codicil to will of H. Ingoldsby, 28 July 1731, NLI, PC 438; Robinson Mss, Gilbert Collection, Ms. 34, p. 141, Dublin Public Library; T. Barnard, 'Introduction', in T. Barnard and B. McCormack (eds.), *The Dublin Tholsel Court records* (Dublin, forthcoming); N. Canny, 'The Irish background to Penn's experiment', in R. S. Dunn and M. P. Dunn (eds), *The world of William Penn* (Philadelphia, 1986), pp. 144, 147; R. Flatman, 'Some inhabitants of the baronies of Newcastle and Upper Cross, Co. Dublin, c. 1650', *Irish Genealogist*, 7 (1989), pp. 496–504; 8 (1990–93), pp. 3–13, 162–9, 498–506; R. Gillespie (ed.), *The first chapter book of Christ Church Cathedral, Dublin, 1574–1634* (Dublin, 1997),

pp. 35, 47, 53, 90, 124, 125, 126; E. P. Shirley, *The history of the county of Monaghan* (London, 1879), pp. 550–1.

48. See below, pp. 243–4.

49. M. Brabazon to M. Brabazon, n.d. [*c*.1705–10], Brabazon Mss, box III, private collection, London.

50. M. Leathes to W. Leathes, 21 Aug. 1717, Suffolk CRO, Ipswich, de Mussenden Leathes Mss, HA 4503/1/2, 235.

51. E. Spencer to F. Price, 24 June 1746, NLW, Puleston Ms. 3580E.

52. E. Peacock, *Index to English-speaking students who have graduated at Leyden University* (London, 1883), p. 23; T. C. Barnard, 'Protestantism, ethnicity and Irish identities, 1660–1760', in T. Claydon and I. McBride (eds), *Protestantism and national identity. Britain and Ireland, c.1650–c.1850* (Cambridge, 1998), pp. 220–2.

53. For the context which produced Cosby's 'Autobiography', P. Cosby to D. S. Cosby, 1 Jan. 1760, Cosby Mss, Stradbally Hall, Co. Laois, calendared in PRONI, T 3829, and cited in D. M. Beaumont, 'The gentry of the King's and Queen's Counties: Protestant landed society, 1690–1760', unpublished Ph.D. thesis, TCD, 2 vols (1999), i, p. 169

54. 'Autobiography of Pole Cosby, of Stradbally, Queen's County, 1703–1737(?)', *Journal of the County Kildare Archaeological Society*, 5 (1906), pp. 174–5.

55. Ibid., p. 254.

56. Rentals of J. Parnell, 1741, 1741–46, Congleton Mss, Southampton UL, Mss. 64/609, 614; M. Parnell to J. Parnell, 27 Nov. 1759, ibid., 614; Beaumont, 'Gentry of the King's and Queen's Counties', i, p. 55.

57. 'Autobiography of Pole Cosby', p. 254.

58. Ibid., p. 253.

59. See below, pp. 259–62.

60. H. Bland to T. Debrisay, 6 Aug. 1751, 26 Sept. 1753, 4 Feb. 1754, 7 Feb. 1756, 10 Oct. 1756, Bland Mss, Blandsfort, Co. Laois. I am grateful to Dr Daniel Beaumont for these references.

61. T. Dolan, History of County Fermanagh, *c.* 1719, in NLI, Ms. 2085, printed in P. Ó Maolagáin, 'An early history of Fermanagh', *Clogher Record*, 1/3 (1955), pp. 131–40; 1/4 (1956), pp. 113–25; 2/1 (1957), pp. 50–70; 2/2 (1958), pp. 280–92; 2/3 (1959), pp. 458–68; 2/4 (1960–61), pp. 42–9; 4/3 (1962), pp. 163–74. Here and in P. Livingstone, *The Fermanagh story* (Enniskillen, 1969), p. 62, the initial T. of the author's name is read as J[ohn]. Further information about some mentioned by Dolan is in J. B. Leslie's notes of members of the Fermanagh militia in 1708, NLI, Ms. 2696.

62. On this theme: T. C. Barnard, 'Integration or separation? Hospitality and display in Protestant Ireland, 1660–1800', in L. W. B. Brockliss and D. S. Eastwood (eds), *A Union of multiple identities: the British Isles, c.1750–c.1850* (Manchester, 1997), pp. 127–46; T. C. Barnard, 'The languages of politeness and sociability in 18th-century Ireland', in D. G. Boyce, R. Eccleshall and V. Geoghegan (eds), *Political discourse in seventeenth- and eighteenth-century Ireland* (2001), pp. 193–221.

63. *Bishop Berkeley's querist in historical perspective*, ed. J. Johnston (Dundalk, 1970); P. H. Kelly, '"Industry and virtue versus luxury and corruption": Berkeley, Walpole and the South Sea Bubble crisis', *Eighteenth-Century Ireland*, 7 (1992), pp. 57–74; P. H. Kelly, 'The politics of political economy in mid-eighteenth-century Ireland', in S. J. Connolly (ed.), *Political ideas in eighteenth-century Ireland* (Dublin, 2000), pp. 105–29; Madden, *Reflections.*

64. Account by Hume, *c.* 1731–32, NLI, Ms. 6054, pp. 7–8.

65. D. Dickson, 'Middlemen', in Bartlett and Hayton (eds), *Penal era and golden age*, pp. 162–85; A. P. W. Malcomson, 'Absenteeism in eighteenth-century Ireland', *Irish Economic and Social History*, 1 (1974), pp. 15–35.

66. W[alter] H[arris], *Remarks on the affairs* (London, 1691).

67. *CARD*, vi, p. 349, 394, 395; R. Day (ed.), 'Cooke's memoirs of Youghal, 1749', *JCHAS*, 9 (1903), pp. 34–63, 105–17; W. Harris, *The history and antiquities of the city of Dublin* (Dublin, 1766), pp. 207–370; C. Smith, *The antient and present state of the county of Cork*, 2nd edn, 2 vols (Dublin, 1774), i, pp. 361–429; G. Wilson, *Historical remarks of the city of Waterford, from 853 to 1270* (Waterford, [1736]).

68. Sir R. Cox, in BL, Add. Ms. 21,127, f. 58.

69. J. L. McCracken, 'The social structure and social life, 1714–60', in T. W. Moody and W. E. Vaughan (eds), *A new history of Ireland*, iv (Oxford, 1986), p. 34, and endorsed in Connolly, *Religion, law and power*, p. 59.

70. Barnard, *Cromwellian Ireland*, pp. 50–89; Dickson, 'Cork region', i, pp. 45–54; ii, pp. 419–519; R. Gillespie, 'The origins and development of an Ulster urban network', *IHS*, 24 (1983), pp. 15–29; B. Graham, 'Urbanization in Ireland during the High Middle Ages, *c.* 1100 to *c.* 1350', in T. Barry (ed.), *A history of settlement in Ireland* (London, 2000), pp. 124–39; B. J. Graham and L. J. Proudfoot, *Urban improvement in provincial Ireland, 1700–1840* (Athlone, 1994); R. J. Hunter, 'Towns in the Ulster plantation', *Studia Hibernica*, 11 (1971), pp. 40–79; R. J. Hunter, 'Ulster plantation towns, 1609–41', in D. W. Harkness and M. O'Dowd (eds), *The town in Ireland: historical studies XIII* (Belfast, 1981), pp. 55–80.

71. W. Petty, *The political anatomy of Ireland* (London, 1691), p. 10.

72. J. R. Hill, *From patriots to Unionists: Dublin civic politics and Irish protestant patriotism, 1660–1840* (Oxford, 1997), pp. 28–9.

73. Monck Mason collections on Dublin, iii, part 1, Dublin Public Library, Gilbert Ms. 68, pp. 151–5.

74. P. Borsay, *The English urban renaissance: culture and society in the provincial town, 1660–1770* (Oxford, 1989); A. Everitt, 'Social mobility in early modern England', *P & P*, 33 (1966), pp. 56–73; A. E. Everitt, *Change in the provinces: the seventeenth century* (Leicester, 1969); G. S. Holmes, *Augustan England: professions, state and society 1680–1730* (London, 1982).

75. E. M. Johnson, *Great Britain and Ireland, 1760–1800* (Edinburgh and London, 1963), pp. 120–78; J. L. McCracken, *The Irish parliament in the eighteenth century* (Dundalk, 1971), pp. 7–13.

76. List of Cork freemen, 22 May 1729, in court book of the Cork Court of D'Oyer Hundred, 1656–1729, transcribed by R. Caulfield, Cork Archives Institute, U/127; register of Cork freemen, 1656–1741, Cork Public Museum, Fitzgerald Park, Cork.

77. *CJIre.*, ii, pp. 381–3; cf. J. L. McCracken, 'Irish parliamentary elections, 1727–1768', *IHS*, 5 (1947), p. 225.

78. List of likely voters, Youghal, 1721, Chatsworth, Lismore Ms. 36/6. Cf. Day (ed.), 'Cooke's memoirs of Youghal, 1749', pp. 112–14; J. Ponsonby to Devonshire [Sept.–Oct.1758], Chatsworth, Devonshire Letters, 380.13.

79. List of voters, Clonakilty, 1725, Chatsworth, Lismore Ms. 36/24; *The Case of Sir Richard Meade, Bart.* ([Dublin, 1725]).

80. Corporation book of Inistiogue, s.d. 9 Nov. 1727, PRONI, D 2685/9/1; list of 1751, NLI, Ms. 8470/9; case of Fownes and Matthews, 25 April 1761, ibid., 8470/1; G. Deyos to Sir W. Fownes, 11 June 1745, ibid., 8470/3.

81. H. Murtagh, *Athlone: history and settlement to 1800* (Athlone, 2000), p. 193.

82. G.H., *A genuine letter from a freeman of Bandon, to George Faulkner* (Dublin, 1755), pp. 11–12; H.G., *A just and true answer to a scandalous pamphlet call'd a genuine letter from a freeman of Bandon* (Dublin, 1755), pp. 6, 15.

83. W. Conner to Sir A. Abdy, 8 May 1758, Chatsworth, Conner letter book, 1749–58; *A letter from a burgess of Monaghan to the parish-clerk of Ardbraccan* (Dublin, 1754), p. 10.

84. W. Conner to Sir A. Abdy, 4 Feb. 1757, Chatsworth, Conner letter book, 1749–58; minute books, Irish revenue commissioners, PRO, CUST 1/91, f. 106v; CUST 1/95, f. 119.

85. T. C. Barnard, 'Considering the inconsiderable: electors, patrons and Irish elections, 1659–1761', in D. W. Hayton (ed.), *The Irish parliament in the eighteenth century: the long apprenticeship* (Edinburgh, 2001), pp. 107–27.

86. A. P. W. Malcomson, 'The Newtown Act of 1748: revision and reconstruction', *IHS*, 18 (1972–73), pp. 313–40.

87. K. Milne, 'The corporation of Waterford in the eighteenth century', in W. Nolan and T. Power (eds), *Waterford: history and society* (Dublin, 1992), pp. 331–50; T. C. Barnard, 'The cultures of eighteenth-century Irish towns', in P. Borsay and L. Proudfoot (eds), *Change, convergence and divergence: provincial towns in early modern England and Ireland*, Proceedings of the British Academy, 108 (2002), pp. 195–222.

88. 'A Briton', *The history of the Dublin election in the year 1749* (London, 1753), pp. 9–10.

89. Hill, *From patriots to Unionists*.

90. W. Clare, 'The Putland family of Dublin and Bray', *Dublin Historical Record*, 54 (2001), pp. 183–209; and below, pp. 161–2, 269.

91. O. M. Goodbody, 'Anthony Sharp: a Quaker merchant of the liberties', *Dublin Historical Record*, 14 (1955), pp. 12–19; R. Greaves, *Dublin's merchant-quaker: Anthony Sharp and the community of Friends, 1643–1707* (Stanford, 1998); D. Hempton, 'Methodism in Irish society', *TRHS*, 5th series, 36 (1986), pp. 117–42; D. Hempton and M. Hill, *Evangelical Protestantism in Irish society, 1740–1890* (London, 1992); K. Herlihy, 'The early eighteenth-century Irish Baptists: two letters', *Irish Economic and Social History*, 19 (1992), pp. 71–2; P. Kilroy, *Protestant dissent and controversy in Ireland, 1660-1714* (Cork, 1994), pp. 25–6, 42, 90.

92. R. Gillespie, 'The Presbyterian revolution in Ulster, 1660–1690', in W. J. Shiels and D. Wood (eds), *The Churches, Ireland and the Irish*, Studies in Church History, 25 (Oxford, 1989), pp. 159–70; R. Greaves, *God's other children: nonconformists and the emergence of denominational churches in Ireland, 1660–1700* (Stanford, 1997); K. Herlihy, 'The Irish Baptists, 1650–1780', unpublished Ph.D. thesis, TCD (1992).

93. J. C. Beckett, *Protestant dissent in Ireland, 1687–1780* (London, 1948).

94. Lists of churchmen and dissenters in Ulster, RIA, Ms. 24 K 19; Lambeth Palace Library, London, Ms. 1742, ff. 49–56; D. W. Hayton, 'Exclusion, conformity and parliamentary representation: the impact of the sacramental test on Irish dissenting politics', in K. Herlihy (ed.), *The politics of Irish dissent, 1650–1800* (Dublin, 1997), pp. 52–73

95. J. Bonnell to J. Strype, 25 Jan. 1698[9], Cambridge UL, Add. Ms. 1, 85; E. Riggs to R. Cox, 26 Dec. 1691, RIA, Ms. 24 G 7; Abp. W. King to Bp. J. Stearne, 25 Sept. 1714, TCD, Ms. 2536, p. 75.

96. *An alphabetical list of the freemen and freeholders of the city of Dublin who polled at the*

election for members of parliament . . . 1749 (Dublin, 1750); J. R. Hill, 'Dublin corporation, Protestant dissent, and politics, 1660–1800', in Herlihy (ed.), *Politics of Irish Dissent*, pp. 34–7.

97. St Werburgh's records, RCB, P. 326/13.1; 326/27.2/102; *Statutes*, iv, p. 427; H. Alcock to A. Mason, 14 June 1718, Villiers-Stuart Mss, Dromana, Co. Waterford, T 3131/B/1/9.

98. N. Alldridge, 'Loyalty and identity in Chester parishes, 1540–1640', in S. J. Wright (ed.), *Parish, church and people: local studies in lay religion, 1350–1750* (London, 1988); D. Eastwood, *Government and community in the English provinces, 1700–1870* (Basingstoke, 1997), pp. 26–56; M. Goldie, 'The unacknowledged republic: office-holding in early modern England', in T. Harris (ed.), *The politics of the excluded, c. 1500–1850* (Basingstoke, 2001), pp. 153–94; S. J. Hindle, 'A sense of place? Becoming and belonging in the rural parish, 1550–1650', in A. Shepard and P. Withington (eds), *Communities in early-modern England* (Manchester, 2000), pp. 96–114.

99. Beaumont, 'Gentry of the King's and Queen's Counties', ii, p. 44.

100. Minutes of Route Presbytery, 1701–6, pp. 8, 68–9, Presbyterian Historical Society, Belfast; Minutes of Connor Session, 1693–1735, s.d. 12 Dec. 1705, 22 April 1711, ibid.; notebook of Samuel Boyce, PRONI, MIC/1, p. 44; J. M. Barkley, *The eldership in Irish Presbyterianism* (Belfast, 1963).

101. For a start, Griffin, *The people with no name*, pp. 9–64. A contrasted view of the involvement of English Quakers in local life is provided by B. Stevenson, 'The social integration of post-Restoration dissenters, 1660–1725', in M. Spufford, *The world of rural dissenters* (Cambridge, 1995), pp. 360–87, and more generally, T. C. Barnard, 'Parishioners, pews and parsons: laypeople and the Church of Ireland, 1647–1780', in R. Gillespie and W. G. Neely (eds), *The laity and the Church of Ireland, 1000–2000: all sorts and conditions* (Dublin, 2002), pp. 70–103; P. Langford, *Public life and the propertied Englishman, 1689–1798* (Oxford, 1991), pp. 71–80.

102. Depositions, 1668, Petworth, Orrery Mss, general series, 12; Abp. M. Boyle to Lord Orrery, 31 Aug. 1678, 23 Nov. 1678, ibid., general series, 29; Orrery to Sir R. Southwell, 29 Oct. 1678, 1, 12 and 26 Nov. 1678, V & A, Orrery Mss, vol. 2; diary of Bp. S. Digby, 1688, Lambeth Palace Library, Ms. 3152, ff. 7v, 19; C. Massy to F. Burton, 29 Feb. 1739[40], 4, 7 and 11 March 1739[40], Chatsworth, Devonshire Letters, 1740–3 273.0–2; P. J. Larkin, '"Popish riot" in south Co. Derry, 1725', *Seanchas Ard Mhacha*, 8 (1975–6), pp. 98–101.

103. Corporation book, Waterford, 1700–27, s.d. 4 Oct. 1704, 26 Feb. 1705[6], 8 Dec. 1707, 25 April 1710, 22 Oct. 1715, 29 Sept. 1716, 21 Sept. 1717, Waterford Municipal Archives; M. Fitzgerald to Lord Grandison, 22 Aug. 1729, 14 Sept. 1729, Villiers-Stuart Mss, Dromana, Co. Waterford, T 3131/C5/45 and 46; Dickson, 'Cork region', ii, pp. 512–18; Day (ed.), 'Cooke's memoirs of Youghal, 1749', p. 63; Mulcahy, *Kinsale*, ii, p. 74; iii, p. 88; vi, p. 23

104. See below, pp. 294–306.

105. Legg, *Synge Letters*, pp. 300, 301.

106. Sir R. Cox to E. Southwell, 24 Oct. 1706, BL, Add. Ms. 38,154, f. 86v.

107. M. Elliott, *The Catholics of Ulster: a history* (London, 2000), pp. 163–210; B. Ó Buachalla, 'Jacobitism and nationalism: the Irish literary evidence', in M. O'Dea and K. Whelan (eds), *Nations and nationalism: France, Britain, Ireland and the eighteenth century context* (Oxford, 1995), pp. 103–16.

2. Peers

1. B. Cunningham, *The world of Geoffrey Keating: history, myth and religion in seventeenth-century Ireland* (Dublin, 2000), pp. 152–8; G. Keating, *Trí Bior-Ghaoithe an Bháis*, ed. O. Bergin (Dublin, 1931), p. 246, quoted in R. Gillespie, 'Negotiating order in early seventeenth-century Ireland', in M. Braddick and J. Walter (eds), *Negotiating power in early modern society* (Cambridge, 2001), p. 196; Seán O Tuama (ed.), *An Duanaire, 1600–1900* (Dublin, 1981), pp. 86, 91; N. Williams (ed.), *Pairlement Chloinne Tomáis* (Dublin, 1981), pp. 22–3.

2. F. G. James, *Lords of the Ascendancy: the Irish House of Lords and its members, 1600–1800* (Dublin, 1995), pp. 99–109; A.P.W. Malcomson, 'The Irish peerage and the Act of Union, 1800–1971', *TRHS*, 6th series, 10 (2000), pp. 289–327.

3. C. Brady, *The chief governors: the rise and fall of reform government in Tudor Ireland, 1536–1588* (Cambridge, 1994), pp. 72–3; J. MacGeoghegan, *Histoire d'Irlande ançienne et moderne*, 3 vols (Paris and Amsterdam, 1758–63 *recte* 1762), ii, pp. 312–23.

4. B. Ó Dálaigh, 'A comparative study of the wills of the first and fourth earls of Thomond', *North Munster Antiquarian Journal*, 34 (1992), pp. 48–63.

5. B. Ó Dálaigh, 'From Gaelic warlords to English country gentlemen', *The Other Clare*, 25 (2001), pp. 40–2.

6. C. R. Mayes, 'The early Stuarts and the Irish peerage', *EHR*, 73 (1958), p. 247.

7. Ibid. p. 245.

8. V. Treadwell, *Buckingham and Ireland, 1616–1628: a study in Anglo-Irish politics* (Dublin, 1998), pp. 104–14.

9. J. Keating to Sir M. Eustace, 11 March 1660[1], PRO, DEL 9/1, p. 383; C. O'Brien to J. Bonnell, 30 Aug. [1709], 30 Sept. [1709], NLI, PC 435.

10. Barnard, 'Sir William Petty' pp. 213–16; J. Keating to M. Eustace, n.d. [1662?], PRO, DEL 8/33, p. 1413; F. W. X. Fincham, 'Letters concerning Sir Maurice Eustace, Lord Chancellor of Ireland', *EHR*, 30 (1920), p. 258; E. F. Tickell, 'The Eustace family and their lands in County Kildare', *Journal of the County Kildare Archaeological Society*, 13 (1958), pp. 318, 321.

11. Bp. G. Stone of Kildare to Dorset, 13 July 1743, PRONI, T 2760/5.

12. C. O. Brien to J. Bonnell, 30 Aug. [1709], 30 Sept. [1709], NLI, PC 435; H. Rose to Sir M. Crosbie, 25 June 1720, ibid., Talbot-Crosbie Mss, folder 44. By the 1720s Conolly was reported to be worth variously £12,000, £13,000 and £15,000 p.a. Bp. W. Nicolson to Abp. W. Wake, 21 Oct. 1721, Christ Church, Wake Ms. 13, f. 288; Bp. H. Downes to same, 4 Feb. 1723[4], ibid., 14, f. 158.

13. M. Coghill to E. Southwell, 8 March 1732[3], 5 April 1733, BL, Add. Ms. 21,123, ff. 24, 33.

14. A. Savile (ed.), *Secret comment: the diaries of Gertrude Savile, 1721–1757*, Kingsbridge Historical Society and Thoroton Society, 41 (1997, for 1994 and 1995), p. 313.

15. D. Cuffe to B. Pratt, 29 June 1757, NLI, Ms. 5245; T. Lloyd to L. Parsons, 3 [?] 1739, Birr Castle, Co. Offaly, Parsons Mss B/4/11; T. Pakenham to W. Smythe, 4 Feb. 1738[9], NLI, PC 436.

16. R. French to W. Smythe, 15 Nov. 1712, NLI, PC 447.

17. J. Swift and T. Sheridan, *The Intelligencer*, ed. J. Woolley (Oxford, 1992), pp. 123–4.

18. Account of Orrery family, NA, M. 2449, p. 135; P. H. to William III, 29 May 1696, Nottingham UL, Portland Mss, PW A 2522.

19. P. Delany, *Twenty sermons on social duties and their opposite vices* (London, 1747), pp. 428, 433; P. Delany, *Sixteen discourses upon doctrines and duties* (London, 1754), p. 235.

20. J. Potter to R. Liddell, 22 July 1745, PRONI, T 3019/665; petition of Athenry and 21 other peers, 1738, ibid., T 3019/196; N. Garnham, 'The trials of James Cotter and Henry, Lord Santry: two case studies in the administration of criminal justice in early eighteenth-century Ireland', *IHS*, 31 (1999), pp. 328–42.

21. D. W. Hayton, 'Ireland and the English ministers, 1707–16: a study of the formulation and working of government policy in the early eighteenth century', unpublished D. Phil. thesis, Oxford University (1975), pp. 99–102.

22. List of House of Lords, 26 June 1719, BL, Add. Ms. 47,127, f. 120v; James, *Lords of the Ascendancy*; J. Falvey, 'The Church of Ireland episcopate in the eighteenth century', unpublished MA thesis, University College, Cork (1995), pp. 14–37; appendix II; [Edmund Sexton Pery], *Letters from an Armenian in Ireland* (London, 1757), pp. 16–17.

23. Abp. H. Boulter to Devonshire, 28 April 1738, Chatsworth, Devonshire Letters, 1737–9, 242.4.

24. Ld. Southwell to J. Brown, 19 Jan. 1767, Palatine Heritage Centre, Rathkeale, Co. Limerick, Southwell-Brown Mss, box 1, bundle 3.

25. Swift and Sheridan, *The Intelligencer*, p. 123.

26. G. Dillon to 'cousin' [?L. Dillon], 30 March 1745, NLI, Ms. 35,746/2.

27. *The present state of Ireland* (London, 1673), pp. 227–9; R. Lawrence, *The Interest of Ireland in its trade and wealth stated*, 2 parts (Dublin, 1682), ii, pp. 164–8.

28. PRO, WO 8/1, ff. 124–4v; 8/2, ff. 50, 108–8v. For the Blayneys, GEC, *Complete peerage*, ii, pp. 186–9.

29. List of pensions, 1713, BL, Add. Ms. 61,637B, f. 13. Cf. R. Cox to E. Southwell, 29 Jan. 1705[6], 21 March 1705[6], ibid., Add. Ms. 38,153, ff. 150v, 176v.

30. Cavan to Bp. W. Smythe of Kilmore, 13 Dec. 1694; Lady Cavan to same, 24 Dec. 1694, NLI, PC 436; Sir R. Cox to Ormonde, 22 Jan. 1706[7], BL, Add. Ms. 38,154, f. 136; petition of Lady Cavan, [1711], Bodleian, Ms. Eng. Hist. C. 41, p. 78; civil list, 1713, BL, Add. Ms. 61,637B, f. 14; civil list, 1715, Bodleian Ms. Eng. Hist. C. 42, p. 140.

31. P. McNally, *Parties, patriots and undertakers: parliamentary politics in early Hanoverian Ireland* (Dublin, 1997), pp. 78, 101, 112; P. McNally, 'Patronage and politics in Ireland, 1714 to 1727', unpublished Ph.D. thesis, Queen's University, Belfast (1993), pp. 198–9.

32. Abp. J. Hoadley to Devonshire, 28 June 1744, Chatsworth, Devonshire Letters, 1744–5, 246.4.

33. J. Potter to R. Wilmot, 9 April 1746; Richmond to Harrington, 19 Aug. 1748; Harrington to Newcastle, 26 Aug. 1748, PRONI, T 3019/734, 1100, 1117.

34. Harrington to Bedford, 3 March 1747[8]; T. Waite to E. Weston, 13 Aug. 1748, Wilmot Mss, PRONI, T 3019/979, 1102.

35. Strangford to Shannon, 5 Dec. 1760; PRONI, D 2707/A1/5/35; same to Dorset, 22 June 1759, ibid., T 2760/35; valuations of Church of Ireland dignities, c. 1750, Lambeth Palace Library, London, Ms. 2168, ff. 127–8; GEC., *Complete Peerage*, xii, pp. 360–1; J. H. Gebbie (ed.), *Introduction to the Abercorn letters* (Omagh, 1972), p. 49.

36. Mountcharles to Hartington, 17 April 1755, Chatsworth, Devonshire Letters, 1752–5, Hartington to Mountcharles, 15 Nov. 1755, ibid., Nov. 1755, 260.183.

37. T. Barnard and J. Fenlon (eds), *Dukes of Ormonde, 1610–1745* (Woodbridge, 2000); R. Gillespie, 'Landed society and the Interregnum in Ireland and Scotland', in R. Mitchison and P. Roebuck (eds), *Economy and society in Scotland and Ireland, 1500–1939* (Edinburgh, 1988), pp. 38–47; R. Gillespie, 'Lords and commons in seventeenth-century Mayo', in R. Gillespie and G. Moran, '*A various county': essays in Mayo history* (Westport, 1987), p. 65; J. H. Ohlmeyer, *Civil war and restoration in three Stuart kingdoms: the career of Randal MacDonnell, marquis of Antrim, 1609–1683* (Cambridge, 1993), pp. 61–5, 276.

38. Ormond to W. Legge, 12 Sept. 1666, Staffordshire CRO, Dartmouth Mss, D(W) 1778/I/I, 201, calendared in HMC, Dartmouth Mss, i, pp. 14–15.

39. Ormond to Sir R. Southwell, 14 and 19 Aug. 1678, 11 Sept. 1678, 21 Jan. 1678[9], 23 April 1679, V & A, Ormonde Mss, 2, ff. 7, 9, 12, 23v–24, 33, 47; Ormonde to H. Aldrich, 31 July 1704, NLI, Ms. 2502/344–5; same to Lords Justice, 11 April 1706, 27 June 1706, ibid., Ms. 993, pp. 17, 73; same to Godolphin, 2 July 1706, ibid., p. 75; Barnard and Fenlon (eds), *Dukes of Ormonde*, pp. 4–6, 37–9; *The case of the children of Coll. John Bourke, commonly called Lord Bophin* (n.p, c.1700).

40. J. H. Ohlmeyer, 'Parliament, political power and the Irish peerage, 1640–1', to be published in Ohlmeyer and Brady (eds), *Argument and power in early modern Ireland* (Cambridge, forthcoming).

41. List of Irish peers, *temp.* Charles II, Bodleian, Carte Ms. 59, ff. 481–2; Ormond to W. Legge, 12 Sept. 1666, Dartmouth Mss, D(W) 1778/I/I, 201; HMC, *Dartmouth Mss*, i, pp. 14–15; GEC, *Complete Peerage*, iv, pp. 516–21; ix, pp. 320–9; M. Blundell (ed.), *Cavalier: letters of William Blundell to his friends, 1620–1698* (London, 1933), pp. 123–5, 229.

42. List of pensions, Bodleian, Carte Ms. 53, f. 649.

43. H.W. E. Petty-Fitzmaurice, marquess of Lansdowne (ed.), *Petty–Southwell Correspondence, 1670–1687* (London, 1928), p. 276.

44. Lawrence, *Interest of Ireland*, ii, pp. 63–6; W. Petty, 'A view of the House of Peers in Ireland', Feb. 1686[7], Bowood House, Petty Papers, F 55; Hugh Phillips, armoury of the Irish peerage, 1681, Cardiff Central Library, Ms. 3. 291.

45. Petty, 'A view of the House of Peers in Ireland', F 55.

46. List of peers, 1721, BL, Add. Ms. 47,127, f. 120v; *A list of the lords spiritual and temporal, together with the knights, citizens and burgesses of the present parliament* (Dublin, 1725). About 1700, ten peers were named as recent converts from Catholicism. Bodleian, Carte Ms. 226, f. 74.

47. Treadwell, *Buckingham and Ireland*, pp. 112–14.

48. Abp. W. King to A. Charlet, 16 Oct. 1714, Bodleian, Ballard Ms. 36, f. 93; N. Canny, *The upstart earl: a study in the social and mental world of Richard Boyle, first earl of Cork, 1566–1643* (Cambridge, 1982); E. Ó Ciardha, '"The Unkinde Deserter" and "The Bright Duke': contrasting views of the dukes of Ormonde in Irish royalist tradition', in Barnard and Fenlon (eds), *The dukes of Ormonde*, p. 190.

49. J. Anderson, *A genealogical history of the house of Yvery*, 2 vols (London, 1742), ii, pp. 428–9.

50. Abp. G. Stone to E. Weston, 25 April 1748, 29 June 1748, PRONI, T 3019/1012, 1063; Harrington to Bedford, 13 March 1749[50], ibid., T 3019/1511; S. Benedetti, *The Milltowns: a family reunion* (Dublin, 1997), pp. 1–5.

51. P. Kelly (ed.), 'The improvement of Ireland', *Analecta Hibernica*, 35 (1992), pp. 83–4.

52. W. Whitshed to Lord Sunderland, 17 Nov. 1714, 16 Dec. 1714, BL, Add. Ms. 61,639, ff. 62v, 66.

53. G. Keating, *The general history of Ireland*, trans. D. O'Connor (London, 1726), appendix, p. [7]; MacGeoghegan, *Histoire d'Irlande*, ii, pp. 317–19.

54. T.C. Barnard, 'Introduction' and 'Aristocratic values in the careers of the dukes of Ormonde', in Barnard and Fenlon (eds), *The dukes of Ormonde*, pp. 1–53, 161–75; J. Dewald, *The European nobility, 1400–1800* (Cambridge, 1996); K. B. Neuschel, *Word of honor: interpreting noble culture in sixteenth-century France* (Ithaca, NY, 1989); E. Schalk, *From valor to pedigree: ideas of nobility in France in the sixteenth and seventeenth centuries* (Princeton, 1986); H.M. Scott (ed.), *The European nobilities in the seventeenth and eighteenth centuries*, 2 vols (London, 1995).

55. T.C. Barnard, 'Crises of identity among Irish Protestants, 1641–1685', *P & P*, 127 (1990), pp. 39–83, reprinted in T. Barnard, *Irish Protestant ascents and descents* (Dublin, 2003); T. Barnard, '1641: a bibliographical essay', in B. MacCuarta (ed.), *Ulster 1641: aspects of the rising* (Belfast, 1993), pp. 173–86; T.C. Barnard, 'Lawyers and the law in later seventeenth century Ireland', *IHS*, 28 (1993), pp. 256–82.

56. Bp. J. Evans of Meath to Palmerston, 11 May 1723, Southampton UL, Broadlands Mss, BR, 4B, 222/2.

57. W. Flower to Palmerston, 29 July 1724, ibid., BR, 4B, 222/6.

58. Payments in England and Ireland for patents, ibid., BR, 4B, 223, 224; Palmerston's narrative of the case of the fees, 1723–24, ibid., BR, 4B, 227; Palmerston to D. Reading, 14 and 19 Feb. 1722[3], 11 and 18 April 1723, 23 May 1723, ibid., BR, 2/4; Ld. Mountjoy to Palmerston, 11 May 1723, ibid., BR, 4/222/3; W. Hawkins to same, 19 May 1724, ibid., BR, 4/222/4.

59. [T. Prior], *A list of the absentees of Ireland* (Dublin, 1729), pp. 2, 5–6, 7.

60. D. T. Andrew, *Philanthropy and police: charity in eighteenth-century London* (Princeton, NJ, 1989), p. 65.

61. These two peers, alone of their order, had been active in relieving the poor of Dublin in 1740. D. Hunter, 'The Dublin audience for Handel and his works, 1741–42', n. 55, forthcoming.

62. Minute book of Mercer's Hospital, 1736–72, Mercer's Library, College of Surgeons, Dublin; minute books, 1731–33, 1733–41, 1741–46, 1758–61, RDS.

63. Grandison to Lord Newport, 2 Jan. 1733[4], Dromana, Co. Waterford, Villiers-Stuart Mss, T 3131/D/5/2; Castledurrow to Sir J. St Leger, 15 July 1738, NLI, Ms. 11,481.

64. W. Colles to F. Bindon, 13 Aug. 1749, NA, Prim Ms. 87.

65. J. Baumann to P. Whichcote, 18 July 1724; J. Kerr to same, 19 Feb. 1724[5], PRO, SP 63/385, 161–2; Lord Ranelagh to T. Coningsby, 27 Oct. 1690, 6 Jan. 1690[1], PRONI, D 638/6/2 and 8; H. Boyle to W. Congreve, 30 April 1691, NLI, Ms. 13,230; Ormonde to Lords Justice, 15 June 1706, ibid., Ms. 993/64; same to same, 9 April 1712, 29 Nov. 1712, 2 Jan. 1712[13], Bodleian, Ms. Eng. Hist. C. 41, pp. 291, 321–2, 339.

66. List of governors, 1679, Bodleian, Carte Ms. 53, f. 162; lists of governors, 1714, PRO, SP 63/371, 17–18, 65–6; H.S. Upton, 'A list of governors and deputy governors of counties in Ireland', *JRSAI*, 55 (1925), p. 36.

67. Lord Perceval to Abp. W. King, 16 Feb. 1719[20]; same to Lord Abercorn, 25 Feb. 1719[20]; Wharton to Perceval, 17 Feb. 1719[20], BL, Add. Ms. 47,029, ff. 14v,

19v–20; F. G. James, 'The Irish lobby in the early eighteenth century', *EHR*, 81 (1966), pp. 544–57; F. G. James, 'The active Irish peers in the early eighteenth century', *Journal of British Studies*, 18/2 (1979), pp. 57–8.

68. Anderson, *A genealogical history of the house of Yvery*, ii, pp. 428–9.

69. Lord Clarendon to Bp. W. Smythe, 16 Nov. 1686, NLI, PC 436/14.

70. Licence for Cork and Burlington, 18 July 1671, ibid., de Vesci Mss, H/8; Ormonde to Lords Justice, 12 Dec. 1706, ibid., Ms 993, p. 164.

71. A. Spurrett to Sir R. Cox, 23 March 1703[4], Chatsworth, Spurrett Letter Book, 1703–4.

72. For Carrickfergus, W. Sacheverell, *An account of the Isle of Man* (London, 1702), p. 124.

73. S. J. Carleton, *Heads and hearths: the hearth money rolls and poll tax returns for County Antrim, 1660–69* (Belfast, 1991), pp. 37, 51, 92, 139, 142, 163. For building activities and circumstances of individuals: R. Loeber, 'Irish country houses and castles in the late Caroline period: an unremembered past recaptured', *Quarterly Bulletin of the Irish Georgian Society*, 16 (1973), p. 35; R. Loeber, *Biographical Dictionary of Architects in Ireland, 1660–1720* (London, 1981), p. 61; Ohlmeyer, *Antrim*; M. Beckett, *Sir George Rawdon* (Belfast, 1935), pp. 163–4.

74. E. MacLysaght (ed.), *Seventeenth-century hearth money rolls with full transcript for County Sligo* (Dublin, 1967), pp. 30, 78. For Collooney and Parke, A. Clarke, *Prelude to restoration in Ireland* (Cambridge, 1999), pp. 224–5, 226–7.

75. S. Pugsley, 'Landed society and the emergence of the country house in Tudor and early Stuart Devon', in T. Gray, M. Rowe and A. Erskine (eds), *Tudor and Stuart Devon: the common estate and government. Essays presented to Joyce Youings* (Exeter, 1992), pp. 96–7; G. Tyack, *Warwickshire country houses in the age of classicism, 1650–1800*, Warwickshire Local History Society, occasional paper, 3 (1980), pp. 3–4, 72, n.3.

76. N. Cooper, *Houses of the gentry* (New Haven and London, 1999), p. 6.

77. T. Laffan, *Tipperary's families: being the hearth money records for 1665–6–7* (Dublin, 1911), p. 70; C. McNeill, 'Hearth money rolls of County Louth', *County Louth Archaeological Journal*, vi (1925–28), p. 183.

78. Census of Elphin, 1749, NA, M. 2466, ff. 1, 337.

79. L. Price, 'The hearth money roll for County Wicklow', *JRSAI*, 61 (1931), pp. 167, 168, 169, 173, 175, 176.

80. G. S. Cary, (ed.), 'Hearth money roll for Co. Dublin, 1664', *Journal of the County Kildare Archaeological Society*, 10 (1922–26), pp. 245–58; 11 (1930–33), pp. 386–466.

81. Inventory of Cork House, 16 Nov. 1645, Chatsworth, Lismore Ms. 28/4; T. Barnard, 'Land and the limits of loyalty: the second earl of Cork and first earl of Burlington (1612–98)', in T. Barnard and J. Clark (eds), *Lord Burlington: architecture, art and life* (London, 1995), p. 175, and sources cited at n. 29.

82. Lord Conway to Lord Finch, 7 Sept. 1678; 5 Oct. 1678, Leicestershire CRO, DG 7/box 4965, Ire. 13; M. H. Nicolson (ed.), *Conway letters* (London, 1930), pp. 202–3, 214, 275.

83. N. T. Burke, 'An early modern Dublin suburb: the estate of Francis Aungier, earl of Longford', *Irish Geography*, vi (1972); 'Rental of langable rents, city of Dublin, 1665', in *The Fifty-Seventh Report of the Deputy Keeper of the Public Records . . . in Ireland* (Dublin, 1936), pp. 528–63.

84. V. Smith to Sir R. Southwell, 21 Sept. 1698, V & A, Ormonde Ms. 4/27/2; Barnard, 'Introduction', in Barnard and Fenlon (eds), *Dukes of Ormonde*, pp. 41–2.

85. *Faulkner's Dublin Journal*, no. 217, 27–30 May 1727, and above p. 26.

86. Anglesey to Orrery, 29 Oct. 1661, 8 March 1661[2], 24 June 1662, Petworth, Orrery Mss, general series, 22; St J. Brodrick to same, 13 July 1669, ibid., general series, 28; Conway to Finch, 30 Nov. 1674, Leicestershire CRO, DG 7/box 4965, Ire. 13; Barnard, 'Land and the limits of loyalty', pp. 193–5; Barnard, 'Introduction', in Barnard and Fenlon (eds), *Dukes of Ormonde*, pp. 23–4; H. M. Colvin, *Biographical dictionary of British architects*, 3rd edn (New Haven and London, 1995), pp. 521–2; C. Knight, 'The Irish in London: post-Restoration suburban houses', *Irish Architectural and Decorative Studies*, 1 (1998), pp. 60–83; Nicolson (ed.), *Conway letters*, pp. 233, 235, 260–1, 285, 291–2.

87. Account and letter book of H. Temple, 1st Viscount Palmerston from 1720, Southampton UL, BR, 2/4; accounts of Palmerston, 1725–56, ibid., BR, 2/6; will of Algernon, earl of Mountrath, 1744, Staffordshire CRO, D 1287/P/373; abstract of will of Diana, countess of Mountrath, 1746, ibid., P/416; part inventory, Mountrath's house, Grosvenor Square, London, 31 July 1766, ibid., P/57; HMC, *Egmont diary*, i, pp. vi, 1; Anderson, *A genealogical history of the house of Yvery*.

88. D. Dickson, 'Capital and country, 1600–1800', in A. Cosgrove, (ed.), *Dublin through the ages* (Dublin, 1988), p. 71.

89. Lease and inventory between R. Murray and Viscount Conyngham, 27 Oct. 1766, NLI, PC 346, box 1; D. Griffin, 'The building and furnishing of a Dublin town house in the 18th century', *Bulletin of the Irish Georgian Society*, 38 (1996–97), pp. 24–39.

90. M. Craig, *Dublin, 1660–1860: a social and architectural history* (Dublin and London, 1952), pp. 131–5; The Georgian Society, *Records of eighteenth-century domestic architecture and decoration in Ireland*, 5 vols (Dublin, 1910–13), i, pp. 14–18; iii, pp. 68–73; iv, pp. 23–32.

91. M. Craig, *The volunteer earl* (London, 1948); J. Kelly, 'A "genuine" Whig and patriot: Lord Charlemont's political career', in M. McCarthy (ed.), *Lord Charlemont and his circle* (Dublin, 2001), pp. 7–37; C. O'Connor, *The pleasing hours: the grand tour of James Caulfield, first earl of Charlemont (1728–1799)* (Cork, 1999).

92. Abp. W. King to Bp. J. Stearne, 16 Sept. 1714, 25 Jan. 1715[16], TCD, Ms. 2536, pp. 60, 180; M. Pilkington, *Poems on several occasions* (Dublin, 1730), pp. iii–iv.

93. GEC, *Complete peerage*, vii, pp. 218–45, 573–8; Delany, *Autobiography*, 1st series, ii, p. 371; Charles Fitzgerald, marquess of Kildare and 4th duke of Leinster, *The earls of Kildare and their ancestors: from 1057 to 1773*, 3rd edn (Dublin, 1858), pp. 276–95; W. Harris, *The history and antiquities of the city of Dublin* (Dublin, 1766), pp. 113–14; D. Griffin and C. Pegum, *Leinster House* (Dublin, 2000).

94. Hearth money roll for Co. Londonderry, 1663, NLI, Ms. 9584, pp. 182–8; Laffan, *Tipperary's families*, pp. 67–9; McNeill, 'Hearth money rolls of Co. Louth', pp. 84–7.

95. Barnard, 'Aristocratic values in the careers of the dukes of Ormonde', pp. 161–76.

96. [? H. Brooke], *Essay on the antient and modern state of Ireland* (Dublin, 1759), p. 81.

97. E. Magennis, *The Irish parliamentary system, 1740–1765* (Dublin, 2000), p. 129; E. P. McParland, 'The office of surveyor-general in Ireland in the eighteenth century', *Architectural History*, 38 (1995), p. 96.

98. W. Henry, *The beauty, deliverances, and security of the British constitution, set forth in a sermon preached in the cathedral church of London-Derry on the first day of August, 1746* (Dublin, 1746), p. 11.

99. A. de la Motraye, *The voyages and travels*, 3 vols (London, 1732), iii, p. 291.

3. *The Quality*

1. S. Povey to W. Smythe, 18 Dec. 1762, NLI, PC 448.

2. St G. Ashe to H. Dodwell, 18 Dec. 1684, Bodleian, Ms. Eng. Lett. C. 29, f. 2v; NLI, MS. 13,229, 6 July 1706; letter book of C. Williamson, Marsh's Library, Ms. Z4.5.16, p. 113; [R. Bulkeley], *The proposal for sending back the nobility and gentry of Ireland* (London, 1690), p. 10; *Faulkner's Dublin Journal*, 13–16 Feb. 1741[2]; J. Hewetson, *Memoirs of the house of Hewetson or Hewson of Ireland* (London, 1901), p. 115.

3. G. Keating, *The general history of Ireland*, trans. D. O'Connor (London, 1726), preface, p. ii.

4. T. Caulfield to K. O'Hara, 19 March 1702[3], NLI, Ms. 20,388; J. H. Gebbie, *An introduction to the Abercorn letters* (Omagh, 1972), p. 64.

5. [G. Hickes?], *The gentleman instructed*, 9th edn (London and Dublin, 1723), sig. [A4v], pp. 435, 443, 471.

6. Abp. H. Boulter to Devonshire, 28 April 1739, Chatsworth, Devonshire Letters, 1737–9, 242.2.

7. Helpful discussions of gentility include: J. P. Cooper; 'Ideas of gentility in early-modern England', in J. P. Cooper, *Land, men and beliefs: studies in early-modern history* (London, 1983), pp. 43–77; J. G. Jones, *Concepts of order and gentility in Wales, 1540–1640* (Llandysul, 1992); G. E. Mingay, *The gentry: the rise and fall of a ruling class* (London, 1976), pp. 1–37; A. Vickery, *The gentleman's daughter: women's lives in Georgian England* (London and New Haven, 1998), pp. 13–37.

8. James Kelly, *Gallows speeches from eighteenth-century Ireland* (Dublin, 2001), pp. 85, 126, 224.

9. Lord Perceval to P. Perceval, 2 Nov. 1721; P. Perceval to Lord Perceval, 14 Nov. 1721, BL, Add. Ms. 47,029, ff. 79, 87v.

10. W. Peard to F. Price, 15 April 1744, NLW, Puleston Ms. 3579E.

11. W. Crosbie to Sir M. Crosbie, 5 April 1745, 14 July 1752, NLI, Talbot–Crosbie Mss, folder 53.

12. R. Waring to S. Waring, 11 and 19 Oct. 1691; same to W. Waring, 23 April 1692, private collection, Co. Down; J. Bayly, 10 Jan. 1735[6], 2 Aug. 1737, 4 March 1739[40], Bayly letter book, private collection, Co. Kildare; M. Coghill to E. Southwell, 27 Sept. 1735, NLI, Ms. 875.

13. J. Ingram to W. Smythe, 6 Dec. 1740, NLI, PC 445.

14. M. Ledwidge to R. Smythe, 1 Sept. 1767, ibid., PC 446.

15. E. Spencer to A. Price, 27 Nov. 1749, NLW, Puleston Ms. 3580E; advertisement in Moore of Newport Pratt Mss, NLI, Ms. 5737; A. Caldwell to S. Bagshawe, 14 March 1752, JRL, B 2/3/249; *Faulkner's Dublin Journal*, 8–11 March 1726[7].

16. M. Smythe to W. Smythe, 21 July 1728, 2 Aug. 1728, 30 Oct. 1731, 11 March 1731[2], NLI, PC 448.

17. P. Delany, *Sixteen discourses upon doctrines and duties* (London, 1754) p. 313. See, too, the treatise of Bishop W. King, *c.* 1696, TCD, Ms. 1042, pp. 42–4.

18. Sir R. Southwell to W. Perceval, 26 Nov. 1699, PRONI, D 906/57.

19. C. Ellison to H. Ellison, 9 Feb. 1729[30], Tyne and Wear Archives, acc. 3419, Ellison Mss, bundle A.18/9.

20. M. Fitzgerald to D. Crosbie, 4 July 1709, TCD, Ms. 3821/117.

21. Crown entry books, City of Dublin, 1748–9, s.d. 5 April 1749, NA. The volume had been stolen from the Dublin house of the squire of Gloster, Trevor Lloyd.

22. [Hickes?], *The gentleman instructed*, 9th edn.

23. T. F. MacCarthy, 'Ulster's Office 1552–1800', unpublished MA thesis, Queen's University Belfast (1983), ch. 5; T. MacCarthy, 'The MacCarthy Mór', *Ulster's Office, 1552–1800* (Little Rock, 1996); G. Holmes, 'Gregory King and the social structure of pre-industrial England', *TRHS*, 5th series, 27 (1977), pp. 41–68; G. D. Squibb, *Precedence in England and Wales* (Oxford, 1981).

24. Hume's account, NLI, Ms. 6054, p. 8; *Retrospections of Dorothea Herbert, 1770–1806* (Dublin, 1988), pp. 186–8.

25. Bills of executors of Bp. Simon Digby, 1720, NLI, French of Monivea papers, envelope 26; L. Parsons to J. Acton, [1740?], Birr Castle, Co. Offaly, Parsons Mss, B/4/25; bill of 11 Aug. 1756, Brabazon Mss, box I, private collection, London; executors' accounts for Viscount Doneraile, 1727, NLI, Ms. 34,112/14; 'Doneraile papers', *Analecta Hibernica*, 15 (Dublin, 1944), pp. 350–1.

26. A. Crossly, 'A collection of arms', Dublin Public Library, Gilbert Ms. 143, ff. 408–8v; list of 'occurrences', BL, Add. Ms. 4815, f. 54; memorial of A. Crossly's will, RD, memorial 46/483/30351; accounts in NA, Chancery salvage, unidentified material, box 31; *An elegy on the much lamented death of Mr Aaron Crossly, herald-painter of Dublin* (Dublin, 1725); P. B. Eustace (ed.), *Registry of Deeds, Dublin, abstracts of wills* (Dublin, 1956), pp. 142–3; 'Some funeral entries of Ireland', *Journal of the Association for the Preservation of the Memorials of the Dead, Ireland*, 8 (1910), p. [220].

27. A. Crossly, *The peerage of Ireland* (Dublin, 1725); list of Guild of St Luke, Dublin, s.d. 8 Nov. 1676, 28 Aug. 1689, 18 Oct. 1690, NLI, Ms. 12,122; proposals of A. Crossly, BL, Add. Ms. 4815, ff. 42, 48.

28. O. Gallagher to O. St George, 22 May 1725, 24 July 1725, PRO, C 110/46, 366, 377; G. Dillon to 'cousin', 30 March 1745, NLI, Ms. 35,746/2; K. Perceval to Lord Perceval, 8 Sept. 1747, BL, Add. Ms. 47,000B, f. 42v; Gebbie (ed.), *Abercorn letters*, pp. 289, 290; J. Lodge, *The peerage of Ireland*, 4 vols (London,1754), i, p. vi.

29. Sir R. Southwell to G. King, 2 Sept. 1689; W. Hawkins to R. Tisdall, 14 May 1698, BL, Add. Ms. 47,151, ff. 231, 258; L. Parsons to J. Acton, [1740?], Birr Castle, Co. Offaly, Parsons Mss. B/4/25.

30. MacCarthy, 'Ulster's Office', pp. 277–80; vestry book, St Mary's, Dublin, 1699–1739, RCB, P. 277/7.1, pp. 11, [416]; minute book, 1731–33, s.d. 25 Nov. 1731, 9 Nov. 1732; minute book, 1733–41, s.d. 22 Nov. 1733, 14 Nov. 1734, 13 Nov. 1735, 11 Nov. 1736, RDS; W. Hawkins to R. Wilmot, 7 May 1745, PRONI, T 3019/628.

31. List of Guild of St Luke, Dublin, s.d. 8 Nov. 1676, 28 Aug. 1689, 18 Oct. 1690, NLI, Ms. 12,122.

32. Note by A. Crossly, 4 Sept. 1721, BL, Add. Ms. 4815, f. 80; memorial of A. Crossly's will, RD, memorial 46/483/30351; *An elegy on the much lamented death of Mr Aaron Crossly, herald-painter of Dublin*; Eustace (ed.), *Registry of Deeds, abstracts of wills*, pp. 142–3; list of Guild of St Luke, Dublin, s.d. 8 Nov. 1676, 28 Aug. 1689, 18 Oct. 1690, NLI, Ms. 12,122.

33. Proposal of Crossly, BL, Add. Ms. 4815, f. 42v.

34. J. F. Bigger, 'The tombs of the Chichesters', *Journal of the Irish Memorials Association*, 11 (1921–25), pp. 113–21; N. Canny, *The upstart earl: a study of the social and mental world of Richard Boyle, first earl of Cork, 1566–1643* (Cambridge, 1982), pp. 9–76; R. Gillespie, 'Irish funeral monuments and social change, 1500–1700', in B. P. Kennedy and R. Gillespie (eds), *Ireland: art into history* (Dublin, 1994), pp. 155–67; A. Harris, 'The funerary monuments of Richard Boyle, earl of Cork', *Church Monuments*, 13 (1998), pp. 70–86; F. McCormick, 'The symbols of death and the tomb of John Foster in Tydavnet, Co. Monaghan', *Clogher Record*, 11 (1983), pp. 273–86.

35. Jones, *Concepts of order and gentility in Wales*, pp. 69–71.

36. K. Simms, 'Charles Lynegar, the O Luinin family and the study of Seanchas', in T. Barnard, D. Ó Cróinín and K. Simms (eds), *'A miracle of learning': studies in manuscripts and Irish learning* (Aldershot, 1998), p. 278, fn. 5; T. Barnard and J. Fenlon (eds), *The Dukes of Ormonde, 1610–1745* (Woodbridge, 2000), p. 7, plate 16; C. Lynegar, genealogy of Brodrick, Mss of Viscount Midleton (I am grateful to Lord Midleton for information about this document); R. Caulfield (ed.), *Autobiography of the Rt. Hon. Sir Richard Cox, Bart.* (London, 1860); D. O'Sullivan, 'A courtly poem for Sir Richard Cox', *Éigse*, 4 (1943–44), pp. 284–7.

37. J. F. Bigger and H. Hughes, 'Armorial sculptured stones of the County Antrim', *Ulster Journal of Archaeology*, 6 (1900), pp. 39–53, 90–104, 162–72, 231–44; 7 (1901), pp. 58–61, 142–57; 8 (1902), pp. 90–3; 9 (1903), pp. 93–6, 131–7; J. F. Bigger, 'Some notes on the architectural and monumental remains of the old abbey church of Bangor, in the county of Down', ibid., 7 (1901), pp. 18–36; F. McCormick, 'A group of eighteenth-century Clogher headstones', *Clogher Record*, 9 (1976), pp. 6–8; F. McCormick, 'A group of tradesmen's headstones', ibid., 10 (1979), pp. 14–19.

38. P. Jenkins, *The making of a ruling class: the Glamorgan gentry 1640–1790* (Cambridge, 1983), p. 199.

39. J. O. Bartley, *Teague, Shenkin and Sawney* (Cork, 1954), pp. 62–3; P. R. Roberts, 'The landed gentry in Merioneth, 1660–1832, with special reference to the estates of Hengwrt, Nannau, Rug and Ynysymaengwyn', unpublished MA thesis, University of Wales (1963), pp. 5–6.

40. C. Falvey to M. Falvey, 3 Jan. 1739[40], Chatsworth, Devonshire Letters, 1740–43, 270.0.

41. N. Ó Muraíle, *The celebrated antiquary, Dubhaltach Mac Fhirbhisigh (c. 1600–1671); his lineage, life and learning* (Maynooth, 1996); R. E. Ward, J. F. Wrynn and C. C. Ward (eds), *Letters of Charles O'Conor of Belanagare* (Washington, DC, 1988), pp. 149, 154, 172–3, 351–2, 359–60, 389, 417, 421, 435–6, 488, 495–6.

42. Peter Francis, *Irish Delftware: an illustrated history* (London, 2000), pp. 65, 100–4, 158–9; colour plate 7; black and white plates 160–1; D.S. Howard, 'Chinese armorial porcelain for Ireland', *Bulletin of the Irish Georgian Society*, 29 (1986), pp. 3–24.

43. By Charles Linegar, now in Kilkenny Castle, partly reproduced in Barnard and Fenlon (eds), *Dukes of Ormonde*, plate 16.

44. Relation of services of Capt. G. Lane, NLI, Ms. 8646/2; W. Domville to W. Legge, [before 1665], Staffordshire CRO, D(W) 1778/V/1148.

45. A. Rochfort to Devonshire, [*c.* 20 May 1757], Chatsworth, Devonshire Letters, May–June 1757, 452.3; R. R. Forlong, *Notes on the history of the family of Rochefort* (Oxford, 1890), pp. 16–17, 19, 30–1.

46. Petition of Robert May to W. Conolly [*c.* 1710], IAA, Castletown deposit, box 55.

47. Reminiscences of M. Jellett, NLI, Ms. 19,745, p. 2.

48. W. Conner to Sir A. Abdy, 5 July 1757, Chatsworth, Conner letter book, 1749–58.

49. H. F. Morris, 'The "principal inhabitants" of County Waterford in 1746', in W. Nolan and T. P. Power (eds), *Waterford: history and society* (Dublin, 1992), pp. 309–10.

50. H. J. Butler and H. E. Butler (eds), *The Black Book of Edgeworthstown and other Edgeworth memories, 1585–1817* (London, 1927), pp. 7–10.

51. Black Book of Edgeworthstown, NLI, Ms. 7361, p. 171. The style of Edgeworth's life is deduced from his account books, ibid., Mss 1507–36.

52. J. Hoppit, 'Attitudes to credit in Britain, 1680–1790', *HJ*, 33 (1990), pp. 305–22; C. Muldrew, 'Interpreting the market: the ethics of credit and community relations in early modern England', *Social History*, 18 (1993), pp. 163–83; S. Shapin, *A social history of truth* (Chicago, 1994).

53. R. Edgeworth, account books, NLI, Mss 1520, p. 154; 1521, pp. 31, 181; 1522, pp. 150, 193, 205; 1524, pp. 152, 249.

54. Black Book of Edgeworth, NLI, Ms. 7361, pp. 185–6; T. Barnard, 'Integration or separation? Hospitality and display in Protestant Ireland, *c.* 1660–1800', in L. Brockliss and D. Eastwood (eds), *A Union of Multiple Identities: the British Isles, c. 1750–1850* (Manchester, 1997), p. 137.

55. Black Book of Edgeworthstown, NLI, Ms. 7361, pp. 172–3.

56. R. Edgeworth, account book, NLI, Ms. 1515, pp. 121, 186, 187.

57. Crown entry books, City of Dublin, 1746–47, s.d. 1 Dec. 1746, 14 Feb. 1746[7], NA.

58. J. Loveday, *Diary of a tour in 1732 through parts of England, Wales, Ireland and Scotland* (Edinburgh, 1890), p. 49.

59. H. & J. Ware, account book, TCD, Ms. 10,528, f. 12v.

60. Ware family history, NLI, Ms. 2563; J. Piers, *Ad majorem Dei gloriam beataeque Virginis Mariae brevis* (Bordeaux, 1631); N. Canny, *Making Ireland British, 1580–1650* (Oxford, 2001), pp. 85–9.

61. H. & J. Ware account book, TCD, Ms. 10,528, ff. 34–5; Ware family papers, NLI, Ms. 116; catalogue of the Revd H. Ware's library, 1766, ibid., Ms. 9885.

62. Will of Sir H. Piers of Tristernagh, 29 July 1691, NLI, Ainsworth report, no. 94, p. 886.

63. T. Cooper, letter of attorney to W. Waring, 27 Sept. 1659, private collection, Co. Down; T. C. Barnard, 'What became of Waring? The making of an Ulster squire' in T. Barnard, *Irish protestant ascents and descents: selected essays* (Dublin, 2003).

64. *Al. Dubl.*, pp. 859, 860.

65. Will of J. Waring, 24 Dec. 1727, PRO, PROB, 11/618, sig. 312; case papers, 12 May 1740, ibid., C 109/230/34.

66. R. Waring to S. Waring, 11 Oct. 1691, Waring Mss, private collection, Co. Down.

67. Memorandum of W. Waring, 22 April 1701, ibid.; grant of crest, 9 June 1701, GO, Dublin, Ms. 103, p. 2.

68. W. Waring to S. Waring, 2 April 1691, 14 Nov. 1696, Waring Mss, private collection, Co. Down.

69. P. Browne, *A letter in answer to a book entituled, 'Christianity not mysterious'* (London, 1697); P. Browne, *Sermons on various subjects*, 2 vols (London, 1749).

70. A. Waring to S. Waring, 1 Oct. 1698; S. Waring to T. Waring, after 1 Oct. 1698; W. Waring to T. Waring, 3 April 1725; T. Waring to W. Waring, 16 April 1725, Waring Mss, private collection, Co. Down.

71. R. Richey, 'Landed society in mid-eighteenth-century County Down', unpublished Ph.D. thesis, Queen's University Belfast (2000), pp. 25–6.

72. [Hickes?], *The gentleman instructed*, p. 8.

73. Dublin Public Library, Robinson Ms. 34, p. 181; NLI, Ms. 5169.

74. Barnard, 'What became of Waring?'

75. G. Macartney to H. Jervis, 18 Dec. 1680, Macartney letter book, formerly in Linen Hall Library, Belfast, now in PRONI; J. Agnew, *Belfast merchant families in the seventeenth century* (Dublin, 1996), p. 54.

76. D. Mussenden to H. Mussenden, 21 May 1737, 31 Dec. 1740, 6 [?] 1742, 3 Jan. 1749[50], 9 Dec.1754, Suffolk CRO, Ipswich, de Mussenden Leathes Mss, HA 403/1/11, 15, 18, 20, 22, 24.

77. Indenture of 2 March 1732[3], ibid., HA 403/1/11, 38; draft will of D. Mussenden, 18 June 1756, PRONI, D 354/166A; R. S. and J. Holmes to D. Mussenden, 30 July 1757, ibid., D 354/336; leases of 1759, ibid., D 354/178, 179; W. Harris, *The antient and present state of the county of Down* (Dublin, 1744), p. 97.

78. Lists of Ulster dissenters and churchmen, Lambeth Palace Library, London, Ms. 1742, ff. 49–56; RIA, Ms. 24 K 19; Agnew, *Belfast merchant families*, pp. 91–104; T. C. Barnard, 'The government and Irish dissent', in K. Herlihy (ed.), *The politics of Irish dissent, 1650–1800* (Dublin, 1997) pp. 9–27; J. R. Hill, 'Dublin corporation, Protestant dissent and politics, 1660–1800', ibid., pp. 28–39; D. W. Hayton, 'Exclusion, conformity and parliamentary representation: the impact of the sacramental test on Irish dissenting politics', ibid., pp. 52–73.

79. S. Burdy, *The life of Philip Skelton*, ed. N. Moore (Oxford, 1914), pp. 17, 231.

80. G. E. Howard, *A compendious treatise of the rules and practice of the pleas side of the exchequer in Ireland*, 2 vols (Dublin, 1759), i, pp. iii–xx.

81. *An alphabetical list of such barristers, attorneys and solicitors, as have taken the oath* (Dublin, 1735).

82. Sir R. Cox, *A charge delivered to the grand-jury . . . for the County of Cork, at Bandon-Bridge, on the Twelfth of July, 1748* (Dublin, 1748), p. 22; G. E. Howard, *A treatise on the rules and practice of the equity side of the exchequer in Ireland*, 2 vols (Dublin, 1760), i, p. xxxvi.

83. Certificate of J. Foster and C. Campbell for Lt. Alex McCulloch, *c.* 1690, Scottish Register Office, Edinburgh, Broughton and Cally Mss, GD 10/498.

84. *Subscribers to the Bank plac'd according to their order and quality* (Dublin, 1721); *A letter to the K——at Arms. From a pretended esquire, one of the subscribers to the Bank* (Dublin, [?1721]).

85. D. M. Beaumont, 'The gentry of the King's and Queen's Counties: Protestant landed society, 1690–1760', unpublished Ph.D. thesis, TCD, 2 vols. (1999), i, pp. 25–33; M. Brennan, 'The changing composition of Kilkenny landowners,

1641–1700', in W. Nolan and K. Whelan (eds), *Kilkenny: history and society* (Dublin, 1990); pp. 161–95; D. Dickson, 'Property and social structure in eighteenth-century south Munster', in L. M. Cullen and F. Furet (eds), *Irlande et France: XVIIIe–XXe siècles: pour une histoire comparée* (Paris, 1980), pp. 129–31; D. Gahan, 'The estate system of County Wexford', in K. Whelan and W. Nolan (eds), *Wexford: history and society* (Dublin, 1987), pp. 210–14; D. Gahan, 'Religion and land tenure in eighteenth-century Ireland: tenancy in the south-east', in R. V. Comerford, M. Cullen, J. R. Hill and C. Lennon (eds), *Religion, conflict and coexistence in Ireland* (Dublin, 1990), pp. 99–114; N. Garnham, 'Local élite creation in early Hanoverian Ireland: the case of the county grand jury', *HJ*, 42 (1999), pp. 623–42; R. Richey, 'County Down', pp. 4, 8.

86. Address of grand jury, justices of the peace and gentlemen, Co. Cavan, 6 Oct. 1724, PRO, SP 63/384, 191; 'Subscriptions towards an exact survey and general map of the County of Meath', *c.* 1750, RCB, D 7/12/1.4; J. H. Andrews, *Shapes of Ireland: maps and their makers, 1564–1839* (Dublin, 1997), pp. 204, 232.

87. J. H. Andrews, 'Charles Vallancey and the map of Ireland', *Geographical Journal*, 132 (1966), pp. 50–9; R. Cox, 'Regnum Corcagiense: or a description of the kingdom of Cork', ed. R. Day, *JCHAS*, 2nd series, 8 (1902), pp. 89–97; D. Dickson, 'A description of County Cork, *c.* 1741', *JCHAS*, 76 (1971), pp. 152–5; S. P. Johnson (ed.), 'On a manuscript description of the city and county of Cork, *cir.* 1685, written by Sir Richard Cox', *JRSAI*, 32 (1902), p. 363; T. Reeves-Smyth, 'Demesnes', in F. H. A. Aalen, K. Whelan and M. Stout (eds), *Atlas of the Irish rural landscape* (Cork, 1997), p. 202.

88. I am grateful to Neal Garnham for these figures of grand jurors, derived from Co. Antrim crown presentment books, 1711–21, 1727–67, PRONI, ANT 4/1/1, 4/1/3; Co. Armagh indictment books, 1735–97, Armagh Public Library; County Donegal grand jury presentments, 1753–62, Donegal County Library, Lifford; Co. Louth presentment book, 1711–33, NLI, Ms. 11,949.

89. J. C. Lyons, *The grand juries of the county of Westmeath from the year 1727 to the year 1853* (Ledenstown, 1853).

90. Commissions of the peace, 1720, NA, M. 2537; 1760, Dublin Public Library, Robinson Mss, Gilbert Ms. 34, 181; 1776–77, NLI, Ms. 5169; Cork commission, BL, Add. Ms. 46,966, ff. 161–2; Dublin commission, NLI, D 22,712; Mayo commissions, Brabazon Mss, private collection, London; Queen's County commission, NLI, D 20,230; Tyrone commission, PRONI, D 1449/10/10; D. M. Beaumont, 'Local office-holding and the gentry of the Queen's County, *c.* 1660–1750', in P.G. Lane and W. Nolan (eds), *Laois: history and society* (Dublin, 1999), p. 438.

91. Hayton, 'Exclusion, conformity and parliamentary representation', pp. 52–73.

92. N. Alldridge, 'Loyalty and identity in Chester parishes, 1540–1840', in S. J. Wright (ed.), *Parish, church and people: local studies in lay religion, 1350–1750* (London, 1988), pp. 89–109; H. R. French, '"Ingenious and learned gentlemen" – social perceptions and self-fashioning among parish elites in Essex, 1680–1740', *Social History*, 25 (2000), pp. 44–66; M. Goldie, 'The unacknowledged republic: office-holding in early modern England', in T. Harris (ed.), *The politics of the excluded, c. 1500–1800* (Basingstoke, 2001), pp. 153–94; J. R. Kent, 'The rural "middling sort" in early modern England, *circa* 1640–1740: some economic, political and socio-cultural characteristics', *Rural History*, 10 (1999), pp. 19–54; P. Laslett, *The world we have lost* (London, 1965), pp. 56–73; D. B. and A. H.

Rutman, *A place in time: Middlesex, County Virginia, 1650–1750* (New York and London, 1984), pp. 143–62.

93. Lists in NA, M. 2537, p. 204; Headford Mss, NLI, Ms. 25,431.

94. R. Cox to E. Southwell, 18 July 1706, 13 Sept. 1706, 29 Oct. 1706, BL, Add. Ms. 38,154, ff. 49, 62, 92.

95. Sir R. Cox to Archdeacon J. Pomeroy, 5 March 1719[20], PRONI, T 2954/2/5; Barnard, 'Cork settlers', p. 343; Caulfield (ed.), *Autobiography of the Rt. Hon. Sir Richard Cox, Bart.*; Dickson, 'Economic history of the Cork region', i, p. 98.

96. A. P. W. Malcomson, 'Report on the Headford papers', NLI special list 238; T. Taylor, account book, NLI, Ms. 25,386; Royal Irish Academy, *Historic Towns Atlas*, i (Dublin, 1996), 'Kells', pp. 4, 7; GEC, *Complete peerage*, vi, pp. 426–7.

97. Bp. R. Howard to H. Howard, 6 Oct. 1730; H. Howard to Bp. R. Howard, 21 Nov. 1730, NLI, PC 227.

98. K. Herlihy, 'The Irish Baptists, 1650–1780', unpublished Ph.D. thesis, TCD (1992), p. 167.

99. V. Treadwell, *Buckingham and Ireland, 1616–1628* (Dublin, 1998), pp. 104–6.

100. J. Alexander to Sir E. Massie, [c. 1661], Gloucestershire CRO, D. 678, Barwick Mss, 5.

101. W.A. Shaw, *The knights of England*, 2 vols (London, 1906), ii, *passim*.

102. Shannon to Devonshire, 12 Feb. 1757, PRONI, D 2707/A1/5/18; H. Walpole to J. Belcher, 4 Aug. 1720, Lincolnshire CRO, ASW 1/B/43; Clanricarde to Hartington, 29 June 1755, Chatsworth, Devonshire Letters, May–July 1755, 415.0.

103. L. L. Peck, 'Beyond the Pale: John Cusacke and the language of absolutism in early Stuart Britain', *HJ*, 41 (1998), p. 141; P. Galloway, *The most illustrious order: the order of St Patrick and its knights* (London, 1999), pp. 11–13.

104. RD, 46/274/28640; 80/147/55277; 105/471/74354; Denbighshire CRO, DD/BK/1, 24; R. McCutcheon, 'Pue's occurrences, 1744–9', *The Irish Genealogist*, 9 (1996), p. 332.

105. S. Pender (ed.), *A 'Census' of Ireland, c. 1659* (Dublin, 1939).

106. Ibid. pp. 149–158; E. P. Shirley, *The history of the county of Monaghan* (London, 1879), pp. 550–1.

107. Dolan, History of County Fermanagh, c. 1719, NLI, Ms. 2085; barony lists of proprietors, Co. Tipperary, c. 1753, PRONI, D1618/18/4.

108. J. C. Walton (ed.), 'Subsidy roll of County Waterford, 1662', *Analecta Hibernica*, 30 (1982), pp. 50–92; Pender (ed.), *A 'Census'*, pp. 610–11.

109. Pender (ed.), *A 'Census'*, pp. 163–88.

110. For descriptions of Clare: J. Frost, *The history and topography of County Clare* (Dublin, 1893); E. MacLysaght, *A short study of a transplanted family in the seventeenth century* (Dublin, 1935); B. Ó Dálaigh (ed.), *The strangers [sic] gaze: travels in County Clare, 1534–1950* (Ennis, 1998), pp. 1–103; C. O'Murchadha, 'Seventeenth-century County Clare: a brief survey', *The Other Clare*, 7 (1983), p. 33.

111. J. Davies, *A discoverie of the true causes why Ireland was never entirely subdued* (London, 1612), p. 171.

112. *The life and errors of John Dunton*, 2 vols (London, 1818), ii, p. 336.

113. BL, Harleian Ms. 3292, f. 30; T. Rundle, *A sermon preach'd . . . the 23d of October 1735*, p. 26; T. C. Barnard, 'The uses of 23 October 1641 and Irish Protestant celebrations', *EHR*, cvi (1991), pp. 898–903.

114. An influential but flawed discussion is in K. Whelan, 'An underground gentry? Catholic middlemen in eighteenth-century Ireland', *Eighteenth-Century Ireland*, 10 (1995), pp. 9–66, reprinted in Whelan, *The tree of liberty: radicalism, Catholicism and the construction of Irish identity 1760–1830* (Cork, 1996), pp. 3–58. For some alternative suggestions: T. C. Barnard, 'The gentrification of eighteenth-century Ireland', *Eighteenth-Century Ireland*, 12 (1997), pp. 137–55.

115. J. G. Barry (ed.), '"The Groans of Ireland"', *The Irish Sword*, 2 (1954–56), p. 134; P. H. Kelly (ed.), 'The improvement of Ireland', *Analecta Hibernica*, 35 (1992), pp. 83–4.

116. Jones, *Concepts of order and gentility in Wales*, p. 126; Roberts, 'The landed gentry in Merioneth', pp. 5–6.

117. Property owners in County Wexford, 1686, Bodleian, Clarendon Ms. 88, ff. 260–5.

118. Roberts, 'The landed gentry in Merioneth', pp. 17–18.

119. 10 William III, c. 8, *Statutes*, iii, pp. 487–96. Cf. A.B., *A letter to the K—— at Arms. From a reputed esquire*. In mid-eighteenth-century England it was reckoned that £40 p.a. enabled the possessor to live creditably. P. Langford, *A polite and commercial people* (Oxford, 1992), pp. 62–3.

120. W. Perceval to A. Charlet, 29 April 1719, Bodleian, Ballard Ms. 36, ff. 109–9v; M. Smythe to W. Smythe, 15 Feb. 1733[4], NLI, PC 448; T. Barnard, 'Integration or separation?', p. 136.

121. C. Price to Mrs Ward, 17 Jan. 1745[6], PRONI, D 2092/1/7, 106.

122. Sir R. Cox to Archdeacon J. Pomeroy, 5 March 1719[20], ibid., T. 2954/2/5.

123. 'Persons who have in 1686 over £2,000 p.a.', Petty Papers, B. 20, now in BL.

124. For comparative figures: B. D. Henning, *The House of Commons, 1660–1690*, 3 vols (London,1983), i, pp. 13–15; Holmes, 'Gregory King and the social structure of pre-industrial England', pp. 54–5, 66–7.

125. List of those who fled from Ireland, 1688, TCD, Ms. 847.

126. D. A. Cronin, *A Galway gentleman in the age of improvement: Robert French of Monivea, 1716–79* (Dublin, 1995), pp. 16–24; L. M. Cullen, 'Economic development, 1691–1750', in T. W. Moody and W. E. Vaughan (eds), *A new history of Ireland. IV Eighteenth-century Ireland, 1691–1800* (Oxford, 1986), pp. 147–50; D. Dickson, 'An economic history of the Cork region', i, pp. 111–13; G. Kirkham, '"No more to be got from the cat but the skin": management, landholding and economic change in the Murray of Broughton estate, 1670–1755', in W. Nolan, L. Ronanyne and M. Dunlevy (eds), *Donegal: history and society* (Dublin, 1995), pp. 357–80; T. P. Power, *Land, politics and society in eighteenth-century Tipperary* (Oxford, 1993) p. 90; L. Proudfoot, 'Landownership and improvement, *ca.* 1700 to 1845', in L. Proudfoot (ed.), *Down: history and society* (Dublin, 1997), pp. 203–38; P. Roebuck, 'Rent movement, proprietorial incomes and agricultural development, 1730–1830', in P. Roebuck (ed.), *Plantation to partition* (Belfast, 1981), pp. 82–101; P. Roebuck, 'Landlord indebtedness in the seventeenth and eighteenth centuries', in J. M. Goldstrom and L. A. Clarkson (eds), *Irish population, economy and society* (Oxford, 1981), pp. 138–53.

127. List of MPs, 1713, BL, Add. Ms. 61,637A.

128. W. Perceval to A. Charlet, 29 April 1719, Bodleian, Ballard Ms. 36, f. 109v.

129. Rental of Blennerhasset, Leighton Hall Ms. 823, box 14, Shropshire CRO, Shrewsbury; F. Lovell to Bp. W. King, 18 March 1692[3], TCD, Ms.

1995–2008/262; R. Rochfort to Lord Strafford, 31 March 1704, BL, Add. Ms. 31,134, f. 24.

130. W. Perceval to Lord Perceval, 14 April 1722, 28 Aug. 1722, BL, Add. Ms. 47,029, ff. 115, 130v; *The case of Richard Connell, an orphan* (n.p., c. 1700); Barnard, 'What became of Waring?'

131. T. Medlycott to E. Southwell, 17 June 1721, BL, Add. Ms. 34,778, f. 51; accounts for 1664, Southwell notebook, NLI, Ms. 14,910; rent receipts, 1670, Boole Library, NUI, Cork, U/20, Kinsale Manorial Papers, 1665–75; rental, 1695, BL, Add. 9714, printed in R. Caulfield (ed.), *The council book of the corporation of Kinsale* (Guildford, 1879), pp. 393–4; Southwell rentals, 1700, Boole Library, NUI, Cork, U/20, Kinsale Manorial Papers, 1698–1764.

132. T. Sheridan and J. Swift, *The Intelligencer*, ed. J. Woolley (Oxford, 1992), p. 207; A. P. I. Samuels (ed.), *The early life, correspondence and writings of the Rt. Hon. Edmund Burke, LL.D.* (Cambridge, 1923), p. 317.

133. T. Pierson to J. Bonnell, 12 March 1719[20], NLI, PC 435.

134. K. Conolly to J. Bonnell, 24 Feb. 1738[9], ibid., PC 434; Hume's account, ibid., Ms. 6054, p. 78.

135. S. Bagshawe to W. Bagshawe, 5 Feb. 1750[1], JRL, B15/1/2.

136. Barnard, 'Robert French of Monivae', p. 289; Cronin, *A Galway gentleman*, pp. 16–24; R. Edgeworth, account books, 1741–42, 1751–52, 1761–62, 1769–70, NLI, Mss 1514, 1519, 1527, 1535; R. Edgeworth, rent books, NA, M. 1503–4; B. T. Balfour to Maj-Gen. Walsh, 23 Jan. 1760, NLI, special list, 416, Holloden papers; accounts, 1738–39, 1751, ibid., Mss 11,922, f. 113v; 10,275.

137. G. Stacpoole, *Some short historical anecdotes, with remarks relative to Ireland*, 4 parts, part 1 (Cork, 1762), p. 31.

138. T. U. Sadleir, 'Manuscripts at Kilboy, Co. Tipperary', *Analecta Hibernica*, 12 (1943), pp. 137–46.

139. T. U. Sadleir, 'The County of Waterford, 1775', *Journal of the Waterford Archaeological Society*, 16 (1913), pp. 49–55.

140. Holmes, 'Gregory King', pp. 67–9; P. H. Lindert and J. G. Williamson, 'Revising England's social tables, 1688–1812', *Explorations in Economic History*, 19 (1982), pp. 385–407; P. Mathias, 'The social structure in the eighteenth century: a calculation by Joseph Massie', *Economic History Review*, 2nd series, 10 (1957–58), pp. 37, 42.

141. Mathias, 'Joseph Massie', p. 42.

142. F. Heal and C. Holmes, *The gentry in England and Wales, 1500–1700* (Basingstoke, 1994), pp. 97–135; J. E. Hollinshed, 'The gentry of south-west Lancashire in the later sixteenth century', *Northern History*, 26 (1990), pp. 82–98; Mingay, *The gentry*, pp. 11–16; Holmes, 'Gregory King', pp. 54–5; Mathias, 'Joseph Massie', pp. 42, 45; C. B. Phillips and J. H. Smith, *Lancashire and Cheshire from A.D. 1540* (Harlow, 1994), pp. 14, 70–2.

143. M. Humphreys, *The crisis of community: Montgomeryshire, 1680–1815* (Cardiff, 1996), pp. 39–41, 60–2, 96–100, 132–5, 215–16, 240, 252–9.

144. Roberts, 'The landed gentry in Merioneth', pp. 17–18, 185.

145. L. Baker-Jones, *Princelings, privileges and power: the Tivyside gentry in the community* (Llandysul, 1999), pp. 36–43; D. W. Howell, *Patriarchs and parasites: the gentry of south-west Wales in the eighteenth century* (Cardiff, 1986), pp. 8–9; B. Howells (ed.), *Early modern Pembrokeshire, 1536–1815* (Haverfordwest, 1987), pp. 299–308, 329–30.

146. Jenkins, *The making of a ruling class*, pp. 48–9; Mingay, *The gentry*, pp. 11–17.

147. L. M. Timperley, 'The pattern of landholding in eighteenth-century Scotland', in M. L. Parry and T. R. Slater (eds), *The making of the Scottish countryside* (London, 1980), pp. 140, 142.

148. R. A. Dodgshon, *From chiefs to landlords: social and economic change in the western highlands and islands, c. 1493–1820* (Edinburgh, 1998), pp. 93–5, 136–7; Timperley, 'The pattern of landholding', pp. 145–50; I. D. Whyte, *Agriculture and society in seventeenth-century Scotland* (Edinburgh, 1979), pp. 29–39; I. D. Whyte and K. A. Whyte, 'Some aspects of the structure of rural society in seventeenth-century lowland Scotland', in T. M. Devine and D. Dickson (eds), *Ireland and Scotland, 1600–1850* (Edinburgh, 1983), pp. 32–40.

149. D. McCrone and A. Morris, 'Lords and heritages: the transformation of the great lairds of Scotland', in T. M. Devine (ed.), *Scottish élites* (Edinburgh, 1994), p. 172.

150. Dodgshon, *From chiefs to landlords*; A. MacInnes, *Clanship, commerce and the House of Stuart, 1603–1788* (East Linton, 1996); S. J. Shaw, *The management of Scottish society, 1707–1764* (Edinburgh, 1983), p. 14.

151. L. M. Cullen, 'Incomes, social classes and economic growth in Ireland and Scotland, 1600–1900', in Devine and Dickson (eds), *Ireland and Scotland, 1600–1850*, pp. 248–60; L. M. Cullen, T. C. Smout and A. Gibson, 'Wages and comparative development in Ireland and Scotland, 1565–1780', in R. Mitchison and P. Roebuck (eds), *Economy and society in Scotland and Ireland, 1500–1939* (Edinburgh, 1988), pp. 105–16.

152. Bartley, *Teague, Shenkin and Sawney*; R. Clyde, *From rebel to hero: the image of the highlander, 1745–1830* (East Linton, 1998); D. W. Hayton, 'From barbarian to burlesque: English images of the Irish, c. 1660–1750', *Irish Economic and Social History*, 15 (1988), pp. 5–31; M. G. H. Pittock, *Celtic identity and the British image* (Manchester, 1999), pp. 20–60.

153. *A dialogue between a secretary of state and a Connaught squier* (Dublin, 1714); *The down-fall of the counts: a ballad* (Dublin, 1746/7); *The north country ordinary opened* (Dublin, 1738/9).

154. K. M. Brown, 'Aristocracy, anglicization and the court, 1603–37', *HJ*, 36 (1993), pp. 543–76; K. M. Brown, 'The origins of a British aristocracy: integration and its limitation before the Union', in S. Ellis and S. Barber (eds), *Conquest and Union: fashioning a British state, 1485–1725* (London, 1995), pp. 222–49; K. M. Brown, 'Scottish identity in the seventeenth century', in B. Bradshaw and P. Roberts (eds), *British consciousness and identity: the making of Britain, 1533–1707* (Cambridge, 1998), pp. 236–58; J. M. Simpson, 'Who steered the gravy train?' in N. T. Phillipson and R. Mitchison (eds), *Scotland in the age of improvement* (Edinburgh, 1970, reprinted 1996), pp. 47–72; Shaw, *Management of Scottish society*, pp. 1–14.

155. Howell, *Patriarchs and parasites*, pp. 39, 48.

156. S. Bagshawe to Lady Caldwell, 22 Feb. 1752, JRL, B 2/3/246; A. Caldwell to S. Bagshawe, [1751], 25 Feb. 1752, 14 March 1752, ibid., B 2/3/244a, 247, 249; W. Gacquin, 'A household account from County Roscommon, 1733–4', in D. A. Cronin, J. Gilligan and K. Holton (eds), *Irish fairs and markets: studies in local history* (Dublin, 2001), p. 107.

157. J. Evelyn, Jr. to J. Evelyn, 26 March 1694, Evelyn Mss, formerly at Christ Church, Oxford; Abp. N. Marsh to T. Smith, 30 Aug. 1698, Bodleian, Smith Ms. 52, f. 67; C. O'Brien to T. Keightley, 17 July 1705, NLI, Inchiquin Mss, no. 1155; Bp. H.

Downes to Abp. W. Wake, 20 May [1716], Christ Church, Wake Ms. 12, f. 55;
W. Yorke to Lord Hardwicke, 11 Oct. 1743, BL, Add. Ms. 35,587, f. 182v.

158. Abp. N. Marsh to T. Smith, 30 Aug. 1698, Bodleian, Smith Ms. 52, f. 67; Bp.
H. Downes to Abp. W. Wake, 20 May [1716], Christ Church, Wake Ms.12, f. 55.

159. C. O'Brien to Sir C. Wyche, 25 April 1700, NA, Wyche Ms., 1/1/172; N. Ogle to
W. Smythe, 28 July 1753, NLI, PC 436; M. Clarke to same, 25 Nov. 1735, 2 Dec.
1735, 8 Oct. 1737, 26 Nov. 1737, ibid., PC 447; M. Ledwidge to same, 1 Jan.
1753, 6 Jan. [?1753], 22 Jan. 1754, ibid., PC 446.

160. J. Potter to R. Liddell, 4 July 1745, PRONI, T 3019/656; Delany, *Autobiography*, 1st
series, iii, pp. 81–2, 87–8, 110, 518.

161. T. Barnard, 'The world of goods and County Offaly in the early eighteenth
century', in T. O'Neill (ed.), *Offaly: history and society* (Dublin, 1998), pp. 371–92;
T. C. Barnard, 'Public and private uses of wealth in Ireland, *c.* 1660–1760', in
J. R. Hill and C. Lennon (eds), *Luxury and austerity: Historical studies XXI* (Dublin,
1999), pp. 66–83.

162. Sir R. Talbot to Sir G. Lane, [1666], NLI, Lane Mss, Ms. 8643/9.

163. Richey, 'County Down', p. 17.

164. M. Tinling (ed.), *The correspondence of the three William Byrds of Westover, Virginia,
1684–1776*, 2 vols (Charlottesville, 1977), i, pp. 438–9.

165. D. Conner to Burlington, 16 April 1736, Chatsworth, Devonshire Letters, 1720–36;
T. Barnard, 'Land and the limits of loyalty: the second earl of Cork and first earl
of Burlington (1612–98)', in T. Barnard and J. Clark (eds), *Lord Burlington:
architecture, art and life* (London, 1995), pp. 168–9; T. C. Barnard, 'Landlords and
urban life: Youghal and the Boyles, 1641–1740', *Newsletter of the Group for the Study
of Historic Settlement*, 5 (1995), pp. 1–5; M. MacCarthy-Morrogh, *The Munster
Plantation: English migration to southern Ireland, 1583–1641* (Oxford, 1986), pp. 141–3,
146–8, 156–7, 168–70, 184–90; T. Ranger, 'The career of Richard Boyle, first earl
of Cork in Ireland, 1588–1643', unpublished D. Phil. thesis, Oxford University
(1958); T. Ranger, 'Richard Boyle and the making of an Irish fortune', *IHS*, 10
(1957), pp. 257–97.

166. Lane, PRO, C 106/104, part 1; ibid., C 106/105, boxes 1 and 2; ibid., C 106/106,
boxes 1 and 2; ibid., C. 106/153, boxes 1 and 2; Sir W. Ellis to Sir C. Wyche, 26
June 1681, NA, Wyche Mss 2/141; rental of Sir W. Ellis, ibid., 2/160; accounts of
H. Temple, 1st Viscount Palmerston, 1727–34, 1735–41, 1742–48, Southampton UL,
BR, 2/7–9; Palmerston rentals, 1723–30, ibid., BR, 2/5; Anglesey rentals, 1713–22,
Oxfordshire CRO, E6/7/E/3.

167. M. Coghill to E. Southwell, 23 March 1734[5], BL, Add. Ms. 21,123, f. 104v; same
to same, 8 and 24 April 1735, NLI, Ms. 875; E. Southwell to M. Coghill, 22 April
1735, 11 Nov. 1735; Dickson, 'Economic history of the Cork region', i, p. 72.

168. R. Lane to Sir G. Lane, received 8 Aug. 1660, NLI, Ms. 8642.

169. O. St George to O. Gallagher, 14 Feb. 1723[4], PRO, C 110/46, 51.

170. Anglesey to Lord Power, 27 Sept. 1670, private collection, Co. Waterford.

171. Bulkeley, *Proposal*, p. 21; *Sr St John Brodrick's vindication of himself* ([London], 1690),
pp. 22–3.

172. J. Smythe to W. Smythe, 25 Oct. 1723, NLI, PC 449.

173. Kelly (ed.), 'The improvement of Ireland', p. 69; Sir R. Southwell to Sir John
Perceval, BL, Add. Ms. 46,961, f. 154v, printed in HMC, *Egmont Mss*, ii, p. 142;
M. Ward to B. Ward, 19 Nov. 1738, PRONI, D 2092/1/7, 265; Sir W. Fownes to
W. Fownes, 8 May 1732, NLI, Ms. 8802; same to same, 19 March 1733[4],

Maidenhall, Co. Kilkenny, Cooke Mss. For similar attitudes in sixteenth- and seventeenth-century Wales: Jones, *Concepts of order and gentility in Wales*, pp. 90, 231; J. G. Jones, *Conflict, continuity and change in Wales, c. 1500–1603* (Aberystwyth, 1999), pp. 154–97.

174. N. Jones to G. Legge, 22 Feb. 1672[3], Dartmouth Mss, Staffs CRO, D 1778/iii/O/19, in HMC, *Dartmouth Mss*, iii, p. 116; R. Aylward to same, 3 Sept. 1678, 5 April 1679, ibid., D 1778/iii/O/19; letters of W. Hovell, 21 March 1683[4], 8 Nov. 1684, 26 May 1685, Hovell letter book, Farmar Mss, private collection, Dublin.

175. H. Conyngham to ?Lady Broughton, 11 Nov. 1704, PRONI, D 2860/5/23; G. Kirkham, '"No more to be got from the cat but the skin"', pp. 357–80.

176. O. St George to O. Gallagher, 14 Feb. 1723[4], PRO, C 110/46, 51.

177. S. J. Connolly, 'Law, order and popular protest in early eighteenth-century Ireland: the case of the Houghers', in P. J. Corish (ed.), *Radicals, rebels and establishments: Historical Studies, XV* (Belfast, 1985), pp. 51–68; E. Magennis, 'In search of the "moral economy": food scarcity in 1756–7 and the crowd', in P. J. Jupp and E. Magennis (eds), *Crowds in Ireland, c. 1720–1920* (Basingstoke, 2000), pp. 189–211.

178. A. P. W. Malcomson, 'Absenteeism in eighteenth-century Ireland', *Irish Economic and Social History*, 1 (1974), pp. 15–35; *Writings of Petty*, i, pp. 46, 185, 193; R. Cox, 'Regnum Corcagiense, or a description of the Kingdom of Cork', ed. R. Day, *JCHAS*, 2nd series, 8 (1902), pp. 70–1; R. Lawrence, *The interest of Ireland*, 2 parts (Dublin, 1682) i, pp. 7–8; F. G. James, 'The Irish lobby in the early eighteenth century', *EHR*, 81 (1966), pp. 544–57.

179. Sir R. Southwell to Sir J. Perceval, 16 May 1682, BL, Add. Ms. 46,959A, ff. 126–31; HMC, *Egmont Mss*, ii, pp. 111–16, 208–11; M. Ward to B. Ward, 19 Nov. 1738, PRONI, D 2092/1/7, 265; *Particulars relating to the life and character of the late Brockhill Newburgh, esq.* (n.p., 1761).

180. Abp. W. King to Bp. W. Nicolson, 3 Feb. 1717[18], TCD, Ms. 2535, p. 77; Bp. R. Howard to H. Howard, 20 March 1728[9], 16 May 1732, NLI, PC. 227; J. Kelly, 'Harvests and hardship: famine and scarcity in the late 1720s', *Studia Hibernica*, 26 (1991–92), pp. 65–105.

181. W. Peard to F. Price, 3 April 1741, 30 July 1745, NLW, Puleston Ms. 3579E.

182. Loveday, *Tour*, p. 32; *The whole works of Sir James Ware*, ed. W. Harris, 2 vols (Dublin, 1764), i, pp. 598–9.

183. R. Howard to H. Howard, 22 March 1734[5], NLI, Ms. 12,149; J. P. Cooper, 'The fortune of Thomas Wentworth, earl of Strafford', in Cooper, *Land, men and beliefs*, pp. 148–75.

184. J. Richardson, *Richardsoniana* (London, 1776), i, p. 268.

185. Hayton, 'From Barbarian to Burlesque', pp. 5–31; D. B. and A. H. Rutman, *A place in time: Middlesex, County Virginia, 1650–1750* (New York and London, 1984), p. 234.

186. Abp. W. King to Sir C. Domville, 3 Feb. 1717[18]; same to E. Southwell, 21 Jan. 1717[18], TCD, Ms. 2535, pp. 62–6, 73–5.

187. J. Bulkeley to J. Bonnell, 9 April 1728, NLI, PC 435; S. R. Lowry-Corry, earl of Belmore, *The history of two Ulster manors* (London and Dublin, 1881), p. 178.

188. Abp. W. King to Lord Fitzwilliam, 9 Aug. 1718, TCD, Ms. 2535, pp. 249–50.

189. R. Molesworth, *Some considerations for the promoting of agriculture, and employing the poor* (Dublin, 1723), pp. 28–9. For Molesworth's sons: D. B. Horn, *British diplomatic representatives, 1689–1789*, Camden Society, 3rd series, xlvi (1932), pp. 74,

79, 80, 123; J. Ingamells, *A dictionary of British and Irish travellers in Italy, 1701–1800* (New Haven and London, 1997), pp. 665–6; E. McParland, *Public architecture in Ireland, 1680–1760* (New Haven and London, 2001), pp. 9–11; M. Wynne, 'Some British diplomats, some grand tourists and some tourists from Great Britain and Ireland in Turin in the eighteenth century', *Studi Piemontesi*, 25/1 (1996), pp. 154–5.

190.   [?Hickes], *The gentleman instructed*, pp. 13, 428–9.

191.   J. Ingram to W. Smythe, 15 Nov. 1743, NLI, PC 445.

192.   R. Pigott to W. Crosbie, 27 Sept. 1757, ibid., Talbot–Crosbie Mss, folder 61.

193.   Paper by 'Philergus' [*c.* 1753], Roden Mss, 17, PRONI, microfilm 147.

194.   R. Howard to T. Taylor, 24 Feb. 1752, NLI, Headford Mss, F/5/17.

195.   Lady A. Crosbie to W. Crosbie, 31 March 1733, TCD, Ms. 3821/194; R. Fitzgerald to Sir M. Crosbie, 19 March 1742, n.s., ibid., 3821/205; J.S. Powell, '*Your humble servant': notes and letters from Portarlington, 1692–1768* (York, *c.* 1992), p. 25.

196.   A. Chetwood to C. Eustace, 14 May 1717, Tickell Mss, private collection, Devon.

197.   G. S. Cotter, *Poems, consisting of odes, songs, pastorals, satyrs, &c.*, 2 vols (Cork, 1788), i, pp. 133–54.

198.   *The Country Gentleman*, 1 (Dublin, 30 March 1726).

199.   E. Southwell to Lord Nottingham, 8 July 1703, 23 Oct. 1703, NLI, Ms. 991/72, 152.

200.   Bp. T. Godwin to Abp. W. Wake, Christ Church, Wake Ms. 12, f. 370; A. Crotty to J. Coughlan, 25 July 1726, Chatsworth, Crotty letter book, 1726; Loveday, *Tour*, p. 47.

201.   W. Molyneux to E. Borlase, 31 Jan. 1679[80], BL, Sloane Ms. 1008, f. 252; [C. Molyneux], *An account of the family and descendants of Sir Thomas Molyneux* (Evesham, 1820).

202.   E. Spencer to F. Price, 6 Dec. 1743, 9 Oct. 1747, NLW, Puleston Ms. 3580E.

203.   S. Hinde, *A sermon preach't before the right honourable the lord mayor of the city of Dublin . . . in the parish church of St Warburghs, the 23. of November. 1671* (Dublin, 1672); P. Delany, *Twenty sermons on social duties and their opposite vices* (London, 1747), pp. 391, 412.

204.   R. Lloyd to F. Herbert, 21 Feb. 1716[17], NLW, Powis Castle deeds, no. 16,060.

205.   T. Wilkinson, *Memoirs of his own life*, 4 vols (York, 1790), i, pp. 163–5.

206.   *Particulars relating to the life and character of the late Brockhill Newburgh, esq.* p. 3.

207.   H. Osborne to E. Darell, [25 March 1700], PRONI, D 162/14.; M. Fitzgerald to D. Crosbie, 4 July 1709, TCD, Ms. 3821/117.

208.   A. Stringer, *The experienced huntsman* (Dublin, 1780), pp. 45, 224.

209.   Lady T. Crosbie to Lady A. Bligh, [1746], PRONI, D 2092/1/6, printed in [D. Fitzgerald], Knight of Glin, 'Three eighteenth-century letters of Lady Theodosia Crosbie's', *Journal of the Kerry Archaeological and Historical Society*, 17 (1984), pp. 76–8.

210.   Lady Midleton to J. Bonnell, 18 March 1730[1], NLI, PC 435.

211.   W. Crosbie to Sir M. Crosbie, 5 April 1742, ibid., Talbot–Crosbie Mss, folder 53.

212.   Lady A. Denny to Lady A. Crosbie, 9 [Feb.] 1747[8], ibid., folder 56.

213.   Lady A. Denny to Lady A. Crosbie, 25 Feb. 1755, ibid., Ms. 20,601; A. Caldwell to S. Bagshawe, 6 July 1759, JRL, B 2/3/297; account book of S. Winter of Agher, NLI, Ms. 3855, s.d. 18 June 1762, 24 June 1763; Delany, *Autobiography*, 1st series, iii, pp. 286, 548, 554; B. Butler, 'Lady Arbella Denny, 1707–1792', *Dublin Historical Record*, 9 (1946–47), pp. 1–20; R. Raughter, 'A natural tenderness: the ideal and

the reality of eighteenth-century female philanthropy', in M. G. Valiulis and
M. O'Dowd (eds), *Women and Irish history. Essays in honour of Margaret MacCurtain*
(Dublin, 1997), pp. 77–9.

214. Lords lieutenants' dinner lists, s.d. 2 Oct. 1763, NLI, Ms. 1468; Lady A. Denny to
?Lady Townshend, 19 July 1768, RCB, Ms. 20/466–7.

215. A. C. Elias, Jr. (ed.), *Memoirs of Laetitia Pilkington* (Athens, Ga. and London, 1997),
i, pp. 22–3; J. Dallway (ed.), *Letters of the late Thomas Rundle, LL.D . . . to Mrs
Barbara Sandys*, 2 vols (Gloucester, 1789), i, pp. cxliv–cxlv.

216. List of 8 May 1760, JRL, Ms. B15/3/7; Lady Powerscourt to dowager countess of
Orrery, 12 Nov. [c. 1684], Petworth, Orrery Mss, general series, 27. Cf. S. E.
Whyman, *Sociability and power in late-Stuart England: the cultural world of the Verneys,
1660–1720* (Oxford, 1999), pp. 87–109.

217. M. Moore to J. Moore, 11 Dec. 1759, Barber Mss, private collection, London.

218. T. Caulfield to K. O'Hara, 18 Nov. 1699, NLI, Ms. 20,388.

219. Marriage settlement, W. Conolly and K. Conyngham, 15 Dec. 1694, IAA,
Castletown deposit, box 47; L. Boylan, 'The Conollys of Castletown: a family
history' *Quarterly Bulletin of the Irish Georgian Society*, 11 (1968), pp. 1–19;
H. Meehan, 'The Conynghams of Slane and Mountcharles', *Donegal Annual*, 51
(1999), pp. 22–35; Mary Blayney's copy of A. Crossly, *The peerage of Ireland*, in
Marsh's Library, pressmark H4.4.20.

220. Lady Eustace to C. Eustace, 23 Nov. [?1728], Tickell Mss, private collection,
Devon.

221. J. Leathes to W. Leathes, 3 and 10 July 1711, 30 May 1721, Suffolk CRO, Ipswich,
de Mussenden Leathes Mss, HA 403/1/6, 4, 5 and 46; A. P. W. Malcomson,
The pursuit of an heiress: aristocratic marriage in Ireland, 1750–1820 (Antrim, 1982).

222. Sir T. Southwell to Lord Coningsby, 29 Nov. 1699, PRONI, D 638/30/15;
Barnard, 'Cork settlers', pp. 350–1.

223. A. Langford to E. Owen, 6 May [1738], UCNW, Penrhos Mss, i, 1087.

224. Duchess of Ormonde to B. Portlock, 12 Feb. 1703[4], NLI, Ms. 2502/222, in
HMC, *7th Report*, appendix, p. 769.

225. Lady Shelburne to W. Conolly, 29 July 1710, IAA, Castletown deposit, box 55.

226. K. Conolly to J. Bonnell, 28 Nov. 1741, NLI, PC 434; M. Coghill to E.
Southwell, 24 April 1735, ibid., Ms. 875; T. C. Barnard, 'Katherine Conolly', in
Barnard, *Irish Protestant ascents and descents*.

227. T. P. C. Kirkpatrick, 'Charles Willoughby, MD', *PRIA*, 36, sect. C (1923), p. 242.

228. Census of Elphin, 1749, NA, M 2466, ff. 397, 422; Abp. W. King, account book,
1700–12, TCD, Ms. 751/2, ff. 116, 165.

229. J. Copping to Sir H. Sloane, 22 Aug. 1741, BL, Sloane Ms. 4057, ff. 68v–69.

230. Abp. J. Hort to Sir M. Crosbie, 14 Aug. 1750, Talbot–Crosbie Mss, NLI, folder
33.

231. C. Royse to J. Brown, [1770s], Palatine Heritage Centre, Rathkeale, Southwell-
Brown Mss, box 1, bundle 1.

232. F. Bellew to Lord Raby, 28 June 1729, 17 July [1729], BL, Add. Ms. 22,228,
ff. 47v, 52v.

233. E. Cooke to M. Cox, [?1726]; Mrs E. Cooke to Mrs Sweet, 17 Oct. 1726,
Maiden Hall, Co. Kilkenny, Cooke Mss.

234. Legg, *Synge Letters*, pp. 155–6, 440.

235. C. Brett to M. Ward, 11 Jan. 1747[8], PRONI, D 2092/1/7,165; cf. Hume's report,
NLI, Ms. 6054, f. 16; Samuel Madden, *Reflections and resolutions proper for the*

gentlemen of Ireland (Dublin, 1738), pp. 47–8; *A letter to a schoolmaster in the country from his friend in town* (Dublin, 1758); B. Kowaleski-Wallace, 'Tea, gender and domesticity in eighteenth-century England', *Studies in Eighteenth-Century Culture*, 23 (1994), pp. 131–45.

236. Letter book of Caesar Williamson, Marsh's Library, Ms. Z4.5.16, p. 93; A. Caldwell to S. Bagshawe, [1751], 25 Feb. 1752, 14 March 1752, JRL, B/2/3/ 244a, 247, 249; H. Crofton to W. Smythe, 17 July 1723, 15 Sept. 1729, NLI, PC 448; F. Crofton to same, 25 May 1727, 8 July 1727, ibid., PC 436; F. Bellew to Lord Raby, 28 June 1729, 17 July [1729], BL, Add. Ms. 22,228, ff. 47v, 52v; K. Benson to J. Bonnell, 4 July 1738, 20 Oct. 1738, NLI, PC 435; J. S. Powell, 'Rethinking Portarlington', *Proceedings of the Huguenot Society of Great Britain and Ireland*, 27 (1999), pp. 246–56; Powell, *'Your humble servant'*, pp. 20, 22.

237. Petition of Anne Butler to Ormond, n.d., NLI, Ms. 2494, f. 54; John Butler to Ormond, n.d., ibid., Ms. 2481, f. 53.

238. A. Spurrett to R. Power, 14, 26 and 28 Sept. 1704, 3 Oct. 1704, Chatsworth, Spurrett letter book, 1703–4.

239. H. Alcock to A. Mason, 10 Oct. 1739, Dromana, Villiers-Stuart Mss, T 3131/B/5/10.

240. H. Crofton to W. Smythe, 17 July 1723, 15 Sept. 1729, 30 May 1734, ibid., PC 448; M. Crofton to same, 27 Dec. 1732, 18 April 1737, 18 May 1741, 21 Oct. 1741, ibid., PC 436; P. Crofton to same, 20 Jan. 1744[5], 26 March 1745, ibid., PC 445.

241. H. Alcock to A. Mason, 10 Oct. 1739, Dromana, Villiers-Stuart Mss, T 3131/B/5/10.

242. S. Povey to W. Smythe, 6 Aug. 1748, 28 Sept. 1748, 26 Oct. 1748, NLI, PC 448.

243. E. Hewetson to Lord Digby of Geashill, 16 Nov. 1756, Dorset CRO, D/SHC, 3C/81.

244. S. Crosse to Lord Castlecomer, 22 Sept. 1766; J. Crosse to Earl Wandesford, 4 Dec. 1770, 1 April 1783, NLI, Ms. 35,561; D. W. Hayton, 'Dependence, clientage and affinity: the political following of the second duke of Ormonde', in T. Barnard and J. Fenlon (eds), *The Dukes of Ormonde, 1610–1745* (Woodbridge, 2000), pp. 221, 227, 229, 235, 241.

245. Burdy, *Life of Philip Skelton*, p. 219.

246. Legg, *Synge letters*, pp. 300–1.

247. W. Perceval to A. Charlet, 29 April 1719, Bodleian, Ballard Ms. 36, ff. 109–9v; B. Badham to ?H. Boyle, 7 Nov. 1731, PRONI, D 2707/A1/11/37.

248. Lunell Memoir, NLI, Ms. 21,521; *The case of Robert Lawe* [Dublin,?1756].

249. J. C. Pilkington, *The real story of John Carteret Pilkington* (London, 1760), p. 74.

250. G. Swift to Sir W. Fownes, 30 June 1757, NLI, Ms. 3889/5.

251. Same to same, 18 Aug. 1757, ibid., Ms. 3889/8.

252. Inventory of L. Delamain, 20 Jan. 1763, TCD, Ms. 2015/395.

4. *Clergy*

1. Bp. R. Howard to H. Howard, 2 Feb. 1735[6], NLI, PC 227.

2. W. Yorke to Lord Hardwicke, 11 Oct. 1743, BL, Add. Ms. 35,587, f. 182; R. Lowth to M. Lowth, 10 May 1755, Bodleian, Ms. Eng. Lett. C. 572, ff. 26–26v.

3. A. C. Elias, Jr. (ed.), *Memoirs of Laetitia Pilkington*, 2 vols (Athens, Ga. and London, 1997), i, pp. 22–3.

4. J. Dallway (ed.), *Letters of the late Thomas Rundle, LL.D . . . to Mrs Barbara Sandys*, 2 vols (Gloucester, 1789), i, pp. cxliv–cxlv.

5. Sir S. Cooke to S. Bagshawe, 24 April 1752, JRL, B 2/3/422.

6. Bp. N. Foy to Bp. W. King, 10 Oct. 1693, TCD, Ms. 1995–2008/301; *Letters written by his excellency Hugh Boulter*, 2 vols (Oxford, 1769–70) i, pp. 210, 223; Richard Barton, *Lectures in natural philosophy* (Dublin, 1751), p. xi. Barton's higher figure included curates and perhaps many schoolmasters and dons at Trinity College. By 1830, the Church of Ireland had 1,625 incumbents. J. C. Erck, *The Irish ecclesiastical register* (Dublin, 1817), p. xxv.

7. T. C. Barnard, 'Improving clergymen, 1660–1760', in A. Ford, J. I. McGuire and K. Milne (eds), *As by law established: the Church of Ireland since the reformation* (Dublin, 1995), pp. 136–51, 257–65; HMC, *Ormonde Mss*, new series, vi, p. 24.

8. D. A. Spaeth, *The Church in an age of danger: parsons and parishioners, 1660–1740* (Cambridge, 2000), p. 30.

9. J. B. Leslie, *Ossory clergy and parishes* (Enniskillen, 1933); J. B. Leslie, *Raphoe clergy and parishes* (Enniskillen, 1940).

10. E. Hughes, 'The professions in the eighteenth century', *Durham University Journal*, 44 (1952), p. 55.

11. W. Owen to J. Owen, 12 Feb. 1674[5], 13 April 1675, UCNW, Penrhos Ms, v, 429, 430; 'Philocurus' to ?Bp. T. Rundle [*c.* 1735], PRONI, D 668/E/38; P. Delany, *Eighteen discourses and dissertations upon various very important and interesting subjects* (London, 1766), p. 234; C. S. King, *A great archbishop of Dublin, William King, D. D.* (London, 1906), pp. 7–8.

12. Autobiography of A. Blair, TCD, Ms. 6447; K. Herlihy, 'The Irish Baptists, 1650–1780', unpublished Ph.D. thesis, TCD (1992), pp. 134–5.

13. B. Lloyd to ?, 24 Oct. 1729, NLW, Puleston Ms. 3576E, 13; J. Kelly (ed.), *The letters of Lord Chief Baron Edward Willes to the earl of Warwick, 1757–62* (Aberystwyth, 1990), p. 94; Legg, *Synge letters*, pp. vii–xxii; *The whole works of Sir James Ware*, ed. W. Harris, 2 vols (Dublin, 1764), i, pp. 598–9.

14. J. Bonnell to J. Strype, 25 Jan. 1697[8], Cambridge UL, Add. Ms. 1/85.

15. Letter of 30 Jan. 1695[6]; certificate of Bp. W. Lloyd on behalf of H. Williams, 1 April 1693; Bp. W. Lloyd to Bp. W. Smythe, 10 April 1693; H. Williams to same, 26 June 1693, NLI, PC 436; Abp. W. King to Bp. W. Ellis, 13 July 1726, TCD, Ms. 750/8/125; proceedings against the Revd V. Needham, 9 Oct. 1724, RCB, P. 276/12.1, p. 82.

16. Revd B. Barrington to Sir A. Acheson, 11 Nov. 1758, PRONI, D 1606/1/20A; S. Madden, *Reflections and resolutions proper for the gentlemen of Ireland* (Dublin, 1738), p. 58.

17. Revd A. Hamilton to Mrs J. Bonnell, 30 Oct. 1741, NLI, PC 435.

18. Barnard, 'Improving clergymen', pp. 136–51.

19. Abp. W. King to F. Annesley, 6 May 1727, TCD, Ms. 750/8, pp. 195–6; Bp. R. Howard to H. Howard, 24 July 1734, NLI, PC 227.

20. Bp. W. Nicolson to Abp. W. Wake, Christ Church, Wake Ms. 12/278; Bp. J. Evans to same, 10 Dec. 1718, ibid., 13/30; C. C. Ellison, 'Bishop Dopping's visitation book, 1682–1685', *Ríoct na Míde*, 4–6 (1971–75); P. Loupès, 'Bishop Dopping's visitation of the diocese of Meath', *Studia Hibernica*, 24 (1984–88), p. 43.

21. 29 Geo II, c. xviii, *Statutes*, vii, pp. 359–75; G. F. A. Best, *Temporal pillars: Queen*

Anne's Bounty, the ecclesiastical commissioners and the Church of England (Cambridge, 1964); E. J. Evans, 'The Anglican clergy of northern England', in C. Jones (ed.), *Britain in the first age of party, 1680–1750* (London and Ronceverte, 1987), pp. 225–8; W. J. Gregory, *Restoration, reformation and reform, 1660–1828: archbishops of Canterbury in their diocese* (Oxford, 2000), pp. 149–54; J. Pruett, *The parish clergy under the later Stuarts* (Urbana, 1978), p. 175; Spaeth, *The Church in an age of danger*, pp. 31–6.

22. *The last and true speech of Mr Sewell, a degraded clergyman* (Dublin,[1740]); *The genuine declaration of Edward Shuel, a degraded clergyman of the Church of Ireland* (Dublin, [1740]). Cf. C. Dickson at Taghmon, visitation of Meath, *c.* 1733, RCB, GS 2/7/3/10, p. 56; E. Lestrange to W. Smythe, 24 May 1746, NLI, PC 449.

23. Executors' accounts for Mrs Elizabeth Vincent, *c.*1669, D. Johnson account book, Birr Castle Archives, A/16.

24. 'Case between Mr Houston and Mr Gifford', PRONI, D 668/E/38; J. B. Leslie, *Derry clergy and parishes* (Enniskillen, 1937), pp. 168, 240, 290.

25. C. Harrison to Bp. W. Smythe, 25 Dec.[?1694], NLI, PC 436; *An elegy on the Reverend Dean Clayton* ([Dublin, 1725]); R. V. Dudley, 'Dublin's parishes, 1660–1729: the Church of Ireland parishes and their role in the civic administration of the city', unpublished Ph.D. thesis, TCD, 2 vols (1995), ii, pp. 329–31; Gregory, *Restoration, reformation and reform*, pp. 146–77; Spaeth, *The Church in an age of danger*, pp. 16–21, 32–6.

26. Revd F. Houston to Bp. A. Smyth, 10–20 Nov. 1757, PRONI, D 668/E/38; Leslie, *Derry clergy and parishes*, p. 240.

27. Proceedings against Needham, RCB, P 276/12/1, pp. 81–8; *Al. Dubl.*, p. 612.

28. S. Foley, *A sermon preached at the primary visitation of his grace Francis [Marsh] lord arch-bishop of Dublin* (London, 1683), p. 18.

29. Revd W. Hansard to Bp. W. Smythe, 5 Aug. 1693, 1696, NLI, PC 436.

30. Revd A. Young to W. Conolly, 15 July 1710, IAA, Castletown deposit, box 57.

31. Revd R. Vaughan to Revd E. Edgeworth, 10 Jan. 1734[5], NA, M. 1502.

32. Revd J. Leathes to W. Leathes, 19 March 1717[18], 1 July 1719, de Mussenden Leathes Mss, Suffolk CRO, Ipswich, HA 413/1/6, 24, 28.

33. Abp. J. Hoadley to E. Walpole, 30 July 1737, Chatsworth, Devonshire Letters, 1737–39 246.0.

34. J. Bonnell to J. Strype, 16 Feb. 1690[1], 13 Feb. 1691[2], Cambridge UL, Add. Ms. 1/67, 68.

35. Huntington Library, Ms. 141398–259, f. 28, quoted in Elias (ed.), *Memoirs of Laetitia Pilkington*, ii, p. 372.

36. E. Maurice to Sir T. Vesey, 31 Jan. [1729]; W. Andrews to same, 18 Jan. 1728[9], de Vesci Mss, NLI; *Fifty-sixth report of the deputy keeper of the public records of Ireland* (Dublin, 1931), p. 384; Leslie, *Ossory clergy and parishes*, pp. 207, 210.

37. Revd J. Smythe to W. Smythe, 1 Oct. 1747, NLI, PC 449.

38. M. Phillips to W. Forward, 3 Jan. 1757, ibid., PC 225 (iv); J. S. Powell (ed.), 'Your humble servant': notes and letters from Portarlington, 1692–1768 (York, n.d.), pp. 29–30; Barnard, 'Improving clergymen', pp. 140–1.

39. J. Tickell to C. Tickell, 3 Oct. 1759; C. Houghton to J. Tickell, 3 Nov. 1759, Tickell Mss, private collection, Devon.

40. Account book of Revd A. Rowan, PRONI, D 1614/3, p. 191; S. T. Carleton (ed.), *Heads and hearths: the hearth money rolls and poll tax returns for Co. Antrim, 1660–1669* (Belfast, 1991), pp. 125–8.

41. Rowan account book, PRONI, D 1614/3, pp. 155, 162, 170, 184, 205; will of Revd A. Rowan, 16 June 1708, ibid., D. 1614/5.
42. Rowan account book, ibid., D 1614/3, pp. 3, 76, 91, 148, 162, 199, 207, 210, 226.
43. Ibid., pp. 172, 183, 185.
44. Ibid., pp. 3, 76, 97, 135.
45. D. A. Chart, 'Account book of the Rev. Andrew Rowan, rector of Dunaghy, Co. Antrim, *c.*1672–1680', *Ulster Journal of Archaeology*, 3rd series, 5 (1942), p. 74.
46. Rowan account book, PRONI, D 1614/3, pp. 157, 158, 172, 199, 212, 221.
47. Story account book, Bingfield, County Cavan; Abp. W. King account books, 1694–1700; 1700–12, TCD, Mss 751/1, f. 51; 751/2, ff. 173, 197; Abp. H. Boulter account book, ibid., Ms. 6399, pp. 93, 117; Revd J. Smythe to W. Smythe, 28 July 1730, NLI, PC 449; Legg, *Synge letters*, pp. 132, 136.
48. Verses by Revd William Young, TCD, Ms. 10,664, pp. 1–50; R. Barton, *Farrago: or, miscellanies in verse and prose* (London, 1739), pp. 81–6.
49. Bp. T. Vesey to J. Smythe, 4 Oct. 1722, NLI, PC 449.
50. W. Preston to E. Southwell, 3 and 17 Dec. 1738, ibid., Ms. 730/11, 12.
51. Same to same, 13 Feb. 1739[40], ibid., Ms. 730/19.
52. Same to W. Lingen, 29 July 1739, ibid., Ms. 730/17.
53. Revd P. Skelton to S. Bagshawe, 14 March 1759, JRL, B 2/3/787; S. Burdy, *The life of Philip Skelton*, ed. N. Moore (Oxford, 1914), pp. 129, 142–3, 169, 175, 176, 196. Cf. Barton, *Farrago*, pp. 81–6.
54. Will of Revd S. Span, Lawder of Bonnybegg Mss, account book from 1759, p. 60, PRONI, D 4123; M. Leathes to J. White, 3 Dec. 1720, Suffolk CRO, HA 403/1/5, 168.
55. J. Cliffe, account book, s.d. 1 Jan. 1780, NA, 1096/8/7.
56. Survey of dioceses, 1693, PRONI, DIO/4/4/4; Bp. E. Woolley to A. Dopping, 24 Oct. 1682, Dopping Mss, 1/33, Armagh Public Library; Bp. Edward Worth's notebook, 1661–69, RCB, Ms. D 14/1.
57. J. C. W. Wylie, *Irish land law* (London, 1975), p. 22.
58. M. Jones to J. Bonnell, 24 Feb. [?1736], or later, NLI, PC 435; J. Smythe to W. Smythe, 26 Dec. 1731, ibid., PC 449; M. Bric, 'The tithe system in eighteenth-century Ireland', *PRIA*, 86, sect. C (1986), pp. 271–87; E. Synge, *Two affidavits in relation to the demands of the tythe-agistment in the diocese of Leighlin* (Dublin, 1736).
59. Survey of Irish dioceses, 1693, PRONI, DIO 4/4/4; N. Foy to W. King, 18 Sept. 1697, ibid., DIO 4/15/2/3.
60. Abp. W. Palliser to Bp. E. Jones, 28 Feb. 1694[5]; same to Bp. W. Lloyd, 1 March 1695[6], Lambeth Palace Library, Ms. 929/66, 67; licence of Lords Justice to Revd W. Jephson, 21 June 1693, ibid., Ms. 942/53; Revd W. Jephson to R. Aldworth, 27 Jan. 1693[4], ibid., Ms. 942/58–9; R. Aldworth to Bp. N. Foy, 20 Feb. 1693[4]; same to Bp. of Cloyne, 20 Feb. 1693[4], ibid., Ms. 942/62, 63; petition of Revd Charles Northcott to Lords Justice of Ireland, n.d.; Abp. W. Palliser to R. Aldworth, 22 Aug. 1694, 6 Oct. 1694, ibid., Ms. 942/67, 68; Abp. W. Palliser to Abp. J. Tillotson, 14 Nov. 1694, ibid., Ms. 942/70; same to Bp. T. Tenison, 30 March 1698, ibid., Ms. 942/143; Bp. N. Foy to Bp. W. King, 28 April 1693, 30 Oct. 1697, 26 Nov. 1697, TCD, Ms. 1995–2008/272, 547, 558; Burlington to R. Power, 20 April 1693, NLI, Ms. 13,226; St Carthage's Cathedral, Lismore, chapter act book, 1663–1829, ff. 28v, 29; D. Grogan, 'Bishop Foy and the cause of reform', *Decies*, 50 (1994), pp. 82–4; M. D. Jephson, *An Anglo-Irish miscellany: some records of the Jephsons of Mallow* (Dublin, 1964), pp. 291–2; W. H. Rennison,

Succession list of the bishops, cathedral and parochial clergy of the dioceses of Waterford and Lismore (Waterford,[1920]), pp. 53, 157.

61. W. Jephson, *A sermon preached in St Andrew's Church, Dublin; on the 5th of November, 1698* (Dublin, 1698), pp. 11, 13–16.

62. R. Davies to Lady Cork, 13 Nov. 1648, Chatsworth, Lismore Ms. 28/10; Lord Cork and Burlington to W. Congreve, 17 May 1692, NLI, Ms. 13,226.

63. Lord Cork and Burlington to W. Congreve, 21 Dec. 1695, NLI, Ms. 13,226; J. Waite to R. Musgrave and T. Baker, 28 July 1707; same to G. Howse, 9 Aug. 1707, Chatsworth, Waite letter book, 1706–8; G. Howse to R. Musgrave, 23 Jan. 1709[10], NLI, Ms. 13,242; correspondence of R. Davies with agents of Lord Cork and Burlington, 1706–7, 1716, ibid., Ms. 13,253.

64. H. Cotton, *Fasti Ecclesiae Hibernicae*, 6 vols (Dublin, 1845–78), i, pp. 196–7, 200, 215, 220, 221–2, 244, 296; W. M. Brady, *Clerical records of Cork, Cloyne and Ross*, 3 vols (Dublin, 1863–64), i, pp. 267–8.

65. Abp. W. King to Bp. J. Moore, 10 Nov. 1704; same to Abp. Sharp of York, 10 Nov. 1704; same to Bp. C. Crow, 9 June 1705, TCD, Ms. 750/3/1, pp. 50, 51, 181; same to same, 6 July 1706, ibid., 750/3/2, p. 35; same to Abp. W. Palliser, 3 July 1705, ibid., 750/3/1, p. 195; Bp. C. Crow to Abp. W. King, 18 Jan. 1705[6], ibid., Ms. 1995–2008/1191; Abp. W. King to Bp. C. Crow, 3 April 1718, ibid., Ms. 2535, p. 144; A. R. Winnett, *Peter Browne: provost, bishop, metaphysician* (London, 1974), pp. 64–7.

66. J. Dennis to ?E. Southwell, 3 Feb. 1708[9]; J. Dennis, account with E. Southwell from 22 Dec. 1708, National Maritime Museum, Greenwich, Southwell Ms. 19/109, 167–8; J. Dennis to E. Southwell, 19 Feb. 1709[10], BL, Add. Ms. 38,152, ff. 35–35v; H. F. Berry, 'Justices of the peace for the county of Cork', *JCHAS*, 3 (1897), pp. 60, 62.

67. R. Caulfield (ed.), *Journal of the Very Rev. Rowland Davies . . . March 8, 1688–9, to September 29, 1690*, Camden Society (London, 1857); R. Davies, *The truly Catholick and old religion* (Dublin, 1716), sig. A3–[A4].

68. R. Davies, *Remarks on a pamphlet entituled Goliath beheaded with his own sword* (Dublin, 1720).

69. R. Davies, *A sermon preach'd in the cathedral church of Cork, on the 30th of January, 1715[16]* [Dublin, 1716].

70. R. Davies, *The right use of riches. A sermon preach'd in the parish church of St Peter's Corke, on Sunday, August the 11th, 1717* (Dublin, 1717); [H. Maule], *Pietas Corcagiensis. Or, a view of the Green-Coat Hospital . . . in the parish of St Mary Shandon, Corke* (Cork, 1721).

71. T. C. Barnard, 'Protestants and the Irish language, 1675–1725', *Journal of Ecclesiastical History*, 44 (1993), pp. 263–5.

72. *Harding's impartial news-letter*, 13 Feb. 1722[3], in Christ Church, Wake Ms. 14/55; A. Best to Shannon, 28 Jan. 1742[3], PRONI, D 2707/B1/34; Cotton, *Fasti*, i, pp. 215, 220–1.

73. Grant to B. Davies, 28 Dec. 1735, BL, Add. Ms. 38,152, ff. 77–8; Berry, 'Justices of the peace for the county of Cork', pp. 60, 62.

74. Boyle Davies, *Protestant unity urg'd in a sermon preach'd in the parish church of St Mary-Shandon in the city of Cork upon apprehension of the late intended invasion* (Dublin, 1719), pp. 6, 10–13.

75. Revd C. Massy to F. Burton, 29 Feb. 1739[40], 7 March 1739[40], Chatsworth, Devonshire Letters, 1740–43, 273.0, 273.2.

76. Same to same, 4 March 1739[40], ibid., 273.1.

77. J. Potter to E. Weston, 27 May 1740, PRO, SP 36/50, 443; ibid., J. Frost, *The history and topography of the county of Clare* (Dublin, 1893), p. 617.

78. D. O'Sullivan, *Carolan: the life, times and music of an Irish harper*, 2 vols (London, 1958), i, p. 112.

79. C. Massy, *A collection of resolutions, queries, &c. wrote on the occasion of the present dispute in the city of Limerick* (Limerick, 1769); E. O'Flaherty, 'Urban politics and municipal reform in Limerick, 1723–62', *Eighteenth-Century Ireland*, 6 (1991), pp. 112–19; T. C. Barnard, *The abduction of a Limerick heiress: social and political relationships in eighteenth-century Ireland* (Dublin, 1998), pp. 37–9.

80. *A letter from a free citizen in Limerick to his friend in Dublin* ([Dublin], 1760), pp. 7–8; [C. Massy], *A collection of resolutions, queries, &c. wrote on the occasion of the present dispute in the city of Limerick* (Limerick, 1769); O'Flaherty, 'Urban politics and municipal reform', pp. 112–19.

81. Minutes of the Barber Surgeons' Company, s.d. 23 July 1750, TCD, Ms. 1447/8/1, f. 113v.

82. R. Richey, 'Landed society in mid-eighteenth-century County Down', unpublished Ph.D. thesis, Queen's University, Belfast (2000), p. 185.

83. J. B. Leslie, *Armagh clergy and parishes* (Dundalk, 1911), p. 54; Leslie, *Raphoe clergy and parishes*, pp. 20–1; *Al. Dubl.*, pp. 360, 362, 363.

84. Leslie, *Raphoe clergy and parishes*, pp. 20–1; Cotton, *Fasti*, iii, p. 364.

85. W. Hamilton, *A discourse concerning zeal, against immorality and prophaneness deliver'd in two sermons in St Michaels Church, Dublin, October 29, and November 26. 1699* (Dublin, 1700), pp. 14–15.

86. T. C. Barnard, 'Reforming Irish manners: the religious societies in Dublin during the 1690s', *HJ*, 35 (1992), pp. 805–38; D. W. Hayton, 'Did the Church of Ireland fail?', in A. Ford et al. (eds), *As by law established: the Church of Ireland since the Reformation* (Dublin, 1995), pp. 166–86, 268–75.

87. W. Hamilton, *The comforts and advantages arising from the belief and consideration of God's governing providence. In a sermon preached in the Cathedral-Church of Armagh, August the 15th 1714* (Dublin, 1714).

88. W. Hamilton to J. Bonnell, 15 Oct. 1720, NLI, PC 435; William Hamilton, *The dangers of popery, and blessings arising from the late revolution, considered in a sermon preached in the Cathedral Church of Armagh. November, 5ᵗʰ MDCCXXII* (Dublin, 1723).

89. W. Hamilton to Mrs J. Bonnell, 4 Feb. 1711[12], 15 March 1711[12], NLI, PC 435; W. Hamilton, *A sermon preach'd before the honourable House of Commons. At St Andrew's Church, Dublin. On Friday the Fifth of November, 1725* (Dublin, 1725).

90. Andrew Hamilton to J. Bonnell, 7 May 1737; Jane Hamilton to same, 11 Oct. 1736, NLI, PC 435.

91. K. Benson to J. Bonnell, 4 July 1738, ibid.

92. A visitor about 1740 noted 'several genteel people and much civility'. Later, the Reverend William Henry lived in the town and boasted of 'maintaining universal hospitality and supporting His Majesty's government' there. Oughton Memoir, NAM, Ms. 8808–38–1, pp. 42, 51–2; W. Henry to D. of Newcastle, 9 Feb. 1767, BL, Add. Ms. 32,980, f. 58; W. Roulston, 'Deeds relating to Strabane and district from the Registry of Deeds in Dublin, 1708–40', *Directory of Irish Family History Research*, 24 (2001), pp. 83–4.

93. K. Benson to J. Bonnell, 4 July 1738, NLI, PC 435; *Faulkner's Dublin Journal*,

29 Sept.–2 Oct. 1753; J. H. Gebbie (ed.), *An Introduction to the Abercorn letters* (Omagh, 1972), pp. 41, 270.

94. Gebbie, *Abercorn letters*, pp. 43, 86.

95. Ibid., pp. 3, 40, 272.

96. K. Simms, 'Frontiers of the Irish church – regional and cultural', in T. Barry, R. Frame and K. Simms (eds), *Colony and frontier in medieval Ireland* (London and Rio Grande, 1995), pp. 178–99.

97. P. Collinson, *The religion of Protestants* (Oxford, 1982), pp. 115–40; Gregory, *Restoration, reformation and reform*, pp. 76–7.

98. A. Hamilton to J. Bonnell, 30 Oct. 1741, NLI, PC 435.

99. W. Hamilton to J. Bonnell, 30 June 1726; A. Hamilton to same, 7 May 1737; K. Benson to same, 4 July 1738, 20 Oct. 1738, NLI, PC 435.

100. Barton, *Lectures in natural philosophy*, p. 95, n.*.

101. Ms. sermon of Archdeacon R. Synge, 25 Nov. 1683, private collection, Greenwich, London.

102. T. Wentworth to A. Nickson, 12 July 1715, 2 Aug. 1715; Sheffield City Libraries, WWM/M 14/13 and 14; payment on 5 March 1713[14], account of A. Nickson with T. Wentworth, ibid., WWM/A 759, p. 383.

103. Observations on Lord Malton's woods in Ireland, 1728, Sheffield City Libraries, WWM/A 766, pp. 7, 17; survey of Lord Malton's Irish lands, 1728, ibid., WWM/A 769, p. 17.

104. Hume's report, NLI, Ms. 6054, pp. 8–9.

105. Bp. R. Howard to H. Howard, 10 Feb. 1732[3], NLI, Ms. 12,149; same to same, 18 Dec. 1735, 2 Feb. 1735[6]; H. Howard to Bp. R. Howard, 15 Jan. 1735[6], NLI, PC 227.

106. K. Quinn, 'The evolution of forestry in County Wicklow from prehistory to the present', in K. Hannigan and W. Nolan (eds), *Wicklow: history and society* (Dublin, 1994), pp. 837–9.

107. Copy of Revd M. Symes's will, 22 Oct. 1750, RCB, GS 2/7/3/35; NLI, report on private collections, no. 95; minute book, Arklow charter school, TCD, Ms. 5598, pp. 2, 3; account book of Ralph Howard, s.d. 28 Aug. 1749, NLI, Ms. 1725; *Al. Dubl.*, p. 797.

108. Account book, Incorporated Schools, 1733–78, TCD, Ms. 5419, pp. 4–6.

109. Valuations of Irish bishoprics and deaneries, Lambeth Palace Library, Ms. 2168, ff. 127–8; S. J. Connolly, *Religion, law and power: the making of Protestant Ireland, 1659–1760* (Oxford, 1992), pp. 180–2; Kelly (ed.), *Letters of Willes*, p. 94; Legg, *Synge Letters*, p. xv.

110. K. Benson to J. Bonnell, 4 July 1738, NLI, PC 435; H. Howard to Bp. R. Howard, 28 Jan. 1734[5], ibid., PC 227.

111. Account book of R. Morgan with Abp. H. Boulter, TCD, Ms. 6399, pp. 39, 41, 59, 131, 135; Lady Carteret to C. Tickell, 11 Jan. 1742[3], Tickell Mss, private collection, Devon; minute book, 1736–72, Mercer's Library, Royal College of Surgeons, Dublin; Abp. J. Ryder to ?A. Hill, 29 March 1758, 6 April 1758, Denbighshire RO, DD/BK/1, 321; P. Delany, *An historical account of the life, and reign of David, King of Israel*, 3 vols (Dublin, 1743), iii, sig. [Dd2v]; E. O'Leary, 'The O'More family of Balyna in the County Kildare, *circa* 1774', *Journal of the Kildare Archaeological Society*, 9 (1918), pp. 325–6.

112. J. Falvey, 'The Church of Ireland episcopate in the eighteenth-century', *Eighteenth-Century Ireland*, 8 (1993), p. 109; D. W. Hayton, 'Ireland and the English

ministers, 1707–1716', unpublished D. Phil. thesis, Oxford University (1975), p. 87; F. G. James, *Ireland in the empire, 1688–1770* (Cambridge, Mass., 1973), p. 131; P. McNally, '"Irish and English interests": national conflict within the Church of Ireland episcopate in the reign of George I', *IHS*, 29 (1995), p. 306.

113. R. Lowth to M. Lowth, 11, 15 March 1755, 16 Sept. 1755, Bodleian, Ms. Eng. Lett. C. 572, ff. 7, 9–9v, 96.

114. Gregory, *Restoration, reformation and reform*, pp. 146–77; Evans, 'The Anglican clergy of northern England', pp. 225–8; Spaeth, *The Church in an age of danger*, pp. 31–6.

115. P. O'Regan, *Archbishop William King of Dublin (1650–1729) and the constitution of church and state* (Dublin, 2000), p. 325.

116. St G. Ashe to H. Dodwell, 16 Feb. 1677[8], 18 Dec. 1684, 23 Feb. 1692[3], Bodleian, Ms. Eng. Lett. C. 29, ff. 1, 2, 20–20v; D. A. Hannigan, 'The University of Dublin, 1685–1750: a study of matriculation records', unpublished MA thesis, St Patrick's College, Maynooth (1995), pp. 25, 49–55, 77–9; R. B. McDowell and D. A. Webb, *Trinity College Dublin, 1592–1952: an academic history* (Cambridge, 1982), pp. 41, 519, n. 16.

117. D. W. Hayton, 'The High Church Party in the Irish Convocation, 1703–1713', in H. J. Real and H. Stover-Leidig (eds), *Reading Swift: papers from the third Münster symposium of Jonathan Swift* (Munich, 1998), pp. 117–40.

118. Abp. W. King to Bp. W. Lloyd, 20 Nov. 1714; same to Bp. J. Stearne, 26 Feb. 1714[15], TCD, Ms. 2536/117, 196; same to A. Charlet, 20 April 1715, Bodleian, Ballard Ms. 8, f. 40v; P. Delany, *An essay towards evidencing the divine original of tythes* (London, 1748); [P. Delany], *The present state of learning, religion, and infidelity in Great-Britain* (London, 1732); P. Delany, *Sixteen discourses upon doctrines and duties, more peculiarly Christian; and against the reigning vanities of the age* (London, 1754).

119. [R. Morres], *A list of the absentees of Ireland*, 3rd edn (Dublin, 1769), p. 10.

120. Williams (ed.), *Correspondence of Swift*, iv, p. 330.

121. E. Echlin to C. Tickell, 14 Feb. 1760, Tickell Mss, private collection, Devon; Barnard, 'Improving clergymen', pp. 138–47.

122. H. F. Berry, *A history of the Royal Dublin Society* (London, 1915), pp. 24–7.

123. Bp. R. Howard to H. Howard, 10 Feb. 1731[2], NLI, PC 227; minute book, 1733–41, s.d. 15 Nov. 1739, 31 Jan. 1739[40], 14 Feb. 1739[40], RDS; J. Copping to Sir H. Sloane, 1 Dec. 1742, BL, Sloane Ms. 4057, ff. 162–2v; M. Dunlevy, 'Samuel Madden and the scheme for the encouragement of useful manufactures', in A. Bernelle (ed.), *Decantations: a tribute to Maurice Craig* (Dublin, 1992), pp. 21–8; D. Fitzgerald, Knight of Glin and E. Malins, *Lost demesnes: Irish landscape gardening, 1660–1845* (London, 1976), pp. 43–4; S. Madden, *A letter to the Dublin-Society on the improving their fund* (Dublin, 1739).

124. Minute book, 1758–61, s.d. 9 and 16 March 1758, 13 and 20 April 1758, 4, 6 and 9 May 1758, 23 and 30 Nov. 1758, 5, 12 and 19 April 1759, 18 Dec. 1760, 16 April 1761, 28 May 1761, RDS; W. Henry to D. of Newcastle, 23 Sept. 1765, BL, Add. Ms. 32,970, ff. 25–5v; Calendar of miscellaneous letters and papers, prior to 1760, s.d. 15 March 1758, NA; W. Henry, *Love of our country* (Dublin, 1756).

125. Minute books, 1733–41, 1741–46, RDS.

126. Minute book, 1736–72, Mercer's Library, Royal College of Surgeons, Dublin.

127. D. T. Andrew, *Philanthropy and police: London charity in the eighteenth century* (Princeton, NJ, 1989), pp. 7–8, 78–81.

128.   H. J. Lawlor, *The Fasti of St Patrick's, Dublin* (Dundalk, 1930), pp. 58, 149, 153, 161, 205.

129.   Indenture, 2 July 1734, NA, D. 7994; *Al. Dubl.*, p. 900; M. E. Burns, *Wilson's Hospital, Multyfarnham: a history from its origin to 1860* (Multyfarnham, 1971), p. 7; Cotton, *Fasti*, ii, pp. 112–13, 138, 143, 178; subscription list to A. Gavin, *A master key to popery* (Dublin, 1724), p. vii.

130.   J. Owen to Abp. W. Wake, 11 Nov. 1725, Christ Church, Wake Ms. 14/302.

131.   H. Maule to Abp. W. Wake, 9 June 1724, 14 July 1724, 19 Nov. 1724, ibid., Wake Ms. 14/202, 204, 223; J. Owen to same, 10 April 1724, 21 Nov. 1724, 23 Feb. 1724[5], 14 April 1725, 18 Sept. 1725, 11 Nov. 1725, ibid., 14/190, 225, 240, 285, 302; Bp. H. Downes to same, 21 Nov. 1724, ibid., 14/225; Barton, *Lectures in natural philosophy*, pp. 111–12.

132.   Visitations, diocese of Limerick, RCB, D 13/1/1–15; licences to schoolmasters, diocese of Clogher, ibid., D.1. 72, 2–5; 28 Henry VIII, *c.*15, clause ix; *Statutes*, i, pp. 119–27; T. C. Barnard, *Cromwellian Ireland: Government and reform in Ireland, 1649–1660* (Oxford, 1975), pp. 183–9; T. Corcoran, *State policy in Irish education* (Dublin, 1916); M. Quane, 'The diocesan schools – 1570–1870', *JCHAS*, 66 (1961), pp. 31–3.

133.   W. Smythe to P. Hare, 26 Aug. 1760; same to R. Smythe, 14 March 1767, 7 April 1767, NLI, PC 446.

134.   List of pupils at Elphin diocesan school, 1730s, ibid., PC 225; J. Ingram to W. Smythe, 3 Sept. 1736, 27 Feb. 1736[7], ibid., PC 445; R. Harvey to Bp. W. Smythe, 29 June 1693, ibid., PC 436/16; R. Lambert to E. Southwell, 9 Feb. 1711[12], BL, Add. Ms. 20,131, f. 13v; J. B. Leslie, list of schoolmasters, NLI, Ms. 2678, p. 4.

135.   J. Aicken, *An address to the magistrates, clergy and learned gentlemen of the city of Dublin* (Dublin, 1698); *A general account of the regulation, discipline, course of study and expences attending the education of youth in the seminary to be opened the 8ᵗʰ day of January, 1759* (Dublin, 1758); *The mountebank schoolmaster*, in BL, pressmark 1890 e 5 (204); D. W. Ressinger (ed.), *Memoirs of the Reverend Jacques Fontaine, 1658–1729*, Huguenot Society of Great Britain and Ireland, new series, 2 (1992), pp. 184, 186–7; T. Sheridan, *An oration pronounced before a numerous body of the nobility and gentry, assembled at the Musick-Hall in Fishamble-Street* (Dublin, 1757).

136.   R. Ratcliff to W. Smythe, 24 Jan. 1748[9], 25 Feb. 1748[9], NLI, PC 449. Cf. Traill autobiography, PRONI, D. 1460/1.

137.   J. D. Harwood to J. Crone, 12 March 1769, Cork Archives Institute, Crone of Byblox Mss, PR3/box 1; R. Walsh, *Two dialogues between a doctor and a lady* (Dublin, n.d.[*c.*1749]), p. ii.

138.   P. Delany, *Twenty sermons on social duties and their opposite vices* (London, 1747), p. 126; W. Mussenden to H. Mussenden, 21 Sept. 1758, Suffolk CRO, de Mussenden Leathes Mss, Ipswich, HA 403/1/11, 1; H. R. Cathcart, 'An help for schoolboys': the choir and grammar schools, 1431–1991* (Dublin, 1991), pp. 6–13; Delany, *Autobiography*, 1st series, iii, p. 16.

139.   W. Perceval to K. O'Hara, 12 Sept. 1717, 21 Nov. 1717, NLI, Ms. 20,385.

140.   Edgeworth, account books, s.d. 11 July 1759, 2 April 1760, 26 May 1760, 12 and 28 June 1760, 18 Oct. 1760, 1 Dec. 1760, ibid., Ms 1525, pp. 97; 1526, pp. 119, 122, 131, 136, 174, 193; accounts, s.d. 11 July 1759, NA, M. 1504, pp. 343–4; *Memoirs of Richard Lovell Edgeworth, Esq.* 2 vols (London, 1820), i, pp. 68–71.

141.   Orrery to L. Beecher, 25 April 1676, Petworth, Orrery Mss, general series, 29;

L. Beecher to dowager countess of Orrery, 17 Nov. 1680, 13 Oct. 1682; J. Hall
to same, 22 April 1682, 13 Dec. 1687, 21 Jan. 1687[8], ibid., general series, 29;
R. Purcell to Orrery, 4 April 1738, Harvard UL, Orrery Mss, Ms. Eng. 218.19;
M. Quane, 'Charleville Endowed School', *JRSAI*, 88 (1958), pp. 28–44; Cork and
Burlington to D. Foulke, 22 Feb. 1693[4], Chatsworth, entry book of Lord Cork
and Burlington's letters, 1693–4; same to W. Congreve, 14 and 23 Feb. 1692[3],
NLI, Ms. 13,226; Lord Burlington to J. Coughlan, 10 March 1728[9], Chatsworth,
Crotty letter book, 1728–9; A. Crotty to Lady Burlington, 23 March 1730[1],
ibid., Devonshire Letters, 200.1; S. Hill to H. Boyle, 5 Nov. 1731, 28 May 1732;
same to Lord Burlington, 5 Nov. 1731, PRONI, D 2707/A1/11, 35, 36, 44; W.
Conner to Sir A. Abdy, 10 Oct. 1750, 3 Nov. 1750, 15 Jan. 1750[1], 6 Dec. 1751,
21 Jan. 1752, Chatsworth, letter book of W. Conner, 1749–58; T. Hewetson to
A. Herbert, 26 Sept. 1764, NA, M. 1854; J. Graves to J. Crone, 6 July 1767, Cork
Archives Institute, Crone of Byblox Mss, PR3/box 1; J. D. Harwood to same, 10
Dec. 1768, 28 Sept. 1771, ibid., box 1; E. Kellett to same, 14 July 1773, ibid., box
1; J. Browne, 'Kilkenny College', *Transactions of the Kilkenny Archaeological Society*, 1
(1849–51), pp. 223–8; T. U. Sadleir, 'The register of Kilkenny School (1685–1800)',
JRSAI, 54 (1924), pp. 55–67, 152–69.

142. Barnard, *Cromwellian Ireland*, pp. 187–8.
143. W. Stannus to W. Leathes, 7 April 1714, 27 Oct. 1714, Suffolk CRO, HA 403/1/7,
      63, 74; J. B. Cunningham, 'William Starrat, surveyor-philomath', *Clogher Record*, 11
      (1983), pp. 214–25; *Poems by Allan Ramsay* (Dublin, 1733), pp. 251–3; W. Starrat,
      The doctrine of projectiles (Dublin, 1730); J. B., *A tutor to arithmetick* (Cork, 1719);
      D. Dickson, 'Philip Ronayne and the publication of his treatise of Algebra', *Long
      Room*, 8 (1973), pp. 13–18; D. Dowling, *Mercantile arithmetic*, 2nd edn (Dublin,
      1766).
144. Visitation of Meath, *c.*1730, RCB, GS 2/7/3/10, p. 64.
145. Churchwardens' accounts, St Michan's, Dublin, 1723–61, RCB, P. 276/8/2;
      disposition of pews, St Michan's Dublin, from 1724, ibid., P. 276/12/2, p. 72.
146. Vestry books, St Catherine's, Dublin, 1693–1730, RCB, P. 117/05/1.2, pp. 324, 332;
      ibid., 1730–67, RCB, P. 117/05/1. 3, p. 5
147. M. Quane, 'Preston Endowed School, Navan', *Ríoct na Míde*, 4 (1968), pp. 50–4;
      M. Quane, 'Ranelagh Endowed School, Athlone', *Journal of the Old Athlone
      Society*, 1 (1969), p. 25; M. Quane, 'Athlone Classical School and Athlone English
      School', ibid., 1 (1970–1), pp. 90–1.
148. L. Beecher to dowager countess of Orrery, 17 Nov. 1680, 13 Oct. 1682; J. Hall to
      same, 22 April 1682, 13 Dec. 1687, 21 Jan. 1687[8], Petworth, Orrery Mss, general
      series, 29; M. Quane, 'Charleville Endowed School', pp. 28–44; Cork and
      Burlington to D. Foulke, 22 Feb. 1693[4], Chatsworth, Cork and Burlington letter
      book, 1693–94; same to W. Congreve, 14 and 23 Feb. 1692[3]; receipt of J.
      Oldfield, 26 March 1705, Chatsworth, Lismore Ms. 35/9.
149. M. Quane, 'Bishop Foy School, Waterford', *JCHAS*, 71 (1966), p. 106.
150. M. Quane, 'Viscount Weymouth's Grammar School, Carrickmacross', *JRSAI*, 86
      (1956), pp. 35–8.
151. Quane, 'Viscount Weymouth's school', pp. 40–2.
152. M. Quane, 'City of Dublin Free School', *JRSAI*, 90 (1960), p. 181.
153. M. Quane, 'Waterford Corporation Free School', *JCHAS*, 64 (1959), p. 91.
154. Mulcahy, *Kinsale*, i, pp. 98, 100, 104, 110, 115, 120; ii, pp. 3, 18; iii, pp. 17, 22, 29,
      39, 43; vi, p. 13; *Al. Dubl.*, p. 86.

155. Mulcahy, *Kinsale*, vi, p. 20.
156. Ibid., p. 60.
157. Ibid., p. 80.
158. Ibid., iii, pp. 38–9; vi, pp. 10–11.
159. Quane, 'Viscount Weymouth's school', pp. 40–2.
160. R. Edgeworth account book, NA, M. 1504, pp. 341–4; Edgeworth, accounts, s.d. 13 April 1752, 18 June 1752, 17 June 1755, 9 Dec. 1755, 30 Jan. 1756, 6 Jan. 1758, 7 and 11 July 1759, NLI, Mss 1520; 1521, p. 198; 1522, pp. 71, 106; 1524, p. 52; 1525, pp. 93, 97; *Memoirs of Richard Lovell Edgeworth, Esq.* 2 vols (London, 1820), i, pp. 62–8; Trevor West, *Midleton College, 1696–1996: a tercentenary history* (Cork, 1996), pp. 7–19.
161. R. Gillespie, 'Church, state and education in early modern Ireland' in M. R. O'Connell (ed.), *O'Connell: education, church and state* (Dublin, 1992), pp. 40–59, 104–7.
162. Lord Burlington to J. Coughlan, 10 March 1728[9], Chatsworth, Crotty letter book, 1728–29; S. Hill to H. Boyle, 5 Nov. 1731, 28 May 1732; same to Lord Burlington, 5 Nov. 1731, PRONI, D 2707/A1/11/35, 36, 44; J. B. Leslie, notes on the clergy, NLI, Ms. 1775, p. 497; M. Quane, 'Raphoe Royal School', *Donegal Annual*, 7 (1967), pp. 155–6.
163. M. Quane, 'Portora Royal School, Enniskillen', *Clogher Record*, 6 (1968), pp. 508–11.
164. J. Ingram to W. Smythe, 3 Sept. 1736, 27 Feb. 1736[7], 6 Dec. 1740, NLI, PC 445/15; J. B. Leslie, notes on clergy, ibid., Ms. 1775, p. 525; *The works in verse of Daniel Hayes, esq.* (London, 1769), p. ix.
165. Sheridan, *An oration*, p. 9.
166. Corporal Todd's journal, Wigan Public Library, EHC/164, pp. 8–10.
167. Mulcahy, *Kinsale*, iii, p. 17.
168. R. Daniel to E. Southwell, 2 Sept. 1738; J. Trotter to same, 30 Sept. 1738; E. Southwell to R. Daniel, [Sept. 1738], same to Dean [?Daniel] of Down, after Sept. 1738, BL, Add. Ms. 20, 131, ff. 99v, 103v, 110, 120.
169. K. C. Balderston (ed.), *The collected letters of Oliver Goldsmith* (Cambridge, 1928), p. 164.
170. Accounts of Primrose Grange, s.d. 15 Dec. 1760, TCD, Ms. 5646; accounts of Ballycastle, ibid., Ms. 5609, p. 34.
171. Ressinger (ed.), *Memoirs of the Reverend Jacques Fontaine*, pp. 184, 186–7.
172. W. Owen to J. Owen, 20 April 1670, 8 Dec. 1671, UCNW, Penrhos Mss, v, 427, 428.
173. M. Higgins to W. King, 7 Dec. 1683, 16 Jan. 1683[4], 3 Aug. 1684, 16 Sept. [?1684], 12 Oct. [?1684], n.d. [c.1684], TCD, Mss 1995–2008/19, 20, 26, 2287, 2288, 2291.
174. Limerick visitations, RCB, D 13/1/1–15.
175. J. McCollin to D. Barret, 24 Dec. 1696, PRONI, T 2529, printed in P. Collins (ed.), *County Monaghan sources in the Public Record Office of Northern Ireland* (Belfast, 1998), p. 17.
176. E. Smith to Governors of his schools in Ireland, [1679]; governors to E. Smith, 3 May 1679; schedule of E. Smith schools, Guildhall Library, London, Ms. 13,823, ff. 52v, 54, 96v.
177. M. Henry, *A sermon preach'd upon occasion of the funeral of the Reverend Daniel Burgess* (London, 1713), p. 33; Quane, 'Charleville Endowed School', pp. 33–4.

178. Visitations of Limerick, 1698, 1708, 1713, 1714, RCB, Ms. D 13/1/2, 10, 14, 15.

179. Visitations of Clogher, 1718–19, 1725, 1747, PRONI, D 242/4, 9, 15.

180. R. Lambert to E. Southwell, 9 Feb. 1711[12], BL, Add. Ms. 20,131, f. 13v.

181. R. Daniel to E. Southwell, 2 Sept. 1738; J. Trotter to same, 30 Sept. 1738; E. Southwell to R. Daniel, [Sept. 1738], same to Dean [?Daniel] of Down, after Sept. 1738, BL, Add. Ms. 20,131, ff. 99v, 103v, 110, 120.

182. Mulcahy, *Kinsale*, vii, p. 28.

183. Visitation of Raphoe, *c*.1730, RCB, Ms. GS 2/7/3/34, pp. 11–12.

184. W. Urwick, *The early history of Trinity College, Dublin, 1591–1660* (London and Dublin, 1892), pp. 67–9, 72.

185. St G. Ashe to H. Dodwell, 13 Aug. 1692, Bodleian, Ms. Eng. Lett. C. 29, f. 18v; Hannigan, 'The University of Dublin', pp. 24–5, 77.

186. J. Waring to W. Waring, 22 July 1703, private collection, Co. Down; Delany, *Autobiography*, 1st series, ii, p. 377; Hannigan, 'The University of Dublin', pp. 57–8.

187. St G. Ashe to H. Dodwell, 13 Aug. 1692, 23 Feb. 1692[3], Bodleian, Ms. Eng. Lett. C. 29, ff. 18v, 20–20v.

188. Account book of J. Griffith, 1683–84, Marsh's Library, Dublin, Ms. Z3.2.4; R. Edgeworth, account books, s.d. 26 May 1760, 9 Dec. 1760, May and June 1761, NLI, Mss 1526, pp. 122, 193; 1527, pp. 67–71, 104, 124, 126; NA, M. 1504, pp. 346–9; accounts of executors of William Vaughan, 1748–60, ibid., M. 4915; Hannigan, 'The University of Dublin', pp. 42–4.

189. St G. Ashe to H. Dodwell, 18 Dec. 1684, 31 March 1685, Bodleian, Ms. Eng. Lett. C. 29, ff. 2v, 4; J. Evelyn, Jr. to J. Evelyn, 29 July 1693, 5 May 1694; Sir C. Wyche to same, 7 Sept. 1693, Evelyn Mss, formerly at Christ Church, Oxford, now in BL, Add. Mss; S. Molyneux to Bp. St G. Ashe, 27 Nov. 1707, 6 Dec. 1707; same to J. Keogh, 29 Nov. 1707, Southampton Civic Archives, D/M, 1/2, pp. 20, 21, 23; R. Howard to H. Howard, 18 Sept. 1707, NLI, PC 227(1); K. T. Hoppen, *The common scientist in the seventeenth century: a study of the Dublin Philosophical Society, 1683–1708* (London, 1970), pp. 53–72.

190. D. Clarke, *Thomas Prior, 1681–1751: founder of the Royal Dublin Society* (Dublin, 1951).

191. Notebook of J. Cousser, Yale University, Beinecke Library, Osborn Music Ms. 16, p. 259.

192. [S. Madden], *A proposal for the general encouragement of learning in Dublin-College* (Dublin, 1731).

193. Minute books, 1731–33, 1733–41, 1741–46, RDS; minute book, 1736–72, Mercer's Library, Royal College of Surgeons, Dublin.

194. Bursars' vouchers, 30 June 1732, TCD, MUN/P/4, 36/31; [W. Maple], *A method of tanning without bark* (Dublin, 1729); minute book, Arklow School, TCD, Ms. 5598, pp. 1, 2, 7; Barnard, 'Improving clergymen', pp. 136–51; P. H. Kelly, 'The politics of political economy in mid-eighteenth-century Ireland', in S. J. Connolly (ed.), *Political ideas in eighteenth-century Ireland* (Dublin, 2000), pp. 105–29.

195. Williams (ed.), *Swift Correspondence*, iv, pp. 91, 104, 170, 271, 298.

196. E. Cooke to Mrs Sweet, 27 July 1727, Cooke Mss, Maidenhall, Co. Kilkenny; J. A. Oughton memoir, NAM, Ms. 8808–36–1, pp. 30–1; Delany, *Autobiography*, 1st series, ii, pp. 416, 559; Legg, *Synge Letters*, pp. 50, 59; *A letter to the young gentlemen of the University of Dublin, on occasion of their late disturbances* (n.p., 1734), pp. 40–1.

197. T. Seele to W. Shaw, [16–18 Oct. 1664], 1 April 1665, TCD, MUN P/1/470, 20, 36.

198. T. Seele to W. Shaw, n.d. [1664], 22 April 1665, ibid., MUN P/1/470, 24, 38.
199. Bp. J. Stearne to Abp. W. King, 23 May 1715, ibid., Mss 1995–2008/1644; H. Howard to same, 16 June 1715, 6 and 23 July 1715, 6 and 30 Aug. [1715], 29 Sept. 1715, 20 Oct. 1715, 31 March 1716, 10 April 1716, ibid., Mss 1995–2008/1665, 1672, 1682, 1695, 1716, 1730, 1738, 1763, 1768; Abp. W. King to H. Howard, 17 Sept. 1715, 6 Oct. 1715, ibid., Ms. 2533, pp. 90, 103; *A true and faithful account of the entry and reception of three extraordinary Irish ambassadors* (London, 1716).
200. J. A. Oughton, autobiography, NAM, Ms. 8808–36–1, p. 29; *Al. Dubl.*, p. 727.
201. Barnard, *Cromwellian Ireland*, pp. 204–5; Hannigan, 'The University of Dublin', pp. 19–21.
202. *A letter to the young gentlemen of the University of Dublin*, pp. 4–6.
203. E. Weston to Abp. G. Stone, 31 March 1747; Abp. G. Stone to E. Weston, 7 April 1747, PRONI, T 3019/852, 855; Lord Shannon to Lord Bedford, 1 Oct. 1758; W. Clement to same, [3 Oct. 1758], Bp. E. Synge to same, [7 Oct. 1758]; Lord Bedford to Lord Shannon, 8 Oct. 1758, ibid., T 2915/6/1, 4, 7 and 9.
204. Abp. J. Vesey, journal, pp. 15, 24, 31, 42, de Vesci Mss, NLI; fragmentary accounts of E. Cliffe, 1732, NA, 1096/8/1; R. Edgeworth, account book, ibid., M. 1504, pp. 346–9; account of C. Boyle with J. Lawson, 16 June 1756, PRONI, D. 2707/A1/1, 81C; accounts of executors of William Vaughan, 1748–60, NA, M. 4915; J. Story, account book, s.d. July 1766, Bingfield, Co. Cavan; W. Smythe to R. Smythe, 24 Oct. 1767, NLI, PC, 446; D. Hannigan, 'The University of Dublin', pp. 8–10, 58–61.
205. W. Owen to J. Owen, 13 April 1675, 30 Aug. 1695, UCNW, Penrhos Mss, v, 430, 444; L. Clayton to R. Huntington, 11 April 1684, Bodleian, Rawlinson Ms. B. 497, f. 6; Bp. W. King to G. Browne, 29 May 1696, TCD, Ms. 750/1, 12; K. Howard to W. Howard, 1 June 1710, 20 March 1713[14], NLI, PC 227.
206. A. Hamilton to J. Bonnell, 30 June 1726, 7 May 1737; K. Benson to same, 27 July 1737, 4 July 1738, NLI, PC 435.
207. W. Conner to H. Boyle, 16 June 1741, PRONI, D 2707/A1/11/75; W. Smythe to R. Smythe, 12 May 1767, NLI, PC 446. Cf. O. Gallagher to O. St George, 11 April 1727, PRO, C 110/46, 479; E. B. Day, *Mr Justice Day of Kerry 1745–1851: a discursive memoir* (Exeter, 1938), pp. 45–6.
208. *A directory of Dublin for the year 1738* (Dublin, 2000), pp. 135–6; McDowell and Webb, *Trinity College Dublin*, p. 41.
209. Boulter, *Letters*, i, pp. 47–8, 51–2, 54–5.
210. Delany, *Autobiography*, 1st series, ii, pp. 465, 552.
211. St G. Ashe to H. Dodwell, 16 Feb. 1677[8], 31 March 1685, 24 Sept. 1685, Bodleian, Ms. Eng. Lett. C. 29, ff. 1, 5, 7; W. Palliser to H. Dodwell, 14 Nov. 1698, ibid., Ms. Eng. Lett. C. 28, f. 37; W. Palliser to W. Perceval, 8 Feb. 1700[1], 22 Aug. 1702, PRONI, D 906/58 & 62.
212. E. Cooke to Mrs Sweet, 27 July 1727, Cooke Mss, Maidenhall, Co. Kilkenny; *A letter to the young gentlemen of the University of Dublin*, pp. 45–7.
213. Bursars' vouchers, 15 Nov. 1768, TCD, MUN/P/4, folder 56/1; W. Smythe to R. Smythe, 12 March 1767, NLI, PC 446; W.S Lewis (ed.), *The correspondence of Horace Walpole*, 48 vols (New Haven, 1937–83), ix, p. 404.
214. Bill of Abraham Walker, 17 March 1743[4], NLI, PC 223(6).
215. Receipts, 17 Dec. 1743, ibid., PC 223(6).
216. Receipts for goods supplied to R. Howard, 1743–44, NLI, PC 223(6); R. Edgeworth, account books, 1760–61, NA, M. 1504, pp. 346–9; NLI, Ms. 1527, pp. 68–71.

217. W. Smythe to R. Smythe, 24 Oct. 1767, NLI, PC 446; F. P. Lock, *Edmund Burke. 1: 1730–1784* (Oxford, 1998), p. 29.

218. *A letter from a school-master in the country from a friend in town, relative to Mr Sheridan's scheme of education* (Dublin, 1758), pp. 6–9, 14–15.

219. W. Smythe to R. Smythe, 4 July 1767, NLI, PC 446; [Morres], *A list of the absentees of Ireland*, 3rd edn, p. 10.

220. 'Epitaph on Francis Andrews', June 1774, NLI, Ms. 25,432.

221. A. Crookshank and D. A. Webb, *Paintings and sculptures in Trinity College Dublin* (Dublin, 1990), p. 12; J. Ingamells, *A dictionary of British and Irish travellers in Italy, 1701–1800* (London and New Haven, 1997), pp. 19–20; McDowell and Webb, *Trinity College Dublin*, pp. 52–3.

222. R. F. Foster, *Modern Ireland 1600–1972* (London, 1988), pp. 172–3; Lock, *Edmund Burke. 1*, pp. 29–52; McDowell and Webb, *Trinity College Dublin*, pp. 53–6.

223. Connolly, *Religion, law and power*, pp. 150–1.

224. 'Report on the state of popery, Ireland, 1731', *Archivium Hibernicum*, 1 (1912), p. 11.

225. T. Daly to H. Owen, 19 April 1694, 23 June 1698; P. Crofts to same, 21 Nov. 1694; C. Daly to same, 24 June 1698, NLW, Powis Castle correspondence, nos. 192, 239, 251, 697; K. O'Shea, *Castleisland: church and people* (Tralee, 1981), pp. 38, 49; Connolly, *Religion, law and power*, pp. 149–59, 264–94.

226. Minute book, 1733–41, s.d. 20 Jan. 1736[7], 10 and 24 Feb. 1736[7], RDS; N. Peacock, diary, s.d. 1 May 1751, 8 July 1751, NLI, Ms. 16,091; J. Pratt, diary, s.d. 17 March 1745[6], Purdon Mss, Cloverhill, Co. Cavan; P. Fagan, *Dublin's turbulent priest: Cornelius Nary, 1658–1738* (Dublin, 1991).

227. T. C. Barnard, 'The government and Irish dissent, 1704–1780' in K. Herlihy (ed.), *The politics of Irish dissent, 1650–1800* (Dublin, 1997), pp. 9–15; lists of conformists and dissenters in Ulster, RIA, Ms. 24 K 19; Lambeth Palace, Ms. 1742, ff. 49–56.

228. R. L. Greaves, *God's other children: Protestant nonconformists and the emergence of denominational churches in Ireland, 1660–1700* (Stanford, 1997), p. 193.

229. *Records of the General Synod of Ulster from 1691 to 1820*, 3 vols (Belfast, 1897), ii, pp. 376, 529–30.

230. Ibid., pp. 501; records of the sub-synod of Derry, 1706–36, pp. 15, 18, 82, 134, Presbyterian Historical Society, Belfast.

231. R. Black to Lord Castlereagh, 27 April 1799; undated paper; paper of 5 Feb. 1799, PRONI, D 3030/741, 742, 743. Cf. I. McBride, '"When Ulster joined Ireland": anti-popery, Presbyterianism and Irish republicanism in the 1790s', *P & P*, 157 (1997), p. 66.

232. Minutes of Princes St Presbyterian Church, Cork, Cork Archives Institute, U 87/3, s.d. 2 and 10 Sept. 1725, 19 June 1757, 16 Feb. 1777, 24 March 1782, 27 Oct. 1796.

233. Cork Baptist Church Book, Cork Baptist Church.

234. P. Griffin, *The people with no name* (Princeton and London, 2001), pp. 86–8.

235. PRONI, D 3030/742.

236. Minutes of Route Presbytery, 1701–6, Presbyterian Historical Society, p. 38; memorandum on house purchase from Mrs Cuthbert, minutes of Princes St Presbyterian Church, Cork, Cork Archives Institute, U 87/3; 'Abstracts of wills', *Irish Ancestor*, 2 (1970), p. 123.

237. Notebook of John Kennedy, Presbyterian Historical Society, Belfast; J. M. Barkley, 'The Presbyterian minister in eighteenth-century Ireland', in [J. L. M. Haire] (ed.), *Challenge and conflict: essays in Irish Presbyterian history and doctrine* (Antrim,

1981), pp. 49–50; M. Brown, *Francis Hutcheson in 1719–1730* (Dublin, 2002);
Gregory, *Restoration, reformation and reform*, p. 77.

238.   I. M. Bishop, 'The education of Ulster students at the University of Glasgow in
       the eighteenth century', unpublished MA thesis, Queen's University, Belfast
       (1987); L. W. B. Brockliss and P. Ferté, 'Irish clerics in France in the seventeenth
       and eighteenth centuries: a statistical study', *PRIA*, 87, sect. C (1987), pp. 527–72;
       Greaves, *God's other children*, pp. 176–7; P. O'Connell, 'The early-modern Irish
       college network in Iberia, 1590–1800', in T. O'Connor (ed.), *The Irish in Europe,
       1580–1815* (Dublin, 2001), pp. 49–64; *Records of the General Synod of Ulster*, ii, pp.
       528–9; T. J. Walsh, *The Irish continental college movement: the colleges at Bordeaux,
       Toulouse and Lille* (Dublin and Cork, 1973).

5. *Professions*

1.   R. Howard to H. Howard, 2 Feb. 1735[6], NLI, PC 227.
2.   L. M. Cullen, 'Catholics' social classes under the penal laws', in T. P. Power and
      K. Whelan (eds), *Endurance and emergence: Catholics in Ireland in the eighteenth
      century* (Dublin, 1990), pp. 57–84; T. P. Power, 'Converts', ibid., pp. 101–28.
3.   G. S. Holmes, 'The professions and social change in England, 1680–1730',
      Proceedings of the British Academy, 65 (1979), pp. 313–54; G. S. Holmes, *Augustan
      England: professions, state and society, 1680–1730* (London, 1982); W. R. Prest (ed.),
      The professions in early modern England (London, 1987); P. Corfield, *Power and the
      professions in Britain, 1700–1850* (London, 1995); R. O'Day, *The professions in early
      modern England, 1450–1800* (Harlow, 2000).
4.   G. E. Aylmer, *The state's servants: the civil service of the English republic, 1649–1660*
      (London, 1973).
5.   P. Borsay, *The English urban renaissance* (Oxford, 1989).
6.   P. Clark, *British clubs and societies, 1580–1800: the origins of an associational world*
      (Oxford, 2000).
7.   P. Fagan, *Catholics in a Protestant Country* (Dublin, 1998).
8.   T. C. Barnard, *Cromwellian Ireland: government and reform in Ireland, 1649–1660*
      (Oxford, 1975), pp. 249–92; J. Crawford, *Anglicizing the government of Ireland: the
      Irish privy council and the expansion of Tudor rule, 1556–1578* (Dublin, 1993);
      N. Garnham, *The courts, crime and the criminal law in Ireland, 1692–1760* (Dublin,
      1996); G. J. Hand, *English law in Ireland, 1290–1324* (Cambridge, 1967); J. McCavitt,
      '"Good planets in their several spheres": the establishment of the assize circuits in
      early seventeenth-century Ireland', *Irish Jurist*, new series, 24 (1989), pp. 248–78;
      H. Pawlisch, *Sir John Davies and the conquest of Ireland: a study in legal imperialism*
      (Cambridge, 1985).
9.   C. Kenny, *The King's Inns and the kingdom of Ireland: the Irish 'Inn of Court'
      1541–1800* (Dublin, 1992); T. P. Power, 'The "Black Book" of the King's Inns', *Irish
      Jurist*, new series, 20 (1985), pp. 139–46.
10.   D. F. Cregan, 'Irish Catholic admissions to the English Inns of Court, 1558–1625',
      Irish Jurist, 5 (1970), pp. 95–114; D. F. Cregan, 'Irish recusant lawyers in politics in
      the reign of James I', ibid., pp. 306–20; J. H. Ohlmeyer, 'Irish recusant lawyers
      during the reign of Charles I', in M. Ó Siochrú (ed.), *Kingdoms in crisis: Ireland in
      the 1640s* (Dublin, 2001), pp. 63–89.

11. T. C. Barnard, 'Lawyers and the law in later seventeenth-century Ireland', *IHS*, 18 (1993), pp. 256–82; C. Kenny, 'The exclusion of Catholics from the legal profession in Ireland, 1537–1829', ibid., 15 (1987), pp. 349–55; Power, 'The "Black Book", pp. 139–46.

12. T. Power, 'Conversions among the legal profession in Ireland in the eighteenth century', in D. Hogan and W. N. Osborough (eds), *Brehons, serjeants and attorneys* (Dublin, 1990), pp. 153–74; Fagan, *Catholics in a Protestant country*, pp. 101–25.

13. Cregan, 'Irish Catholic admissions', pp. 95–114; Cregan, 'Irish recusant lawyers', pp. 306–20.

14. K. Howard to W. Howard, 19 Feb. 1708[9], 28 Feb. 1709[10], 6 and 22 March 1709[10], 26 May 1709, 19 June 1711, 15 Dec. 1713, 3 April 1714, 8 July 1714, NLI, PC 227; R. French to W. Smythe, 29 May 1712, 23 Dec. 1712, 10 Nov. 1713, ibid., PC 447.

15. R. Cox to E. Southwell, 29 Nov. 1695, Bristol Record Office, Ms. 12,694(1), 52; K. Howard to W. Howard, 31 Aug. 1710, NLI, PC 227; R. Edgeworth, account books, 1720–34, ibid., Mss 1507–1510; P. Earle, *The making of the English middle class, 1660–1730* (London, 1991), pp. 60–1; E. Hughes, *North-country life in the eighteenth century. I. The north-east, 1700–1850* (London, New York and Toronto, 1952), p. 82; Williams (ed.), *Swift Correspondence*, v, p. 138.

16. Barnard, 'Lawyers and the law in later seventeenth-century Ireland', pp. 262–3.

17. *An alphabetical list of such barristers, attorneys and solicitors, as have taken the oath* (Dublin, 1735).

18. G. E. Howard, *Queries relative to the several defects and grievances in some of the present laws of Ireland*, 2nd edn (Dublin, 1761), pp. 17–19; G. E. Howard, *A compendious treatise of the rules and practice of the pleas side of the Exchequer in Ireland*, 2 vols (Dublin, 1759) i, p. iii–xx; *An alphabetical list . . .* ; W. N. Osborough, 'The regulation of the admission of attorneys and solicitors in Ireland', in Hogan and Osborough (eds), *Brehons, serjeants and attorneys*, pp. 101–51.

19. R. Gillespie, 'Finavarra and its manor court in the 1670s', *The Other Clare*, 25 (2001), pp. 47–8.

20. Barnard, 'Lawyers and the law', pp. 275–6.

21. A. Brodrick to St J. Brodrick, 11 Nov. 1684, Surrey CRO, Midleton Papers, Ms. 1248/1, f. 202v; Lord Capell to Portland, 6 Nov. 1695, Nottingham UL, Portland Mss, PW A 252; Bp. R. Howard to H. Howard, 27 Feb. 1727[8], NLI, PC 227.

22. Cases in King's Bench, 1687 and Exchequer, 1692, PRONI, T 2825/B/3/1; case, 8 March 1687[8], ibid., T 2825/B/1/12; case, 13 Feb. 1701[2], ibid., B/1/38; Conolly's fees, ibid., B/3/4 (Michaelmas, 1687); B/3/5 (Easter and Trinity 1694), account with J. Hamilton, 1695–95, ibid., B/5/26.

23. W. Conolly to corporation of Londonderry, 21 Nov. 1691, 26 Dec. 1691, 21 Jan. 1692[3], PRONI, D 1449/12, 6, 7, 11; same to W. Crookshank, 8 April 1693, ibid., 17; same to J. Harvey, 27 May 1701, ibid., 33; Londonderry corporation minute book, 1688–1704, s.d. 27 Nov. 1690, 27 Jan. 1690[1], 14 Feb. 1690[1], 15 Jan. 1691[2], 2 May 1693, PRONI, LA 79/2A/2.

24. Receipts and papers as deputy alnager, ibid., T 2825/B/5/3, 7, 9, 12, 14, 19, 20, 23, 25.

25. M. Coghill to E. Southwell, 13 June 1728, ibid., T 2534/2; P. McNally, *Parties, patriots and undertakers: parliamentary politics in early Hanoverian Ireland* (Dublin, 1997), pp. 88–117.

26. Marriage settlement of K. Conyngham and W. Conolly, 15 Dec. 1694, IAA,

Castletown deposit, box 47; L. Boylan, 'The Conollys of Castletown: a family history', *Quarterly Bulletin of the Irish Georgian Society,* 11 (1968), pp. 1–19; J. G. Simms, *The Williamite confiscation in Ireland, 1690–1703* (London, 1956), pp. 126–7, 141, 150, 155.

27. M. Jones to J. Bonnell, 13 Jan [*c.*1735], NLI, PC 435.

28. Abp. W. Palliser to H. Dodwell, 4 June 1703, Bodleian, Ms. Eng. Lett. C. 28, f. 62; H. Dodwell to Abp. W. Palliser, 19 June 1703, Bodleian, Cherry Ms. 23, p. 135; *Schemes from Ireland for the benefit of the body natural, ecclesiastical and politick* (Dublin, 1732), p. 27.

29. D. Mussenden to H. Mussenden, 6 [?]1742, Suffolk CRO, Ipswich, de Mussenden Leathes Mss, HA 403/1/11, 20.

30. F. Bernard, account book, 1719–28, Cork Archives Institute, Doherty Mss, U/137; F. Bernard to H. Prittie, 15 Oct. 1729, NLI, Ms. 29,810/1; F. E. Ball, *The judges of Ireland,* 2 vols (New York, 1926), ii, pp. 199, 200; John Stevenson, *Two centuries of life in County Down, 1600–1800* (Belfast and Dublin,1920), pp. 283–339.

31. *Memoirs of Richard Lovell Edgeworth, Esq.,* 2 vols (London, 1820), i, pp. 21, 230; Barnard, 'Robert French of Monivea', pp. 273–4; *KIAP,* pp. 150, 179.

32. R. Edgeworth, account books, 11 and 13 June 1737, 4 Dec. 1737, 29 April 1752, 2 April 1760; 11 Dec. 1769, NLI, Mss 1512, pp. 28, 62; 1519, p. 226; 1526, p. 119; 1535, p. 280.

33. R. Edgeworth, account books, s.d. 20 Feb. 1733[4], ibid., Ms. 1510.

34. Black Book of Edgeworth, ibid., Ms. 7361, p. 2; Southwell notebook, BL, Egerton Ms. 1628, f. 13v; Sir R. Southwell to Sir J. Perceval, 21 Dec. 1685, BL, Add. Ms. 46,962, f. 166; HMC, *Egmont Mss,* ii, pp. 171–2.

35. R. Cox to E. Southwell, 29 Nov. 1695, Bristol Record Office, Ms. 12,694(1), 52.

36. Abp. W. King to S. Foley, 27 Dec. 1707, 27 Jan. 1707[8], 28 Feb. 1707[8], 20 Jan. 1711[12], TCD, Mss 750/3/2, pp. 171, 181, 189; 750/4, p. 6.

37. R. Cox to E. Southwell, 29 Nov. 1695, Bristol Record Office, Ms. 12,694(1), 52.

38. D. Mussenden to H. Mussenden, 31 Dec. 1740, 6 [?] 1742, de Mussenden Leathes Mss, Ipswich, HA 403/1/15, 18.

39. J. Perceval to Sir R. Southwell, 28 May 1676; P. Perceval to same, 15 Dec. 1676, BL, Add. Ms. 46,953, ff. 74, 205; Sir R. Southwell to Sir W. King, 5 Oct. 1683; Sir W. King to Sir R. Southwell, 6 and 15 June 1684, 24 Oct. 1684, NLI, Ms. 664; J. Anderson, *A genealogical history of the house of Yvery,* 2 vols (London, 1742), ii, p. 369.

40. Sir W. Fownes to W. Fownes, 8 May 1732, NLI, Ms. 8802/1.

41. J. Prendergast to Ormond, [n.d.?1670s], ibid., Ms. 2485/318.

42. D. Hannigan, 'The University of Dublin, 1685–1750: a study of the matriculation records', unpublished MA thesis, St Patrick's College, Maynooth (1995), p. 62; D. Lemmings, *Gentlemen and barristers: the Inns of Court and the English Bar 1680–1730* (Oxford, 1990), pp. 18–19.

43. K. Howard to W. Howard, 26 May 1709, 31 Aug. 1710, NLI, PC 227; R. Cox to E. Southwell, 29 Nov. 1695, Bristol Record Office, Ms. 12,694(1), 52.

44. D. Mussenden to H. Mussenden, 9 Dec. 1754, de Mussenden Leathes Mss, Ipswich, HA 403/1/11, 22.

45. G. E. Howard, *Almeyda: or, the rival kings* (Dublin, 1769), sig. [A1].

46. [Francis Boyle], Viscount Shannon, *Moral essays and discourses* (London, 1690), pp. 121, 125, 127. For his own financial difficulties, see Shannon to D. Muschamp, 8 March 1666[7], NLI, de Vesci Mss, H/26. Similar opinions expressed by Lord

Anglesey to unknown, 13 March 1683[4], Bodleian, Clarendon Ms. 88, f. 50;
R. Ridge to A. Brabazon, 24 Nov. 1722, Barber Mss, private collection, London,
box III; Bp. R. Howard to H. Howard, 6 Jan. 1731[2], NLI, PC 227; *CARD*, iv, p.
125.

47. J. Smythe to W. Smythe, 7 Jan. 1723[4], NLI, PC 449; Palmerston to D. Reading,
21 Feb. 1722[3], 18 April 1723, 4 May 1723, Southampton UL, BR, 2/4; same to
R. Roberts, 12 Aug. 1732, ibid., BR, 2/7; R. Langrishe to Countess of
Middlesex, 3 July 1757, PRONI, D 2707/B1/43; *The Censor*, 3 (Dublin, 10–17
June 1749), 4 (17–24 June 1749), 19 (30 Sept.–7 Oct. 1749); 27 (28 April 1750–5
May 1750); G. E. Howard, *Treatise on the rules and practice of the equity side of the
Exchequer*, 2 vols (Dublin, 1760), i, p. xxviii; *The life and character of Harvey, the
famous conjuror of Dublin* (Dublin, 1728), pp. 21–2; *A list of the fees of the several
officers of the Four Courts* (Dublin, 1734); *Proposals humbly offered . . . for remedying
the great charge and delay of suits at law and in equity*, 6th edn (Dublin, 1725); 8th
edn (Dublin, 1727); *Statutes*, iv, pp. 458–9, 4 Geo. I, c. viii.

48. *Queries proposed for the consideration of the publick, concerning the lawyer and the
alderman* (n.p., n.d. [1730s]).

49. J. Evelyn, Jr. to J. Evelyn, 18 June 1695, Evelyn Mss, formerly at Christ Church,
Oxford, now in BL, Add. Mss.

50. Barnard, 'Lawyers and the law', pp. 262–3; *An alphabetical list . . .*

51. C. Brooks, 'Professions, ideology and the middling sort in the late sixteenth and
early seventeenth century', in J. Barry and C. Brooks (eds), *The middling sort of
people: culture, society and politics in England, 1550–1800* (Basingstoke, 1994), pp.
113–15; C. Brooks, *Pettyfoggers and vipers of the commonwealth: the 'lower branch' of the
legal profession in early modern England* (Cambridge, 1986); R. Robson, *The attorney
in eighteenth-century England* (Cambridge, 1959).

52. G. E. Howard, *Queries relative to the several defects and grievances in some of the
present laws of Ireland*, 2nd edn (Dublin, 1761), pp. 17–19; Howard, *A compendious
treatise of the rules and practice of the pleas side of the exchequer in Ireland*, i, p. iii–xx;
An alphabetical list . . . ; Osborough, 'The regulation of the admission of attorneys
and solicitors in Ireland', pp. 101–51.

53. *CARD*, iv, pp. 125, 248, 390.

54. *CARD*, vi, *passim*.

55. Ibid., pp. 247, 259, 295, 297, 304–5, 371, 480, 499, 502, 510, 539–40.

56. *CARD*, iv, pp. 531–2.

57. *CARD*, v, p. 393.

58. T. Dalrymple, precedent book, TCD, Ms. 874; *KIAP*, p. 117.

59. *CARD*, iv, p. 125; v, pp. 226–7, 500.

60. Belturbet municipal records, formerly NA, M. 3573; Cork freemen's register, Cork
Public Museum; court book of Askeaton, NLW, Cottesmore deeds, B.10; *The
Limerick Directory* (Limerick, 1769), p. 40; T. S. Smyth, *The civic history of the town of
Cavan* (Dublin, 1938), p. 172.

61. E. Malone to E. Malone, 16 Sept. 1701, Brabazon Mss, private collection, London,
box III; J. Meade to Sir R. Southwell, 4 July 1688, NUI, Cork, Boole Library,
U/20, Kinsale Manorial Papers, 1676–92; account book of John Crone, 1747–56,
Cork Archives Institute, Crone of Byblox Mss, PR3, box 2; H. Temple to
L. Roberts, 3 Feb. 1721[4], 14 May 1724; same to D. Reading, 21 Feb. 1722[3],
Southampton UL, BR, 2/4; J. Brett to M. Ward, 25 April 1726, PRONI, D 2092/
1/3, 193; E. T. Martin (ed.), *The Ash Mss., written in the year 1735, by Lieut.-Col.
Thomas Ash* (Belfast, 1890), p. 14.

62. Abraham Nickson, accounts 1713–20, pp. 374, 383–4, 390, 398, 404, 409, 426, Sheffield City Archives, WWM/A 759; A. Nickson, trespass book, 1713–20, pp. 6–7, ibid., WWM/A 765; Abp. W. King, account book, 1715–23, TCD, Ms. 751/3, ff. 21, 29; 2nd earl of Cork, account book, 1684–91, s.d. 26 Aug. 1684, NLI, Ms. 6300; notebook of Howell Ellis, UCNW, Gwyneddon Ms. 18, pp. 190, 201; A Spurrett to J. Coughlan, 19 Oct. 1704, Chatsworth, Spurrett letter book, 1703–4; account book of J. Pickard, *c.* 1731–49, Dorset CRO, D/BLX/B1; account book of J. Pickard, from 1737, ibid., B5; J. Usher to W. Abdy, 21 Nov. 1743, NLI, Ms. 1743; account book of John Crone, 1747–56, Cork Archives Institute, PR 3, Crone of Byblox Mss, box 2; W. Bolton to J. Howlin, 12 July 1755, NA, M. 2663; fee book of Bartholomew Cliffe, attorney in Dublin, from 1766. Carlow County Library, Vigors Mss; Barnard, 'Lawyers and the law', p. 267, and sources cited in note 38 there.

63. 'Alexander the Coppersmith', *Remarks upon the religion, trade, government, police, customs, manners and maladys of the city of Corke* (Cork, 1737), pp. 34–42; Howard, *Queries*, pp. 17–19; Howard, *A treatise*, i, pp. iii–xx; G. E. Howard, *The Miscellaneous Works, in verse and prose*, 3 vols (Dublin, 1782), i, pp. xxviii–xxix.

64. Barnard, 'Lawyers and the law', p. 277.

65. N. Jones to G. Legge, 5 Dec. 1671, 8 March 1672[3]; R. Piersse to same, 29 Jan. 1673[4], Staffs CRO, D (W) 1778/iii/O/19; *KIAP*, p. 253.

66. Establishment book of Irish Revenue, 1747, PRO, CUST 20/115; Howard, *Miscellaneous Works*, i, pp. ix–xlix.

67. Palmerston to J. Pocklington and J. St Leger, 15 Feb. 1725[6]; same to Lord Chief Baron Dalton, 15 Feb. 1725[6], Southampton UL, BR, 2/4; *A collection concerning the family of Yarner of Wicklow* (n.p, 1870); *KIAP*, p. 424.

68. Account books for Conna, Co. Wicklow, NLI, Mss 3857, 3858; F. E. Ball, *A history of the County Dublin*, part iii (Dublin, 1905), pp. 11, 107; letter book of J. Pickard, s.d. 11 May 1738, Dorset CRO, D/BLX, B18.

69. Minute books, 1731–33, s.d. 17 Feb. 1731[2], 9 Nov. 1732; 1741–46, s.d. 20 June 1745, 31 Oct. 1745, RDS; marriage articles for L. Roberts and B. Putland, 15 Feb. 1745[6], RD, 121/292/82975; NLI, Ainsworth report, no. 48, pp. 805–7; account book of J. Pickard, Dorset CRO, D/BLX, B1, ff. 15v–16; R. McCutcheon, 'Pue's occurrences, 1744–9', *The Irish Genealogist*, 9 (1996), p. 330.

70. Lord Palmerston to R. Roberts, Southampton UL, 12 Jan. 1741[2], BR, 2/8. Cf. E. Warren to W. Flower, 29 March 1726, NLI, Ms. 11,481/9.

71. J. Harington, *Oceana*, ed. J. Toland (Dublin, 1737), subscription list; James Fleming, *A collection of all the Irish and English statutes* (Dublin, 1741), list of subscribers.

72. J. Pickard to R. Nelson, 19 Dec. 1746, Dorset CRO, letter book of J. Pickard, D/BLX, B 18; account book of J. Pickard, f. 161v, ibid., D/BLX, B1; minute book of Mercer's Hospital, 1736–72, s.d. 16 Dec. 1749, Mercer's Library, College of Surgeons, Dublin; *KIAP*, p. 361; *A directory of Dublin for the year 1738* (Dublin, 2000), p. 70.

73. B. Colles to W. Flower, 5 Oct. 1732, NLI, Ms. 11,481/8; J. Pickard to B. Colles, 21 Dec. 1736, Dorset CRO, letter book of J. Pickard, D/BLX, B 18; account book of J. Pickard, ff. 72–3, ibid., D/BLX, B1; W. Colles to B. Colles, 11 March 1746[7], 22 Jan. 1749[50], 5 April 1766, 14 June 1766, NA, Prim Ms. 87; *An alphabetical list . . .* p. 13; *KIAP*, p. 92.

74. J. Agnew, *Belfast merchant families in the seventeenth century* (Dublin, 1996), pp. 55–7, 184–5, 328–9.

75. W. Nugent to F. Anderson, 18 Jan. 1710[11], NA, M. 3271(1); O. Gallagher to O. St George, 4 and 20 Feb. 1724[5], 11 March 1724[5], 12 and 19 July 1726, 13 June 1730, 23 Feb. 1730[1]; F. Anderson to same, 20 Nov. 1724, 19 March 1725[6], PRO, C 110/46, 319, 325, 327, 360, 433, 435, 763, 749, 952; F. Anderson, bill of costs with O. St George, 1723–29, ibid., C 110/46, 607; J. Pickard to F. Anderson, 7 March 1737[8], 5 Dec. 1738, letter book of J. Pickard, D/BLX, B 18; J. Brett to M. Ward, 25 April 1726, PRONI, D 2092/1/3, 193; E. Warren to W. Flower, 29 March 1726, NLI, Ms. 11481/9; *KIAP*, p. 7; *An alphabetical list . . .* , p. 12; *A directory of Dublin for the year 1738*, p. 2.

76. Palmerston to F. Anderson, 19 Jan. 1726[7], Southampton UL, BR, 2/4; same to same, 8 Nov. 1740; same to R. Roberts, 22 Dec. 1741, ibid., BR, 2/8.

77. H. Hatch to Lord Palmerston, 5 Dec. 1741, ibid., BR, 142/1/11; J. L. Napper to W. Smythe, 1 March 1737, n.s., NLI, PC 436.

78. Vestry book of St Bride's, Dublin, 1662–1742, RCB, P. 327/3/1, p. 309; T. C. Barnard, *The abduction of a Limerick heiress: social and political relationships in mid-eighteenth-century Ireland* (Dublin, 1998), esp. pp. 22, 32; McCutcheon, 'Pue's occurrences', p. 374.

79. R. Bell, *A description of the condition and manners . . . of the peasantry of Ireland* (London, 1804), p. 32.

80. Vestry minutes of St Michan's, Dublin, RCB, P. 276/4/1, p. 117; *KIAP*, p. 491.

81. R. Morgan to Abp. W. Wake, 20 July 1724, 10 Aug. 1724, Christ Church, Wake Ms. 14/208, 210; accounts of Morgan with Abp. H. Boulter, TCD, Ms. 6399; Mss account of the O'More family of Balyna, Co. Kildare, c. 1774, pp. 10–11, 26, private collection, Co. Kildare; *KIAP*, p. 350.

82. Barnard, *Cromwellian Ireland*, p. 248; T. W. Belcher, *Memoir of John Stearne, M. & J.U.D., S.F.T.C.D.* (Dublin, 1865), p. 23; *Family of Yarner*; R. Gillespie, 'Reverend John Yarner's notebook: religion in Restoration Dublin', *Archivium Hibernicum*, 52 (1998), pp. 30–41.

83. Will of A. Yarner, esq., 22 July 1703, Southampton UL, BR, 138/1; Lord Palmerston to H. Hatch, 8 Feb. 1734[5], ibid., BR, 2/7.

84. Petition of W. Henderson, after 25 Oct. 1718, Marsh's Library, Ms. Z3.1.1.

85. Palmerston to J. Pocklington and Sir J. St Leger, 15 Feb. 1725[6]; same to Lord Chief Baron Dalton, 15 Feb. 1725[6], Southampton UL, BR, 2/4.

86. *Faulkner's Dublin Journal*, no. 1635, 13–16 Feb. 1741[2]; *KIAP*, p. 522.

87. *Faulkner's Dublin Journal*, no. 112 [*recte* 122], 25 June 1726. Cf. Palmerston to R. Roberts, 14 Feb. 1739[40], 13 April 1740, Southampton UL, BR, 2/8.

88. R. Cooke to O. St George, 4 June 1727; O. Gallagher to same, PRO, C 110/46, 285, 489; *KIAP*, p. 99.

89. Notes on the militia, Co. Down, c.1719, PRONI, D 2092/1/3, 30. He was also a Protestant dissenter.

90. Mulcahy, *Kinsale*, ii, p. 38. Cf. ibid., p. 68; vi, pp. 23, 52, 84, 89, 95; vii, pp. 26–7.

91. *The Limerick Directory* (Limerick, 1769), pp. 39–40; B. Ó Dálaigh (ed.), *Corporation book of Ennis* (Dublin, 1990), pp. 403–6. Cf. ibid., pp. 21, 259.

92. Barnard, *Abduction*, esp. pp. 23, 28.

93. Account book of John Crone, 1747–56, Cork Archives Institute, PR 3, Crone of Byblox Mss, box 2; B. de Breffni, 'Letters of John Crone of Doneraile, Co. Cork, 1763–81', *Irish Ancestor*, 14/2 (1982), pp. 74–82; *KIAP*, pp. 11–12. See, too, the fee book of Bartholomew Cliffe, attorney in Dublin, from 1766. Carlow County Library, Vigors Mss; L. A. Clarkson, 'Armagh, 1770: a portrait of an urban

community', in D. Harkness and M. O'Dowd (eds), *The town in Ireland: Historical studies*, xiii (Belfast, 1981), p. 90.

94. List of property-owners, Co. Wexford, 1686, Bodleian, Clarendon Ms. 88, ff. 260–5; Dolan, History of Fermanagh, NLI, Ms. 2085; fees to W. Westby, 2 April 1717, accounts of A. Nickson with T. Wentworth, 1713–20, Sheffield City Archives, WWM/A 759, p. 407; brief for W. Westby, 14 May 1729, Gunning Mss, Northants CRO, G (H) 27; exchequer bill, 4 Nov. 1746, Hampshire CRO, 43M48/2813, 2819; T. U. Sadleir, 'Manuscripts at Kilboy', *Analecta Hibernica*, 12 (1943), pp. 137–44; T. U. Sadleir, 'The county of Waterford, 1775', *Journal of the Waterford Archaeological Society*, 16 (1913), pp. 50–5.

95. Census of Elphin, NA, M. 2466.

96. Paper of Sir J. Shaen, June 1693, BL, Harleian Ms. 4892, ff. 87–89v; civil list of 1715, Bodleian, Ms. Eng. Hist. C. 42, pp. 177–80; F. Bernard to H. Prittie, 15 Oct. 1729, NLI, Ms. 29,810/1; M. Coghill to E. Southwell, 13 June 1728, PRONI, T 2534/2; *CSPIre., 1660–2*, pp. 524–5; ibid., *1665–9*, pp. 73–4.

97. J. Potter to Devonshire, 17 July 1739, Chatsworth, Devonshire Letters, 1737–39, 252.3; J. Coughlan to T. Baker, 20 Nov. 1711, NLI, Ms. 13,242.

98. A. R. Hart, *A history of the king's serjeants at law in Ireland* (Dublin, 2000).

99. Clarendon to Sunderland, 16 Feb. 1685[6], PRO, SP 63/351, 161; W. Longueville to T. Hales, 30 March 1686, 2 July 1686, Somerset CRO, DD/BR/ely, C 1509, 3/11; Sir T. Hales to T. Hales, 4 July 1686, ibid., 3/10; R. Cox to E. Southwell, 9 May 1704, BL, Add. Ms. 38,153, f. 52; G. D. Burtchaell, *Members of parliament for the county and city of Kilkenny* (Dublin, 1888), p. 66.

100. W. Howard to unknown, 13 Sept. 1718; same to Webster, 4 Oct. 1718; same to P. Whichcote, 13 Nov. [1718]; same to Lord Midleton, 20 Dec. 1718, NLI, PC 227.

101. A. Clarke, 'Patrick Darcy and the constitutional relationship between Ireland and Britain', in J. H. Ohlmeyer (ed.), *Political thought in seventeenth-century Ireland* (Cambridge, 2000), pp. 35–55; P. H. Kelly, 'Recasting a tradition: William Molyneux and the sources of *The case of Ireland . . . stated* (1698)', ibid., pp. 83–106.

102. Howard, *Miscellaneous works*, i, pp. xxxi–xxxix; [R. French], *The constitution of Ireland, and Poyning's Laws explained* (Dublin, 1770).

103. J. Kelly (ed.), *The letters of Lord Chief Baron Edward Willes to the earl of Warwick, 1757–62* (Aberystwyth, 1990), pp. 101, 120; Edgeworth accounts, s.d. 27 March 1724, 21 July 1724, 4 and 5 April 1726, 14 July 1733, 29 and 31 March 1734, 23–24 April 1734, 21–22 March 1734[5], 21–22 Aug. 1739, 13 July 1742, 5 Oct. 1742, NLI, Mss 1508, pp. 108, 132; 1509, p. 49; 1510, pp. 78, 104, 106; 1511, p. 27; 1513, p. 46; 1515, pp. 173, 192; R. French, account book, s.d. 8 Sept. 1744, ibid., Ms. 4919, p. 64.

104. R. French to W. Smythe, 29 May 1712, 24 Oct. 1713, n.d.[1713], NLI, PC 447.

105. Notebook of Howell Ellis, 1682–88, p. 31, UCNW, Gwyneddon Ms. 18; R. French to W. Smythe, 24 Oct. 1713, n.d.[1713], NLI, PC 447; O. Gallagher to O. St George, 11 and 20 Feb. 1724[5], PRO, C 110/46, 321, 325; F. Anderson to same, 13 March 1724[5], ibid., 331; A. Nickson, accounts 1713–20, pp. 374, 383–4, 390, 398, 404, 409, 426, Sheffield City Archives WWM/A 759; J. Pratt, diary, s.d. 1, 2 and 9 Aug. 1746, Purdon Mss, Cloverhill, Co. Cavan; C. Caldwell to revenue commissioners, 22 Oct. 1744, PRO, CUST 112/10.

106. D. Lemmings, *Professors of the law: barristers and English legal culture in the eighteenth century* (Oxford, 2000).

107. Invitation to T. Dalrymple, 13 Aug. 1757, precedent book, TCD, Ms. 874.

108. R. Edgeworth, account books, s.d. 6, 13 and 16 Feb. 1733[4], NLI, Ms. 1510, pp. 94, 95.

109. R. Wilson to E. Wilson, 21 June 1757, 2 July 1757, ibid., special list no. 416.

110. P. French, case book, *c.* 1705, ibid., Ms. 4917; R. Cox, case book, ibid., Ms. 4245; R. Edgeworth, account books, 1720–34, ibid., Mss 1507–10; T. Kingsbury to F. Price, 24 June 1742, NLW, Puleston Ms. 3584E; legal notebooks, TCD, Mss 657, 1170; 'Acton papers', *Analecta Hibernica*, 25 (1967), p. 4; A. Pardailhé-Garabrun, *The birth of intimacy* (Oxford, 1991), p. 215; M. Pollard, *Dublin's trade in books, 1550–1800* (Oxford, 1989), p. 215.

111. T. C. Barnard, 'Learning, the learned and literacy in Ireland, *c.*1660–1760', in T. C. Barnard, D. Ó Cróinín and K. Simms (eds), *'A miracle of learning': studies in manuscripts and Irish learning* (Aldershot, 1998), pp. 209–35; T. Barnard, 'The uses of reading: private and public pleasures', in B. Cunningham and M. Kennedy (eds), *The experience of reading: Irish historical perspectives* (Dublin, 1999), pp. 60–77.

112. E. Matthews to Mrs J. Hamilton, 6 and 13 Dec. 1726, Clwyd CRO, Ruthin, Brynkinalt Mss, Irish estates, DD BK/I, 477, 478; J. Hawkshaw to F. Price, 7 Oct. 1736, 2 March 1737[8], NLW, Puleston Ms. 3576E/7, 8; C. Caldwell to J. Pickard, 13 June 1745, Dorset CRO, D/BLX/B 19; J. Pickard to M. White, 29 June 1734; same to J. Barne, 28 Nov. 1734; same to S. White, 7 July 1736, 9 March 1737[8]; same to E. Foley, 19 Feb. 1736[7]; same to R. Marshall, 14 Nov. 1738; same to I. Hussey, 17 Nov. 1739, J. Pickard, letter book, 1734–38, Dorset CRO, D/BLX, B 18; R. Edgeworth, accounts, Nov. 1720 and Feb. 1720[1], Jan.–Feb. 1732[3], June 1734, NLI, Mss 1507, pp. 32–5; 1510, pp. 39–41, 138–40; T. Kingsbury to F. Price, 8 Sept. 1744, NLW, Puleston Ms. 3584E; A. C. Elias, Jr. (ed.), *Memoirs of Laetitia Pilkington* (Athens, Ga. and London, 1997), i, pp. 22–3, 72–80; Laurence Whyte, *Poems* (Dublin, 1740), list of subscribers, pp. ii–xix; Williams (ed.), *Swift Correspondence*, iv, pp. 170, 175–6, 271, 298, 338.

113. Cregan, 'Irish Catholic admissions', pp. 95–114; Cregan, 'Irish recusant lawyers', pp. 306–20.

114. Bp. T. Otway to D. Muschamp, 13 Jan. 1682[3], NLI, de Vesci Mss, J/20; visitations of diocese of Limerick, 1707–10, RCB, D 13/1/9–12; E. Duffy, 'Valentine Greatrix, the Irish stroker', in K. Robbins (ed.), *Religion and humanism*, Studies in Church History, xvii (Oxford, 1981), pp. 251–73.

115. Papers of Thomas Arthur, BL, Add. Ms. 31,885, ff. 8–13; M. Lenihan, 'The fee-book of a physician of the seventeenth-century', *Journal of the Kilkenny and South-East of Ireland Archaeological Society*, new series, 6 (1867); notebook of W. Petty, s.d. 13 Nov. 1657, TCD, Ms. 2947, p. 68.

116. Accounts of R. Edgeworth, 20 May 1755, NLI, Ms. 1521, p. 192; *Memoirs of Richard Lovell Edgeworth*, i, pp. 57–62.

117. F. P. Lock, *Edmund Burke. 1: 1730–1784* (Oxford, 1998), pp. 74–5, 90, 204.

118. Roger Morice, Ent'ring Book, Dr Williams' Library, London, 2, p. 403; V. Ferguson to H. Sloane, BL, Sloane Ms. 4037, f. 74v; D. Cumyng to H. Sloane, 2 May 1699, 5 May 1702, ibid., Sloane Mss 4037, ff. 263–4; 4038, f. 341; Abp. W. King to D. Cumyng, 31 Aug. 1710, TCD, Ms. 2531, p. 195; A. Hamilton to Sir H. Sloane, 10 Aug. 1721, BL, Sloane Ms. 4046, f. 112; H. Howard to T. Howard, 19 Sept. 1724, NLI, PC 225; Paull, account book, openings 3, 15, 21, ibid., PC 13,991; R. Wilson to O. St George, 16 May 1730, PRO, C 110/48/922; *Analecta Hibernica*, 15 (1944), p. 377; J. Boyse, *The works*, 2 vols (London, 1728), i,

pp. 315–16; *The case of Sir Patrick Dun and Dr Cumming, physicians* ([Dublin, c.1705]); *A collection of pamphlets containing the way and manner of inoculating the small-pox . . . to which is added, a letter by Dr D. Cumyng* (Dublin,1722), pp. 1–2; HMC, *Ormonde Mss*, new series, viii, pp. 86–8; *Records of the General Synod of Ulster from 1691 to 1820*, 3 vols (Belfast, 1897), ii, p. 7; R. W. Innes Smith, *English-speaking students of medicine at the university of Leyden* (Edinburgh, 1932), p. 60.

119. 'Salutation' in PRONI, D 552/B/4/1/1, p. 4; W. Waring to S. Waring, 24 March 1696[7], 10 and 21 April 1697; A. Hill to S. Waring, 29 Oct. 1707, private collection, Co. Down; V. Ferguson to H. Sloane, 10 Aug. 1715, BL, Sloane Ms. 4044, ff. 84–4v; NA, Prerogative will book, 1728–9, ff. 260–1; Agnew, *Belfast merchant families*, pp. 71, 188.

120. Notebooks of J. Kennedy, Presbyterian Historical Society, Belfast.

121. J. Fleetwood, *A history of medicine in Ireland* (Dublin, 1951); J. Kelly, 'The emergence of scientific and institutional medical practice in Ireland, 1650–1800', in E. Malcolm and G. Jones (eds), *Medicine, disease and the state in Ireland, 1650–1940* (Cork, 1999), pp. 22–39; J. H. D. Widdess, *A history of the Royal College of Physicians of Ireland, 1654–1693* (Edinburgh and London, 1963).

122. C. Ward to M. Ward, 21 Nov. 1723, PRONI, D 2092/1/2, 41.

123. Innes Smith, *English-speaking students of medicine at the university of Leyden*; E. Peacock, *Index to English speaking students who have graduated at Leyden University* (London, 1883); E. A. Underwood, *Boerhaave's men at Leyden and after* (Edinburgh, 1977), pp. 24–5, 189–90.

124. Autobiography of Adam Blair, TCD, Ms. 6447; will of J. Hayman, 10 April 1777, NLI, D 13,351–13,422(46).

125. J. Trotter to E. Southwell, 4 Aug. 1750, BL, Add. Ms. 9713, f. 135v; A. Hamilton to J. Bonnell, 30 June 1726, NLI, PC 435; J. Lane, 'The role of apprenticeship in eighteenth-century medical education in England', in W. F. Bynum and R. Porter (eds), *William Hunter and the eighteenth-century medical world* (Cambridge, 1985), pp. 57–103.

126. V. Ferguson to H. Sloane, 10 May 1700, BL, Sloane Ms. 4038, f. 14; J. McBride to same, 30 Dec. 1700, 16 July 1701, 16 Jan. 1701[2], 28 Jan. 1705[6], 3 Nov. 1713, ibid., 4038, ff. 117, 189, 289; 4040, f. 122; 4043, f. 202; M. Prince to same, 2 Oct. 1732, 9 July 1737, n.d., ibid., 4052, f. 192; 4055, f. 134; 4060, f. 130; R. McBride to same, 3 Oct. 1740, 31 March 1741, 4056, f. 317; 4057, f. 14.

127. A. MacGregor, 'The life, character and career of Sir Hans Sloane', in A. MacGregor (ed.), *Sir Hans Sloane: collector, scientist, antiquary, founding father of the British Museum* (London, 1994), pp. 11–13.

128. T. W. Belcher (ed.), *Records of the King's and Queen's College of Physicians* (Dublin, 1866); Minute Book of Mercer's Hospital, 1736–72, Mercer's Library, College of Surgeons, Dublin.

129. NLI, Ainsworth report, no. 208; J. C. McWalter, *A history of the worshipful company of apothecaries of the city of Dublin* (1916).

130. Barnard, *Cromwellian Ireland*, p. 242; T. W. Belcher, *Memoir of Sir Patrick Dun* (Dublin, 1866); T. W. Belcher, *Memoir of John Stearne* (Dublin, 1865); T. P. C Kirkpatrick, 'Charles Willoughby, M.D.', *PRIA*, sect. C, 36 (1923), pp. 239–48; 'Sir Thomas Molyneux, M.D., F.R.S.', *Dublin University Magazine*, 18 (1841), pp. 314–26, 472–90, 604–13, 744–51.

131. J. Loveday to T. Hearne, 9 July 1732, Bodleian, Rawlinson Letters, 15, f. 129; E. Ford to K. O'Hara, 30 March 1717, NLI, Ms. 20,385.

132. Fagan, *Catholics in a Protestant country*, pp. 77–84.
133. Petty notebook, TCD, Ms. 2947; H. W. E. Petty-Fitmaurice, *The life of Sir William Petty, 1623–1687* (London, 1895), pp. 18–22
134. Ormond to Arran, 16 Feb. 1683[4], Bodleian, Carte Ms. 220, f. 19.
135. V. Ferguson to H. Sloane, 14 July 1691, BL, Sloane Ms. 4036, f. 106; D. Cumyng to same, 2 May 1699, ibid., Sloane Ms. 4037, f. 263; T. Proby to M. Adams, 3 July 1721, minute book, Dublin Company of Barber Surgeons, TCD, Ms. 1447/8/1, f. 159v; R. McBride to Sir H. Sloane, 31 March 1741, BL, Sloane Ms. 4057, f. 14; J. Adlecron to S. Bagshawe, 31 March 1753, JRL, B 2/2/28.
136. Calendar of departmental correspondence, 1741–59, s.d. 20 Jan. 1742[3], NA.
137. H. Owen and J. E. Griffith, 'The diary of William Bulkeley of Brynddu, Anglesey', *Transactions of Anglesey Antiquarian Society and Field Club* (1931), pp. 46, 52; G. N. Evans, *Social life in mid-eighteenth-century Anglesey* (Cardiff, 1936), pp. 100, 103.
138. Visitations of diocese of Limerick, 1707–10, RCB, D 13/1/9–12; *The Limerick Directory*, p. 39; R. Hayes, 'Some notable Limerick doctors', *North Munster Antiquarian Journal*, 1 (1937), pp. 113–19.
139. Will of John Martin, 29 June 1786, Kirkpatrick transcripts, Royal College of Physicians, Dublin; Hayes, 'Some notable Limerick doctors', p. 117.
140. Cork Freeman's Register, 1656–1741, Cork Public Museum, s.d. 1656; C. J. F. MacCarthy, 'Patrick Blair, M.D.', *JCHAS*, 90 (1985), pp. 104–19; J. Wolveridge, *Speculum matricis Hybernicum* (London, 1670), sig. A3–sig. [a6].
141. N. Delacherois to D. Delacherois, 27 Dec. 1773, NAM, London, 7805–63.
142. Census of Elphin, 1749, NA, M. 2466, f. 167; T. Pakenham to W. Smythe, n.d., NLI, PC 449; H. Murtagh, *Athlone: history and settlement to 1800* (Athlone, 2000), pp. 188–9.
143. J. Rutter to H. Goold, 8 Nov. 1672, Petty Papers, BH 14/43, now BL. Add. Ms. 72,861; Bp. H. Downes to Abp. W. Wake, 9 July 1717; Bp. J. Evans to same, Christ Church, Wake Ms. 12, ff. 161, 190v; J. Smythe to W. Smythe, 10 Dec. 1716, 18 Feb. 1728[9], 21 Oct. 1729, NLI, PC 449; R. Howard to H. Howard, 28 Jan. 1728[9], 18 Sept. 1729, 28 Nov. 1729, 15 Dec. 1729, ibid., PC 227; J. Copping to Sir H. Sloane, 1 Dec. 1742, BL, Sloane Ms. 4057, f. 162; Legg, *Synge Letters*, pp. 8–9, 332.
144. J. Smythe to W. Smythe, 22 Nov. 1749, NLI, PC 449.
145. Bond of A. Brabazon and T. Vero, 4 July 1716; bill of T. Vero, 1716; list of A. Brabazon's creditors, *c.*1723, Barber Mss, private collection, London, box III; account book of T. Butler, 1722, NLI, French of Monivea Mss, envelope 25.
146. R. Robinson to W. Smythe, 19 June 1744, 23 July 1749, 2 Dec. 1760, NLI, PC 447.
147. P. Dun to H. Sloane, 15 Jan. 1705[6], 14 March 1705[6], BL, Sloane Ms. 4040, ff. 110–11, 137–8; E. Southwell to same, 26 Aug. 1708, ibid., Sloane Ms. 4041, f. 194; Lady E. Southwell to same, 9 Sept. 1708, ibid., Sloane Ms. 4041, f. 200; E. Southwell to same, 6 Oct. 1740, ibid., Sloane Ms. 4056, f. 319.
148. Lady E. Southwell to H. Sloane, 9 Sept. 1708, BL, Sloane Ms. 4041, f. 200.
149. J. Hamilton to H. Sloane, 3 July 1697, ibid., Sloane Ms. 4036, f. 326; V. Ferguson to same, 14 May 1698, ibid., Sloane Ms. 4037, ff. 73–4; A. Hamilton to same, 10 Aug. 1721, ibid., Sloane Ms. 4046, f. 112.
150. 'Dr Mead's letter about my case', 1 Dec. 1742, Story account book, 1742–50, Bingfield, Co. Cavan.
151. HMC, *Various collections*, viii, pp. 303–4.

152. R. Wood to Sir W. Petty, 28 April 1674, BH, Petty Papers, 6, series ii, now BL, Add. Ms. 72,850; Mountrath to H. Sloane [?1690s], BL, Sloane Ms. 4058, f. 177.

153. Sir R. Bulkeley to M. Lister, 1 July 1693, 25 Aug. 1693, 28 Feb. 1699[1700], Bodleian, Lister Mss. 3, f. 41; 36, ff. 56, 62; T. C. Barnard, 'Reforming Irish manners: the religious societies in Dublin during the 1690s', *HJ*, 35 (1992), pp. 805–38.

154. J. Evelyn, Jr, to John Evelyn, 7 Sept. 1693, Evelyn Mss, formerly Christ Church, now in BL; D. Clarke, accounts for W. Smythe, s.d. 27 July 1708, NLI, PC 443.

155. Census of Elphin, 1749, NA, M 2466. I am grateful to Mary-Lou Legg for abstracting these figures.

156. Inventory of Dr John McKeogh, 25 May 1751, Killaloe Consistory Court papers, BL, Add. Ms. 31,882, ff. 187–8v.

157. E. Herbert to ?F. Herbert, 6 Oct. 1707, NLW, Powis Castle correspondence, no. 809; R. Purcell to Lord Perceval, 20 Dec. 1743, BL, Add. Ms. 47,001B, f. 41.

158. Account book of Abp. H. Boulter, TCD, Ms. 6399, p. 135.

159. Petition of P. Ronayne, 1714, NLI, D 25,804.

160. Edgeworth accounts, 23 Sept. 1744, NLI, Ms. 1516, p. 131.

161. Edgeworth accounts, 10 Aug. 1733, 21 and 25 May 1743, 14 July 1743, ibid., Mss. 1510, p. 79; 1516, pp. 34, 48.

162. Marsh's Library, Dublin, Ms. Z3.1.1, cxxvi.

163. Abp. W. King, account book, 1715–23, TCD, Ms. 751/3, ff. 11, 53, 71, 96, 119, 141v, 147v.

164. T. Kingsbury to F. Price, 2 Sept. 1743, NLW, Puleston Ms. 3584E.

165. Same to same, 17 Dec. 1739, 3 Oct. 1740, 11 Dec. 1744, ibid., Puleston Ms. 3584E.

166. K. Conolly to J. Bonnell, 14 April 1744, NLI, PC 434.

167. Abp. W. King, account book, 1700–12, TCD, Ms. 751/2, f. 217.

168. K. Conolly to Lady A. Conolly, 1 June 1745, IAA, Castletown deposit, box 76; same to same, 8 March 1745[6], TCD, Ms. 3974/52.

169. Williams (ed.), *Swift Correspondence*, iv, p. 323; Lady Carteret to C. Tickell, 10 Dec. 1733, Tickell Mss, private collection, Devon.

170. K. Conolly to J. Bonnell, 24 Sept. 1739, 30 Oct. 1742, NLI, PC 434.

171. V. Ferguson to H. Sloane, 14 May 1698, BL, Sloane Ms. 4037, f. 74.

172. G. D. Burtchaell, 'The family of Grattan', *Irish Builder*, 30 (1888), pp. 225–6; M. Quane, 'Portora Royal School, Enniskillen', *Clogher Record*, 6 (1968), p. 508.

173. Innes Smith, *English-speaking students of medicine at the university of Leyden*, p. 101; Underwood, *Boerhaave's men*, pp. 80, 175; Widdess, *History of the Royal College of Physicians of Ireland*, pp. 239–40.

174. He is not mentioned in Underwood, *Boerhaave's men*; cf. H. Boerhaave to W. Smythe, 1733, NLI, PC 449; R. Black, travel journal, PRONI, T 1073/2.

175. B. Lloyd to B. Parry, 21 Dec. 1735, NLW, Puleston Ms. 3576E.

176. T. Kingsbury to F. Price, 31 May 1740, ibid., Among the books to which he subscribed were: M. Chomell, *Dictionaire oeconomique*, ed. and trans. R. Bradley (Dublin, 1727), i; *An Universal History* (Dublin, 1744).

177. T. Kingsbury to F. Price, 31 May 1740, NLW, Puleston Ms 3584E.

178. T. Kingsbury to F. Price, 19 April 1746, Thomas Kingsbury, Jr. to J. Buchan, 22 Jan. 1750[1], ibid., see below, pp. 209–10.

179. R. Edgeworth accounts, 29 June 1733, 1, 3 and 5 July 1733, 9 March 1733[4], 31 Jan. 1734[5], 14 Nov. 1739, 12 Dec. 1739, 23 Sept. 1744, NLI, Mss. 1510, pp. 77, 103; 1511, p. 20; 1513, pp. 67, 70; 1514, p. 131.

180. R. Edgeworth accounts, 29 May 1733, NLI, Ms. 1510, p. 73; Lady Carteret to C. Eustace, 10 Dec. 1733, Tickell Mss, private collection, Devon.

181. Elias (ed.), *Memoirs of Laetitia Pilkington*, i, p. 16.

182. Ibid., pp. 77–9, ii, p. 465; John Carteret Pilkington, *The real story of John Carteret Pilkington* (London, 1760), pp. 1–14.

183. E. Spencer to F. Price, 13 May 1748, NLW, Puleston Ms. 3580E; Mrs E. Kingsbury to Mrs A. Price, 13 March 1755, 14 June 1755, Ibid. Puleston Ms. 3584E; same to same, 5 July 1754, 28 May 1756, ibid., Puleston deeds, nos. 735, 1184; genealogical notes on Kingsburys, RCB, Ms. 30/275.

184. K. Howard to W. Howard, 28 Feb. 1709[10], 31 Aug. 1710, NLI, PC 227.

185. Poor Book, St Michan's, Dublin, 1723–34, RCB, P. 276/8.1, p. 52.

186. T. C. Barnard, 'The Hartlib circle and the origins of the Dublin Philosophical Society', *IHS*, 19 (1974), pp. 60–1, 69; D. Clarke, *Thomas Prior, 1681–1751: founder of the Royal Dublin Society* (Dublin, 1951); K. T. Hoppen, *The common scientist in the seventeenth century: a study of the Dublin Philosophical Society, 1683–1708* (London, 1970), pp. 104–12; minute books, 1731–33, 1733–41, RDS.

187. H. Dodwell to Abp. W. Palliser, 19 June 1703, Bodleian, Cherry Ms., p. 135; J. Stearne, *De Obstinatione, opus posthum* (Dublin, 1672) (the copy in Bodleian, 8vo Rawlinson 1070, has additional notes by the editor, Henry Dodwell); Belcher, *John Stearne*, p. 23.

188. W. O'Sullivan, 'John Madden's manuscripts', in V. Kinane (ed.), *Essays on the library of Trinity College Dublin* (Dublin, 1999); F. Madan, *The Madan family and Maddens in Ireland and England* (Oxford, 1933).

189. V. Ferguson to H. Sloane, 14 July 1691, 4 Feb. 1697[8], BL, Sloane Mss 4036, f. 106; 4037, f. 25.

190. Minutes of Physico-Historical Society, RIA, Ms. 24 E 28; printed account of Physico-Historical Society, 8 Jan. 1749[50], Marsh's Library, G4.2.34, item 30; C. Smith, histories of Clare, Limerick and Tipperary, RIA, Mss 24 G 9; W. Fraher, 'Charles Smith, 1715–1762: pioneer of Irish topography', *Decies*, 53 (1997), pp. 33–44.

191. Minutes of the 'Medico-Politico-Physico-Classico-Ethico-Puffical Society', 1756–67, RIA, Ms. 24 K 31; J. Rutty, *An essay towards a natural, experimental and medicinal history of the mineral waters of Ireland* (Dublin, 1757); Underwood, *Boerhaave's men*, pp. 47–8.

192. Hayes, 'Some notable Limerick doctors', p. 119; A. De Valera, 'Antiquarian and historical investigations in Ireland in the eighteenth century', unpublished MA thesis, NUI (1978), pp. 186–7; R. E. Ward, J. F. Wrynn and C. C. Ward (eds), *Letters of Charles O'Conor of Belanagare* (Washington, DC, 1988), pp. 173, 222–3, 226–7, 255, 289; S. O' Halloran, *A general history of Ireland*, 2 vols (London, 1778); Rutty, *An essay*, subscription list.

193. S. O'Halloran to J. Brown, 31 March 1788, Palatine Heritage Centre, Rathkeale, Co. Limerick Southwell-Brown Mss, box 1, bundle 5; same to unknown, 2 Dec. 1779, in W. Betham's copy of O'Halloran, *A general history of Ireland*, now Bodleian, pressmark Gough Ireland, 40, 19; RIA, Ms. 24 K 31, p. 92; paper of S. O'Halloran, 8 June 1762, ibid., Ms. 24 E 5, no. 60.

194. B. Lloyd to B. Parry, 21 Dec. 1735, NLW, Puleston Ms. 3575D.

195. P. Dun to H. Sloane, 10 May 1705, 26 Jan. 1705[6], 14 March 1705[6], BL, Sloane Ms. 4040, ff. 110–11, 124–5, 137–8; V. Ferguson to same, 23 July 1700, ibid., Sloane Ms. 4038, ff. 38–9; T. Molyneux to same, 22 Feb. 1700[1], 29 Aug. 1702, 10 May 1706, ibid., Sloane Mss, 4038, f. 140; 4039, f. 18; 4040, f. 164; D. Cumyng to same, 5 May 1702, ibid., Sloane Ms. 4038, f. 341.

196. Brilliana Rawdon to H. Sloane, 26 Sept. 1703, ibid., Sloane Ms. 4039, f. 190v. Cf. E. C. Nelson, 'Sir Arthur Rawdon (1662–1695) of Moira: his life and letters, family and friends, and his Jamaican plants', *Proceedings and Reports of the Belfast Natural History and Philosophical Society*, 2nd series, 10 (1977–82), pp. 30–52; E. C. Nelson, 'Hellen Rawdon – My Booke', *Linen Hall Review*, 4/1 (1987), pp. 12–13.

197. Abp. W. King to Sir H. Sloane, 5 Oct. 1725, 27 Nov. 1727, BL, Sloane Mss. 4048, f. 67; 4049, f. 66; TCD, 750/8, 35–6; A. Griffiths, 'Sir Hans Sloane (1660–1753)', in A. Griffiths (ed.), *Landmarks in print collecting* (London, 1996), pp. 21–42; John Rowlands, 'Prints and drawings', in MacGregor (ed.), *Sir Hans Sloane*, pp. 245–62.

198. E. Perceval to Sir H. Sloane, BL, Sloane Ms. 4049, f. 75; M. Reilly to same, 20 July 1728, ibid., Sloane Ms. 4049, f. 206; G. Cunningham to same, ibid., Sloane Ms. 4050, ff. 114, 175; Bp. J. Hort to Sir H. Sloane, 9 Oct. 1735, ibid., Sloane Ms. 4054, ff. 112v–113v; J. Taaffe to same, 5 Feb. 1735[6], ibid., Sloane Ms. 4054, ff. 173, 269; J. Copping to same, 31 Jan. 1738[9], 22 Aug. 1741, ibid., Mss 4056, f. 39; 4057, ff. 68–9.

199. Bill for medals, 1729, NLI, Ms. 8390/1; H. Howard to R. Howard, 2 Aug. 1726; R. Howard to H. Howard, 18 Feb. 1730[1], 2 Dec. 1735, 2 March 1735[6], H. Howard to R. Howard, 29 Sept. 1737, ibid., PC 227; R. Barton, *Lectures in natural philosophy* (Dublin, 1751), pp. xii, 96; *Some memoirs of the life and writings of Dr Richard Mead* (London, 1755); Elias (ed.), *Memoirs of Laetitia Pilkington*, i, pp. 194–6.

200. H. Ingoldsby to W. Smythe, 11 May 1725, NLI, PC 445; H. Howard to Bp. R. Howard, 29 Sept. 1737, ibid., PC 227; 'Dr Mead's letter about my case', 1 Dec. 1742, Story account book, 1742–50, Bingfield, Co. Cavan.

201. D. Coakley, *Dr Steevens' Hospital* (Dublin, 1992); P. Gatenby, *Dublin's Meath Hospital 1753–1996* (Dublin, 1996); T. C. P. Kirkpatrick, *History of Dr Steevens' Hospital, Dublin, 1720–1920* (Dublin, 1924); T. C. P. Kirkpatrick and H. Jellett, *The book of the Rotunda Hospital* (London, 1913); J. B. Lyons, *The quality of Mercer's: the story of Mercer's Hospital, 1734–1991* (Dublin, 1991); E. Malcolm, *Swift's Hospital: a history of Swift's Hospital Dublin, 1745–1989* (Dublin, 1989); T. G. Moorhead, *A short history of Sir Patrick Dun's Hospital* (Dublin, 1942); Eoin O'Brien, (ed.), *The Charitable Infirmary, Jervis Street, 1718–1987* (Dublin, 1988); I. C. Ross (ed.), *Public virtue, public love: the early years of the Lying-in Hospital: the Rotunda* (Dublin, 1986); J. H. D. Widdess, *The Charitable Infirmary, Jervis Street, 1718–1968* (Dublin, 1968).

202. N. M. Cummins, *Some chapters of Cork medical history* (Cork, 1957), pp. 1–4; Widdess, *History of the Royal College of Physicians of Ireland*, p. 69.

203. Waterford corporation book, 1700–27, s.d. 10 Feb. 1708[9], Waterford Municipal Archives; T. Gogarty (ed.), *Council book of the corporation of Drogheda, 1649–1734* (Drogheda, 1915), pp. 143–4, 304.

204. R. Edgeworth, accounts, s.d. 16 Oct. 1767, NLI, Ms. 1533, p. 241; E. Southwell, memorandum book, BL, Egerton Ms. 1630, ff. 6, 33; J. H. Gebbie (ed.), *An introduction to the Abercorn letters* (Omagh, 1972), pp. 303–5; Kelly, 'Scientific and institutional practice', p. 31; E. Parkinson, *The City of Downe from its earliest days* (Belfast and London, 1928), p. 93; *Rules for the governing and regulating of the*

County of Kildare Infirmary (Dublin, 1770); 5 George III, c. cxx; 7 George III, c. viii, *Statutes,* ix, pp. 376–83, 514–15.

205. B. Boydell, *Rotunda music in eighteenth-century Dublin* (Dublin, 1992); B. Boydell, *A Dublin musical calendar, 1700–1767* (Dublin, 1988), p. 267.

206. The principal exception was Bartholomew Mosse, the male midwife behind the development of the Lying-In Hospital and Rotunda. A. Browne, 'Bartholomew Mosse, 1712–59: founder and first master', in A. Browne (ed.), *Masters, midwives and ladies-in-waiting: the Rotunda Hospital, 1745–1995* (Dublin, 1995), pp. 1–20.

207. Malcolm, *Swift's Hospital,* pp. 50–1.

208. Underwood, *Boerhaave's men,* pp. 79, 144.

209. Minute book, Mercer's Hospital, 1736–72, Mercer's Library, Royal College of Surgeons, Dublin.

210. Legg, *Synge Letters,* pp. 21, 24; T. Mozeen, *A collection of miscellaneous essays* (London, 1762), p. 71.

211. Abp. W. King, account book, 1701–12, TCD, Ms. 751/2.

212. He was styled esquire in St Mary's, Dublin, vestry book, 1699–1739, RCB, P. 277/7.1, p. 15.

213. J. Madden and T. Molyneux to unknown, BL, Sloane Ms. 1786, ff. 152–3; Bp. T. Lindsay to A. Charlet, 4 Oct. 1713, Bodleian, Ballard Ms. 8, f. 63; Evans, *Social life in mid-eighteenth-century Anglesey,* p. 100; Hoppen, *The common scientist,* pp. 44–5; Owen and Griffith, 'Diary of William Bulkeley', p. 52.

214. 'Portrait of an English lady in Dublin in the late eighteenth century', NA, M. 6810, pp. 10–11; R. Edgeworth, accounts, memo in NLI, Ms. 1535; Magdalen Asylum register from 1766, RCB, 551/1/1, no. 44; P. Guinness, 'The meeting book of the County of Kildare Knot of the Friendly Brothers of St Patrick, 1758–1791', *Journal of the County Kildare Archaeological Society,* forthcoming.

215. J. S. Powell (ed.), *'Your humble servant': notes and letters from Portarlington, 1692–1768* (York, n.d.), p. 24.

216. Minutes of Grand Lodge of Munster [copy], s.d. 22 Aug. 1728, Cork Archives Institute, U/177; bill of G. van Leewen, 2 Aug. 1727, NLI, Ms. 34,112/14; 'Doneraile papers', *Analecta Hibernica,* xv (Dublin, 1944), p. 351; Elias (ed.), *Memoirs of Laetitia Pilkington,* ii, pp. 454–5; Pilkington, *Real story,* pp. 12–16, 33–41.

217. Cork D'Oyer hundred book, 1656–1729, s.d. 1697, Cork Archives Institute, U/127.

218. Inventory of J. Bentley, 12 Dec. 1760, TCD, Ms. 2015/388. See, too, will of a Clonmel apothecary in W. P. Burke, *History of Clonmel* (Waterford, 1907), p. 328.

219. Corporation book of Limerick, BL, Add. Ms. 19,859, f. 31; rental of Limerick, c.1672, Petworth, Orrery Mss, general series, 15.

220. Legg, *Synge Letters,* p. xxxviii; M. Reynolds, 'The Boileau and Boyd apothecary jars', *Irish Pharmacy Journal,* 60/9 (1982), pp. 300–2; *A directory of Dublin for the year 1738,* p. 100.

221. Census of Elphin, NA, M. 2466, f. 388. On the apothecaries' trade: J. G. L. Burnby, 'Apprenticeship records', *Transactions of the British Society for the History of Pharmacy* (1977); J. G. L. Burnby, *A study of the English apothecary from 1660–1760,* Medical History, supplement 3 (1983).

222. Cork freemen's register, 1656–1741, s.d. 23 May 1656, 25 April 1657, 29 Oct. 1657, 10 May 1682, 16 Sept. 1697, 24 Dec. 1735, 3 May 1736, 24 Jan. 1738[9], Public Museum, Cork. For the guild of barber surgeons and apothecaries in Cork, ibid.,

s.d. 29 Oct. 1657; court book of Court of D'Oyer Hundred, Cork, 1656–1729, transcribed by R. Caulfield, Cork Archives Institute, U/127. For its incorporation at Kinsale in 1746, Mulcahy, *Kinsale*, vi, p. 62.

223. J. Barry, 'Publicity and the public good: presenting medicine in eighteenth-century Bristol', in W. F. Bynum and R. Porter (eds), *Medical fringe and medical orthodoxy, 1750–1850* (London, 1987), pp. 29–39; R. Porter, *Health for sale: quackery in England, 1660–1850* (Manchester, 1989).

224. Bills of T. Quinn, 25 Oct. 1722; W. Walker, 19 Dec. 1722, private collection, Co. Down.

225. *Pharmacopola Circumforaneus; or the horse doctor's harangue to the creduluous mob* (Dublin, [c.1740]); *Faulkner's Dublin Journal*, no. 370, 7–11 Jan. 1728[9], 14–18 Jan. 1728[9], 8–11 Feb. 1728[9], 18–22 Dec. 1733; *Dublin Courant*, 12–16 June 1744; *The Censor*, 21 (Dublin, 4–11 Nov. 1749).

226. *Solid reasons humbly offer'd to the consideration of the publick; for castrating physicians, quack-doctors, &c.* (Dublin, 1725).

227. *CARD*, xi, p. 494.

228. 1 George III, c. xiv, *Statutes*, vii, pp. 848–58.

229. Minute book of Barber Surgeons, 1703–57, TCD, Ms. 1447/8/1; transactions, Apothecaries' Guild, 1747–95, s.d. 30 Nov. 1747, 29 March 1750, 28 Dec. 1750, 27 Dec. 1753, 3 Jan. 1760, Apothecaries' Hall, Dublin.

230. Census of Elphin, 1749, NA, M. 2466, pp. 397, 399; order book, Primrose Grange, Sligo, 1757–90, s.d. 29 Oct. 1759, 4 Jan. 1762, TCD, Ms. 5646.

231. Minutes of the Physico-Historical Society, s.d. 5 Aug. 1745, RIA, Ms. 24 E 28.

232. Account books, Cork and Burlington estate, 1671–73, s.d. 5 March 1672[3], 2 and 10 Nov. 1685, 17 Aug. 1686, NLI, Mss 6274, 6300.

233. Accounts of J. Halfpenny, 20 July 1714, 11 Sept. 1728; H. and B. Bathorn, 24 June 1734, 1 Feb. 1741[2]; H. O'Hara, 27 Dec. 1740, NLI, Ms. 11,469/5. For evidence of apothecaries closer to Castle Durrow, list of freemen of St Canice's corporation, Kilkenny, 1731, RCB, D 11.1.1. For payments to Dr John Martin, apothecary: F. Bernard, account book, 1719–28, pp. 164, 216, Cork Archives Institute, Doherty Mss, U/137.

234. Account of J. Halfpenny, 11 Sept. 1728; account of H. O'Hara, 19 March 1739[40], NLI, Ms. 11,469/5.

235. Census of Elphin, 1749, NA, M. 2466; *The Limerick Directory*, p. 39.

236. J. Wight, journal, s.d. 12 April 1752, Friends' Historical Library, Dublin.

237. Minute book of Barber Surgeons, 1703–57, TCD, Ms. 1447/8/1, f. 79.

238. C. Lucas, *Pharmacomastix* (Dublin, 1741), pp. 29, 31–5, 70–2, 78.

239. Ibid., pp. 7, 11, 14, 25–6.

240. Transactions, Apothecaries' Guild, 1747–95, s.d. 31 Jan. 1748[9], 29 July 1755, 6 Dec. 1756, Apothecaries' Hall, Dublin.

241. [H. Brooke?] *Essay on the antient and modern state of Ireland* (Dublin, 1759), p. 87.

242. W. Stephens to Sir H. Sloane, 21 March 1737[8], BL, Sloane Ms. 4055, f. 302.

243. Papers of the Medico-Philosophical Society, s.d. 26 April 1767, RIA, Ms. 24 E 6, p. 147.

244. Accounts of 1st Viscount Rosse, from 1680, s.d. 16 Nov. 1680; Birr Castle Archives, Co. Offaly, A /1/143; A Spurrett to J. Coughlan, 19 Oct. 1704, Chatsworth, Spurrett letter book, 1703–4; Abp. W. King, accounts, TCD, Ms. 751/3, ff. 7, 21, 100v, 143; Abp. W. King to Bp. C. Crow, 3 April 1718, ibid., Ms. 2535, p. 142; J. Ussher to W. Abdy, 21 Nov. 1743, NLI, Ms. 1743; Somerset

Lowry-Corry, earl of Belmore, *The history of the Corry family of Castlecoole* (London and Dublin, 1891), pp. 239, 241, 245.

245. Account of Mrs Hamilton, 9 April 1675, account book of D. Johnson, Birr Castle Archives, A/16; R. Edgeworth accounts, 12–18 April 1733, May 1733, 13 and 19 April 1743, 21 and 25 May 1743, 13 June 1743, 14 July 1743, NLI, Mss 1510, pp. 48, 71; 1515, pp. 237, 240; 1516, pp. 34, 39, 41

246. Accounts of executors of Elizabeth Vincent, [1669], account book, D. Johnson, Birr Castle Archives, A/16; R. Dudley , 'Dublin's parishes, 1660–1729: the Church of Ireland parishes and their role in the civic administration of the city', unpublished Ph.D. thesis, Trinity College, Dublin, 2 vols (1995), ii, pp. 329–31.

6. Offices and Office-holders

1. Petition to Abp. W. King, [1720s], Marsh's Library, Dublin, Ms. Z3.1.1, cxx.
2. Civil list, 1720, Bodleian, Rawlinson Ms. B. 511; E. Magennis, *The Irish political system, 1740–1765* (Dublin, 2000), pp. 47–9.
3. F. Alen to W. Conolly, 21 March 1723[4], IAA, Castletown deposit, box 53; civil list, 1720, Bodleian Library, Rawlinson Ms. B. 511.
4. J. Seyers to Sir H. Sloane, 9 April 1735, BL, Sloane Ms. 4054, f. 30.
5. Minute book, Primrose Grange school, 1757–90, s.d. 19 Feb. 1759, TCD, Ms. 5646.
6. D. W. Hayton, 'Ireland and the English ministers, 1707–1716', unpublished D. Phil. thesis, Oxford University (1975), pp. 42–65; Magennis, *Irish political system*, pp. 40–60; J. C. Sainty, 'The secretariat of the chief governors of Ireland, 1690–1800', *PRIA*, 77 sect. C, (1997), pp. 1–33.
7. E. Warren to W. Flower, 29 March 1726, NLI, Ms. 11,481/9.
8. P. McNally, *Parties, patriots and undertakers: parliamentary politics in early Hanoverian Ireland* (Dublin, 1997), p. 91; Magennis, *Irish political system*, p. 47.
9. *CJIre*, iv, part 2, pp. cclxi–cclxvii.
10. Minute book, Navan turnpike trust, 1730–36, NLI, Ms. 25,448; minute book, Nobber turnpike trust, 1734–36, ibid., Ms. 25,451; C. Conron to H. Boyle, 18 Dec. 1731, PRONI, D 2707, A1/1/3; *CJIre*., iv, part 2, p. ccxci; E. O'Leary, 'Turnpike roads of Kildare, Queen's County, etc. in the eighteenth century', *Journal of the Kildare Archaeological Society*, 7 (1912–14), pp. 120, 122.
11. [James Corry], *Precedents and abstracts from the journals of the trustees of the linen and hempen manufactures of Ireland* (Dublin, 1784), pp. 130, 131.
12. Ibid., pp. 5, 13, 95, 102.
13. *CJIre*., viii, part ii, p. ccccxcviii.
14. R. Cox to E. Southwell, 19 Jan. 1706[7], BL, Add. Ms. 38,154, f. 132; B. Taylor to Lord Perceval, 9 Sept. 1715, ibid., Add. Ms. 46,966, f. 104; W. M. Brady, *Clerical and parochial records of Cork, Cloyne and Ross*, 3 vols (London, 1864), i, pp. xlviii.
15. T. Barnard, 'Introduction', in T. Barnard and B. McCormack (eds), *The Dublin Tholsel Court records* (Dublin, forthcoming).
16. Barnard, 'Sir William Petty', pp. 201–17; H. E. Butler and H. Butler, *The Black Book of Edgeworthstown* (London, 1927), pp. 7–16; N. Canny, *Making Ireland British, 1580–1650* (Oxford, 2001), pp. 254–62; T. Cooke, *The early history of the town of Birr* (Dublin, 1875), pp. 35–51; R. Loeber, 'Preliminaries to the Massachusetts Bay Colony: the Irish ventures of Emanuel Downing and John Winthrop, senior', in

T. Barnard, D. Ó Cróinín and K. Simms (eds), *'A miracle of learning': studies in Irish manuscripts and learning. Essays in honour of William O'Sullivan* (Aldershot, 1998), pp. 164–200; H. W. E. Petty-Fitzmaurice, marquess of Lansdowne, *The life of Sir William Petty* (London, 1895); T. O. Ranger, 'Richard Boyle and the making of an Irish fortune, 1588–1691', *IHS*, 10 (1957), pp. 257–97.

17. J. G. Simms, *The Williamite confiscation in Ireland, 1690–1703* (London, 1956), pp. 126–7, 141, 150, 155.

18. W. Robinson to Sir N. Armorer, 24 Dec. 1682, Staffs CRO, D (W) 1778/iii/O/19; W. Perceval to A. Charlet, 5 Feb. 1712[13], Bodleian, Ballard Ms. 36, f. 8; Ormonde to Nottingham, 16 Oct. 1703, NLI, Ms. 991; R. Loeber, *A biographical dictionary of architects in Ireland* (London, 1981), pp. 88–97; E. P. McParland, *Public architecture in Ireland 1680–1760* (New Haven and London, 2001), pp. 19, 56–7.

19. T. Prior, *A list of the absentees of Ireland* (Dublin, 1729), pp. 10–11; [R. Morres], *A list of the absentees of Ireland*, 2nd edn (Dublin, 1767), pp. 8–9; *A list of the absentees of Ireland*, 3rd edn. (Dublin, 1769), p. 10; J. C. Sainty, 'A Huguenot civil servant: the career of Charles Delafaye, 1677 to 1762', *Proceedings of the Huguenot Society of London*, 22 (1970–76), pp. 398–413.

20. J. J. Cartwright (ed.), *The Wentworth papers, 1705–1739* (London, 1882) p. 516; Prior, *Absentees*, p. 11.

21. HMC, *Ormonde Mss*, n.s, vii, p. 135.

22. Abp. G. Stone to E. Weston, 7 Jan. 1748[9]; T. Waite to same, 27 Dec. 1748, 18 Jan. 1748[9]; T. Carter to Harrington, 19 Jan. 1748[9], 1 Feb. 1748[9], PRONI, T 3019/1236, 1240, 1242, 1266; Magennis, *Irish political system*, pp. 34, 37.

23. Indenture between Thomas Carter, the elder and younger, and E. Southwell, 14 Nov. 1717, NA, D 9353; HMC, *Egmont diary*, i, p. 462; J. Owen to Mrs A. Owen, 7 March 1725[6], UCNW, Penrhos Mss, i, 840.

24. Carteret to Newcastle, 15 July 1725, PRO, SP 63/385, 281, 283; J. Pocklington to Abp. W. Wake, 1 May 1725, Christ Church, Wake Ms. 14, f. 260.

25. J. Owen to Mrs A. Owen, 18 Feb. 1725[6], 7 March 1725[6], UCNW, Penrhos Mss, i, 838, 840.

26. B. Browne to H. Boyle, 8 Feb. 1731[2], PRONI, D 2707/A/1/3, 42.

27. T. Carter to H. Boyle, 26 Feb. 1731[2], ibid., 43A.

28. J. Dennis to Mr Forth, 9 Sept. 1722, Boole Library, NUI, Cork, Ms U/20, Kinsale Manorial papers, 1698–1764.

29. Warrant and appointment of R. Southwell, 1664, BL, Add. Ms. 38,861, ff. 9, 14; R. Southwell to ?R. Southwell, the elder, Petty Papers, 9, f. 7, now BL, Add. Ms. 72,852; Sir W. Petty to Lady Petty, 14 July 1683, Petty Papers, 5/109, now BL, Add. Ms. 72,856; letters patent for reversion to Charles Dering as auditor-general of Ireland, 9 Nov. 1678, Kent Archives Office, U 1713/C1.52; C. Dering to E. Southwell, 6 and 25 May 1697, 19 June 1697, ibid., C4.22–4; *CSP, Domestic, 1672–3*, p. 321; HMC, *Egmont Mss*, ii, pp. 3, 5, 26, 31, 60–2, D. M. Gardener, 'The work of the English privy council 1660–1679 (with respect to domestic affairs)', unpublished D.Phil. thesis, Oxford University (1992), p. 243.

30. W. Petty to Brooke, 19 Jan. 1674[5], Petty Papers, 19, p. 325, now BL, Add. Ms. 72,858.

31. Barnard, 'Cork settlers', pp. 339–40.

32. Sainty, 'Secretariat of the chief governors of Ireland' pp. 1–30; list of office-holders, *c.* 1695, NLI, Inchiquin Ms, no. 983.

33. Annotated civil list, BL, Add. Ms. 61,637B, f. 7; indenture, 14 Nov. 1717, NA, D 9353; Sainty, 'Secretariat of the chief governors of Ireland', pp. 11, 13–15, 30.

34. Annotated civil list, BL, Add. Ms. 61,637B, f. 5; list of Irish establishment, 1688–1727, NA, M. 2537; T. C. Barnard, 'Land and the limits of loyalty: the second earl of Cork and first earl of Burlington (1612–1745)', in T. Barnard and J. Clark (eds), *Lord Burlington: architecture, art and life* (London, 1995), p. 190.

35. L. A. Clarkson and E. M. Crawford, *Ways to wealth: the Cust family of eighteenth-century Armagh* (Belfast, 1985); P. McNally, *Parties, patriots and undertakers: parliamentary politics in early Hanoverian Ireland* (Dublin, 1997), pp. 88–117.

36. Grant, 1670, Staffordshire CRO, D (W) 1778/I/I, 298; Essex to Arlington, 10 March 1673[4], Bodleian, Add. Ms. C. 34, f. 51v; order, 23 March 1673[4], ibid., Rawlinson Ms. B. 492, f. 119v; accounts of Thomas Domville, clerk of hanaper in Chancery, 1684–85, ibid., Clarendon Ms. 88, f. 159; receipts, Hanaper Office, 1706–7, Clwyd CRO, Ruthin, Brynkinalt Mss, DD/BK/I, 407; annotated civil list, BL, Add. Ms. 61,637B, f. 8.

37. T. C. Barnard, 'Lawyers and the law in late seventeenth-century Ireland', *IHS*, 28 (1993) pp. 274–7; W. Temple, *Observations upon the United Provinces of the Netherlands*, ed. G. N. Clark (Oxford, 1972).

38. Account book, H. Temple, 1712–21, Southampton UL, BR, 2/2, ff. 9–12v.

39. H. Temple to J. Addison, 28 Oct. 1714; same to L. C. J. Whitshed, 6 Nov. 1714; same to Lord Chief Baron Dean, 8 Jan. 1714[15], ibid., BR, 2/2B, ff. 14, 14v, 16.

40. H. Temple to Lord Chief Baron Dean, 10 Feb. 1714[15], ibid., BR, 2/2B, f. 16.

41. H. Temple to W. Yarner, 10 Feb. 1714[15]; same to Riley, 10 April 1715; same to D. Reading, 23 Aug. 1715, ibid., BR, 2/2B, ff. 16v, 20, 22v.

42. Palmerston to Sir R. Walpole, 21 Aug. 1740, 18 Oct. 1740, ibid., BR, 2/8; calendar of departmental correspondence, 1741–59, s.d. 17 Aug. 1742, NA.

43. H. Temple to Lord Chancellor Brodrick, 29 March 1715, Southampton UL, BR, 2/2B, f. 19.

44. H. Temple to Sir H. Echlin, 15 March 1714[15], ibid., BR, 2/2B, f. 17v; Palmerston to L. Roberts, 10 Feb. 1725[6], ibid., BR, 2/4.

45. Palmerston to J. Pocklington and J. St Leger, 15 Feb. 1725[6], same to LCB. Dalton, 15 Feb. 1725[6], ibid., BR, 2/4.

46. Palmerston to Mrs Hill, 10 and 22 Feb. 1725[6], L. Roberts, 3 March 1725[6], 14 April 1726, ibid., BR, 2/4; *A collection concerning the family of Yarner of Wicklow* (n.p., 1870).

47. Palmerston to A. Hill, [12] Jan. 1741[2], Southampton UL, BR, 2/8.

48. Account book, 1756–57, Irish accounts, ibid., BR, 2/12.

49. H. Temple to Lord Chief Baron Dean, 10 Feb. 1714[15]; same to F. Shrigley, 12 April 1715, 1 Oct. 1715; same to W. Flower, 13 Oct. 1715; ibid., BR, 2/2B; same to W. Yarner, 2 Jan. 1723[4]; same to J. Pocklington and J. St Leger, 15 Feb. 1725[6], same to Lord Chief Baron Dalton, 15 Feb. 1725[6], ibid., BR, 2/4; account book, 1725–56, s.d. 1731, ibid., BR, 2/6, f. 26v.

50. H. Temple to Lord Chancellor Brodrick, 12 March 1714[15]; same to W. Flower, 19 Nov. 1715, ibid., BR, 2/2B, ff. 17, 26.

51. E. Warren to W. Flower, 29 March 1726, NLI, Ms. 14,481.

52. H. Temple to D. Reading, 12 Feb. 1714[15], 28 Jan. 1717[18], 7 Feb. 1718[19]; same to F. Shrigley, 19 Feb. 1714[15]; same to Lord Chief Baron Dean, 12 March 1714[15]; same to Sir H. Echlin, 15 March 1714[15]; same to Abp. W. King, 22 March 1714[15]; same to J. Beecher, 29 March 1715, 30 Aug. 1715; same to

Vincent, 30 Aug. 1715; same to R. Michelburne, 15 Sept. 1715, Southampton UL, BR, 2/2B, ff. 16v–23v, 37v, 44; same to L. Roberts, 10 Feb. 1725[6], ibid., BR, 2/4.

53. H. Temple to J. Beecher, 1 March 1715[16], same to R. Vincent, 12 April 1716, ibid., BR, 2/2B, ff. 28v, 29v; same to L. Roberts, 3 Feb. 1721[2], 14 May 1724, ibid., BR, 2/4; same to E. Warren, 30 May 1727; same to R. Roberts, 7 Aug. 1733, ibid., BR, 2/7.

54. H. Temple to J. Beecher, 27 Oct. 1715, 29 Dec. 1716; same to D. Reading, 19 Nov. 1715, ibid., BR 2/2B, ff. 25v, 26, 32v; same to F. Anderson, 19 Jan. 1726[7], same to E. Warren, 7 Feb. 1726[7], ibid., 2/4; same to R. Roberts, 17 Oct. 1730; same to Jane Yarner, 27 Oct. 1733, ibid., BR, 2/7.

55. Henry Temple account book, 1712–21, ibid., BR, 2/2, f. 1; D. Reading to H. Temple, 22 Oct. 1715, ibid., BR, 141/3/6; NLI, Ainsworth reports on private collections, no. 95, pp. 931, 932, 943.

56. H. Temple to D. Reading, 11 Oct. 1712, 12 Feb. 1714[15], 14 March 1714[15], Southampton UL, BR, 2/2B, ff. 6v, 16v, 18.

57. H. Temple to D. Reading, 15 Sept. 1715, ibid., BR, 2/2B, f. 23v; same to same, Sept. 1721, ibid., BR, 2/4; accounts, 1717, Temple account book, 1712–21, ibid., BR, 2/2, f. 56.

58. Palmerston to D. Reading, 20 March 1724[5], 15 June 1725; same to Lord Chancellor West, 15 July 1725, ibid., BR, 2/4.

59. H. Temple to D. Reading, 19 Feb. 1718[19], 21 March 1718[19], ibid., BR 2/2B, ff. 44v, 45; same to L. Roberts, 8 and 10 Feb. 1725[6], ibid., BR, 2/4; D. Reading to H. Temple, 25 Nov. 1715, 17 July 1716, ibid., BR, 4/221a, 221b.

60. Lord Bellasyse to D. Reading, 16 Aug. 1712, 11 Nov. 1712; Lord Berkeley to same, 30 May 1713, 9 March 1713[14], NLI, Ms. 21,778; rental of Wharton's Irish estate, 1717, IAA, Castletown deposit, box 37.

61. J. Owen to Anne Owen, 7 March 1725[6], UCNW, Penrhos Mss, i, 840.

62. Some of its elements can be traced in the will of T. Flower, 4 May 1700, Southampton UL, BR, 138, B.91; *A collection concerning the family of Yarner*; Henry Temple's letter books, Southampton UL, BR, 2/2, 4 and 7.

63. H. Temple to L. Roberts, 22 Aug. 1719, Southampton UL, BR, 2/2B, f. 47.

64. Constitution of the Irish Exchequer, BL, Add. Ms. 18,022, f. 90v.

65. D. Reading to H. Temple, 17 July 1716, Southampton UL, BR, 4/221b.

66. H. Temple account book, 1712–21, ibid., BR, 2/2B, f. 64v.

67. H. Temple to D. Reading, 5 Jan. 1715[16], 26 July 1716, 9 April 1717, 7 Jan. 1717[18], ibid., BR, 2/2B, ff. 27, 30v, 33v, 37; accounts, 1717, ibid., BR, 2/2, f. 56.

68. H. Temple to D. Reading, 7 Jan. 1717[18], 21 March 1718[19], 26 Sept. 1719, ibid., BR, 2/2B, f. 37v, 45, 47v; L. Roberts to Palmerston, 31 March 1726, ibid., BR, 141/2/3C.

69. Palmerston to R. Roberts, April 1732, ibid., BR, 2/7.

70. H. Temple to D. Reading, 26 Sept. 1719; same to L. Roberts, 26 Jan. 1719[20], ibid., BR, 2/2B, ff. 47v, 49; same to Carteret, 8 May 1727; same to R. Roberts, 19 Oct. 1727, 12 Aug. 1729, 9 Feb. 1730[1], same to H. Hatch, 2 Dec. 1727; same to T. Burgh, 12 May 1730, ibid., BR, 2/7.

71. *CJIre.*, iv, pt 2, pp. cxxi–cxxii.

72. Calendar, miscellaneous letters and papers before 1760, s.d. 17 July 1755, NA.

73. H. Temple, 1st Viscount Palmerston, account book, 1717–25, Southampton UL, BR, 2/3. The Broadlands estate, bought in 1736, cost £21,000. Palmerston accounts, 1756, ibid., BR, 2/10, p. 23.

74. Memorandum and account book, 1725–56, ibid., BR, 2/6, f. 61v.

75. Accounts, ibid., BR, 2/2, 2/4, 2/7–9.

76. H. Temple to D. Reading, 9 April 1717, ibid., BR, 2/2B, f. 33v; same to R. Roberts, 14 Aug. 1731, ibid., BR 2/7.

77. Report on Riall Mss, NLI, Ainsworth reports, 48, p. 805; Royal Commission on Ancient and Historic Monuments, *An inventory of the ancient monuments in Anglesey* (London, 1937), p. 141.

78. R. Gwynne to Lord Tyrone, 27 Jan. 1676[7], private collection, Co. Waterford; HMC, *Egmont Mss*, ii, p. 25; B. Cunningham and R. Gillespie, 'The cult of St David in Ireland before 1700', in J. R. Guy and W. G. Neely (eds), *Contrasts and comparisons: studies in Irish and Welsh church history* (Llandysul, 1999), pp. 27–42.

79. W. Owen to J. Owen, 30 Aug. 1695, UCNW, Penrhos Mss, i, 444; W. Stephens to same, 5 Nov. 1701, ibid., v, 557; J. Owen to Mrs Wynne, 29 June 1722, NLW, Bodewryd letters, 171.

80. E. Warren to W. Flower, 29 March 1726, NLI, Ms. 11481; L. Roberts to Palmerston, 31 March 1726, Southampton UL, BR, 141/2/3C.

81. Ormonde to Lords Justice, 22 April 1706, NLI, Ms. 993, p. 27; R. Lascelles, *Liber munerum publicorum Hiberniae*, 2 vols (London, 1824–30), ii, p. 67; M. J. McEnery and R. Refaussé (eds), *Christ Church deeds* (Dublin, 2001), p. 427.

82. Irish establishment, BL, Add. Ms. 61,637B, f. 5v; D. Reading to H. Temple, 25 Nov. 1715, Southampton UL, BR, 4/221a.

83. H. Temple to D. Reading, 1 April 1718, Southampton UL, BR, 2/2B, f. 39v; same to L. C. B. Dalton, 15 Feb. 1725[6]; same to R. Roberts, 24 Nov. 1739, ibid., BR, 2/8; *CJIre.*, iv, part 2, p. lxx.

84. H. Temple to L. Roberts, 8 June 1721, 16 Nov. 1725; same to J. Pocklington, 24 Jan. 1726[7], Southampton UL, BR, 2/4; Report on Riall Mss, NLI, Ainsworth reports, 48, p. 805; Lascelles, *Liber munerum*, ii, p. 68.

85. Palmerston to H. Hatch, 10 Feb. 1725[6]; same to L. Roberts, 10 Feb. 1725[6], 3 March 1725[6]; same to L. C. B. Dalton, 19 Jan. 1726[7], Southampton UL, BR, 2/4; *A collection concerning the family of Yarner*, pp. 6, 8.

86. Palmerston to R. Roberts, 19 Jan. 1726[7], Southampton UL, BR, 2/4.

87. Palmerston to R. Roberts, 12 Jan. 1741[2], ibid., BR, 2/8.

88. Letter book of Jocelyn Pickard, 11 May 1738; Dorset CRO, D/BLX, B18; *Pue's Occurrences*, 18–21 July 1747; F. E. Ball, Mss notes for history of County Dublin, vol. 1, RSAI, Dublin; deed between J. Helsham, B. Roberts, J. Maddock and L. Roberts, 19 Aug. 1749, RD, 213/573/143058.

89. Crown entry books, Co. Dublin, 12 Dec.1743, NA.

90. Lease of C. and M. Edwards to R. Roberts, RD, 51/453/34327; deed between R. Roberts, H. Kenny and J. Richards, ibid., memorial 54/442/36359; marriage articles of L. Roberts and B. Putland, 15 Feb. 1745[6], ibid., 121/292/82975; deed between R. Roberts, J. Maddocks, R. Donovan, C. P. Edwards, O. Edwards, etc, 10 Sept. 1753, ibid., 165/247/111000; marriage settlement of M. Chamberlain and D. Roberts, 27 April 1742, ibid., 165/428/112620; deed of R. Roberts, C. Edwards and O. Edwards, 29 Nov. 1753, ibid., 180/532/121702; deed of L. Roberts, B. Nunn and J. Nunn, 28 Oct. 1758, ibid., 196/279/130006; NLI, Ainsworth report, no. 48, pp. 805–7; account book for Old Conna, NLI, Ms. 3857; F. E. Ball, *A history of the county Dublin*, part iii (Dublin, 1905), pp. 56, 107.

91. Ball, *County Dublin*, iii, p. 11; *Pue's Occurrences*, 55/12 (1758).

92. Minute book 1731–33, 3 and 17 Feb. 1731[2], 9 Nov. 1732; minute book, 1733–41,

9 Nov. 1738; minute book, 1741–46, 21 Jan. 1741[2], 29 March 1744, 31 Oct. 1745, RDS.

93. Marriage settlement of Dr William Roberts and Catherine, daughter of Dr Philip Ridgate, 1728, NLI, reports on private collections, no. 48, p. 805; Calendar of departmental correspondence, 1741–59, s.d. 14 May 1745, NA; *A catalogue of books, being the library of the late Philip Ridgate, esq, LL.D* (Dublin, 1746); Putland library catalogue, NLI, Mss 4185–7.

94. Palmerston to R. Roberts, 22 Dec. 1741, 12 Jan. 1741[2], 20 Feb. 1741[2]; same to H. Hatch, 20 Feb. 1741[2], ibid., BR, 2/8; same to R. Roberts, 6 April 1742; same to L. Roberts, 26 Nov. 1747, Ibid., BR, 2/9; account book of J. Pickard, Dorset CRO, D/BLX, B1, ff. 15v–16.

95. R. McCutcheon, 'Pue's occurrences, 1744–9', *Irish Genealogist*, 9 (1996), p. 330.

96. Palmerston to R. Roberts, 26 April 1735, 24 July 1735, 9 and 20 March 1735[6], 28 Aug. 1736; same to Baron Wainwright, 26 April 1735, 23 Feb. 1735[6], 22 Dec. 1740, Southampton UL, BR, 2/8; *The case of Oswald Edwards* (Dublin, 1740), p. 9.

97. Palmerston to R. Roberts, 9 Oct. 1736, Southampton UL, BR, 2/8; J. Burward to J. Usher, 7 March 1737[8], NLI, Ms. 13,251(1).

98. A. Crotty to Burlington, 1 March 1735[6], Chatsworth, Devonshire Letters, 1720–36, 200.3.

99. HMC, *Various collections*, vi, p. 59; division list on the motion to expel Arthur Jones Nevill from the House of Commons, JRL, Ms. B15/3/6, in which Roberts voted for Nevill's expulsion; *An address from the independent electors of the county of Westmeath, to Anthony Malone, esq.* (London, 1754), p. 15.

100. Palmerston to Hartington, 31 July 1755, Chatsworth, Devonshire Letters, May–July 1755, 419.0; Hartington's dinner lists, s.d. 25 Jan. 1756, NLI, Ms. 1466.

101. R. Roberts to Palmerston, 25 May 1737, Southampton UL, 142/2/3C; *Statutes*, vi, pp. 149–70 (7 Geo. II, c. xxvi); viii, pp. 549–50 (31 Geo. II, c. xii); *Case of Oswald Edwards*; *a first letter from R- R-s, esq; to the creditors of Burton's Bank* (Dublin, 1752); R. Roberts, *A state of the case* (?Dublin, 1752).

102. J. Burward to J. Usher, 18 Feb. 1737[8], 7 March 1737[8], NLI, Ms. 13251/1.

103. Palmerston to R. Roberts, 26 Jan. 1737[8], 8 April 1738, 27 Aug. 1738, 4 Sept. 1739, 15 Jan. 1739[40], Southampton UL, BR, 2/8; same to same, 18 Jan. 1742[3], 19 April 1743, 4 Sept. 1743, ibid., BR, 2/9.

104. Palmerston to R. Roberts, 4 Sept. 1739, 16 Dec. 1740, ibid., BR, 2/8.

105. Palmerston to R. Roberts, 26 Jan. 1737[8], 31 March 1744, ibid., BR, 2/8; 2/9.

106. Valuation of R. Roberts's estate, 10 Jan. 1758, ibid., BR, 143/3/4.

107. J. Hatch to Palmerston's executors, 19 Jan. 1758, ibid., BR, 3/104; E. Corkran to Palmerston, 11 Dec. 1759, ibid., BR, 143/1; leases of R. Roberts to M. Chamberlain, J. Hatch, M. Dalley and A. Williams, 26 and 27 June 1757, RD 187/391/125641.

108. L. Roberts to Lord Palmerston, 31 March 1726, Southampton UL, BR 142/2/3C, and below, pp. 229, 235.

109. Bp. R. Howard to H. Howard, 28 Nov. 1729, NLI, PC 227; Palmerston to H. Hatch, 13 Nov. 1735, 11 Jan. 1736[7], 19 March 1736[7], Southampton UL, BR, 2/8; rough minutes, 1758–61, f. 1v, RDS; T. Barry to H. Hatch, 16 May 1758, NLI, Ms. 11,327/8; *Al. Dubl*, p. 380; *KIAP*, p. 218.

110. J. Brett to M. Ward, 25 April 1726, PRONI, D 2092/1/3, 193.

111. Letter book of Jocelyn Pickard, 7 March 1737[8], 5 Dec.1738, Dorset CRO, D/BLX/B18.

112.   *An alphabetical list of such barristers, attorneys and solicitors as have taken the oath*
       (Dublin, 1735).

113.   R. Wilson to E. Wilson, 21 June 1757, 2 July 1757, NLI, special list 416. For later
       competition for the place of chief remembrancer: A. Kavanaugh, *John Fitzgibbon,
       earl of Clare* (Dublin, 1997), pp. 134, 153.

114.   J. Potter to T. Corbett, 1 March 1742[3]; W. Shiel to same, 22 Dec. 1744, PRO,
       ADM 1/3990.

115.   J. Hawkshaw to same, 24 Feb. 1742[3], ibid.

116.   *KIAP*, p. 219.

117.   J. Potter to T. Corbett, 15 March 1742[3], PRO, ADM 1/3990; T. U. Sadleir,
       'Manuscripts at Kilboy', *Analecta Hibernica*, 12 (1943), p. 139.

118.   GO, Ms. 173, p. 86; J. B. Leslie, Dublin clerical succession lists, ii, p. 439, RCB,
       Ms. 61/2/4/2; B. Boydell, *Music at Christ Church before 1800: documents and
       selected anthems* (Dublin, 1999), pp. 92, 95, 96, 97, 100, 102, 132–4, 136–7, 139, 157,
       251.

119.   J. Hawkshaw to F. Price, 7 Oct. 1736, 2 March 1737[8], 3 Oct. 1738, 1 Sept. 1743,
       1 March 1743[4], NLW, Puleston Mss 3576E, 3585C, 3587E.

120.   J. Potter to T. Corbett, 1 March 1742[3], PRO, ADM 1/3990.

121.   J. Potter to T. Corbett, 1 March 1742[3]; W. Shiel to same, 22 Dec. 1744, ibid. For
       the death of Hawkshaw, see McCutcheon, 'Pue's Occurrences', p. 316. On the
       jurisdiction, Sir W. Petty, March 1677[8], Bodleian, Rawlinson Ms. A. 191, ff.
       174–6.

122.   H. Baillie to T. Corbett, 30 March 1745, 10 Feb. 1746[7], 2 May 1747, PRO, ADM
       1/3990; same to Bedford, 18 Jan. 1757, PRONI, T 2915/1/14.

123.   E. King to Dr S. Foley, *c.* 1690, records of St Werburgh's Dublin, RCB, P.
       326/27/3/76.

124.   Ann Murray to M. Evelyn, 14 Jan. 1705[6], Evelyn Mss, unbound Mss, formerly
       in Christ Church, Oxford.

125.   W. Blair to N. Clements, 16 and 18 Dec. 1756, 10 Feb. 1757, 15 March 1757,
       TCD, Ms. 1741/14, 15, 18, 21.

126.   M. Coghill to E. Southwell, 27 Sept. 1735, NLI, Ms. 875; will of M. Coghill, 23
       March 1735[6], PRO, PROB, 11/695, 74; HMC, *Egmont diary*, ii, p. 397; J. H.
       Coghill, *The family of Coghill, 1377–1879* (Cambridge, [1879]), pp. 23–6; B. C. A.
       Windele, 'A genealogical note on the family of Cramer or Coghill', *JCHAS*, 2nd
       series, 16 (1910), pp. 66–81.

127.   J. Bayly to G. Dodington, 1 Jan. 1735[6], letter book of John Bayly, 1735–44,
       Clements Mss, Co. Kildare; HMC, *Various collections*, vi, p. 55.

128.   J. Bayly to G. Dodington, 10 Jan. 1735[6], 24 May 1736, 31 July 1736, 2 Aug.
       1737, 4 March 1739[40], letter book of John Bayly, 1735–44.

129.   M. Coghill to E. Southwell, 27 Sept. 1735, 9 and 28 Oct. 1735, NLI, Ms. 875;
       R. Jocelyn to R. Jocelyn, 31 Dec. 1744, PRONI, Mic. 147/3.

130.   *CARD*, viii, pp. 121; ix, p. 251; J. R. Hill, *From patriots to unionists: Dublin civic
       politics and Irish Protestant patriotism, 1660–1840* (Oxford, 1997), p. 395. The artist
       was Francis Bindon.

131.   J. Potter to R. Wilmot, 1 July 1746, PRONI, T, 3019/771.

132.   *Statutes*, iv, pp. 458–9 (4 Geo. I, c. viii).

133.   Conolly list, PRONI, T 2825/A/1/8A.

134.   Queen Anne to Ormonde, 22 June 1711, Bodleian, Ms. Eng. Hist. C. 41, f. 164;
       Ormonde to Dartmouth, 22 June 1711, PRO, SP 63/376, 50–1; Hayton, 'Ireland

and the English ministers', pp. 108–9, 179, 184–6; Magennis, *Irish political system*, pp. 83–4.

135. E. Southwell to M. Coghill, 5 March 1735[6], NLI, Ms. 875; W. Henry to Abp. J. Herring, 21 Dec. 1753, BL, Add. Ms. 35,592, f. 230.

136. M. L. Legg, 'Money and reputations: the effects of the banking crises of 1755 and 1760', *Eighteenth-Century Ireland*, 11 (1996), pp. 74–87.

137. J. Digby to Lord Digby, 22 April 1760, Dorset CRO, D/SHC, 3C/81; F. Trench to S. Bagshawe, 6 Nov. 1759, JRL, B 2/3/808.

138. 29 Geo II, c. xvi, 33 Geo II, c. xiv, *Statutes*, vii, pp. 334–5, 736–43.

139. W. Perceval to A. Charlet, 5 Feb. 1712[13], Bodleian, Ballard Ms. 36, f. 80; Loeber, *Biographical dictionary of architects in Ireland*, pp. 88–97.

140. Thrift index of Dublin freemen, Dublin City Archives; W. Clare, 'The Putland family of Dublin and Bray', *Dublin Historical Record*, 54 (2001), pp. 183–209.

141. L. M. Cullen, 'Landlords, bankers and merchants: the early Irish banking world, 1700–1820', *Hermathena*, 135 (1983), pp. 25–44; M. MacCarthy-Morrogh, 'Credit and remittance: monetary problems in early seventeenth-century Munster', *Irish Economic and Social History*, 14 (1987), pp. 5–19.

142. *CJIre.*, ii, appendix, p. clxxii; iii, appendix, pp. ccxxxi–ccxxxiii; NLI, Ms. 2487, pp. 429–34; PRO, SP, 63/382, pp. 25–8; Clare, 'The Putland family', pp. 183–209.

143. NLI, Ms. 2487, pp. 429–34; *CJIre.*, iii, appendix, pp. ccxxxi–ccxxxiii; PRO, SP 63/382, 25–8.

144. *An elegy for Thomas Putland, banker, of Dublin* (Dublin, 1721); Clare, 'The Putland family', pp. 183–209; see below, p. 269.

145. Bp. W. Nicolson to Abp. W. Wake, 13 July 1725, Christ Church, Wake Ms. 14/275; C. D., *A letter from a brother-prisoner to the honourable John Pratt, esq . . . upon his confinement in four-court marshalsea, on the ninth day of June, 1725* (Dublin, 1725); J. W., *Second letter to the honourable Captain P[rat]t, from a gentleman formerly in an office under him* ([Dublin, 1725]); Williams (ed.), *Swift Correspondence*, iii, pp. 64, 73.

146. J. Pratt, final account, 7 June 1725, IAA, Castletown deposit, box 46.

147. P. McNally, 'Patronage and politics in Ireland, 1714 to 1727', unpublished Ph.D. thesis, Queen's University, Belfast (1993), p. 74; McNally, *Parties, patriots and undertakers*, p. 131. Cf. A. Saville (ed.), *Secret comment: the diaries of Gertrude Saville, 1721–1757*, Kingsbridge History Society and Thoroton Society (1997), p. 33.

148. Carteret to Newcastle, 8 June 1725, PRO, SP 63/385, 138; Bp. W. Nicolson to Abp. W. Wake, 27 Aug. 1725, Christ Church, Wake Ms. 14/281.

149. Bp. T. Godwin to Abp. W. Wake, 21 May 1726, Christ Church, Wake Ms. 14/263.

150. Affidavit of W. Whitshed, 18 Feb. 1724[5], PRO, SP, 63/385, 54. For links between the Conollys and Pratt, J. Hamilton to K. Conolly, 18 May 1723, IAA, Castletown deposit, box 54.

151. Minute books, 1731–33; 1733–41, RDS; M. Kelleher, list of members of RDS.

152. J. P. McDermott, 'An examination of the accounts of James Moore, esq., land agent and collector of port fees at Newport Pratt, Co. Mayo, 1742–1765', unpublished MA thesis, St Patrick's College, Maynooth (1994).

153. Abp. W. King to E. Southwell, 17 Aug. 1725; same to F. Annesley, 26 Nov. 1725, TCD, Ms. 750/8/20, 54.

154. J. Pratt, 'final account', 7 June 1725, IAA, Castletown deposit, box 46; Carteret to Newcastle, 6 July 1725, PRO, SP 63/385, 263; unknown to Newcastle, 16 Nov. 1725, House of Lords RO, Tickell Mss, iv; *CJI*, viii, part ii, p. cliv.

155. J. Evelyn, Jr. to J. Evelyn, 29 May 1693, Evelyn Mss, formerly at Christ Church, Oxford, now in BL.

156. P. McNally, 'The Hanoverian accession and the Tory party in Ireland', *Parliamentary History*, 14 (1995), pp. 270–3.

157. M. Hall to M. and W. Leathes, 10 May 1705, de Mussenden Leathes Mss, Suffolk CRO, HA 403/1/7; W. Leathes to Hugh Eccles, 2 April 1721; same to Sir J. Eccles, 2 April 1721; same to W. Conolly, 2 Aug. 1721; ibid., HA 403/1/5; J. Mussenden to W. Leathes, 22 Nov. 1724, and note on same by Sir J. Eccles, 24 Nov. 1724, ibid., HA 403/1/6; J. Agnew, *Belfast merchant families in the seventeenth century* (Dublin, 1996), p. 224; Clarkson and Crawford, *Ways to wealth*, pp. 26, 42–3.

158. Rental of Ormonde properties, 1689, NLI, Ms. 2562; Ormonde estates, 1720, PRO, FEC 1/870, p. 8; S. Synge to T. Medlycott, Nov. 1691, BL, Add. Ms. 28,877, f. 188; E. Southwell to Lords Justice, 29 July 1711, Bodleian, Ms. Eng. Hist. C. 41, f. 182.

159. J. Evelyn, Jr. to J. Evelyn, Nov. 1695; F. Roberts to J. Evelyn, Jr., 11 April 1696, Evelyn Mss, Christ Church, Oxford, now in BL, Add. Mss; will of John, 18th earl of Kildare, 19 March 1704[5], PRONI, D 3168/K/1/1; correspondence of T. Medlycott with E. Southwell, 1703–27, BL, Add. Ms. 34,778; Ormonde to Lord Godolphin, 10 May 1704, NLI, Ms. 2502/381; annotated civil list, BL, Add. Ms. 61,637B, f. 6; E. Southwell to M. Coghill, 10 May 1735, 20 Dec. 1735, NLI, Ms. 875; will of T. Medlycott, 9 Aug. 1732, PRO, PROB, 11/691, 218; *CARD*, vi, pp. 52–3; B. D. Henning, *History of the House of Commons, 1660–90*, 3 vols (London, 1983), pp. 336–7; K. T. Hoppen, *The common scientist in the seventeenth century: a study of the Dublin Philosophical Society* (London, 1970), pp. 121, 127, 175, 177, 181, 192; R. Sedgwick (ed.), *History of Parliament, 1715–1754*, 2 vols (London, 1970), ii, pp. 250, 384–5; HMC, *Various collections*, vi, p. 56.

160. J. Forth to T. Medlycott, 10 Oct. 1718, letter book of J. Forth, NLI, Ms. 16,007, 64.

161. J. Evelyn, Jr. to J. Evelyn, 18 June 1695, Evelyn Mss, formerly at Christ Church, now in BL.

162. For the salary, raised from £800 to £1,000 to qualify commissioners to sit in the English parliament, BL, Add. Ms. 61,637, f. 38; J. Evelyn, Jr, to J. Evelyn, 23 Jan. 1696[7], 15 and 21 April 1697, in Evelyn Mss, formerly at Christ Church, now in BL.

163. M. Coghill to ?E. Southwell, 11 Nov. 1732, PRONI, T 2534.

164. M. Coghill to E. Southwell, 11 Nov. 1735, NLI, Ms. 875; will of M. Coghill, 23 March 1735[6], PRO, PROB, 11/695, 74.

165. Correspondence with W. and K. Conolly, 1720s, IAA, Castletown deposit, box 53.

166. J. Ponsonby to Sir. T. Taylor, 16 March 1759, NLI, Headfort Papers, F/5/46; minute book, revenue commissioners, s.d. 1761, 17 Dec. 1765, PRO, CUST 1/67, f. 65; 1/89, f. 100.

167. Memorial of Sir R. Deane to Bedford, 20 Feb. 1758, PRONI, T 2915/4/21.

168. J. Leslie to Sir M. Crosbie, 10 Jan. 1752, 14 Feb. 1752, NLI, Talbot-Crosbie Mss, folder 37; E. Spencer to F. Price, 18 Jan. 1744[5]; same to Mrs A. Price, 1 Sept. 1760, NLW, Puleston Ms. 3580E.

169. Revenue commissioners to Sunderland, 13 Jan. 1714[15], letter book of James Forth, NLI, Ms. 16,007, p. 8.

170. Minute book of revenue commissioners, s. d. 29 Oct. 1760, PRO, CUST 1/66, f. 12v. Manuals such as J. Ballard, *Gauging unmasked* (Dublin, 1761) and *Tables calculated for the use of the revenue officers of Ireland* (n.p., n.d.) offered instruction.

171. Order of 8 Dec. 1739, minute book of revenue commissioners, 1739–41, PRO, CUST 1/31, p. 8; D. B. Horn, *British diplomatic representatives, 1689–1789*, Camden Society, 3rd series, xlvi (1932), p. 123.

172. Revenue commissioners to Lord Molesworth, 13 Oct. 1718, letter book of J. Forth, NLI, Ms. 16,007, pp. 65–6.

173. Civil list, 1720, Bodleian, Rawlinson Ms. B. 511; minute book of revenue commissioners, s.d. 19 May 1761, PRO, CUST 1/68, f. 32v.

174. J. Forth to T. Coplestone, 2 Jan. 1728[9], NLI, Ms. 16,007, pp. 182–3.

175. Ormonde to Irish revenue commissioners, 5 April 1712, Bodleian, Ms. Eng. Hist. C. 41, f. 289.

176. Revenue commissioners to Sunderland, 13 Jan. 1714[15], letter book of J. Forth, NLI, Ms. 16,007.

177. Orrery correspondence with B. Badham, 1723–27, NLI, Ms. 4177; R. Purcell to Orrery, 24 Jan. 1737[8], Harvard UL Ms. Eng. 218.19; Orrery to unknown 2 Jan. 1743[4], TCD, Ms. 3821/212; E. Boyle, countess of Cork and Orrery (ed.), *The Orrery Letters*, 2 vols (London, 1903), i, p. 127; Dickson, 'Economic history of the Cork region', i, p. 118, C. M. Tenison, 'Cork MPs', *JCHAS*, 1 (1895), p. 41. At his death in 1744, a neighbour was reassured that 'I never could hear that he attempted to pass for a honest man'. E. Spencer to F. Price, 24 July 1744, NLW, Puleston Ms. 3580E.

178. B. Badham to ?H. Boyle, 7 Nov. 1731, PRONI, D 2707/A/1/11, 37.

179. Clarkson and Crawford, *Ways to wealth*, pp. 26, 34–43.

180. G. Wahab to J. Evelyn, 4 March 1692[3], 13 May 1693, 27 June 1693, 9 Feb. 1693[4], Evelyn Mss, formerly at Christ Church, now in BL.

181. M. Ní Mhurchadha, ' "Sober, active and bred to the sea": the customs service in Fingal, 1684–1765', unpublished M.A. thesis, St Patrick's College, Maynooth (1998), pp. 84–91; G. Wauchope, *The Ulster branch of the family of Wauchope, Wauhope, Wahab, Waughop, etc.* (London, 1929).

182. Notebook relating to Loughreagh revenue district, 1696, 1697, RIA, Ms. 12 A 29; D. Dickson, 'The account book of a Kerry revenue official', *Journal of the Kerry Archaeological and Historical Society*, 6 (1973), pp. 76–82.

183. Mulcahy, *Kinsale*, vii, p. 42.

184. Census of Elphin, 1749, NA, M. 2466, ff. 396–421; minute book of revenue commissioners, s.d. 10 and 17 June 1762, PRO, CUST 1/72, ff. 35v, 58; parish register of St Peter's, Drogheda, 1747–72 (copy), NA, M. 5127.

185. J. Barry to R. Power, 14 Sept. 1703, NLI, Ms. 13,247; *CJIre.*, ii, p. 756.

186. Minute books of revenue commissioners, s.d. 22 Dec. 1755, 19 March 1756, 1 Oct. 1757, 23 Nov. 1757, 18 April 1760, 8 Sept. 1760, 20 July 1764, 8 Aug. 1764, 22 Jan. 1765, 24 May 1765, 25 June 1765, 15 Aug. 1765, 5 Oct. 1765, 10 March 1766, 28 April 1766, 27 Jan. 1767, PRO, CUST 1/57, ff. 54, 133; 1/61, ff. 22–2v, 59; 1/64, f. 63v; 1/65, f. 8v; 1/82, ff. 150v–51; 1/83, f. 28; 1/85, ff. 26v–27; 1/86, f. 113v; 1/87, ff. 7, 110v–111; 1/88, f. 83v; 1/90, f. 97; 1/91, ff. 116–16v; 1/95, f. 91.

187. J. Wight, journal, s.d. 28 Aug. 1754, Friends' Historical Library, Dublin; Corporal Todd's journal, Wigan Public Library; minute book of revenue commissioners, s.d. 18 Nov. 1754, PRO, CUST 1/55, f. 58; B. Molesworth to T. Waite, 24 June 1754, Calendar of miscellaneous letters and papers before 1760, NA; A. J.

Fetherstonhaugh, 'The true story of the two chiefs of Dunboy', *JRSAI*, 5th series, I (1894), pp. 35–43, 139–49; N. Garnham, *The courts, crime and the criminal law in Ireland, 1692–1760* (Dublin, 1996), p. 37; R. A. Williams, *The Berehaven copper mines*, 2nd edn (Kenmare, 1993), pp. 31–2.

188. J. Waller to E. Southwell, 20 Jan. 1701[2]; memorandum, 29 Dec. 1708; B. Townshend to H. Beecher and J. Dennis, 8 Feb. 1708[9]; same to E. Southwell, 23 Feb. 1708[9], National Maritime Museum, Southwell Ms. 19; L. M. Cullen, 'The smuggling trade in Ireland in the eighteenth century', *PRIA*, 67, sect. C (1967), pp. 149–75.

189. Orders of 18 Aug. 1747, 24 April 1758, April 1761, 14 Aug. 1762, 10 Nov. 1763, minute books of revenue commissioners, PRO, CUST 1/43, p. 22; 1/61, f. 146; 1/67, f. 155; 1/73, ff. 34v–35; 1/79, ff. 63–3v.

190. Lunnell, Memoir, NLI, Ms. 21,521; B. MacMahon, *The story of Ballyheigue* (Ballyheigue, 1994), pp. 75–81.

191. Calendar of departmental correspondence, 1741–59, 6 March 1759, 20 April 1759, NA; minute books of revenue commissioners, s.d. 18 Jan. 1755, 14 and 28 Feb. 1755, 26 Jan. 1758, 17 Oct. 1760, 17 May 1766, PRO, CUST 1/55, ff. 100, 120v, 131; 1/61, f. 97; 1/65, f. 144; 1/92, f. 14.

192. Minute books of revenue commissioners, s.d. 24 April 1756, 4 June 1756, 10 and 13 Aug. 1757, 25 and 29 Aug. 1758, 22 Sept. 1759, 26 March 1760, 5 and 15 April 1760, 2 and 29 Oct. 1760, 8, 21, 24 and 26 Nov. 1760, 7, 14, 20, 21 and 31 Jan. 1761, 16 March 1761, 4 and 9 April 1761, 19 Feb. 1763, 15 April 1763, 21 Feb. 1764, 7, 20 and 26 June 1764, 13 and 16 July 1764, 28 Sept. 1764, 23 Nov. 1764, 28 Feb. 1765, 30 April 1765, 6 and 10 May 1765, 9 Sept. 1765, 7 and 17 Dec. 1765, PRO, CUST 1/59, ff. 50v, 52–2v, 140, 145v; 1/62, ff. 112, 116; 1/63, f. 115v; 1/64, ff. 28, 29, 44v, 58; 1/65, ff. 93v–94; 1/66, ff. 12, 13v–14, 18v, 25, 35, 69v–70, 76, 82v, 95v, 132v, 136v, 151–51v; 1/75, f. 103; 1/76, f. 98v; 1/80, ff. 90v, 92v–93; 1/82, ff. 45, 60, 76, 129–9v, 134, 136; 1/83, f. 124v; 1/84, ff. 64–4v; 1/85, f. 98v; 1/86, ff. 56–6v, 73v, 86v–7; 1/88, f. 16; 1/89, ff. 83v, 100.

193. Minute books of revenue commissioners, s.d. 1766, PRO, CUST 1/92, ff. 163–3v.

194. Magennis, *Irish political system*, pp. 62–108; C. I. McGrath, *The making of the eighteenth-century Irish constitution: government, parliament and the revenue, 1692–1714* (Dublin, 2000); J. I. McGuire, 'The Irish parliament of 1692', in T. Bartlett and D. W. Hayton (eds), *Penal era and golden age: essays in Irish history, 1690–1800* (Belfast, 1979), pp. 1–21; D. O'Donovan, 'The money bill dispute of 1753', ibid., pp. 55–87.

195. J. Waller to E. Southwell, 1 Nov. 1698, 13 Dec. 1698, BL, Add. Ms. 38,150, ff. 117v, 127; ibid., Add. Ms. 61,637B, ff. 35, 36v; R. Lloyd to F. Herbert, 14 Aug. 1717, NLW, Powis Castle correspondence, no. 16062; Bp. J. Evans to Abp. W. Wake, 6 July 1717; Abp. W. King to same, 19 Aug. 1717, Christ Church, Wake Ms. 12, ff. 187, 203; F. Bernard to E. Southwell, 24 Dec. 1725, BL, Add. Ms. 9713, f. 84; M. Ronayne to Grandison, 3 Oct. 1729, Dromana, Villiers-Stuart Mss, T 3131, C/5/48; J. Smythe to W. Smythe, 20 Nov. 1742, NLI, PC 449; *Advice to the patriots of the Coomb, the Liberties and the suburbs of Dublin, lately assembled in Parliament* (Dublin, 1759), pp. 8–9.

196. E. Magennis, 'Coal, corn and canals: the dispersal of public moneys, 1695–1772', in D. W. Hayton (ed.), *The Irish parliament in the eighteenth century: the long apprenticeship* (Edinburgh, 2001), pp. 71–86.

197. *The secret history and memoirs of the barracks of Ireland*, 2nd edn (London, 1747), p. 23.

198. Kilkenny corporation book, 1690–1717, s.d. 23 March 1715[16]; *CARD*, vi, p. 134; vii, pp. 286–7, 293–4; Waterford corporation book, s.d. 22 Jan. 1717[18], Waterford Municipal Archives.

199. Accounts of Youghal corporation, 1665, 1667, 1685, Cork Archives Institute, U/138/1821; 'Manuscripts of the old corporation of Kinsale', *Analecta Hibernica*, 15 (1944), pp. 177, 180, 181; D. Townshend, 'Notes on the council book of Clonakilty', *JCHAS*, 2nd series, 1 (1895), pp. 352–3, 452, 518; 2 (1896), p. 33, 34, 130, 134; Mulcahy, *Kinsale*, i, p. 116; ii, pp. 3–5, 76; iii, pp. 3, 13, 38, 55, 56, 59–60, 62; vii, pp. 8, 13, 46, 58, 79; vi, p. 25; Waterford corporation book, 1700–27, s.d. 30 June 1701, 26 Feb. 1705[6], 3 April 1712; B. Ó Dálaigh (ed.), *Corporation book of Ennis* (Dublin, 1990), pp. 63, 97, 117, 120–1.

200. *CARD*, iv, pp. 365, 373; vi, p. 67

201. Ibid., iii, pp. 41, 48, 49, 67, 132, 166, 197, 219, 222, 241, 242, 250.

202. Ibid., vi, pp. 189, 208, 230.

203. Ibid., iii, p. 504; iv, p. 107; vi, p. 541, 545.

204. Ibid., iii, pp. 415, 417, 493; iv, p. 68.

205. Kilkenny corporation book, 1690–1717, s.d. 10 Feb. 1698[9]; Youghal corporation accounts, 1684–85, Cork Archives Institute, U/138, 1821; *CARD*, vi, pp. 208, 230; R. Caulfield (ed.), *The council book of the corporation of Cork* (Guildford, 1876), p. 231; T. Gogarty (ed.), *Council book of the corporation of Drogheda, 1649–1734* (Drogheda, 1915), pp. 136, 174, 175–6.

206. Limerick corporation book, BL, Add. Ms. 19,859, f. 37v.

207. Ó Dálaigh (ed.), *Ennis*; p. 114; poor book, St Michan's, Dublin, 1723–34, RCB, P. 276/8.1, p. 114.

208. Mulcahy, *Kinsale*, iii, p. 56; vi, pp. 40, 65, 89.

209. V. Smith to J. Ellis, 30 June 1691; J. Baxter to same, 23 Nov. 1691, BL, Add. Ms. 28,877, ff. 56, 193; Belturbet municipal records, s.d. 22 Feb. 1708[9], formerly NA, M. 3572; Youghal corporation accounts, 1685, Cork Archives Institute, U/138/1821; *A just and true relation of Josias Bateman's concern* (n.p., c. 1732); Mulcahy, *Kinsale*, vi, p. 48; Townshend, 'Clonakilty', ii, pp. 134–5.

210. Mulcahy, *Kinsale*, vi, p. 47; vii, p. 96.

211. Corporation book of Atherdee, 1661–87, s.d. 29 Sept. 1662, Public Library, Dundalk; Waterford corporation book, 1700–27, s.d. Jan. 1702[3], Waterford Municipal Archives; Gogarty, *Drogheda*, pp. 88–9, 116; Mulcahy, *Kinsale*, i, p. 116; Townshend, 'Clonakilty', pp. 449–50, 518.

212. Lease to O. Silver, 29 Sept. 1664, Youghal Municipal Records, U/138, G7, Cork Archives Institute; Barnard, 'Cork settlers', p. 345; M. Seoighe, *The story of Kilmallock* (Kilmallock, 1987), pp. 154–6; Tenison, 'Cork MPs', p. 276.

213. Will of E. Singleton, 15 Aug. 1709, NLI, reports on private collections, no. 195; Gogarty, *Drogheda*, pp. 207, 245, 250, 292, 296, 299, 307.

214. H. Boyle to Lord Burlington, 17 Aug. 1731, Chatsworth, Devonshire Letters, 1720–36 205.0; parish register of St Peter's, Drogheda, 1747–72 (copy), s.d. 12 Nov. 1759, NA, M. 5127; F. E. Ball, *The Judges of Ireland*, 2 vols (London and New York, 1926), ii, pp. 130–1, 136–7, 139–40; C. Casey, 'J. Ravell's "A Map of the Town and Suburbs of Drogheda 1749"', *Journal of County Louth Archaeological and Historical Society*, 22 (1992), p. 361; Delany, *Autobiography*, 1st series, p. 557.

215. C. Crofts to Sir R. Southwell, 3 June 1690, 18 July 1690, RIA, 24 G 3/3, 24 G 4/36.

216. Waterford corporation book, 1700–27, s.d. 24 June 1712, Waterford Municipal Archives.

217. Ormonde to Lords Justices, 28 Feb. 1712[13], Bodleian, Mss. Eng. Hist. C. 42, 13.

218. *CARD*, viii, pp. 343–4; *KIAP*, p. 193.

219. J. S. Rabbitte, 'Galway corporation Ms. C.', *Journal of the Galway Archaeological and Historical Society*, 11 (1921), pp. 84, 101, 103, 110–11; 12 (1922), pp. 9–11, 21.

220. Ibid., 11, p. 90; 12, p. 33.

221. Mulcahy, *Kinsale*, vii, pp. 16, 57.

222. R. Marshall to E. Lee, 27 Sept. 1737, NA, 1079/6/5; brief of R. Malone, [1737], NA, 1079/6/7(b); F. E. Ball, 'Robert Marshall', *JCHAS*, 2nd series, 3 (1897), pp. 263–74.

223. Barnard, 'Cork settlers', pp. 342–5; T. Barnard, 'Lawyers and the law in late seventeenth-century Ireland', *IHS*, 28 (1993), p. 268.

224. L. G. Pine (ed.), *Burke's genealogical and heraldic history of the landed gentry of Ireland*, 4th edn (London, 1958), pp. 380–2; Townshend, 'Clonakilty', ii, pp. 81, 134, 174.

225. Rabbitte, 'Galway corporation Ms. C.', 11, p. 100.

226. Waterford corporation book, 1700–27, s.d. 6 Dec. 1701, 14 Aug. 1714, Waterford Municipal Archives; Barnard, 'Cork settlers', pp. 342–5; R. Caulfield (ed.), *Autobiography of Rt. Hon. Sir Richard Cox, Bart.* (London, 1860), pp. 11–13; *KIAP*, pp. 34, 106.

227. J. Waite to T. Baker and C. Musgrave, 29 May 1708, Chatsworth, J. Waite letter book, 1708–10.

228. Minute book, corporation of Athy, s.d. 15 May 1746, 1 July 1746; PRONI, D 3078/4/2; *KIAP*, p. 15.

229. *CARD*, viii, p. 121; ix, pp. 310, 348, 365; J. R. Hill, *From patriots to unionists: Dublin civic politics and Irish Protestant patriotism, 1660–1840* (Oxford, 1997), p. 395.

230. Barnard, 'Introduction', in Barnard and McCormack (eds), *Dublin Tholsel records*; R. V. Dudley, 'Dublin's parishes, 1660–1729: the Church of Ireland parishes and their role in the civic administration of the city', unpublished Ph. D. thesis, TCD, 2 vols (1995), i, pp. 83–5, 86, 90; R. Gillespie, *Thomas Howell and his friends: serving Christ Church Cathedral, Dublin, 1570–1700* (Dublin, 1997), pp. 14–15.

231. Appointments in the diocese of Clogher, RCB, D.1. 72.

232. Vestry book, St John's, Dublin, 1660–1702, RCB, P. 328/5.2, p. 151.

233. Churchwardens' accounts, Ballymodan [Bandon], 1694–1780, s.d. 7 April 1729, RCB, P. 140.7; vestry book of Agher, s.d. 27 March 1751, NLI, Ms. 5246; vestry book, Kells, s.d. 25 April 1729, 26 March 1751, 26 March 1754, 1 April 1755.

234. Vestry book, St Catherine's, Dublin, 1693–1730, RCB, P. 117/5/1.2, ff. 326, 360, 380v; Churchwardens' accounts, St Michan's, Dublin, 1723–61, ibid., P. 276/8/2, pp. 306, 409; vestry book, St Bride's, Dublin, 1662–1742, ibid., P. 327/3/1, p. 235.

235. Proctors' accounts, St Patrick's Cathedral, Dublin, 1718–35, s.d. 1718, 20 Nov. 1719, 26 May 1722, RCB, C. 2.1.10 (1); vestry book, St Bride's, Dublin, 1662–1742, ibid., P. 327/3.1, p. 174; vestry book, St John's, Dublin, accounts, 1747, 1757, ibid., P. 328/5.2; vestry book, St Michan's, Dublin, ibid., P. 276/4.1, p. 148.

236. Vestry book, Carlow, 1669–1762, s.d. 29 April 1724, RCB, P. 317/5.1; J. Loughlin, accounts with Lord Castledurrow, s.d. 25 March 1740, NLI, Ms. 11,463.

237. Vestry book, St Catherine's, Dublin, 1693–1730, RCB, P. 117/5/2, p. 360; Masters' accounts, Weavers' Company, s.d. 1697–98, RSAI.

238. Minutes of the Barber Surgeons' Company, Dublin, 1703–57, s.d. 2 May 1709, 25 April 1720, 22 July 1749, TCD, Ms. 1447/8/1, ff. 3v, 34, 106v.

239. Extracts from records of the Dublin Holy Trinity (Merchants') Guild, s.d. 10 Jan. 1668[9], Dublin Public Library, Gilbert Ms. 78; account book, Guild of St Anne's, s.d. May 1709, RIA, Ms. 12 P 1.

240. Minute book, Goldsmiths' Company, Assay Office, Dublin Castle.

241. Transactions, Apothecaries' Guild, 1747–95, s.d. 30 June 1747, 29 Dec. 1748, Apothecaries' Hall, Dublin.

242. Ormonde to Lords Justice, 17 April 1711, Bodleian, Ms. Eng. Hist. C. 41, f. 125; appointments of W. Langton and W. Dobyns, 5 March 1710[11], 12 May 1711; of R. England, 15 June 1711, PRO, SP 34/30/31A; SP 34/31/23C; SP 34/33/4A; Lord Castledurrow to Sir St J. Leger, 15 July 1738, NLI, Ms. 11481/11; R. Purcell to Lord Perceval, 27 July 1746, BL, Add. Ms. 47,002A, f. 55; R. Blair, 'An analysis of the Donegal grand jury presentments, 1753–1762', *Donegal Annual*, 36 (1984), p. 62; W. M. Brady, *Clerical and parochial records of Cork, Cloyne and Ross*, 3 vols (London, 1864), i, xlviii, xlix, li.

243. H. Murtagh, *Athlone: history and settlement to 1800* (Athlone, 2000), p. 189.

244. P. Whichcote to R. Liddell, 28 Jan. 1745[6], PRONI, T 3019/724.

245. Petition of P. Whichcote to George I, *c.* 1725, PRO, SP 63/385, 159–61.

246. Mr Baumann to P. Whichcote, 18 July 1724; J. Kerr to same, 25 July 1724, 19 Feb. 1724[5], PRO, SP, 63/385, 161–2.

247. Prior, *Absentees*, p. 11.

248. Petition from south Munster to Lord Cork and Burlington, 1 May 1728, PRONI, D 2707/A1/1, 11B.

249. G. Aylmer, *The state's servants* (London, 1973), pp. 326–43; L. W. B. Brockliss, 'The professions and national identity', in L. W. B. Brockliss and D. S. Eastwood (eds), *A union of multiple identities: the British Isles, c. 1750-c. 1850* (Manchester, 1997), pp. 9–28.

250. Palmerston to R. Roberts, 31 Aug. 1740, 24 Jan. 1744[5], Southampton UL, BR, 2/8; 2/9.

251. List of 72 MPs 'in employment', PRONI, T 2825/A/1/8A; E. Southwell to M. Coghill, 5 March 1735[6], NLI, Ms. 875; division list to expel Nevill, JRL, Ms. B15/3/6; W. Henry to Abp. T. Herring, 21 Dec. 1753, BL, Add. Ms. 35,592, f. 230; *An address from the influenc'd electors of the county and city of Galway* (London, 1754), p. 14.

252. Court book of Kilmallock corporation, NLI, Ms. 9451, pp. 8, 21, 45; list of those taking the oaths, Belturbet Municipal Records, s.d. 7 Aug. 1715, formerly NA, M. 3572; C. Lennon, *The lords of Dublin in the age of reformation* (Dublin, 1989), pp. 48, 101, 196; S. Pender (ed.), *Council books of the corporation of Waterford, 1662–1700* (Dublin, 1964), pp. 34, 41–2; Townshend, 'Clonakilty', p. 349.

253. Vestry book of Carlow parish, 1669–1762, s.d. 31 Jan. 1715[16], RCB, P. 317/5/1.

254. P. D. Vigors (ed.), 'Extracts from the old corporation books of New Ross, Co. Wexford', *JRSAI*, 5th series, 11 (1901), p. 59. Cf. R. Herbert, 'The antiquities of the corporation of Limerick', *North Munster Antiquarian Journal*, 4 (1945), p. 95; H. F. Hore (ed.), 'A chorographic account of the southern part of the County of Wexford, written, anno 1684, by Robert Leigh', *Journal of the Kilkenny and South-East of Ireland Archaeological Society*, new series, 2 (1858–59), pp. 452–3.

255. R. Caulfield (ed.), *The council book of the corporation of Youghal* (Guildford, 1878), plate 8; K. B. Dillow, 'The social and ecclesiastical significance of church seating arrangements and pew disputes, 1500–1740', unpublished D. Phil. thesis, University

of Oxford (1990), pp. 152–4. Cf. R. Tittler, *Architecture and power: the town hall and the English urban community, c. 1500–1640* (Oxford, 1991), pp. 98–156.

256. M. Goldie, 'The unacknowledged republic: office-holding in early modern England', in T. Harris (ed.), *The politics of the excluded, c. 1500–1850* (Basingstoke, 2001), pp. 153–94; S. J. Hindle, 'A sense of place? Becoming and belonging in the rural parish, 1550–1650', in A. Shepard and P. Withington (eds), *Communities in early-modern England* (Manchester, 2000), pp. 96–114; S. Rappaport, *Worlds within worlds: structures of life in sixteenth-century London* (Cambridge, 1989), pp. 175–83.

7. Soldiers and Sailors

1. E. Spencer to F. Price, 18 Jan. 1744[5]; same to Mrs A. Price, 25 Sept. 1749, NLW, Puleston Ms. 3580E; establishment books, Irish Revenue, PRO, CUST 1/56, f. 152; CUST 20/123.

2. J. Smythe to W. Smythe, 14 June 1710, 13 Aug. [?1711], NLI, PC 449; Abp. W. King to J. Trotter, 4 July 1726, TCD, Ms. 750/8, 118.

3. C. S. King (ed.), *A great archbishop of Dublin* (London, 1906), pp. 315–16.

4. R. Waring to S. Waring, 11 and 19 Oct. 1691; same to W. Waring, 23 April 1692, private collection, Co. Down; Charles Dalton, *George the First's army, 1714–1727*, 2 vols (London, 1910), i, pp. 186, 229, 329.

5. L. M. Cullen, 'The Irish diaspora of the seventeenth and eighteenth centuries', in N. P. Canny, (ed.), *Europeans on the move* (Oxford, 1994), pp. 190–6; J. Cunningham, *A history of Castle Caldwell and its families* (Monaghan, c. 1980); H. Murtagh, 'Irish soldiers abroad, 1600–1800', in T. Bartlett and K. Jeffery (eds), *A military history of Ireland* (Cambridge, 1996), pp. 294–314.

6. E. Southwell to Lord Nottingham, 8 July 1703, PRO, SP 63/363/385; S. Bagshawe to W. Bagshawe, 10 Feb. 1749[50], JRL, Bagshawe of Ford Mss, B 2/3/226; A. J. Guy (ed.), *Colonel Samuel Bagshawe and the army of George II, 1731–1762* (London, 1990), p. 18.

7. T. Denman, '"Hibernia officina militum": Irish recruitment to the British regular army, 1660–1815', *The Irish sword*, 20 (1996), pp. 149–59; K. P. Ferguson, 'The army in Ireland from the Restoration to the Act of Union', unpublished Ph.D. thesis, TCD, 2 vols (1981); A. J. Guy, 'The Irish military establishment, 1660–1776', in Bartlett and Jeffery (eds), *A military history of Ireland*, p. 219.

8. J. A. Houlding, *Fit for service: the training of the British army, 1715–1795* (Oxford, 1981), pp. 50–4; *Rules, orders, powers and directions for the good government and preservation of the barracks and redoubts for quartering the army in Ireland* (Dublin, 1726); *The secret history and memoirs of the barracks of Ireland*, 2nd edn (London, 1747).

9. For half-pay officers, see Census of Elphin, NA, M. 2466, f. 43.

10. Abp. G. Stone to E. Weston, 21 Oct. 1748, PRONI, T 3019/1172.

11. P. McNally, 'Patronage and politics in Ireland, 1714 to 1727', unpublished Ph.D. thesis, Queen's University, Belfast (1993), p. 113.

12. J. Waller to E. Southwell, 22 Nov. 1698, 12 and 21 Jan. 1698[9], BL, Add. Mss 38,150, f. 121; 38,151, ff. 3v, 9; letter book of earl of Drogheda and Abp. N. Marsh, 1700–3, s.d. 23 and 26 Feb. 1701[2], NLI, Ms. 16,210; list of

barrack-masters, 1703, TCD, Ms. 1179; establishment of George I, 25 March 1715, Bodleian, Ms. Eng. Hist. C. 42, ff. 218v–19.

13. K. M. Brown, 'From Scottish lords to British officers: state building, élite integration and the army in the seventeenth century', in N. MacDougall (ed.), *Scotland and war, A.D. 79–1918* (Edinburgh, 1991), pp. 133–69; I. F. Burton and A. N. Newman, 'Sir John Cope: promotion in the eighteenth-century British army', *EHR*, 78 (1963), pp. 655–68; J. Hayes, 'Scottish officers in the British army, 1714–1763', *Scottish Historical Review*, 37 (1958), pp. 23–33.

14. G. S. Holmes, *Augustan England: professions, state and society 1680–1730* (London, 1982), p. 266; R. B. McDowell, *Ireland in the age of imperialism* (Oxford, 1979), p. 62; Guy, 'Irish military establishment', p. 219.

15. T. Sheridan and J. Swift, *The Intelligencer*, ed. J. Woolley (Oxford, 1992), p. 12; Swift, *The Examiner*, 13 (2 Nov. 1710).

16. J. A. Oughton, autobiography, NAM, Ms. 8808–36–1, p. 54. Cf. *The Censor*, 21 (Dublin, 14–21 Oct. 1749).

17. R. French, notes for a parliamentary speech, *c.* 1769, NLI, French of Monivea Mss, envelope 83. Cf. J. Waller to E. Southwell, 13 Dec. 1698, BL, Add. Ms. 38,150, f. 127v.

18. [H. Brooke?], *An essay on the antient and present state of Ireland* (Dublin, 1759), p. 88.

19. S. J. Conway, 'War and national identity in the mid-eighteenth-century British Isles', *EHR*, 116 (2001), pp. 863–93.

20. G. E. Howard, *The miscellaneous works*, 3 vols (Dublin, 1782), i, p. xxxvi.

21. Commission of Ormonde as lord-lieutenant, 1703; Queen Anne to Ormonde, 26 March 1703, NLI, Ms. 991, pp. 1–4, 47.

22. M. Coghill to E. Southwell, 8 Dec. 1727, BL, Add. Ms. 21,122, f. 36v.

23. T. C. Barnard, 'Scotland and Ireland under the later Stewart monarchy', in S. G. Ellis and S. Barber (eds), *Conquest and Union: fashioning a British state, 1485–1725* (Harlow, 1995), pp. 254–7, 265–70; McNally, 'Patronage and politics', p. 24.

24. H. Boyle to Harrington, 18 Feb. 1748[9], 7 May 1749; Harrington to H. Boyle, 1 June 1749, PRONI, T 3019/1268, 1331, 1337; Abp. G. Stone to E. Weston, 7 Jan. 1748[9]; T. Waite to same, 18 Jan. 1748[9]; T. Carter to Harrington, 19 Jan. 1748[9], 1 Feb. 1748[9], 25 April 1749, ibid., T 3019/1236, 1240, 1242, 1266, 1327.

25. D. A. Baugh, *British naval administration in the age of Walpole* (Princeton, 1965), pp. 93–146; J. Childs, *The army of Charles II* (London, 1976), pp. 203–9; J. Childs, *The army, James II and the Glorious Revolution* (Manchester, 1980), pp. 58–76.

26. Lord Robartes to Sir O. Bridgeman, 19 and 23 Oct. 1669, Staffordshire CRO, Bradford Mss, D. 1287/18/3; Barnard, 'Introduction' and 'Aristocratic values' in T. Barnard and J. Fenlon (eds), *The dukes of Ormonde, 1610–1745* (Woodbridge, 2000); pp. 9–11, 167–9; P. A. Morris, 'Ormond's army: the Irish standing army, 1640–1669, with special reference to the personnel and administration after the Restoration', unpublished Ph.D. thesis, Vanderbilt University (1980).

27. J. Methuen to unknown, 6 Nov. 1697, PRO, SP 63/359, 375; E. Southwell to Nottingham, 8 July 1703, ibid., SP 63/363, 384–5; R. Cox to E. Southwell, 9 May 1704, BL, Add. Ms. 38,153, f. 52v; J. Dryden, *Fables ancient and modern; translated into verse from Homer, Ovid, Boccace, & Chaucer* (London, 1700), sig. B[1]–[C1v].

28. J. A. Oughton, autobiography, NAM, 8808–36–1, pp. 65–6; S. Bagshawe, fragmentary journal, 1740–42, JRL, B 15/3/1; S. Bagshawe to W. Bagshawe, 12 Nov. 1743, ibid., B 2/3/90; J. Copping to Sir H. Sloane, 15 Feb. 1741[2], BL,

Sloane Ms. 4057, f. 109; Fr. White, Annals of Limerick, NLI, Ms. 2714, pp. 134–5; C. O'Hara, journal, 1, 6 and 28 Feb. 1758, 11 March 1758, 10 May 1758, ibid., Ms. 20,389.

29. List of disbanded officers, 22 March 1688[9], BL, Add. Ms. 28,938, f. 314.

30. R. Waring to S. Waring, 4 Sept. 1690; same to W. Waring, 23 April 1692, private collection, Co. Down; G. Bonnivet to H. Sloane, 5 Aug. 1703, BL, Sloane Ms. 4039, f. 167; Nottingham to Ormonde, 11 and 16 Sept. 1703, National Maritime Museum, Phillips-Southwell Mss, SOU/15; life of H. Hawley, NAM, Ms. 7411–24–101, pp. 12–13; Barnard, 'Introduction', in Barnard and Fenlon (eds), *Dukes of Ormonde*, pp. 6–7, 9–10, 12, 28–9, 38, 48; D. W. Hayton, 'Dependence, clientage and affinity: the political following of the second duke of Ormonde', ibid., pp. 214, 228, 231–3, 238–9. For evidence about one captain of foot's commission to George Wandesford, 22 July 1715; notebook of G. Wandesford, 1715, NLI, Ms. 35,460.

31. J. K'eogh, *A vindication of the antiquities of Ireland* (Dublin, 1748), pp. 96–7.

32. F. Hamilton to Sir A. Conyngham, 30 Dec. 1690, IAA, Castletown deposit, box 54.

33. For accounts of the war by those from Ireland: R. Stearne, journal, NAM, Ms. 6807/392; NLI, Ms. 4166; R. Kane, *Campaigns of King William and Queen Anne* (London, 1745); R. Parker, *Memoirs of the most remarkable transactions from the year 1683, to 1718* (London, 1747). An alternative perspective is offered by S. Burrell (ed.), *Amiable renegade: the memoirs of Captain Peter Drake 1671–1753* (Stanford and London, 1960).

34. R. Waring to S. Waring, 1 March 1689[90]; A. Brownlow to J. Peers, 25 Jan. 1689[90], private collection, Co. Down; *Al. Dubl.*, p. 859.

35. R. Waring to W. Leathes, 28 Dec. 1714, 11 and 15 April 1715, 15 May 1715, 20 March 1715[16], 22 March 1716[17], 3 June 1717, 17 Aug. 1717, 21 Sept. 1717, de Mussenden Leathes Mss, Suffolk CRO, Ipswich, HA 403/1/1, 97, 108, 114, 117, 118; 403/1/2, 214, 225, 234, 237.

36. Diary of E. Bouhéreau, Marsh's Library, Ms. Z2.2.2, s.d. 1 Oct. 1709, 29 Jan. 1714, 3 Aug. 1715, 3 Feb. 1716, 17 May 1716, 30 Aug. 1716, 20 June 1717, 16 July 1718, 16 Dec. 1718, 31 March 1719.

37. E. P. Alexander (ed.), *The journal of John Fontaine: an Irish Huguenot son in Spain and Virginia 1710–1719* (Charlottesville, Va, 1974), p. 37; D. W. Ressinger (ed.), *Memoirs of the Reverend Jacques Fontaine, 1658–1728*, Huguenot Society of Great Britain and Ireland, new series, 2 (1992), pp. 188–9. On Slane, see GEC, *Complete peerage*, xii, part 1, pp. 19–20.

38. Ressinger (ed.), *Memoirs of the Reverend Jacques Fontaine*, p. 189.

39. E. T. Martin (ed.), *The Ash Mss, written in the year 1735, by Lieut.-Col. Thomas Ash* (Belfast, 1890), p. 23.

40. Accounts of Capt. A. Ussher, 1708–14, NLI, Ms. 10,186; receipt of J. Boesnier to Capt. A. Ussher, 5 Nov. 1727, ibid., Ms. 10,186; E. Hubbart to unknown, 23 March 1718[19], ibid., Ms. 10,175.

41. Receipt of J. Ussher to Capt. Ussher, 25 March 1739, ibid., Ms. 10,185/1.

42. G. Bonnivet to Sir C. Wyche, 6 Aug. 1702, NA, Wyche Ms. 1/1/270; same to H. Sloane, 24 June 1703, BL, Sloane Ms. 4039, f. 153.

43. W. Peard to F. Price, 7 Aug. 1741, NLW, Puleston Ms. 3579E; E. Spencer to F. Price, 10 and 20 Dec. 1748, ibid., Ms. 3580E; memorial of Sir R. Deane and others to Bedford, 20 Feb. 1758, PRONI, T 2915/9/1.

44. E. Spencer to F. Price, 9 Nov. 1745, 15 May 1746, 5 Jan. 1747[8], 16 Feb. 1747[8], 13 May 1748, NLW, Puleston Ms. 3580E.

45. Minute books, Irish revenue commissioners, PRO, CUST, 1/56, f. 152; 60, ff. 77, 84; 1/61, ff. 103v, 142, 146v; 1/81, ff. 54, 118; 1/82, f. 71v; 20/123.

46. E. Spencer to F. Price, 3 Oct. 1746, NLW, Puleston Ms. 3580E; order of 28 March 1757, PRO, CUST 1/60, f. 29.

47. M. Hall to W. Leathes, 18 Sept. 1705, Suffolk CRO, HA 403/1/7, 16.

48. R. Edwards to F. Price, 13 April 1742, NLW, Puleston Ms. 3577E.

49. Memorial of C. Irvine to Lord Townshend, [after 1714], TCD, Mss 1995–2008/2408.

50. M. A. Rudd, *Records of the Rudd family* (Bristol, 1920), p. 121.

51. Abp. W. King to E. Southwell, 9 Oct. 1708, TCD, Ms. 2531/2; C. Irvine to Abp. W. King, 19 Oct. 1711, ibid., Mss 1995–2008/1411; Abp. W. King to C. Irvine, 10 Aug. 1727, ibid., Ms. 750/9, pp. 4–6.

52. Abp. W. King to C. Irvine, 4 Oct. 1709, 11 Feb. 1710[11], 13 March 1717[18], ibid., Mss 750/11/1, pp. 116, 313; 750/11/3, pp. 113–14.

53. Abp. W. King to C. Irvine, 1 March 1721[2], ibid., Ms. 750/7, pp. 79–80.

54. Abp. W. King to C. Irvine, 3 April 1718, 1 March 1721[2], 3 July 1722, 28 Aug. 1722, ibid., Mss 750/11/3, pp. 140–1; 750/7, pp. 79–80, 148–9, 203; ibid., 2535/140; R. Cox to E. Southwell, 4 and 10 Dec. 1705, BL, Add. Ms. 38,153, ff. 122, 124.

55. W. Jephson to Sir R. Southwell, 4 Aug. 1690, RIA, Ms. 24 G 5/27.

56. K. Conolly to J. Bonnell, 20 March 1732[3], NLI, PC 434.

57. E. Spencer to F. Price, 13 May 1748, NLW, Puleston Ms. 3580E.

58. C. Conran to Lord Perceval, 13 Feb. 1740[1], BL, Add. Ms. 47,009A, f. 92.

59. E. Spencer to F. Price, 16 Feb. 1747[8], NLW, Puleston, Ms. 3580E.

60. Abp. W. King to C. Irvine, 1 March 1721[2], TCD, Ms. 750/7, pp. 79–80.

61. E. Spencer to F. Price, 13 May 1748, NLW, Puleston Ms. 3580E; E. Hewetson to Lord Digby of Geashill, 16 Nov. 1756, Dorset CRO, D/SHC, 3C/81.

62. Lord Robartes to Sir O. Bridgeman, 9, 13, 19, 23 and 30 Oct. 1669, Staffordshire CRO, D 1287/18/3; Barnard, 'Sir William Petty', p. 211.

63. H. Conyngham to Lady Murray of Broughton, 2 Oct. 1703; same to A. Murray, 4 Sept. 1704, 11 Nov. 1704, PRONI, D 2860/5/16, 21, 223; T. Knox to A. Murray, 6 June 1704, 22 July 1704, ibid., D 2860/4/10, 11; Ormonde to Marlborough, [March 1704]; same to T. Earle, 6 and 22 July [1704], NLI, Ormonde Mss, Ms. 2502/297, 327, 337; M. Hall to W. Leathes, 18 Sept. 1705, Suffolk CRO, HA 403/1/7, 16; K. Howard to W. Howard, 3 April 1711, NLI, PC 227; 'The autobiography of Pole Cosby, of Stradbally, Queen's County 1703–1737(?)', *Journal of the County Kildare Archaeological and Historical Society*, 5 (1906–8), p. 84; HMC, *Ormonde Mss*, new series, viii, pp. 107, 115, 116.

64. Rudd, *Records of the Rudd family*, p. 121; S. G. P. Ward (ed.), 'The letters of Captain Nicholas Delacherois, 9th Regiment', *Journal of the Society for Army Historical Research*, 51 (1973), pp. 4–13.

65. A. Bruce, *The purchase system in the British army, 1660–1871* (London, 1980), pp. 18–36.

66. Bedford to Sir E. Walpole, 11 April 1758, PRONI, T 2915/4/36.

67. Bruce, *Purchase system*, pp. 25, 34–5; Houlding, *Fit for service*, pp. 9–57.

68. R. Waring to W. Waring, 11 Oct. 1691, private collection, Co. Down; A. J. Guy, *Oeconomy and discipline: officership and administration in the British army, 1714–63* (Manchester, 1985), pp. 92–3.

69. R. Waring to W. Waring, 23 Feb. 1696[7], private collection, Co. Down.

70. F. Hamilton to Abp. W. King, 7 Sept. 1715, TCD, Ms. 1995–2008/1721.

71. M. Leathes to W. Leathes, 27 May 1720, Suffolk CRO, HA 403/1/2, 288; R. Waring to W. Leathes, 24 June 1720, 22 May 1721, ibid., HA 403/1/2, 291; 403/1/7, 93; same to same, 16 and 30 June 1721, ibid., HA 403/1/2, 307, 308; T. C. Barnard, 'What became of Waring? The making of an Ulster squire', in T. Barnard, *Irish protestant ascents and descents: selected essays* (Dublin, 2003).

72. K. Howard to W. Howard, 3 April 1711, 22 Oct. 1713; H. Howard to R. Howard, 28 Feb. 1726[7], NLI, PC 227.

73. W. Waring to S. Waring, 9 Feb. 1698[9], PRONI, D 659/73; R. Waring to S. Waring, 12 May 1699, private collection, Co. Down.

74. S. Waring to W. Waring, 23 Feb. 1698[9], 16 Sept. 1699, [11 Nov. 1699], private collection, Co. Down; W. Waring to S. Waring, 23 March 1698[9], 29 April 1699, 19 Aug. 1699, PRONI, D 659/53, 65, 66.

75. S. Waring to W. Waring, 16 Sept. 1699, private collection, Co. Down.

76. J. Waring to W. Waring, 12 June 1703; same to S. Waring, 8 Jan. 1701[2]; R. Waring to S. Waring, 27 March 1701, ibid.,

77. Abp. W. King to T. Foley, 18 March 1709[10], TCD, Ms. 2531/161.

78. Bruce, *Purchase system,* pp. 23–5, 33.

79. Fragment of S. Bagshawe's journal, s.d. 10 and 12 Feb. 1741[2], JRL, B 2/2/19.

80. J. Smythe to W. Smythe, 10 Oct. 1741, NLI, PC 449.

81. J. Belcher to R. Wilmot, 2 June 1750, PRONI, T 3019/1599; J. Adelcron to S. Bagshawe, 30 Dec. 1752, JRL, B 2/2/19.

82. H. Lambart to N. Clements, 23 [May] 1745, 25 July 1745; H. Gore to same, 5 July [1745], TCD, Ms. 1471/25, 28, 30; N. Clements to R. Wilmot, 14 July 1747; same to Harrington, 14 July 1704, PRONI, T 3019/916, 917; T. S. Smyth, *The civic history of the town of Cavan* (Dublin, 1938), p. 30.

83. H. Lambart to N. Clements, 28 Sept. 1745, 9 Jan. 1745[6], TCD, Ms. 1741/33, 37.

84. R. Waring to W. Leathes, 22 March 1716[17], 3 June 1717, Suffolk CRO, HA 403/1/2, 214, 225.

85. R. Purcell to Lord Perceval, 19 Oct. 1747, 12 Nov. 1747, BL, Add. Ms. 47,002A, ff. 129, 133v.

86. P. Rawson to Lord Gowran, 12 and 19 Aug. 1709, 24 May 1712, 26 July 1712, 26 Dec. 1717, NA, M. 3189, 3190, 3195, 3196, 3200.

87. Guy, *Oeconomy and discipline,* pp. 91–4, 140–1.

88. N. Delacherois to D. Delacherois, 10 May 1768, NAM, 7805–63; J. Hayes, 'Two soldier brothers of the eighteenth century', *Journal of the Society of Army Historical Research,* 40 (1962), p. 153; P. Mathias, 'The social structure in the eighteenth century: a calculation by Joseph Massie', *Economic History Review,* 2nd series, 10 (1957–58), pp. 37, 42–3.

89. H. Lambart to N. Clements, 9 Jan. 1745[6], TCD, Ms. 1741/37; E. Spencer to Mrs A. Price, 25 Sept. 1749, NLW, Puleston Ms. 3580E.

90. S. Bagshawe to W. Bagshawe, 2 June 1743, JRL, B 2/3/88; same to Lady Caldwell, 22 Feb. 1752, 9 June 1752, ibid., B 2/3/246, 255; J. Adlecron to S. Bagshawe, 11 April 1752, ibid., B 2/2/3; S. Bagshawe to Sir J. Caldwell, 9 June 1752, 3 Feb. 1754, ibid., B 2/3/375, 387; Guy (ed.), *Colonel Samuel Bagshawe,* pp. 94–6.

91. N. Delacherois to D. Delacherois, 24 July 1757, 9 Aug. 1757, NAM, 7805–63.

92. R. Hautenville to W. Cope, 28 June 1770, 6 July 1770, 17 Aug. 1770, 4 Sept. 1770, undated [before Nov. 1770], 1 Dec. 1771, NLI, Ms. 1715.

93. H. Brown to J. Brown, 10 Nov. [*c.* 1777], Palatine Heritage Centre, Rathkeale, Co. Limerick, Southwell-Brown Mss, box 1.

94. Memoir of H. Thomson, *alias* Burnside, Bodleian, Ms. Eng. Hist. d 155, ff. 108v–9.

95. R. Waring to S. Waring, 4 Sept. 1690, 19 Oct. 1691; same to W. Waring, 23 April 1692, 23 Feb. 1696[7], private collection, Co. Down; R. Waring to W. Leathes, 20 March 1715[16], 11 and 22 April 1715, 15 May 1715, de Mussenden Leathes Mss, Suffolk CRO, HA 403/1/1, 108, 114, 117, 118.

96. E. Herbert to A. Herbert,[1762], NA, M. 1857.

97. B. Boyle to H. Boyle, 19 Dec. [?1728], PRONI, D 2707, A1/11/8B.

98. K. Conolly to J. Bonnell, 15 March 1719[20], NLI, PC 434.

99. K. Howard to W. Howard, 26 Feb. 1711[12], ibid., PC 227.

100. R. Cox to E. Southwell, 29 Nov. 1695, Bristol Record Office, Ms. 12964(1), 52.

101. Sir C. Porter to T. Coningsby, 2 Jan. 1693[4], De Ros Mss, PRONI, D 638/18/7.

102. Bp. T. Milles to Abp. W. King, 23 July 1718, 9 and 18 Aug. 1718, 1, 10 and 15 Sept. 1718, TCD, Mss 1995–2008/1864, 1867, 1869, 1874, 1875, 1877; Abp. W. King to Bp. T. Milles, 29 July 1718, 7 Aug. 1718, ibid., Ms. 2535, pp. 235, 244; T. C. Barnard, 'Athlone, 1685; Limerick, 1710: religious riots or charivarias?', *Studia Hibernica*, 27 (1993), pp. 61–75; T. Barnard, *The Abduction of a Limerick heiress: social and political relationships in eighteenth-century Ireland* (Dublin, 1998), pp. 17–19.

103. H. Brown to J. Brown, 28 Feb. [*c.* 1777], 12 Nov. 1778, Southwell-Brown Mss, box I.

104. N. Delacherois to D. Delacherois, 28 April 1770, NAM, 7805–63.

105. N. Delacherois to S. Delacherois, 12 Dec. 1766; same to D. Delacherois, 13 May 1771, ibid., 7805–63.

106. N. Delacherois to D. Delacherois, 23 July 1770; same to S. Delacherois, 29 Sept. 1770, undated fragment of same to either D. or S. Delacherois, [1770], ibid., 7805–63.

107. N. Delacherois to D. Delacherois, 22 Nov. 1757, 22 Jan. 1770, ibid., 7805–63.

108. Same to same, 20 March 1767, ibid., 7805–63.

109. H. Oxburgh to Sir L. Parsons, 10 Oct. 1687, Birr Castle Archives, A/1/149; H. Hatch to Lord Palmerston, 20 Aug. 1733, Southampton UL, BR, 142/1/3; *CSP, Irel, 1669–70*, p. 228; M. Byrne, 'The development of Tullamore, 1700–1921', unpublished M. Litt. thesis, TCD (1979), p. 41; R. Gillespie, 'Small towns in early modern Ireland', in P. Clark (ed.), *Small towns in early modern Europe* (Cambridge, 1995), p. 160; E. P. McParland, *Public architecture in Ireland, 1680–1760* (New Haven and London, 2001), pp. 123–43.

110. Parish register, 'B', St Mary's, Church of Ireland rectory, Youghal; parish register, 1681–1820, St Multose, Kinsale; vestry book, Carlow, 1669–1762, s.d. 9 April 1708, RCB, P. 317/5.1, p. 101; parish register, Drogheda, 1747–72 (copy), NA, M. 5127; H. Murtagh, *Athlone: history and settlement to 1800* (Athlone, 2000), p. 170; Rules and Orders of the Incorporated Society, 1735–79, s.d. 12 May 1762, TCD, Ms. 5301, p. 46.

111. Rules and Orders of the Incorporated Society, 1735–79, s.d. 1 Dec. 1756, TCD, Ms. 5301, p. 36; accounts and roll, Ballycastle Charter School, Sligo, s.d. 14 Dec. 1763, ibid., Ms. 5609.

112. *Charter for incorporating the Hibernian Society, in Dublin, for maintaining, educating and apprenticing, the orphans and children of soldiers in Ireland, for ever* (Dublin, 1769),

pp. 3–4; minutes of Connor Session, s.d. 17 May 1704, Presbyterian Historical Society, Belfast.

113. S. Bagshawe to T. Waite, 10 April 1753, JRL, B 2/2/730.
114. Thomson memoir, Bodleian, Ms. Eng. Hist. d. 155, ff. 38v–39.
115. Ibid., ff. 108v–109.
116. N. Delacherois to D. Delacherois, 24 July 1757, NAM, Ms. 7805–63.
117. Same to same, 3, 22 and 24 May 1757, 9 June 1757, 20 Sept. 1757, ibid., Ms. 7805–63.
118. N. Delacherois to D. Delacherois, 17 March 1772, ibid., 7805–63.
119. T. G. H. Green (ed.), 'Diary of a journey from the south of Ireland in 1761 and 1762', *The Antiquary*, 36 (1900), pp. 203–6, 342–6, 366–70.
120. S. Wood, . . . *By dint of labour and perseverance . . . A journal recording two months in northern Germany kept by Lieutenant-Colonel James Adolphus Oughton*, Society for Army Research, special publications, no. 14 (1997), pp. 1–5.
121. Instructions of Queen Anne to Ormonde, 3 Nov. 1710, Bodleian, Ms. Eng. Hist. C. 41, f. 98; E. Southwell to Dartmouth, 12 Oct. 1711, ibid., f. 217; J. S. Kelly, '*That damn'd thing call'd honour': duelling in Ireland* (Cork, 1995), pp. 47–8.
122. J. A. Oughton, autobiography, NAM, Ms. 8808–36–1, pp. 54–5, 59; S. H. Dorman, 'The Kinsale Knot of the Friendly Brothers of S. Patrick, AD 1754–1856', *JCHAS*, 19 and 20 (1913–14), pp. 178–83; P. Guinness, 'The meeting book of the County of Kildare Knot of the Friendly Brothers of St Patrick, 1758–1791', *Journal of the County Kildare Archaeological Society*, forthcoming; Kelly, '*That damn'd thing call'd honour*', pp. 65–6.
123. J. A. Oughton, autobiography, NAM. 8808–36–1, pp. 42, 45, 46, 47, 50, 73–4, 82.
124. S. Bagshawe to W. Bagshawe, 24 Nov. 1741, 2 June 1743, 27 Sept. 1743, JRL, B 2/3/81, 88, 89; S. Bagshawe, fragmentary autobiography, ibid., B 15/3/1.
125. S. Bagshawe to Mrs Bagshawe, 12 Sept. 1740, ibid., B 2/3/77; C. Bagshawe to S. Bagshawe, 1 Aug. 1755, 23 Sept. 1755, ibid., B 2/3/20, 24, 25.
126. S. Bagshawe to C. Caldwell, 5 and 12 July 1751, ibid., B 3/1/3, 6; same to J. Caldwell, 9 June 1752, ibid., B 2/3/375; same to T. Waite, 10 April 1753, ibid., B 2/2/730; same to F. Trench, 25 Sept. 1753, ibid., B 2/3/799; J. Adlecron to S. Bagshawe, 11 April 1752, ibid., B 2/2/3.
127. E. Weston to Sir Hugh Williams, UCNW, Baron Hill Mss, no. 5682; Sir H. Williams to unknown, 20 Aug. 1762, 6 June 1763, ibid., nos. 5728, 5731; Guy, *Colonel Samuel Bagshawe*, pp. 12–13; Hayes, 'Two soldier brothers', pp. 150–6; Wood, . . . *By dint of labour and perseverance*.
128. C. Ellison to H. Ellison, 13 July 1730, 15 Aug. 1730, Tyne and Wear Archives, Newcastle, acc. 3419, Ellison Mss, bundle A 18/13 and 14; settlements of Hebburn estate, Co. Durham, 12 June 1723; mortgage of Hebburn estate, 9 Nov. 1724, ibid., acc. 3415, Cotesworth Mss, CA 14/75 and 79; Hayes, 'Two soldier brothers', pp. 150–6.
129. C. Ellison to H. Ellison, 13 Aug. 1733, Tyne and Wear Archives, acc. 3419, Ellison Mss, A 18/19.
130. C. Ellison to H. Ellison, 15 Dec. 1730, 18 Sept. [1731], 13 Aug. 1733, 14 Nov. 1733, 16 Feb. 1733[4], 19 March 1733[4], 25 Oct. 1735, 3 April 1736, ibid., Ellison Mss, A 18/15, 17, 19–22, 30, 32; schedule of repayments from C. Ellison to G. Liddell, 9 Nov. 1734, ibid., acc. 3415, Cotesworth Mss, CA 14/87.
131. C. Ellison to H. Ellison, 14 July 1739, ibid., Ellison Mss, A 18/48.
132. C. Ellison to H. Ellison, 25 Dec. 1739, ibid., Ellison Mss, A 18/51.

133. C. Ellison to H. Ellison, 19 March 1733[4], 22 Nov. 1734, ibid., Ellison Mss, A 18/22 and 25.

134. C. Ellison to H. Ellison, 6 and 30 Aug. 1729, 6 April 1733, 14 Nov. 1733, 10 June 1735, 6 June 1738, ibid., Ellison Mss, A 18/6, 7, 18, 20, 28, 42.

135. C. Ellison to H. Ellison, 25 Aug. 1735, ibid., Ellison Mss, A 18/29.

136. C. Ellison to H. Ellison, 14 July 1739, ibid., Ellison Mss, A 18/48.

137. Cunningham, *The Caldwells of Castle Caldwell*, pp. 46–68.

138. C. Ellison to H. Ellison, 6 Oct. 1738, 5 June 1739, Tyne and Wear Archives, acc. 3419, Ellison Mss, A 18/43 and 47.

139. Indenture, 25 Aug. 1778, ibid., Cotesworth Mss, CA 14/94; Hayes, 'Two soldier brothers', pp. 150–6.

140. C. Ellison to H. Ellison, 15 Dec. 1730, 13 Aug. 1733, 14 Nov. 1733, 4 Sept. 1736, 3 April 1739, Tyne and Wear Archives, acc. 3419, Ellison Mss, A 18/17, 19, 20, 38, 45; Sir H. Liddell to H. Ellison, 21 Oct. 1739, ibid., Ellison Mss, A 31/13; Oughton, autobiography, NAM, Ms. 8808–36–1, p. 64.

141. C. Ellison to H. Ellison, 5 June 1739, 29 Sept. 1739, 25 Dec. 1739, Tyne and Wear Archives, acc. 3419, Ellison Mss, A 18/47, 49, 51.

142. C. Ellison to H. Ellison, 31 Jan. 1761, 27 April 1763, ibid., A 21/22 and 46.

143. Barnard, 'What became of Waring?'

144. F. Bernard, account book, 1719–28, Cork Archives Institute, Doherty Mss, U/137; M. Coghill to E. Southwell, 14 Dec. 1728, BL, Add. Ms. 21,122, f. 61v; F. E. Ball, *The Judges in Ireland*, 2 vols (London and New York, 1926), pp. 199, 200; John Stevenson, *Two centuries of life in County Down, 1600–1800* (Belfast and Dublin, 1920), pp. 283–339; above, pp. 120, 126.

145. W. Henry, 'Hints towards a natural and typographical[*sic*] history of the Counties Sligo, Donegal, Fermanagh and Lough Erne', NA, M. 2533, pp. 371–4; army list, 1702, PRO, WO 64/1, p. 93; army list, 1715, ibid., WO 64/3, p. 16; list of officers, *c.* 1710–33, ibid., WO 64/8, p. 37; O. Wynne to O. Wynne, 3 Oct. 1752; Lord G. Sackville to same, 23 Oct. 1752, PRONI, MIC/666/D/7/2; W. Guthrie Jones, *The Wynnes of Sligo and Leitrim* (Manorhamilton, 1994). Wynne was said to have 'a numerous clan of relations that follow him'. M. Coghill to E. Southwell, 30 Dec. 1727, BL Add. Ms. 21,122, f. 37.

146. G. Kirkham, '"No more to be got from the cat but the skin": management, landholding and economic change in the Murray of Broughton estate, 1670–1755', in W. Nolan, L. Ronayne and M. Dunlevy (eds), *Donegal: history and society* (Dublin, 1995), pp. 357–80; H. Meehan, 'The Conynghams of Slane and Mountcharles', *Donegal Annual*, 51 (1999), pp. 22–35.

147. Debts owed to H. Conyngham, 13 May 1704; A. Cairnes to W. Conolly, 25 Sept. 1712, IAA, Castletown deposit, box 57.

148. Assignment by A. Brodrick and J. Macartney to W. Conolly, 1 Jan. 1703[4], Clwyd CRO, Ruthin, Brynkinalt Mss, D/BK/I, 228; J. G. Simms, *Williamite confiscation in Ireland, 1690–1703* (London, 1956), p. 155.

149. Debts owed to H. Conyngham, 1704–06; A. Knox to W. Conolly, 15 Sept. 1719, 3 March 1719[20], IAA, Castletown deposit, box 57.

150. GEC, *Complete peerage*, iii, pp. 410–11.

151. H. T. Crofton, *Crofton memoirs* (York, 1911), pp. 203–4; 'Abstracts of wills', *Irish Ancestor*, 5 (1973), p. 55.

152. H. Crofton to W. Smythe, 22 April 1723, NLI, PC 448.

153. J. Fleming to K. O'Hara, 5 Jan. 1716[17], ibid., Ms. 20,385; Dalton, *George the First's army*, ii, pp. 181, 316–17, 350, 389.

154. Army list, 1724, PRO, WO 64/8, p. 37; petition of T. Crofton, 9 March 1742[3], TCD, Ms. 3575/53.

155. W. A. S. Hewins (ed.), *The Whiteford Papers* (Oxford, 1898), p. 10.

156. H. Crofton to W. Smythe, 11 June 1736, NLI, PC 448.

157. L. M. Cullen, 'Economic development, 1691–1750' and '1750–1800', in T. W. Moody and W. E. Vaughan (eds), *A new history of Ireland. IV. Eighteenth-century Ireland 1691–1800* (Oxford, 1986), pp. 148–50, 177–8; Dickson, 'Economic history of the Cork region', i, pp. 111–13; P. Roebuck, 'Rent movement, proprietorial incomes and agricultural development, 1730–1830', in P. Roebuck (ed.), *Plantation to partition* (Belfast, 1981), pp. 90, 98; P. Roebuck, 'The economic situation and function of substantial landowners, 1600–1815: Ulster and lowland Scotland compared', in R. Mitchison and P. Roebuck (eds), *Economy and society in Scotland and Ireland 1500–1939* (Edinburgh, 1988), pp. 81–92.

158. H. Crofton to W. Smythe, 26 Nov. 1728, 13 Sept. 1730, 12 Oct. 1730, 20 March 1730[1], NLI, PC 448.

159. Bp. W. Nicolson, diary, s.d., 15 May 1725, Cumbria County Library, Carlisle; agreements of 9 Feb. 1710[11]; 19 and 20 June 1721, RD 60/182/40435; 28/533/18640; H. Howard to R. Howard, 17 April 1730, 20 Sept. 1733, 2 Jan. 1734[5], 15 Nov. 1735, 4 Dec. 1735; R. Howard to H. Howard, 25 April 1730, 1 Feb. 1734[5], 20 Nov. 1735, NLI, PC 227; H. Potterton, *Irish church monuments, 1570–1880* (Belfast, 1975), fig. 13, pp. 90–1; The Georgian Society, *Records of domestic architecture and decoration in Ireland*, 5 vols (Dublin, 1910–13), ii, pp. 53, 59; *Hiberniae Notitia* (Dublin, 1723), p. 51.

160. C. Casey and A. Rowan, *The buildings of Ireland. North Leinster* (London, 1993), pp. 485–7.

161. J. Dobbin to Sir W. Fownes, [1735], NLI, Ms. 8802.

162. 'Autobiography of Pole Cosby', pp. 253–4; D. M. Beaumont, 'The gentry of the King's and Queen's Counties: Protestant landed society, 1690–1760', unpublished Ph.D. thesis, TCD, 2 vols (1999), i, pp. 55, 81.

163. H. Crofton to W. Smythe, 23 Jan. 1726[7], 30 May 1734, NLI, PC 448; P. Crofton to same, 6 Oct. 1726, 20 Oct. 1734, ibid., PC 445.

164. P. Crofton to W. Smythe, 29 March 1736, 17 April 1736, 30 May 1736, 6 Dec. 1736, 30 June 1739, 21 May 1740, 3 Nov. 1741, NLI, PC 445; H. Cotton, *Fasti Ecclesiae Hibernicae*, 6 vols (Dublin, 1851–1878), i, pp. 227, 392; Crofton, *Crofton memoirs*, p. 205.

165. H. Crofton to W. Smythe, 17 April 1729, NLI, PC 448; R. Crofton to unknown, 20 June 1734, 18 Nov. 1734, ibid., PC 436.

166. J. Crofton to W. Smythe, 6 Oct. 1731, 27 Dec. 1732, NLI, PC 436; J. Smythe to W. Smythe, 26 Dec. 1731, 7 March 1731[2], 31 March 1732, 2 Sept. 1732, 13 April 1733, ibid., PC 449; G. Wills to J. Crofton, 7 Sept. 1742, ibid., PC 436; Census of Elphin, 1749, NA, M. 2466, f. 115; *Faulkner's Dublin Journal*, 28 June 1746; above p. 269.

167. H. Crofton to W. Smythe, 17 July 1723, NLI, PC 448; and above, p. 77.

168. Ward (ed.), 'Letters of Captain Nicholas Delacherois', p. 6.

169. H. Crofton to W. Smythe, 26 Aug. 1728, 30 May 1734, 15 Sept. 1735, NLI, PC 448; P. Crofton to same, 30 June 1739, ibid., PC 445.

170. N. Delacherois to D. Delacherois, 12 Dec. 1766, 20 March 1767, NAM, 7805–63.

171. Account of Lt. George Knox with Major-General H. Conyngham, *c.* 1706, IAA, Castletown deposit, box 57; inventory of goods belonging to W. Conyngham, 20 Dec. 1710, ibid., box 55.

172. Jean Agnew, *Belfast merchant families in the seventeenth century* (Dublin, 1996), pp. 228–31.

173. M. Leathes to W. Leathes, 10 July 1702, Suffolk CRO, HA/403/1/1, 2; W. Stannus to same, 17 May 1703, ibid., HA 403/1/71; army list, 1702, PRO, WO 64/1, p. 242; army list, 1709, ibid., WO 64/2, p. 32; army list, 1715, ibid., WO 64/3, p. 46; army list, 1717, WO 64/4, p. 88; C. Dalton, *George the First's Army*, p. 159.

174. Accounts of W. Leathes as paymaster, Royal Artillery of Ireland, 1712–21, Suffolk CRO, HA 403/1/8; R. Stearne to W. Leathes, 13 April 1713, 17 May 1715, ibid., HA 403/1/7, 15, 49; R. Parker to same, 12 June 1708, ibid., HA 403/1/7, 25.

175. W. Leathes to Lord Castlemaine, 17 Jan. 1720, 7 Feb. 1720, 2 April 1721, 29 Nov. 1721, 22 April 1722; same to F. Hamilton, 9 March 1720, 19 May 1720, ibid., HA 403/1/5, 12, 32, 49, 90, 182, 253, 270; accounts of W. Leathes with Lord Castlemaine and J. Craggs, ibid., HA, 403/1/8, openings 85, 86; R. Waring to W. Leathes, 9 March 1724[5], ibid., HA 403/1/3, 393.

176. M. Leathes to W. Leathes, 15 or 16 Sept. 1715, ibid., HA 403/1/1, 134; inventory of W. Leathes's London house, 15 July 1727, ibid., HA 403/1/7, 122; J. H. Druery, *Historical and topographical notices of Great Yarmouth* (London, 1826), pp. 208–10; A. W. Moore, *Dutch and Flemish painting in Norfolk* (London, 1988), pp. 20–1, 72, 111–12, fig. 20; Christ Church Mansion, Ipswich, *The William Leathes collection* [Ipswich, 1992].

177. K'eogh, *A vindication of the antiquities of Ireland*, pp. 96–7; Guy, *Oeconomy and discipline*, pp. 102–7, 116.

178. H. Howard to R. Howard, 28 Feb. 1726[7], NLI, PC 227.

179. Guy, *Oeconomy and discipline*, pp. 91–4; Mathias, 'A calculation by Joseph Massie', pp. 37, 42–3; Holmes, *Augustan England*, pp. 263–72; above, pp. 59–65.

180. J. S. Shaw, *The management of Scottish society, 1707–1764* (Edinburgh, 1983), pp. 6–9; R. Clyde, *From rebel to hero: the image of the highlander, 1745–1830* (East Linton, 1998).

181. N. Delacherois to D. Delacherois, 8 Oct. 1764, NAM, 7805–63.

182. N. Delacherois to D. Delacherois, 17 July 1765, 20 March 1767; same to S. Delacherois, 12 Dec. 1766, ibid., 7805–63; Ward (ed.) 'Letters of Captain Nicholas Delacherois', pp. 10–11.

183. N. Delacherois to D. Delacherois, 29 June 1767, 10 May 1768, NAM, 7805–63.

184. N. Delacherois to D. Delacherois, 22 Dec. 1769, NAM, 7805–63.

185. N. Delacherois to D. Delacherois, 4 and 12 March 1770, NAM, 7805–63.

186. N. Delacherois to D. Delacherois, 28 April 1770, NAM, 7805–63.

187. N. Delacherois to D. Delacherois, 27 Dec. 1773, NAM, 7805–63.

188. J. Evelyn, Jr, to J. Evelyn, 27 June 1693, Evelyn Mss, formerly at Christ Church, Oxford, now in BL; T. C. Barnard, 'An Anglo-Irish industrial enterprise: iron-making at Enniscorthy, Co. Wexford, 1657–1692', *PRIA*, 85, sect. C (1985), p. 140; T. C. Barnard, 'Sir William Petty as Kerry ironmaster', ibid., 82, sect. C (1982), p. 26; J. de Courcy Ireland, *Ireland and the Irish in maritime history* (Dun Laoghaire, 1986).

189. D. D. Aldridge, 'Admiral Sir John Norris 1670 (or 1671)–1749: his birth and early service, his marriage and his death', *Mariner's Mirror*, 51 (1965), pp. 74–8; Baugh,

British naval administration, pp. 93–146; B. S. Capp, *Cromwell's navy* (Oxford, 1989); J. D. Davies, *Gentlemen and tarpaulins: the officers and men of the Restoration navy* (Oxford, 1991); Holmes, *Augustan England*, pp. 274–87.

190. J. Kelly to E. Southwell, 15 Oct. 1712; T. Nevin to same, 25 April 1721, BL, Add. Ms. 20,131, ff. 15, 51; M. Coghill to E. Southwell, 23 Oct. 1736, 10 May 1737, NLI, Ms. 856.

191. E. Southwell to J. Burchet, 12 March 1711[12], PRO, ADM 1/3989.

192. E. Southwell to J. Burchet, 15 and 27 Aug. 1711, 12 March 1711[12], ibid.; R. L. DiNardo and D. Syrett, *The commissioned sea officers of the Royal Navy, 1660–1815*, Naval Records Society, occasional publications, 1 (1994), p. 237.

193. J. Tom to E. Southwell, 9 Feb. 1704[5], H. Hawley to same, 1 April 1705, E. Southwell to Sir R. Meade, 30 April 1737, NUI, Cork, Boole Library, U/20, Kinsale Manorial Papers, 1698–1764; Southwell memorandum book, 1750–52, BL, Egerton Ms. 1630, f. 27; E. Southwell to Sir H. Cavendish, *c.* 1752, BL, Add. Ms. 9714, f. 138; DiNardo and Syrett, *Commissioned sea officers*, p. 440; W. M. Brady, *Clerical and parochial records of Cork, Cloyne and Ross*, 3 vols (London, 1864), i, pp. 194–5.

194. Southwell memorandum book, 1750–52, BL, Egerton Ms. 1630, f. 39; DiNardo and Syrett, *Commissioned sea officers*, p. 445.

195. W. Bowler to unknown, 27 Nov. 1748, BL, Add. Ms. 9714, f. 168; Southwell memorandum book, BL, Egerton Ms. 1630, ff. 2, 37v, 39v, 52; DiNardo and Syrett, *Commissioned sea officers*, p. 216.

196. J. Kelly to Sir H. Sloane, 31 March 1718, BL, Sloane Ms. 4045, f. 106.

197. R. Cox to E. Southwell, 26 Dec. 1706, BL, Add. Ms. 38,154, f. 122v; DiNardo and Syrett, *Commissioned sea officers*, p. 102.

198. J. Dawson to J. Burchet, 2 and 19 June 1711, 17 March 1712[13], 5 May 1713, PRO, ADM 1/3989.

199. G. Saunders to Abp. W. King, 27 Nov. 1708, 9 Aug. 1709, 18 Nov. 1714, TCD, Ms. 1995–2008/1123, 1309, 1326; Abp. W. King to W. King, 22 Nov. 1711, Jan. 1711[12], ibid., Ms. 750/11/1, pp. 371, 380; same to Lord Gowran, 21 Dec. 1717; same to Adm. M. Aylmer, 21 Dec. 1717; same to C. Irvine, 13 March 1717[18]; same to R. Findlay, 3 April 1718, ibid., Ms. 2535/44, 46, 113, 146; Abp. W. King to G. Tollet, 22 Nov. 1711, same to Capt. G. Saunders, 22 Nov. 1711; same to W. King, 22 Nov. 1721, ibid., Ms. 2531/161, 371, 372; Abp. W. King to C. Irvine, 3 April 1718, ibid., Ms. 750/11/3, pp. 140–1.

200. Abp. W. King, account book, May and June 1708, May 1710, ibid., Ms. 751/2, ff. 199, 205, 245; G. Saunders to Abp. W. King, 14 Feb. 1714[15], 29 Oct. 1718, 12 Jan. 1722[3], ibid., Mss 1995–2008/1754, 1887, 2024; 750/8/105; Abp. W. King to W. King, 10 Sept. 1720, 14 Feb. 1720[1], 26 May 1722, 22 Jan. 1722[3], 14 Feb. 1722[3], 1 Nov. 1726, ibid., Mss 750/6/1, pp. 116–17, 195; 750/7, pp. 120, 284–5, 301; 750/8, p. 157; same to Col. C. Irvine, 24 Dec. 1717, ibid., Ms. 750/11/3, 47; same to same, 10 Aug. 1727, ibid., Ms. 750/9, pp. 4–6; DiNardo and Syrett, *Commissioned sea officers*, p. 258.

201. Aldridge, 'Admiral Sir John Norris', pp. 177–8; F. J. Aylmer, *The Aylmers of Ireland* (London, 1931), pp. 168–94; Davies, *Gentlemen and tarpaulins*, pp. 36–7, 65, 185–6.

202. Davies, *Gentlemen and tarpaulins*, pp. 36–7.

203. Abp. W. King to C. Irvine, 24 Dec. 1717, TCD, Ms. 750/11/3, p. 47; H. McDonnell, 'Irishmen in the Stuart navy, 1660–90', *The Irish Sword*, 16 (1985),

pp. 87–104; J. D. Davies, 'More light on Irishmen in the Stuart navy', ibid., 16 (1986), pp. 326–7.

204. A. Brodrick to St J. Brodrick, 11 Nov. 1684, Surrey CRO, Midleton Mss, 1248/1, f. 202v.

205. J. O'Brien to H. Boyle, 20 June 1731, PRONI, D 2707/A/1/3/4; M. Coghill to E. Southwell, 27 March 1733, 23 Nov. 1733, BL, Add. Ms. 21,123, ff. 28v, 75.

206. Sir W. Abdy to W. Conner, 9 Jan. 1757, Chatsworth, Conner letter book, 1749–58; portrait, Christie's, London, *The Irish sale*, 19 May 2000, lot 105; DiNardo and Syrett, *Commissioned sea officers*, p. 47.

207. Commission to H. Prittie, 28 Sept. 1741, NLI, Ms. 29,806/134; DiNardo and Syrett, *Commissioned sea officers*, p. 366.

208. J. H. Gebbie, *An introduction to the Abercorn letters* (Omagh, 1972), pp. 57–8.

209. T. Colley to Lord Digby, 22 June 1763, Dorset CRO, D/SHC, 3C/81; cf. T. Barry to H. Hatch, 16 May 1758, NLI, Ms. 11,327/8.

210. R. Purcell to Perceval, 29 Oct. 1747, BL, Add. Ms. 47,002A, f. 131v.

211. R. Purcell to Perceval, 19 Oct. 1747, 12 Nov. 1747, 17 Dec. 1747, ibid., Add. Ms. 47,002A, ff. 129, 133v, 143; DiNardo and Syrett, *Commissioned sea officers*, p. 369. For the academy at Portsmouth and its indifferent reputation: Baugh, *British naval administration*, pp. 99–100.

212. St J. Browne to S. Bagshawe, 30 June 1758, JRL, B2/3/562.

213. T. Herbert to A. Herbert, 28 Oct. 1756, NA, M. 1857; DiNardo and Syrett, *Commissioned sea officers*, p. 215.

214. PRO, ADM 33/685, quoted in N. A. M. Rodger, *The wooden world: an anatomy of the Georgian navy*, pbk edn (London, 1988), p. 156.

215. W. Peard to F. Price, 20 Sept. 1748, 1 Nov. 1748, NLW, Puleston Ms. 3579E; DiNardo and Syrett, *Commissioned sea officers*, p. 352.

216. D. Clarke, *Arthur Dobbs, Esquire, 1689–1765* (Chapel Hill, NC, 1957); A. Dobbs, *An essay on the trade and improvement of Ireland* (Dublin, 1729).

217. W. Henry, 'Hints towards a natural and typographical[sic] history of the Counties Sligo, Donegal, Fermanagh and Lough Erne', NA, M. 2533, p. 418.

218. E. Southwell to M. Coghill, 23 Aug. [1736], 22 Feb. 1736[7], NLI, Ms. 876; J. S. Curle, *The Londonderry plantation, 1609–1914* (Chichester, 1986), p. 132.

219. 'Itinerarium Londinense', BL, Add. Ms. 27,951, f. 63v; A. P. W. Malcomson, 'The Irish peerage and the Act of Union', *TRHS*, 6th series, 10 (2000), pp. 303–4; P. J. Marshall, *East India fortunes: the British in Bengal in the eighteenth century* (Oxford, 1976), pp. 238–9.

220. K. Conolly to J. Bonnell, 24 Feb. 1738[9], NLI, PC 434.

221. E. Herbert to A. Herbert, 17 April 1764, NA, M. 1857.

222. E. Herbert to A. Herbert, 17 April 1764, 24 May 1764, ibid., M. 1857; Writers' petitions, India Office Records, J/1/5, ff. 310–13.

223. M. Prince to Sir H. Sloane, n.d. [c. 1740], BL, Sloane Ms. 4060, f. 130.

224. J. Spranger to J. Bonnell, 10 Jan. 1705[6], NLI, PC 435.

225. J. Smythe to W. Smythe, 10 Oct. 1741, 20 Nov. 1742, 22 Nov. 1749, 11 Aug. 1750, ibid., PC 449.

226. F. P. Lock, *Edmund Burke. I. 1730–1784* (Oxford, 1998), pp. 23, 24.

227. Gebbie, *Abercorn letters*, p. 307.

228. Writers' petitions, J/1/1–8, India Office Records; L. M. Cullen, 'Scotland and Ireland, 1600–1800: their role in the evolution of British society,' in

R. A. Houston and I. D. Whyte (eds), *Scottish society, 1500–1800* (Cambridge, 1986), pp. 233–4.

229. M. Coghill to E. Southwell, 3 Jan. 1729[30], BL, Add. Ms. 21,122, f. 104; H. C. Lawlor, *A history of the family of Cairnes or Cairns* (London, 1906); A. Nesbitt, *History of the family of Nisbet or Nesbit in Scotland and Ireland* (Torquay [1898]); R. Nesbitt, *History of the Nesbitt family sometime resident in the townland of Corglass . . . County Monaghan* (Belfast, 1930); J. H. Stevenson, 'Arnold Nesbitt and the borough of Winchilsea', *Sussex Archaeological collections*, 129 (1991), pp. 183–93.

230. A. Uniacke to S. Bagshawe, 20 Oct. 1755, JRL, B 2/3/452.

231. J. A. Oughton, autobiography, NAM, 8808–3–1, p. 88.

232. Delany, *Autobiography*, 1st series, ii, p. 310.

233. E. Spencer to F. Price, 5 April 1746, NLW, Puleston Ms. 3580E.

234. J. Wight, journal, s.d. 22–23 May 1752, 11 June 1752, 3 March 1756, Friends' Historical Library, Dublin.

235. D. Balle to J. Dawson, 6 Feb. 1702[3], J. Dawson to E. Southwell, 27 Feb. 1702[3], 19 March 1702[3], PRO, ADM 1/3989.

236. J. Franklin to Lords Justice, 7 Feb. 1707[8], ibid.; Baugh, *British naval administration*, pp. 159–61.

237. T. Waite to S. Bagshawe, 4 Aug. 1753, JRL, B2/2/732; J. Wight, journal, s.d. 11 and 15 Feb. 1755, 4 March 1755, Friends' Historical Library, Dublin.

238. Examination of B. Nonnen, 18 Feb. 1741[2]; J. Potter to Duncannon, 10 April 1742, PRO, ADM 1/3990; same to Legge, 1 Feb. 1739[40], PRONI, T 3019/225.

239. Examinations of T. Keightley and S. Todd, 9 April 1742; J. Potter to Duncannon, 10 April 1742, same to T. Corbett, 21 Sept. 1742, PRO, ADM 1/3990.

240. Lady A. Conolly to Lord Strafford, 31 Oct. [?1733], IAA, Castletown deposit, box 76.

241. J. Wight, journal, s.d. 9 Jan. 1755, Friends' Historical Library, Dublin; J. Fitzgerald, *Cork Remembrancer* (Cork, 1783), p. 169.

242. J. Wight, journal, s.d. 7 July 1755, Friends' Historical Library, Dublin.

243. J. Tidmarsh to Lord Brandon, 5 June 1762, NLI, Talbot-Crosbie Mss, folder 67; same to same, 1 June 1762, TCD, Ms. 3821/251; D. Lauder to same, 1 June 1762, ibid., 252.

244. Thomson memoir, Bodleian, Ms. Eng. Hist. d. 155, f. 39v.

245. Bp. W. Nicolson to Abp. W. Wake, 4 March 1721[2], Christ Church, Wake Ms. 13, f. 325.

246. Calendar of presentments, 1698–1813, s.d. 8 June 1706, NA.

247. Ibid., s.d. Jan. 1724[5], NA; T. Pearce to T. Clutterbuck, 28 Nov. 1725, House of Lords RO, Tickell Mss, iv; *A true state of present affairs in Limerick* (London, 1726); Barnard, *Abduction of a Limerick heiress*, pp. 18–19; E. O'Flaherty, 'Urban politics and municipal reform in Limerick', *Eighteenth-Century Ireland*, 6 (1991), pp. 112–19.

248. M. Broughton to T. Tickell, 9 Sept. 1727, House of Lords RO, Tickell Mss, vi; Cumberland papers, C 44/98, 99, Royal Archives, Windsor, quoted in Guy, *Oeconomy and discipline*, p. 41.

249. G. Sealy to S. Bagshawe, 31 March 1753; S. Bagshawe to G. Sealy, 31 March 1753, JRL, B 2/3/782 and 783; S. Bagshawe to T. Waite, 3 and 10 April 1753, ibid., B 2/2/727, 730; same to W. Lushington, 3 April 1753, ibid., B 2/2/727; T. Waite to S. Bagshawe, 7 April 1753 (two letters), ibid., B 2/2/728 and 729; J. Adelcron to same, 7 and 10 April 1753, ibid., B 2/3/30 and 31; J. Wight, journal, s.d. 8, 22–23,

24 and 28 May 1752, 11 June 1752, 12, 14 and 18 May 1753, Friends' Historical Library, Dublin; Calendar of miscellaneous letters and papers prior to 1760, s.d. 20 April 1759, NA.

250. Lord Essex to Lord Arlington, 16 May 1674, Bodleian, Add. Ms. C. 34, f. 118v; Wilmot-Horton Mss, W. H. 2945, 470, quoted in E. Magennis, 'Politics and administration in Ireland during the Seven Years' War, 1756–63', unpublished Ph.D. thesis, Queen's University, Belfast (1996), p. 195; T. C. Barnard, 'Lawyers and the law in late seventeenth-century Ireland', *IHS*, 28 (1993), p. 257.

251. Calendar of departmental correspondence, s.d. 6 March 1759, 20 April 1759, 20 May 1759, 1 June 1759, 1 and 4 Dec. 1759; NA, Calendar of miscellaneous letters and papers, s.d. 22 Aug. 1748, NA; paper by M. Ward, PRONI, D 2092/1/4/38; M. M. B. Ní Mhurchadha, *The customs and excise service in Fingal, 1684–1765: 'Sober, active and bred to the sea'* (Dublin, 1999), pp. 25–41; see above, pp. 167–9.

252. Bp. T. Godwin to Abp. W. Wake, Christ Church, Wake Ms. 12, f. 370; A. Crotty to J. Coughlan, 25 July 1726, Chatsworth, Crotty letter book, 1726; M. Pratt to B. Pratt, 21 Oct. 1745, NLI, Ms. 5245; J. Loveday, *Diary of a tour in 1732 through parts of England, Wales, Ireland and Scotland* (Edinbugh, 1890), p. 47.

253. H. Bland, *A treatise of military discipline*, 5th edn (London, 1753), sig. [A4]–[A5].

254. T. C. Barnard, 'Protestantism, ethnicity and Irish identities, 1660–1760', in T. Claydon and I. McBride (eds), *Protestantism and national identity: Britain and Ireland, c. 1650–1850* (Cambridge, 1998), pp. 206–35; D. W. Hayton, 'Anglo-Irish attitudes: changing perceptions of national identity among the Protestant Ascendancy in Ireland, ca. 1690–1750', *Studies in eighteenth-century culture*, 17 (1987), pp. 145–57; D. W. Hayton, 'From barbarian to burlesque: English images of the Irish, c. 1660–1750', *Irish Economic and Social History*, 15 (1988), pp. 5–31.

8. Agents

1. Massareene to Newdegate, 26 Jan. 1690[1], Warwickshire CRO, CR 136/B 298.

2. *Writings of Petty*, i, pp. 46, 185, 193; R. Cox, 'Regnum Corcagiense; or a description of the kingdom of Cork', ed. R. Day, *JCHAS*, 2nd series, 8 (1902), pp. 70–1; R. Lawrence, *The interest of Ireland*, 2 parts (Dublin, 1682), i, pp. 80–9; *Statutes*, i, pp. 84–9 (28 Henry VIII, c. iii).

3. A. P. W. Malcomson, 'Absenteeism in eighteenth-century Ireland', *Irish Economic and Social History*, 1 (1974), pp. 15–35.

4. Sir R. Cox to E. Southwell, 6 Sept. 1716, BL, Add. Ms. 38, 157, f. 147; R. Barton, *Some remarks, towards a full description of Upper and Lower Lough Lene* (Dublin, 1751); R. Barton, *A dialogue, concerning some things of importance to Ireland* (Dublin, 1751); Cox, 'Regnum Corcagiense', pp. 67, 70–1; *The Dublin Society's weekly observations* (Dublin, 1739), pp. 6–8; T. Dunne, '"A gentleman's estate should be a moral school": Edgeworthstown in fact and fiction, 1760–1840', in R. Gillespie and G. Moran (eds), *Longford: essays in county history* (Dublin, 1991), pp. 95–122; H. Maule, *A sermon preached in Christ-Church, Dublin . . . on Tuesday, the twenty-third day of October, 1733* (Dublin, 1733), p. 21.

5. *Dublin Journal*, 8–11 Dec. 1733.

6. T. C. Barnard, 'An Anglo-Irish industrial enterprise: iron-making at Enniscorthy, Co. Wexford, 1657–1692, *PRIA*, 85, sect. C (1985), pp. 116–21, 139–42; Barnard,

'Robert French of Monivea', p. 279; Barnard, 'Sir William Petty as Kerry ironmaster', ibid., 82, sect C (1982), p. 17; W. H. Crawford, *The management of a major Ulster estate in the late eighteenth century* (Dublin, 2001); T.O. Ranger, 'Richard Boyle and the making of an Irish fortune, 1588–1614', *IHS*, 10 (1957), pp. 257–97.

7. Lord Strafford to Ormond, 8 Aug. 1674, BL, Add. Ms. 33,589, f. 252; J. Hall, will, 5 March 1687[8]; codicil, 6 July 1689, PRO, PROB 11/405, 100; donors' book, TCD, Ms. 571, f. 4; Barnard, 'Cork settlers', pp. 341–2; T. W. Belcher, *Memoir of John Stearne, M. & J.U.D., S.F.T.C.D.* (Dublin, 1865), p. 23; M. Quane, 'Dr Jeremy Hall endowed schools, Limerick', *North Munster Antiquarian Journal*, 11 (1968), pp. 47–50; E. Wilson, 'Dr Jeremiah Hall and his charities', *Transactions of the Halifax Antiquarian Society* (1956), pp. 1–10.

8. L. Roberts to Lord Palmerston, 31 March 1726, Southampton UL, BR 142/2/3c; H. Hatch to same, 17 July 1729, ibid., BR 142/1/2; R. Howard to H. Howard, 28 Nov. 1729, NLI, PC 227; Thrift index of Dublin freemen, Dublin City Archives; vestry book, St Bride's, Dublin, RCB, P. 327/3/1, f. 252; marriage settlement of H. Hatch of Cushionstown, Co. Dublin, and Dorothy Reading, 1719, NLI, reports on private collections, no. 104, p. 1063.

9. E. Kingsbury to Alicia Price, 27 June 1757, NLW, Puleston Ms, 3584E; T. Kingsbury to R.P. Price, 9 Aug. 1770, ibid., Ms. 3584E; R. Edgeworth, account book, NLI, Ms. 1534, p. 360.

10. M. Coghill to E. Southwell, 14 Dec. 1728, BL, Add. Ms. 21,122, f. 61v–62; G. Bennett, *The history of Bandon* (Cork, 1869), pp. 561–5.

11. W. Eustace to C. Tickell, 12 July 1740, Tickell Mss, private collection, Devon.

12. W. Burnett to unknown, 2 Feb. 1757; Jeremy Digby to Lord Digby of Geashill, 3 June 1760; John Digby to same, 19 April 1761, Dorset CRO, D/SHC, 3C/81.

13. John Digby to Lord Digby of Geashill, 22 April 1760, 19 April 1761; H. Lyons to same, 22 April 1761, 19 May 1761; T. Colley to same, 26 May 1761, Digby Mss, Dorset CRO, D/SHC, 3C/81.

14. T. Kingsbury to F. Price, 23 April 1737, 3 Dec. 1737, 5 April 1746; E. Kingsbury to A. Price, 22 Dec. 1753; T. Kingsbury, Jr. to John Buchan, 22 Jan. 1750[1]; same to A. Price, 4 Sept. 1756; same to R. P. Parry, 9 Aug. 1770, NLW, Puleston Ms. 3584E.

15. Letter and account book of H. Temple, 1712–21, Southampton UL, BR, 2/2, f. 1.

16. E. Rorke to Lord Digby of Geashill, 7, 13 and 27 March 1717, Dorset CRO, D/SHC, 3C/81.

17. E. Herbert to ?F. Herbert, 6 Oct. 1707, NLW, Powis Castle correspondence, no. 809; R. Lloyd to F. Herbert, 21 Jan. 1717[18], ibid., deeds, no. 16,065; 'the knot tied', ibid., no. 14,960.

18. R. Lloyd to F. Herbert, 9 Feb. 1716[17], 13 May 1718, NLW, Powis Castle deeds, nos. 16,058, 16,067. On the Herberts in Kerry: N.P. Canny, *Making Ireland British, 1580–1650* (Oxford, 2001), pp. 142–5, 150–3, 158–9; Sir William Herbert, *Croftus sive de Hibernia liber*, ed. A. Keaveney and J.A. Madden (Dublin, 1992); G. H. Orpen, *The Orpen family* (London and Frome, 1930), pp. 146, 159; W. J. Smith (ed.), *Calendar of Herbert correspondence* (Dublin and Cardiff, 1993).

19. R. Lloyd to F. Herbert, 21 Jan. 1717[18], NLW, Powis Castle deeds, no. 16,065; J. Jackson to R. Baldwin, 27 May 1731, 9 and 28 June 1731, NLW, Powis Castle correspondence, nos. 912–14.

20. H. Wood, 'Sir William Petty and his Kerry estate', *JRSAI*, 64 (1934), pp. 22–40.

21. R. Orpen to Lady Shelburne, 1 April 1692, RIA, Ms. 12. I. 2: cf. C. Daly to H. Owen, 13 April 1694, NLW, Powis Castle correspondence, no. 191.

22. T.C. Barnard, 'Sir William Petty', p. 214; G. J. Lyne, 'Land tenure in Kenmare and Tuosist, 1696–c.1716', *Kerry Archaeological and Historical Society Journal*, 10 (1977), pp. 19–54; G. J. Lyne, 'Land tenure in Kenmare, Bonanne and Tuosist, 1720–1770', ibid., 11 (1978), pp. 25–55.

23. Orpen, *The Orpen family*, pp. 51–2, 64–5; [R. Orpen], *An exact relation of the persecutions, robberies, and losses sustained by the Protestants of Killmare, in Ireland* (London, 1689).

24. D. R. Hainsworth, *Stewards, lords and people: the estate steward and his world in later Stuart England* (Cambridge, 1992), pp. 54–5; D. W. Howell, *Patriarchs and parasites: the gentry of south-west Wales in the eighteenth century* (Cardiff, 1986), pp. 214–15; Melvin Humphreys, *The crisis of community: Montgomeryshire, 1680–1815* (Cardiff, 1996), pp. 96–125; P. Roebuck, 'The making of an Ulster great estate: the Chichesters, barons of Belfast and viscounts of Carrickfergus, 1599–1648', *PRIA*, 79, sect. C (1979), pp. 150–2; P. Roebuck, 'Landlord indebtedness in Ulster in the seventeenth and eighteenth centuries' in J. M. Goldstrom and L.A. Clarkson (eds), *Irish population, economy and society* (Oxford, 1981), pp. 150–1.

25. Dickson, 'Economic history of the Cork region', i, pp. 225–30; L. Proudfoot, *Urban patronage and social authority* (Washington, DC, 1995), pp. 94, 97–9.

26. J. Burward to J. Ussher, 7 March 1737[8], NLI, Ms. 13,251.

27. Hainsworth, *Stewards, lords and people*; E. Hughes, 'The eighteenth-century estate agent', in H.A. Cronne, T.W. Moody and D. B. Quinn (eds), *Essays in British and Irish history* (London, 1949), pp. 185–99.

28. E. Weston to R. Wilmot, 6 March 1749[50], PRONI, T 3019/1504.

29. J. Kelly, 'Harvests and hardship: famine and scarcity in Ireland in the later 1720s', *Studia Hibernica*, 26 (1992), pp. 65–105; P. H. Kelly, 'The politics of political economy in mid-eighteenth-century Ireland', in S. J. Connolly (ed.), *Political ideas in eighteenth-century Ireland* (Dublin, 2000), pp. 105–29.

30. D. Beaumont, 'The gentry of the King's and Queen's Counties: Protestant landed society, 1690–1760', unpublished Ph. D. thesis, TCD, 2 vols (2000), i, pp. 123–5.

31. *A bibliography of the publications of the Royal Dublin Society from its foundation in the year 1731*, 2nd edn (Dublin, 1953).

32. N. Peacock diary, NLI, Ms. 16,091.

33. W. Waring to W. Layfield, 9 July 1691, 25 Sept. 1691, 29 March 1692, Waring Mss, private collection, Co. Down; Sir J. Temple to H. Temple, 16 March 1695[6], Southampton UL, BR, 5/22; Juliana, Countess of Burlington to R. Power, R. Bagge and T. Baker, 23 Oct. 1705, NLI, Ms. 13,231.

34. W. Perceval to K. O'Hara, 25 May 1718, NLI, Ms. 20,385; T. Barnard and J. Fenlon (eds) *The dukes of Ormonde, 1610–1714* (Woodbridge, 2000), pp. 153–9, 167, 171; T. P. Power, *Land, politics and society in eighteenth-century Tipperary* (Oxford, 1993), pp. 88–100, 222–3, 331–3.

35. D. W. Hayton, 'Dependence, clientage and affinity: the political following of the second duke of Ormonde', in Barnard and Fenlon (eds.), *The dukes of Ormonde*, pp. 213–22; Power, *Eighteenth-century Tipperary*, pp. 119–26.

36. Rental of 2nd duke of Ormonde, 1689, NLI, Ms. 2562; rentals of 2nd duke of Ormonde, May 1713, Sept. 1713, PRO, FEC 1/846; 1/965.

37. R. Bagge to H. Boyle, 2 Aug. 1731, PRONI, D 2707/A1/1/36.

38. T. U. Sadleir, 'Manuscripts at Kilboy', *Analecta Hibernica*, 12 (1943), pp. 144–7.

39. T. O. Ranger, 'The career of Richard Boyle, first earl of Cork, in Ireland, 1588–1643', unpublished D. Phil. thesis, University of Oxford (1959); Ranger, 'Richard Boyle and the making of an Irish fortune', pp. 257–97.

40. Sir R. Southwell to Sir J. Perceval, BL, Add. Ms. 46,961, f. 154v, printed in HMC, *Egmont Mss*, ii, p. 142; J. Bateman, *A just and true relation of Josias Bateman's concern* [*c.*1732], p. iii.

41. Burlington to W. Congreve, 7, 21 and 30 July 1691, NLI, Ms. 13,226; Cork and Burlington accounts, ibid., Ms. 6300; T. C. Barnard, 'Land and the limits of loyalty: the second earl of Cork and the first earl of Burlington (1612–98)', in T. Barnard and J. Clark (eds), *Lord Burlington: architecture, art and life* (London, 1995), p. 172.

42. Burlington to W. Congreve and R. Power, 12 Nov. 1698, ibid., Ms. 13,227.

43. Juliana, Countess of Burlington to R. Power, R. Bagge and T. Baker, 23 Oct. 1705, ibid., Ms. 13,231.

44. Andrew Crotty, account book, 1726–32, opening 47, Chatsworth.

45. J. Burward to J. Ussher, 17 Feb. 1738[9], Chatsworth, Lismore Ms. 36/81; 'Ussher papers', *Analecta Hibernica*, 15 (1944), p. 75.

46. R. Purcell to Lord Perceval, 19 Oct. 1747, BL, Add. Ms. 47,002A, f. 129; J. Wight journal, s.d. 6 March 1752, Friends' Historical Library, Dublin; P. O'Connor, *Exploring Limerick's past: an historical geography of urban development in county and city* (Coolanoran, 1987), pp. 65–7.

47. Deposition, Feb. 1719[20], Donegal accounts, IAA, Castletown deposit, box 52; wills of O. McCausland, 7 Oct. 1721, and J. McCausland, 5 Aug. 1728, NLI, PC 345, box 2; will of W. Conolly, 1729, ibid., PC 348, box 2; R. McCausland to W. Conolly, 21, 23 and 25 Nov. 1728, TCD, Ms. 3974/8, 9 and 11; C. McCausland to ?T. Conolly, 9 Nov. 1765, IAA, Castletown deposit, box 37; E. T. Martin (ed.), *The Ash Mss., written in the year 1735, by Lieut.-Col. Thomas Ash* (Belfast, 1890), p. 21.

48. H. Owen, description of Castleisland, 1686, NLI, Ms. 7861, f. 155; H. Hatch to Lord Palmerston, 15 Sept. 1733, Southampton UL, BR 42/1/4; H. Hatch to Lord Blundell, 7 Feb. 1746[?7], PRONI, D 607/A/12.

49. D. Conner to Burlington, 16 April 1736, Chatsworth, Devonshire Letters, 1720–36 238.0; Proudfoot, *Urban patronage and social authority*, pp. 89–101.

50. L. Proudfoot, 'Landlord motivation and urban improvement on the duke of Devonshire's Irish estates, *c.* 1792–1832', *Irish Economic and Social History*, 18 (1991), pp. 7–8.

51. Cork and Burlington, account books, s.d. 5 May 1685, NLI, Mss 6902, 6300.

52. Burlington to W. Congreve, 8 Aug. 1691; same to R. Power, 20 Oct. 1691, 4 Feb. 1691[2], 20 April 1693, ibid., Ms. 13,226.

53. For others securing the appointment of agents as justices of the peace: accounts of Abp. M. Boyle, s.d. 16 June 1671, ibid., de Vesci Ms, H/2; W. Petty to J. Crookshank, 30 Oct. 1677, 13 Nov. 1677, McGill UL, Osler Ms. 7612; C. Daly to H. Owen, 13 April 1694, NLW, Powis Castle correspondence, no. 191; H. Temple to Lord Midleton, 22 Nov. 1722, Southampton UL, BR 2/4; Lord Palmerston to B. Byrne, 22 Oct. 1723, 11 March 1724[5], ibid., BR 2/4; O. Gallagher to O. St George, 14 Nov. 1727, PRO, C 110/46, 519.

54. J. Waite to T. Baker, 21 Sept. 1708, 28 Oct. 1708, 3 Feb. 1708[9], 12 March 1708[9], 17 May 1709; same to R. Musgrave, 6 Nov. 1708, Chatsworth, Waite Letter Book, 1708–10.

55. H. Temple to Lord Midleton, 22 Nov. 1722; same to L. Roberts, 18 Dec. 1722, Southampton UL, BR, 2/4.

56. T. Page to Sir G. Lane, 11 and 29 June 1664, 9 and 20 July 1664, NLI, Ms. 8643; R. Lascelles, *Liber munerum publicorum Hiberniae*, 2 vols (London, 1824–30), ii, pp. 135–6; F. E. Ball, 'Some notes on the households of the dukes of Ormonde', *PRIA*, 38 sect. C, (1928), pp. 8–9, 16; HMC, *Ormonde Mss*, new series, iii, p. 316.

57. Ball, 'Notes on the households of the dukes of Ormonde', p. 17.

58. Diary of 2nd earl of Cork, s.d. 21–29 Nov. 1660, 1 Dec. 1660, 4, 15 and 21 Jan. 1660[1], 20 Feb. 1660[1], 30 March 1661, 10 July 1661, 22 Aug. 1661, 1 and 3 Oct. 1661, 10 and 11 Dec. 1662, 23 Jan. 1662[3]; customs officers at Limerick, 1 Aug. 1661; T. Batty to Cork, 2 Aug. 1661, Chatsworth, Lismore Ms. 32/12, 14; L. Gostelow to same, 4 and 18 Jan. 1661[2], ibid., Lismore Ms. 32/55 and 61; *CSPI Ire., 1660–2*, pp. 28, 200–1, 214, 289; Barnard, 'Land and the limits of loyalty', p. 190.

59. Diary of 2nd earl of Cork, s.d. 20, 21 Nov. 1660, 11 Dec. 1660, 15 Jan. 1661[2], 1 July 1665, 29 Sept. 1665, Chatsworth, Lismore Mss; Lord Ranelagh to T. Coningsby, 27 Oct. 1690 and 24 Feb. 1690[1], PRONI, D 638/6/2 and 8; HMC, *Ormonde Mss*, new series, v, p. 517.

60. W. Gostelow, *Charles Stuart and Oliver Cromwell united* (London, 1655), p. 82.

61. L. Gosteloe to Cork, 5 and 11 Feb. 1661[2], Chatsworth, Lismore Ms. 32/65 and 68; same to same, 23 June 1663, NLI, Ms. 13,228; St Carthage's Cathedral, Lismore, chapter book, 1663–1829, f. 18v.

62. Cork and Burlington, account book, 1684–91, s.d. 23 April 1685, 5 May 1685, NLI, Ms. 6300; H.F. Berry, 'Justices of the peace for the county of Cork', *JCHAS*, 2nd series, 3 (1897), p. 60.

63. G. Deyos to earl of Arran, [*c.*1682], NLI, Ms. 2482/101.

64. L. Beecher to Cork, Aug. 1661, Chatsworth, Lismore Ms. 32/32; account book, 1672–75, s.d. 3 Nov. 1673, 17 Oct. 1674, NLI, Ms. 6273; Essex to Arlington, 13 Aug. 1674, Bodleian, Add. Ms. C. 34, f. 162v; Barnard, 'Cork settlers', p. 341; T. Birch (ed.), *The works of the honourable Robert Boyle*, 5 vols (London, 1745), v, pp. 469–70.

65. Ormonde to commissioners of Irish revenue, 5 April 1712, Bodleian, Ms. Eng. Hist. C. 41, f. 289.

66. Arrears of rent at 23 Sept. 1661, Chatsworth, Bolton Abbey Ms. 281.

67. Cork and Burlington to D. Foulke, 14 Nov. 1695, Chatsworth, Cork and Burlington letter book, 1695–96; depositions taken before D. Foulke, 26 Nov. 1707, NLI, Ms. 13,254; Berry, 'Justices of the peace for county Cork', p. 60.

68. Burlington to W. Congreve, 4 Aug. 1692, NLI, Ms. 13,226; D. Foulke to unknown, 7 Feb. 1692[3], ibid., Ms. 13,249; G. Roche, letter book, s.d. 1 May 1672, 5 June 1672; Ibid., Ms. 7177; Barnard, 'Cork settlers', p. 339.

69. Burlington to D. Foulke, 22 Feb. 1693[4], 9 Oct. 1694, Chatsworth, Burlington's Irish letters, 1693–94; agreement with D. Foulke, 9 Oct. 1694, ibid., Londesborough Mss, box I (v) 15, Irish letter book, 1694.

70. A. Spurrett to T. Baker, 27 April 1704, Chatsworth, Spurrett letter book, 1703–4.

71. J. Waite to D. Foulke, 27 Feb. 1710[11], NLI, Ms. 13,254; *A just and true relation of Josias Bateman's concern*, p. 12.

72. Cork and Burlington to W. Congreve, 29 Oct. 1696, Chatsworth, Cork and Burlington letter book, 1696; same to Congreve, 10 April 1697, NLI, Ms. 13,226.

73. R. Bagge, accounts from 1690, NLI, Ms. 6903; R. Bagge to Burlington, 22 May 1697, 16 Sept. 1697; unknown to Bagge, 21 Dec. 1697, ibid., Ms. 13,235.

74. Burlington to W. Congreve, 22 July 1697, ibid., Ms. 13,226.

75. R. Bagge and J. Walsh to Cork and Burlington, 24 Dec. 1695, ibid., Ms. 13,235; Cork and Burlington to W. Congreve, R. Power and R. Bagge, 4 Aug. 1696, Chatsworth, Cork and Burlington letter book, 1696.

76. Cork and Burlington to R. Bagge, 25 June 1696, 28 July 1696, Chatsworth, Cork and Burlington letter book, 1696.

77. Burlington to W. Congreve, 18 Sept. 1694, NLI, Ms. 13,226.

78. W. Congreve to unknown, 6 July 1706, ibid., Ms. 13,229; A. Spurrett to W. Congreve, 16 May 1704, Chatsworth, Spurrett letter book, 1703–4.

79. 1st Lord Burlington to Congreve, 8 June 1697, NLI, Ms. 13,226; 2nd Lord Burlington to Congreve and Power, 12 Nov. 1698, ibid., Ms. 13,227; A. Spurrett to R. Bagge, 26 Dec. 1704, Chatsworth, Spurrett letter book, 1703–4.

80. A. Crotty to Burlington, 8 July 1725, Greater London RO, Q/CML/10/1.

81. Rental for 1699–1700, Chatsworth.

82. A. Spurrett to R. Bagge, 5 Sept. 1704, 26 Dec. 1704; same to Smith, 6 Jan. 1704[5], Chatsworth, Spurrett letter book, 1703–5; J. Waite to J. Coughlan, 10 Feb. 1706[7], 25 Nov. 1707; same to T. Baker, 19 June 1707, ibid., J. Waite letter book, 1706–8; J.M. Walcott to J. Ussher, 18 Feb. 1743[4], ibid., Ms. 13,251.

83. R. Bagge to H. Boyle, 24 Nov. 1736, ibid., Ms. 13,235.

84. R. Bagge's account to 23 May 1727, PRONI, D 2707/B9/IC; another copy in NLI, Ms. 13,235; *Al. Dubl.* p. 31.

85. R. Bagge's account to 23 May 1727, PRONI, D 2707/B9/IC; R. Bagge to H. Boyle, 24 Nov. 1736, NLI, Ms. 13,235.

86. Minute book, revenue commissioners, PRO, CUST 1/61, f. 4v; W. H. Rennison, *Succession list of the bishops, cathedral and parochial clergy of the diocese of Waterford and Lismore* (Waterford, [1920]), pp. 68, 79, 138, 141, 143, 152, 175, 178, 194, 197, 203, 208, 219.

87. Letter of 9 Nov. 1707, NLI, Ms. 13,254; C. Smith, *The antient and present state of the county and city of Waterford* (Dublin, 1746), p. 35.

88. Burlington to R. Power, 19 Nov. 1695, Chatsworth, Cork and Burlington letter book, 1695–96; Burlington to W. Congreve, 13 March 1693[4], ibid., Lismore Ms. 34/59; same to W. Congreve and D. Foulke, 19 Nov. 1695, NLI, Ms. 13,226; J. Waite to R. Musgrave and T. Baker, 19 June 1707, Chatsworth, Waite letter book, 1706–8.

89. R. Bagge to H. Boyle, 2 Aug. 1731, PRONI, D 2707/A1/3/36.

90. Burlington to W. Congreve, 3 Dec. 1692, NLI, Ms. 13,226.

91. Burlington to R. Power, 25 Jan. 1693[4], Chatsworth, entry book of Lord Cork and Burlington's letters, 1693–94; J. Waite to R. Musgrave, 29 Oct. 1706, ibid., J. Waite letter book, 1706–8; trustees of jointure estate, Bodleian, Rawlinson Ms. A. 492, f. 12.

92. Bill of Roger Power, 1704–6, Chatsworth, Lismore Ms. 35/48.

93. J. Waite to R. Power, 11 Feb. 1706[7], Chatsworth, Waite letter book, 1706–8; *CJIre.*, ii, p. 323; T. Barnard, 'Considering the inconsiderable', in D. W. Hayton (ed.), *The Irish Parliament in the eighteenth century* (Edinburgh, 2001), pp. 113–15.

94. A. Spurrett to Turner, 24 Aug. 1704; same to J. Coughlan, 19 Oct. 1704; Chatsworth, Spurrett letter book, 1703–5; Bennett, *Bandon*, pp. 563–4; and see above, p. 210.

95. Accounts of G. Roche, 1661–63, s.d. 22 April 1663, Chatsworth, Bolton Abbey Ms. 279; accounts of W. Congreve, 1664, ibid., Londesborough Mss box 1 (v). It is possible that the earl had first encountered the Congreves, royalists in Staffordshire, when he soldiered in that county during the 1640s. William Congreve may not have remained continuously in the Boyles' service from the 1660s to 1690. However, his garrison duties as a lieutenant at Youghal, Carrickfergus and Kilkenny in the intervening decades were compatible with an agency for Burlington. J. C. Hodges, *William Congreve the man: a biography from new sources* (New York and London, 1941), pp. 4–5, 7–12, 30–3, 55–6.

96. Burlington to W. Congreve, 11 Jan. 1693[4], Chatsworth, Lismore Ms. 34/46. Cf. list of army officers, 22 March 1688[9], BL, Add. Ms. 28,938, f. 314v.

97. Burlington to W. Congreve, 8 March 1693[4], Chatsworth, Burlington letter book, 1693–94; same to same, 22 Sept. 1696, ibid., Burlington letter book, 1696.

98. Burlington to W. Congreve, 19 Sept. 1692, 22 July 1697, NLI, Ms. 13,226.

99. Burlington to W. Congreve, 11 March 1692[3], ibid., Ms. 13,226; H. Boyle to W. Congreve, 25 Oct. [1692], ibid., Ms. 13,230.

100. R. Bagge to H. Boyle, 2 Aug. 1731, PRONI, D 2707/A1/3/36; same to same, 24 Nov. 1736, NLI, Ms. 13,235.

101. Burlington to W. Congreve, 10 April 1697, 8 June 1697, NLI, Ms. 13,226; C. Congreve to W. Congreve, 18 April 1694, ibid., Ms. 13,230; E. Villiers to same, 3 Jan. 1693[4], ibid., R. Bagge to Burlington, 22 May 1697, ibid., Ms. 13,235; Hodges, *William Congreve the man*, pp. 14–21; *Al. Dubl.*, p. 168; Smith, *Waterford*, p. 374.

102. E. Villiers to ?W. Congreve, 3 Jan. 1693[4], NLI, Ms. 13,230.

103. B. Burke, *Burke's genealogical and heraldic history of the landed gentry of Ireland*, 4th edn (London, 1955), pp. 173–4; J. Burke, *A genealogical and heraldic history of the commoners of Great Britain and Ireland*, 4 vols (London, 1833), i, pp. 15–16; Rennison, *Succession list*, p. 162.

104. A. Spurrett to R. Musgrave, 26 May 1705, Brynmor Jones Library, Hull, DD LO/11/27; Barnard, 'Land and the limits of loyalty', p. 179; GEC, *Complete baronetage*, 6 vols (London, 1900–9), v, pp. 406–7; D. Dickson, 'Foreword', in R. Musgrave, *Memoirs of the different rebellions in Ireland*, 4th edn (Fort Wayne, Indiana, and Enniscorthy, 1995), p. iii.

105. Cork and Burlington, account book, 1686–88, s.d. 16 March 1688[9], NLI, Ms. 6303; account book, 1684–91, s.d. 27 Oct. 1691, ibid., Ms. 6300.

106. Burlington to W. Congreve, 13 July 1697, ibid., Ms. 13,226; Barnard, 'Cork settlers', pp. 349–50.

107. Burlington to W. Congreve, R. Power and D. Foulke, 28 April 1694, NLI, Ms. 13,226.

108. J. Waite to R. Musgrave, 22 and 25 Nov. 1707, 17 Jan. 1707[8], Chatsworth, Waite letter book; cf. A. Spurrett to R. Power, 23 March 1703[4], ibid., Spurrett letter book.

109. J. Waite to D. Foulke, 25 Nov. 1707, ibid., Waite letter book, 1706–8.

110. H. Boyle to J. Coughlan, 27 Sept. 1710; letter of attorney of H. Boyle to R. Power and J. Coughlan, 28 Feb. 1705[6]; instructions of H. Boyle to W. Snow and J. Coughlan, 27 June 1710, Chatsworth, letters of William Snow; *KIAP*, p. 104.

111. A. Spurrett to Turner, 24 Aug. 1704; same to J. Coughlan, 19 Oct. 1704, Chatsworth, Spurrett letter book, 1703–5; J. Waite to J. Coughlan, 25 Nov. 1707, ibid., Waite letter book, 1706–8; A. Crotty to J. Coughlan, 22 July 1726; same to

J. Uniacke, 28 July 1726, ibid., Crotty letter book, 1726; J. Burward to Sir W. Abdy, 20 Jan. 1739[40], 21 Nov. 1743, NLI, Ms. 7179; W. Abdy to J. Ussher, 2 Feb. 1739[40], Chatsworth, Lismore Ms. 36/98.

112. J. Waite to Myers, 24 July 1707; same to D. Foulke, 28 Feb. 1707[8]; same to J. Coughlan, 6 March 1707[8], Chatsworth, Waite letter book, 1706–8; J. Coughlan to R. Musgrave, 22 Nov. 1712, 4 Dec. 1712, NLI, Ms. 13,242; A. Crotty to J. Coughlan, 22 July 1726, Chatsworth, Crotty letter book, 1726.

113. T. P. Power, 'Converts', in T. P. Power and K. Whelan (eds), *Endurance and emergence: Catholics in Ireland in the eighteenth century* (Dublin, 1990), pp. 101–27; L. M. Cullen, 'Catholic social classes under the penal laws', ibid., 57–84; K. Whelan, *The tree of liberty* (Cork, 1996), pp. 3–56.

114. Register of Lismore parish, St Carthage's Cathedral, Lismore, Co. Waterford,

115. *Al. Dubl.*, pp. 161, 183; Rennison, *Succession list*, pp. 142, 165–6, 194, 175, 177, 196; I. Gervais to Sir A. Abdy, Aug. 1755, Chatsworth, Devonshire Letters, Aug–Oct 1755, 387.4.

116. *A just and true relation of Josias Bateman's concern*, pp. 4, 6–7, 14, 16.

117. J. Burward to J. Ussher, 28 Oct. 1739, Chatsworth, Lismore Ms. 36/91.

118. Subscribers to Meath County map, *c.* 1750, RCB, D7/12/1/4; roll and accounts, Ardbraccan charter school, s.d. 20 June 1752, TCD, Ms. 5597; J. B. Leslie's abstract of will of Bp. H. Maule, 5 Dec. 1757, NLI, Ms. 2678, p. 12; M. Bence-Jones, 'The empty grandeurs of Ardo', *Country Life Annual* (1968), pp. 126–8; W. Fraher, 'Ardo House', *Decies*, 24 (1983), pp. 25–8; H. F. Morris, 'The "principal inhabitants" of County Waterford in 1746', in T. Power and W. Nolan (eds), *Waterford: history and society* (Dublin, 1992), pp. 324–5.

119. Cork and Burlington to W. Congreve, 4 Sept. 1694, Chatsworth, Londesborough Mss, box I (v) 15.

120. J. Waite to R. Musgrave, 22 Nov. 1707, 26 Feb. 1707[8], Chatsworth, Waite letter book, 1706–8; same to T. Baker and R. Musgrave, 29 May 1712, NLI, Ms. 13,242.

121. *A just and true relation of Josias Bateman's concern*, p. 18; cf. A. Crotty to H. Simpson, 12 Oct. 1728, Chatsworth, Bolton Abbey Mss.

122. A. Crotty to Burlington, 14 Nov. 1731, Chatsworth, Devonshire Letters, 1720–36, 200.2; Crotty account book, 1726–32, opening 47, Chatsworth.

123. J. Waite to R. Musgrave, 13 Jan. 1707[8], Chatsworth, Waite letter book, 1706–8.

124. M. Coghill to E. Southwell, 8 April 1735, 7 Oct. 1735, NLI, Ms. 875; W. Conner to Sir A. Abdy, 30 Oct. 1756, Chatsworth, William Conner letter book, 1749–58; J. Burward to J. Ussher, 4 March 1737[8], NLI, Ms. 13,251; same to same, 10 Oct. 1738, 2 Jan. 1738[9], Chatsworth, Lismore Ms. 36/63, 72; Sir W. Abdy to ?J. Burward, 22 Dec. 1739, ibid., Lismore Ms. 36/94; M. Fitzgerald to Lord Grandison, Dromana Villiers-Stuart Mss, T 3131/C/3/6B.

125. J. Burward to J. Ussher, 18 Feb. 1737[8], NLI, Ms. 13,251.

126. J. Parker to J. Ussher, 26 Oct. 1745, ibid.

127. W. Conner to Sir A. Abdy, 30 Oct. 1756, Chatsworth, W. Conner letter book, 1749–58.

128. A. Crotty to H. Simpson, 10 May 1726, Chatsworth, Bolton Abbey Mss; same to Burlington, 1 March 1735[6], ibid., Devonshire Letters, 1720–36, 200.3; Sir W. Abdy to J. Ussher, 1 Dec. 1741, ibid., Lismore Ms. 36/105; same to W. Conner, 20 June 1749, NLI, Ms. 13,251; W. Conner to Sir A. Abdy, 30 Oct. 1756, 8 Dec. 1756, Chatsworth, W. Conner letter book, 1749–58.

129. Covenant of 18 March 1725[6], Denbighshire RO, Brynkinalt Mss, DD/BK/I, 24; bond of A. Crotty and D. Crotty, F. Bernard account book, 1719–28, p. 97, Cork Archives Institute, Doherty Mss, U/137; J. Ainsworth (ed.), *The Inchiquin manuscripts* (Dublin, 1961), pp. 152–9.

130. W. Taylor to Lord Perceval, 21 Sept. 1731, BL, Add. Ms. 46,982, f. 69; W. Peard to F. Price, 20 May 1746, 27 June 1746, NLW, Puleston Ms. 3579E.

131. A. Crotty and J. Coughlan to Lord Grandison, 13 May 1734, Villiers-Stuart Mss, T 3131/C/7/10; A. Crotty to same, 6 Feb. 1734[5], ibid., T 3131/C/7/11.

132. W. Peard to F. Price, 15 April 1744, NLW, Puleston Ms. 3579E.

133. A. Crotty to P. Gould, 23 Sept. 1726, Chatsworth, Crotty letter book, 1726.

134. A. Crotty to Burlington, 14 Nov. 1731, ibid., Devonshire Letters, 1720–36, 200.2.

135. A. Crotty to H. Boyle, 30 May 1727, PRONI, D 2707/A1/1/8.

136. *A just and true relation of Josias Bateman's concern*, p. 35.

137. A. Crotty to W. Snow, 22 July 1729, Chatsworth, Crotty letter book, 1728–29.

138. A. Crotty to H. Boyle, 22 Dec. 1730, PRONI, D 2707/A1/1/20.

139. RD, 46/274/28640; 80/147/55277; 105/471/74354; Denbighshire RO, DD/BK/I, 24.

140. R. McCutcheon, 'Pue's occurrences, 1744–9', *Irish Genealogist*, 9 (1996), p. 332.

141. J. Clark, ' "His zeal is too furious": Lord Burlington's agents', in E. Corp (ed.), *Lord Burlington: the man and his politics: questions of loyalty* (Lewiston and Lampeter, 1998), pp. 182–93; Morris, ' "Principal inhabitants" in 1746', pp. 322–3.

142. *A just and true relation of Josias Bateman's concern*, pp. 4, 6, 7–11.

143. E. Weston to R. Wilmot, 6 March 1749[50], PRONI, T 3019/1504.

144. M. Ronayne to Lord Grandison, 30 Aug. 1730, Villiers-Stuart Mss, T 3131/C/5/65.

145. H. Temple to T. Corkran, 28 Nov. 1719, Southampton UL, BR, 2/2; Census of Elphin, NA, M. 2466, f. 397; T. O'Rorke, *The history of Sligo: town and county*, 2 vols (Dublin, 1889), i, p. 226.

146. H. Temple to L. Roberts, 7 April 1719, 22 Aug. 1719; same to T. Corkran, 28 Nov. 1719, Southampton UL, BR, 2/2.

147. Will of Lewis Corkran, 4 March 1737[8], PRO, PROB, 11/689, 114; T. Truxes, *Irish-American trade, 1660–1783* (Cambridge, 1988), pp. 87–8.

148. Palmerston to F. Corkran, 27 Jan. 1731[2], Southampton UL, BR, 2/7; F. Corkran to Palmerston, 6 Nov. 1739, 2 Jan. 1740[1], ibid., BR, 143/1; Palmerston to E. Corkran, 28 Jan. 1748[9], ibid., BR, 2/9; Edward Corkran to same, 24 Feb. 1758, 11 Dec. 1759, 20 Feb. 1761, ibid., BR, 143/1.

149. H. Hatch to Palmerston, 20 Aug. 1733, ibid., BR, 142/1/2; [James Corry], *Precedents and abstracts from the journals of the trustees of the linen and hempen manufactures of Ireland* (Dublin, 1784), p. 135; McCutcheon, 'Pue's occurrences', p. 359.

150. H. Temple to Revd J. Fontainer, 26 May 1715; same to J. Beecher, 23 Aug. 1716, Southampton UL, BR, 2/2B; same to T. Corkran, 5 Jan. 1720[1], 29 Nov. 1722, 23 July 1723, 22 Nov. 1723, 31 Dec. 1724, 11 March 1724[5], ibid., BR, 2/4; same to Bp. R. Howard, 18 Jan. 1731[2], ibid., BR, 2/7; O'Rorke, *History of Sligo*, i, pp. 331–2; W. G. Wood-Martin, *History of Sligo, county and town*, 3 vols (Dublin, 1892), iii, pp. 129–30.

151. Lady A. Herbert to H. Owen, 3 Dec. 1698, NLW, Powis Castle correspondence, nos. 252, 254; observations on E. Herbert's accounts, 1715, ibid., deeds, no. 14,779.

152. Rental, Annesley (Viscounts Valentia and earls of Anglesey) estates, 1713–21, Oxon CRO, E6/7/E/3.

153. Rental, Lord Digby of Geashill, 1711–12, Dorset CRO, D/SHC, 3C/81.

154. [R. Morres], *A list of the absentees of Ireland* (Dublin, 1767), p. 5; J. H. Gebbie, *An introduction to the Abercorn letters* (Omagh, 1972), p. 287.

155. J. Kelly (ed.), *The letters of Lord Chief Baron Edward Willes to the earl of Warwick, 1757–62* (Aberystwyth, 1990), p. 59.

156. R. Purcell to Lord Perceval, 29 Oct. 1747, BL, Add. Ms. 47,002A, ff. 131–1v.

157. Letter of attorney of H. Morton to W. Waring, 7 May 1658; T. Cooper to W. Waring, 19 and 27 Sept. 1659; letter of attorney from T. Cooper to same, 27 Sept. 1659, private collection, Co. Down; letter of attorney of A. Smith to W. Waring, 17 Feb. 1659[60], PRONI, D 695/43; T. Cooper to A. Smith, 3 Dec. 1659; W. Waring to same, 10 Jan. 1659[60], 17 April 1660; R. Lawrence to W. Waring, 5 Feb. 1674[5]; same to R. Trueman, 30 Dec. 1679; draft letter of W. Waring to R. Lawrence, [1675], private collection, Co. Down.

158. W. Waring to A. Smith, 26 Dec. 1665; A. Smith to W. Waring, 5 Aug. 1664, 18 May 1665, 5 June 1668, private collection, Co. Down; W. Waring to W. Layfield, 2 Aug. 1673, 26 and 27 June 1674, 16 March 1674[5], PRONI, D 695/10, 13A, 13B, 89; same to same, 5 Sept. 1690, 9 July 1691, 25 Sept. 1691, 29 March 1692; W. Layfield to W. Waring, 10 Nov. 1691, 7 May 1692, 19 Sept. 1693, 21 Feb. 1694[5], private collection, Co. Down.

159. S. Waring to W. Waring, 19 Feb. 1698[9]; W. Waring to S. Waring, 20 Feb. 1698[9]; list of W. Waring's lands, c. 1696, private collection, Co. Down.

160. J. Blennerhasset and E. Herbert to H. A. Herbert, 30 April 1730, Powis Castle correspondence, no. 895; K. O'Shea, *Castleisland: church and people* (Tralee, 1981), p. 16.

161. A. Crotty, account book, 1726–32, openings 62–64, Chatsworth; list of lands sold, 28 Aug. 1729, PRONI, D 2707/B9/6.

162. Report of J. Allen, H. Sankey, E. Roberts and E. Reader, 30 April 1678, Guildhall Library, London, E. Smith's book relating to his charities in Ireland, Ms. 13,823; copy of E. Smith's will, 9 May 1690, ibid., Ms. 13,829, pp. 29–30; J. Damer to T. Lockington, 20 Sept. 1709, ibid., Ms. 13,830, bundle 3.

163. Rental of 1688, with Damer as tenant of a Tipperary farm for £59 10s.: Guildhall Library, London, Ms. 13,830, bundle 12.

164. J. Damer to N. Hawes, 31 May 1694; same to J. Reeves, 24 Dec. 1696, ibid., Ms. 13,827, ff. 98, 102v.

165. R. Reading to N. Hawes, 23 April 1685, ibid., Ms. 13,830, bundle 9.

166. J. Damer to J. Reeves, 16 Jan. 1700[1], ibid., Ms. 13,823, f. 105; same to T. Lockington, 21 July 1709, 20 Sept. 1709, 23 March 1709[10], ibid., Ms. 13,830, bundle 3.

167. J. Damer to F. Brerewood, 28 March 1702, ibid., Ms. 13,830, bundle 1; words to be engraved on silver cup, [1702], ibid., Ms. 13,830, bundle 2.

168. G. Macartney to Sir J. Allen, 27 Sept. 1680, PRONI, Macartney letter book, 1679–81; Cork and Burlington to W. Congreve, 20 Dec. 1694, Chatsworth, Burlington letter book, 1694–95; H. Temple to D. Reading, 9 April, 1717, Southampton UL, BR 2/2; Palmerston to R. Roberts, 14 Aug. 1731, ibid., BR, 2/7; Peacock's journal, NLI, Ms. 16,091, s.d. 23 May 1745.

169. BL, printed ballad on death of Damer, 1720.

170. L. M. Cullen, *Anglo-Irish trade, 1660–1800* (Manchester, 1968), pp. 187–204;

Dickson, 'Economic history of the Cork region', i, pp. 53–4, 218–21; ii, pp. 505–9; M. MacCarthy-Morrogh, 'Credit and remittance: monetary problems in early seventeenth-century Munster', *Irish Economic and Social History*, 14 (1987), pp. 5–19.

171. Dr J. Hall to T. Lockington, 15 July 1712; S. Martin to same, 25 Oct. 1712; Abp. W. King to F. Annesley, 6 May 1718, Guildhall Library, London, Ms. 13,830. Cf. Palmerston to J. Hatch, 31 July 1756, Southampton UL, BR, 2/12.

172. H. Boyle to R. Power and J. Coughlan, 27 Sept. 1705; W. Snow to J. Coughlan, 24 June 1710; letter of attorney from H. Boyle to W. Snow, 28 June 1710, Chatsworth, W. Snow letter book.

173. A. Crotty to Burlington, 8 July 1725, Greater London RO, Q/CML/10/1–2.

174. A. Best to Lady Shannon, 19 Oct. 1728, 25 March 1729, 3 May 1729, PRONI, D 2707/B1/12B, 12C, 12F.

175. A. Best to Lady Shannon, 3 May 1729; same to Lord Shannon, 7 June 1739; Lord Duncannon to same, 9 June 1739; ibid., D 2707/B1/12F, 20, 21.

176. Note on PRONI, D 602/A/23, quoted in W.A. Maguire, 'Missing persons: Edenderry under the Blundells and Downshires, 1707–1922', in W. Nolan and T. P. O'Neill (eds), *Offaly: History and Society* (Dublin, 1998), p. 522.

177. H. Hatch to Lord Blundell, 18 Oct. 1746, 18 Nov. 1746, PRONI, D 607/A/23. A decade later, this murmuring had not been entirely silenced. One widespread practice which Hatch hoped to eradicate was to allow an agent himself to be tenant for some of the lands that he was overseeing. The agent valued the holding, set the rent and deterred any from bidding against him. Same to same, 7 Feb. 1746[7], ibid.

178. *A just and true relation of Josias Bateman's concern*, pp. iii, 18–19, 28–9.

179. Burlington to G. Howse and T. Forster, 3 Dec. 1695, Chatsworth, Cork and Burlington letter book, 1695–96.

180. *A just and true relation of Josias Bateman's concern*, pp. 10–11.

181. Ibid., pp. 30–3. For Bateman as a tenant at Tallow in 1695: Cork and Burlington to unknown, 21 Sept. 1695, Chatsworth, Cork and Burlington letter book, 1695–96.

182. S. Hill to Burlington, 5 Nov. 1731; same to H. Boyle, 28 May 1732, PRONI, D 2707/A1/11/36 and 44.

183. Hume's report, *c.* 1730, NLI, Ms. 6054, f. 11.

184. D. Dickson, 'Middlemen', in T. Bartlett and D. W. Hayton (eds), *Penal age and golden era: essays in Irish history, 1690–1860* (Belfast, 1979), pp. 162–85.

185. Lord Strafford to Lords Justice, 19 Oct. 1694, NA, Wyche Ms, 1/1/110; day book, Irish accounts, 1707–13, Sheffield City Archives, WWM/A 758, p. 229; survey of Lord Malton's Irish estate, 1728, ibid., WWM/A 769, pp. 11–12.

186. Irish accounts, 1707–13, ibid., WWM/A 758, pp. 225, 231; accounts, 1713–20, ibid., WWM/A 759, p. 397; trespass book, s.d. 15 July 1719, ibid., WWM/A 765.

187. T. Wentworth to A. Nickson, 25 June 1717, ibid., WWM/M14/27a.

188. Survey of Lord Malton's Irish estate, 1728, ibid., WWM/A 769, p. 11.

189. Hume's report, NLI, Ms. 6054, p. 7.

190. Irish accounts, 1707–13, Sheffield City Archives, WWM/A 758, pp. 221, 246, 247; Nickson's accounts, 1703–20, ibid., WWM/A 759, pp. 380, 382, 385, 388, 392–3, 400–1, 403, 420, 427.

191. Inventory of John Nickson, late of Killinure, 17 July 1730, NA, salvaged Chancery Pleadings, box 4.

192. R. Lloyd to W. Hickman, n.d.[*c.* 1715], NLW, Powis Castle correspondence, no. 903.

193. R. Lloyd to W. Hickman, n.d., and 27 April 1717, ibid., Powis Castle correspondence, no. 904; ibid., Powis Castle deeds 16,070; A. Herbert to E. Herbert, 3 Aug. 1715; same to Francis Herbert, 20 Jan. 1716[17], ibid., Powis Castle correspondence, nos. 820, 835; H. A. Herbert to E. Herbert, 16 March 1716[17], ibid., no. 837; E. Herbert to F. Herbert, 25 Oct. 1717, 18 Dec. 1717, ibid., no. 843.

194. R. Lloyd to F. Herbert, 14 April 1717, NLW, Powis Castle deeds, no. 16,061.

195. R. Lloyd to F. Herbert, 9 Feb. 1716[17], ibid., Powis Castle deeds, no. 16,058.

196. Paper, *c.* 24 March 1715[16], R. Lloyd to F. Herbert, 12 June 1716, ibid., Powis Castle deeds, nos. 16,043, 16,050.

197. E. Herbert to ?F. Herbert, 6 Oct. 1707, ibid., Powis Castle correspondence, no. 809.

198. R. Lloyd to F. Herbert, 2 Nov. 1715, ibid., Powis Castle correspondence, no. 821.

199. R. Lloyd to F. Herbert, 25 June 1715, ibid., Powis Castle deeds, no. 16,049; H. Owen, description of Castleisland, 1686, NLI, Ms. 7861, f. 156v.

200. ?J. Ussher to J. Burward, 21 Nov. 1743, NLI, Ms. 7180.

201. H. Hatch to Palmerston, 20 Aug. 1733, 15 Sept. 1733, Southampton UL, BR 142/1/3, 4.

202. H. Conyngham to A. Murray, 4 Sept. 1704, 11 Nov. 1704, PRONI, D 2860/5/21 and 23.

203. G. Kirkham, ' "No more to be got off the cat but the skin": management, landholding and economic change on the Murray of Broughton estate, 1670–1755', in W. Nolan, L. Ronayne and M. Dunlevy (eds), *Donegal: history and society* (Dublin, 1995), pp. 357–74; H. Meehan, 'The Conynghams of Slane and Mountcharles', *Donegal Annual*, 51 (1999), pp. 22–35; D. Verschoyle, 'Background to a hidden age', ibid., 6 (1965), pp. 110–20.

204. Lady Shelburne to A. Murray, 20 June 1705, 13 April 1706, 7 Dec. 1706, PRONI, D 2860/3, 11 and 16; T. Knox to same, 1 Nov. 1706, ibid., D 2860/4/20.

205. H. Owen, description of Castleisland, 1686, NLI, Ms. 7861, ff. 154–165v; R. Lloyd to F. Herbert, 25 June 1715, NLW, Powis Castle deeds, no. 16,049.

206. R. Lloyd to F. Herbert, 2 Nov. 1715, NLW, Powis Castle correspondence, no. 821.

207. H. Hatch to Lord Palmerston, 17 July 1729, 5 Dec. 1741, 22 March 1742[3], Southampton UL, BR 142/1/2, 11, 12; same to Lord Blundell, 18 Oct. 1746, 18 Nov. 1746, 7 Feb. 1746[7], PRONI, D 607/A/23; N.T. Burke, 'Dublin, 1600–1800: a study in urban morphogenesis', unpublished Ph.D. thesis, TCD (1972), pp. 232–45, 290–306.

208. *The adventures and metamorphoses of Queen Elizabeth's pocket-pistol, late of Charles-Fort, near Kinsale* (?Dublin, 1756); Barnard, 'Considering the inconsiderable', pp. 120–1; *A narrative of the dispute in the corporation of Kinsale* (Dublin, 1756), pp. 7–8, 11, 13, 19.

209. PRONI, D 356/8, quoted in R. Richey, 'Landed society in mid-eighteenth-century County Down', unpublished Ph.D. thesis, Queen's University, Belfast (2000) p. 70; E. Parkinson, *The city of Downe from its earliest days* (Belfast, 1927), p. 67.

210. Delany, *Autobiography*, 1st series, ii, p. 576.

211. Peacock diary, s.d. 27 April 1748, 4 May 1748, NLI, Ms. 16,091.

212. Southwell notebook, 1750–52, BL, Egerton Ms. 1630, ff. 2, 39, 77; J. Trotter to

E. Southwell, 18 April 1757, BL, Add. Ms. 20,131, f. 127v; A. Crookshank and [D. Fitzgerald], Knight of Glin, *The painters of Ireland* (London, 1978), p. 86.

213. J. Perceval to Lord Perceval, 20 Aug. 1731, BL, Add. Ms. 46,982, f. 104v.

214. R. Purcell to Lord Perceval, 19 and 29 Oct. 1747, 12 Nov. 1747, 17 Dec. 1747, ibid., Add. Ms. 47,002A, ff. 129, 131–1v, 133v, 143; J. Wight, journal, s.d. 6 March 1752, Friends' Historical Library, Dublin; Berry, 'Justices of the peace for county Cork', p. 65.

215. Revd R. Purcell to Lord Egmont, 7 May 1768, RCB, Ms. 20/766.

216. Orpen, *The Orpen family*, pp. 68–9, 148–54, 167–74.

217. Mitchell to Blundell, 12 June 1746, PRONI, D 607/A/23; Maguire, 'Missing persons', pp. 518, 522–3.

218. T. Barry to H. Hatch, 16 May 1758, NLI, Ms. 11,327/8.

219. Palmerston to H. Hatch, 13 Nov. 1735, 11 Jan. 1736[7], 19 March 1736[7], Southampton UL, BR 2/8; rough minutes, 1758–61, f. 1v, RDS; *Al. Dubl.*, p. 380; *KIAP*, p. 218.

220. Sir R. Southwell to H. Sloane, 4 Nov. 1693, BL, Sloane Ms. 4036, ff. 157–7v; B. Banfield to Sir R. Southwell, 20 Sept. 1695, ibid., Add. Ms. 9714, f. 122.

221. W. Fitzwilliam to Viscount Fitzwilliam, 12 March 1761, NA, Pembroke estate papers, 96/46/1/2/7; correspondence of E. Fagan with same, 1761–71, ibid., 97/46/1/2/8, 38–119.

222. E. MacAulay, 'Some problems of the Fitzwilliam estate during the agency of Barbara Verschoyle', *Irish Architectural and Decorative Studies*, 2 (1999), pp. 98–117.

223. Cork and Burlington to W. Congreve, 28 Aug. 1697, 2 Oct. 1697, Chatsworth, Lismore Ms. 34/135, 137.

224. Accounts of L. Gosteloe and G. Roche, 1677–81, s.d. 23 March 1677[8], 13 June 1678, 4 March 1678[9], 26 April 1681, NLI, Ms. 6902; accounts, 1684–91, s.d. 13 June 1684, 27 Jan. 1684[5], 25 March 1685[6], ibid., Ms. 6300; accounts of R. Bagge, 1690–91, s.d. 26 Jan. 1690[1], ibid., Ms. 6903.

225. S. Wilson to M. St George, 22 Aug. 1730, PRO C 110/48, 916; O. Gallagher to O. St George, 11 March 1724[5], 13 April 1725, 30 Oct. 1725, 11 Dec. 1725, 14 Jan. 1726[7], ibid., C 110/46, 327, 362, 404, 406, 410; bill of S. Wilson, 9 May 1734, IAA, Castletown deposit, box 55.

226. H. Temple to D. Reading, 1 Jan. 1722[3], Southampton UL, BR 2/4.

227. Hume report, NLI, Ms. 6054, p. 16; *A letter to a schoolmaster in the country from his friend in town relative to Mr Sheridan's scheme of education* (Dublin, 1758), pp. 10, 14.

228. R. Richey, 'County Down', pp. 66–7.

229. H. Owen, description of Castleisland, 1686, NLI, Ms. 7861, ff. 155, 163v.

230. Legg, *Synge Letters*, pp. xviii–xix; C. Varley, *A new system of husbandry*, 3 vols (York, 1770), iii, pp. 31–2, 78–9; [Charles Varley], *The modern farmer's guide by a real farmer* (Glasgow, 1768), pp. xliii–xlv.

231. A. Young, *A tour in Ireland*, ed. C. Maxwell (Cambridge, 1925), pp. xiv–xv.

232. L. Baker-Jones, *Princelings, privileges and power: the Tivyside gentry in their community* (Llandysul, 1999), pp. 75–8; Howell, *Patriarchs and parasites*, pp. 55–7; Humphreys, *Montgomeryshire, 1680–1815*, pp. 136–7.

233. R. Orpen to Lady Shelburne, 1 April 1692, RIA, Ms. 12. I. 2; Orpen, *The Orpen family*, pp. 87–97, 98–106. Cf. C. Daly to H. Owen, 13 April 1694, NLW, Powis Castle correspondence, no. 191. It prefigured uncannily the show of the high sheriff in Kerry in 1732. C. Smith, *The antient and present state of the County of Kerry*, new edn (Dublin and Cork, 1979), pp. 258–9.

9. The Middle Station

1. R. V. Dudley, 'Dublin's parishes, 1660–1729: the Church of Ireland parishes and their role in the civic administration of the city', unpublished Ph.D. thesis, TCD, 2 vols (1995), i, p. 118; vestry book, St Michan's, Dublin, 1724–60, s.d. 6 May 1725, RCB, P. 276/4.1, p. 11; account book, Holy Trinity, Cork, 1664–1710, s.d. 14 Feb. 1680[1], RCB, P. 527/7.1, p. 81; W. H. Dundas, *Enniskillen: parish and town* (Dundalk and Enniskillen, 1913), pp. 36, 162–4.

2. C. Whittingham to Abp. W. King, 18 March 1708[9], TCD, Ms. 1995–2008/1316.

3. Minutes of Route Presbytery, 1701–6, p. 8, Presbyterian Historical Society, Belfast.

4. K. B. Dillow, 'The social and ecclesiastical significance of church seating arrangements and pew disputes, 1500–1640', unpublished Oxford D.Phil. thesis (1990), pp. 87–168; J. Livesey, 'Acton church seating arrangements', *Transactions of the Historic Society of Lancashire and Cheshire*, 64 (1912), pp. 289–91; J. Popplewell, 'A seating plan for North Nibley church in 1629', *Transactions of the Bristol and Gloucestershire Archaeological Society*, 103 (1985), pp. 179–84.

5. Vestry book, St Peter's Dublin, 1686–1736, RCB, P. 45/6.1, pp. 65–75; N. T. Burke, 'An early modern Dublin suburb: the estate of Francis Aungier, earl of Longford', *Irish Geography*, 6 (1972), pp. 369–76; G. A. Forrest, 'The extent and character of Huguenot settlement and speculation in the Aungier estate, 1708–1779', unpublished BA thesis, TCD (1988).

6. Vestry book, St Paul's, Dublin, 1698–1750, RCB, P. 273/6.1, pp. 9, 12.

7. Ibid., pp. 44–5.

8. N. T. Burke, 'Dublin, 1600–1800: a study in urban morphogenesis', unpublished Ph.D. thesis, TCD (1972), pp. 91, 117, 140, 185–6, 197, 212–13, 234–5, 283–4.

9. Vestry book, St Mary's, Dublin, 1699–1739, RCB, P. 277/7.1, pp. 40, 54, 179–81.

10. Vestry book, St Catherine's, Dublin, 1693–1730, ibid., P. 117/5.2, p. 30.

11. M. Ronan (ed.), 'Archbishop Bulkeley's visitation of Dublin, 1630', *Archivium Hibernicum*, 8 (1941), pp. 56–98.

12. Register of pews, St Werburgh's, Dublin, 1719–1828, RCB, P. 326/13.1.

13. Ibid.

14. *Statutes*, iv, p. 427.

15. Register of pews, St Werburgh's, Dublin, 1719–1828, s.d. 23 April 1760, RCB, P. 326/13.1.

16. Vestry book, St Paul's, Dublin, 1698–1750, ibid., P. 273.6.1, pp. 9, 12, 43.

17. 'The disposition and settlement of seats', St Michan's, Dublin, 1724, ibid., P. 276/12.2; assignment of pew to J. Parnell, 10 July 1724, Southampton UL, Ms. 64, Congleton Mss, 1/2; N. Alldridge, 'Loyalty and identity in Chester parishes, 1540–1640', in S. J. Wright (ed.), *Parish, church and people: local studies in lay religion* (London, 1988), pp. 93–7; Dillow, 'The social and ecclesiastical significance of church seating arrangements', pp. 107–8.

18. Revd W. Perceval, memorandum book, St Michan's, Dublin, RCB, P. 276/12, pp. 151–3.

19. Cess applotment book, St Michan's, ibid., P. 276/10.1; vestry book, St Michan's, Dublin, 1724–60, s.d. 26 Feb. 1724[5], 25 Feb. 1725[6], 23 Feb. 1726[7], 21 Feb. 1726[7], 23 Feb. 1726[7], 21 Feb. 1727[8], 27 March 1733, ibid., P. 276/7/1.

20. Monck Mason's collections for the city of Dublin, transcribed in 1867 for J. T. Gilbert, iii, part 1, Dublin Public Library, Gilbert Ms. 68, pp. 151–5.

21. J. Bonnell to J. Strype, 25 Jan. 1698[9], Cambridge UL, Add Ms. 1, 85; Abp. W. King to Bp. J. Stearne, 25 Sept. 1714, TCD, Ms. 2536, p. 75; Bp. W. Nicolson to Abp. W. Wake, 17 June 1718, Christ Church, Wake Ms. 12, f. 278.

22. Monck Mason's collections, iii, part 1, Dublin Public Library, Gilbert Ms. 68, pp. 151–5; Dudley, 'Dublin's parishes', i, pp. 27–60; ii, pp. 272–89.

23. Abp. W. King to F. Annesley, 9 June 1711, TCD, Ms. 2531, p. 341; same to T. Wentworth, 13 Oct. 1713, ibid., Ms. 750/4, p. 214; same to unknown, 14 May 1714, ibid., Ms. 750/4/2, 47; same to J. Spranger, 3 March 1718[19], ibid., Ms. 750/5, 127; same to H. Maule, 8 May 1722, ibid., Ms. 750/7, 105; Palmerston to L. Roberts, 16 Nov. 1725, Southampton UL, BR, 2/4.

24. Vestry book, St Bride's, Dublin, 1663–1702, RCB, P. 327/4.1.

25. Vestry books, St John's, Dublin, 1660–1710, 1711–62, ibid., P. 328/5. 2 and 3; R. Gillespie (ed.), *The vestry records of the parish of St John the Evangelist, Dublin, 1595–1658* (Dublin, 2002), pp. 11–12.

26. F. X. McCorry, *Lurgan: an Irish provincial town, 1610–1970* (Lurgan, 1993), pp. 18, 20.

27. R. Caulfield, 'Annals of St Mary, Shandon', p. 11, St Finbarre's Cathedral, Cork; 'Dr Caulfield's antiquarian notes', *JCHAS*, 2nd series, 10 (1904), p. 268.

28. Vestry book of St Catherine's, Dublin, 1657–92, RCB, P. 117/5/1.1, pp. 155, 343, 357; Dudley, 'Dublin's parishes', i, pp. 86–96; R. Gillespie, 'The Rev. Dr John Yarner's notebook: religion in Restoration Dublin', *Archivium Hibernicum*, 52 (1998), pp. 30–1; J. T. Boulton, *Neighbourhood and society: a London suburb in the seventeenth century* (Cambridge, 1987), pp. 140–3; D. Eastwood, *Government and community in the English provinces, 1700–1870* (Basingstoke, 1997), pp. 30–1, 42–9; S. Hindle, 'A sense of place? Becoming and belonging in the rural parish, 1550–1650', in A. Shepard and P. Withington (eds), *Communities in early modern England* (Manchester, 2000), pp. 96–114; K. Wrightson and D. Levine, *Poverty and piety in an English village: Terling, 1525–1700* (New York and London, 1979), pp. 103–9.

29. Vestry book, St Catherine's, Dublin, 1693–1730, RCB, P. 117/5/1.2, pp. 47–51, 66–7.

30. Vestry book, St Mary's, Dublin, 1699–1739, s.d. 23 Dec. 1713, ibid., P. 277/1.2, p. 88.

31. Vestry book, St Mary's, Dublin, 1699–1739, s.d. 28 Feb. 1722[3], ibid., P. 277/1.2, p. 167.

32. Vestry book, St Michan's, Dublin, 1724–60, ibid., P. 276/4.1; list of churchwardens, St Michan's, ibid., P. 276/12.1, p. 191; vestry book, St Paul's, Dublin, 1698–1750, RCB, P. 275/6.1.

33. W. Gacquin, *Roscommon before the famine: the parishes of Kiltoom and Cam, 1749–1845* (Dublin, 1996), pp. 12–24.

34. C. O'Hara, observations, s.d. 1757/8, NLI, Ms. 20,397.

35. G. Stacpoole, *Some short historical anecdotes, with remarks, relative to Ireland*, 4 parts, part 1 (Cork, 1762), pp. 37, 70, 83.

36. R. Gillespie (ed.), *The first chapter book of Christ Church Cathedral, Dublin, 1574–1634* (Dublin, 1997), pp. 35, 47, 53, 90, 124, 125, 126; E. P. Shirley, *The history of the county of Monaghan* (London, 1879), pp. 550–1.

37. Robinson Mss, Dublin Public Library, Ms. 34, p. 141.

38. *A letter from Sir Richard Cox, Bart. to Thomas Prior, Esq.* (Dublin, 1749), p. 43; *A letter to a member of the Irish Parliament relative to the present state of Ireland* (London,

[1755]), p. 9; M. Whyte, *An inquiry into the causes of our want of tillage in Ireland: with some hints for establishing a yeomanry* (Dublin, 1755); above, pp. 7–9.

39. T. C. Barnard, 'Fishing in seventeenth-century Kerry: the experience of Sir William Petty', *Journal of the Kerry Archaeological and Historical Society*, 14 (1981), pp. 14–25; N. Canny, *Making Ireland British, 1580–1650* (Oxford, 2001), pp. 310–15, 339–44, 352–3, 359–61; M. MacCarthy-Morrogh, *The Munster plantation: English migration to southern Ireland 1583–1641* (Oxford, 1986), pp. 230–40.

40. T. C. Barnard, 'Sir William Petty as Kerry ironmaster', *PRIA*, 82, sect. C (1982), pp. 1–32.

41. P. Francis, *Irish Delftware: an illustrated history* (London, 2000), p. 10; P. Francis, '"The Glass-Maker's Memoirs": George Minty's "Crusonian" adventures in Ireland, 1746–1757', *Journal of Glass Studies*, 42 (2000), pp. 113–31.

42. T. C. Barnard, 'An Anglo-Irish industrial enterprise: iron-making at Enniscorthy, Co. Wexford, 1657–92', *PRIA*, sect. C, 85 (1985), pp. 101–44.

43. W. Henry, 'Natural and typographical history', NA, M. 2533, pp. 408–11; R. Barton, *A dialogue concerning some things of importance to Ireland; particularly to the county of Ardmagh* (Dublin, 1751), sig. [A3], pp. 13–14, 17–18; C. Smith, *The antient and present state of the county and city of Cork*, 2nd edn, 2 vols (Dublin, 1774), i, pp. 211–13, 253–6, 307.

44. *Writings of Petty*, i, 146, and n. 1.

45. N. B. Harte, 'The economics of clothing in the late seventeenth century', *Textile History*, 22 (1991), pp. 285, 290–1.

46. J. Bulkeley to J. Bonnell, 4 April 1721, NLI, PC 435; K. Conolly to same, 7 March 1740[1], ibid., PC 434.

47. Lists of brethren, Weavers' Company, 1693–1722; accounts for 1696 and 1707, Masters' accounts, 1691–1714, Weavers' Company, RSAI.

48. Petition of master, wardens and brethren of corporation of clothiers and stuff weavers to Clarendon, *c.* 1686, Bodleian, Clarendon Ms. 88, ff. 290–1; lists of brethren, 1693–1722, 1722–43, 1746–64; minute book, Weavers' Company, 1734–60, RSAI.

49. Depositions for Queen's County, 1642, TCD, Ms. 821, ff. 55–55v, 84v, 90–90v, 180; T. C. Barnard, 'The Hartlib circle and the cult and culture of improvement in Ireland', in M. Greengrass, M. Leslie and T. Raylor (eds), *Samuel Hartlib and universal reformation* (Cambridge, 1994), pp. 283–9; G. Boate, *Irelands natural history* (London, 1652), pp. 73, 89, 97–8, 134–7, 162; R. Loeber, 'Preliminaries to the Massachusetts Bay Colony: the Irish ventures of Emanuel Downing and John Winthrop, sr.', in T. Barnard, D. Ó Cróinín and K. Simms (eds), '*A Miracle of Learning*': *studies in Irish manuscripts and learning. Essays in honour of William O'Sullivan* (Aldershot, 1998), pp. 165–99.

50. MacCarthy-Morrogh, *The Munster plantation*, pp. 230–40.

51. T. King, *Carlow, the manor and town, 1674–1721* (Dublin, 1997), pp. 34, 44; B. Ó Dálaigh (ed.), *Corporation book of Ennis* (Dublin, 1990), pp. 362–3; E. P. Shirley (ed.), 'Extracts from the journal of Thomas Dineley, esq . . . ', *Journal of the Kilkenny and South-East of Ireland Archaeological Society*, 4 (1862–63), pp. 41, 47.

52. T. C. Barnard, 'Interests of Ireland', in C. Brady and J. Ohlemeyer (eds), *Argument and power in early modern Ireland* (Cambridge, forthcoming).

53. Grants to C. Lovett, 17 July 1677, 1 Aug. 1677; petition of Mrs C. Lovett, after 1690, Southampton UL, BR, 150; Sir J. Temple to H. Temple, 23 May 1696, ibid.,

BR, 5/22; *CSPD, 1691–92*, pp. 321–2; HMC, *Ormonde Mss*, new series, iv, p. 156; R. Lawrence, *The interest of Ireland in its trade and wealth stated*, 2 parts (Dublin, 1682), i, sig. *4v; ii, p. 189; A. Longfield, 'History of tapestry making in Ireland in the seventeenth and eighteenth centuries', *JRSAI*, 68 (1938), pp. 92–9.

54. W. Hovell to unknown, 11 Dec. 1683, 5 Feb. 1683[4], 7 March 1683[4], 8 April 1684, 24 June 1684; same to J. Houblon, 22 April 1684, Hovell letter book, 1683–88, Farmar Mss, private collection, Dublin. Langton had hedged his bets by obtaining the reversions to the clerkship of the peace for Counties Cork and Waterford in 1668. W. M. Brady, *Clerical and parochial records of Cork, Cloyne and Ross*, 3 vols (London, 1864), i, p. xlix; *CSP, Ire. 1666–69*, p. 633.

55. W. Hovell to unknown, 28 Dec. 1683, Hovell letter book, 1683–88, Farmar Mss, private collection Dublin.

56. Deposition of J. Langton, 1642, TCD, Ms. 823, f. 51; Canny, *Making Ireland British*, p. 343. Cf. T. Barnard, 'The world of goods and County Offaly in the early eighteenth century', in T. P. O'Neill and W. Nolan (eds), *Offaly: history and society* (Dublin, 1998), p. 387.

57. P. Melvin (ed.), 'Paul Rycaut's memoranda and letters from Ireland, 1687–1687', *Analecta Hibernica*, 27 (1972), p. 132.

58. W. Hovell to J. Houblon, 4 Jan. 1683[4], Hovell letter book, 1683–88, Farmar Mss, Dublin.

59. R. Langrishe to Lady Shannon, 28 Jan. 1743[4], PRONI, D 2707/B1/34.

60. Armiger genealogy, GO, Ms. 810/20; Chatsworth, 29 Sept. 1695, letter book, 1695–96; ibid., 21 Sept. 1696, letter book, 1696, lease of G. Sealy and W. Meade, 19 April 1744, RD, 114/280/78946; mortgage of W. Coughlan with G. Sealy, 20 April 1749, ibid., 158/150/105293; indenture, 26 July 1756, ibid., 186/92/123339; lease of G. Sealy with J. Sealy, 27 and 28 April 1770, ibid., 277/600/180864; indenture, 26 Feb. 1774, ibid., 301/137/199397; agreement of G. Sealy and R. Sealy, 15 Aug. 1780, ibid., 359/45/240832; T. Barnard, 'The cultures of eighteenth-century Irish towns', in P. Borsay and L. Proudfoot (eds), *Change, convergence and divergence: provincial towns in early modern England and Ireland*, Proceedings of the British Academy, 108 (2002), pp. 195–222; E. Peacock, *Index to English speaking students who have graduated at Leyden University* (London, 1883), p. 88.

61. J. Perceval to Lord Perceval, 11 June 1731, BL, Add. Ms. 46,982, f. 98v; also above, pp. 201, 234–5.

62. Lawrence, *Interest of Ireland*, i, sig. *4; ii, pp. 104, 189.

63. W. H. Crawford, 'The social structure of Ulster in the eighteenth century', in L. M. Cullen and F. Furet (eds), *Irlande et France, XVIIe–XXe siècles: pour une historie rurale comparée* (Paris, 1980), pp. 117–27; W. H. Crawford, 'Drapers and bleachers in the early Ulster linen industry', in L. M. Cullen and P. Butel (eds), *Négoce et industrie en France et en Irlande aux xviiie et xixe siècles* (Paris, 1980), pp. 113–19; W. H. Crawford, 'The evolution of the linen trade in Ulster before industrialisation', *Irish Economic and Social History*, 15 (1988), pp. 32–53; W. H. Crawford, 'The political economy of linen: Ulster in the eighteenth century', in C. Brady, M. O'Dowd and B. Walker (eds), *Ulster: an illustrated history* (London, 1989), pp. 134–57; M. W. Dowling, *Tenant right and agrarian society in Ulster, 1600–1780* (Dublin, 1999).

64. P. Griffin, *The people with no name: Ireland's Ulster Scots, America's Scots Irish, and the creation of a British Atlantic world, 1689–1764* (Princeton and London, 2001), pp.

37–64; I. MacBride, *Scripture politics: Ulster Presbyterians and Irish radicalism in the late eighteenth century* (Oxford, 1998).

65. E. Magennis, 'A Presbyterian insurrection: reconsidering the Hearts of Oak disturbances of July 1763', *IHS*, 31 (1998), pp. 165–87.

66. Minute books, revenue commissioners, PRO, CUST 1/91, f. 106v; ibid., CUST 1/95, f. 119; W. Conner to A. Abdy, 4 Feb. 1757, Chatsworth, letter book of W. Conner; 'Ant. Constitution', *A short and easy method of reducing the exorbitant pride and arrogance of the city of Dublin* (London, 1748), p. 24; G. H., *A genuine letter from a freeman of Bandon, to George Faulkner* (Dublin, 1755), pp. 11–12; T. C. Barnard, 'Considering the inconsiderable: electors, patrons and Irish elections, 1659 to 1761', in D. W. Hayton (ed.), *The Irish parliament in the eighteenth century: the long apprenticeship* (Edinburgh, 2001), pp. 107–27.

67. Sir M. Crosbie to H. A. Herbert, 15 Oct. 1736, NLW, Powis Castle correspondence, no. 916.

68. Hume's report, NLI, Ms. 6054, p. 104.

69. H. Hatch to Palmerston, 20 Aug. 1733, 5 Dec. 1741, Southampton UL, BR, 142/1/3, 11; Palmerston to H. Hatch, 17 Aug. 1736, ibid., BR 2/8; M. Ward to Palmerston, 23 April 1763, ibid., BR, 143/3; Census of Elphin, 1749, NA, M. 2466, ff. 396–421; J. Brush to W. Smythe, 30 Nov. 1741, 7 and 19 April 1742, 22 May 1742, NLI, PC 449.

70. J. Thompson to W. Smythe, 18 Nov. 1749, NLI, PC 445; J. Cooley to same, 28 Feb. 1756, ibid., PC. 446; W. Smythe to unknown, 12 Jan. 1754, ibid., PC 449; draft petitions of W. Smythe to Linen Board, [?1750s], ibid., PC 449.

71. Nash to ?R. Smythe, [1750s], ibid., PC 444.

72. *A letter from Sir Richard Cox, Bart. to Thomas Prior, Esq; shewing, from experience, a sure method to establish the Linen-Manufacture* (Dublin, 1749); *A letter from Sir Richard Cox, Bart. To the high sheriff of the county of Cork relative to the present state of the linen-manufacture in that county* (Dublin, 1759).

73. M. D. Jephson, *An Anglo-Irish miscellany: some records of the Jephsons of Mallow* (Dublin, 1964), p. 370; *Seasonable advice to Protestants, containing some means of reviving and strengthening the Protestant interest* (Cork, 1745), pp. 7–9; Smith, *Cork*, i, pp. 58–9.

74. A. Young, *A tour of Ireland*, 2 vols (Dublin, 1780), i, p. 386.

75. Barnard, 'Robert French of Monivea', pp. 271–96; D. A. Cronin, *A Galway gentleman in the age of improvement* (Blackrock, 1995), pp. 25–41.

76. Hume report, NLI, Ms. 6054, p. 16; *A letter to a schoolmaster in the country from his friend in town relative to Mr Sheridan's scheme of education* (Dublin, 1758), pp. 10, 14.

77. Robert Bell, *A description of the condition and manners . . . of the peasantry of Ireland* (London, 1804), p. 32.

78. T. C. Barnard, 'The gentrification of eighteenth-century Ireland', *Eighteenth-Century Ireland*, 12 (1997), pp. 137–55; *The Censor*, 6 (Dublin, 1–8 July 1749); S. J. Connolly, *Religion, law and power* (Oxford, 1992), pp. 63–4, 129–30; D. Dickson, 'Middlemen', in T. Bartlett and D. W. Hayton (eds), *Penal era and golden age: essays in Irish history, 1690–1800* (Belfast, 1979), pp. 162–85; K. Whelan, 'An underground gentry? Catholic middlemen in eighteenth-century Ireland', *Eighteenth-Century Ireland*, 10 (1995), pp. 9–66, reprinted in Whelan, *The tree of liberty: radicalism, Catholicism and the construction of Irish identity 1760–1830* (Cork, 1996), pp. 3–58. Cf. P. Ramsey, *Tudor economic problems* (London, 1966), pp. 153–4; R. H. Tawney, *The agrarian problem in*

the sixteenth century (London, 1912); R. B. Westerfield, *Middlemen in English business, particularly between 1660–1760* (New Haven, Conn., 1915).

79. Barnard, 'Gentrification of eighteenth-century Ireland'; Connolly, *Religion, law and power*, pp. 63–4, 129–30; Dickson, 'Middlemen', pp. 162–85; Whelan, 'Underground gentry?', pp. 3–58.

80. C. Eustace to C. Tickell, 23 Nov. [1728], Tickell Mss, private collection, Devon; E. Spencer to F. Price, 16 Oct. 1747, NLW, Puleston Ms. 3580E; J. Wight, journal, s.d. 26 May 1753, Friends' Historical Library, Dublin; L. Whyte, *Poems* (Dublin, 1740), pp. vii–viii.

81. Dolan, History of County Fermanagh, *c.* 1719, NLI, Ms. 2085; Bell, *Description of the peasantry of Ireland*, pp. 35–6.

82. M. Mascuch, 'Social mobility and middling self-identity: the ethos of British autobiographies, 1600–1750', *Social History*, 20 (1995), pp. 45–61. Cf. H. B. Hancock (ed.), '"Fare weather and good helth [*sic*]": the journal of Caesar Rodeney, 1727–1729', *Delaware History*, 10 (1962), pp. 33–70.

83. Lucas journal, 1739–41, NLI, Ms. 14,101; B. Ó Dálaigh *Ennis in the eighteenth century: portrait of a community* (Dublin, 1995), pp. 31, 48–51; B. Ó Dálaigh, D. A. Cronin and P. Connell (eds), *Irish townlands* (Dublin, 1998), pp. 99–104.

84. GEC, *Complete baronetage*, 6 vols (London, 1900–9), iv, pp. 213–14; Barnard, 'Cork settlers', pp. 342–3; R. C. B. Oliver, 'The Hartstonges and Radnorshire', *Transactions of the Radnorshire Society*, 43 (1973), table 3; 44 (1974), p. 30; N. Peacock, journal, 1740–51, NLI, Ms. 16,091, s.d. 27 Feb. 1742[3], 23 May 1743, 7 Feb. 1743[4], 17 Aug. 1744, 25 Oct. 1744, 27 June 1746, 24 July 1746, 25 July 1747, 30 May 1748, 25 July 1748, 23 July 1751, 13 Aug. 1751.

85. NLI, Ms. 16,084, f. 30; ibid., Ms. 16,091, s.d. 19 April 1742, 5 and 7 Oct. 1742; will of H. Widenham, 2 Aug. 1719, PRONI, D 3196/K/1/2; tripartite indenture, 23 Oct. 1725, ibid., D 3196/K/2/2; S. Lewis, *A topographical dictionary of Ireland*, 2 vols (London, 1837), ii, p. 87.

86. NLI, Ms. 16,091, s.d. 17 Aug. 1745.

87. Ibid., s.d. 1–4 May 1744, 23 May–2 June 1745.

88. Ibid., s.d. 24 Nov. 1745.

89. My identification of Nicholas Peacock as the diarist rests on the mention of his marriage, ibid., s.d. 7 and 9 May 1747, which is confirmed in H. W. Gillman, 'Index to the marriage licence bonds of the diocese of Cork and Ross, Ireland', *JCHAS*, 2nd series, 3 (1896–97), p. 23.

90. NLI, Ms. 16,091, s.d. 25 Dec. 1745. For this usage, see N. Tadmor, 'The concept of the household family in eighteenth-century England', *P & P*, 151 (1996), pp. 111–39.

91. NLI, Ms. 16,091, s.d. 27 March 1745.

92. Ibid., s.d. 5 June 1749, 18 Aug. 1749, 13 Aug. 1751.

93. Ibid., s.d. 25 July 1744.

94. E. Spencer to F. Price, 24 June 1746, NLW, Puleston Ms. 3580E.

95. D. Dickson, 'The demographic implications of Dublin's growth', in R. Lawton and R. Lee (eds), *Urban population development in western Europe from the late eighteenth to the early-twentieth century* (Liverpool, 1989), pp. 178–87; D. Dickson, '"Centres of motion": Irish cities and popular politics', in L. Bergeron and L. M. Cullen (eds), *Culture et pratiques politiques en France et en Irlande XVIe–XVIIIe siècle* (Paris, 1991), p. 106; P. Fagan, 'The population of Dublin in the eighteenth century with particular reference to the proportions of Protestants and

Catholics', in *Eighteenth-Century Ireland*, 6 (1991), pp. 12–56, reprinted in P. Fagan, *Catholics in a Protestant country: the papist constituency in eighteenth-century Dublin* (Dublin, 1998), pp. 31–7, 43–5; H. Murtagh, *Athlone: history and settlement to 1800* (Athlone, 2000), p. 199.

96. J. Barry, 'Introduction', in J. Barry and C. Brooks (eds), *The middling sort of people: culture, society and politics in England, 1550–1800* (Basingstoke, 1994), pp. 1–27; H. R. French, 'Social status, localism and the "middle sort of people" in England, 1620–1750', *P & P*, 166 (2000), pp. 66–99; H. R. French, '"Ingenious and learned gentlemen" – social perceptions and self-fashioning among parish élites in Essex, 1680–1740', *Social History*, 25 (2000), pp. 44–66; J. Kent, 'The rural "middling sort" in early modern England, *circa* 1640–1740: some economic, political and socio-cultural characteristics', *Rural History*, 10 (1999), pp. 19–54; S. Rappaport, *Worlds within worlds: structures of life in sixteenth-century London* (Cambridge, 1989), pp. 162–284; A Shepard, 'Manhood, credit and patriarchy in early modern England, *c.* 1580–1640', *P & P*, 167 (2000), pp. 75–106.

97. For its earlier settlement: M. O'Dowd, *Power, politics and land: early modern Sligo, 1568–1688* (Belfast, 1991).

98. Census of Elphin, 1749, NA, M. 2466, pp. 396–421; H. Hatch to Palmerston, 20 Aug. 1733, 13 Oct. 1737, 5 Dec. 1741, Southampton UL, BR/142/1/3, 6, 11; J. Irwin to same, 13 June 1738, ibid., BR, 140/5; Palmerston to H. Hatch, 19 June 1744, 5 Aug. 1744, ibid., BR 2/9; proposals for Sligo estate, 1768, ibid., BR/142/2/3b.

99. J. Irwin to Palmerston, 30 Jan. 1738[9], Southampton UL, BR, 143/3; W. Henry, 'Natural and typographical history', NA, M. 2533, pp. 364–9; memoir of J. A. Oughton, NAM, 8808.36.1, pp. 46–7, 50.

100. Census of Elphin, NA, M. 2466, pp. 166–75; Murtagh, *Athlone*, pp. 180–9.

101. Belturbet corporation records, s.d. 31 March 1680, formerly NA, M. 3573; Corporation book of Limavady, s.d. 6 June 1668, PRONI, D 663/2; L. A. Clarkson, 'The city of Armagh in the eighteenth century', in A. J. Hughes and W. Nolan (eds), *Armagh: history and society* (Dublin, 2001), pp. 559–82; King, *Carlow, the manor and town*, pp. 46–9, 50–2; H. F. Morris, 'The registers of Waterford cathedral (Church of Ireland) 1655/6–1706/7', *The Irish genealogist*, 6 (1982), pp. 276–7; J. G. A. Prim, 'Documents connected with the city of Kilkenny militia in the seventeenth and eighteenth centuries', *Proceedings and Transactions of the Kilkenny and South-East of Ireland Archaeological Society*, 3 (1854–55), pp. 254–7, 272; W. J. Smyth, 'Towns and town life in mid-seventeenth County Tipperary', *Tipperary Historical Journal* (1991), p. 167. More generally: R. Gillespie, 'Small towns in early modern Ireland', in P. Clark (ed.), *Small towns in Europe* (Cambridge, 1995), pp. 148–65; R. Gillespie, 'The small towns of Ulster, 1600–1700', *Ulster Folklife*, 36 (1990), pp. 23–30; MacCarthy-Morrogh, *The Munster plantation*, pp. 253–60.

102. P. Borsay (ed.), *The eighteenth-century town: a reader in urban history, 1688–1820* (London, 1990); P. Corfield, *The impact of English towns, 1600–1800* (Oxford, 1982); C. B. Estabrook, *Urbane and rustic England: cultural ties and social spheres in the provinces, 1660–1780* (Manchester, 1998); J. Patten, *English towns, 1500–1700* (Folkestone, 1978), pp. 282–90; J. F. Pound, 'The social and trade structure of Norwich, 1525–1575', *P & P*, 34 (1966), pp. 49–69.

103. H. Dingwall, *Late seventeenth-century Edinburgh: a demographic study* (Aldershot, 1994), pp. 36–7, 56, 64, 70, 77–9, 128–62; D. W. Howell, *Patriarchs and parasites: the*

gentry of south-west Wales in the eighteenth century (Cardiff, 1986), pp. 187–90; M. Humphreys, *The crisis of community: Montgomeryshire, 1680–1815* (Cardiff, 1996), pp. 23–7; M. Lynch, 'Continuity and change in urban society, 1500–1700', in R. A. Houston and I. D. Whyte (eds), *Scottish society 1500–1800* (Cambridge, 1989), pp. 85–117; I. D. Whyte, 'Scottish and Irish urbanization in the seventeenth and eighteenth centuries: a comparative perspective', in S. J. Connolly, R. A. Houston and R. J. Morris (eds), *Conflict, identity and economic development: Ireland and Scotland, 1600–1939* (Preston, 1995), pp. 14–28.

104. Barnard, 'The worlds of goods and County Offaly', pp. 371–92; W. H. Crawford, 'The patron or festival of St Kevin at the seven churches, Glendalough, Co. Wicklow, 1813', *Ulster Folklife*, 32 (1986), pp. 38–46; W. H. Crawford, 'Provincial town life in the early nineteenth century: an artist's impressions', in B. P. Kennedy and R. Gillespie (eds), *Ireland: art into history* (Dublin and Niwort, 1994), pp. 43–59; W. H. Crawford, 'A Ballymena business in the late eighteenth century', in J. Gray and W. McCann (eds), *An uncommon bookman: essays in memory of J. R. R. Adams* (Belfast, 1996), pp. 23–33.

105. J. R. Farr, *Hands of honor: artisans their world in Dijon, 1550–1650* (Ithaca, NY, 1988), pp. 161–2; J. Hoppit, 'The use and abuse of credit in eighteenth-century England', in N. McKendrick and R. B. Outhwaite (eds), *Business life and public policy: essays in honour of D. C. Coleman* (Cambridge, 1986), pp. 64–78; J. Hoppit, 'Attitudes to credit in Britain, 1680–1790', *HJ*, 33 (1990), pp. 305–22; C. Muldrew, *The economy of obligation* (Basingstoke, 1998), pp. 123–95. Cf. *A letter from an old merchant to his son* (Dublin, 1753), pp. 13–17.

106. T. Coningsby to C. Fox, Aug. 1690, Dorset CRO, Fox-Strangeways Mss, D/FSI, box 238, bundle 15.

107. T. C. Barnard, *Cromwellian Ireland* (Oxford, 1975), pp. 50–89; T. C. Barnard, 'Settling and unsettling Ireland: the Cromwellian and Williamite revolutions', in J. H. Ohlmeyer (ed.), *Ireland from independence to occupation, 1640–1660* (Cambridge, 1995), pp. 265–91.

108. Will of S. Hayman, proved 12 Jan. 1672[3]; inventory of S. Hayman, 8 July 1673, NLI, D. 13,351–13,422, items 15, 30; inventory of Elizabeth Hayman, 27 March 1677, ibid., item 35; will of J. Hayman, 10 April 1777, ibid., item 46; notebook of George Hayman, 1685–86, Somerset CRO, DD/X/HYN, 1; Barnard, 'Cork settlers', pp. 345–7.

109. For Colles: minute book, 1731–33, s.d. 3 Feb. 1731[2], RDS; Colles correspondence, NA, Prim Ms. 87; D. Dickson, 'Inland city: reflections on eighteenth-century Kilkenny', in W. Nolan and K. Whelan (eds), *Kilkenny: history and society* (Dublin, 1990), pp. 339–40; J. Hill, 'Davis Ducart and Christopher Colles: architects associated with the Custom House at Limerick', *Irish architectural and decorative studies*, 2 (1999), pp. 118–45; J. C. J. Murphy, 'The Kilkenny marble works', *Old Kilkenny Review*, 2 (1949), pp. 14–19. For Knox, J. Irwin to Lord Palmerston, 30 Jan. 1738[9], Southampton UL, BR 143/3; ledger of Kane and La Touche, NLI, Ms. 2785, p. 3; J. A. Oughton, memoir, NAM, Ms. 8808.36.1, p. 50; notebook of J. Thomson, *c.* 1698–1765, NLI, Ms. 3131, p. 213.

110. Cork and Burlington to W. Congreve, 25 Jan. 1693[4], Chatsworth, Lismore Ms. 34/48; W. Waring to S. Waring, 20 Feb. 1696[7], 24 March 1696[7], 27 March 1697, 24 April 1697, 17 and 25 July 1697, Waring Mss, private collection, Co. Down.

111. K. Conolly to J. Bonnell, 23 June 1740, NLI, PC 434; J. Arbuckle to J. Black, 28 Aug. 1737, PRONI, T 1034/4; J. V. Beckett, *Coal and tobacco: the Lowthers and the economic development of West Cumberland, 1660–1760* (Cambridge, 1981), p. 111; E. Hughes, *North-country life in the eighteenth century. II. Cumberland and Westmorland, 1700–1830* (London, 1965), p. 32; cf. C. Muldrew, 'Interpreting the market: the ethics of credit and community relations in early modern England', *Social History*, 18 (1993), pp. 169–82.

112. G. Macartney to W. Barron, 24 Sept. 1662; same to J. Thurston, 26 Sept. 1662; same to D. Arthur, 21 Sept. 1664; same to H. Lavie, 14 June 1679, 23 Nov. 1680, Macartney letter books, now in PRONI.

113. G. Macartney to D. Arthur, 20 Aug. 1664; same to J. Delap, 15 Sept. 1680; same to A. Perry, 13 Aug. 1680, Macartney letter books.

114. G. Macartney to J. Chandler, 9 Nov. 1664; same to R. Huish, 18 Nov. 1665; same to J. Zuille, 2 April 1666; same to P. Lombard, 5 May 1680; same to Sir J. Allen, 23 July 1680, 25 May 1681; same to E. Lumm, 26 Jan. 1680[1], Macartney letter books.

115. G. Macartney to Sir J. Allen, 3 Aug. 1680, Macartney letter book; J. Agnew, *Belfast merchant families in the seventeenth century* (Dublin, 1996), pp. 143–54.

116. W. Waring to R. Lawrence, draft [1674]; R. Lawrence to W. Waring, 5 Feb. 1674[5]; W. Waring to W. Layfield, 5 Sept. 1690; same to S. Waring, 27 March 1697, Waring Mss, private collection, Co. Down; T. Barnard, 'What became of Waring?' in T. Barnard, *Irish Protestant ascents and descents* (Dublin, 2003).

117. W. Hovell to J. Perry, 16 Dec. 1684, Hovell letter book, 1683–88, Farmar Mss, private collection, Dublin.

118. J. Wight, journal, s.d. 2 Dec. 1754, 18 Feb. 1755, Friends' Historical Library, Dublin; *Memoirs of the life, religious experiences and labours in the gospel of James Gough, late of the city of Dublin* (Dublin, 1781), pp. 106–9; R. L. Greaves, *Dublin's Merchant-Quaker: Anthony Sharp and the community of Friends, 1643–1707* (Stanford, 1998), pp. 204–22; *An account of the life of Joseph Pike of Cork* (London, 1837), pp. 59–66; *An account of the life of that ancient servant of Jesus Christ, John Richardson* (London, 1757), pp. 198–9; B. Stevenson, 'The social and economic status of post-Restoration dissenters', in M. Spufford (ed.), *The world of rural dissenters, 1520–1725* (Cambridge, 1995), pp. 342–4; R. T. Vann and D. Eversley, *Friends in life and death: the British and Irish Quakers in the demographic transition* (Cambridge, 1992), p. 162.

119. J. Gill, journal, 1674–1741, Friends' Historical Library, Dublin.

120. G. Bewley to J. Hudson, 'first day of 12th month' 1733; E. Chamberlain to same, 25 Oct. 1733, PRO, C 105/1; S. White to J. Coneley, 15 Nov. 1735, NLI, Ms. 34,025/1.

121. J. Wight, journal, s.d. 23 July 1756, Friends' Historical Library, Dublin.

122. J. Gill, journal, 1674–1741, ibid.; will of J. Gill, 22 Nov. 1741, and inventories, ibid., MM II. L.2, 127–45, 212–214; P. B. Eustace and O. Goodbody (eds), *Quaker records, Dublin. Abstracts of wills* (Dublin, 1957), p. 45.

123. G. Macartney to W. Dickson, 13 Jan. 1665[6]; same to D. Arthur, 12 March 1666[7]; same to T. Papillon, 13 Dec. 1679; same to Sir H. Jervis, 13 Dec. 1679, 7 July 1680; same to E. Harrison, 3 Jan. 1679[80]; same to M. Scott, 7 Aug. 1680, Macartney letter books; W. Hovell to J. Perry, 16 Dec. 1684; same to T. Putland, 17 and 24 Feb. 1684[5], Hovell letter book, private collection, Dublin.

124. G. Macartney to Sir H. Jervis, 15 Sept. 1680; same to Lady Antrim, 18 Jan. 1680[1], Macartney letter book.

125. G. Macartney to J. Sloane, 12 May 1679, 30 April 1679, 27 April 1681; same to Sir J. Allen, 15 Jan. 1680[1], ibid.
126. W. Hovell to T. Putland, 24 Aug. 1686, Hovell letter book.
127. W. Hovell to J. Houblon, 4 Aug. 1685, 26 May 1685; same to T. Putland, 29 Oct. 1686, ibid.
128. W. Hovell to T. Putland, 29 May 1685, ibid.
129. P. Delany, *Twenty sermons on social duties and their opposite vices* (London, 1747), p. 255. *Observations on the conduct of Messrs. W[illco]cks and D[awson], late bankers of the city of Dublin* (Dublin, [1755]), p. 5. See, too: W. Leathes to J. Mussenden, 18 May 1720, Suffolk CRO, Ipswich, de Mussenden Leathes Mss, HA 403/1/5, 88; L. Biggar to D. Mussenden, 13 March 1756, PRONI, D 354/1045; F. Trench to S. Bagshawe, 9 Sept. 1758, JRL, B 2/3/805.
130. *The Ouzel Galley: rules and regulations with lists of members* (Dublin, 1859), pp. 7–8, 17–21; L. M. Cullen, *Princes and pirates: the Dublin Chamber of Commerce, 1783–1983* (Dublin, 1983), pp. 25–33.
131. A. Hill to D. Mussenden, 22 March 1757, 1 Feb. 1759, PRONI, D 354/334, 348; papers relating to D. Mussenden, 1 March 1759, ibid., D 354/1010, 1016; *The conduct of Messrs. Daniel Mussenden, James Adair, and Thomas Bateson . . . impartially examined* (n.p., 1759), pp. 4, 19; J. Agnew (ed.), *Funeral register of the First Presbyterian Church of Belfast, 1712–1736* (Belfast, 1995), p. 20.
132. G. Johnston to D. Mussenden, 2 Aug. 1755, 7 Nov. 1757, 4 Jan. 1758, PRONI, D 354/680, 750, 751; W. Benson to same, 16 April 1755, 10 and 29 April 1756, ibid., 873, 895, 1047; Marsden and Benson to same, 10 and 17 June 1756, 7 Sept. 1756, ibid., 908, 909, 922; W. Richardson to same, 24 March 1763, ibid., 597; lease of 2 Nov. 1763, ibid., 351; P. Francis, *Irish Delftware: an illustrated history* (London, 2000), pp. 153, 169–70; T. M. Truxes (ed.), *Letter book of Greg and Cunningham, 1756–57. Merchants of New York and Belfast*, Records of social and economic history, British Academy, new series, 28 (Oxford, 2001), pp. 20, 107.
133. Francis, *Irish Delftware*, pp. 169–70.
134. N. Delacherois to D. Delacherois, 20 March 1767, NAM, 7805–63.
135. J. Wight, journal, s.d. 13 July 1754, Friends' Historical Library, Dublin; 'Prerogative will of Edward Hoare, 1709', *Journal of the Irish Memorials Association*, 12 (1926–31), pp. 159–61; 'Letters of James H. Watmough to his wife, 1785', *Pennsylvania Magazine of History and Biography*, 29 (1905), pp. 31–5.
136. D. Mussenden to H. Mussenden, 16 Jan. 1743[4], 9 Dec. 1754, 17 June 1758, Suffolk CRO, HA 403/1/11, 21, 22, 28; draft will of D. Mussenden, 18 June 1756, PRONI, D 354/166A.
137. Orrery to Essex, 4 June 1672, BL, Stowe Ms., printed in O. Airy (ed.), *Essex papers 1672–79*, Camden Society (London, 1890), p. 7; cf. Sir G. Rawdon to Lord Conway, 30 Aug. 1680, PRO, SP 63/339, 128, quoted in Agnew, *Belfast merchant families*, p. xvii, n. 1.
138. Lawrence, *The interest of Ireland*, i, p. 7.
139. W. Waring to S. Waring, 7 Aug. 1697, private collection, Co. Down; F. Bellew to Lord Raby, 28 June 1729, BL, Add. Ms. 22,228, f. 47.
140. E. Spencer to Mrs A. Price, 25 Sept. 1749, NLW, Puleston Ms. 3580E.
141. E. Malone to E. Malone, 16 Sept. 1701, Brabazon Mss, private collection, London, box III.
142. W. Hovell to T. Putland, 17 Nov. 1685, Hovell letter book, 1683–88, Farmar Mss, private collection, Dublin.

143. L. M. Cullen, *Anglo-Irish trade, 1660–1800* (Manchester, 1968), p. 78; D. Dickson, 'The place of Dublin in the eighteenth-century Irish economy', in T. M. Devine and D. Dickson (eds), *Ireland and Scotland, 1600–1850. Parallels and contrasts in economic and social development* (Edinburgh, 1983), pp. 179, 190, n. 9.

144. J. Wright to T. Proby, 22 and 30 Oct. 1716; T. Proby to J. Wright, 22 Oct. 1716, minute book of Barber Surgeons' Company, TCD, Ms. 1447/8/1, ff. 159v–60v, 161; ibid., s.d. 12 and 19 Oct. 1741, f. 78v.

145. Minute book, Court of D'Oyer Hundred, Cork, 1656–1729, NUI, Cork, Boole Library, Ms. U/127; charters, Youghal guilds, 1656, Cork Archives Institute, Youghal corporation records, U/138, G1–3; minute book, corporation of Limerick, BL, Add. Ms. 19,859, f. 74; freedom of nine Waterford guilds granted to A. Mason, 18 and 19 Oct. 1738, Dromana, Villiers-Stuart Mss, T 3131/S/13; R. Day (ed.), 'Cooke's memoirs of Youghal, 1749', *JCHAS*, 2nd series, 9 (1903), p. 42; E. M. Fahy, 'The Cork Goldsmiths' Company, 1657', *JCHAS*, 58 (1953), p. 33; T. Gogarty (ed.), *Council book of the corporation of Drogheda. I. 1649–1734* (Drogheda, 1915), pp. 46, 52; P. Higgins, 'Ancient guilds or fraternities of the city of Waterford', *Journal of the Waterford and South East of Ireland Archaeological Society*, 5 (1899), p. 161; Mulcahy, *Kinsale*, v, p. 10.

146. For the range of apprenticeship fees in mid-eighteenth-century England, from £300 for a merchant and banker to £10 for a card-maker, see J. Lane, 'The role of apprenticeship in eighteenth-century medical education in England', in W. F. Bynum and R. Porter (eds), *William Hunter and the eighteenth-century medical world* (Cambridge, 1985), pp. 68–9, 73; Rappaport, *Worlds within worlds*, pp. 232–8, 291–322.

147. N. Plunkett to H. Plunkett, 5 Jan. 1713[14], NA, 1075/30/1.

148. J. H. Andrews, *Plantation acres: an historical study of the Irish land surveyor* (Belfast, 1985), pp. 224–66.

149. E. Hewetson to Lord Digby, Dorset CRO, DD/SHC, 3C/81; Revd J. Smythe to W. Smythe, 7 May 1728, NLI, PC 449; Legg, *Synge Letters*, pp. 121, 337, 351; G. N. Nuttall-Smith, *The chronicles of a Puritan family in Ireland [Smith (formerly) of Glasshouse]* (Oxford, 1923), pp. 38, 41–3.

150. M. Combe to W. Leathes, 22 June 1714, Suffolk CRO, HA, 403/1/7/61.

151. John Caldwell to S. Bagshawe, 15 Aug. 1751, JRL, B 2/3/409; J. B. Cunningham, 'The port of Ballyshannon', *Donegal Annual*, 52 (2000), pp. 9–10; Cullen, *Princes and pirates*, p. 28.

152. H. Caldwell to S. Bagshawe, 2 May 1752, 23 Jan. 1752, JRL, B/2/3/341, 342.

153. S. Bagshawe to H. Caldwell, 17 March 1753, H. Caldwell to S. Bagshawe, 3 April 1753, ibid., B 2/3/343, 344.

154. S. Bagshawe to H. Caldwell, 17 March 1753, H. Caldwell to S. Bagshawe, 3 April 1753, ibid., B 2/3/343, 344; Sir J. Caldwell to same, 1 Oct. 1755, 20 July 1757, ibid., B 2/3/389, 345; J. B. Cunningham, *A history of Castle Caldwell and its families* (Monaghan, c. 1980), pp. 119–27.

155. Rappaport, *Worlds within worlds*, pp. 302–3.

156. The number of guilds was raised to 25 with the establishment in 1747 of the Apothecaries' Company: M. Clark and R. Refaussé (eds), *Directory of historic Dublin guilds* (Dublin, 1993); J. R. Hill, *From patriots to unionists: Dublin civic politics and Irish protestant patriotism 1660–1840* (Oxford, 1997), pp. 389–90.

157. Mulcahy, *Kinsale*, v, pp. 10–11.

158. A. P. W. Malcomson, ' "The parliamentary traffic of this country" ', in Bartlett and

Hayton (eds), _Penal age and golden era_, pp. 137–61; Barnard, 'Considering the inconsiderable', pp. 107–27.

159. _An alphabetical list of the freemen and freeholders of the city of Dublin who polled at the election for members of parliament . . . 1749_ (Dublin, 1750).

160. 'A Briton', _The history of the Dublin election in the year 1749_ (London, 1753), p. 9.

161. Waterford corporation book, 1700–27, Waterford Municipal Archives, s.d. 10 Feb. 1708[9], 25 April 1710, 27 June 1711, 3 April 1712, 28 Feb. 1714[15], 2 Oct. 1715; K. Milne, 'The corporation of Waterford in the eighteenth century', in W. Nolan and T. P. Power (eds), _Waterford: history and society_ (Dublin, 1992), p. 331.

162. Barnard, 'The cultures of Irish towns', pp. 195–222; cf. J. Barry, 'Provincial town culture, 1640–1780: urbane or civic?' in J. Pittock and A. Wear (eds), _Interpretation and cultural history_ (Basingstoke, 1991), pp. 199–223; J. Barry, 'Civility and civic culture in early modern England: the meanings of urban freedom', in P. Burke, B. Harrison and P. Slack (eds), _Civil histories: essays presented to Sir Keith Thomas_ (Oxford, 2000), pp. 181–96; R. Sweet, 'Freemen and independence in English borough politics, c. 1770–1830', _P & P_, 161 (1998), pp. 84–115.

163. Bail books, Dublin Tholsel Courts, 1651–52, 1693–94, 1699–1700, Dublin City Archives, C1/J/4/1–3; M. Clark (ed.), 'Roll of members of the Dublin Guild of Carpenters, 1656', _Irish Genealogist_, 8 (1992), p. 334.

164. Bail books, Dublin Tholsel courts, 1651–52, 1693–94, 1699–1700, Dublin City Archives, C1/J/4/1–3; register of apprentices, King's Hospital, Palmerston, Co. Dublin, Ms. 181; M. Clark (ed.), 'List of principal inhabitants of the City of Dublin, 1684', _Irish Genealogist_, 8 (1990), pp. 49–57.

165. _An alphabetical list of the freemen and freeholders of the city of Dublin . . . 1749._

166. Transcribed documents of the Holy Trinity or Merchants' Guild, 1438–1824, s.d. 18 Jan. 1663[4], 28 April 1679, Dublin Public Library, Gilbert Ms. 78.

167. Lists of brethren, Weavers' Company, 1693–1722, RSAI; minute book, Weavers' Company, 1734–60, s.d. 1 July 1734, RSAI.

168. Minute book, Barber Surgeons' Company, 1703–57, s.d. 13 July 1734, TCD, Ms. 1447/8/1, f. 67v.

169. Rappaport, _Worlds within worlds_, pp. 238–84.

170. Minute book, Weavers' Company, 1734–60, s.d. 2 Oct. 1749, RSAI.

171. Minute book, Limerick Masons, 1747–57, Limerick Civic Museum; minute book of Barber Surgeons, 1703–57, s.d. 30 Aug. 1703, 16 July 1711, 20 Feb. 1712[13], 28 Feb. 1714[15], 13 Oct. 1718, 24 Nov. 1720, 20 Oct. 1723, 23 April 1750, 7 Jan. 1757, TCD, Ms. 1447/8/1, ff. 5v, 7v, 13–14, 30, 35, 40v, 111v, 153v, 164v; Masters' accounts, Weavers' Company, 1691–1714, RSAI.

172. Ledger labelled, 'Quarter Brothers, no. 10', Weavers' Company, ibid.

173. Minute book, 1734–60, Weavers' Company, ibid.

174. Petition on behalf of the 'poor societies belonging to the clothing trade' from W. Dames to Abp. W. King, 6 June 1728, Marsh's Library, Ms. Z3.1.1, clxiv; case of the undertakers and journeymen broad cloth weavers to Abp. W. King, ibid., clxv; E.B., _The defence of the whole society of wool-combers of the city and liberties of the city of Corke, upon their turn-out_ (Cork, 1722); H. N[elson], _A poem in honour of the antient and loyal society of the journey-men-taylors, who are to dine at the King's Inns, on Monday the 25th inst., July; 1726_ (Dublin, [1726]); H. Nelson, _Poem on the procession of journeymen tailors, July the 28th, MDCCXXIX_ ([Dublin, 1729]); H. Nelson, _A poem in praise of the loyal and charitable society of journeymen tailors, who are to dine at the King's Inns, this present Monday the 28th of July 1729_ (Dublin,

[1729]); *CARD*, xi, pp. 496–8; I. W. Archer, *The pursuit of stability: social relations in Elizabethan London* (Cambridge, 1991), pp. 100–48; Rappaport, *Worlds within worlds*, pp. 238–42; J. Ward, *Metropolitan communities: trade guilds, identity and change in early modern London* (Stanford, 1997), pp. 125–43.

175. W. Hovell to J. Houblon, 4 Jan. 1683[4], Hovell letter book, 1683–88, Farmar Mss, private collection, Dublin.

176. Minute book, 1734–60, Weavers' Company, s.d. 1 April 1745, 1 May 1747, 1 April 1748, 2 July 1753, 1 Oct 1753, RSAI.

177. Calendar of presentments, Co. Dublin, 12–18 May 1750, 27 July 1752, NA; minute book, 1734–60, Weavers' Company, s.d. 1 Oct. 1753; *To the honourable committee appointed to enquire into the causes of the disputes between masters and journeymen, the reply of the journeymen stocking-makers of the city of Dublin . . . 18ᵗʰ of December, 1749* ([Dublin, 1749]); *The case of the journeymen sheermen of the city of Dublin briefly and impartially stated*, in PRONI, D. 562/1338; *By order of the Right Honourable Robert Ross, Lord Mayor of the City of Dublin* (Dublin, 1749), ibid., D 562/1328; A.W., *The clothier's letter to the inhabitants of the Liberties* (Dublin, 1759); below, pp. 284–6.

178. Bp. J. Evans to Abp. W. Wake, 8 April [1721], Christ Church, Wake Mss, 13/242; Legg, *Synge Letters*, p. 184.

179. Vestry book, St Catherine's, Dublin, 1693–1730, s.d. 6 Jan. 1718[19], 19 Jan. 1724[5], RCB, P. 117/5/1.2, opening 362.

180. Masters' accounts, 1691–1714, Weavers' Company, RSAI; *The memorial of the master clothiers, whose names are hereunto subscribed* in PRONI, D 562/1337.

181. R. Dudley, (ed.), 'The Cheney letters, 1682–1685', *Irish Economic and Social History*, 23 (1996), pp. 107, 110; O. Goodbody, 'Anthony Sharp, wool merchant, 1643 to 1707, and the Quaker Community in Dublin', *Journal of the Friends' Historical Society*, 48 (1958), pp. 36–50; Greaves, *Dublin's Merchant-Quaker*, p. 13.

182. W. Hovell to J. Houblon, 8 Nov. 1684, 6 Jan. 1684[5], 9 Oct. 1685, Farmar Mss, private collection, Dublin; *Writings of Petty*, i, p. 146, n. 1.

183. W. Alloway letter book, from 1695, Somerset CRO, DD DN/463, ff. 76–8, 81, 87, 89, 92, 110, 152, 157, 161–3, 167–70, 173–4, 180–2, 188, 194, 196, 205; cf. D. Dickson, 'Huguenots in the urban economy of eighteenth-century Dublin and Cork' in C. E. J. Caldicott, H. Gough and J. P. Pittion (eds), *The Huguenots and Ireland: anatomy of an emigration* (Dun Laoghaire, 1987), pp. 330–1.

184. D. Johnson, account book, from 1669, Birr Castle, Ms. A/16; Thrift list of freemen, Dublin City Archives; *CARD*, iv, pp. 20–1.

185. Will of John Barlow, 8 Feb. 1688[9], Marsh's Library, Dublin, Ms. Z2.1.7, 61.

186. Will of George Craford, 2 April 1690, ibid., Ms. Z2.1.7, 78.

187. *An elegy on the much lamented death of Alderman Ford* ([Dublin, 1725]).

188. Inventory of W. Stowell, 1701, NA, Chancery pleadings, unidentified material, box 14; Proctors' accounts, Christ Church, Dublin, nos. 23, 26, RCB, C. 6/1/15.1.

189. Petition of John Molyneux to Lords Justice, [?1720s], Marsh's Library, Ms. Z3.1.1, xxxii; vestry book, St Catherine's, Dublin, 1693–1730, s.d. 19 April 1720, accounts, 1720, 1724, RCB, P. 117/5/1.2.

190. Dudley, 'Dublin's parishes', ii, pp. 252–3; Thrift index of freemen, Dublin City Archives, s.v. Daniel Molyneux, freeman, merchants' company, 1722; grand jury list, city of Dublin, 13 April 1743, NA, Crown entry books.

191. Abp. W. King, account book, s.d. April 1723, TCD, Ms. 751/3, f. 149; bills of D. and W. Molyneux, 29 March 1743, 12 Dec. 1743, Castletown deposit, box 52, IAA.

192. J. Crofton to W. Smythe, 6 Oct. 1731, NLI, PC 436; Census of Elphin, 1749, NA, M 2466, f. 115; H. T. Crofton, *Crofton Memoirs* (York, 1911), p. 114. He may be the John Crofton, freeman of Dublin, 1736, via Smiths' Company, Thrift index of freemen, Dublin City Archives.

193. Belturbet municipal records, apprenticeship indenture, 12 Sept. 1699, s.d. 12 Dec. 1704, accounts for 1711, NA, M. 3572; G. Fennell, *A list of Irish watch and clock makers* (Dublin, 1963), p. 31.

194. Thrift index of Dublin freemen, Dublin City Archives, s.v. George Putland, smith (1649); Thomas Putland, smith (1671); W. Hovell to J. Houblon, 15 Dec. 1685, Hovell letter book, Farmar Mss, private collection, Dublin.

195. Thrift index of Dublin freemen, Dublin City Archives, s.v. Thomas Putland, merchant (1714); John Putland 'esquire', merchant (1762); George Putland, 'esquire', merchant (1769); *Al. Dubl.*, p. 687; *An alphabetical list of the freemen and freeholders of the city of Dublin . . . 1749*, p. 84; L. Clare, 'The Putland family of Dublin and Bray', *Dublin Historical Record*, 54 (2001), pp. 183–209; Hill, *From patriots to unionists*, p. 179, n. 67; *John Putland and others, appellants . . . to be heard at the Bar of the House of Lords . . . third day of April.1725* [Dublin, 1725]; J. Putland and T. Debrisay, *To the honourable the knights, citizens and burgesses in parliament assembled* [Dublin, 1755].

196. Monck Mason collections, ii, part 3, Dublin Public Library, Gilbert Ms. 67, p. 544; minute book, Dublin Goldsmiths' Company, 1731–58, pp. 60, 125, 127, 171, 220–1, 323, Assay Office, Dublin Castle; masters' accounts, 1691–1714, Weavers' Company, s.d. 1701–2, 5 Aug. 1707, RSAI; extracts from records of the Tailors' Guild, 1296–1723, Dublin Public Library, Gilbert Ms. 80, pp. 82, 86, 87; minute book, Dublin Barber Surgeons' Company, 1703–57, TCD, Ms. 1447/8/1, ff. 58, 67v–68, 72v, Monck Mason, collections on Dublin, NA, M. 2549, pp. 7–9, 123–6; minute book, Limerick Masons' Guild, 1747–57, s.d. 8 Oct. 1753, 24 May 1755, Limerick City Museum; Barnard, 'Cultures of Irish towns', pp. 195–222; R. Caulfield (ed.), *The council book of the corporation of Kinsale* (Guildford, 1879), p. 214; M. Lenihan, *Limerick: its history and antiquities* (Dublin, 1866), pp. 355–6.

197. Minute book, corporation of Kilkenny, 1690–1717, s.d. 29 Sept. 1690, 7 Feb. 1695[6], 4 June 1697, 1 Oct. 1697, 1 Nov. 1697, 23 Feb. 1702[3]; court book, corporation of Kilmallock, loose paper at front, 1699, NLI, Ms. 9451, pp. 8, 21, 45.

198. Minute book, Guild of St Anne, s.d. 1671–72, 26 July 1694, 13 Aug. 1700, 27 July 1703, 27 July 1708, RIA, Ms. 12 D 1, pp. 435, 600, 619, 620, 621; account book, Guild of St Anne, *passim*, ibid., Ms. 12 P. 1; minute book, 1734–60, Weavers' Company, s.d. 1 April 1740, RSAI; P. McNally, *Parties, patriots and undertakers: parliamentary politics in early Hanoverian Ireland* (Dublin, 1997), p. 24; Nelson, *A poem in praise of the loyal and charitable society of journeymen tailors*; H.N., *A poem in honour of the antient and loyal society of journey-men-taylors*.

199. Council book, corporation of Kilkenny, 1656–86, s.d. 8 Oct. 1662, 17 Jan. 1680[1]; ibid., 1690–1717, s.d. 29 Sept. 1690, 10 Jan. 1700[1], 27 Jan. 1715[16].

200. Minute book, 1734–60, Weavers' Company, s.d. 2 July 1750, RSAI.

201. Minute book, Dublin Florists' Company, 1747–67, s.d. 17 June 1763, RIA, Ms. 24 E 374; transcripts of Tailors' Guild documents, 1296–1753, Dublin Public Libraries, Gilbert Ms. 80. pp. 85, 91; accounts, 1711–12, 1713–14, 1714–15, Masters' accounts, 1691–1714, Weavers' Company, RSAI.

202. Transcripts from St Luke's Guild of Cutlers, Stainers, Painters and Stationers, s.d. 15 April 1712, 8 Aug. 1730, Dublin Public Library, Gilbert Ms. 81, pp. 32, 35; transcripts of Merchants' Guild documents, 1296–1753, s.d. 16 July 1683, 14 Jan. 1683[4], 4 July 1684, 12 Oct. 1691, pp. 166, 167, 169, 171; council book, corporation of Kilkenny, 1690–1717, s.d. 20 June 1701.

203. Masters' accounts, Weavers' Company, s.d. 17 Feb. 1703[4], RSAI; minute book, Barber Surgeons' Company, 1703–57, s.d. 23 July 1750, TCD, Ms. 1447/8/1, f. 113v.

204. Barnard, 'Settling and unsettling Ireland', pp. 274–6.

205. Corporation book, Waterford, 1700–27, s.d. 4 Oct. 1704, 26 Feb. 1705[6], 8 Dec. 1707, 25 April 1710, 22 Oct. 1715, 29 Sept. 1716, 21 Sept. 1717, Waterford Municipal Archives; M. Fitzgerald to Lord Grandison, 22 Aug. 1729, 14 Sept. 1729, Villiers-Stuart Mss, Dromana, Co. Waterford, T 3131/C5/45 and 46; Dickson, 'Economic history of the Cork region', ii, pp. 512–18; Day (ed.), 'Cooke's memoirs of Youghal, 1749', p. 63; Mulcahy, *Kinsale*, ii, p. 74; iii, p. 88; vi, p. 23.

206. D. Dickson 'Catholics and trade in eighteenth-century Ireland: an old debate revisited', in Power and Whelan (eds), *Endurance and emergence: Catholics in Ireland in the eighteenth century*, pp. 85–100.

207. E. Malone to E. Malone, 16 Sept. 1701, private collection, Brabazon Mss, box III; Conran pedigree, GO, Dublin, Ms. 169, p. 290; C. Lennon, *The lords of Dublin in the age of reformation* (Dublin, 1989), p. 239.

208. D. W. Hayton, 'Exclusion, conformity, and parliamentary representation: the impact of the sacramental test on Irish dissenting politics', in K. Herlihy (ed.), *The politics of Irish dissent* (Dublin, 1997), pp. 52–73.

209. Dickson, 'Huguenots in the urban economy', pp. 330–1.

210. *An alphabetical list of the freemen and freeholders of the city of Dublin; A letter to the freemen and freeholders of the city of Dublin, who are Protestants of the Church of Ireland as by law established* (n.p, [?1728]).

211. Vestry book, Monasterosis, RCB, P. 484/5.1, p. 52; D. M. Beaumont, 'The gentry of the King's and Queen's Counties: Protestant landed society, 1690–1760', unpublished Ph.D. thesis, TCD, 2 vols (1999), ii, pp. 43–4, figure 10.

212. W[alter] H[arris], *Remarks on the affairs* (London, 1691), p. 32.

213. C. Bagshawe to S. Bagshawe, 23 Sept. 1755, JRL, B 2/3/25; F. Trench to same, 9 Feb. 1758, ibid., B 2/3/802; Bp. J. Browne to same, 29 April 1758, ibid., B 2/3/559; E. Caldwell to same, 29 June 1758, ibid., 2/3/318; Delany, *Autobiography*, 1st series, iii, p. 281.

214. Sir S. Cooke to S. Bagshawe, 12 Jan. 1753 *recté* 1754, 31 July 1755, JRL, B 2/3/429, 434; S. Bagshawe to Sir S. Cooke, 1 Aug. 1757, ibid, B 2/3/437; C. Bagshawe to same, 23 Sept. 1755, ibid, B 2/3/25; F. Trench to same, 9 Feb. 1758, ibid, B 2/3/802.

215. E. T. Martin (ed.), *The Ash Mss., written in the year 1735, by Lieut.-Col. Thomas Ash* (Belfast, 1890).

216. J. Owen to Mrs Wynne, 29 June 1722, NLW, Bodewyrd letters, 171; K. Conolly to J. Bonnell, 26 July 1739, NLI, PC 434.

217. 'The autobiography of Pole Cosby, of Stradbally, Queen's County, 1703–1737(?)', *Journal of the County Kildare Archaeological and Historical Society*, 5 (1906–8), pp. 317–24, 423–30; S. J. Connolly, *Religion, law and power: the making of Protestant Ireland, 1660–1760* (Oxford, 1992), pp. 62–5; Legg, *Synge Letters*, p. 415.

218. P. Delany, *Sixteen discourses upon doctrines and duties* (London, 1754), p. 235.

219. *An address to the people of England and Ireland . . . more particularly adapted to the electors of the County of Limerick* (Dublin, 1783), pp. v, 13, quoted in S. Small, 'Republicanism, patriotism and radicalism: political thought in Ireland, 1776–1798', unpublished Oxford D. Phil. thesis, (1998), p. 150.

220. J. R. Hill, 'Corporate values in Hanoverian Dublin and Edinburgh', in S. J. Connolly, R. A. Houston and R. J. Morris (eds), *Conflict, identity and economic development: Ireland and Scotland, 1600–1939* (Preston, 1995), pp. 114–24.

221. Capt. Cobbe, 16 Dec. 1738, Physico-Historical Society papers, Armagh Public Library, G. II 23.

222. For views of the distinctive ethos: P. Borsay, *The English urban renaissance* (Oxford, 1989); P. Gauci, *The politics of trade: the overseas merchant in state and society, 1660–1720* (Oxford, 2001); R. Grassby, *The business community of seventeenth-century England* (Cambridge, 1995). An admiration for the 'free state' of Hamburg among Protestants from Ireland is apparent in R. Black, travel journal, 1727, PRONI, T 1073/2. More generally, M. Heinemann, *Patriots and paupers: Hamburg, 1712–1830* (New York and Oxford, 1990), pp. 3–73; T. Barnard, *The Grand Figure: material worlds of Ireland, 1641–1770* (forthcoming), ch. 10.

223. *Faulkner's Dublin Journal*, 10–14 Oct. 1727; *The Censor*, 22 (Dublin, 21–28 Oct. 1749).

224. Stacpoole, *Some short historical anecdotes*, part i, pp. 19, 83.

225. J. Barry, 'Introduction', in Barry and Brooks (eds), *The middling sort of people*, pp. 20–5; French, '"Ingenious and learned gentlemen"', pp. 44–66; French, 'Social status, localism and the "middle sort of people"', pp. 66–98; Kent, 'The rural "middling sort" in early modern England', pp. 19–43; Mascuch, 'Social mobility and middling self-identity', pp. 45–61.

226. R. Fitzpatrick, account book, NLI, Ms. 3000, p. 62; Abp. W. King, account book, 1700–12, TCD, Ms. 751/2, ff. 80–100; bills of 1726, 4 Oct. 1727, 10 Aug. 1728, 8 Oct. 1739, 1742, NLI, Mss 11,468; 11,467; M. Clark, 'Dublin piped water accounts, 1704/5', *Irish Genealogist*, 9 (1994), p. 86.

227. C. Cox, 'Women and business in eighteenth-century Dublin: a case study', in B. Whelan (ed.), *Women and paid work in Ireland, 1500–1930* (Dublin, 2000), pp. 30–43; M. Pollard, *A dictionary of the members of the Dublin book trade* (London, 2000), pp. 134–6, 279–80.

228. Barnard, 'Cork settlers', p. 350.

229. Green Coat School minute book, St Ann's Church, Cork; accounts of St John's, Dublin, RCB, P. 328/12.1.

230. P. Earle, 'The female labour market in London in the late seventeenth and early eighteenth-centuries', *Economic History Review*, 2nd series, 42 (1989), pp. 328–53; M. R. Hunt, *The middling sort: commerce, gender and the family in England, 1680–1780* (Berkeley, Los Angeles and London, 1996), pp. 73–100, 125–46; M. Prior, 'Women and the urban economy', in M. Prior (ed.), *Women in English society, 1500–1800* (London, 1985), pp. 93–117.

231. Minute book, Guild of St Anne's, RIA, Ms. 12 D 1.

232. Barnard, *The Grand Figure*, ch. 11; P. Borsay, '"All the town's a stage": urban ritual and ceremony, 1660–1800, in P. Clark (ed.), *Country towns in pre-industrial England* (Leicester, 1981), pp. 228–58; N. Rogers, *Crowds, culture and politics in Georgian Britain* (Oxford, 1998), pp. 21–57, 216–44; N. Rogers, 'Crowds and political festival in Georgian England', in T. Harris (ed.), *The politics of the excluded, c. 1500–1800* (Basingstoke, 2001), pp. 233–64.

233. Bursars' accounts, 1685–86, TCD, MUN, P/4/2/4, P/4/3/7 and 8; *CARD*, v, p. 513.

234. D. Conner to Lord Burlington, 16 April 1736, Chatsworth, Devonshire Letters, 1720–36, 238.0.

235. Somerset R. Lowry-Corry, earl of Belmore, *The history of two Ulster manors of Finagh in the County of Tyrone and Coole, otherwise Manor Atkinson, in the county of Fermanagh* (London and Dublin, 1881), pp. 163, 178.

236. *CARD*, vi, pp. 132, 275, 342, 372, 500–1.

237. Ormonde to Lords Justice, 23 May 1713, Bodleian, Ms. Eng. Hist. C. 42/52.

238. Margaret Humphrey to Devonshire, 25 Nov. 1739; same to unknown, 8 Nov. 1749, C. Litton Falkiner papers, RIA, Ms. 12 F 50; accounts of Dorset and Devonshire, 1730–41, s.d. 30 Dec. 1734, Dublin Public Library, Gilbert Ms. 199; Calendar of departmental correspondence, 1741–59, s.d. 24 Dec. 1744, NA.

239. Lord Cork and Burlington to W. Congreve, 28 Aug. 1697, 2 Oct. 1697, Chatsworth, Lismore Ms. 34/135, 137.

240. W. Colles to M. Archdale, 17 April 1756, NA, Prim Ms. 87; will of R. Edgeworth, 20 March 1770, ibid., T. 5555.

241. Abp. W. King to Mrs H. Ormsby, 24 June 1710, 2 Sept. 1710, 10 Feb. 1710[11], TCD, Ms. 2531, pp. 181, 196, 312.

242. Abp. W. King to B. Foley, 2 Sept. 1710, 2 Jan. 1710[11], ibid., Ms. 2531, pp. 196–7, 302.

243. Abp. W. King to B. Foley, 8 May 1711, ibid., Ms. 2531, p. 334.

244. Poor book, St Michan's, Dublin, 1723–34, RCB, P. 276/8.1, pp. 5, 6, 52, 262.

245. Ibid., p. 11.

246. Ibid., pp. 57, 58, 68, 101.

247. S. Nash, 'Prostitution and charity: the Magdalen Hospital: a case study', *Journal of Social History*, 17 (1983–84), pp. 617–28.

248. Register of Magdalen Asylum, from 1766, nos. 2, 16, 19, 22, 24, 26, 29, 83, 94, 100, RCB, Ms. 551/1/1.

249. Deposition of M. Purdon, NLI, PC 438/7; M. Smith to F. Price, 13 March 1738[9], NLW, Puleston Mss 3579E/173.

10. The Lower People

1. R. Cox to E. Southwell, 24 Oct. 1706, BL, Add. Ms. 38,154, f. 86v; Roger Boyle, earl of Orrery, *An answer to a scandalous letter lately printed and subscribed by Peter Walsh* (London, 1662), p. 65; I. Mann, *A sermon preached at Christ Church, Dublin, on the 15th of May 1774 before . . . Earl Harcourt, president; and the rest of the Incorporated Society of Dublin* (Dublin, 1775), p. 17; D. W. Hayton, 'Ireland and the English ministers, 1707–16', unpublished D. Phil., University of Oxford (1975), p. 23. The passage is from Joshua, 9: 21, 23. It was applied to attorneys in the context of the 'commonwealth of law'. Alexander the Coppersmith, *Remarks upon the religion, trade, government, police, customs, manners and maladys of the city of Cork* (Cork, 1737), p. 40. For another satirical application, 'Ant. Constitution', *A short and easy method of reducing the exorbitant pride and arrogance of the city of Dublin* (London, 1748), p. 35. Archbishop King credited the Catholics in James II's time with wishing to reduce Protestants to this condition. W. King, *State of the Protestants of Ireland under the late King James's government* (London, 1691), p. 18.

2. Autobiography of J. Traill, PRONI, D 1460/1; list of property owners in Ulster, *c.*1720, RIA, Ms. 24 K 19.

3. Legg, *Synge Letters*, p. 447.

4. T. C. Barnard, 'Planters and policies in Cromwellian Ireland', *P & P*, 61 (1973), pp. 32–69; P. C. Mancall, 'Native Americans and Europeans in English America, 1500–1700', in N. P. Canny (ed.), *The origins of empire* (Oxford, 1998), pp. 328–50; T. W. Moody, 'The treatment of the native population under the scheme for the plantation of Ulster', *IHS*, 1 (1939), pp. 59–63.

5. V. Gookin, *The great case of transplantation in Ireland discussed* (London, 1655), p. 17.

6. *Writings of Petty*, i, 146, and n.1.

7. *Reasons humbly offered for passing heads of a bill for the building of new-churches in the city of Dublin, &c.* ([Dublin,?1725]), p. 2.

8. Ormond to Sir R. Southwell, 19 Nov. 1678, V & A, Ormonde Mss, 2, f. 22; Sir R. Cox to W. Harris, 23 April 1741, papers of the Physico-Historical Society, Armagh Public Library; *Seasonable advice to Protestants*, 2nd edn (Cork, 1745), p. 25.

9. *Abstract of the number of Protestant and Popish families in the several counties and provinces of Ireland* (Dublin, 1736); S. J. Connolly, *Religion, law and power: the making of Protestant Ireland, 1660–1760* (Oxford, 1992), p. 146.

10. L. M. Cullen, 'Catholics under the penal laws', *Eighteenth-Century Ireland*, 1 (1986), pp. 23–36; L. M. Cullen, 'Catholic social classes under the penal laws', in T. P. Power and K. Whelan (eds), *Endurance and emergence: Catholics in Ireland in the eighteenth century* (Dublin, 1990), pp. 57–84; K. Whelan, 'An underground gentry? Catholic middlemen in eighteenth-century Ireland', *Eighteenth-Century Ireland*, 10 (1995), pp. 7–68, reprinted in K. Whelan, *The tree of liberty* (Cork, 1996).

11. *Writings of Petty*, i, pp. 141–4.

12. D. Dickson, C. Ó Gráda and S. Daultrey, 'Hearth tax, household size and Irish population change, 1672–1821', *PRIA*, 82, sect. C (1982), pp. 125–55.

13. C. O'Hara, observations, NLI, Ms. 20,397.

14. L. M. Cullen, T. C. Smout and A. Gibson, 'Wages and comparative development in Ireland and Scotland, 1565–1780', in R. Mitchison and P. Roebuck (eds), *Economy and society in Scotland and Ireland 1500–1939* (Edinburgh, 1988), pp. 105–16; D. W. Howell, *The rural poor in eighteenth-century Wales* (Cardiff, 2000), pp. 66–81; L. Kennedy and M. W. Dowling, 'Prices and wages in Ireland, 1700–1850', *Irish Economic and Social History*, 24 (1997), pp. 62–104; S. R. Lowry-Corry, earl of Belmore, *The history of the Corry family of Castlecoole* (London and Dublin, 1891), p. 276; V. Pollock, 'Contract and consumption: labour agreements and the use of money in eighteenth-century rural Ulster', *Agricultural History Review*, 43 (1995), pp. 19–33; V. Pollock, 'The household economy in early rural America and Ulster: the question of self-sufficiency', in H. T. Blethen and C. W. Wood (eds), *Ulster and North America: transatlantic perspectives on the Scotch-Irish* (Tuscaloosa and London, 1997), pp. 61–75.

15. Census of Elphin, NA, M. 2466; *Abstract of the number of Protestant and Popish families*.

16. W. Gacquin, *Roscommon before the famine. The parishes of Kiltoom and Cam, 1749–1845* (Dublin, 1996), pp. 12–24.

17. M. Campbell, '"Of people too few or too many": the conflict of opinion on population', in W. A. Aiken and B. D. Henning (eds), *Conflict in Stuart England: essays in honour of W. Notestein* (London, 1960), pp. 169–202.

18. D. T. Andrew, *Philanthropy and police: London charity in the eighteenth century* (Princeton, NJ, 1989); S. Cavallo, *Charity and power in early modern Italy: benefactors and their motives in Turin, 1541–1789* (Cambridge, 1995); S. Cavallo, 'The motivations of benefactors: an overview of approaches to the study of charity', in J. Barry and C. Jones (eds), *Medicine and charity before the welfare state* (London, 1991), pp. 46–62; C. Lis and H. Soly, *Poverty and capitalism in pre-industrial Europe* (Brighton, 1979); P. Slack, *From reformation to improvement* (Oxford, 1999), pp. 81–3.

19. Abp. W. King to Bp. W. Nicolson, 21 Feb. 1717[18], TCD, Ms. 2535/84.

20. *Writings of Petty*, i, pp. 146–7.

21. P. Francis, *Irish Delftware: an illustrated history* (London, 2000), p. 10.

22. D. Dickson, 'The place of Dublin in the eighteenth-century Irish economy', in T. M. Devine and D. Dickson (eds), *Scotland and Ireland: parallels and contrasts in economic and social developments* (Edinburgh, 1983), p. 182.

23. *Some thoughts on the tillage of Ireland* (Dublin, 1738), pp. 29–30; *A brief review of the rise and progress of the Incorporated Society* (Dublin, 1744), p. 11.

24. N. Canny, *Making Ireland British, 1580–1650* (Oxford, 2001), pp. 315–16.

25. R. Lawrence, proposals for works at Chapelizod, Oct. 1668, Bodleian, Carte Ms. 36, f. 523; report on Lawrence's petition, *c.* 1669, ibid., Carte Ms. 160, f. 36v; T. C. Barnard, 'An Anglo-Irish industrial enterprise: iron-making at Enniscorthy, Co. Wexford, 1657–1692', *PRIA*, 85, sect. C (1985), p. 141; T. C. Barnard, 'Sir William Petty as Kerry ironmaster', ibid., 82, sect. C (1982), p. 26; T. C. Barnard, 'Interests of Ireland: the "fanatic zeal and irregular ambition" of Richard Lawrence', in C. Brady and J. H. Ohlmeyer (eds), *Argument and power in early modern Ireland* (Cambridge, forthcoming).

26. Sir T. Southwell to Lord Coningsby, 6 Aug. 1699, PRONI, D 638/30/9; cf. C. Crofts to ?Sir R. Southwell, 2 June 1699, BL, Add. Ms. 21,133, f. 39; A. Lawton to R. Hoare, 14 Aug. 1696; T. Morrish to same, 18 April 1697, PRO, C 104/12, box 1, letter book of R. Hoare, ff. 24, 110v.

27. Dickson, 'Economic history of the Cork region', ii, pp. 558–65.

28. J. McVeagh (ed.), *Richard Pococke's Irish tours* (Dublin, 1995), pp. 97, 103.

29. J. Buckley, 'Account of some Irish state proclamations (1744–1756)', *JCHAS*, 40 (1935), p. 89.

30. L. A. Clarkson, 'The Carrick-on-Suir woollen industry in the eighteenth century', *Irish Economic and Social History*, 16 (1989), pp. 23–41.

31. J. Potter to R. Wilmot, 2 July 1741, PRONI, T 3019/306; 'The proclamations issued by the lord-lieutenant and council of Ireland, 1618 to 1875', *The twenty-third report of the deputy keeper of the public records in Ireland* (Dublin, 1891), p. 66.

32. Abp. W. King to Abp. W. Wake, 23 March 1720[1], Christ Church, Wake Ms. 13, f. 240; Abp. W. King, account book, s.d. March 1720[1], TCD, Ms. 751/3, f. 41; vestry book, St Catherine's, Dublin, 1693–1730, RCB, P. 117/05/1.2, pp. 339–40, 345, 351.

33. Vestry book of St Catherine's, 1657–92, RCB, P. 117/05.01.1, pp. 285, 307, 319, 343, 355.

34. Bp. J. Evans to Abp. W. Wake, 8 April 1721, Christ Church, Wake Ms. 13, f. 241.

35. Bp. T. Lindsay to A. Charlet, 4 Oct. 1713, Bodleian, Ballard Ms. 8, f. 64v.

36. E. Southwell to Lord Dartmouth, 10 Sept. 1711, PRO, SP 63/376, 366.

37. Proceedings of 8 July 1752, Crown entry book, County Dublin, 1750–52, NA.

38. J. Perceval to Lord Perceval, 11 June 1731, BL, Add. Ms. 46,982, f. 98; J. Wight, journal, s.d. 1 and 18 May 1752, Friends' Historical Library, Dublin; W. Colles to

B. Colles, 1766, NA, Prim Ms. 87; W. H. G. Bagshawe, *The Bagshawes of Ford* (London, 1886), p. 335; J. Fitzgerald, *The Cork remembrancer* (Cork, 1783), p. 166; M. Lenihan, *Limerick: its history and antiquities* (Dublin, 1866), p. 342.

39. J. Wight, journal, s.d. 21 Dec. 1754, Friends' Historical Library, Dublin.

40. J. Kirby to S. Bagshawe, 2 April 1762, JRL, B 15/1/38; J. S. Donnelly, Jr, 'The Whiteboy movement, 1761–5', *IHS*, 21 (1978–79), pp. 20–55; J. Kelly (ed.), 'The Whiteboys in 1762: a contemporary account', *JCHAS*, 94 (1989), pp. 19–26.

41. Minute book, 1734–60, Dublin Weavers' Company, s.d. 3 Nov. 1742, 25 March 1743, RSAI; W. Colles to B. Colles, 20 Feb. 1743[4], NA, Prim Ms. 87; *Censor*, 16 (Dublin, 9–16 Sept. 1749).

42. Minute book, 1734–60, Dublin Weavers' Company, s.d. 1 April 1745, 1 April 1748; 'The proclamations issued by the lord-lieutenant and council of Ireland, 1618 to 1875', pp. 67, 68, 69, 70; *CARD*, viii, pp. 137–8, 176–7, 374–5, 511–13; ix, p. 393.

43. Minute book, 1734–60, Weavers' Company, 1734–60, s.d. 1 April 1748, 8 July 1748, 1 July 1751, 17 Aug. 1752, 2 July 1753.

44. *The case of the journeymen sheermen of the city of Dublin briefly and impartially stated* ([Dublin,?1749]), in PRONI, D 562/1338.

45. Kennedy and Dowling, 'Prices and wages', pp. 77, 79; F. D'Arcy, 'Wages of labourers in the Dublin building industry, 1667–1918', *Saothar*, 14 (1989), pp. 18–19.

46. Minute book, Barber Surgeons' Company, 1703–57, TCD, Ms. 1447/8/1, f. 153v.

47. Belmore, *History of the Corry family*, p. 276; *The secret history and memoirs of the barracks of Ireland*, 2nd edn (London, 1747), p. 32.

48. P. Delany to M. Ward, 1 June 1746, PRONI, D 2092/1/7, 133.

49. Register of Magdalen Asylum, from 1766, nos. 2, 16, 19, 22, 24, 26, 29, 83, 94, 100, RCB, Ms. 551/1/1.

50. M. Deane to J. Clane, 20 Feb. 1682[3], Cork Archives Institute, Ms. U/138/B, Youghal corporation records.

51. T. B., *A letter to the inhabitants of Dublin and the Liberty* (Dublin, 1759), pp. 3–6.

52. Bp. J. Evans to Abp. W. Wake, 8 April 1721, Christ Church, Wake Ms. 13, f. 241; K. Conolly to J. Bonnell, 22 Sept. 1741, NLI, PC 434.

53. Vestry book, Union of Kells, s.d. 30 Sept. 1741, 13 July 1742, 5 April 1743, 26 April 1748, RCB, P. 192/5.1, pp. 53, 59, 79.

54. Vestry book, Union of Kells, s.d. 6 Oct. 1742, 4 April 1749, ibid., P. 192/5.1, pp. 59, 81.

55. Accounts for 1720, 1724, 1727, 1729, vestry book, 1693–1730, St Catherine's, Dublin, ibid., P. 117/05/1.2, pp. 340, 365, 375, 390.

56. Accounts for 1724, vestry book, 1693–1730, St Catherine's, Dublin, ibid., P. 117/5/1.2, pp. 360, 365.

57. Vestry book, 1730–67, St Catherine's, Dublin, ibid., P. 117/5/1.3; Monck Mason's collection for Dublin, iii, part 1, Gilbert Ms. 68, pp. 151–2; houses in Dublin, 1701–5, TCD, Ms. 888/2, 262; houses in Dublin, 20 July 1719, BL, Add. Ms. 47,127.

58. Vestry books, 1660–1710, 1711–62, St John's, Dublin, RCB, P. 328/5.2 and 3.

59. Petition of W. Dames to Abp. W. King, 6 June 1728, Marsh's Library, Ms. Z3.1.1, item clxiv; case of undertakers and journeymen, broadcloth weavers, c.1728, ibid., item clxv; petition of J. Gallaway and others on behalf of undertakers and journeymen broadcloth weavers, c. 1728, ibid., item clxvi; petition on behalf of

silk and worsted weavers of Dublin, 1720s, ibid., item clxvii; *To the honourable the committee appointed to enquire into the causes of the disputes between masters and journeymen, the reply of the journeymen stocking-makers of the city of Dublin* ([Dublin, 1749]).

60. E. B., *The defence of the whole society of wool-combers of the city and liberties of the city of Corke* (Cork, 1722).

61. P. Delany to M. Ward, 1 June 1746, PRONI, D 2092/1/7, 133; P. Delany, *An essay towards evidencing the divine original of tythes* (London, 1748), pp. 6–8.

62. *The Dublin Society's weekly observations* (Dublin, 1739), pp. 187–9.

63. P. Delany to M. Ward, 1 June 1746, PRONI, D 2092/1/7, 133; R. Barton, *A dialogue concerning some things of importance to Ireland; particularly to the County of Ardmagh* (Dublin, 1751), pp. 11–14, 17–18; Delany, *An essay towards evidencing the divine original of tythes*, pp. 6–8.

64. Masters' accounts, 1691–1714, Dublin Weavers' Company, s.d. 7 Sept. 1702, RSAI; J. Barry, W. Power and T. Sheridan to W. Howard, n.d. [1727], NLI, PC 223; W. Preston to E. Southwell, 13 Feb. 1739[40], 2 March 1739[40], ibid., Ms. 730/19 and 20; T. Kingsbury to F. Price, 31 May 1740, NLW, Puleston Ms. 2584E; W. Colles to B. Colles, 14 June 1766, NA, Prim Ms. 87; J. Wight, journal, s.d. 25 July 1752, Friends' Historical Library, Dublin; Barnard, 'Cork settlers', pp. 349–50; Legg, *Synge Letters*, pp. 190, 295.

65. S. Clark and J. Donnelly (eds), *Irish peasants: violence and political unrest, 1780–1914* (Manchester, 1983); S. J. Connolly, 'The Houghers: agrarian protest in early eighteenth-century Ireland', in C. H. E. Philpin (ed.), *Nationalism and popular protest in Ireland* (Cambridge, 1987), pp. 38–51; T. P. Power, *Land, politics and society in eighteenth-century Tipperary* (Oxford, 1993), pp. 174–220.

66. Trespass book, from 7 Nov. 1713, Sheffield City Archives, WWM/A 765. Of the offenders, fourteen had English and eleven Irish names.

67. Lord Roscommon to Lord Cork and Burlington, 23 Jan. 1665[6], BL, Althorp Ms. B 5.

68. T. C. Barnard, 'An Anglo-Irish industrial enterprise: iron-making at Enniscorthy, Co. Wexford, 1657–1692', *PRIA*, 85, sect. C (1985), pp. 140–2; 'A descriptive account of the County of Kildare in 1682, by Thomas Monk', *Journal of the County Kildare Archaeological Society*, 6 (1910), p. 344; T. O. Ranger, 'The career of Richard Boyle, first earl of Cork, in Ireland, 1558–1643', unpublished D. Phil. thesis, University of Oxford (1959), p. 131.

69. E. Richardson to T. Seele, 1 Feb. 1664[5], TCD, MUN, P/1/469, 19.

70. D. B. Quinn, *The Elizabethans and the Irish* (Ithaca, NY, 1966), pp. 15, 17, 70–1, 84–5.

71. J. Kelly (ed.), *The letters of Lord Chief Baron Edward Willes to the earl of Warwick, 1757–62* (Aberystwyth, 1990), pp. 75–6.

72. W. O'Sullivan, 'William Molyneux's geographical collections for Kerry', *County Kerry Archaeological Journal*, 4 (1971), p. 37.

73. W. F[ownes], *Methods proposed for regulating the poor* (Dublin, 1725), p. 16.

74. R. Lloyd to F. Herbert, 2 Nov. 1715, NLW, Powis Castle correspondence, no. 821; Abp. W. King to Abp. W. Wake, 2 June 1719, Christ Church, Wake Ms. 13, f. 62; same to E. Southwell, 30 Jan. 1728[9], 8 March 1728[9], TCD, Ms. 750/9, pp. 104, 111; Lord Palmerston to E. Corkran, 5 Dec. 1728, 9 Aug. 1729; same to H. Hatch, 26 April 1729, Southampton UL, BR, 2/7; J. Wight, journal, s.d. 30 May 1753, Friends' Historical Library, Dublin; 'A descriptive account of the County of

Kildare in 1682, by Thomas Monk', p. 344; *Seasonable advice*, pp. 18–23; G. Story, *An impartial history*, 2 vols (London, 1693), ii, pp. 320–1.

75. T. C. Barnard, 'The languages of politeness and sociability in 18th-century Ireland', in D. G. Boyce, R. Eccleshall and V. Geoghegan (eds), *Political discourse in seventeenth- and eighteenth-century Ireland* (Basingstoke, 2001), pp. 193–221; J. Brett, *A friendly call to the people of the Roman Catholick religion in Ireland* (Dublin, 1757), p. 12; [W. Bruce], *Some facts and observations relative to the fate of the late Linen Bill* (Dublin, 1753), p. 21; N. Foy, *A sermon preached in Christ's-Church, Dublin; on the 23d of October, 1698* (Dublin, 1698), pp. 27–8; H. Maule, *A sermon preached in Christ-Church, Dublin . . . on Tuesday, the twenty-third day of October, 1733* (Dublin, 1733), p. 21.

76. I. Hont, 'The language of sociability and commerce: Samuel Pufendorf and the foundations of "Four Stages Theory"', in A. Pagden (ed.), *The languages of political theory in early modern Europe* (Cambridge, 1987), pp. 253–76.

77. 'An account of the barony of O'Neiland, Co. Armagh in 1682', *Ulster Journal of Archaeology*, 4 (1898), p. 241.

78. Gookin, *The great case of transplantation*, p. 17; J. Logan, 'Tadgh O Roddy and two surveys of County Leitrim', *Breifne*, 4 (1971), p. 333; 'The County of Kildare in 1682, by Thomas Monk', p. 344; *The Dublin Society's weekly observations*, pp. 11, 118–19, 192; *Some thoughts on the tillage of Ireland*, pp. 27–30, 34–5, 47.

79. Bp. E. Synge to T. Seele, 8 Jan. 1674[5], TCD, MUN/P/1/469, 37.

80. G. Swift to Sir W. Fownes, 16 May 1757, 30 June 1757, NLI, Ms. 3889/4 and 5; S. Meade to Sir M. Crosbie, 4 Feb. 1752, ibid., Talbot-Crosbie Mss, folder 37.

81. Report of Lord Herbert to the lord-lieutenant on the state of Kerry, 27 May 1673, printed in M. F. Cusack, *A history of the kingdom of Kerry* (London, 1871), pp. 282–7; another copy in Petty Papers, D.14, now in BL, Add. Mss; Lord Herbert to Essex, 21 Feb. 1673[4], BL, Stowe Ms. 204, f. 209v; Sir F. Brewster to Ormond, 2 May 1685, Bodleian, Carte Ms. 217, ff. 148–9.

82. T. Hutchins to T. Herbert, 8 April 1762, NA, M. 1857; D. Lauder to Lord Brandon, 10 April 1762, TCD, Ms. 3821/248.

83. J. Wight, journal, s.d. 20 June 1752, 13 Jan. 1753, 28 March 1753, 16 June 1753, Friends' Historical Library, Dublin.

84. Henry, 'Natural history', NA, M. 2533, pp. 348–9, 370, 409–11, 431; C. Smith, account of Co. Tipperary, 1760, RIA, Ms. 24 G 9, pp. 277–85; J. H. Andrews, *Shapes of Ireland: maps and their makers, 1564–1839* (Dublin, 1997), pp. 1–213; Barton, *Dialogue*, sig. [A3], pp. 11, 15–16.

85. [R. Barton], *Some remarks, towards a full description of Upper and Lower Lough Lene, near Killarney, in the County of Kerry* (Dublin, 1751), p. 8; Barton, *Dialogue*, sig. [A3], pp. 21–2; C. Smith, *The ancient and present state of the county of Kerry*, reprinted edn (Dublin and Cork, 1979), pp. 52–3.

86. Barton, *Upper and Lower Lough Lene*, sig. [a2]–[A2v], pp. 7–8, 13–14.

87. [G. Rye], *Considerations on agriculture* (Dublin, 1730), pp. 84–5.

88. W. Henry, *Love of our country* (Dublin, 1756), p. 19.

89. Henry, 'Natural history', NA, M. 2533, p. 348.

90. R. Hedges to Sir R. Cox, 20 Oct. 1704; same to J. Dawson, 22 Oct. 1704, Bodleian, Ms. Top. Ireland, C.2, ff. 27, 29; N. Delacherois to D. Delacherois, 4 March 1770, 28 April 1770, NAM, 7805–63; T. Barnard, *The Abduction of a Limerick Heiress: social and political relationships in eighteenth-century Ireland* (Dublin, 1998), pp. 24–31; *Seasonable advice*, p. 14.

91. Description of Co. Wicklow, *c.*1739, Armagh Public Library, papers of Physico-Historical Society.

92. Bp. R. Clayton to E. Weston, 31 May 1748, 4 Sept. 1748, PRONI, T 3019/1048, 1128; Delany, *Autobiography*, 1st series, ii, p. 490.

93. *The Censor*, 11 (Dublin, 5–12 August 1749).

94. J. C. Walton, 'Two descriptions of County Waterford in the 1680s. ii Sir Richard Cox's account', *Decies*, 36 (1987), p. 30.

95. A. Crotty to A. de Wilstar, 28 July 1726, Chatsworth, Crotty letter book, 1726; Williams (ed.), *Swift Correspondence*, iv, p. 413.

96. N. Delacherois to D. Delacherois, 4 March 1770, 28 April 1770, NAM, 7805–63.

97. W. C. Abbott (ed.), *The writings and speeches of Oliver Cromwell*, 4 vols (Cambridge, Mass., 1937–47), ii, pp. 196–205.

98. O'Sullivan, 'Molyneux's geographical collections', p. 45.

99. *The Dublin Society's weekly observations*, p. 192.

100. C. O'Hara, Observations, NLI, Ms. 20,397.

101. E. Fitzpatrick to Sir S. Fox, 9 Jan. 1713[14], Dorset CRO, Fox-Strangeways Mss, D/FSI, box 254; E. Fitzpatrick to Sir S. Fox, 16 Oct. 1713; receipt of P. French to J. Digby, 12 June 1714; account of E. Fitzpatrick and P. French with J. Digby, ibid., box 237, bundle 3; conveyance of Sir S. Fox to E. Fitzpatrick and P. French, 24 Dec. 1713, ibid., box 134; J. Digby to J. Ward, 27 Sept. 1720, ibid., box 254.

102. J. Digby to W. Smythe, 14 and 25 Jan. 1744[5], NLI, PC 445/13; J. Digby, notes of proceedings relating to Aran Islands, 4 May 1738, Dorset CRO, D/FSI, Fox-Strangeways Mss, D/FSI box 134; R. Fitzpatrick to M. Ward, 11 Aug. 1727, ibid., box 134.

103. R. J. S. Hoffman (ed.), *Edmund Burke, New York agent with his letters to the New York Assembly and intimate correspondence with Charles O'Hara*, Memoirs of the American Philosophical Society, 41 (Philadelphia, 1956), p. 283.

104. Memoir of H. Thomson, Bodleian, Ms. Eng. Hist. d. 155, f. 111.

105. J. A. Oughton, Autobiography, NAM, 8808–36–1, pp. 45, 87.

106. Ibid., p. 48.

107. C. Bagshawe to S. Bagshawe, 23 Sept. 1755, JRL, B 2/3/25; S. Bull to W. Smythe, 5 July [?1720s], NLI, PC 444; W. Crosbie to Sir M. Crosbie, 26 April 1753, ibid., Talbot-Crosbie Mss, folder 53; P. Delany to T. Tickell, 14 Aug. 1736, Tickell Mss, private collection, Devon; E. Echlin to C. Tickell, 7 Oct. 1754, ibid.; J. Hamilton to J. Bonnell, 16 April 1733, 5 May 1733, NLI, PC 435; T. Harrison to J. Strype, 5 and 28 Aug. 1718, Cambridge UL, Add. Ms. 9/261, 262; W. Henry, 'Natural history', NA, M. 2533, p. 389; Bp. E. Smythe of Down and Connor to W. Smythe, 24 Sept. 1709, NLI, PC 445; C. Bagshawe to S. Bagshawe, 23 Sept. 1755, JRL, B2/3/25; A. Uniacke to same, 20 Oct. 1755, ibid., B2/3/452; A. Carpenter (ed.), *Verse in English from eighteenth-century Ireland* (Cork, 1998), pp. 265, 277; *Faulkner's Dublin Journal*, 12–16 June 1733; Kelly (ed.), *Letters of Willes*, p. 40; Delany, *Autobiography*, 1st series, ii, p. 547; iii, p. 594.

108. R. Barton, *Lectures in natural history* (Dublin, 1751), p. 169; Delany, *Autobiography*, 1st series, iii, pp. 16–17, 511–21, 594.

109. Kelly (ed.), *Letters of Willes*, p. 91; E. MacLysaght, *Irish life in the seventeenth century*, 2nd edn (Shannon, 1969), pp. 321–63.

110. K. Howard to W. Howard, 18 April 1710, NLI, PC, 227; S. Ormsby to Sir J. Temple, 12 Feb. 1701[2], Southampton UL, BR, 141/2/3d; unknown to J. Evelyn,

13 Feb. 1693[4], Evelyn Mss, box VII, formerly at Christ Church, Oxford; H. Murtagh, *Athlone: history and settlement* (Athlone, 2000), p. 165.

111. Petitions to 2nd duke of Ormonde, RIA, Ms. 12 W 24.

112. Census of Elphin, 1749, NA, M. 2466, f. 377.

113. Ibid., ff. 1, 63, 175, 208, 336, 363, 417, 434.

114. J. T. Cliffe, *The world of the country house in seventeenth-century England* (New Haven and London, 1999), appendix; J. J. Hecht, *The domestic servant in eighteenth-century England* (London, 1956), p. 7; B. Hill, *Servants: English domestics in the eighteenth century* (Oxford, 1996), p. 29; D. W. Howell, *Patriarchs and parasites: the gentry of south-west Wales in the eighteenth century* (Cardiff, 1986), p. 183; P. Jenkins, *The making of a ruling class: the Glamorgan gentry, 1640–1790* (Cambridge, 1983), p. 198; A. Vickery, *The gentleman's daughter: women's lives in Georgian England* (New Haven and London, 1998), p. 134; R. G. Wilson and A. Mackley, *Creating paradise: the building of the English country house, 1660–1880* (London, 2000), p. 371.

115. Bp. W. Nicolson, account books, 1721, 1723, Cumbria County Library, Carlisle.

116. R. Edgeworth, account books, 1764–65, 1767, 1768, 1769, NLI, Mss 1528; 1533, pp. 321–6; 1534, pp. 341–6; 1535, pp. 345–51.

117. S. Madden, *Reflections and resolutions proper for the gentlemen of Ireland* (Dublin, 1738), p. 63; Sir F. Brewster, *A discourse concerning Ireland* (London, 1698), pp. 18–20.

118. M. Ledwidge to W. Smythe, 15 Sept. 1731, NLI, PC 446; A. Kussmaul, *Servants in husbandry in early modern England* (Cambridge, 1981).

119. Petty's calculations and disbursements from 21 Aug. 1685 to 21 Oct. 1685, Petty Papers, 8/56, 60, 71, now BL, Add. Ms. 72,857.

120. Bp. W. King, account book, 1693–1700, TCD, Ms. 751/1, f. 35.

121. Abp. W. King, account book, 1700–12, ibid., Ms. 751/2, ff. 157v–8, 174.

122. Ibid., f. 222.

123. W. Flower, accounts, 1726–49, NLI, Ms. 11,463.

124. R. Howard, accounts, 1748–88, ibid., Ms. 1725.

125. James and Revd Henry Ware, account book, TCD, Ms. 10,528, ff. 15v, 25.

126. *Writings of Petty*, i, p. 144.

127. K. Conolly to J. Bonnell, 9 Dec. 1729, NLI, PC 434; J. Bulkeley to same, 24 Jan. 1729[30], ibid., PC 435; F. Burton to same, 26 Jan. 1729[30], 23 Feb. 1729[30], ibid., PC 434.

128. K. Conolly to J. Bonnell, 30 July 1721, ibid., PC 434; M. Jones to same, 11 Aug. 1733, ibid., PC 435. Two running footmen would be included in the entourage of Lord Kerry in 1732. C. Smith, *The antient and present state of the county of Kerry*, new edn (Dublin and Cork, 1979), p. 258.

129. P. Fagan, *Catholics in a Protestant country: the papist constituency in eighteenth-century Dublin* (Dublin, 1998), pp. 18, 22, 37, 49–51.

130. J. Whitelaw, *A note on the population of Dublin* (Dublin, 1805); Fagan, *Catholics in a Protestant country*, p. 52.

131. Clarkson, 'The Carrick-on-Suir woollen industry in the eighteenth century', p. 32; L. A. Clarkson, 'The demography of Carrick-on-Suir, 1799', *PRIA*, 87, sect. C (1987), p. 35; L. A. Clarkson, 'An anatomy of an Irish town: the economy of Armagh, 1770', *Irish economic and social history*, 5 (1978), pp. 31–5, 45.

132. Census of Elphin, 1749, NA, M. 2466; Murtagh, *Athlone*, pp. 180–1.

133. P. Delany, *Twenty sermons on social duties and their opposite vices*, 2nd edn (London, 1747), pp. 185–6, 190, 193.

134. Ibid., p. 228.

135. Legg, *Synge Letters*, pp. 383–4.

136. Ibid., pp. 203, 235.

137. B. Bacon, *A sermon preach'd at St Andrew's Dublin before the honourable House of Commons, on Sunday the twenty-third of October, 1743* (Dubin, 1743), p. 12; J. Dane, *The reformation protected by the providence of God* (London, 1710), p. 7; R. Lambert, *A sermon preach'd to the Protestants of Ireland, now residing in London* (London, 1708), p. 11; Maule, *A sermon preached in Christ-Church, Dublin . . . on Tuesday, the twenty-third day of October, 1733*, pp. 8, 23; J. Stoughton, *The greatest good, or the greatest evil* (London, 1717), p. 20; J. Travers, *A sermon preached in St Andrew's Church Dublin before the honourable the House of Commons the twenty third of October, 1698* (Dublin, 1698), p. 3.

138. R. French, account book, NLI, Ms. 4919; Legg, *Synge Letters*, pp. 185, 234, 240–1.

139. C. O'Hara, wages book, NLI, Ms. 16,705, pp. 28–9.

140. R. Edgeworth, account books, 1741–42; 1748–49; 27 Dec. 1749; 1764; 1768; 1769, NLI, Mss 1515, pp. 162, 213; 1518, p. 195; 1528, p. 157; 1534, p. 343; 1535, p. 345.

141. R. French, account book, NLI, Ms. 4919; Barnard, 'Robert French of Monivea', p. 288; D. A. Cronin, *A Galway gentleman in the age of improvement: Robert French of Monivea, 1716–1779* (Dublin, 1995), p. 24.

142. F. Bernard, account book, 1719–28, p. 216, Cork Archives Institute, Doherty Mss, U/137; R. Edgeworth, account book, 1756–57, s.d. 14 May 1756, NLI, Ms. 1522, p. 143; S. Waring, 'A book of entrys of servants' wages', p. 8, Waring Mss, private collection, Co. Down; account of St Paul with W. Flower, 9 May–9 Aug. 1726, NLI, Ms. 11,468.

143. J. & H. Ware, household book, TCD, Ms. 10,528, ff. 84–6, 182v, 185v.

144. Ibid., f. 184v.

145. Ibid., ff. 183–4.

146. Abp W. King, account book, 1715–23, ibid., Ms. 751/3, ff. 123, 127, 131, 137, 141v, 149.

147. R. Edgeworth, account books, 1763–64, 1769, 1770, s.d. 2 Jan. 1764, 29 June 1769, 1770, NLI, Mss 1530, p. 165; 1535, p. 205; 1536, p. 333.

148. M. Gilleland to H. Sloane, 9 May 1691, BL, Sloane Ms. 4036, f. 112; M. Burgh to W. Smythe, 7 Dec. 1746, NLI, PC 446.

149. Conolly accounts, Castletown, 1767, TCD, Ms. 3953, f. 108v.

150. K. Conolly to J. Bonnell, 3 April 1740, NLI, PC 434; M. Jones to same, 24 Feb. [?1736], 30 Jan. [1740 or 1741], ibid., PC 435.

151. H. Alcock to Sir J. Mason, 14 June 1718, Dromana, Co. Waterford, Villiers-Stuart Mss, T 3131/B/1/9.

152. Will of 2nd earl of Cork and 1st earl of Burlington, PRO, PROB 11/448/251; will of T. Flower, 4 May 1700, Southampton UL, BR, 138, B.91; will of B. Span, 6 Nov. 1718, Lawder of Bonnybegg Mss, formerly property of Capt. Turner, Great Rissington, Gloucestershire, now PRONI, D 4123; codicil to will of H. Ingoldsby, 28 July 1731, NLI, PC 438; M. Burgh to W. Smythe, n.d. [?1740s], ibid., PC 446; will of Bp. F. Hutchinson, PRONI, D 3860/D/7; executors' accounts, estate of W. Handcock, 1759, NA, Sarsfield-Vesey Mss, account nos. 78 and 81; J. Ainsworth (ed.), *The Inchiquin manuscripts* (Dublin, 1961), p. 511; M. V. Conlon, 'Some old Cork charities', *JCHAS*, 48 (1943), p. 91; E. R. McC. Dix, 'Will of a Limerick printer of the eighteenth century', *Journal of the North Munster*

Antiquarian Society, 2 (1911–13), pp. 45–6; C. S. King (ed.), *A great archbishop of Dublin. William King, D.D., 1650–1729* (London, 1906), pp. 44–5.

153. K. Conolly to J. Bonnell, 21 Sept. 1742, NLI, PC 434; J. Pery to Lady A. Crosbie, 16 Oct. 1752, TCD, Ms. 3821/221; Delany, *Autobiography*, 1st series, iii, pp. 166–7.

154. K. Conolly to Lady A. Conolly, 6 Jan. 1746[7], IAA, Castletown deposit, box 76; same to J. Bonnell, 14 Dec. 1731, NLI, PC 435; C. Smythe to W. Smythe, 9 April 1749, ibid., PC 445; J. Cooley to same, 23 Jan. 1737[8], 8 Feb. 1737[8], and undated, ibid., PC 446; J. Smythe to W. Smythe, 'Monday night', 'Tuesday morning', [?1740s], ibid., PC 449; R. Smythe to R. Smythe, [1750s], ibid., PC 448.

155. K. Conolly to Lady A. Conolly, 6 Jan. 1746[7], IAA, box 76; same to J. Bonnell, 14 Dec. 1731, NLI, PC 435.

156. Legg, *Synge Letters*, p. 271. Cf. M. Jones to J. Bonnell, 11 Aug. 1733, NLI, PC 435.

157. B. T. Balfour, account book, 1737–68, NLI, Ms. 11,920; F. Bernard, account book, 1719–28, pp. 93, 95, 140–1, 143, 145, 190, Cork Archives Institute, Doherty Mss. U/137; R. French, account book, NLI, Ms. 4919; J. and H. Ware, household book, TCD, Ms. 10,528; wages of servants of Bp. R. Howard, 1732, NLI, PC 223; account book, 1759–72, Lawders of Bonnybegg, Co. Leitrim, PRONI, D 4123; O'Hara, servants' wages book, 1743–63, Nymphsfield, Co. Sligo, NLI, Ms. 16,705; S. Waring, 'A book of entrys of servants' wages', Waring Mss, private collection, Co. Down; J. Garry, 'Townland survey of County Louth: supplementary notes to townland survey of Beaulieu', *Journal of County Louth Archaeological Society*, 22 (1992), pp. 414–16.

158. Ormond servants, list of 20 April 1665, Bodleian, Carte Ms. 145, p. 177; lists of Ormond servants, NLI, Ms. 2487, pp. 97–101; household book of marquess of Kildare (later duke of Leinster) from 1758, Ramsden, Oxfordshire, Mss. of duke of Leinster; Conolly servants' book and wage receipts, Castletown, TCD, Mss. 3942–3; Barnard, 'Cork settlers', p. 337.

159. Edgeworth account books, 1746–47, 1755–56, s.d. 9 Aug. 1746; 25 Sept. 1755, NLI, Mss 1517, p. 229; 1522, p. 43; B. T. Balfour, accounts, ibid., Ms. 11,920.

160. Garry, 'Townland survey of County Louth', p. 414.

161. St Leger family, servants' book, NLI, Ms. 34,112/10.

162. O'Hara wages book, ibid., Ms. 16,705, p. 13.

163. H. Ingoldsby to W. Smythe, 8 Feb. 1723[4], ibid., PC 445; M. Ledwidge to same, [?], and 8 April 1738, ibid., PC 446; O'Hara accounts, ibid., Ms. 16,705, p. 13; R. Edgeworth, account book, 1741–42, s.d. 31 Aug. 1741, ibid., Ms. 1515, p. 59.

164. Bagshawe, *Bagshawes of Ford*, p. 328.

165. H. Ingoldsby to W. Smythe, 8 Feb. 1723[4], NLI, PC 445; examination of B. Nonnen, 18 Feb. 1741[2]; J. Potter to Duncannon, 10 April 1742, PRO, ADM 1/3990; same to Legge, 1 Feb. 1739[40], PRONI, T 3019/225; Barnard, 'Cork settlers', pp. 309–65; T. C. Barnard, 'Gardening, diet and "improvement" in late seventeenth-century Ireland', *Journal of Garden History*, 10 (1990), pp. 71–85.

166. Lord Drogheda, account book, s.d. 28 July 1754, NLI, Ms. 9470.

167. S. Waring, 'A book of entrys of servants' wages', p. 9. Waring Mss, private collection, Co. Down.

168. Abp. W. King, account book, 1700–12, TCD, Ms. 751/2, ff. 175v, 215, 223; Bp. J. Stearne to Abp. W. King, 25 June 1715, ibid., Ms. 1995–2008/1666; King, *A great archbishop*, p. 44; O. St George to W. Conolly, 15 Oct. 1723, IAA, Castletown deposit, box 53.

169. J. Stearne, will, 7 March 1744[5], PRONI, DIO 4/9/5/1/1.

170. 'Abstracts of wills', *Irish Ancestor*, 5/1 (1973), p. 55; Brewster, *A discourse concerning Ireland*, pp. 18–20; L. F. McNamara, 'Some matters touching Dromoland: letters of father and son, 1758–59', *North Munster Antiquarian Journal*, 18 (1986), p. 67.

171. E. Echlin to C. Tickell, 4 Jan. 1755, Tickell Mss, private collection, Devon.

172. M. Luddy (ed.), *The diary of Mary Mathew* (Thurles, 1991), p. 1.

173. S. J. Connolly, 'A woman's life in mid-eighteenth-century Ireland: the case of Letitia Bushe', *HJ*, 43 (2000), pp. 433–51.

174. J. C. Sainty, 'A Huguenot civil servant: the career of Charles Delafaye, 1677 to 1762', *Proceedings of the Huguenot Society of London*, 22 (1970–76), p. 410; W. Conolly to C. Delafaye, 13 Aug. 1717, PRO, SP 63/376; K. Conolly to C. Tickell, 2 July 1734, Tickell Mss, private collection, Devon; accounts of Dorset and Devonshire, s.d. 30 Dec. 1734, Dublin Public Library, Gilbert Ms. 199; M. Humphrey to Devonshire, 25 Nov. 1739, C. Litton Falkner Mss, RIA, Ms. 12 F 50; Calendar of departmental correspondence, 1741–59, s.d. 24 Dec. 1744, NA.

175. Account book of Abp. H. Boulter, TCD, Ms. 6399, s.d. 21 July 1727.

176. W. Colles to Revd. M. Archdall, 17 April 1756, NA, Prim Ms. 87.

177. E. Bullingbrooke and J. Belcher, *An abridgement of the statutes of Ireland* (Dublin, 1754), pp. 789–93; Delany, *Twenty sermons*, p. 220; M. Dutton, *The law of masters and servants in Ireland* (Dublin, 1723), p. 80.

178. Ware account book, TCD, Ms. 10,528, ff. 91, 98, 102, 109; Vigors account book, 1711–22, s.d. 7 June 1721, 7 Feb. 1721[2], 22 Dec. 1722, Carlow County Library; S. Waring, 'A book of entrys of servants' wages', p. 20, Waring Mss, private collection, Co. Down; *The Censor*, 27 (28 April–5 May 1750); Dutton, *The law of masters and servants*, p. 81; *Faulkner's Dublin Journal*, 29 Nov.–3 Dec. 1726, 3–6 Dec. 1726.

179. Ware account book, TCD, Ms. 10,528, ff. 93, 94, 101, 107, 114, 117, 119–24, 128–9, 132, 134–7, 143–4, 148–50, 158, 160.

180. *Faulkner's Dublin Journal*, 17 May 1726, 28 Feb.–1 March 1726[7]; Madden, *Reflections*, p. 13; John Richardson, *The great folly, superstition and idolatry of pilgrimage in Ireland* (Dublin, 1727), p. 63.

181. K. Conolly to J. Bonnell, 11 June 1719, NLI, PC 434; C. Campbell to K. Conolly, 20 Feb. 1712[13], IAA, Castletown deposit, box 54.

182. Confession of Capt. John Meagher, *c.*1690, RIA, Ms. 24 G 5/62.

183. G. H. Bell [John Travers], (ed.), *The Hamwood papers of the ladies of Llangollen and Caroline Hamilton* (London, 1930), p. 10.

184. Madden, *Reflections*, p. 63.

185. W. F[ownes], *Methods proposed for regulating the poor* (Dublin, 1725), p. 8.

186. St Leger, accounts, s.d. 1767, NLI, Ms. 34,112/10.

187. J. S. Kelly, 'Infanticide in eighteenth-century Ireland', *Irish economic and social history*, 19 (1992), pp. 9, 11–14, 22–3.

188. *A letter from a residing member of the Society in Dublin* (Dublin, 1721), p. 32; 'Dublin, St Andrew's vestry' [Dec.1725], in Marsh's Library, Ms. Z1.1.3, item 97; W. Hogan and L. Ó Buachalla, 'The letters and papers of James Cotter, junior, 1689–1720', *JCHAS*, 68 (1963), p. 95.

189. W. Smythe to R. Smythe, 26 May 1752, NLI, PC 445; R. Smythe to R. Smythe, 23 Sept. 1760, ibid., PC, 448.

190. Census of Elphin, 1749, NA, M. 2466; Murtagh, *Athlone*, p. 181.

191. Marsh's Library, Ms. Z1.1.13, item 97; *The state and case of the native servants most humbly offered to the consideration of the publick* (Dublin, 1750).

192. Waterford corporation book, 1700–27, s.d. 26 Sept. 1712, 22 May 1713, 24 Aug. 1713, Waterford Municipal Archives.

193. Minute book, Corresponding Society in London of the Incorporated Society, 1735–43, s.d. 11 April 1740, 19 May 1740, TCD, Ms. 5302, ff. 112v, 115v.

194. R. Smythe to R. Smythe, 4 Oct. 1760, NLI, PC 448.

195. *Faulkner's Dublin Journal*, 18–22 July 1727.

196. M. Ledwidge to W. Smythe, 8 and 15 April 1738, NLI, PC 446.

197. R. Allen to H. Boyle, 18 Dec. 1732, PRONI, D 2707/A1/1, 51.

198. K. Conolly to J. Bonnell, 9 July 1742, NLI, PC 434.

199. *A letter from a residing member of the society in Dublin*, p. 39.

200. Register of Magdalen Asylum, from 1766, RCB, Ms. 551/1.1, nos. 54, 70, 82, 83, 85, 92.

201. Order book, Primrose Grange school, Sligo, 1757–90, s.d. 4 Oct. 1758, 19 Feb, 1759, 4 Oct. 1769, TCD, Ms. 5646; minute book, Green Coat School, Shandon, St Mary's Church, Cork.

202. W. King to J. Bonnell, 1 Dec. 1693, TCD, Mss 1995–2008/316.

203. Legg, *Synge Letters*, p. 115.

204. G. Mathew to K. O'Hara, 15 Feb. 1717[18], NLI, Ms. 20,385.

205. M. Ledwidge to W. Smythe, 15 Sept. 1743, 22 June 1745, NLI, PC 446; same to R. Smythe, 24 June 1760, ibid., PC 446; W. Smythe to same, 26 May 1752, ibid., PC 445; T. Pakenham to W. Smythe, 17 May 1750, ibid., PC 436; certificate of J. Paull on behalf of James Huston, gardener, 5 July 1753, ibid., PC 449; R. Butterfield to W. Smythe, 31 July 1753, 25 Aug. 1753, ibid., PC 449; C. Rowley to? W. Smythe, 14 Oct. [?1740s]; ?W. Smythe to C. Rowley, n.d., ibid., PC 444; W. Gibson to Sir E. O'Brien, 9 June 1759; J. Phelan to same, 9 June 1759, ibid., Inchiquin Mss, no. 2034; H. J. Thomson to Mrs Smythe, 3 Dec. 1768, ibid., PC 445; certificate of W. Lawder on behalf of Denis Keegan, coachman, 24 Feb. 1767, Lawder of Bonnybegg Mss, now PRONI, D 4123.

206. P. Brett to Mrs O'Hara, 14 Nov. 1718, NLI, Ms. 20,385.

207. M. Ledwidge to R. Smythe, 24 June 1760, ibid., PC 446.

208. Legg, *Synge Letters*, p. 193.

209. A. Langford to E. Owen, 6 May [1738], UCNW, Penrhos Ms. i, 1087.

210. Lawder of Bonnybegg, account book from 1759, p. 32, PRONI, D 4123; R. Smythe to Mrs R. Smythe, 3 Dec. 1768, NLI, PC 445.

211. R. Smythe to Mrs R. Smythe, 11 Dec. 1768, ibid.

212. Deposition of J. Story, 28 April 1686, NUI, Cork, Boole Library, Ms. U/20, Kinsale Manorial Papers, 1676–92.

213. Register of Magdalen Asylum, RCB, Ms. 551/5.1, no. 97.

214. Ibid., no. 94.

215. R. Smythe to Mrs Smythe, 23 March 1768, NLI, PC 445.

216. Jemmet Browne, *A sermon preach'd in Christ-Church, Dublin . . . the 18th of December, 1745* (Dublin, 1746), p. 10; *By-Laws agreed to and confirmed by the Hibernian Society* (Dublin, 1775), p. 31; Delany, *Twenty sermons*, pp. 98–100; Hogan and Ó Buachalla, 'The letters and papers of James Cotter, junior', p. 95.

217. Delany, *Twenty sermons*, p. 220; Dutton, *The law of masters and servants*, p. 80.

218. Act book, cathedral chapter of Cloyne, s.d. 29 May 1735, RCB, C.12/2.1; 'The autobiography of Pole Cosby, of Stradbally, Queen's County 1703–1737 (?)', *Journal of the County Kildare Archaeological and Historical Society*, 5 (1906–8), p. 170.

219. Vestry book, St Peter's, Dublin, RCB, 1686–1736, P. 45/6.1, p. 73; vestry book, St Bride's, Dublin, 1662–1742, ibid., P. 327/3/1, p. 164; vestry book, St Mary's, Dublin, 1699–1739, ibid., P. 277/7.1, pp. 179–82; list of seats at St Werburgh's, Dublin, 1716, ibid., P. 326/3/102.

220. R. Dudley (ed.), 'The Cheney letters, 1682–85', *Irish Economic and Social History*, 23 (1996), p. 112.

221. Delany, *Twenty sermons*, p. 225.

222. E. Synge to A. Dopping, 5 Aug. 1683, Armagh Public Library, Dopping Ms. I/36; Bp. N. Foy to Bp. W. King, 28 April 1693, TCD, Mss 1995–2008/272; W. Beveridge, *A sermon concerning the excellency and usefulness of the Common Prayer* (Dublin, 1698), sig. A2v; E. Edgeworth, *Morning and evening prayers for private families*, 3rd edn (Dublin, 1733), pp. 11–12; E. Synge, *A discourse of confirmation*, 5th edn (London, 1768), p. 5; *The Church-Catechism explain'd*, 7th edn (Dublin, 1713).

223. F. Hutchinson, account book, s.d. 23 March 1729[30], 4 March 1733[4], PRONI, DIO 1/22/2; R. Edgeworth account book, NLI, Ms. 1507, p. 26; Peacock diary, s.d. 17 March 1740[1], 17 March 1741[2], 16 March 1744[5], 17 March 1746[7], 17 March 1748[9], 17 March 1749[50], 17 March 1750[1], ibid., Ms. 16,091.

224. I. K. Ben-Amos, *Adolescence and youth in early modern England* (New Haven and London, 1994); P. Griffiths, *Youth and authority: formative experiences in England, 1560–1640* (Oxford, 1996), pp. 147–69; S. Rappaport, *Worlds within worlds: structures of life in sixteenth-century London* (Cambridge, 1989), pp. 232–8, 291–322.

225. Palmerston to L. Roberts, 14 May 1724, Southampton UL, BR, 2/4.

226. W. Hovell to J. Perry, 16 and 24 Dec. 1684, Farmar Mss, private collection, Dublin, Hovell letter book; T. Barnard, 'What became of Waring?' in T. Barnard, *Irish Protestant ascents and descents* (Dublin, 2003); J.M. Price, *Perry of London: a family and firm on the seaborne frontier, 1615–1753* (Cambridge, Mass., 1992), pp. 16–18, 93–4, 114–19.

227. W. Stannus to W. Leathes, 7 April 1714, 27 Oct. 1714, 7 May 1716, Suffolk CRO, Ipswich, de Mussenden Leathes Mss, HA 403/1/7, 63, 74, 78.

228. *The last speech and dying words of Charles Donnell of the city of Dublin, gent.* (Dublin, 1712).

229. T. Batty to Sir R. Browne, 18 Aug. 1674, Christ Church, Oxford, Evelyn Mss, Browne Letters, box A–C, now in BL.

230. W. Hamilton to J. Bonnell, 30 June 1726, NLI, PC 435.

231. C. Brett to M. Ward, 25 April 1726, PRONI, D 2092/1/3, 193.

232. N. Plunkett to H. Plunkett, 5 Jan. 1713[14], NA, 1075/30/1.

233. Indenture of 22 Nov. 1684, ibid., 992/612/21.

234. Journal of Abp. J. Vesey, pp. 15, 24, 31, 42, de Vesci Mss, NLI, G/2; E. Malone to E. Malone, 16 Sept. 1701, Brabazon Mss, private collection, London; W. Stannus to W. Leathes, 7 April 1714, 27 Oct. 1714, Suffolk CRO, HA 403/1/7, 63, 74; diary of E. Bouhéreau, s.d. 14 Feb. 1717, Marsh's Library, Ms. Z2.2.2.

235. M. Stritch to Sir E. O'Brien, 12 March 1763, NLI, Inchiquin Mss, folder 2065, printed in P. Francis, *Irish Delftware: an illustrated history* (London, 2000), p. 177.

236. Will of Grace Kempston, 9 May 1723, Acton Mss, Co. Dublin, NLI, microfilm p. 4529.

237. W. Stephens to J. Owen, 27 [?] 1718[19], UCNW, Penrhos Mss i, 558; J. Owen to A. Owen, 14 Dec. 1725, ibid., Penrhos Mss, i, 837; same to W. Owen, 1 Jan. 1725[6], ibid., v, 397.

238. Palmerston to L. Roberts, 3 Feb. 1721[2], 14 May 1724, Southampton UL, BR, 2/4.

239. Petition of Hugh Speke to Lord Chancellor C. Phipps, 12 Feb. 1710[11], Flintshire CRO, DD BK/1, 443.
240. H. Johnston to J. Moore, 21 May 1763; accounts, s.d. 22 Nov. 1764, NLI, Ms. 5737.
241. Mulcahy, *Kinsale*, v, pp. 10–11.
242. M. Pollard, *A dictionary of members of the Dublin book trade, 1550–1800* (London, 2000), pp. xxx–xxxii, based on NLI, Ms. 12,131.
243. Register of Cork freemen, 1656–1741, Cork Public Museum; list of apprenticeship fees, Cork, 1763–1770, Cork Archives Institute, Ms. U/5; Caulfield's transcript of Cork apprenticeship enrolments, 1756–1801, ibid., Ms. U/225; Belturbet corporation records, s.d. 1671, 1672, 1674, 1679, 12 Sept. 1699, formerly NA, M. 3572; R. Caulfield (ed.), *The council book of the corporation of Cork* (Guildford, 1876), p. 226; R. Day (ed.), 'The council book of Bandon Bridge, 1765–1840', *JCHAS*, 2nd series, 12 (1906), p. 97.
244. *CARD*, iii, p. 577, iv, pp. 38, 400, 425, 528; v, pp. 164, 189, 509; vi, pp. 137–41, 151–2, 184, 379–80; Mulcahy, *Kinsale*, iii, p. 88.
245. Masters' accounts, Dublin Weavers' Company, 1691–1714, s.d. 3 March 1697[8]; minute book, Weavers' Company, 1734–60, s.d. 3 Nov. 1742, 1 July 1751, RSAI; list of quarter-brothers, Weavers' Company, RSAI; C. D. A. Leighton, *Catholicism in a Protestant kingdom: a study of the Irish* ançien régime (Basingstoke, 1994), pp. 67–85; M. Wall, *Catholic Ireland in the eighteenth century*, ed. G. O'Brien (Dublin, 1989), pp. 61–72.
246. *Faulkner's Dublin Journal*, 12 July 1726, 3–6 Dec. 1726, 15–18 Dec. 1733.
247. Petition of Hugh Speke to Lord Chancellor Phipps, 12 Feb. 1710[11], Flintshire CRO, DD BK/1, 443.
248. List of apprenticeship enrolments, Cork, 1756–1801, Cork Archives Institute, U/225; Day (ed.), 'Council book of Bandon Bridge', p. 97.
249. Minute book, Goldsmiths' Company, 1667–1731, s.d. 9 May 1695, Assay Office, Dublin.
250. Accounts, 1669–1739, King's Hospital, Palmerston, Co. Dublin, Ms. 1; F. R. Falkiner, *The foundation of the hospital and free school of King Charles II, Oxmantown Dublin* (Dublin, 1906); 'King's Hospital manuscripts', *Analecta Hibernica*, 15 (1944), pp. 327–30; L. Whiteside, *A history of the King's Hospital* (Dublin, 1985), pp. 5–22.
251. R. V. Dudley, 'Dublin's parishes, 1660–1729: the Church of Ireland parishes and their role in the civic administration of the city', unpublished Ph.D. thesis, TCD, 2 vols (1995), i, p. 192; Legg, *Synge Letters*, pp. 21, 156, 160, 226, 257, 280, 341; petition of J. Molyneux, [1720s], Marsh's Library, Ms Z3.1.1, item xxxii.
252. 'King's Hospital manuscripts', p. 329.
253. Accounts of St John's School, Dublin, RCB, P. 328/12.1; *A hymn to be sung by the charity-children of St Andrew's Dublin . . . 21 Feb. 1730/1* (Dublin, 1730/1).
254. Register of apprentices, King's Hospital, Palmerston, Ms. 181.
255. Accounts of N. Cormick with Sir T. Vesey, 1719–20, NLI, de Vesci Mss, J/21, J/26.
256. Green-Coat School minute book, St Ann's Church, Shandon, s.d. 11 Dec. 1721, and memorandum; TCD, Ms. 2014/255; [H. Maule], *Pietas Corcagiensis* (Cork, 1721), p. 72.
257. Register of Green Coat School; D. Dickson, '"Centres of motion": Irish cities and popular politics', in L. Bergeron and L. M. Cullen (eds), *Culture et pratiques politiques en France et en Irlande XVIe–XVIIIe siècle* (Paris, 1991), p. 6.
258. Register of Foy's School, RCB, Ms. 523.

259. Ibid; B. Kirby, 'Civic politics and parliamentary representation in Waterford city, 1730–1807', unpublished Ph.D. thesis, NUI, Maynooth (2002), pp. 80–106; also small figure – 366 – of Protestants in one parish in 1826: *Waterford Mirror*, 21 Jan. 1826, cited in M. Tanner *Ireland's holy wars* (New Haven and London, 2001), p. 235.

260. On the Sligo school at Primrose Grange, T.C. Barnard, 'Protestants and the Irish language, c.1675–1725', *Journal of Ecclesiastical History*, 44 (1993), pp. 261–3. For another venture, M. V. Conlon, 'Register of the boys of St Stephen's hospital, Corke', *JCHAS*, 2nd series, 62 (1957), pp. 46–55.

261. Rules and orders, Incorporated Society, 1735–79, s.d. 25 Jan. 1734[5], 3 Jan. 1745[6], 4 May 1757, 21 Dec. 1757, 12 May 1762, 1 Nov. 1769, 2 Feb. 1774, TCD, Ms. 5301, pp. 5, 13, 38, 46, 57, 70; order book, Primrose Grange, 1757–90, s.d. 12 Nov. 1760, 15 Dec. 1760, 2 July 1776, 19 July 1777, ibid., Ms. 5646.

262. K. Milne, *The Irish Charter Schools, 1730–1830* (Dublin, 1997), p. 46.

263. Abp. J. Hort of Tuam, S. Hutchinson and R. Downes to the Corresponding Society, London, 23 April 1743, minute book, Corresponding Society, London, 1735–43, TCD, Ms. 5302, f. 177v–178.

264. Rules and orders, Incorporated Society, 1735–79, s.d. 24 May 1769, ibid., Ms. 5301, p. 56.

265. *Faulkner's Dublin Journal*, 13–16 Feb. 1741[2].

266. Order book, Primrose Grange, 1757–90, TCD, Ms. 5646.

267. Bp. H. Maule to W. Smythe, 22 Feb. 1736[7], 26 March 1745, NLI, PC 449; J. Smythe to same, 9 April 1747, ibid., PC 449.

268. Accounts and roll, Ardbraccan Charter School, TCD, Ms. 5597.

269. School roll, Arklow Charter School, ibid., Ms. 5598.

270. Accounts and roll, Ballycastle School, ibid., Ms. 5609; C. Dallat, 'Ballycastle's eighteenth-century industries', *The Glynns*, 3 (1975), pp. 7–13.

271. Rules and orders, Incorporated Society, 1735–79, s.d. 30 Jan. 1765, TCD, Ms. 5301, p. 51.

272. Vestry book, St Catherine's, Dublin, 1693–1730, RCB, P. 117/5.2; accounts of St John's School, Dublin, ibid., P. 328/12.1; D. W. Hayton, 'Did Protestantism fail in early eighteenth-century Ireland? Charity schools and the enterprise of religious and social reformation, c. 1690–1730', in A. Ford, J. I. McGuire and K. Milne (eds), *As by law established: the Church of Ireland since the Reformation* (Dublin, 1995), pp. 168, 184.

273. RCB, P. 326/27/3/76.

274. Accounts, 1726, 1729, vestry book, St Catherine's Dublin, 1693–1730, RCB, P. 117/5.2, pp. 375, 390.

275. Contract of John and Joseph Gregory with Countess of Orrery, 1 Jan. 1667[8], Petworth, Orrery papers, general series, 10.

276. Will of E. Sweetman, Co. Dublin, 25 March 1700, NLI, Ainsworth report, no. 50, p. 842.

277. Abp. W. King, account book, 1715–23, TCD, Ms. 751/3, f. 91.

278. 'Autobiography of Pole Cosby', p. 317.

279. K. Conolly to J. Bonnell, 12 June 1733, NLI, PC 434; receipt of J. Loughlan to W. Flower, 22 April 1726; receipt of same to Lord Castledurrow, 1 March 1733[4], NLI, Ms. 11,468/2; B. Fitzgerald (ed.), *Correspondence of Emily, duchess of Leinster*, 3 vols (Dublin, 1949–57), i, pp. 141, 147–8.

280. Deposition of J. Story, 28 April 1686, NUI, Cork, Boole Library, Ms. U/20, Kinsale manorial papers, 1676–92.

281. N. Plunkett to H. Plunkett, 5 Jan. 1713[14], NA, 1075/30/1.

282. W. Waring to S. Waring, 7 Aug. 1697, private collection, Co. Down.

283. Weavers' Company, minute book, 1734–60, s.d. 1 July 1751, RSAI.

284. S. Pike to Lord Grandison, 15 March 1744[5], Dromana, Co. Waterford, Villiers-Stuart Mss, T3131/C/7/27.

285. Francis, *Irish Delftware*, p. 53.

286. *CARD*, iv, p. 38; vi, pp. 130–1, 184, 379–80; Pollard, *Dublin book trade*, p. xxviii.

287. J. Owen to A. Owen, 14 Dec. 1725, UCNW, Penrhos Mss, i, 837; same to W. Owen, 1 Jan. 1725[6], ibid., v, 397; *A memoir of Mistress Ann Fowkes (née Geale) . . . with some recollections of her family* (Dublin, 1892), p. 32; T. Harrison, *A funeral sermon on Mordecai Abbott, esq.* (London, 1700), pp. 44–7; K. Herlihy, 'The Irish Baptists, 1650–1780', unpublished Ph.D. thesis, TCD (1992), pp. 88, 135, 159; J. Piggott, *A funeral sermon upon the sad occasion of the death of Mordecai Abbott, Esq.* (London, 1700), p. 78.

288. 'Mallow testamentary records', *Irish Ancestor*, 1 (1969), p. 58.

289. O. Gallagher to O. St George, 10 Nov. 1724, PRO, C 110/46, 348.

290. *Faulkner's Dublin Journal*, no. 225, 24–27 June 1727. Cf. ibid., 23–26 June 1733, 13–16 Feb. 1741[2]; *Dublin Courant*, 12–16 June 1744.

291. Minute book, Goldsmiths' Company, 1667–1731, s.d. 9 and 12 Nov. 1694, 1 May 1696, 1 May 1702, Assay Office, Dublin.

292. Pollard, *Dublin book trade*, p. xxx.

293. Autobiography of J. Traill, PRONI, D 1460/1.

294. Mulcahy, *Kinsale*, v, p. 10; A.W., *The clothiers' letter to the inhabitants of the Liberties* (Dublin, 1759), p. 3.

295. P. Fagan, 'The Dublin Catholic mob (1700–1750)', *Eighteenth-Century Ireland*, 4 (1989), pp. 133–41.

296. *CARD*, iv, pp. 537–8, 539–40.

297. T. C. Barnard, 'Reforming Irish manners: the religious societies in Dublin during the 1690s', *HJ*, 35 (1992), pp. 805–38.

298. Rules and orders of the Incorporated Society, 1735–79, 2 Feb. 1774, TCD, Ms. 5301, p. 70.

299. Ben-Amos, *Adolescence and youth in early modern England*, pp. 183–207; S. Brigden, 'Youth and the English Reformation', *P & P*, 95 (1982), pp. 37–67; Griffiths, *Youth and authority*, pp. 161–9; Rappaport, *Worlds within worlds*, pp. 289–322; S. Smith, 'The London apprentices as seventeenth-century adolescents', *P & P*, 61 (1973), pp. 97–123.

300. Mulcahy, *Kinsale*, vi, p. 92.

301. J. S. Kelly (ed.), *Gallows speeches from eighteenth-century Ireland* (Dublin, 2001), pp. 49, 88, 93, 94–5, 117, 126, 224–5.

302. St G. Ashe to H. Dodwell, 24 May 1687, Bodleian, Ms. Eng. Lett. C. 29, f. 12; R. Howard to H. Howard, 18 March 1730[1], NLI, PC 227; J. Wight, journal, s.d. 26 April 1755, Friends' Historical Library, Dublin; H. Thomson, memoir, Bodleian, Ms. Eng. Hist. d. 155, f. 39v; D. Lauder to Lord Brandon, 8 and 19 June 1762; J. Tidmarsh to same, 5 June 1762, NLI, Talbot-Crosbie Mss, folder 67; same to same, 1 June 1762, TCD, Ms. 3821/251; T. C. Barnard, 'Athlone, 1685; Limerick, 1710: religious riots or charivaris?', *Studia Hibernica*, 27 (1993), pp. 61–75.

303. *Writings of Petty*, i, pp. 144, 146.

304. D. Dickson, 'In search of the old Irish poor law', in R. Mitchison and P. Roebuck (eds), *Economy and society in Scotland and Ireland 1500–1939* (Edinburgh,

1988), pp. 149–59; Dudley, 'Dublin's parishes, 1660–1729', i, pp. 164–209; R. Dudley, 'The Dublin parishes and the poor', *Archivium Hibernicum*, 53 (1999), pp. 80–94.

305. Vestry book, St John's, Dublin, s.d. 28 Nov. 1670, RCB, P. 328/5.1, f. 30.

306. St Werburgh's records, ibid., P. 326/27/3/83.

307. Lord Cork and Burlington to W. Congreve, 29 Dec. 1691, 25 June 1692, 4 Aug. 1692, 15 Sept. 1692, 28 Feb. 1692[3], NLI, Ms. 13,226; J. Waite to R. Musgrave, 21 June 1712, ibid., Ms. 13,242.

308. Unknown to J. Waite, 25 Jan. 1711[12], 18 March 1711[12], NLI, Ms. 13,255/4; H. Boyle to W. Conner, 3 April 1753, Chatsworth, Lismore Ms. 36/126.

309. Orders and rules for almshouses at Castlemartyr [*c*.1680], Petworth, Orrery Mss, general series, 7; contract for Maryborough almshouses, *c*.1684, NLI, de Vesci Mss, H/17; B. Power, *White knights, dark earls: the rise and fall of an Anglo-Irish dynasty* (Cork, 2000), pp. 7–8.

310. Indenture of 12 April 1698, NA, M. 6252.

311. Will of James Knight, 21 Feb. 1725[6], PRONI, D 3168/2/7; Monck Mason's collections, Dublin Public Library, Gilbert Ms. 67, p. 726.

312. B. Gurrin, 'Populating a parish: changing population trends in the civil parishes of Delgany, Kilcoole and Kilmacanoge between 1666 and 1779', unpublished MA dissertation, NUI, Maynooth (1999), p. 85.

313. Vestry book of Ballymodan, s.d. 16 Nov. 1697, 25 April 1712, RCB, P. 140/7.

314. D. Muschamp to T. Fitzgerald, 21 Jan. 1692[3], de Vesci Mss, H/2.

315. Dudley, 'The Dublin parishes and the poor', p. 92; T. Gogarty (ed.), *Council book of the corporation of Drogheda. I. 1649–1734* (Drogheda, 1915), p. 309; R. Malcolmson, *Carlow vestries in olden times* (Carlow, 1870), p. 15.

316. D. Dickson, *Arctic Ireland* (Dundonald, 1997); M. Drake, 'The Irish demographic crisis of 1740–41', in T. W. Moody (ed.), *Historical Studies*, vi (1968), pp. 101–24.

317. Ballymodan vestry book, s.d. 7 April 1740, RCB, P. 140/7.

318. R. Dudley, 'Dublin's parishes, 1660–1729', i, p. 175.

319. Poor book, St Michan's, Dublin, 1723–34, RCB, P. 276/8.1, pp. 8, 10, 117, 189, 262, 271, 313.

320. Poor book, St Michan's, Dublin, 1723–34, ibid., P. 276/8.1, pp. 19–20, 57.

321. Vestry accounts of St Bride's, Dublin, 1663–1702, ibid., P. 327/4.1; Dudley, 'Dublin's parishes, 1660–1729', i, p. 189.

322. Poor book, St Michan's, Dublin, 1723–34, RCB, P. 276/8.1, p. 6; Monck Mason's collections for Dublin, iii, part 1, Dublin Public Library, Gilbert Ms. 68, pp. 151–2.

323. *CARD*, iv, pp. 29, 156–7, 212; v, p. 253; vi, pp. 90–1, 179, 292.

324. Accounts, 1680–1, vestry book, St Catherine's, Dublin, 1657–92, RCB, P. 117/5/1.1; accounts, 1724, vestry book, St Catherine's, Dublin, 1693–1730, ibid., P. 117/5/1.2; Dudley, 'Dublin's parishes, 1660–1729', i, pp. 167, 205–6; *CARD*, v, pp. 586–7.

325. Minutes of Connor session, 1693–1735, s.d. 12 Dec. 1705, 22 April 1711, Presbyterian Historical Society, Belfast; notebook of Revd S. Boyse, PRONI, MIC 139/1, p. 44; notes on Catholics' and dissenters' charities, Monck Mason Mss, 1, part 2, pp. 239–48, Dublin Public Library, Gilbert Ms. 63.

326. 'Dr Caulfield's annals of the parish church of St Maria de Shandon, now St Ann's, Cork', *JCHAS*, 2nd series, 10 (1904), p. 271; Caulfield's annals of St Mary, Shandon, p. 12, St Fin Barre's Cathedral, Cork.

327. Annals of St Mary's, Shandon, p. 5, St Fin Barre's Cathedral, Cork; vestry book, St Peter's Cork, s.d. 24 Jan. 1749[50], NLI, Ms. 764; Waterford corporation book, 1700–27, s.d. 26 Feb. 1705[6], Waterford Municipal Archives; W. H. Dundas, *Enniskillen: parish and town* (Dundalk and Enniskillen, 1913), pp. 53–4; *Statutes*, 11 & 12 Geo III.

328. Mulcahy, *Kinsale*, vii, p. 5.

329. Ibid., vi, p. 6.

330. Ibid., vi, pp. 10–11, 20, 46, 67; vii, pp. 23–4, 64, 79, 93, 96–8.

331. Accounts for 1705–6, Masters' accounts, Weavers' Company, 1691–1714, RSAI; minute book, Weavers' Company, 1734–60, s.d. 1 Jan. 1734[5], 1 Jan. 1736[7], 2 Oct. 1738, RSAI; minute book, Guild of St Anne's, s.d. 27 July 1702, 26 July 1703, 11 Nov. 1706, 26 July 1708, 26 July 1709, 27 July 1713, 26 July 1746, 4 Nov. 1760, RIA, Ms. 12 D 1; list of pensioners, minute book, Goldsmiths' Company, 1667–1731, Assay Office, Dublin; note on M. Chamberlain, 9 Oct. 1694, Evelyn Mss, box vii, formerly at Christ Church, Oxford, now in BL.

332. Minute book, Lodge 138, Coleraine, 1753–72, s.d. 27 Dec. 1760, 6 Jan. 1763, 7 Nov. 1765, 29 May 1769, PRONI, D 668/O.

333. Minute book, Lodge 138, Coleraine, 1753–72, s.d. 2 June 1757, ibid.

334. Memorandum book of Revd F. Houston and Revd R. Hezlett, PRONI, D 668/E/38.

335. E. Nicholson, *A supplement to the method of charity-schools, for Ireland* (Dublin, 1714), p. 25.

336. Abp. W. King to J. Kane, 10 May 1726, TCD, Ms. 750/8, p. 96; Dudley, 'Dublin's parishes, 1660–1729', i, pp. 171–5; J. Robins, *The lost children: a study of charity children in Ireland* (Dublin, 1980).

337. J. Kelly, 'The emergence of scientific and institutional medical practice in Ireland, 1650–1800', in E. Malcolm and G. Jones (eds), *Medicine, disease and the state in Ireland, 1650–1940* (Cork, 1999), pp. 22–39; and above, pp. 137–8.

338. Dudley, 'Dublin's parishes 1660–1729', i, pp. 164–73.

339. List of city poor, 20 March 1725[6], Marsh's Library, Dublin, Ms. Z3.1.1, cxlviii.

340. K. Conolly to J. Bonnell, 29 Jan. 1739[40], 9 July 1742, NLI, PC 434.

341. Same to same, 4 Aug. 1740, 22 Sept. 1741, ibid., PC 434.

342. J. Wight, journal, s.d. 19 July 1756, Friends' Historical Library, Dublin.

343. K. Conolly to J. Bonnell, 15 Jan. 1738[9], NLI, PC 434; S. Burdy, *The life of Philip Skelton*, ed. N. Moore (Oxford, 1914), p. 219; P. Delany, *Sixteen discourses upon doctrines and duties* (London, 1754), pp. 223–7, 233.

344. K. Conolly to J. Bonnell, 4 Feb. 1729[30], NLI, PC 434.

345. J. Loughlin, accounts, s.d. 25 March 1739, ibid., Ms. 11,463.

346. Account book, Incorporated Society, 1733–78, TCD, Ms. 5419, pp. 74, 144.

347. Abp. W. King to H. Temple, 27 Nov. 1718, ibid., Ms. 750/5, p. 69.

348. Howell, *Rural poor*, pp. 93–115; M. Humphreys, *Crisis of a community: Montgomeryshire, 1680–1815* (Cardiff, 1996), p. 55.

349. Sir P. Perceval, accounts, 1679, 1680, BL, Add. Ms. 47,037, ff. 42v, 44v; Abp. W. King, account book, 1700–12, TCD, Ms. 751/2, ff. 199, 221v, 266; expenses at funeral of Lady Domville, 19 Dec. 1712, NLI, Ms. 9381/11; payments for Bishop Charles Carr of Killaloe, account book of John Smith, PRONI, D 668/D/1, pp. 1, 5; J. Smythe to W. Smythe, 12 Feb. 1740[1], ibid., PC 449; accounts of R. Howard, 1748–50, NLI, Ms. 1725; R. Edgeworth, accounts, s.d. April–May 1756, ibid., Ms. 1522, pp. 131–2; S. Winter, diary, s.d. 19 June 1762, July 1762, 24 Sept.

1763, 29 Oct. 1763, ibid., Ms. 3855; [T. Dawson], *A letter from a country gentleman in the province of Munster to his grace the Lord Primate of All Ireland* ([Dublin, 1741]), p. 6.

350. 'Autobiography of Pole Cosby', p. 433.

351. Sir P. Perceval, accounts, 1680, BL, Add. Ms. 47,037, f. 48v; C. O'Hara, observations, NLI, Ms. 20,397; Belmore, *History of the Corry family*, p. 276; Cullen et al., 'Wages and comparative development in Ireland and Scotland, 1565–1780', pp. 105–16; D'Arcy, 'Wages of labourers in the Dublin building industry, 1667–1918', pp. 18–19; Kennedy and Dowling, 'Prices and wages in Ireland, 1700–1850', pp. 62–104; Pollock, 'Contract and consumption', pp. 19–33; Pollock, 'The household economy in early rural America and Ulster', pp. 61–75.

352. P. Griffin, *The people with no name* (Princeton, 2000), pp. 65–97; G. Kirkham, 'Ulster emigration to North America, 1680–1720', in Blethen and Wood (eds), *Ulster and North America: transatlantic perspectives*, pp. 76–97.

353. Sir A. Rawdon to H. Sloane, 24 June 1691, BL, Sloane Ms. 4036, f. 105.

354. C. O'Hara, observations, NLI, Ms. 20,397; R. F. Mackay (ed.), *The Hawke papers: a selection, 1743–1771*, Navy Records Society, 129 (1990), p. 161.

355. H. Caldwell to S. Bagshawe, 3 Jan. 1762, JRL, B2/3/362; PRO, WO 27/5, cited in S. J. Conway, 'War and national identity in the mid-eighteenth-century British Isles', *EHR*, 116 (2001), p. 878.

356. Sir J. Caldwell to S. Bagshawe, 1 Feb. 1760, JRL, Ms. B2/3/398.

357. Rules and orders, Incorporated Society, 1735–79, TCD, Ms. 5301, pp. 46–7; Board book, Incorporated Society, 1761–75, ibid., Ms. 5225, pp. 13, 20.

358. J. Walton, 'The earliest Presbyterian register of Waterford', *Irish ancestor*, 13 (1981), pp. 94–8.

359. St Multose's church, Kinsale, register, 1683–1820; St Mary's church, Youghal, register B (from 1727); register, Drogheda parish church, 1747–72, NA, M. 5127.

360. E. Ó hAnnracháin, 'Corkmen in the Hôtel des Invalides', *JCHAS*, 105 (2000), pp. 129–54; E. Ó hAnnracháin, 'Irish veterans in the Invalides: the Tipperary contingent', *Tipperary Historical Journal* (1998), pp. 158–89.

361. Census of Elphin, 1749, NA, M. 2466, ff. 43, 52–3.

362. PRO, WO 118/45; account of out-pensioners of Chelsea Hospital in Ireland, PRONI, T 3019/955; Census of Elphin, NA, M. 2466, f. 43; Legg, *Synge Letters*, p. 134.

363. G. E. Howard, *Queries relative to several defects and grievances in some of the present laws of Ireland*, 2nd edn (Dublin, 1761), p. 48.

364. Register of Magdalen Asylum, RCB, Ms. 551/1.1; S. Nash, 'Prostitution and charity: the Magdalen Hospital: a case study', *Journal of Social History*, 17 (1983–84), pp. 617–28.

365. Register of inmates of the Magdalen Hospital, Dublin, RCB, Ms. 551/1.1.

366. T. Barnard, '"Parlour entertainment for an evening": histories of the 1640s', in M. Ó Siochrú (ed.), *Kingdoms in crisis: Ireland in the 1640s* (Dublin, 2001), pp. 20–43.

367. E. Nicholson, *A method of charity-schools* (Dublin, 1712), pp. 27–8; Nicholson, *A supplement to the method*, pp. 5–6, 14–15.

368. S. J. Connolly, 'Unnatural death in four nations: contrasts and comparisons', in S. J. Connolly (ed.), *Kingdoms united? Great Britain and Ireland since 1500: integration and diversity* (Dublin, 1999), pp. 200–14; N. Garnham, 'How violent was eighteenth-century Ireland?', *IHS*, 30 (1997), pp. 377–92; N. Garnham, 'The

criminal law 1692–1760: England and Ireland compared', in Connolly (ed.), *Kingdoms united?*, pp. 215–24.

369. T. C. Barnard, 'The world of goods and County Offaly in the early eighteenth century', in T. P. O'Neill and W. Nolan (eds), *Offaly: history and society* (Dublin, 1998), pp. 371–92; W. H. Crawford, 'A Ballymena business in the late eighteenth century', in J. Gray and W. McCann (eds), *An uncommon bookman: essays in memory of J.R.R. Adams* (Belfast, 1996), pp. 22–33; L. M. Cullen, 'Incomes, social classes and economic growth in Ireland and Scotland, 1600–1900', in T. Devine and D. Dickson (eds), *Ireland and Scotland, 1600–1850* (Edinburgh, 1983), pp. 248–60; Pollock, 'Contract and consumption', pp. 19–33; Pollock, 'The household economy in early rural America and Ulster', pp. 61–75.

370. S. Hinde, *A sermon preach't before the right honourable the lord mayor of the city of Dublin . . . the 23. of November 1671* (Dublin, 1672), pp. 2–5, 9, 23–4, 30–1.

371. E. Synge, *Universal beneficence* (Dublin, 1721), pp. 31–2; R. Clayton, *The religion of labour* (Dublin, 1740), pp. 16–17; Delany, *Twenty sermons*, p. 391.

372. Poor book, St Michan's, Dublin, 1723–34, RCB, P. 276/8.1, p. 105.

373. J. Boyse, *Sermons* (Dublin, 1708), pp. 92, 96.

374. Building accounts for Abp. E. Synge's palace at Tuam, NLI, Ms. 2173; Bp. E. Synge to Abp. W. Wake, 9 April, 1716; Abp. W King to same, 8 May 1716; Abp. E. Synge to same, 15 Jan. 1716[17], 27 Sept. 1717, 16 April 1720, 22 Aug. 1721; Bp. T. Godwin to same, 28 April 1720, Christ Church, Wake Mss, 12, ff. 33v, 48v, 108, 427v; 13, ff. 166, 171, 264; J. Potter to R. Wilmot, 3 May 1741, PRONI, T 3019/295.

11. Conclusion: Ranks and Rankings

1. J. Devereux, *Mr Devereux's letter to the inhabitants of St Catherine's parish* ([Dublin], 1740).

2. Corporation book, Waterford, 1700–27, s.d. 4 Oct. 1704, 26 Feb. 1705[6], 8 Dec. 1707, 25 April 1710, 22 Oct. 1715, 29 Sept. 1716, 21 Sept. 1717, Waterford Municipal Archives; M. Fitzgerald to Lord Grandison, 22 Aug. 1729, 14 Sept. 1729, Dromana, Co. Waterford, Villiers-Stuart Mss, T. 3131/C5/45 and 46; R. Day (ed.), 'Cooke's memoirs of Youghal, 1749', *JCHAS*, 2nd series, 9 (1903), p. 63; Mulcahy, *Kinsale*, ii, p. 74; iii, p. 88; vi, p. 23; Census of Elphin, NA, M. 2466, pp. 26, 69, 82, 92, 95, 99, 100, 125, 141, 153.

3. N. Garnham, 'Local élite creation in early Hanoverian Ireland: the case of the county grand jury', *HJ*, 42 (1999), pp. 623–42.

Index